Industrial Location

The real duty of the economist is not to explain our sorry
reality, but to improve it. The question of the best location
is far more dignified than determination of the actual one.

There is no scientific and unequivocal solution
for the location of the individual firm, but only
a practical one: the test of trial and error.

Wherever something new is being created, and thus in
settlement and spatial planning also, the laws revealed through
theory are the sole economic guide to what *should* take place.

> August Lösch, *The Economics of Location*

Industrial Location

An Economic Geographical Analysis

David M. Smith

Associate Professor of Geography
University of Florida

John Wiley & Sons, Inc.

New York · London · Sydney · Toronto

Copyright © 1971 by John Wiley & Sons, Inc.

All rights reserved. Published simultaneously in Canada.

No part of this book may be reproduced by any means, nor transmitted, nor translated into a machine language without the written permission of the publisher.

Library of Congress Catalogue Card Number: 71-139280

ISBN 0-471-80185-2

Printed in the United States of America

10 9 8 7 6 5 4 3 2

Preface

This book resulted from more than a decade of personal involvement in matters relating to industrial location. It reflects a variety of interests and experiences—as a student, research worker, professional planner, consultant, and university teacher on both sides of the Atlantic. Like any book, it also reflects the time in which it was conceived and written. It was completed at the end of the two decades in which economics discovered space and regions and geography discovered statistics, models, and paradigms. This has been a period of great innovation and excitement in location analysis, with new techniques, ideas, and structures of knowledge introduced and debated at length. Much of the geographer's traditional dogma has been questioned, some has been discarded, and the new thinking gradually has become the conventional wisdom.

Thus this book should reflect an era of considerable progress in the study of industrial location as a geographical problem. But it also reflects some of the uncertainty that inevitably accompanies a period of intellectual innovation. Particularly, it reveals uncertainty concerning how far location theory can ever adequately account for the complex reality of the industrial world, and how far some of the critical variables can ever be measured with any kind of precision. It also reveals uncertainty as to how far some existing approaches may require substantial modification in the near future. The next geographical revolution may still be a long way off, but there is a clear trend toward even greater emphasis on "behavioral" aspects of location decision making and the beginnings of a movement toward a closer professional involvement with conditions of human welfare, social justice and the quality of the environment. Both these emergent themes find some expression in this book; they may become the dominant themes of the 1970s.

Of all the influences that led to the writing of this book, the first remains the most important. As a teacher at the University of Nottingham in the late 1950s, Eric Rawstron brought to the attention of his students the work of Weber, Hoover, Lösch, Isard, and Greenhut at a time when they were largely unknown in British geography, and he first stimulated my curiosity in this field. Elements of his ideas and teaching figure prominently in some sections of this book. Another major influence has been the undergraduates at Manchester University who took my first courses in industrial geography, and the graduate students who have worked with me at Southern Illinois University; many ideas have been much improved by the critical scrutiny of these individuals. I am particularly grateful to Professor E. M. Hoover (University of Pittsburgh), Gerald Karaska (Clark University), Denis Fair (University of the Witwatersrand), Ronald Beazley (Southern Illinois University), Francois Gay (University of Rouen), Ian Hamilton (London School of Economics), and Ronald Reifler (The Fantus Company, Chicago) for reading certain sections in draft and for their helpful comments and suggestions.

Most of the book was written while on the faculty of the Geography Department at Southern Illinois University. I am grateful to this institution for its support, particularly with respect to secretarial, computer, and cartographic facilities. With the exception of the diagrams, the illustrations in this book were prepared in the Cartographic Laboratory at the University, under the supervision of Dan Irwin and Tso-Hwa Lee, and the results are a tribute to their efficiency and art. Tso-Hwa Lee has also helped with a number of computer programming problems. More than twenty of the maps were generated by computer using the SYMAP system developed at Harvard University, and much of the credit for whatever merit these illustrations possess goes to Phil Frankland who worked in the Cartographic Laboratory as my assistant. The secretarial staff of the Geography Department deserve a special mention for meeting an almost impossible deadline for the typing of the final manuscript, and for their efforts in making sense of my strange combination of English and American spelling.

Finally, I must thank my family for an unusual degree of tolerance toward one for whom the creative process is not always the most tranquil of experiences. As always, they provided a constant reminder of life's more important realities.

David M. Smith

Carbondale, Illinois, 1970

Contents

INTRODUCTION		1
1 THE APPROACH		5
	1.1 Observation and Description	6
	1.2 Explanation and Theory	10
	1.3 The Approach to Industrial Location Analysis	15

PART ONE

The Variables in Industrial Location — 23

2 SOME PRELIMINARY MATTERS		25
	2.1 The Factors of Production, Input Combination, and Cost Structure	26
	2.2 Cost Structures Illustrated	29
3 THE MAJOR INPUTS		32
	3.1 Land	32
	3.2 Capital	37
	3.3 Materials and Power	41
	3.4 Labor	45
	3.5 State and Local Taxes	52
	3.6 Enterprise	54
4 SUPPLY AND DEMAND, MARKET AND PRICE		57
	4.1 The Interaction of Supply and Demand	57
	4.2 The Market	62
	4.3 Pricing Policies	66

5 TRANSPORTATION   69

    5.1 Methods of Transportation   69
    5.2 The Structure of Freight Rates   71

6 SOME OTHER CONSIDERATIONS   82

    6.1 Agglomeration and External Economies   82
    6.2 Public Policy and Planning   88
    6.3 Historical Accident and Personal Preference   89
    6.4 Some Concluding Remarks   92

PART TWO
Approaches to Theory, and Models of Industrial Location   95

7 INDUSTRIAL LOCATION THEORY: SOME GEOGRAPHICAL CONTRIBUTIONS   97

    7.1 Early Geographical Approaches   97
    7.2 Economic-Base Theory   100
    7.3 Rawstron's Three Principles   102
    7.4 The Behavioral Approach   105
    7.5 Other Recent Developments   109

8 INDUSTRIAL LOCATION THEORY: THE ECONOMIST'S CONTRIBUTION   112

    8.1 Alfred Weber   113
    8.2 Tord Palander   119
    8.3 Edgar Hoover   125
    8.4 August Lösch   130
    8.5 Locational Interdependence   137
    8.6 Melvin Greenhut   143
    8.7 Walter Isard   148
    8.8 Some Other Recent Contributions   156

9 OPERATIONAL MODELS OF INDUSTRIAL LOCATION   159

    9.1 The Development of Operational Models   159
    9.2 Some Models in Current Use   162

9.3		An Industrial Location Model Illustrated	164
	a.	The Structure of the Model	166
	b.	Applications	169

PART THREE

Industrial Location Theory: A Synthesis 177

10 BASIC PRINCIPLES 181

11 THE VARIABLE-COST MODEL 188

11.1	Extending the Classical Variable-Cost Framework	188
11.2	The Initial Variable-Cost Model	191
11.3	Some Variations on the Initial Model	197
11.4	Cost Surfaces and Spatial Margins in Industrial Location Theory	205

12 RELAXING SOME ASSUMPTIONS IN THE VARIABLE-COST MODEL 207

12.1	Entrepreneurial Skill	207
12.2	Locational Subsidy	210
12.3	External Economies	211
12.4	Substitution between Inputs	212
12.5	Scale of Production	222
12.6	Personal Considerations	231

13 INTRODUCING THE DEMAND FACTOR 236

13.1	Factors Affecting Demand and Revenue	237
13.2	Spatial Variations in Demand and Revenue	242
13.3	A More Complex Situation	248
13.4	Revenue, Cost, and the Profit Surface	259

14 INTRODUCING THE TIME DIMENSION 262

14.1	Changes in the Spatial Cost/Revenue Situation	262
14.2	The Evolution of Industrial Location Patterns	269

PART FOUR

Some Empirical Applications   275

15   THE IDENTIFICATION OF COST SURFACES   279

    15.1   Land-Cost Surfaces   280
    15.2   Building-Cost Surfaces   282
    15.3   Material-Cost Surfaces   284
    15.4   Labor-Cost Surfaces   288
    15.5   Taxation Surfaces   292

16   THE MARKET, AND AREAL VARIATIONS IN DEMAND   296

    16.1   The Aggregate Travel (Transport Cost) Model   297
    16.2   The Market Potential Model   301
    16.3   Market Areas   304

17   MORE COMPLETE ANALYSES OF COMPARATIVE LOCATIONAL ADVANTAGE   312

    17.1   Comparative-Cost Studies   312
    17.2   The Anatomy of a Comparative-Cost Analysis   320
    17.3   Combining Cost and Demand Factors   325
    17.4   Three Selected Empirical Studies   330
         a.   Lindberg on the Swedish Paper Industry   330
         b.   Törnqvist on the Swedish Light Clothing Industry   337
         c.   Kennelly on the Mexican Steel Industry   341

18   THREE CASE STUDIES   346

    18.1   The Iron and Steel Industry in the United States   346
         a.   The Prewar Cost Situation   349
         b.   New England as a Possible Location for an Integrated Iron and Steel Works   352
         c.   The National Cost Pattern in 1950   354
         d.   Conclusions   360
    18.2   The Location of an Electrical Appliance Plant   361
         a.   The Comparative-Cost Analysis   362
         b.   The Market-Area Analysis   367

18.3	The Location of a Branch of the Electronics Industry	374
	a. Constructing the Cost Surfaces	376
	b. Explaining the Location of the Electronic Equipment Industry	383
18.4	Concluding Remarks	387

PART FIVE

Some Alternative Approaches 391

19 CORRELATION AND REGRESSION ANALYSIS 393

19.1	Methods	394
19.2	Multiple Correlation and Regression Analysis	397
19.3	Illustrations of Multiple Correlation and Regression Analysis	400
	a. McCarty et al. on the Location of the Machinery Industry	400
	b. Stafford on the Paperboard Container Industry	404

20 LINEAR PROGRAMMING 406

20.1	Basic Linear Programming Formulations	407
20.2	Some Practical Applications	415
	a. The Location of a Single Firm	416
	b. Interregional Commodity Flows and the Allocation of Production	417
	c. The Dual and Location Rent	420

21 INPUT-OUTPUT ANALYSIS 423

21.1	Input-Output Tables and Their Uses	423
21.2	An Illustration from the United States Input-Output Tables	431

PART SIX

Industrial Location, Economic Development and Public Policy
437

22 REGIONAL PROBLEMS AND PROBLEM REGIONS 441

xii CONTENTS

23 REGIONAL INDUSTRIAL DEVELOPMENT PLANNING — 447

    23.1 Industrial Location Policy Instruments — 449
    23.2 The Spatial Strategy of Industrial Development Planning — 452
    23.3 Predicting the Impact of Industrial Development — 458

24 ILLUSTRATIONS OF INDUSTRIAL DEVELOPMENT PLANNING STRATEGY — 463

    24.1 Great Britain — 463
    24.2 France — 467
    24.3 The United States — 469
    24.4 Southern Italy — 473
    24.5 Poland — 475

25 INDUSTRIAL LOCATION, LAND USE, AND CITY PLANNING — 480

    25.1 The Local Demand for Industrial Land — 481
    25.2 The Areal Allocation of Industrial Land — 485

26 LOCATION THEORY AND INDUSTRIAL DEVELOPMENT PLANNING — 492

    26.1 The Neoclassical Theoretical Approach — 493
    26.2 Scale, Agglomeration, Linkages, and Industrial Complex Analysis — 501
    26.3 Risk, Uncertainty, and the Behavior of the Firm — 507

27 ON INDUSTRIAL LOCATION AND SOCIAL WELL-BEING — 511

BIBLIOGRAPHY — 519

INDEX — 543

Industrial Location

Introduction

An understanding of the nature and operation of economic systems is one of the most important contemporary intellectual requirements. This is not only to satisfy man's natural curiosity in a world that is becoming more and more complex from an economic point of view but also to provide a sound basis for the planned development that is becoming increasingly necessary in advanced nations as well as those in earlier stages of economic growth. The study of spatial aspects of economic systems belongs to that nebulous borderland between economics and geography, partially occupied by regional science. It is a subject that transgresses the conventional boundaries of our rather arbitrary divisions of knowledge. Nevertheless, there is one field of inquiry which is exclusively concerned with the study of spatial aspects of economic systems and that is economic geography.

Economic geography is a well established branch of geographical inquiry. But it is a very broad field, embracing agriculture, extractive industry, manufacturing and the provision of services, and also such related matters as transportation and trade. Many of these topics have now become virtually separate fields of study, with their own methodology, favored techniques, and body of literature. The increasing fragmentation of spatial economic analysis into narrow specializations is unfortunate in some respects, since it diverts attention from the objective of developing a comprehensive view of the space economy as an integrated whole. But this trend seems to be an inevitable result of the present need for more exact knowledge and deeper understanding of specific aspects of spatial behavior. It seems to be a necessary preliminary to the ultimate development of an all-embracing theory of the way man organizes his activities on the face of the earth.

The recognition of industrial location as a distinct field within spatial economic analysis is partly an outcome of this increasing topical specialization. The study of industrial location is clearly one of the most important branches of economic geography, with many practical implications for public policy as well as offering enormous scope for academic research. Yet in recent years this subject has been somewhat overshadowed by the disproportionate attention given to certain aspects of urban geography and other lines of inquiry that happen to be in vogue. This is unfortunate, because the nature and complexity of the industrial world is such that neither a broad training in human or economic geography nor a deep immersion in the mysteries of central place theory or regression analysis is an adequate preparation for work on problems of industrial location. The comparative neglect of industrial location is reflected in the current textbooks, which generally cover this subject with undue brevity and with insufficient attention to theory. The increasing interest in industrial location on the part of economists has not yet produced an alternative to the conventional geographical treatments, despite some very important specialist texts and some more general books on regional economic analysis. There is thus an urgent need for a framework of reference for the study of industrial location, which has due regard for the increasing attention being given to theoretical matters in geographical inquiry.

The purpose of this book is to provide such a framework. It has been designed and written with the requirements of advanced undergraduate and graduate education in mind, although it may not be too difficult for some courses at the introductory level. It should be suitable for students in economics, business and planning, as well as in geography. But the aim has been to offer something more than a college textbook, since the approach to industrial location analysis developed here embodies techniques and concepts that are of direct relevance to regional and urban planning at a practical level. There is also much that could help the businessman in making decisions on plant location and related matters such as product distribution. This book, therefore, should have something to offer to those concerned with industrial location in public service and private business, as well as the student, teacher, and research worker.

The existing literature on industrial location reveals two divergent approaches. The geographer, with his traditional concern for the "real world," has emphasized empirical inquiry and the search for generalization through case studies, while the economist has preferred a much more theoretical approach with a high degree of abstraction. This book attempts a compromise. Great stress is placed on location theory, but the need to keep this relevant to the solution of practical problems is borne in mind throughout, even when the analysis may appear far removed from reality. The theoretical sections make extensive use of the kind of graphic models favored in economics texts, but these parts of the book should cause little distress to students with only slight background in economics. No mathematics is required other than a knowledge of elementary algebra. Many real-world illustrations are used to demonstrate various techniques and concepts, and there are a number of substantial case studies. Readers familiar with the more conventional geographical texts will find comfort in the large number of maps that have been used.

After an introductory chapter, the book is divided into six parts. Part One discusses the factors affecting industrial location, identifying the variables that must be incorporated into theory. Part Two considers various geographical and economic contributions to theory and model building, and is followed by an attempt at a theoretical synthesis (Part Three). Part Four illustrates some aspects of the practical application of theory in geographical research. Part Five offers a brief review of some alternative approaches to industrial location analysis. Part Six pursues the connection between industrial location and economic development planning, and considers the relevance of existing theory in this context.

Students and teachers using this book as a text in courses on industrial location (or industrial geography) will find that the degree of difficulty of the material varies considerably. Some of the contents (such as Parts One, Four, and Six) should be easily assimilated at the introductory level, while other sections (such as some of Part Three) may extend even advanced graduate students. However, with appropriate guidance from the instructor this book should serve as basic reading for courses at the introductory, intermediate, and graduate levels.

1

The Approach

Every industrial establishment has a location. Each factory occupies a portion of the earth's surface, and stands in a certain spatial relationship to other factories and other economic phenomena. As the participants in a specific industry make their locational decisions, selecting some places for development in preference to others, an areal distribution pattern emerges. It may be concentrated or dispersed; it may tend toward regularity or take on a more random form. Each industry adopts its own distinctive areal distribution, and the assemblage of all these patterns makes up the complex reality of the industrial space economy. Attempting to understand industrial location patterns, and the individual decisions embodied in them, constitutes the fundamental task of the field of inquiry which is the subject of this book.

Industrial location analysis may thus be defined as the study of the spatial arrangement of industrial activity. The term *industrial location analysis* is preferred to the more conventional expressions of *industrial geography* or *the geography of manufacturing* to emphasize the analytical nature of the approach adopted in this book. The concern here is with the general circumstances determining industrial location, and not with offering interpretations of particular distribution patterns.

The study of the spatial arrangement of industrial activity goes somewhat beyond the analysis of areal distribution patterns and individual locational decisions, however. It is also very much concerned with the areal variations in industrial character which arise from the different spatial forms adopted by different activities. Some cities and regions have one leading industry while others produce a wide variety of goods. Some show a rapid rate of industrial growth while others are in decline. And, in some areas, industrial activity is the dominant source of livelihood, while in others agriculture, mining, or the provision of services may be of much greater importance. The explanation of these and other similar circumstances forms an important part of industrial location analysis.

Whatever the precise nature of the problem under review, the locational decision of the single businessman or firm is of critical importance in the search for the reasons behind what is observed. The location pattern of any industry is the product of a large number of individual decisions, made as firms react in different ways to different economic circumstances (and sometimes to the same circumstances) in pursuit of their own business or personal objectives. The approach set down in this book, particularly in the theoretical chapters, focuses more on the locational choice of the single entrepreneur, or decision-making unit, than on the patterns adopted by the location of entire industries. This microtheoretical approach seems the most effective way toward the fuller understanding of the wider industrial space economy at the present stage in the development of this field of inquiry. It also helps to emphasize that it is the way economic circumstances affect human behavior rather than some abstract geometry of spatial form which is the ultimate object of our curiosity.

At the outset it is useful to make a distinction between observation and description, on the one hand, and explanation and theory, on the other. The processes of observation and description are concerned with the collection and ordering of data while explanation and theory are directed toward the interpretation and understanding of the industrial world as it is perceived. The emphasis in this book is very much on the development and application of theory, and the main concern of this chapter is to provide a brief introduction to some general questions relating to explanation and theory in industrial location analysis. But before this is attempted, some comments on observation and description are required to stress the significance of these aspects of inquiry and to make brief suggestions on the way in which the subject matter can be structured.

1.1 OBSERVATION AND DESCRIPTION

The kind of empirical investigations conducted under the heading of industrial location analysis may be divided into two broad categories. First, there are *systematic* studies of the location of a single set of spatially distributed phenomena such as participants in a particular industry or employees engaged in a given activity. These studies can be on a world, national, regional, or local scale. Second, there are *areal* studies, which are concerned with the industrial character or structure of specific areas and how they differ from one another. A comparison between the employment structures of a group of cities or counties would come under this heading. These two categories are not, of course, entirely independent of one another, and many studies contain elements of both. There are also investigations that focus on changes, in either a systematic or an areal context, instead of a static account of industrial location or structure. And there are some that are concerned with specific industrial problems such as local employment opportunity, the feasibility of development in a particular location, or the impact of a new plant on an area's economy. The distinction between the systematic view and the areal view is nevertheless sufficiently important to act as a framework for some initial observations on the nature of the data with which the student of industrial location generally works.

Observation and description are essential prerequisites to explanation in any scientific investigation. The description serves to identify the problem, or that which is to be explained, and has as its starting point a set of observations. The form that the data take may be explained by referring to Figure 1.1, which comprises a number of cells in each of which may be deposited some piece of information or observation. Each column of the matrix represents an industry, or specific class of phenomena, while each of the rows comprises an areal unit for which data have been compiled. In the systematic study of the present location of a single industry the set of observations will take the form of a single column in a two-dimensional matrix which represents the total industrial information available for the areas under review at that time. A comparison between the location of the first industry with that of another will involve another column of information. An areal study of industrial structure will make use of a row in the matrix, and other rows will be used as structural comparisons are made with other areas. Each point of time for which information can be compiled has its own set of data, and these can be thought of as being stacked behind the one relating to the present, to form a three-dimensional matrix. Information relating to changes over time (for example, the percentage growth rates of industries by areas) can be organized in matrix form in the same way as the other data.

Thinking of data in the form illustrated in Figure 1.1 helps to focus on a number of important problems connected with the process of observation. First, there is the way in which the totality of industrial activity is split up, or how information is ordered along the horizontal axis of the matrix. Individual industries may be defined in a variety of ways, but the usual bases are similarity of material or product. Thus the engineering

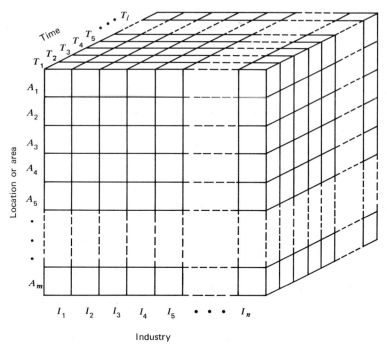

Figure 1.1. The general form of the data matrix in spatial analysis. (*Source.* Based on Berry, 1964.)

industry or the food industry comprise a group of firms producing broadly the same type of goods, while the terms leather industry or cotton industry stress the nature of the material as the unifying element. In most cases the investigator has an official or standard industrial classification laid down for him, but the question of what level of aggregation is appropriate still arises.

The second problem is that of deciding on appropriate areal units for the collection of data. This relates to the vertical axis of the matrix in Figure 1.1. Information may be available for different sets of areas (for example, states, counties, and individual urban places), and a choice must be made in relation to the detail required. For some kinds of statistical analysis the size and shape of the data-collection units may be a critical matter, and there are great advantages to the use of a regular system, such as grid squares, if data can be compiled on this basis.

Third, the time or time period to be investigated must be decided. If the investigation is of "the present," the latest date for which reliable information can be found must be determined. If the inquiry involves tracing the historical evolution of a location pattern, the dates in the past for which information is to be sought have to be decided, often partly on the basis of data availability. If the study is one of industrial growth rates over time, the period under review must be chosen with great care, in relation to position in the business cycle and other considerations likely to effect the validity of year-to-year comparisons.

These three sets of decisions all relate to one of the most important questions in the initial stage of any scientific inquiry—that of *classification*. The definition of industries involves the classification of the phenomena, the choice of areal units involves the classification of space, and the decision as to the datum point or periods to be covered is in effect a temporal classification. The function of a classification is to organize observations in a meaningful way. Thus the vast range of industrial activities is grouped into categories on the basis of similar properties, just as animals are grouped into species or man into races, so as to order information on a large number of individual entities in a way that will assist further inquiry. Information on a number of factories may be amalgamated for statistical purposes on the basis of geographical proximity in order to reduce the number of observations to be considered to more manageable proportions. And the continuum of time, like that of space, may be divided into intervals to simplify the process of historical inquiry. The kind of classification used in each case will be a product of the specific problem under investigation; some will generate a need for more detailed areal or temporal classifications than others, in the same way that some will focus on narrower ranges of industrial activities than others.

The final question raised by Figure 1.1 is how to fill the individual cells of the data matrix with information. This involves *measurement*, which may be defined as the assignment of numbers to objects, events, or situations according to some rule. In industrial location analysis measurement involves giving numerical values to areas, or points, in relation to the magnitude of the occurrence of whatever activity, or groups of activities, is being investigated. The selection of the appropriate property or criterion that determines the units of measurement is very important, since there may be a choice between alternatives such as value added in the process of manufacture, number of employees, size of payroll, and number of plants. As in the case of classification, the selection of the measurement rules to be applied in any specific case will depend on the nature of the inquiry being carried on and the conceptual framework on which it rests.

Once the appropriate systems of classification have been set up, and the means of measurement chosen, the necessary information can be compiled. It is only then that the process of observation has been completed and the inquiry can move on to description. The function of description in a scientific context is to set down perceptions of the world, or observations, in a formal way. In industrial location studies this can be a statement of the industry's distribution, or the region's varying industrial structure. The conventional method of geographical description is the map, on which the observed distribution of industrial activity can be illustrated quantitatively in a variety of ways. But distribution patterns shown on maps are liable to subjective interpretation, and it is often necessary to supplement them with statistics of various kinds. Whatever precise means of description are chosen, it is important that they should give an accurate and objective view. The application and development of techniques aimed at the more exact depiction and measurement of industrial location patterns are therefore very important, and have been greatly assisted by the increasing attention to quantitative methods in geographical inquiry.

Questions relating to observation, classification, and descriptive techniques cannot be considered further, except for occasional passing references in some subsequent chapters. A thorough treatment would require a volume on its own. However, a useful discussion of many of the general issues raised above can be found in McCarty and Lindberg (1966), while particulars of the numerical methods in current use for describing areal distribution patterns are available in the standard geographical texts on quantitative techniques (for example, Berry and Marble, 1967; Garrison and Marble, 1967; Cole and King, 1968; and King, 1969).

1.2 EXPLANATION AND THEORY

Having established and set down the facts, how are they to be explained? How might it be possible to predict the values in individual cells, and in complete columns and rows, of the matrix described above? This raises a number of fundamental issues relating to the conduct of scientific inquiry, which have yet to be resolved to the satisfaction of every philosopher. Many books have been written on explanation and theory. A number of them have been written specifically for the social or behavioral scientist, and geography has recently achieved the distinction of a volume of its own on the subject of explanation (Harvey, 1969). The present book clearly is not the place to try to resolve philosophical difficulties; all that will be attempted here is to set down certain features of the way explanations are conventionally sought in social science, relating this to the construction of industrial location theory.

The role of explanation in scientific inquiry has been well expressed by

Meehan (1968, 97): "the fundamental cognitive task is to create patterns that can be imposed upon the incoming stream of perceptions in ways that will create understanding of what is being perceived and expectations that will follow—and that will suggest ways in which man can intervene to alter the course of events for his own ends." The basic procedure is to try to explain individual observations, or facts, as instances of the operation of general tendencies or laws, and to relate and explain these laws by means of theories. The search for explanations involves proceeding from narrow generalizations to ones that are successively broader in scope, until ultimately all facets of human behavior can be incorporated within the same theoretical system.

In the analysis of industrial location the process of explanation is concerned with the elucidation of specific locations and distribution patterns empirically observed, and with the creation of a theoretical framework relating to this particular aspect of man's economic behavior. The various problems involved in arriving at an explanation can best be introduced by considering a simple imaginary situation. Suppose that ten plants are operating in a certain industry in a given region *ABCD* (Figure 1.2). How is the choice of location to be explained?

A sensible way to proceed would be to attempt to establish a spatial association between the phenomena to be explained and some other phenomena of a kind likely to be causally related to it. Suppose it was observed that each of the ten plants was located beside a railroad station (Figure 1.2). It would then be possible to make an *empirical generalization* of the form "all x's are y's" or "if x then y" ($x \rightarrow y$), that is, all plants (of this type in this region) are beside railroad stations. But in the search for an explanation this does not necessarily take the inquiry very far. The observation of a spatial association between two phenomena, no matter how carefully established and precisely stated, is not proof of a causal relationship. Even if this seems likely, as in the present case, there may be no indication of which is the cause and which the effect; which came first—the railroad stations that attracted the factories, or the factories that generated the need for the stations?

Suppose that further inquiries reveal that the railroad stations did in fact come first. This lends weight to the hypothesis that the factory locations are such because of the prior existence of the stations, but this is still not necessarily true because these ten places might also be the sources of a required material for example, the presence of which has nothing to do with the railroad. Therefore, to test the hypothesis, the investigator asks each factory owner why he located where he did. The answer is, in every case, that it was "because of the presence of the railroad station." On the basis of this, a further generalization might be stated to the effect

12   THE APPROACH

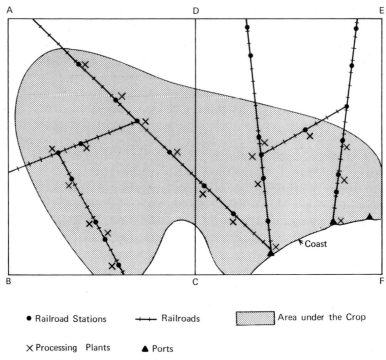

- Railroad Stations
- + Railroads
- ▨ Area under the Crop
- × Processing Plants
- ▲ Ports

Figure 1.2.   An imaginary industrial location problem.

that all plants are located where they are because of the *necessary condition* of the existence of railroad stations. But how far have the locations really been explained even now? Each individual observation has been shown to be an instance of a general condition, but is the generalization that relates factory sites causally to the position of railroad stations really understood? It is known that the one is where it is because the other is there, but it is not known why the factory has to be beside the station, or even whether it really has to be there.

If the region being studied is taken to be the entire universe, then a statement of the form "all x's are y's, all y's are x's" could be made—all factories are beside stations and all stations are beside factories. This might be written as the conditional statement "if x then y, if y then x," or $x \leftrightarrow y$. In these circumstances it might reasonably be claimed that the presence of a station is a *necessary and sufficient condition* for the location of a factory, since the two phenomena are invariably associated spatially. Although this still begs the question of why, the invariable association of two phenomena in this way is good prima facie evidence for a causal relationship. In industrial location analysis, as in other branches of social science, establishing such necessary and sufficient conditions is much more difficult than the discovery of conditions which are necessary for a particular outcome but not sufficient to guarantee it.

To complicate matters a little, suppose the investigation is extended into an adjoining region (CDEF in Figure 1.2), and that ten additional factories are found. Eight are beside railroad stations but two are at ports, and in this new region there are some stations that do not have factories beside them. The previous generalization now no longer holds as a universal truth, and the original "explanation" of the factory locations has to be revised.

To proceed further clearly requires a greater *understanding* of the situation in which locational choices are made. When the two regions are examined together a tendency for plants to concentrate in the southwest can be observed, a fact that is not explained by the distribution of railroad stations. All but two of the stations without nearby factories are found in the northeast, while the remaining two are near the ports. Faced with this increasingly complex problem the investigator now decides that he needs to know more about the factors affecting industrial location in general before he can formulate an adequate explanation, and he reads a little location theory. This tells him of the importance of such matters as access to materials and the market, and leads him to look at the twenty plants in a different light. He is now able to see them not simply as industrial buildings that happen to exist near railroad stations but as functional entities, processing a crop in the surrounding area and marketing the resulting product. He finds that the lack of plants in the northeast is associated with the absence of the crop which forms the material, and that in the area around the port it is more profitable to export the product by ship than to serve the home market via the railroad.

A fuller explanation may thus be constructed as follows. The crop-processing plants (x) are located beside the railroad stations (y) within the area where the crop is grown (z), except where the export market is preferred to the domestic market (q) in which case a port location (p) is chosen (that is, $x \to y$ if z unless q; if q, $x \to p$). It is further found that, given information on the yield of each field under the crop, knowledge of the market situation, and the location of railroad stations, a simple representation, or *model*, of the economic system can be constructed which is capable of accurately predicting the size as well as the location of the twenty plants. Because there are no exceptions to the general conclusion, and because the investigator is unaware of the world beyond his two-region isolated state, he claims his finding as a universal truth or *law*.

This discussion raises the important question of the distinction between empirical generalizations and laws. An empirical generalization, whether it relates to the spatial association of two phenomena or any other observation of the world, simply records what has been found to be true, and does not tell us that things necessarily have to be this way. Because ten plants all happen to be beside railroad stations it does not mean that an eleventh has to be, since the observed association may have been simply the result of chance. Without understanding why, there is no reason other than previous observation to expect an additional or new plant to adopt the same kind of location. The repeated discovery of the same condition may provide good grounds for hypothesizing a causal relationship, however, even if there is as yet no a priori reason for expecting this. The term law implies a causal relationship, or the establishment of necessary conditions for the presence of some phenomena. The discovery that in certain circumstances a railroad station really is a necessary condition for the setting up of a processing plant not only offers an explanation of the location of the plants but also makes possible the prediction that providing the stipulated circumstances remain unchanged an additional plant will be beside a station. Laws are universal propositions that state our convictions as to what must be true. Unlike other generalizations, they should be derivable from other laws and should be consistent with existing theory.

Leaving aside for the moment the question of how far the discovery of such laws can be expected in the study of industrial location, it is now time to consider the place of *theory* in the search for explanation and understanding. A theory may be thought of as a system of knowledge which relates things to each other in a meaningful way. It can place laws in some kind of connection with one another, thus helping to explain the laws in the same way that laws explain facts by relating them to other facts. And it can also incorporate general knowledge of the variables relevant to a particular field of inquiry, and how they interact to produce specific outcomes.

Some recourse to the existing body of theory, in the sense just indicated, is necessary during any empirical investigation. Any attempt to explain a specific industrial location or pattern implies some knowledge of how locations are arrived at in general. At the most sophisticated level, this knowledge may comprise an interconnected set of precisely formulated principles concerning the nature of and relationship between the various factors affecting plant location. At its most elementary level, it may be no more than vague general knowledge which forms a conscious or unconscious basis for intuitive judgment in the absence of a more rigorous theoretical framework. Whatever their nature, theories help to direct inquiries: "Without a theory, however provisionally or loosely formulated, there is only a miscellany of observations, having no significance either in themselves or over against the plenum of fact from which they have been arbitrarily or accidentally selected" (Kaplan, 1964, 268).

Thus, attempts to explain the world as it is observed inevitably involve some kind of theory. The reason for something is known if it can be fitted into an established pattern or set of generalizations, or if it can be deduced from other known truths. The hypothesis that the location of a given industry can be explained in a certain way may be verified by showing that it is consistent with the observed facts of the situation, and that such an explanation is supported by the existing body of theory. The repeated observation of conditions that cannot be reconciled with location theory as presently constituted would call into question the soundness of the theory and the propositions on which it rests.

As a concluding comment on the subject of explanation, the following remarks which develop an analogy between an explanation and a map may be instructive to the geographical reader:

A map records the results of observations, using conventional rules and symbols; it tells us what to expect when certain landmarks are sighted. No map records *everything* in an empirical situation; the map chosen for use should suit the purpose of the user. Maps, like explanations, structure a particular situation from a given point of view. And maps, like explanations, must be altered to include new experience or changes in the situation. Given a purpose, and some knowledge of the way in which the map was prepared, some criticism of the adequacy of the map can be made before the map is used. In the end, the value of the map must be tested by use" (Meehan, 1968, 98).

A similar analogy between maps and theories has been suggested by Toulmin (1953, 105–110); both help us to find our way around a range of phenomena, but their use requires a certain amount of expertise. The ultimate test of any explanation, or theory, is whether it is effective— whether it really does explain and help us towards understanding.

1.3 THE APPROACH TO INDUSTRIAL LOCATION ANALYSIS

The way has now been prepared for a more direct discussion of the problems of explanation and the development of theory in the study of industrial location. A convenient place to start is the manner in which scientific inquiry is commonly conducted. This is sketched in Figure 1.3, and the various stages represented are as follows.

1. The identification of the phenomena, area, or problem to be investigated. The nature of the topic may arise from perceptual experience

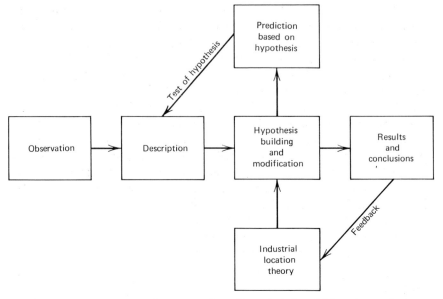

Figure 1.3. An approach to research problems in industrial location analysis.

(that is, an initial observation of some empirical situation that arouses curiosity), or it may involve the examination of some concept or hypothesis derived from the existing body of location theory.

2. Observation, or the collection of data. This stage includes the various classification and measurement decisions, and some preliminary sifting and processing of data.

3. The description of the observed pattern of industrial location, structure, or change, in cartographic or statistical form. This becomes a statement of the explanatory problem.

4. The development of an explanatory hypothesis, based on observed spatial associations or other empirical relationships, on a priori reasoning from theory, or on a combination of the two. This may have been derived from an initial *working hypothesis,* used simply to get the inquiry going and refined to produce the *test hypothesis*—a formal statement of what is thought might be true.

5. The testing of the hypothesis. This generally involves predicting what should be found (for example, what form the industrial location pattern, structure, or change should adopt if the hypothesis is true), and comparing this with the actual situation. This is the stage at which a model might be used to test the consequences of the hypothesis and the theory on which it rests. Testing may lead to the modification of the hypothesis until either an adequate explanation has been constructed or the line of inquiry has to be abandoned as erroneous or inconclusive.

THE APPROACH 17

6. If the hypothesis has been verified, a fact has been established. It may take the form of a statement to the effect that the location of the industry is a specified function of certain variables, with the rider that this explains a given proportion of the observed pattern. If the result can be regarded as a general truth rather than restricted in its validity to a particular case, it may be said to constitute a universal law.

The approach outlined above, and summarized in Figure 1.3, is of course only one way of looking at the organization of scientific research. However, it does seem particularly appropriate for industrial location analysis. Some alternative approaches are described in other texts, for example in Harvey (1969, 32–6).

These formal scientific procedures cannot always be applied in practice, of course. Lack of data may mean that it is difficult or impossible to measure certain critical variables, and there are many cases where data are so limited or imprecise that not even a very simple quantitative model can be constructed to test the hypothesis. But whatever explanatory approach is adopted—whether it involves a sophisticated model or simply a loose verbal argument—it must rest on some kind of theoretical foundation. This is why location theory is included in Figure 1.3 feeding into the investigation at the hypothesis-building stage. And the expectation is that the results of the inquiry, if the research has been properly designed, will provide some kind of feedback into theory.

The discussion of the place of theory in locational analysis raises a number of important issues. One of them is the question of the scientific status of locational studies, and of human geography in general, which has still not been resolved to the satisfaction of everyone. On the one hand it is argued that it is possible to formulate laws or principles relating to the spatial arrangement of phenomena, and that a geography capable of this is truly scientific. On the other hand it is held that all geographical phenomena are unique, in location if in no other respect, and that because it is possible to go no further than explaining each individual case on its merits geography cannot produce general truths as a passport to scientific status.

This problem has been discussed at length by Hartshorne (1939, 1959), Bunge (1962), Haggett (1965), Harvey (1969), and others. There now seems to be fairly widespread agreement that the uniqueness of areally distributed phenomena is not a logical barrier to the derivation of generalizations or lawlike statements concerning locational behavior. Uniqueness does not imply that *nothing* is shared with other individuals, only that *not everything* is common to them. So geographical inquiry is now generally conducted on the assumption that there are laws to be discovered.

The basic problem in working toward the formulation of laws or general principles of industrial location, and the development of a body of theory, is that man is the ultimate object of the inquiry. The student of industrial location, whether he calls himself a geographer, economist, or regional scientist, is attempting to understand human behavior in a specific economic context. The location of every industrial plant, and its place in the wider economic system, is the product of a decision taken by an individual or group, which possesses the important human quality of free will. As soon as the exercise of free will is recognized in locational behavior, as in all human affairs, it becomes difficult to envisage any hard and fast laws relating to the spatial arrangement of industrial phenomena. But free will is not incompatible with the formulation of some kind of general statements; there is no a priori reason why locational choices freely made should not exhibit some regularity. Such statements may be of the form of *quasi laws*, or generalizations known to have exceptions. If it is not possible at the moment to explain the minority of exceptional cases, "it surely does not follow that we know nothing at all, or even that what we know is nothing like a law" (Kaplan, 1964, 97). These quasi laws do not state rigid, invariable relationships of the "if x then y" form. They are general statements of tendencies involving high but not perfect correlation between variables, or representing the mean response of individuals to a given set of circumstances. They do not permit the exact prediction of individual behavior, but they should indicate a high degree of probability that the outcome of a particular situation will be of a specified form.

All this is reflected in the growing use in locational analysis of *probabilistic* models, as opposed to the *deterministic* models which hold that events are entirely predictable from certain known conditions or relationships.

Experiences in the field of economics are of special relevance to the development of generalization, laws, and theory in industrial location analysis, and some brief illustrations may be helpful. Consider the very simple assertion that a rise in the price of a good will lead to a fall in its consumption. No economist believes that a price rise is a necessary or sufficient condition for a fall in consumption, but the statement is still a useful general guide to the relationship between two variables. Consider the slightly more complex and formal relational statement made in the equation $D = f(PYT)$, where D is demand for a good, P is its price, Y is income, and T the point in time (that is, demand is a function of price, income, and time). The substitution of numbers in this equation is never likely to give more than an approximate prediction of the volume of demand in any specific situation, but this does not mean that the statement is of no interpretive value. A perfect prediction is possible only if all the variables affecting the result can be built into the equation, and ultimately loaded with accurate empirical data.

The essential procedure of the economist, and the theorist in other behavioral sciences, is to simplify or idealize the real situation to the extent that meaningful statements can be made about what will happen in certain circumstances. Examples of this simplification are the assumptions of the economically rational entrepreneur, perfect competition and a spaceless economy in much microeconomic theory, or of uniform transportation rates and fixed demand in some location theory. Such devices simplify the complex reality that the behavioral scientist faces. If the generalizations or theories that result may seem very broad and sweeping, the assumptions on which they rest can be relaxed as more is known about the phenomena in question, and as the scientist's technical capacity to formulate multivariate models improves.

McNee (1959, 191) has summarized the value of economic theory as follows.

Economics has attained great intellectual heights in the building of abstract models, though these models have not always been tested in the real world. Perhaps many of them are not testable. Nevertheless these models are of great value in interpreting, if not predicting, economic behavior in the real world. As guiding hypotheses, they are superior to anything else thus far developed in the social sciences.

If the economist has been so successful in producing a body of theory relating to what and how much people will produce or purchase in given circumstances, and at what price, the problems involved in theorizing about where units of production are located may not be as forbidding as some of the geographical literature may suggest. Perhaps the geographer has been too ambitious in his search for the grand, all-embracing theory, failing to step back far enough from the real world to simplify the problem down to bare essentials as the economist does. Perhaps this is an inevitable outcome of the geographer's traditional and deep-rooted preference for generalization via empirical experience, as against the more abstract approach from which the economist has gained so much.

A body of theory can be developed in two ways. These are generally referred to as the *deductive* and *inductive* approaches. The deductive approach starts from a set of basic propositions and proceeds by logical reasoning to deduce the consequences. In the field of industrial location, such an approach might begin with the proposition that people go into business to make as much money as possible and that their success will be determined by the interaction of specified variables, from which certain generalizations concerning the forms adopted by an industrial location pattern might be deduced. Such generalizations, which might be stated as laws, are shown to be the logical consequences of the initial propositions. The soundness of these generalizations is subject to empirical testing, and their failure to conform with reality may reveal weaknesses in the assumptions or in the logical structure of the theory.

The inductive approach stresses the search for generalization through empirical inquiry. The observation of a spatial association, such as that between processing plants and railroad stations in the imaginary case above, may lead to the discovery of a causal relationship, and the study of other industries may produce generalizations concerning the causal factors responsible for their particular location patterns. The relating of these generalizations to each other, and to other established general truths, constitutes a theoretical system.

The most effective way toward the more complete understanding of industrial location at the present time appears to be through a largely deductive theoretical approach. This must inevitably lean heavily on economic theory for its methods of construction as well as for its substance. It may well be, as Harvey (1967, 1969) convincingly argues, that geographical theory is essentially derivative, concerned with elaborating economic, sociological, political, and psychological theory in a spatial context. Thus, industrial location theory generally attempts to deduce the spatial form adopted by industrial activity from the postulates of economics. The observation by McCarty (1940, xiii) that "economic geography derives its concepts largely from the field of economics and its methods largely from the field of geography" is still generally applicable to the study of industrial location.

The rather abstract deductive approach to the development of theory does have its dangers, however. As Isard (1956, viii) recognized, such theoretical deliberations have the habit of turning in on themselves, tending to grow more and more remote from the real world. This is why great importance is attached here to the development of *operational models* from industrial location theory. At the present time, great stress is being placed on the role of models in geographical inquiry (for example, Haggett, 1965; Chorley and Haggett, 1967), but any precise meaning the term model once may have had has been obscured by the current tendency to dignify almost any explanatory or descriptive device with this label. Broadly speaking, anything may be regarded as a model of something else if it replicates it in a way that makes the study of the one useful in trying to understand the other. But it may be better to think of models in a more restricted sense, as the formal expression of theory in which the relevant variables and the relationship between them are specified. When fed with the appropriate empirical data, such a model should be capable of generating an outcome that can be compared with the situation observed in the real world. The capacity of a model to replicate reality constitutes a test of the validity of the theory from which the model has been derived.

The inductive approach must be pursued along with the development of deductive theory, however. This involves the identification of empirical regularities and relationships broad enough in their validity to warrant the status of laws or quasi laws. The kind of spatial regularities which may be found in the industrial world can be divided into three types: (1) interval laws, relating to the distances separating phenomena of the same class—for example, the distance between grain elevators along a railroad line; (2) laws stating relationships between the occurrence of phenomena and distance from some fixed point, like the relationship between land costs and distance from a city center; and (3) pattern laws, which find phenomena in a certain spatial form, such as the hexagonal net of central place theory. These generalizations can usefully be concerned with properties of the variables affecting plant location, for example with spatial variations in the cost of inputs, as well as with the occurrence of the factories themselves. Other generalizations or laws may involve the precise statement of observed relationships between the location of certain activities and specific independent variables. Initially, few of these general statements can be expected to be of universal validity in the sense of being applicable to all parts of the world, but, as McCarty (1954, 101) has suggested, geography can find great use for principles that are applicable to only a relatively small part of the earth's surface. In the course of time, and as the principles are refined, they should take on a wider generality in the areal sense. But at present the achievement of universality through generalizations applicable to all times and places is a very long way away (McCarty and Lindberg, 1966, 46).

It is important to stress the inseparability of the deductive and inductive approaches. In locational analysis, as in most other fields, there has been a constant interplay between the two (Smith, Taaffe, and King, 1968, 14). Deductive theory needs frequent reference to the real world if it is to have any practical interpretive value, just as empirical inquiry directed toward lawlike statements must feed on more abstract theory. The emphasis on the deductive approach here arises from the belief that the application of this kind of theory is at present the most fruitful way of advancing the understanding of industrial location. Decades of empirical research have failed to produce the kind of generalizations or laws necessary to form the building blocks of a theory of industrial location based on the inductive approach, and one of the reasons for this has been the inadequate conceptual basis of most of the case studies. Yet there is a substantial body of abstract theory already in existence, and capable of extension, which has not been sufficiently tested in the arena of empirical inquiry.

This book is thus concerned primarily with an exposition of industrial location theory which is of a rather abstract nature. But a major objective is also to give operational meaning to theoretical concepts in order to demonstrate their application in empirical inquiry and in a practical problem-solving context. The empirical applications may seem rather tentative and unsatisfactory at times, as is inevitable in a field of inquiry still in its infancy. But it is only by continually crossing and recrossing the bridge between theory and the real industrial world that knowledge and understanding can be advanced. And it is only when substantial advances in this direction have been made that man can use planned industrial development as a more effective and predictable means of achieving his economic and social objectives.

PART ONE

The Variables in Industrial Location

Industrial activity is seldom if ever found evenly spread over the earth's surface, or distributed in an apparently random fashion. There may be relatively small areas with patterns of this kind, but generally some grouping of plants occurs, with manufacturing typically concentrated in certain localities. These concentrations may take the form of an isolated industrial town in a predominantly rural area, groups of neighboring towns, or more extensive regional agglomerations. Why do such concentrations of industrial activity take place, and why do they occur where they do?

When individual towns or industrial districts are examined, their economic character is found to vary one from another. Some places have a wide range of industries, including ones that are closely related to each other and some that may have little or no connection with other local activities. Other places have a narrower industrial base, and may concentrate largely on one industry or group of related trades. Why are these differences found, and what determines the industrial structure of particular cities, regions, or nations?

The study of specific industries reveals wide variation in their distribution patterns. Some are dispersed in a fairly regular manner throughout whole regions or countries, with no area standing out as being particularly important. Others may be highly concentrated, perhaps largely confined to one region, one city, or even a certain section of a city. Many industries show entirely different patterns of distribution at different points in time; some are contracting from an earlier era of greater prosperity, while others may show vigorous growth and a tendency to disperse to new locations. Why do different industries adopt different patterns, and what makes these patterns change through time?

Attempts to plan industrial development raise similar questions. Some parts of the world appear to be favorable locations for the establishment of new industry, while in other areas there seems to be no future for modern manufacturing activities. Some firms are found to be highly mobile, and can be successfully directed to a variety of new locations, but others would quickly fail if moved any distance from their present sites. Why is it that the future industrial potential of all places is not the same, and why is it that some activities have more locational mobility than others?

These, put very simply, are some of the basic explanatory problems that the student of industrial location faces. These are the problems toward which empirical research is directed, many of them having important practical implications in the fields of development planning, resource allocation, and public policy. And these are the sort of questions that industrial location theory should be able to help to answer, by guiding research toward a fuller understanding of the plant location decision and the spatial economic context within which it is made. The development of a theoretical framework for industrial location analysis is the major objective of this book. But before attempting this, some elementary facts about the forces influencing industrial location must be introduced, along with a necessary minimum of industrial economics and elementary microeconomic theory.

Part One thus serves the purpose of identifying the relevant independent variables in industrial location analysis. The objective is to examine the causal factors in the plant-location decision in a very general way, with appropriate illustrations. First, there is a brief discussion of some preliminary matters, including the combination of inputs and the concept of cost structure (Chapter 2). Chapter 3 covers the major inputs in the production process, and Chapter 4 deals with the effect of the market. Chapter 5 examines transportation. Chapter 6 reviews some other considerations, including the effect of externalities, public policy, and the personal factor in location decision making.

2

Some Preliminary Matters

Manufacturing involves changing the utility of goods and hence increasing their value. The necessary materials have to be assembled at the plant, along with the factors of production required to undertake the process of manufacture. Then the materials are converted into the finished product, or output, which is subsequently shipped to the consumer. Transportation enters the picture both at the stage of material assembly and for the distribution of the finished product (Figure 2.1).

In setting up a factory a manufacturer must make three decisions, or sets of decisions, which will together determine success or failure: (1) the *scale* of operations, including how much is to be produced and at what price it is to be offered to the consumer; (2) the *technique* to be adopted, which involves the selection of the appropriate combination of factors of production; and (3) the *location* of the factory.

The choice of location cannot be considered in isolation from scale and technique, since they are all interrelated (Figure 2.1). Different scales of operation may require different locations to give access to markets of different sizes, and if the location decision is made first this may have an important bearing on the output that the firm can reasonably expect to sell. Different techniques will favor different locations, as firms tend to gravitate toward cheap sources of the factors that they require in the largest quantities, and location itself can influence the combination of factors and hence the technique adopted. Scale and technique similarly affect each other, but this is of less direct importance in the present context than the reciprocal relationship between scale and location, on the one hand, and technique and location, on the other.

The two major sets of economic variables influencing industrial location are thus those relating to technique and those relating to scale. The

26 THE VARIABLES IN INDUSTRIAL LOCATION

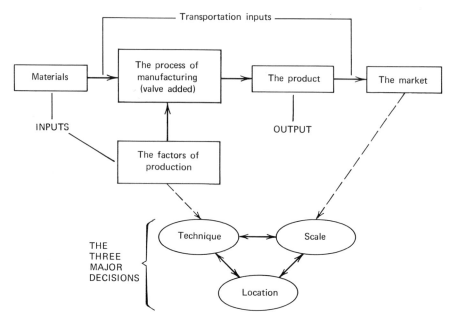

Figure 2.1. The manufacturing process and the three major decisions.

former will be considered in the remainder of this chapter and in the discussion of the major inputs in the chapters that follow, while the latter will be dealt with in detail in Chapter 4. The way these variables affect and are affected by location is very important, and its introduction here helps to emphasize at the outset the interrelationship of the different decisions the businessman has to make. His success may not be determined by choice of location alone, but technique and scale as they influence profits cannot be divorced from location.

2.1 THE FACTORS OF PRODUCTION, INPUT COMBINATION, AND COST STRUCTURE

To produce any commodity, the businessman, or *entrepreneur*, must assemble at one point the necessary *factors of production*. They are conventionally listed as land, labor, capital, and enterprise, and they may be combined in different proportions for different industries. Some activities are *labor intensive*, using a large amount of labor in relation to other factors; some are *capital intensive*, perhaps highly mechanized with large quantities of physical plant per worker; some make more extensive use of land than others; and so on. Generally, some *substitution* between factors

SOME PRELIMINARY MATTERS 27

of production is possible, particularly between labor and capital, and firms in the same industry may find it profitable to employ different combinations of factors in different locations or for different volumes of output.

How an entrepreneur might decide his combination of factors in a simplified situation is illustrated in Figure 2.2. Assume that a firm uses two factors of production X and Y (say, capital and labor). One unit of X costs him $10, as does one unit of Y, so for $100 he can buy 10 units of X, 10 of Y, or some combination of the two, such as 5 units of each. The various combinations of the two factors that can be purchased with

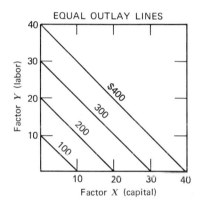
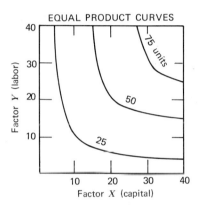

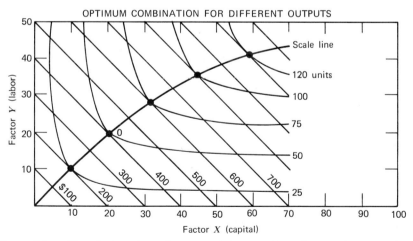

Figure 2.2. The choice of combination of factors of production (or inputs), in relation to outlay and scale.

given sums of money are shown as *equal outlay lines*. Next, the combinations of factors that will enable a given output to be achieved are identified and are plotted as *equal product curves*. These are typically convex to the origin of the graph, reflecting the fact that there is a necessary minimum requirement for each factor of production; for example, 50 units of output can be produced from any of the combinations of factors indicated by the appropriate equal product curve, which shows that although some substitution between factors is possible a minimum of about 15 units of capital and 15 units of labor is needed. The optimum or least-cost combination of factors can now be found by putting the equal outlay lines and equal product curves together. For any scale of output, the optimum combination of factors is revealed by the point where the appropriate equal product curve is tangential to the lowest value equal outlay line. In Figure 2.2 the 50 equal product curve touches the $400 equal outlay line at O, which represents 19 units of labor and 21 units of capital, this being the combination of factors that costs least for the required output. Any other point on the 50 equal product curve will be above the $400 line, and will increase costs, while any movement along the $400 line (for example, down, toward more capital) will reduce output by moving off the 50 units curve. The points of tangency for different scales of production can be joined to form a *scale line* (sometimes termed an *expansion path*), which here indicates a tendency for the proportion of capital to labor to rise with output. This illustration includes only two of the necessary factors, but the principles involved in deciding the overall combination will be the same.

The supply of factors of production is closely related to their *mobility*. The concept of the mobility of factors can be thought of as applying between different activities as well as spatially, but it is in the latter context that it is particularly important in industrial location analysis. Whether factors are geographically immobile, imperfectly mobile (that is, transportable at a cost), or perfectly mobile (that is, ubiquitous) will obviously influence their availability to an entrepreneur at a given location.

It will be clear that the combination of factors of production, and their availability from place to place, will have a very important bearing on the choice of a factory site. But in industrial location analysis it is seldom convenient to base an explanatory study on the four conventional categories of land, labor, capital, and enterprise. These are too broad, and it is generally necessary to subdivide some if not all of them in order to identify precisely the major influences at work on locational choice. This introduces the concept of *input combination*, with the term input used to denote any item on which expenditure is incurred in the manufacture and distribution of the product. For any firm or industry, the combination of inputs can be categorized in whatever manner is most meaningful in relation to the locational decision; for example, in some cases it may be necessary to divide the materials item into a large number of different categories, while in other situations the recognition of different grades of labor with their particular skills may be important.

As in the case of the factors of production, the combination of inputs will vary from industry to industry, from firm to firm, and from place to place. In order to identify these variations it is necessary to have some common unit of measurement so that the importance of different items can be compared, and this is provided by monetary cost. The *cost structure* of any industry or firm thus indicates the relative cost of the required quantity of the various inputs needed to produce a given output, or to operate a plant over a given period of time. These values are generally referred to as the *input coefficients*. The concepts of cost structure and input combination are of great importance to industrial location analysis, as will be shown in subsequent chapters.

2.2 COST STRUCTURES ILLUSTRATED

As a specific illustration of cost structures, the annual (1963) expenditures on the major inputs are listed in Table 2.1 for six American industries. These have been selected to demonstrate the variety of input combinations that may be found. The first two are examples of material orientation, with wheat accounting for more than half the total value of shipments in flour milling, and expenditure on ores only a little short of 50 percent in primary zinc manufacture. The manufacture of dresses is highly labor intensive, with a long tradition of using large quantities of cheap female labor rather than adopting extensive mechanization. The newspaper industry illustrates another kind of labor intensive activity, with a very large salaries item in addition to the wages of production workers. The manufacture of industrial gases is of interest as one of the few cases in which capital expenditure accounts for a high proportion of total annual costs, while the lace industry shows a rough balance between labor and material costs.

As the figures in Table 2.1 suggest, the importance of any single cost item can vary considerably from industry to industry. A detailed analysis of the 1947 U.S. *Census of Manufacturing* (Chicago and Eastern Illinois Railroad, 1953), although now rather dated, provides some interesting information on this subject. The study was based on the four-digit level of the industrial classification, which contained 452 categories at that time,

Table 2.1 The Cost Structure of Selected Industries in the United States, 1963 (Millions of Dollars)

1. *Flour Milling*		2. *Manufacturing Primary Zinc*	
Wages	95	Wages	36
Salaries, etc.	43	Salaries, etc.	12
Capital	23	Capital	5
Energy and fuels	15	Energy and fuels	19
Wheat	1313	Zinc ores, etc.	135
Other materials	687	Other materials	17
Value of shipments	2177	Value of shipments	282
3. *Dresses (Contractors)*		4. *Newspapers*	
Wages	320	Wages	935
Salaries, etc.	26	Salaries, etc.	850
Capital	4	Capital	135
Energy and fuels	4	Energy and fuels	27
Materials	23	Newsprint	889
		Other materials	273
Value of shipments	465	Value of shipments	4484
5. *Industrial Gases*		6. *Lace Goods*	
Wages	33	Wages	16
Salaries, etc.	34	Salaries, etc.	4
Capital	94	Capital	1
Electricity	31	Energy and fuels	1
Fuels	6	Cotton yarn	4
Materials	127	Man-made fibers	9
		Other materials	7
Value of shipments	425	Value of shipments	53

Source. *Census of Manufacturing*, 1963, Vol. II. Wages refer to payment to production workers, while salaries etc. are the rest of the 1963 payroll. The capital item represents expenditure on new plants and machinery in 1963. Note: the items listed here do not necessarily represent the total value of shipments.

and examined the proportion of total value of shipments accounted for by four broad groups of inputs. In the first—materials, parts, containers and supplies—the highest proportion was in tobacco stemming and redrying with 92.3 percent, while the minimum was 2.9 percent in miscellaneous structural clay products; the median percentage was 46.6. For fuels and purchased electric energy the range was from 37 percent in blast furnaces to 0.1 percent in book publishing and printing, and the median was just under 1 percent. Production workers wages varied from 67.8 percent in the manufacture of earthenware food utensils to 7.7 in book publishing, with a median of 42 percent. Finally the salaries of nonproduction workers

Table 2.2 The Cost Structure of a Typical Small Steel-Products Manufacturer in Alternative Ontario Locations

	Percentages of Total Spatially Variable Costs				
Location	Labor	Transportation	Utilities	Land and Building	Local Taxes
Barrie	36.6	32.2	17.1	8.7	5.4
Brampton	42.4	24.8	18.2	9.4	5.3
Georgetown	41.8	26.6	20.6	8.8	2.2
Lindsay	38.6	30.9	19.7	7.0	3.8
Orangeville	35.3	33.4	19.8	7.5	4.1
Preston	38.0	28.8	19.6	7.7	5.8
Stratford	36.8	33.4	19.7	7.5	2.7

Source. The Fantus Company, location consultants (unpublished data). The figures refer to the early 1960s, and are based on a labor force of 22, a 10-acre site, a 30,000 sq ft building, and amortization over 20 years. Because of roundings the figures for each location may not add up to exactly 100.

reached a maximum of 39.1 in the production of aircraft propellers to a lowest value of 2.2 in linseed oil mills; the median percentage was 12.1.

Table 2.2 illustrates the way in which the cost structure of a particular firm can vary between locations. This example is based on the requirements of a manufacturing concern in the steel products industry, and shows the percentage distribution of costs among five spatially variable input categories in seven Ontario cities. The proportion accounted for by labor costs can be seen to vary from a high of 42.4 percent down to 35.3 percent while transportation, which is generally less important than labor in percentage terms, has a greater variation—from 33.4 to 24.8 percent. The costs of utilities and of land and building vary much less between alternative locations, but in local taxes, the smallest item, the variations are more extreme in relative terms than for any of the other inputs. The differences in proportions reflect variations between the seven cities in the cost of the inputs in question.

Further illustrations of cost structures will be found in later chapters, where the place of this concept in industrial location analysis will be examined more extensively.

3

The Major Inputs

This chapter reviews the major inputs required in the production process. For convenience, these are considered under the general headings of land, capital, materials and power, labor, state and local taxes, and enterprise. The purpose is to introduce some elementary facts concerning these inputs, and to determine how far it is possible to generalize about their spatial incidence.

3.1 LAND

The need for land goes far beyond simply requiring ground on which to put the factory. The land occupied by the physical plant is of course very important, and may be hundreds of acres in the case of, say, an iron and steel works or an oil refinery, but the plant itself often occupies a relatively small part of the land area that the firm owns. Land is also needed for such purposes as the storage of materials and finished products, the parking of cars and trucks, and internal vehicular circulation, and few firms now put up a factory without making sure they have enough room to expand.

Firms with large requirements for land will obviously find it more easily in some places than in others. It will be particularly difficult to find (and costly to acquire) in and around big cities where undeveloped land is scarce and competition from other users is strong. Many existing firms in urban areas have less space than they need, and expansion may be economically impossible. Also it may be prevented by land-use zoning laws. Even outside urban areas, amenity issues such as the preservation of green belts and areas of outstanding natural beauty may prevent industry from occupying otherwise suitable land.

For many firms a particular kind of site may be required, with certain special physical attributes. For example, textile manufacturing during the early stages of the Industrial Revolution needed water-power sites, and often also a place where the configuration of the land facilitated the building of a dam for storing water. These features could, of course, be created anywhere given sufficient capital, but it reduced the initial outlay if they already existed naturally. Access to water for use in industrial processes, and proximity to a river, canal, or lake into which effluence can be deposited, is still a major consideration for many firms. Level land may be important for industries with extensive areas of plant, and some firms need a very solid site, preferably with bedrock near the surface, to support special equipment. Services such as sewers, gas and electricity connections, and good road access can also be regarded as desirable physical attributes of land.

The cost of land varies considerably from place to place, and the geographical pattern that it adopts is often quite complex. But enough research has been done on land values to permit some broad generalizations. A basic distinction can be made between the pattern observed over a whole country or other extensive piece of territory, where fairly regular changes in land costs may be observed over long distances, and the situation in individual cities or metropolitan areas where much more dramatic local variations are likely to be found.

As an illustration of broad regional variations within a nation, Table 3.1 lists average costs of land in nine subdivisions of England and Wales. The highest costs are in Greater London, as might be expected, with a figure almost twice that of any other area. Then come the three other parts of the metropolitan core of southeast England. In the Midlands and the peripheral regions, including Wales, average land costs are considerably lower, seldom reaching half the figure in any of the core areas. The general impression of the relationship between cost and distance is of a peak represented by Greater London, with costs falling away rapidly at first and then evening out to form a fairly regular curve. But the figures in Table 3.1 represent the averages of samples, within which the cost of land varies considerably with the quality and exact location of the site. For example, in Greater London the range is from less than £ 10,000 per acre to over £ 75,000; in the Midlands it is from £ 1500 to £ 31,000; and in the Northwest the range is £ 2000 to over £ 18,000. Thus the fairly regular decrease away from London when viewed at a broad regional level, although a useful generalization, is very much a simplified picture of reality when intraregional cost variations are taken into account.

As a second example, this time relating specifically to land for indus-

Table 3.1 The Average Cost of Land Developed for Residential Purposes in England and Wales, 1966-1967

Region	Houses (£ per Acre)	Low-Rise Apartments (£ per Acre)
Metropolitan Core		
Greater London	27,783	42,685
Southeastern counties	12,749	19,809
Southern counties	11,368	21,764
Bedfordshire, Essex, and Hertfordshire	15,328	23,015
Midlands and Peripheral Areas		
Midlands	6,135	14,713
Southwest	5,222	12,129
Yorkshire and Humberside	4,282	10,107
Northwest	4,282	8,130
Wales	2,296	10,136

Source. National Building Agency (1968). The figures are based on a sample of 392 projects, and are considered representative of prices paid by private land purchasers.

trial purposes, Table 3.2 presents cost data for a selection of Canadian cities. The cities are listed from east to west, top to bottom of the table. The highest prices are in Montreal and the major Ontario industrial cities, but by the time the smaller cities of western Ontario are reached the figure has fallen considerably. The lowest costs are in the interior

Table 3.2 Two Estimates of the Cost of Improved Industrial Land in a Selection of Canadian Cities

City	For a 5–15 Acre Site (Dollars/Acre)[a]	For a 10 Acre Site (Dollars/Acre)[b]
Montreal, Que.	30,000–50,000	30,000–40,000
Toronto, Ont.	20,000–35,000	20,000–30,000
Hamilton, Ont.	10,000–18,000	10,000–15,000
Stratford, Ont.	2,000– 3,000	No data
Windsor, Ont.	5,000–10,000	5,000– 7,500
Winnipeg, Man.	4,000– 8,000	4,500– 6,500
Portage la Prairie, Man.	1,000– 2,000	1,000– 2,000
Regina, Sask.	3,500– 5,500	3,500– 5,500
Saskatoon, Sask.	3,500– 5,500	3,000– 5,000
Edmonton, Alb.	3,000–10,000	7,000–10,000
Red Deer, Alb.	2,000– 4,000	No data
Calgary, Alb.	5,000–11,000	5,000– 8,000
Vancouver, B.C.	6,000–12,000	6,000–11,000

[a] Source. Noyes Development Corporation (1965).
[b] Source. The Fantus Company, 1962 (unpublished data).

plains, as exemplified by Portage la Prairie and Red Deer, with somewhat higher figures in the larger cities such as Winnipeg, Calgary, and Edmonton. On the west coast the data for Vancouver indicate an increase compared with the cities of the interior. The broad national pattern in Canada thus compares closely with that revealed in England and Wales, being described fairly accurately by a curve with its peak at Montreal, falling rapidly to even out over the prairies, and with perhaps a slight upturn as the west coast is reached. But again this obscures the extent of local variation in the cost of industrial land (as indicated in Table 3.2).

How far is it possible to generalize about the pattern of land costs at a more local level, within the major city or metropolitan area? Figure 3.1 shows a very broad profile for London, based on average costs of residential sites in five-mile distance bands from Charing Cross in the city center. A peak of almost £ 90,000 per acre is found in the inner band, falling to less than one half of this figure in the next band. Then the profile begins to flatten out, to rise slightly between 20 and 25 miles from the city center where pressure for good-quality residential development in outer suburbia conflicts with the designated green belt. A similar curve is shown in Figure 3.1 for Okayama, Japan. In this case the data are for narrower distance bands around the peak value point, and stress the very steep fall in land values over short distances in the inner part of the city.

There is ample evidence to suggest that the general form of the London and Okayama land-cost profiles is common to many other cities. For example, the profile for Chicago in the 1950s, as illustrated by Colin Clark (1967, 384), shows a very steep fall away from downtown prices of about $100 per square foot to level off at around $1 three to four miles out, and even replicates London's upturn as the suburbs are reached. Other studies that support the general impression of a strongly marked concave profile include those of van Cleef (1949) on Denver and Knoss (1962) on Topeka. Variations in the cost of land with distance from the city center can thus be described fairly accurately by a straight line on a graph where distance is plotted on an arithmetic scale and cost on a logarithmic scale (Clark, 1967, Chapter IX).

In the discussion of broad regional land-cost variations, above, it was stressed that generalized profiles hide a large amount of local or intraregional variation. The same is true at the level of the individual city. The decline in land values away from the city center is not characterized by a smooth curve when examined in detail; instead, it comprises an irregular profile that generally declines with distance from the peak but that is interrupted by minor elevations or local peaks. More specifically, ridges of higher values radiate from the central peak along major traffic arteries, with the back of each ridge falling with distance from the

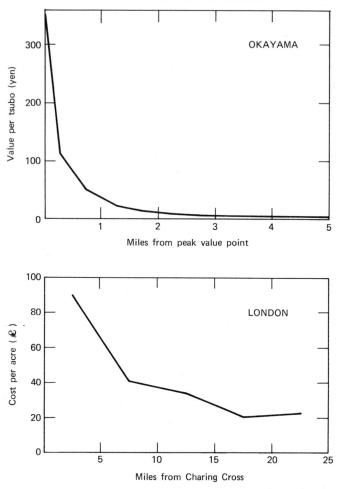

Figure 3.1. Generalized land-cost profiles for Greater London, England, and Okayama, Japan. (*Sources of Data.* National Building Agency, 1968, 13, for London, and Hawley, 1955, Table 3, for Okayama.)

central peak. Between each ridge are troughs of varying elevation and depth, separated from each other by circumferential ridges connecting the radial ridges. Local land-value peaks are formed where the radial and circumferential ridges intersect (Garner, 1966, 19–20). An interesting graphic illustration of this kind of pattern will be found in Berry et al (1963, 14; see also Garner, 1967, 337).

Whatever the exact details of the urban land-cost pattern, it is clear that the price a manufacturer will have to pay for a factory site will vary within a very wide range in most cities. This can be illustrated by figures for the cost of a ten-acre industrial site in different parts of the New York metropolitan region (Hoover and Vernon, 1959, 259). Information on a selection of sites in 1957 revealed the highest costs in the Bronx, with a median of $1,100,000, in Queens ($870,000), and in Brooklyn ($850,000). But even within these areas there were extreme local variations in cost, from $1,300,000 to $950,000 in the Bronx, $1,750,000 to $550,000 in Queens, and from $1,300,000 to $450,000 in Brooklyn. At the bottom end of the scale, median costs of between $50,000 and $30,000 were found in Rockland, Morris, and Monmouth.

How far do these variations, and others that may exist at an intercity or interregional level, really influence the manufacturer's choice of location? Although the cost of land is often a major item in the initial expenditure involved in setting up a factory, it is insignificant in most industries when costed over a long period, or when rent is expressed as a proportion of total production costs. Although this leads many observers to conclude that the cost of land is of little importance when compared with other major inputs, there are some who feel that greater practical and theoretical emphasis should be placed on land costs (for example, Logan, 1966). It is certainly true that a firm with average land needs will not be particularly sensitive to quite substantial variations in the cost of comparable sites, especially if the higher-cost locations have advantages with respect to access to more important inputs. But sites that are otherwise highly desirable may have to be eliminated because of the prohibitively high cost of land. This is generally true of many city center locations, where the manufacture is unable to outbid commercial users for land around the peak value point. So, even if the cost of land is relatively insignificant as a determinant of plant location among a number of possible sites, there may be some where the price that other users are prepared to pay will effectively exclude any form of manufacturing.

3.2 CAPITAL

The term capital in its broadest sense refers to all things deliberately made by man for use in the production process. This section deals with a number of related matters, which fall under the general heading of capital. They include both financial capital and the fixed capital represented by the physical plant.

Financial capital is needed before land or any of the other inputs can be acquired. Obtaining capital is generally no problem for the large modern industrial corporation, whose activities are financed internally from retained earnings and depreciation reserves, and externally in the national money market through the issue of shares. This has tended to weaken the locational influence of local capital supplies for the large well-established national concern (Thompson, 1968, 54). But for small firms and those just starting up, local supplies of capital may be very important, both as sources of commercial credit for working capital and as equity money. This kind of capital may be obtainable easier in some places than others; for example, a man going into business for the first time may be able to get backing from friends and relatives in his home town, as well as from local banks where his personal capabilities and credit standing are known, but if he went to another city he might be refused support. As Chinitz (1961, 285) has remarked, "The cost of transferring confidence may be high enough to give us a capital-supply function which has distance as an important independent variable." Particular kinds of activities may be easier to finance in some places than in others; in the textile industry in Britain at the time of the Industrial Revolution, for example, innovations in machinery got financial backing easier in existing textile manufacturing towns than in places less familiar with the likely profit and risk involved (Smith, 1962; 1965, 64).

An important feature that distinguishes financial capital from the land input is mobility. Funds are in fact perfectly mobile, and it is areal differences in risk that prevent uniform interest rates and introduce an element of immobility (Beckmann, 1968, 101). Since land is of course perfectly immobile, capital can move to the right piece of land but the reverse is impossible.

Capital can be obtained in any location, provided that a high enough return is offered, but rates appear not to differ very much in advanced industrial nations. During the course of a number of plant-location studies for clients, the Fantus Company calculated the average annual financing cost, including principal and interest, for a selection of American and Canadian cities and found no significant relationship with either the location of the cities or their size (unpublished data). The figures ranged from 9.31 percent in Charlottesville, Virginia, to 7.92 percent in the Kentucky cities of Elizabethtown and Cynthiana, but of the thirty-four cities examined only eight had figures outside the range 8.30 to 8.60. The largest place, the Chicago metropolitan area (1960 population 6,743,000), was found to have an annual financing cost of 8.30 percent, which was exactly the same as in Bentonville, Arkansas, the smallest place considered (3600 people in 1960). The cost of financial capital is thus not very influential in locational choice in the modern industrial state.

Turning now to *fixed capital equipment*, this is much more like land than monetary funds in terms of spatial mobility. Machinery, buildings, and other kinds of physical plant are usually permanently fixed in space. Most industrial buildings are for all practical purposes perfectly immobile, and because in certain circumstances they have the capacity to attract the more mobile factors of capital and enterprise after they have been vacated by their original owners, they tend to perpetuate existing industrial location patterns by successive reoccupation. This is part of the tendency sometimes referred to as *industrial inertia*.

To a firm setting up in business or looking for room for expansion the presence of an existing building ready for immediate occupation may be a major and even a deciding factor in the choice of location. This is particularly true if the cost of the existing factory is substantially less than the cost of a new one. Examples of new firms reoccupying old premises could no doubt be found in any industrial town or city, but there are a few instances where vacant premises have existed in such large numbers that the economic structure and prospects of entire regions have been affected. An illustration is provided by the former cotton-manufacturing region of Lancashire in England, where the rapid decline of the textile trade during the past half century has led to the vacation of many hundreds of mill buildings, which can be obtained very cheaply indeed. A survey conducted in 1962 (Holt, 1964) showed that of 622 mills closed in the region since 1951, 414 had been converted to other uses by 1962 and an additional 63 had been partially converted, leaving only 145 vacant or demolished. The reoccupation of Lancashire mills must be one of the most extensive industrial recolonizations in history, having brought many replacement industries to a region very much in need of new employment opportunities.

Other examples of the same thing readily come to mind. In New England the reoccupation of textile mills has taken place on a scale comparable with Lancashire. Many of the mills and warehouses of Nottingham in England, at one time the thriving center of the world's lace trade, have been taken over by other activities since the collapse of the lace industry in the 1920s. Clothing manufacturing is often located in converted premises in the relatively low rental areas of urban blight around the city center. And many industries with a small size of plant and a low degree of mechanization can exist quite happily and profitably in any small workshop where the rent is low; for example, in Birmingham, England, highly specialized industrial districts making jewelry and quality sporting guns respectively grew up in former residential areas around the city center during the nineteenth century (Wise, 1950; Smith, 1964).

By providing cheap premises, the conversion or reoccupation of an existing building often enables a firm to enter business in circumstances where the cost of a new factory would have been prohibitive. Old premises thus serve the useful function of "industrial nurseries" (Freeman and Rodgers, 1966, 145). But many if not most firms need new premises built to their own specific requirements. They may need to accommodate special machinery or create certain physical conditions like high humidity in spinning mills or clean air in a plant making precision instruments.

The cost of factory construction may vary from place to place, and this can have an important bearing on the locational choice of a firm where construction costs form a significant element in total cost or in the initial investment. There is some evidence to show that the cost of factory construction can vary geographically in a fairly regular fashion. The total cost indexes published regularly for the United States and Canada by the F. W. Dodge Company (1969) and others show very significant regional variations. Lowest costs are found in the southern states of Alabama, North Carolina, and Virginia, and in certain parts of eastern Canada, while the highest figures are in the major manufacturing belt. The geographical pattern revealed by these figures is illustrated in detail in a later chapter (Figure 15.2). They tend to follow a similar pattern to that of average wage levels, which suggests that local construction costs are rather sensitive to the prevailing cost of labor. But in their investigation of the New York metropolitan area, Hoover and Vernon (1959, 257–261) found that local wage rates did little to explain differences from place to place in construction costs, and felt that these would have to be accounted for by factors that elude precise measurement, such as the productivity of labor and special requirements (for example, sidewalk protection and site enclosure). Whatever the detailed reasons, it seems fair to conclude that the general position of a possible plant location within a country or major metropolitan area may have quite an important bearing on construction costs.

The other major item of fixed capital is the machinery and other equipment placed in the factory in order to perform the manufacturing process. The amount and technical complexity of this plant will vary greatly between industries and between firms. In some places machinery may be easier to obtain, repair, and replace than in others, since cities concentrating on a particular activity often have specialized machine makers to serve it. And there may be situations where the cost of machinery varies slightly between different suppliers. But any really significant differences are likely to be a result of the freight cost to the factory site, a matter more conveniently dealt with in Chapter 5 on transportation.

3.3 MATERIALS AND POWER

All manufacturing activities require *materials*, since the essence of an industrial process is the conversion of something into a good which has greater utility. Materials may be of an extractive nature (like iron ore, stone, or timber) or they may be goods manufactured elsewhere (like the components that an engineering firm may purchase from outside). Some activities, like metal smelting or cotton spinning, use a very small number of materials, sometimes only one of any importance, whereas others, like the manufacture of motor cars, may require components from hundreds of separate suppliers. Materials vary enormously in such aspects as bulk, weight, and perishability, and some need special means of transport as well as handling and storage facilities at the factory.

Materials are not evenly spread over the earth's surface. Their distribution is a major determinant of plant location, which has been emphasized by geographers for a long time and also occupies an important place in some of the economic approaches to industrial location theory. The effect of the material inputs is, in fact, so familar that little elaboration is required, and the discussion here is confined to a few summary comments.

Assembling materials and components at the factory is in most industries a large and continuing item of expenditure. In Table 3.3 the cost of materials as a proportion of the total value of shipments is listed for the major industry groups in the United States, with figures for the payroll included for comparison. The industries are arranged in order of the relative size of the materials item, which ranges between a maximum of almost 80 percent down to 35 percent. In one half of the industries, materials account for more than 50 percent of the total value of shipments, and in none does the payroll come to more than the cost of materials. In all American industry material costs account for $2\frac{1}{2}$ times that of the payroll.

The expenditure incurred in acquiring materials involves both the cost of extraction or production and the cost of transporting them to the factory. The cost of extracting a mineral or manufacturing a component will affect locational choice only if there are significant variations in the price at different sources. It appears to be increasingly the case for such variations to be reduced or eliminated, sometimes by agreements within the supplying industry, and there is also the important tendency for the large corporation (in automobiles, for example) to extend its ownership to include major sources of material so that the supply and

Table 3.3 The Importance of the Cost of Materials as Compared with the Payroll in Major American Industries, 1963

Major Industry Group	Cost as a Percentage of Total Value of Shipments	
	Materials	Payroll
Petroleum and coal products	79	7
Food	68	13
Tobacco	63	7
Textiles	61	22
Transportation equipment	59	21
Primary metals	57	22
Lumber and wood	56	26
Apparel	55	25
Paper	55	21
Leather	51	29
Fabricated metal products	49	28
Rubber and plastics	49	26
Furniture and fixtures	48	30
Miscellaneous	46	28
Chemicals	45	16
Machinery (excluding electrical)	44	31
Electrical machinery	43	31
Stone, clay, and glass products	43	26
Printing and publishing	36	34
Instruments	35	32
All industries	55	22

Source. *Census of Manufacturing,* 1963.

price are completely within its control. Thus, in very many instances, the cost of materials at source can be ignored as an influence on plant location. This leaves transport costs, which can be a vital matter not only in selecting the location for the factory but also in deciding between alternative sources of raw materials and components. The discussion of transportation and freight rates is reserved for Chapter 5. Another consideration, which has an important bearing on what a manufacturer has to pay for his materials, is the pricing policy of the supplier. If a uniform delivered price is adopted, as is often the case today, the cost of the material to the manufacturer will of course be the same anywhere, and the effect of that particular input as an influence on the choice of plant location need not be considered (see Chapter 4, Section 4.3).

Because of their dependence on transportation charges, the cost of materials can vary with distance from their source in a fairly regular and predictable manner. Specific illustrations are given in a number of the case studies presented in Part Four, and Chapter 5 on transportation contains examples of the spatial structure of commodity freight rates.

Sources of power, like materials, can exercise an important influence on plant location. There are very few modern industries that do not use some form of powered machinery, although the amount and type of energy needed will of course vary from industry to industry and from firm to firm according to the nature of the activity conducted and the kind of technology applied. Power can be produced in a number of different ways and from a variety of sources, and the geography of energy supply and demand is a very important feature of the spatial structure of any industrial economy (Manners, 1964).

Electricity is the main source of motive power in most industries today. Electricity is much more geographically mobile than water power and steam power (the earlier forms of industrial energy), since it can be transmitted from one place to another at relatively little cost. This means that over fairly large areas the cost of electricity may not vary much if there are no significant differences in local production costs, and in these circumstances its influence on plant location will be negligible. In Britain and some other small countries the transmission of electricity through a national grid makes this source of energy virtually ubiquitous for most practical industrial purposes, and the cost of electricity can often be ignored in making the locational decision.

But there are cases where the availability of large supplies of cheap power has a very important influence on industrial location. Certain metallurgical and chemical industries, such as aluminum and copper processing and the production of fertilizers, are especially sensitive to the cost of power, and some areas that can produce electricity very cheaply have been able to attract important manufacturing industries of this type. The development of aluminum production in the Pacific Northwest of the United States, in the Tennessee Valley, and in the St. Maurice and Saguenay river valleys in Canada are examples. Similar developments have taken place in Europe; for instance, at Fort William in Scotland and in the French Alps. Generally such places derive their power-cost advantage from the capacity to produce hydroelectricity.

It is extremely difficult to offer specific generalizations concerning the geographical pattern of electricity costs. Each country, and often each region, has its own distinctive pattern arising from local circumstances and, to further complicate matters, it is common for users of large quantities to be offered lower rates than other consumers. However, when the pattern of electricity costs for industrial users in the United States is mapped (Figure 3.2) some interesting features emerge. The lowest costs are in the Pacific Northwest around Tacoma and Eugene, and from there

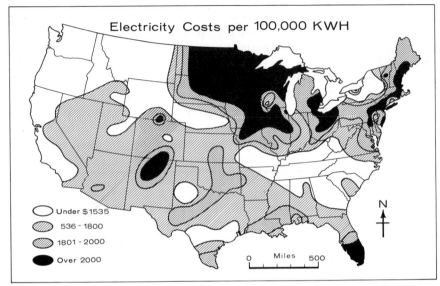

Figure 3.2. Monthly electricity costs for industrial users with a billing demand of 500 kilowatts. (*Source.* Highsmith and Northam, 1968, 312. © by Harcourt Brace & Jovanovich Inc. Adapted from *World Economic Activity* by permission of the publishers.)

a major low-cost zone extends eastward almost continuously to the south Atlantic coast. North of this trough, costs rise fairly steeply, the only exception being most of New York state, including the area near Niagara. But the extreme high or low figures apply only to relatively small areas and, in most of the United States, the monthly cost of electricity for industrial users is shown to be $1500–$2000 per kilowatt-hour.

The historical tendency has been for sources of power to play a steadily decreasing role in industrial location, since electricity has replaced the less mobile water and steam power. This seems likely to continue as means of transmitting electricity over long distances become more efficient, although the effect of technological changes (like the increasing use of atomic power) is hard to predict. However, there are always likely to be some areas that have a particular attraction for certain industries by virtue of local circumstances which allow power to be generated relatively cheaply.

3.4 LABOR

Labor is needed to operate any industrial plant, but the amount and type required vary from industry to industry and firm to firm. In the case of a motor-vehicle factory, an iron and steel works or a petro-chemicals complex, for example, many thousands will be employed, whereas some viable enterprises can still be operated by the owner and a couple of apprentices. Some industries need a highly skilled labor force, some a large clerical and managerial staff, and others need many unskilled manual workers. In some industries the labor input is a large cost item (it accounts for more than a quarter of the total value of shipments in more than half the major industry groups in the United States—see Table 3.3), while for other activities it may be of only minor importance.

The distinctive labor requirements of particular industries make some places more suitable locations than others. A firm needing a big labor force with a large range of skills obviously will find this easier to obtain in a major metropolitan area than in a small town. If workers with a specific skill are needed, a location in one region or city might suggest itself on the grounds of an existing concentration on a particular activity; traditional familiarity with industries can be an advantage to a firm seeking a particular kind of labor, if only because less expenditure on training is involved. Some industries may need a predominantly female work force, in which case a location in a mining region or other area where male employment predominates might be sought and a textile town avoided, while a firm looking for a large supply of relatively unskilled male workers would avoid a mining region or a town dominated by a big steel works.

If the right kind of workers are not available at a location that is otherwise attractive, it may be possible to obtain them from other areas or from other local employers, since labor is mobile both geographically and in terms of occupation. A firm can attempt to attract workers from one place to another by providing attractive wages or conditions of employment, just as it may try to build up a labor force by enticing workers from neighboring plants. In these days of uniform wage rates negotiated by trade unions, active competition between firms through wage differentials is often difficult, but it certainly has been important in the past. Today a firm wishing to get more labor may incur additional costs not so much in higher wages paid as in expenditure on fringe benefits, welfare, and recreational facilities. If for other reasons, such as access to materials or sources of power, a relatively isolated location is chosen for the plant, it may be necessary to incur the expense of building houses or other accommodation to attract the necessary labor. This is what happened in the Industrial Revolution in the cotton industry, when the need for water power took mills into the largely unpopulated valleys of the Pennines in Britain and New England in the United States, leading to the erection of some of the first company towns.

Variations from place to place in labor costs can assume critical importance in the modern industrial system, where the level of wages paid and the supply of labor may be beyond the control of the individual firm, and it is often possible to identify clear and fairly regular differences within specific nations. This can be conveniently illustrated by selected data for the United Kingdom (Table 3.4). Average hourly earnings in all manufacturing decrease fairly steadily from maximum figures in southeast England and the Midlands outward to the peripheral regions of the Southwest, northern England, Scotland, and Northern Ireland, with Wales as the only major exception to this trend. In vehicle manufacturing there is the same general trend, although here the highest earnings by far are in the Midlands, while in the chemical industry some of the highest figures are in the Northwest and in the Northern region. The regional ranges in average hourly earnings reach a maximum of 31.7 d (pence) in vehicles and a minimum of 18.3 d in chemicals.

Despite the interesting patterns revealed by these figures, it is always rather dangerous to interpret areal variations in earnings as indicative of real differences in labor costs. As the published commentary to the figures in Table 3.4 states: "In view of the wide variations, as between different industries, in the proportions of skilled and unskilled workers, and in the opportunities for extra earnings from overtime, night-work and payment-by-results schemes, the differences in average earnings

Table 3.4 Regional Variations in Average Earnings (Pence per Hour) in Selected Industries in the United Kingdom, October 1966

Region	Chemicals	Vehicles	Textiles	All Manufacturing
London and Southeastern	109.0	125.9	103.4	114.7
Eastern and Southern	120.0	126.0	102.4	114.2
Southwestern	110.5	118.9	95.9	105.9
Midlands	104.1	138.2	111.0	115.2
Yorkshire and Humberside	101.7	107.2	92.3	101.7
Northwestern	118.7	114.8	92.3	105.8
Northern	115.9	111.5	108.2	108.9
Wales	117.3	115.0	114.8	117.5
Scotland	111.8	115.8	88.5	106.0
Northern Ireland	109.6	109.2	86.4	95.7
United Kingdom	113.0	127.7	97.3	110.8

Source. *Ministry of Labour Gazette,* February 1967. The figures refer only to men, aged 21 and over. The pence are as before the UK currency decimalization.

shown in this table should not be taken as evidence of, or as a measure of, disparities in the ordinary rates of pay prevailing in different industries for comparable classes of workpeople employed under similar conditions" (*Ministry of Labour Gazette,* February 1967, 120). For example, the high earnings in the vehicle industry in the Midlands partially reflects the overtime worked. Nevertheless, in many industries the manufacturer can expect to pay somewhat more for comparable types of labor in some regions than others, and in the United Kingdom it is generally the prosperous regions of southeast England and the Midlands where the higher costs are incurred.

The identification and interpretation of areal variations in the cost of labor may be considered in more detail with reference to the United States. In Figure 3.3 average earnings of production workers in manufacturing have been interpolated as a continuous surface from data for about 150 urban areas. The pattern shows a general tendency for fairly regular changes across the nation, from the relatively low wage levels in the South to the high figures in northern and western regions. But there are a number of interesting local variations to the trend, including the narrow belt of high wages along the Texas and Louisiana Gulf Coast, and the relatively low average wages in New England and parts of the eastern end of the major manufacturing belt. In interpreting this map, and others compiled on a similar basis, keep in mind that the control points are spaced in an irregular manner, with the larger number in the east tending to produce a more detailed pattern there than in the western half of the nation.

What does this map really mean, in terms of the comparative economic advantage of different parts of the country as locations for manufacturing industry? A lower average wage level in an area does not necessarily imply that a new firm will face lower labor costs there, since differences in wages that exist on average may not exist in the skill and industry group from which the new firm must hire. In addition, productivity differences may offset differences in wages and, in any case, the hiring activities of the newcomer may raise local wage rates if the firm is large and the qualified labor in the area is small. Of particular importance is the fact that low average wages may simply be a reflection of a local specialization in industries where there is characteristically a relatively low rate of pay.

This last problem can be overcome by calculating average wage levels on the basis of some uniform industrial composition, thus eliminating variations in the structure of employment. Wonnacott (1963, 16–17) attempted this by states for the year 1958 by applying the individual

48   THE VARIABLES IN INDUSTRIAL LOCATION

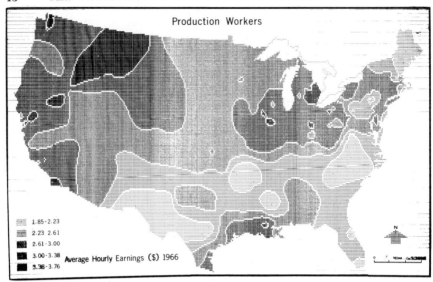

Figure 3.3. Average hourly earnings of production workers in manufacturing industry, December 1966. (*Source of Data.* U.S. Department of Labor, *Employment and Earnings and Monthly Report on the Labor Force*, February, 1967.) *Note.* This is the first of a number of similar maps in this book prepared by using the SYMAP computer mapping system developed at Harvard University.

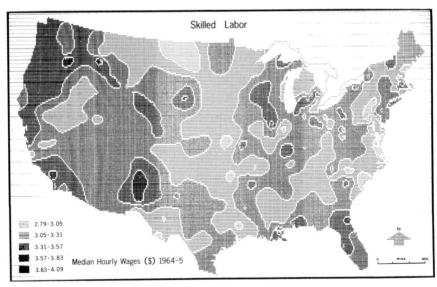

Figure 3.4. Median hourly wage rates for selected occupational groups representative of skilled labor (labor grade 13), 1964–1965. (*Source of Data.* Army-Air Force Wages Board.)

THE MAJOR INPUTS 49

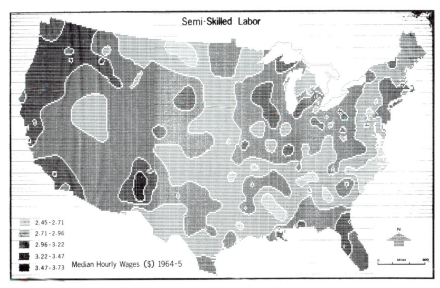

Figure 3.5. Median hourly wage rates for selected occupational groups representative of semiskilled labor (labor grade 10), 1964–1965. (*Source of Data.* Army-Air Force Wages Board.)

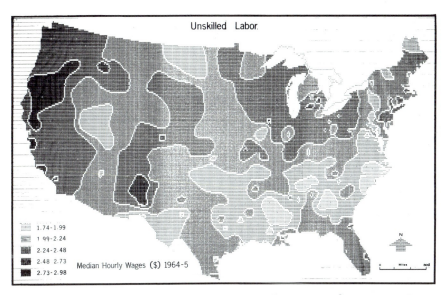

Figure 3.6. Median hourly wage rates for selected occupational groups representative of unskilled labor (labor grade 5), 1964–1965. (*Source of Data.* Army-Air Force Wages Board.)

industrial wage rates in each state to the employment structure of each state. How some of these standardized figures relate to the actual published average wage levels may be illustrated briefly by comparing the actual averages for 1958 with state averages calculated on the basis of the employment structure in Illinois. The low-wage states on the basis of the actual average also have low averages when the Illinois structure is assumed, and the high wage states are broadly the same on both measures, but there are some important differences between the two sets of figures. At the bottom end of the scale, the fifteen states with the lowest actual average wages all have higher rates on the basis of the Illinois structure. The largest difference is in Georgia, where the actual average of $1.55 an hour is raised to $1.85 by the application of its individual industrial rates to the structure of Illinois, where there are more employed in relatively highly paid activities. At the other end of the scale the effect of the standardization is less clear, since a number of states with a high actual average have an even higher figure when the Illinois structure is assumed, but in many cases the figure is lower because the state in question has a "better" structure than Illinois in terms of well-paid industries. For example, Michigan, with its motor industry, has an average of $2.65 on the basis of its own structure, but only $2.52 when the Illinois structure is assumed. In general the elimination of the structural variable pulls up the rates in the lower states, including practically the whole of the South, and depresses them in many of the higher pay states. It thus reduced the interstate variability in average wages; the range in the actual averages is from $1.46 to $2.65 while the application of Illinois structure makes it $1.59 to $2.56.

The published figures for state average wage rates can thus exaggerate areal variations in the cost of labor. But even after the effect of structure is removed a clear geographical pattern of variation remains, not vastly different from the one illustrated in Figure 3.3. The application of the same sort of standardizing procedure to average wage rates in individual cities would be interesting, particularly if nonstructural considerations such as labor productivity and reliability could be built into the calculation, but the analysis presented here is sufficient to emphasize that an overall average wage level may not be closely indicative of variations from place to place in what any given firm looking for a new location can expect to pay, but that it may provide a broad indication.

To the manufacturer looking for a cheap labor location, the prevailing cost of particular grades of labor is likely to be much more important than the overall average wage rates. Areal differences may be far greater in the lower grades of skills (Fulton, 1960), which means that the firm needing a large number of unskilled workers may be more sensitive to the cost of labor in choosing his location than one which uses more skilled workers, other things being equal. To illustrate the geographical pattern of wage rates for different classes of labor, three maps have been prepared from information compiled for 250 cities distributed throughout the United States (Figures 3.4, 3.5, and 3.6). The patterns shown are broadly indicative of areal variations in the cost of skilled, semiskilled, and unskilled labor. Of particular interest is the gradual breakdown of the distinction between the South as a low-wage area and parts of the northern and western regions at the other extreme, with the progression up the labor skills. The wages of unskilled workers appear to be subject to a more systematic areal variation than is the case with the skilled jobs, where the variations are often of a more local significance. However, it is not difficult to detect some similarity between the three maps at a very broad regional level.

The similarity in the form of the labor-cost surfaces illustrated in this section raises the question of how far is it possible to set down some generalizations regarding spatial variations in the cost of this vital factor of production. Although it is very doubtful whether enough research has yet been done in different parts of the world to produce any precise empirical generalizations of widespread validity, sufficient is known to suggest some similarities with the form of land-cost surfaces, as described earlier in this chapter. As in the case of land, the cost of labor is subject to broad variations over large areas, which may display a degree of regularity. And as with land, these broad trends may be interrupted by local cost peaks representing the major cities or other places where the demand for labor is high enough to force up wage rates. The cost of labor is certainly not subject to the same extreme local variations as may exist in the urban land market, but often intercommunity variations in wage rates are greater than interarea or interregional variations (Fulton, 1955). Labor, like land also displays local qualitative differences, which always makes it difficult to generalize in precise cost terms regarding the comparative advantage of alternative locations.

Just how important is the cost or availability of labor as an influence on plant location today? It is clear that on paper the total cost of production in some industries is highly sensitive to areal differences in wage rates; in a study of the competitive position of Minnesota, a high labor cost state, it has been shown that in industries such as lumber, furniture, and primary metals total costs in many of the southern states are more than 10 percent lower than in Minnesota because of wage differences alone (Wonnacott, 1963, 8–10). But there are considerable divergences of opinion on how far differences of this kind really affect industrial location. Stevens and Brackett (1967), in their review of the literature, conclude that few industries appear heavily influenced by wage levels in their locational decisions, although the supply of needed skills may be of substantial importance. Wilbur Thompson (1968, 54–55) emphasizes that the spread of unionism is a big step toward spatially invariate labor costs, and that although areal differences in productivity may remain the tendency toward automation should reduce the opportunity for variations in worker skill and effort to a point where the quantity or quality of output is not significantly altered. Such developments as these should substantially reduce the relative importance of labor in the locational decision. But some take the opposite view; Britton Harris (1968, 400) feels that the relative importance of labor force assembly is increasing by comparison with the transportation costs of inputs and outputs, and in relation to site costs, and a recent United Nations inquiry by the Economic Commission for Europe (1967) also stresses the important and growing influence of the labor factor, particularly in the many nations where labor supply has been very tight in recent years.

The overall influence of the labor factor on plant location is thus difficult to evaluate. Increasing mechanization, automation, and the tendency to substitute capital for labor may well be reducing the importance of labor in the modern industrial nation. But significant local advantages with respect to cost, quantity and quality still exist. The increasing sophistication of industrial processes is reducing the need for unskilled labor in many industries, but the presence of workers with special technical skills can now give some areas big labor advantages. And on a world scale there are still many areas where the low cost of labor is the main competitive industrial advantage, particularly in the developing countries of Africa and Asia.

3.5 STATE AND LOCAL TAXES

Wherever a firm locates, it is generally liable to some form of taxation on its plant or revenue. This may be levied by some local authority such as the city or county, by the state or some other upper-tier authority, or by the nation, and often a firm is taxed at all three levels. If the rate of taxation is the same in all sections of a given country, it will have no bearing on locational choice, just as a local or state corporation tax will not affect the competitive position of alternative locations within the area in question. But any geographical variations in the rate of taxation will affect a firm's total outlay, and may thus exercise some influence on the locational decision. In the present context, taxes are an additional cost; the subsidy of certain locations, which can be regarded as negative taxation or an addition to revenue, is best considered in the context of public policy and development planning (see Part Six).

In recent years a large volume of literature has accumulated on the subject of the influence of state and local taxes on plant location in the United States (for example, Floyd, 1952; Thompson, 1957b; Stopler, 1958; Due, 1961; and Williams, 1967). This appears to be more a reflection of the American businessman's distaste and distrust for something that he considers as disturbing free market mechanisms than an indication of the real importance of areal differences in taxation rates as an influence on comparative locational advantage. Most studies have looked at differences between the states, and the general conclusion is that relatively high business tax levels do not have the disastrous effect on industrial development often attributed to them (Due, 1961, 171). Two studies that have attempted to measure the correlation between state and local taxes, on the one hand, and industrial growth rates, on the other, both conclude that tax levels are not important determinants of industrial location and expansion (Bloom, 1955; Thompson and Matilla, 1959). And Wonnacott (1963), in his general study of interstate differences in manufacturing costs, found that, on average, variations in tax costs are roughly one-tenth of the variations in the cost of labor, marketing, and transportation.

The most obvious differences from place to place in the level of taxation are to be found within the major metropolitan area. A detailed study of the New York region in the latter part of the 1950s (Campbell, 1958; Hoover and Vernon, 1959), based on sample firms and locations, found that taxes could be up to three times as high in some parts of the metropolitan region as in others. Sixty-four locations were selected within the region and, for each, the various taxes in operation were applied to the appropriate data for twenty-five actual firms. The average level of taxation at each location was then expressed as an index, with 100 representing the average level for all firms at all locations. The highest figures were found in Jersey City (160.1), Union City (141.3), and Newark (140.6), all in New Jersey, with slightly lower figures in New York City and the Bronx, while the lowest indexes were in New Jersey on the western edge of the metropolitan area. The general impression was of tax levels reaching a peak in the core of the region, and falling away toward the fringe in a rather asymmetrical fashion. The pattern is thus closely similar to that which the cost of land or labor could be expected to display, although the range of the tax bill in alternative locations is less than in land costs and more than in wage rates. Similar though less detailed studies of other metropolitan areas support the general finding of a significantly lower level of taxation in peripheral or suburban areas compared with the central city (for example, Strasma, 1959).

These local tax differentials can be expected to have some bearing on industrial location. In a single metropolitan area the cost of most other inputs may vary from place to place only to a minor degree, thus increasing the significance of differences in taxation levels. And if substantial variations in the cost of labor and land, for example, do exist these are likely to reinforce the trend indicated by the taxation figures rather than oppose it. Differences in the level of business taxation, with or without the assistance of other cost variations, are likely to favor the decentralization of industrial activity within the major metropolitan area. There is certainly some strong evidence to support his contention in New York City, where the effect of tax levels on decentralization is so clear that it has had a major influence on recent tax policy in both the city and the peripheral areas (Netzer, 1968, 445).

Tax differences within the metropolitan area seem to be somewhat more important than the differences between cities. As in the case of individual states, there may be isolated examples of a firm disregarding some locational options because of the tax situation, but intercity differences in the anticipated tax bill are more often submerged by variations in the cost of other inputs or of supplying the market. Williams (1967), in a study of Minnesota's tax position, came to this same general conclusion.

State and local taxes are thus generally a relatively unimportant influence on industrial location. Very seldom do they make up a large share of total costs, though there may be occasional instances where this is the case and where firms are therefore more than usually sensitive to geographical variations in taxation levels. Most empirical inquiries agree that tax policy has relatively little effect on location unless carried to extremes or working in combination with other factors (Stevens and Brackett, 1967, 10). But there is also evidence that taxes may assume a disproportionate significance in the minds of some businessmen, their irrationality perhaps reflecting personal political bias (Karaska and Bramhall, 1969, 17). Businessmen may also feel that other local conditions can be inferred from high levels of taxation, since they may be viewed as indicative of local attitudes toward industry (Campbell, 1958), as reflecting the "image" of an area and its past treatment of business (Wonnacott, 1963), or as an important indicator of the prevailing "business climate" in a community (Due, 1961). When the final decision is made, such subjective concepts as the local business climate may have a greater influence on the choice of location for a factory than more direct evidence of cost penalties or savings.

3.6 ENTERPRISE

The skill with which the various inputs are combined to produce some good is dependent on business enterprise. Broadly, this term embraces the contribution of the management at the policy-making level. In the earlier stages of modern industrial development the entrepreneurial function was generally performed by one man, who was typically the founder of the firm, the major bearer of risk, and the main profit taker. This is still the case today in many relatively small firms, but in the large corporation the decision making has tended to shift from the old-style entrepreneur to what Galbraith (1967) has termed the technostructure; that is, the upper management group whose technical, scientific, and business skill run the corporation but whose financial stake in its success may be very small. In a large firm it may now be very difficult in practice to distinguish the real decision makers from other managerial workers, and to allocate expenditure on particular employees as between the labor and enterprise categories. This is not an important practical matter, but it does emphasize that the single entrepreneur of classical economic theory, guiding the fortunes of his firm with single-minded attention to his personal profits, is becoming a figure of the past, to be submerged by a growing breed of anonymous "organization men."

No matter who performs the entrepreneurial functions of the organization and management of a firm's affairs, the skill with which this is done will have a vital bearing on business success or failure. Among the many decisions that must be made is of course the choice of location, involving the balancing of the various considerations discussed in this and subsequent chapters, and the assessment of such nebulous concepts as the local business climate. Good decision makers are therefore very important to a firm, and because they are easier to obtain in some places than others their availability can influence the location of a new plant or branch factory which expects to attract or locally recruit some of its upper-level managerial employees. For example, in Britain it is often said that high-caliber executives can be attracted to firms in the London area easier than to other regions, and that they need substantially higher salaries to induce them to bear the discomforts and lack of social life thought to exist in the northern industrial cities. And in the United States the residential preferences of the management have certainly had a bearing on the development of some industrial activity in Florida and California. In general, the takeover by the technostructure seems likely to increase the importance of such considerations as the residential preference of those performing the entrepreneurial function; compared with the old-style entrepreneur, the modern management group who collectively make the locational decision may attach much greater significance to finding a place where they can realize the contemporary middle-class way of life with all its embellishments.

As was indicated in Section 3.4, the growing need for highly skilled managerial employees at all levels may bestow considerable locational advantages on areas best able to supply them. For example, a firm requiring a range of managerial personnel with specific technical skills is far more likely to find them in a major city than in a small town. And certain places with a good university or business school may seem attractive locations in these days when appointments to decision-making posts in industry are often made direct from the ranks of the faculty or graduate school.

The location of enterprise can affect industrial development in other rather different ways. Chinitz (1961, 284) has argued that the supply of entrepreneurs is a function of certain local social characteristics which are heavily influenced by an area's traditional economic specializations; a highly competitive industry, like apparel manufacturing, is likely to breed more local entrepreneurs than an industry like steel which is organized along oligopolistic lines. Some existing concentrations of manufacturing can be partly explained by the fact that at one time they were centers of mechanical innovation, or the homes of particularly skilled or enterprising individuals; for example, the North Staffordshire Potteries in England owed much of their emergence as a specialized industrial region during the late eighteenth century to the technical advances initiated by Josiah Wedgwood and others. And there are many places where the presence of a prominent firm can be ascribed to the fact that it was the home of a particularly enterprising businessman, who could have been equally successful in many other towns; the establishment of motor manufacturing by Ford in Detroit and by Morris in Oxford are familiar illustrations. Further consideration of this and related matters is reserved for Chapter 6, Section 6.3, which deals with the personal factor in industrial location.

In summary, although the availability of enterprise is seldom a major locational influence today, there are cases where it is important, or where it has been important at some stage in the past. And it must not be forgotten that the skill of the entrepreneur may determine whether a particular location is suitable, since a good businessman may be able to succeed in a place where others would fail—a matter which will be returned to when some of the theoretical implications of differences in entrepreneurial skill are discussed in Part Three, Section 12.1.

4

Supply and Demand, Market and Price

When all the necessary inputs have been assembled, with an appropriate degree of entrepreneurial skill, the manufacturing process can begin. Then the product has to be sold. This raises the related question of how much to produce, what price to charge, and how and where to market the output. These are all matters that have an important bearing on the locational decision, since different scales of operation and different pricing policies may require different locations, and for many firms today access to the market is regarded as the dominant consideration in choosing a site for a factory.

4.1 THE INTERACTION OF SUPPLY AND DEMAND

How does the firm decide what quantity to produce? Assuming that the objective is to make as much money as possible, the output at which total revenue exceeds total cost by the greatest amount will be chosen. In producing any good, total profits will tend to rise as output increases, until the point is reached where unit cost begins to exceed unit revenue. This point represents the profit-maximizing output, where *marginal cost* equals *marginal revenue*. The marginal cost is the cost of producing one additional unit and the marginal revenue is the price obtainable for it, and as long as the revenue from making one more of the good is greater than the production cost involved, further profit will be added to the total. As soon as marginal cost begins to exceed marginal revenue, total profits will be reduced, and there is nothing to gain from continuing to increase production.

Understanding the implications of all this requires some knowledge of the shape of a firm's cost and demand curves. There is a discussion of these matters in most introductory texts on microeconomic theory, but its relevance to some of the theoretical location analysis introduced in subsequent chapters justifies a brief treatment here. What follows also helps to emphasize the interrelationship between locational choice and other decisions the firm has to make.

A *cost curve* expresses the relationship between the cost of production and volume of output. A firm's total costs will include expenditure on the acquisition of the various inputs referred to in the previous chapter, plus the cost of marketing. When they are divided by output, this gives the average cost per unit. The average cost usually falls with *economies of scale*, but eventually a point is reached where the plant becomes too large to be fully efficient, and *diseconomies of scale* set in. As the cost of producing additional units rises the average cost begins to rise, so the average cost curve is characteristically U-shaped.

A simple illustration will help to explain this. Table 4.1 lists cost data

Table 4.1 Imaginary Data to Illustrate the Relationship between Cost, Revenue, and Profits at Different Levels of Output[a]

Output	MC	AC	TC	MR	AR	TR	TP
1	30	30	30	24	24	24	−6
2	10	20	40	22	23	46	6
3	5	15	45	20	22	66	21
4	3	12	48	18	21	84	36
5	2	10	50	16	20	100	50
6	4	9	54	14	19	114	60
7	9	9	63	12	18	126	63
8	17	10	80	10	17	136	56
9	28	12	108	8	16	144	36
10	42	15	150	6	15	150	0
11	70	20	220	4	14	154	−66
12	140	30	360	2	13	156	−204

[a] MC = marginal cost, AC = average cost, TC = total cost, MR = marginal revenue, AR = average revenue, TR = total revenue, and TP = total profit. Values in all but the output column are in monetary units and may be read as dollars.

for an imaginary firm, showing that the cost of producing an additional unit falls with economies of scale until an output of 5 is reached. Then marginal cost rises, and at 8 units the average cost begins to increase. The figures are plotted in Figure 4.1 to derive the two cost curves. The marginal cost curve remains below average cost while the average is falling sharply, then moves up to intersect the average cost curve at its

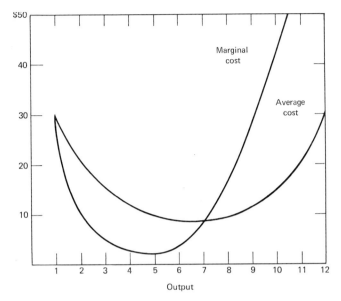

Figure 4.1. Average and marginal cost curves for an imaginary firm.

lowest point. The general forms of these curves and their relationship to each other will be the same irrespective of the data used.

Table 4.1 also shows revenue data, from which the *demand curves*, or *revenue curves*, can be constructed (Figure 4.2). Average revenue per unit is seen to decrease as output rises, since purchasers will be prepared to pay a higher price for something that is scarce than for a plentiful commodity. The marginal revenue line keeps below average revenue for reasons that are obvious from an examination of the data.

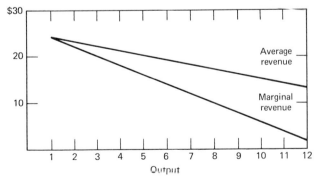

Figure 4.2. Average and marginal revenue curves for an imaginary firm.

The slope of the demand (average revenue) curve, and whether it is really a curve or a line, expresses the *elasticity of demand*. This measures the extent to which demand is sensitive to a change in price. The elasticity of demand is calculated by dividing the proportionate change in the amount demanded by the proportionate change in price, or alternatively from the expression

$$\text{elasticity of demand} = \frac{dq}{q} \div \frac{-dp}{p},$$

where q is the quantity demanded, p is the price, dq is the change in demand, and dp is the change in price. Where the result is 1.0 (for example, a 10 percent fall in price increases demand by 10 percent) there is unit elasticity, where a small change in price leads to a big change in sales demand is relatively elastic, and where demand varies little with price changes it is said to be inelastic. Elasticity of demand varies at different points on the demand curve, except for a hyperbole convex to the origin of the graph, which has constant unit elasticity. The extremes are a horizontal demand curve, indicating infinitely elastic demand or the sale of any quantity at a given constant price, and a vertical curve indicating infinitely inelastic or constant demand. But usually the demand curve slopes down from left to right (Figure 4.2). The elasticity of a demand curve is important in location analysis, and assumptions as to its nature are stated or implicit in any theoretical framework.

The cost and revenue curves for this imaginary firm can now be combined to show how the most profitable output is arrived at (Figure 4.3). As stated above, maximum profits will be made where marginal revenue (MR) equals marginal cost (MC), as it is here where total revenue (TR) exceeds total cost (TC) by the greatest amount. The diagram shows that $MR = MC$ just after an output of 7 units is reached, so 7 is the optimum output. Here average cost (AC) is $9, and the price, or average revenue (AR), is $18. The average profit at this point is the vertical distance between AR and AC, which is $9. When this is multiplied by the output, total profit becomes $63 (that is, the area of the shaded part of Figure 4.3), which corresponds with the figure listed in Table 4.1. A production of more or less than 7 units will reduce the total profit that can be made.

This is only one method of analyzing the scale decision in a simple diagramatic way. In fact, it corresponds with the economic theorist's analysis of *imperfect competition*, which is a situation where firms compete with each other to some extent but each has a degree of

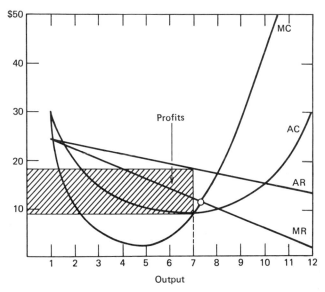

Figure 4.3. The optimum output for an imaginary firm under conditions of imperfect competition, as derived from the cost and revenue curves.

monopolistic control over part of the market. The above-normal profits possible in this partially monopolistic situation are protected by restrictions on the freedom of new firms to enter the industry and compete them away. A downward sloping demand curve is assumed in this situation, compared with the horizontal demand curve used in the analysis of *perfect competition,* where no monopoly profits are made. Since costs conventionally include the so-called normal profits that can be expected in a nonmonopolistic situation, the optimum output (or the firm's *equilibrium* position) is achieved under perfect composition where MC = MR and AC = AR. If unit revenue exceeds unit cost to provide supernormal profits, then in the perfectly competitive situation postulated in theory new firms will enter the industry until all excess profits are competed away.

The relevance to industrial location of cost and demand curves, output and price, and perfect or imperfect competition may not be immediately obvious. But these matters assume very great importance when it is appreciated that the scale of production influences the locational decision, and that the cost and demand curves may differ in different locations. Furthermore, conditions of imperfect as opposed to perfect competition are implicit in a space economy, where location alone can bestow certain monopoly advantages. These considerations and their place in industrial location theory are discussed in more detail in Parts Two and Three.

4.2 THE MARKET

The general importance of access to the market as a factor affecting industrial location has been recognized for a long time. And there is evidence that in many industries the significance of the market is growing in relation to such considerations as the cost of labor and materials. Freed from the original necessity of being on a coalfield or other source of power or raw material, many firms now show a distinct preference for a location in or near one of the major metrolopitan regions, such as the northeastern Megalopolis of the United States and the southeastern corner of England around Greater London. The market is not the only attraction of a metropolitan location, but the large, concentrated, and relatively affluent body of consumers found in the city, together with its large industrial market, is certainly one of the main reasons for relatively rapid industrial growth in and around the major urban areas.

In addition to this, there is the general tendency for industry to pay more attention to the market and its manipulation than was the case in earlier stages of industrial development. At one time goods were produced to satisfy a known demand, this being the classical response of the entrepreneur in the free market, but today it is often the case that a market is created by advertising without which effective demand for the product would not exist. The amount of expenditure on sales promotion necessary to generate and sustain demand for a new consumer good today, together with the large initial capital investment involved in most new industrial enterprises of this kind, makes the achievement of a large volume of sales of critical importance. Such a market may be easier found and more efficiently served in some locations than in others. As Chisholm (1966, 147) has remarked: "To maximize profits in an imperfectly competitive world, easy access to a large market may permit scale economies to be achieved that will more than offset the cost of assembling and processing materials that are greater than in other possible locations."

The effect of the demand factor on industrial location, and how the market relates to other causal factors, is the subject of extensive discussion in the theoretical chapters in Parts Two and Three. The remainder of this section is confined to some very general observations on the ways in which the market can operate as an influence on locational choice.

These influences may conveniently be divided into two categories: (1) the nature of the market, and (2) the cost of supplying it.

For any product the volume of sales and the price obtainable, as reflected in the consumers demand curve, may be subject to geographical variations. Demand will obviously vary from place to place according to the nature of the product and the number, type, and distribution of potential customers. For some products a location in an area of relatively high per capita income or purchasing power may be an advantage; a manufacturer of washing machines, electric carving knives, portable barbecue stoves, and other necessities of the modern American way of life would clearly achieve more sales in Texas than Mexico, and more in Westchester County than Harlem. For other industries (such as baking and, at one time, brewing) the main thing is to have a secure local market with a steady and predictable demand. If a manufacturer requires a market with an assured minimum volume of sales, his choice of location may be restricted to cities of a given size, and his decision may also be strongly influenced by the location of competitors and their likely reaction to his entry into the industry. All these and many other considerations are relevant to the effect of the nature of the market on plant location, with different areas offering different volumes of sales, different prices and total revenues, and perhaps also different elasticities of demand.

The manner in which the volume of sales that can be expected in a given area or from a given location may be calculated will be discussed in detail in Chapter 13. But one brief illustration here will further emphasize the importance of areal variations in the demand for different kinds of goods. In Figure 4.4 some retail sales statistics for the United States are mapped by states on a per capita basis to show how personal expenditure on all goods and on food products varies between the states. Total retail sales show a clear geographical pattern, with the highest per capita sales in the west and in the major manufacturing belt of the northeast, while the lowest figures are in the South. Sales of food per head of population tend to follow a similar pattern, but with a less obvious distinction between high- and low-spending areas. Maps such as these clearly show that potential sales for a given product can vary considerably within one nation, and this is bound to influence industrial location.

Some firms may be more interested in the spending habits of individual cities, however, and these will not necessarily reflect the spending habits of the state to which they belong. Hecock and Rooney (1968), in their research on the geography of consumption in the United States, have studied annual family expenditure in sixty-six cities, and find that for all goods the cities in the northeast and the west are the biggest spenders.

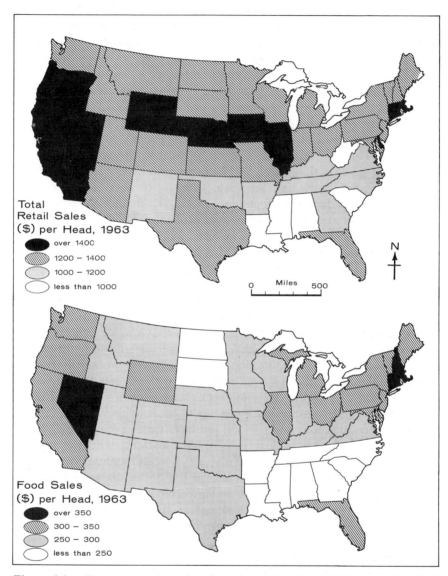

Figure 4.4. Two aspects of retail trade in the United States, 1963: per capita sales in all retail establishments and in food stores. (*Source of Data. Statistical Abstract of the United States,* 1967.)

Some of the north-central cities are the lowest spenders, including Green Bay, Wisconsin, and Cincinnati, while urban centers in the South represent intermediate spending habits. But these figures, like those for state total retail sales in Figure 4.4, hide important variations in spending on specific goods. For example, in the food category, Hecock and Rooney show the peaks of expenditure to be in the east and west coast cities, with considerable intercity variations in the north-central cities and expenditure uniformly well below the national average in the South. Further research along these lines can be expected to provide more much-needed empirical information on the geography of consumption, which has such an important bearing on how the demand factor affects industrial location.

The second of the two ways in which the market can influence plant location is through its effect on costs. Finished products have to be transported to the consumer, and in many industries the outgoing freight bill can be a substantial addition to the cost incurred in acquiring the necessary inputs and conducting the process of manufacture. Proximity to the market if it is spatially concentrated, or a central location if customers are dispersed, can thus be an advantage and, to some firms, a necessity. As the cost of distribution, like the cost of many materials, is almost entirely accounted for by transportation charges, further discussion of this and related matters is postponed until the next chapter, where patterns of freight rates are illustrated.

But the transport cost involved in distributing the product to the consumer is not the only item of expenditure involved in marketing. In some industries, large sums of money are spent on advertising and other forms of sales promotion, and although this is not generally a spatially variable cost item there are circumstances where it may be related to the choice of location. For example, more advertising may be needed in a highly competitive market than in one where the firm has a monopoly, and because of existing habits or preferences people in some areas may need more persuasion as to the virtues of a new product than they might in other areas. However, these considerations are far less likely to be important enough to determine the choice of a factory than is the cost of transporting the product.

The nature of the market and its geographical distribution can thus affect a manufacturer's profits both through his costs and through the price he can obtain for his product. Consequently the overall influence of the market in relation to other factors which have a bearing on locational choice in any specific situation is often very hard to evaluate precisely. The difficulty of generalizing about the operation of the market, and of integrating the demand factor into theoretical approaches to industrial location, will become apparent from later chapters.

4.3 PRICING POLICIES

The earlier discussion of a firm's cost and demand curves suggested that the price charged for a good should be a function of the demand for it and the cost of supplying it. The price should in theory vary from place to place in accordance with differences in these two independent variables. But in the real world this is seldom the case. A firm is highly unlikely to be constantly altering the price it charges in some part of the market with every slight fluctuation in demand, and although some firms may charge a higher price to distant customers who are more costly to supply, it is more likely that no such discrimination will take place. Pricing policies are very important in industrial location analysis for two reasons: (1) the price charged to any group of customers can influence the volume of sales, which in turn can influence choice of plant location; and (2) the customer of one firm may be a manufacturer in another industry, so the price the first one charges for his product will affect the cost of the material or component the second firm is buying in.

The simplest way to sell a product is to adopt a uniform delivered price over the entire market. This is known as the *c.i.f.* (cost, insurance, freight) pricing system, and it means, in effect, that the producer pays all the costs involved in getting the product to the consumer and spreads this over all customers irrespective of their location. In many advanced industrial nations (like the United States and the United Kingdom) this pricing system is much more common than is generally supposed. The evidence has been carefully examined by Chisholm (1966, 182–201), who notes, among other observations, that British Oxygen supplies about 95 percent of the United Kingdom's domestic market for certain industrial gasses at a uniform price despite the fact that transportation can make up a quarter of the total cost of these products, that many important industrial commodities including fertilizers and chemicals are generally sold c.i.f., and that as early as the 1940s a variety of goods ranging from aluminum to rayon yarn and sheet brass to electric turbine generators were being sold at a nationally uniform price in the United States. Even when some discrimination against distant customers is practiced, it is often the case that a uniform price is charged over broad zones of a country.

The tendency to charge a uniform delivered price, which appears to be increasing, is very important to industrial location because it means that proximity to sources of certain materials and components may be of no advantage. There is nothing to be gained from building a metal goods factory next to the supplier of sheet steel if the material can be obtained at the same price in a better location some distance away. The adoption of a uniform delivered price is also important to the sales side of a firm, because it enables prices to be kept down in distant markets where volume of sales would be low or nonexistant if the customer had to pay the whole of the freight cost. The c.i.f. pricing system in effect enables the producer to pass on part of the real cost of supplying distant consumers to those who are closer to the factory.

The usual alternative to a uniform delivered price is the *f.o.b.* (free-on-board) plant pricing system. In this case the price is established at the plant and the customer pays the transfer cost of getting the product from there to his location. Thus the farther away from the point of production a customer is, the higher the delivered price he has to pay. It is in these circumstances that the structure of freight charges becomes so important in determining the price of materials, components, or finished products in alternative locations. An f.o.b. plant pricing system, when applied to the supply of some industrial input, will make proximity to the source of supply a relevant consideration when plant-location decisions are being made, whereas this can be ignored if a c.i.f. pricing policy is in operation. When applied to the pricing of the firm's output, an f.o.b. system will generally have the effect of limiting the market area for the product, as the price will be higher for distant customers than it would be under c.i.f. pricing, although the exact outcome in any specific case will depend, among other things, on the price elasticity of demand.

A less frequent method of pricing, but one that has attracted much attention in the literature, is the *basing-point* system. Under this system, all production of a certain commodity is regarded as originating from a single point, a uniform price at the factory is set for all producers irrespective of their costs, and the price quoted to any customer is this price plus the cost of transportation that would have been incurred if the consignment had originated at the basing point. If the basing point is central to the market, this system will tend to create the agglomeration of production around that point, other things being equal. The base-price plus system tends to protect the competitive advantage of firms at the basing point, and attracts consumer industries there if the product in question is some commodity like steel which forms an input for other manufacturers. The basing-point system has been used extensively in the United States where multiple basing-point arrangements are also sometimes adopted (Machlup, 1949).

The best-known example of the basing-point price system is undoubtedly the "Pittsburgh plus" arrangement applied for some time to the marketing of steel in the United States. Under this system all steel consignments irrespective of where they were produced were charged to the consumer as if originating from Pittsburgh, a device that protected the Pittsburgh manufacturers from competition from locations with lower production costs. The precise effect of the Pittsburgh plus arrangement on the location of the steel industry before this particular basing-point system was abolished by law is a matter of some controversy, but it certainly had a restricting effect on the industrial development of parts of the South, which were prevented from taking full advantage of the low-cost steel being produced in Birmingham, Alabama. The basing-point system made steel-using firms near Birmingham pay more for their material than their competitors near Pittsburgh had to pay (Stocking, 1954).

This brief discussion of pricing policies should indicate the importance of these matters to plant location, with respect to both obtaining materials and supplying the market. Without some knowledge of the pricing arrangement in operation, highly erroneous conclusions can be arrived at in attempts to explain specific industrial location patterns. The significance of the different systems and, in particular, the difference between c.i.f. and f.o.b. pricing will be considered further in some of the theoretical treatments in succeeding chapters.

5

Transportation

Transportation is often considered to be the most important single determinant of plant location. This is less true than it has been historically, but transportation is still a major factor in the location of many industries. Transport charges affect both what a firm has to pay for its materials and the cost of sending the finished product to the market; like pricing policies, they thus operate on both the input and the output sides of an industry. The importance of the total ingoing and outgoing freight bill varies considerably from industry to industry; for example, raw-material assembly costs may exceed 30 percent of the total cost of manufacturing pig iron, and the delivery of finished steel involves freight charges that are on average more than 10 percent of the base price, while in cotton textiles the freight-cost advantages of southeastern mills as against New England with respect to supplies of raw cotton represents a cost saving of less than one percent (Fulton and Hoch, 1959, 57–58). However, there are very few firms that can ignore the transportation factor in making their locational choice, and for many the total freight bill will be the largest difference between costs at alternative sites. The spatial structures of freight charges are thus of vital significance to industrial location analysis, but before this is discussed some brief remarks on the choice of means of transportation are required.

5.1 METHODS OF TRANSPORTATION

A firm wishing to move any commodity from one point to another generally has a choice, with respect both to the route and the method of transportation used. The increase in the range of choice through time is one of the most important aspects of the advance of modern technology over the past two centuries. When the Industrial Revolution began in Europe in the latter part of the eighteenth century goods had to be moved slowly and laboriously along very poor roads unless natural waterways existed, and this was a major obstacle to any kind of industrial development that involved the assembly of large volumes of bulky inputs. The canal era improved the situation, but the choice of route was still severely restricted and unless a manufacturer could obtain a site beside the waterway or at the terminal he had the problem of trans-shipment and the use of roads for part of the journey. The introduction of railroads not only improved the speed and reliability of overland transportation but also led to the creation of a much more flexible spatial system of movement. There was also, in the course of time, a greater possibility for a manufacturer to site his plant with direct access to the rail route than was the case with the canals. The increasing use of road transportation, made possible by the internal combustion engine and by the construction of modern highway systems, has taken this flexibility a stage further, giving practically every factory the opportunity for direct access to most customers and many sources of material without the necessity for trans-shipment from one means of transport to another en route.

The past few decades have been especially important in terms of new developments in transportation. The highways of many industrial nations have been extensively modernized, and a number of important innovations have been introduced, including the use of pipelines for moving bulky commodities like petroleum and oil, and the development of container systems that greatly facilitate the transfer of goods from road to rail and rail to ship. Again, the effect of all this is to increase the flexibility of the system and enlarge the choice of service available to the manufacturer. The more efficient transportation becomes, as measured by decreasing costs of overcoming distance, the more freedom the manufacturer has to locate his plant with regard to criteria other than freight costs.

The choice of route and method of transportation are closely interrelated. Between most cities in a modern industrial nation there is at least a choice of rail or road, and often a waterway and the possibility of air transport in addition. Sometimes both the general location and the exact site of a factory are determined by other considerations, and the transportation decisions follow from this, but very often the nature of the materials or product require a particular kind of transportation, and the availability of whatever service this happens to be can have a vital bearing on locational choice.

The nature of the material or product to be moved can affect the means of transport required in a number of ways. It is well known that bulky goods of relatively low value, such as iron ore and coal, can be moved cheapest by waterway, while to justify air transportation a commodity must have a very high value in relation to its weight and volume. If it is important to move the goods quickly, then rail would be preferred to road over anything but a short distance, and road would be preferred to a waterway. Some goods may require special facilities such as refrigeration or careful handling, and some means of transportation may be equipped to provide this additional service while others are not.

The distance over which the goods have to be moved is also an important consideration. It is a well-established generalization that for most commodities trucking is the cheapest means of transportation over short distances, railroads are cheaper over medium distances, while waterways are preferred for very long hauls (Hoover, 1948, 20; Thoman, Conkling, and Yeates, 1968, 118; and Karaska, 1969, 23). The reason for this is found in the characteristics of the terminal charges and line-haul charges as they vary between the three methods. Motor trucks have the lowest terminal and overhead costs but the highest line-haul costs per unit of distance, water transport has the highest terminal costs but a relatively low line-haul rate, and the railroads occupy an intermediate position. This is illustrated in Figure 5.1, where the intersection of the vertical axis indicates the terminal charge for each of the three methods of transport, and the slope of the lines give a rough impression of the relationship between line-haul cost and distance.

In general, then, the nature of the commodity to be moved and the distance involved will decide the method of transportation. Given specific sources of material and the location of the market, the necessary means of transportation may then suggest certain sites suitable for the manufacturing unit. But the final choice between the alternatives, of which there may be many, can only be made when the transport costs likely to be incurred at each are related to local advantages with respect to other costs.

5.2 THE STRUCTURE OF FREIGHT RATES

The attribute of great complexity can be applied to a number of matters dealt with in previous chapters, but probably none so clearly warrant this description as the structure of freight rates. The charge levied for a particular transport service is the product of a large number of variables (for a full discussion, see one of the more specialized works

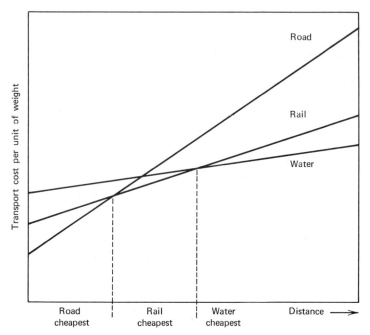

Figure 5.1. A generalized comparison between the cost of using different methods of transportation.

on the subject: for example, Daggett and Carter, 1947; Daggett, 1950; Fair and Williams, 1959; and Sampson and Farris, 1966). All that can be offered here are a number of broad generalizations, which are mainly directed toward the way in which freight rates vary with distance and how this affects the cost of obtaining or supplying goods in different locations. These comments refer specifically to the United States, but the conclusions are broadly representative of the situation existing in any nation. The emphasis is on road and rail transportation, which are the two methods of moving goods most commonly adopted at a local, regional and national level; international maritime and airfreight rates are not considered.

There are three general kinds of freight-rate structures, known respectively as postage-stamp rates, blanket rates, and mileage rates. Whichever of these is in operation in any particular situation will have an important bearing on what is charged for a commodity in different places, assuming an f.o.b. plant price system is in operation, quite irrespective of what the actual rates are. The kind of rate structure is thus highly relevant to plant location.

A *postage-stamp rate* is the simplest possible structure for transport charges. As the name implies, it involves a uniform rate irrespective of distance, like the charge levied by the post office to deliver a letter anywhere within the country. The transport cost of goods shipped on this kind of arrangement will of course have no effect on industrial location, since it is a spatial constant.

A *blanket rate* is similar to a postage-stamp rate, but in this case a different uniform rate is adopted in different zones. The blanket rate customarily rises with the distance of the zone from the origin of the shipment. This kind of rate structure is more common than is often supposed, and has the same effect on plant location locally or regionally as does the postage-stamp rate nationally. Its use in transcontinental rail movements dates back into the nineteenth century, and the present zone patterns are often the product of a long process of evolution. The zones can vary in size from several states to a cluster of points around a single metropolitan area, and they also vary in shape and in their relationship to topographical features (Sampson, 1961, 40–41). Blanket rates have the big advantage to the operating concern that they greatly simplify rate quotations and the publication of tariffs, because between many origins and destinations the charge is the same. An illustration of a blanket rate structure is provided by Figure 5.2, which shows the cost of shipping lumber from the northwest corner of the United States.

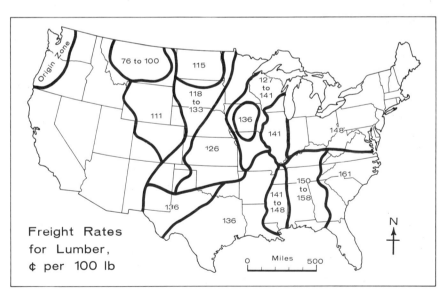

Figure 5.2. An illustration of a blanket freight-rate structure: lumber rates from Western Oregon and Washington to various zones in the United States. (*Source.* Sampson, 1961, 45, Map 1.)

Notice in this case, that there is some variation in the rates quoted for some of the zones but, in most of them, there is a uniform change.

The most common method of charging for transportation in most countries is by a *mileage rate*, whereby cost is related to distance moved from the point of origin. It is important to make a distinction between two separate elements in the rate under this system—the terminal cost and the line-haul cost. The *terminal cost* includes expenses incurred at each end of the journey, comprising the cost of loading and unloading, the preparation and handling of documents, and any other overheads. Because these costs arise irrespective of the distance that the consignment is moved, they are fixed for a given type and quantity of goods. The *line-haul cost* is that part of the total charge which is related to the distance travelled. Because of the constant nature of the terminal charge, the total cost of transporting a certain quantity over a given unit of distance decreases with the length of the haul, since the overheads are being spread over a larger number of miles.

Under a mileage-rate system the cost of moving any consignment of goods is related to three variables: the distance to be covered, the nature of the goods, and the quantity, weight, or volume to be shipped. The simplest way of relating the rate to distance is to establish a constant charge per unit of distance, so that any transport cost (x) would take the form $x = a + by$, where a is the constant terminal charge, b is the line-haul charge per unit of distance, and y is the total distance covered. But, in practice, the line-haul charge is seldom a linear function of distance because the normal arrangement is for the charge per mile to be reduced as the length of the haul increases. This accentuates the tapering affect of the terminal charge on the total rate per mile (that is, terminal plus line-haul charges), and means that the cost/distance profile typically starts off relatively steep and then tends to even off with distance from the point of origin.

The kind of goods moved on any transport system are subject to enormous variations. They differ in their physical characteristics, dimensions, weight, value, method of packing, liability to damage, perishability, and so on, and the shipper will tend to charge a higher rate for some goods than for others depending on the precise nature of the service they require. Thus there exists a complex system of freight rates, which for any transport agency will reflect such things as the competition for specific kinds of business and any specialized service they offer with respect to certain commodities, as well as the general nature of different kinds of goods. In the United States, the rates are generally determined by what is called *the classification*. This involves allocating a class number to every conceivable kind of good and applying a different rate to each class. Class 100 represents the "average" good, less than 100 indicates a commodity needing less than average care, attention, or other special services, while class numbers of more than 100 apply to more fragile goods the shipment of which involves the carrier in more than usual time, trouble, or effort. In addition, *commodity rates* may exist for certain items, generally those which move in large quantities between specific points. There may also be *service tariffs*, payable for services other than the line-haul movement of goods.

A typical set of freight-cost profiles for transportation by truck is shown in Figure 5.3. These indicate the increase in charges with the

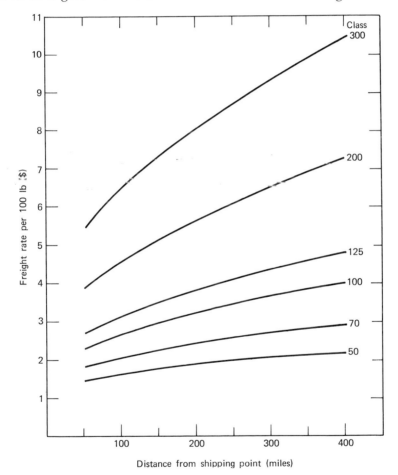

Figure 5.3. Truck freight costs related to distance, for different classes of goods. (*Source of Data.* Summary of public carrier tariffs, in Sears Roebuck mailorder catalog, 1967.)

higher class of goods, and also the tapering off with distance referred to above. Class 300 covers such fragile items as fireplaces and boats; Class 200 includes certain types of furniture, metal ladders (an awkward shape), and pipes and pipe fittings made out of fiber or plastic; Class 125 has within it such less delicate goods as steel bathtubs, kitchen cabinets, certain insulating material, and television and radio sets (fragile but well packaged). The kind of goods that qualify for Class 100 are bicycles, fiberglass panels, certain types of electrical and other machinery, and steel lavatories. Class 70 includes boilers, furnaces, and many kinds of metal goods, while at the bottom of the scale illustrated in Figure 5.3, with the lowest transport costs, are such Class 50 goods as steel fencing, fertilizers, and iron and steel pipes. As the graph shows, the range of charge is considerable; it costs almost five times as much to send a boat to the customer at a given distance than to send a consignment of fertilizer of equivalent weight.

The cost of transportation almost invariably will increase with an increase in the amount shipped. But the increase may not be a regular one, since the rate per ton on a large consignment is very often less than on a small one. And freight rates are generally lower for rail carload (CL) or road truckload (TL) quantities than they are for less-than-carload (LCL) or less-than-truckload (LTL) quantities. Profiles of charges for consignments of different weights as transported by truck are illustrated in a highly generalized way in Figure 5.4. The less-than-proportional increase in cost as weight rises is fairly clear; for example, it costs $24 to ship 400 lb over a distance of 1000 miles but only $43 for 800 lb. The profiles for 200 lb and 5 lb show that there may be a minimum charge irrespective of distance for small shipments; the charge for 200 lb is $5.50 whether the distance is 50 miles or 150 miles, and for a shipment as small as 5 lb the same charge is levied as far as 600 miles. This illustration is based on weights far smaller than most manufacturers are concerned with, but in industrial transportation the same considerations apply. Another interesting feature of Figure 5.4 is the very obvious tapering off of the profiles with large distances. The charges rise fairly steeply for approximately the first 500 miles, but after this an additional 100 miles adds very little to the total freight bill.

In view of the importance of freight rates to industrial location it is perhaps surprising that relatively little empirical work has been conducted on the identification of transport-cost profiles and patterns. There are many studies of economic development in which the structure of freight rates has been examined along with other factors, and there is the interesting work of Alexander and others concerned with the mapping of transport costs in the American midwest (Alexander, 1944; Alexander,

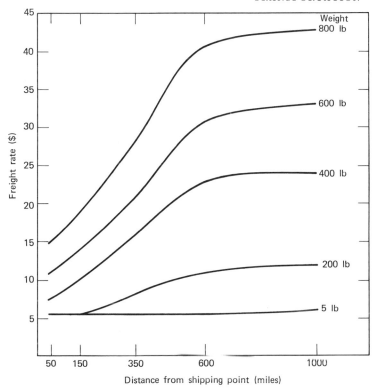

Figure 5.4. Truck freight costs related to distance, for different weights of shipments. (*Source of Data.* Summary of public carrier tariffs, in Montgomery Ward mailorder catalog, 1968.)

Brown, and Dahlberg, 1958; and Russell, 1959). But still there is not enough published research on the geography of transport costs to provide a sound basis for much more than the broad generalizations offered in the preceding paragraphs.

As one illustration of actual transport-cost patterns, some maps from a series in the *Atlas of Illinois Resources* (1960, Section 4) are reproduced in Figure 5.5. Maps *a* and *b* compare the cost of shipping different classes of goods by rail from Chicago and show how much closer the isolines are for Class 70 than for the much more cheaply transported Class 35 goods. Map *c* shows a similar pattern for Class 35 from East St. Louis as the one for Chicago in map *a* while map *d* emphasizes the more expensive nature of truck transportation from Chicago for this class when compared with rail. Map *e* enables a similar comparison to be made for East St. Louis.

One of the reasons for the scarcity of useful empirical work on the

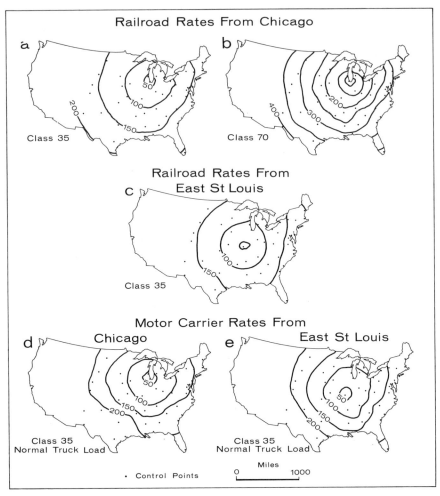

Figure 5.5. Illustrations of transport-cost patterns, for goods shipped from Chicago and East St. Louis. (*Source. Atlas of Illinois Resources,* Section 4 Transportation, 1960, 7 and 26. Printed by authority of the State of Illinois.)

geographical patterns of transport costs is the extreme complexity of freight-rate schedules in practice. Cost gradients are seldom as simple and regular as those illustrated in Figures 5.3 and 5.4. Instead of adopting a smooth curve they usually rise in a series of steps, since the carrier will quote the same rate for a given stretch of line rather than change it with every railroad station or for every mile of road distance. The rate is thus constant between certain points, with the steps tending to become longer with increasing distance from the point of origin. Two profiles illustrated in Figure 5.6 give a good impression of cost/distance

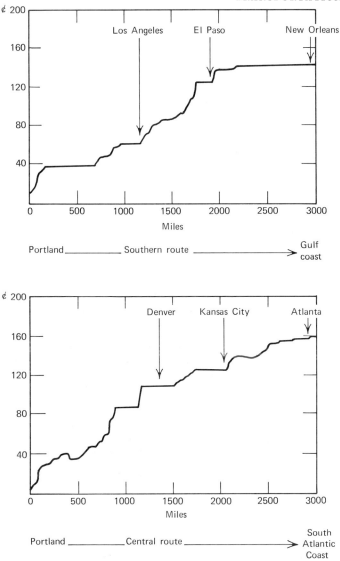

Figure 5.6. Freight-rate profiles for the transportation of lumber and plywood from Portland, Oregon, across the United States via the Central Route to the South Atlantic Coast and via the Southern Route to the Gulf coast. (*Source.* Sampson, 1961, 40–41, Charts 2 and 3.)

relationships in reality. Both show transcontinental rates for the cost of shipping lumber and plywood from the Pacific northwest. The irregular stepping, suggesting a combination of mileage rates and blanket rates, is fairly typical of the situation facing many industries.

Another complication that tends to distort the regularity of a transport-cost gradient is the *break of bulk point*. This occurs if the goods have to be transferred from one carrier to another, or trans-shipped from, say the railroad to a canal barge. When this happens, additional costs will be incurred, similar to another terminal charge in the course of the journey, and this results in a marked step in the cost profile. Such points often attract manufacturers, who avoid additional costs by locating there rather than have their product or materials proceed across the break of bulk point. Additional complications, which can only be mentioned in passing here, include special back-haul rates if the carrier is assured of a return cargo, stopover or in-transit privileges that a customer may be given, and all manner of deals that the carrier may make with favored customers for one reason or another.

One final influence on freight rates that must not be overlooked is competition between carriers. If there are alternative ways of moving goods between two points, competition will tend to keep rates down. But if one carrier has a monopoly over a route he can charge a relatively high price and this may enable him to lower charges over routes along which he does have competition. There are many examples of freight-rate discrimination of this kind in the United States, where the cost of moving some commodities between certain places may be considerably greater or less than the intervening distance would suggest.

An illustration of this is provided by rates for the shipment of phosphate rock for the production of fertilizers from mines in the vicinity of Tampa, Florida. Rates by rail to six cities are listed in Table 5.1, which indicates

Table 5.1 An Illustration of Freight-Rate Discrimination: The Movement of Phosphate Rock from the Tampa District in Florida

Destination	Miles from Tampa	Freight Rate (Dollars/Ton)	Rate per Ton/Mile (Cents)
Norfolk, Virginia	802	4.95	0.62
Lynchburg, Virginia	781	7.40	0.95
Knoxville, Tennessee	679	7.44	1.10
Greensboro, North Carolina	667	7.44	1.11
Montgomery, Alabama	464	6.33	1.37
Pensacola, Florida	462	4.25	0.97

Source. Common Carrier Conference of Domestic Water Carriers (1964, 16–20). The rates are for 1963.

substantial differences in the charge per mile. The rate to Norfolk, on the Virginia coast, is only .62¢ per mile compared with about 1¢ in locations inland, and the rate to Pensacola on the Gulf Coast is .40¢ per mile below that to Montgomery, which is almost exactly the same distance from the mines. The explanation is that the railroad faces competition from water transportation along the coasts, while there is no realistic alternative to rail for moving this bulky material to the other markets. This situation would clearly have an important bearing on the locational decision of a new fertilizer manufacturer, since Norfolk and Pensacola would offer a big saving on the freight bill. Other examples of similar discriminatory practices are to be found where rivers such as the Mississippi and Ohio provide cheap transport for bulky goods, with which the railroads can only compete by lowering their normal rates along the river routes and making it up through high rates elsewhere (Common Carrier Conference of Domestic Water Carriers, 1964).

The determination of transport costs is thus subject to all manner of complicating factors. These make the simple textbook cost/distance profiles less likely to occur in practice than might at first be supposed. Nevertheless, transport-cost patterns are generally more predictable than those of most other manufacturing costs, and it is often not too much of a distortion to depict them as a fairly regular function of distance from the point of origin.

6

Some Other Considerations

The preceding chapters covered the major industrial inputs, the marketing factor, and the effect of transportation. But there are still other influences at work—economic, institutional, and personal—distorting the spatial patterns of comparative advantage created by the variables already discussed, and often having the final say when the locational choice is made. These other considerations may be conveniently grouped under three headings: (1) agglomeration and external economies, (2) public policy and planning, and (3) the element of personal preference or historical accident.

6.1 AGGLOMERATION AND EXTERNAL ECONOMIES

The areal concentration of industrial activity often provides firms with collective benefits that they would not be able to enjoy in an isolated location. These take the form of *external economies,* as opposed to the internal economies that a manufacturer may create within his own organization. Nourse (1968, 85–90) suggests a classification of agglomeration economies into four types: (1) transfer economies arising from savings in transport costs because of the proximity of different firms, (2) internal economies of scale large enough for some single firms to create a town or city, (3) immobile external economies of scale to the firm which arise from the expansion of its own industry in a particular place, and (4) the external economies of scale available to many industries which reduce costs as different industries grow up in one place. The concern here is with the last two of these types—the case of an agglomeration involving one industry or a group of closely related activities, and the more general question of the advantages that a firm in any industry may gain from locating in some large urban-industrial complex like a major city or metropolitan region. To the former type the term *economies of localization* is sometimes applied, while the latter are described as *urbanization economies*.

The advantages to a new firm of a location among other firms engaged in the same activity are fairly obvious. An existing industrial concentration may contain a pool of labor with particular skills, or special educational institutions geared to the needs of the industry in question, both of which will help the firm to reduce the cost of training its workers. Firms may also join together to develop a research institute, a marketing organization, and other collective facilities that individual manufacturers would be unable to provide for themselves. In addition, a city or region specializing in one industry will often have machine makers and repairers, suppliers of components, containers and so on, and other industries ancillary to the main one and providing goods and services for it. All these benefits of agglomeration, when added together, may offer a firm considerable cost advantages over alternative locations.

A good example of this kind of situation is provided by the textile-manufacturing center as it typically developed during the nineteenth century. A town specializing in the production of a particular kind of fabric would generally also contain firms manufacturing and repairing the looms, and others providing bleaching, dying, and finishing facilities. The labor force would be accustomed to women taking a job, and girls from a relatively early age would be familiar with the idea (and soon the practice) of minding a machine in a mill. In the course of time the town might set up a technical college in which there would be departments training people in textile design, the maintenance of machinery, and other skills related to the local industry. If the place or the industry was important enough some kind of marketing organization might also emerge, such as the old Cotton Exchange in Manchester, center of the British cotton industry.

Not all agglomerations demonstrate such a range of advantages. In many cases the benefits from a location in a specialized industrial town may be confined to the local availability of just a few of the goods and services that may be required. A footwear manufacturer may get his cardboard boxes and certain tools locally, but the bulk of his inputs may come from outside. The pottery manufacturer may obtain transfers for applying designs to his product and certain chemicals needed in the manufacturing process from local suppliers but his clay may come from many miles away. The clothing manufacturer may be able to buy his labels, ribbons and packaging materials in the same city, but his fabric might come from a textile manufacturer elsewhere. However complex or however simple, these *inter-industry linkages* can have a very important bearing on locational choice and on the successful growth of certain manufacturing centers.

There is a fairly close relationship between the economies of localization arising in a particular industry and the prevailing size of plant. Small firms generally have more to gain from a location in an existing industrial concentration than have large ones, who can create economies internal to themselves which others have to obtain externally. Thus the manufacture of clothing, for example, is typically concentrated in restricted areas (as in New York, and in London, Leeds, and Manchester in England) where advantage can be taken of proximity to suppliers of buttons, trimmings and so on, the pool of skilled labor, and the interchange of ideas on design so necessary in a fashion trade. Other examples are the manufacture of jewelry and quality sporting guns in Birmingham, England, where each developed in a distinctive quarter of the inner city along with suppliers of certain materials, components and services (Wise, 1950). Sometimes the existence of external economies in a particular city will make a location there a virtual necessity for the small or average-sized firms in an industry, while the larger ones will have a greater freedom of choice. This was the case in the machine-lace industry in England in the nineteenth century, when most firms located in and around the city of Nottingham where the machine makers, finishers, skilled labor and marketing facilities existed, but a few were able to survive in the West Country, well away from the main concentration, by virtue of a large-scale organization which enabled them to develop internally what others enjoyed as external economies in Nottingham (Rawstron, 1958a).

The second aspect of agglomeration as a factor affecting industrial location relates to the advantages that arise in any large urban-industrial area, and that are potentially available to any firm irrespective of the industry to which it belongs. Since the literature on the subject of the relationship between city size and industrial growth is too extensive for even a superficial review here, all that is attempted is a general discussion of why a location in or near a large city appears to have certain attractions for many firms, compared with a location in a smaller community.

The main advantages of a large city or industrial region arise from the existence of a relatively well-developed *infrastructure*. This term covers such things as highways, railroad lines and termini, airports, utilities, commercial facilities, educational institutions, research organizations, and many other services that might not exist or would be less well developed in a smaller place. These advantages may appear to be of a rather intangible nature, but they often express themselves directly through the reduced cost of specific inputs. Isard (1956) illustrates economies of scale with urban size hypothetically, in a diagram reproduced here as Figure 6.1. This shows economies rising as city size increases to a certain point, beyond which diseconomies of scale begin to operate. Isard shows transportation economies, labor economies, and total economies falling fairly steeply after a population of about 100,000 has been reached, but there is as yet no general empirical support for such a specific optimal city size. As Isard points out, the situation varies betwen industries and between individual manufacturers, and we are thrown back on the simple statement that for each firm there are attracting and repelling forces for a location in cities of different sizes (Isard, 1956, 188).

With respect to specific inputs, it is possible to offer some generalizations about the effect of city size. Certain materials and supplies may be cheaper in larger cities than in small ones, by virtue of their local production or the good transportation facilities the major city enjoys, and economies of scale can be expected to make power cheaper as the size of the local market increases (Figure 6.1). Wages are generally

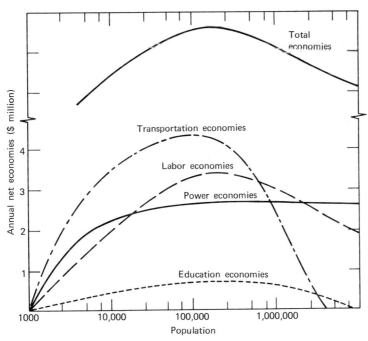

Figure 6.1. Hypothetical economies of scale with urban size. (*Source.* Isard, 1956, 187, Figure 35. Reprinted from *Location and Space Economy* by permission of the MIT Press, Cambridge, Mass. © 1956 by The Massachusetts Institute of Technology.)

higher in large cities than in small ones (Fuchs, 1967, 24), but this is often offset by higher productivity and by the wider range of choice of personnel that the big city offers. However, very high wage rates and strong competition for labor in a prosperous city may raise the real cost of labor and lead to the kind of diseconomies suggested in Isard's diagram. Large urban areas are particularly favorable locations with respect to access to managerial skills since, as Thompson (1968, 55; see also 1965, 44–51) has remarked, they are more than proportionately places of creative entrepreneurship.

But for some inputs a location in a large city is no advantage, and it may even increase costs. As an illustration of this, Figure 6.2 shows the cost of land, building, and financing in a sample of twenty-seven cities in the eastern United States and Canada. They range in size from Chicago (6,750,000 population) and Toronto (1,500,000) to Columbia City, Indiana (4800) and Orangeville, Ontario (4500), and in location from Palm Beach, Florida to Barrie, Ontario, from New Brunswick, New Jersey to Pawhuska, Oklahoma. In the case of land costs there is a fairly clear tendency for the price that has to be paid for an improved industrial site to increase with city size up to about 60,000 population, after which there appears to be no relationship between the two. In the case of building costs the relationship can only be described as random, while the cost of financing (principle plus interest rate costed over twenty years) is

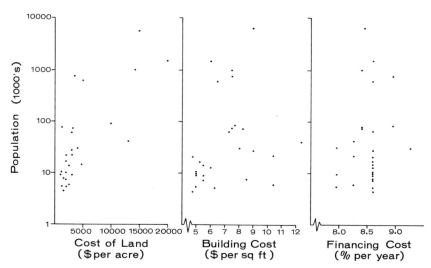

Figure 6.2. The relationship between city size and the cost of land, building and finance, based on a sample of United States and Canadian cities. (*Source of Data.* The Fantus Company, Chicago.)

almost exactly the same in more than half the cities studied, with random fluctuations about the modal figure of $8.60.

These generalizations have no claim to universal validity, nor will they necessarily be true for the whole of the United States or any other country. Indeed, much more empirical inquiry must be undertaken before the relationship between the size of a city and the real cost of industrial inputs can be fully understood. But the previous paragraphs should indicate that this is not a simple matter. For access to certain inputs the advantage of a location in a major urban area may be fairly clear and easily measured, but the main benefits of agglomeration may arise from a mass of intangible and probably immeasurable factors, which the manufacturer almost instinctively knows (or imagines) will increase his efficiency or lower his total costs.

Thus far, this section has concentrated on the advantages of a large urban area, but the disadvantages must not be overlooked. In addition to the higher price that a firm may have to pay for certain inputs, such as land, taxes, and perhaps labor, those who locate in the city must also contend with such problems as traffic congestion and lack of space, which are becoming increasingly important as diseconomies of scale in the modern urban world. Indeed, the forces of *deglomeration* are leading many firms to leave the inner city for what they consider to be better sites outside.

Nevertheless, the balance of advantage still appears to favor the city. The continuing growth of industrial activity in certain highly developed regions, such as the major manufacturing belt of the United States, the southeastern corner of England, and the Paris-Randstadt-Ruhr triangle in northwestern Europe, is clear evidence of this, and seems justified from a purely economic point of view. But regional and urban planners are becoming increasingly concerned about this kind of development, pointing out that the external economies of an individual plant are counterbalanced by the growing social costs of the expansion of big metropolitan areas (Economic Commission for Europe, 1967, 39). In this context, some remarks by Wilbur Thompson (1968, 60) are highly pertinent:

The larger places have a clear and sizable advantage in such areas as cheaper and more flexible transportation and utility systems, better research and development facilities, a more skilled and varied labor supply, and better facilities for educating and retraining workers. Further, these economies of scale are captured by private business as lower private costs; at the same time private business is able to slough off on society various social costs that its presence imposes, such as its addition to traffic congestion and air pollution. If, then, the external diseconomies of business-created noise, dirt, congestion, and pollution are some increasing function of city size and/or density, factor market prices are biased in favor of larger urban areas, and understate the true marginal costs of production in the metropolis. In the absence of sophisticated public policy and the even more sophisticated public management that would be needed to implement price reform, factor markets so biased promote urban growth and great size.

In other words, if the manufacturer in the city had to bear his share of the social costs of agglomeration, a location in a major urban area might look far less attractive than it does at present. The current public interest in the environmental pollution issue is drawing increasing attention to the fact that private industry is passing some of its real costs of operation onto the rest of the community, a problem which is by no means confined to the cities. This leads to the question of public policy and planning as influences on industrial location.

6.2 PUBLIC POLICY AND PLANNING

Planning of one kind or another is an important factor affecting industrial location in many countries today. This matter will be introduced only very briefly here, since it is discussed in detail in Part Six.

National and local government bodies may set out to influence industrial location when they believe that certain economic, social, or strategic objectives can be achieved more readily by planning than by leaving manufacturers to locate where they please. Industrial location may be influenced in two ways. First, freedom of choice of site may be restricted through land-use zoning or by some tax penalty in an area where new industrial development is to be prevented or discouraged. Second, governments can encourage firms to go to certain areas which need new development by offering financial inducements in the form of a loan, subsidy, or tax incentive. In countries where industry is state-owned, or where the positive direction of industry to selected areas is possible, public action can modify existing location patterns speedily and effectively. In a free-enterprise economy the adjustment is likely to be less rapid and predictable, since whatever the national government may think is best for the nation, and whatever inducements they offer, locational decisions are still subject to the capriciousness of the individual entrepreneur.

How far public bodies should influence business decisions such as choice of plant location is a very difficult question. It depends on the values of the society involved, their basic objectives, and how they rate such things as the freedom of the individual enterprise against the welfare of the majority. It also depends on the magnitude of the problems which exist. Another difficult issue is the extent to which a carefully planned pattern of industry is likely to be more efficient in a purely economic sense than the collective decisions of individual businessmen or corporations pursuing their own objectives. But whatever the pros and cons of planning as against unregulated private capitalism, it seems certain that matters of public policy will become steadily more important as influences on industrial location in most countries as the social and economic benefits of national, regional, and local planning become increasingly obvious.

6.3 HISTORICAL ACCIDENT AND PERSONAL PREFERENCE

An investigation of any industry reveals cases of plant locations that cannot be explained by obvious economic factors. The choice of one site over possible alternatives might seem to be entirely a matter of chance, with historical accident or the personal whim of the entrepreneur as the only possible explanations.

The term *historical accident* in this context covers a number of random factors. Some places have a particular industry by virtue of the accident of birth of the founder of a business: the automobile factories of Ford at Detroit and Morris at Oxford, England, have been previously mentioned, and hundreds of others with similar origins could be added. For example, the city of Nottingham in England owes the existence of two of its largest businesses—Players Tobacco and the Boots pharmaceutical concern—to two local entrepreneurs who had the initiative to build big manufacturing corporations out of the small shop that they started with. Another accidental factor is the invention of some kind of revolutionary process or machinery, which may lead to the growth of an industry in a particular city. Sometimes there is a greater probability that the invention will take place in a specific region, where a more primitive form of the industry in question is already in existence, but which of a number of places within the region produces the inventor is often purely a matter of chance. Industrial concentrations that owe their origin partly to local ingenuity of this kind are quite common in the older industrial districts of Western Europe, examples from Britain being the manufacture of knitwear and lace in the East Midlands and the fine china industry of Stoke-on-Trent. Other important industries can be explained by their founders settling in a particular place simply because they liked the look of it, and then building up a business there which could have been equally successful in a number of other locations. The random factor in the diffusion of industrial innovation can also have a bearing on the spatial pattern of the adoption of new techniques, with some places and some entrepreneurs being more receptive to change than others.

This leads to the question of the personal preference of the entrepreneur as an influence on the location of industry. This is of course closely bound up with historical accident, and is difficult to distinguish entirely from the general availability of entrepreneurial skill as discussed in Chapter 3. The influence of the personal factor in business behavior may be looked at in two ways: through its effect on the location of new plants and through its effect on the mobility of existing industry.

The man who sets up his factory in a particular place because it is close to a good golf course is a celebrated figure in the literature of industrial location. The number of decisions that have really been influenced by this specific consideration is questionable, but there is a mass of empirical evidence that such matters do enter into the decision-making process at some stage, and that for many plants they may determine the precise choice of location. For example, in a survey of new industrial development or expansion schemes in Atlanta between 1946 and 1955 Chapman and Wells (1958) found personal reasons cited by eleven of the forty-nine firms as factors influencing the choice of this particular city as a location. Overall, personal factors ranked fourth behind the market, transportation facilities, and labor. In a survey of the factors determining business decisions in Michigan, Katona and Morgan (1950, 1952) interviewed executives of 188 plants, and found that enough of these to represent 51 percent of the state's employees listed personal reasons of some kind for their original location in Michigan. The most frequent response to the question of how the firm happened to locate in Michigan rather than another state was that the founder lived in Michigan when the plant was first opened. In an investigation into the influence of personal factors in the location of small manufacturing plants, Malinowski and Kinnard (1961) took a random sample of small firms in the Hartford, Connecticut, area and found that of a total of 359 reasons mentioned by executives for location at their specific site, 44 were purely personal. The personal reasons included proximity to home and family, personal attachment to the area, and important contacts. Malinowski and Kinnard concluded that personal factors certainly play a role in the locational decision, but as a secondary factor; 45 percent of executives mentioned them, but only 16 percent put them among the most important reasons.

More studies of this kind could be cited, but these are enough to emphasize the general importance of personal factors. The main conclusion appears to be that economic factors probably establish a broad region within which a location will be considered, while personal factors operate at a secondary level in the decision-making process, narrowing down the choice to a few communities or perhaps to a single location. This matter will be discussed again in a more theoretical context in Part Three, Chapter 12.

Once a plant has been built, personal factors as well as the immobility of fixed capital may prevent a relocation, even if this seems desirable on other economic grounds. In addition to leaving familiar surroundings, a move involves an increase in managerial effort while it is planned and undertaken, with some degree of risk and uncertainty as to the outcome. Some manufacturers may simply prefer to stay put, no matter how much an alternative location may seem to be an attractive economic proposition. The attitude of the small businessman in this situation, and probably many businessmen with larger plants, is well summarized in the following imaginary statement (Eversley, 1965, 108):

I am all right where I am. I am making a living. The home trade suits me. I don't like to move to a new location, it might be worse there. More income means higher taxes. Moving is a bother. Here I know where I am—suppliers, customers, workpeople, council officials, transport agents. If I move I might be richer, but I might be poorer. I know of a chap who went bankrupt after he moved. I am too old to think of expanding very much. We've got all we need. If I move out of reach of toolmakers, repairers, suppliers . . . I might have to pre-plan production. They might make me adopt stock control, progress chasing, introducing computing or accounting staff.

Such attitudes make an important contribution to industrial inertia, or the preservation of the status quo, and help to give existing industrial location patterns a degree of stability and permanence that economics alone may not justify.

The influence of personal considerations and other apparently random factors makes the general explanation of industrial location even more difficult than it might otherwise be. This is closely connected with the broader problem of interpreting the evident suboptimal nature of much corporate decisionmaking in the modern world, when it is viewed entirely in the context of financial profits. These are the kind of difficulties that lead some observers to despair of the usefulness of any attempts at theorizing in the field of industrial location, and to fall back on the explanation of individual cases as the best that scientific endeavor can achieve. But others take a more enterprising view, as expressed by Andrews and Brunner (1962/3, 72):

The location of a particular factory may have been precisely determined because it suited the managing director's desire for convenient access to a certain golf course, or because his wife wanted the week-end home to be in the Lake

District. The question is not whether such a factor is, or is not, important in the individual case, but whether any particular factor of this kind has systematic effects upon economic variables.

Recent literature in location analysis clearly indicates a growing awareness of and interest in "behavioral" aspects of decision making. The social scientist, in industrial location as in any other field, cannot forever regard the capriciousness of man as an inconvenience, to be assumed away in the theories he constructs. Instead, it should be seen as a permanent challenge to him to devise theory that truly reflects the nature of man.

6.4 SOME CONCLUDING REMARKS

Part One has taken a broad look at the various factors influencing industrial location. The entrepreneur or corporation has to assemble at the factory site the necessary inputs, combine them in an appropriate manner for the process of manufacture, and then send the finished goods to the market. Transportation plays a vital role in connecting the factory with the rest of the economic system, making possible the movement of materials, fuels, energy, labor and finished products. Scale and price enter the picture as functions of the interaction of the forces of supply and demand, influencing the choice of location and in turn being themselves influenced by it. External economies, government action, and all manner of fortuitous and personal circumstances can also play a part in the complex process of locational decision making. All these variables have necessarily been described in a fairly elementary way, and certainly without any claim to comprehensive treatment, but hopefully enough information has been provided to make the transition into more theoretical and abstract thinking a relatively painless process.

In looking at the location problem in general, or in the context of a particular industry, some of the variables considered will be more important than others. Many attempts have been made to discover empirically the relative importance of the various location factors, largely through questionnaire or interview surveys of the behavior of individual firms. But these inquiries are seldom designed in a way which would insure that the findings are relevant to anything other than a restricted number of firms in a particular area, and the results, taken together, are remarkable only for the divergence of the observations presented.

Actually the relative importance of different causal factors varies in space and through time as well as between industries and individual firms. At some points in time and space, industrial location may have been dominated by one primary consideration, such as the need for water power in the early stages of the Industrial Revolution in Britain and the eastern part of the United States, or access to supplies of coal throughout much of the nineteenth century in the emerging industrial nations of Europe and North America. But at the same time water power and coal meant nothing to large parts of the world, where the primitive form of manufacturing industry that existed was almost entirely geared to the local market. As technology has progressed in the advanced nations, energy has become much more mobile and transportation more efficient, and the market, skilled labor and externalities appear to be increasing their relative importance in these countries. In the emerging industrial nations of the present century, however, the need to utilize basic raw materials, unskilled labor, and cheap sources of power makes these factors still very important.

These trends are very significant in attempting to understand the changing circumstances in which industrial location decisions are made. In most existing geographical texts, great emphasis is placed on transportation and access to raw materials, but there is considerable evidence from Western Europe (for example, Economic Commission for Europe, 1967) and North America (for example, Management and Economics Research Inc., 1967) to suggest that their importance is being reduced. As industrial processes have become more sophisticated, the value added at the plant has tended to increase its importance relative to the value of the material inputs. Improvements in transportation have lessened the friction of distance and, in any case, industry is becoming more dependent on relatively mobile materials drawn from other manufacturing industries. The bulky and highly localized raw materials, so important in earlier stages of industrialization, no longer exert the same pull on plant location. One exception to the general trend is in the supply of water for industrial purposes, which still imposes stringent restrictions on locational choice for industries like electricity generation where water is a major input.

The decrease in the importance of transportation and materials has been accompanied by an increase in the significance of labor supply and the market. Although unionization and national wage legislation can be expected to reduce spatial variations in wage rates, this is sometimes a slow process, and differences in the skills and reliability of labor can still create substantial variations in real labor costs, as was suggested in Chapter 3. The growing importance of the market as a factor in industrial location is associated with the desire of the large-scale manufacturer of both consumer goods and industrial components to be near a major concentration of consumers.

Earlier in this chapter reference was made to the influence of external economies of agglomeration and urbanization on industrial location. This is undoubtedly a factor of growing importance in many industries, a condition reflected in the current interest in the effect of industrial linkages on plant location (for example, Britton, 1969; Richter, 1969; Striet, 1969; Wood, 1969). With the pull of the market, externalities go a long way toward explaining the continuing concentration of manufacturing in the major metropolitan regions. But there is also some evidence of a trend in another direction. Some of the external economies usually found in major industrial agglomerations are becoming more mobile geographically; for example, information can now be transmitted very efficiently over long distances with advances in telecommunications and computer technology, and a carefully developed industrial park in a small town can offer many of the services that a firm could expect to find in a metropolitan area. There has thus been some movement of industry in modern industrial nations from the inner city to nearby suburban communities and beyond to some smaller towns.

These, very briefly, are some of the current trends. As technological advances continue to be made, there will no doubt be further changes in the relative importance of the location factors in different parts of the world. And the possibility of changes in the general importance of the location decision as a factor in the success of a business must not be overlooked. The increasing spatial mobility of some of the critical inputs appears to be widening the choice of location in many industries, and hence expanding the possibility of location decisions being made on grounds other than those of economics.

PART TWO

Approaches to Theory, and Models of Industrial Location

Having identified the variables involved in industrial location analysis, the next step is to determine how they can be integrated into some kind of theoretical framework. This should help to clarify how the variables relate to each other, and how their significance can vary from case to case. Ideally, such a theory should be universal in its validity in space and time, and should be capable of generating operational models and testable hypotheses for use in empirical inquiry.

The development of industrial location theory has occupied the attention of both geographers and economists. But their respective approaches have differed, the geographer being mainly concerned with arriving at generalization through case studies with a largely intuitive conceptual base, while the economist has shown a greater interest in a more formal, abstract, or deductive theoretical approach with a relatively small empirical content. Part Two offers a broad view of the literature in both fields. Chapter 7 examines briefly a very limited selection of geographical contributions. Chapter 8 takes a more extended look at the work of the economists who have been concerned with industrial location theory. Chapter 9 provides an introduction to the development of operational models. These three chapters serve both as an exposition of the various approaches taken in the development of theory and models in industrial location analysis and as background for the synthesis attempted in Part Three.

7

Industrial Location Theory: Some Geographical Contributions

The geographer's traditional predisposition toward the empirical investigation of the real world has tended to limit his contribution to industrial location theory. His case studies have provided an enormous body of factual knowledge concerning the location of specific industries, but few geographical inquiries have been framed in a way likely to lead to conclusions of relevance beyond the narrow topical and spatial context of the actual problem under review. Even fewer studies have had the formulation of general principles as their primary aim.

The treatment of the geographer's theoretical contribution here is therefore highly selective. It deals only with work that appears to have made a direct and significant contribution to the *general* understanding of industrial location. No attempt is made to discuss geographical theory relating to such matters as settlement patterns, diffusion of innovation, spatial interaction, and the location of other economic activities, despite their obvious connections with the location of industry.

7.1 EARLY GEOGRAPHICAL APPROACHES

Until the 1950s, few geographers were concerned with theoretical matters. They were generally satisfied with explaining industrial location patterns as a response to the physical environment, or with describing their historical evolution. Most geographers were aware of the influence of raw materials, transportation, labor, the market, and so on, but few had any understanding of how these factors really operated. Consequently, the findings of these early studies (particularly those with an environmentalist bias) were usually highly restricted in their validity and, on occasions, were quite erroneous. Their contribution toward a theory or principles of plant location was very limited.

One of the few geographers to consider the location problem in more general terms at this time was Richard Hartshorne (1926, 1927). He advanced the then revolutionary view that *the factor of relative location* is a more important influence on economic activity than physical factors such as relief, soil, drainage, and climate. He recognized the need for a general method by which the importance of various factors influencing the location of manufacturing in particular places could be evaluated, and which could also help find the best location for new plants.

The first major geographical contribution to location theory was that of Walter Christaller (1933), with his work on *central place theory*. Christaller was not primarily interested in industrial location, nor was his viewpoint entirely geographical. His aim was to find out whether there might be laws that determine the number, size, and distribution of towns and cities. Arguing from certain initial assumptions, Christaller deduced a geometrically regular pattern of central places (service centers) and complimentary regions. Illustrations of this are unnecessary here, since they can be found in most of the standard texts in urban geography (for example, Murphy, 1966).

Despite the failure of some elements to withstand empirical testing, Christaller's model is generally recognized as a valuable formal statement of the spatial arrangement of towns as service centers under certain simplified conditions. As such, it is a useful guide to the pattern likely to be adopted by manufacturing industry in a special demand situation, where production is punctiform in location and serving a market of areal extent. But it fails to encompass the development of belts of industrial concentration and the agglomeration tendencies that are so important a part of the modern industrial world. Central place theory is a theory of the location of tertiary activities, as Berry and Pred (1961, 6) have stressed; it is relevant to manufacturing as a special case, which can be expected to represent reality only in circumstances where rather special market conditions exist.

Most of the early economic geographers were understandably reticent about stating their ideas concerning industrial location as formal laws or general principles. A major exception was George Renner (1947, 1950). Renner classified industry into extractive, reproductive, fabricative, and facilitative, and stated that to undertake any of these, six ingredients are required: raw materials, market, labor (including management), power, capital, and transportation. He formulated a general principle of industrial location (Renner, 1947, 169):

> An industry tends to locate at a point which provides optimum access to its ingredients or component elements. If all these component elements be juxtaposed, the location of the industry is predetermined. If, however, they occur widely separated, the industry is so located as to be most accessible to that element which would be the most expensive or difficult to transport and which, therefore, becomes the locative factor for the industry in question.

This principle, though generally applicable, operates in a different way with each of the four classes of industry. *The law of location for fabricative industries* (that is, manufacturing) reads as follows (Renner, 1947, 181):

> Any manufactured industry tends to locate at a point which provides optimum access to its ingredient elements. It will, therefore, seek a site near to:
> (a) *Raw Materials*, if it uses perishable or highly condensible raw substances or
> (b) *Market*, where the processing adds fragility, perishability, weight, or bulk to the raw materials, or where its products are subject to rapid changes in style, design, or technological character or
> (c) *Power*, where the mechanical energy costs of processing are the chief item in the total cost or
> (d) *Labor*, where its wages to skilled artisans are a large item in the total cost.

Renner also considers what he terms industrial simbiosis. *Disjunctive simbiosis* is where it is advantageous for unlike industries to exist together without any "organic" connection; for example, the silk textile industry drawing female labor from the families of miners and steelworkers in some Pennsylvania towns. *Conjunctive simbiosis* occurs when different industries in an area have an organic connection, such as one providing material for another. This tendency for industry to develop symbiotically may ultimately lead to a big regional concentration of industry, to which Renner applies the expression *conindustrialization*.

Thus there is much good sense in Renner's statements, which bring together many of the variables discussed in Part One of this book. The main criticism is his failure to penetrate the economic forces behind his laws (Murata, 1959). For example, he neglects to emphasize that an industry's "point of optimum access to its ingredient elements" is a product of spatial cost variation, and his industrial symbiosis and conindustrialization are merely elaborate expressions for externalities and agglomeration tendencies. Nevertheless, by putting his notions down in a formal way Renner performed a useful service, particularly for the great majority of geographers unaware of the more rigorous theoretical work of some economists available by this time.

7.2 ECONOMIC-BASE THEORY

The search for generalization through empirical inquiry within a fairly simple conceptual framework typifies much of the work of the geographer in industrial location analysis. One of the most fruitful applications of this approach has been in the investigation of the urban economic base. Economic-base theory involves making a distinction between industries producing for the population of the city itself and those producing for an external market. The *basic industries* are those that produce for export, while those that serve the local market are termed *nonbasic industries*.

The first attempt to analyze the industrial structure of cities in this way was made in the 1930s, and the idea was soon taken up by a number of geographers (see Alexander, 1954; Murphy, 1966). Once the technical problem of separating goods exported from those sold locally is overcome, total figures for value of production or employment in the basic and nonbasic sectors, respectively, can be calculated for any city or region. Then the B/N *ratio* can be found, which takes the form $1:x$ where x is nonbasic employment divided by basic employment. This ratio tends to vary between 1:0.5 and 1:2, with big cities having a higher figure (that is, more nonbasic or city-serving industry because of their greater self-sufficiency). Some writers have claimed that this ratio has analytical value in the interpretation of urban economic structure (Alexander, 1954), but others have criticized the concept on the grounds that the ratio is difficult if not impossible to find in practice, and that in any case no precise significance can be attached to the figure (Blumenfeld, 1955).

The B/N ratio is, of course, purely a descriptive device, of no value in itself in explaining why specific industries are represented as they are in particular cities. But the *minimum requirement approach* to economic-base theory, as developed by Ullman and Dacey (1960), is of some value as a predictive device. This approach is based on the proposition that in any city of a given size there is a minimum requirement for every industry, needed to satisfy local demand, and that employment in excess of this can be equated with the basic or export sector. The minimum requirement is found empirically by simply examining the employment structure of towns of the appropriate size and seeking the smallest representation of the industry in question. This is then taken to be the minimum requirement, although extreme low values may be disregarded (Alexandersson, 1956).

The nonbasic employment, as derived from the minimum requirement technique, tends to increase with the size of the city. The values are such that when the proportion of total employment in the nonbasic sector is plotted against the logarithm of the population of the city size class there is a linear relationship, and the minimum requirements for individual industries increase in a similar manner (Table 7.1). Once

Table 7.1 Minimum Percentages Employed in Selected Activities in Cities of Varying Size Classes in the United States, 1950

Size Class (Population)	All Industries	Manufacturing	Construction	Wholesale and Retail
Over 1,000,000	56.7	7.2	4.6	16.9
300,000–800,000	48.6	6.8	4.1	15.6
100,000–150,000	43.1	6.2	3.8	13.5
25,000–40,000	39.8	2.7	3.2	14.9
10,000–12,500	33.2	2.2	2.5	13.0
2,500–3,000	24.0	2.8	1.8	8.6

Source. Ullman and Dacey (1962, 123). The figure for all industries is the sum of the "minimum requirement" of every individual industry, and thus represents nonbasic employment. The figures for each size class are based on a sample of 38 cities, except the over 1,000,000 category where there are 14.

these relationships have been established, the nonbasic industrial structure of a city of any size can be predicted simply by reading off the the minimum requirement for each industry from graphs or by using the regression equations, and when these are subtracted from the actual employment figures for each industry in the city the residual is the basic or export sector. The main conceptual problem here is that there is no reason (other than the previous empirical findings) why the economic base for any town should be as predicted, and special local circumstances may make the town deviate considerably from the expected economic character. The minimum requirement should, in fact, be thought of as minimum expectation; cities do not necessarily require specific amounts of any industry, although observation might suggest that a certain minimum can be expected.

If it is possible to overcome the operational problems involved, economic-base theory can help to explain industrial location by identifying within the industrial structure of a city components producing for different markets. The nonbasic sector is that which can be explained as a response to demand generated internally, while the surplus, which may be substantial in relatively few branches of industry, indicates those activities that the city produces for sale outside. The export industries can then be subjected to further analysis to find out why they should occur in this particular place.

Another approach related to economic-base theory is the development of empirical generalizations concerning the observed association between industrial structure and city size. This is implicit in the minimum-requirement approach, and has been taken further by a few writers. For example, Czamanski (1964, 1965) has attempted to develop a theory of industrial location and urban growth, which would enable the amount of industry of different types to be predicted for a city of given size, with the parameters of his model derived empirically from a study of the industrial structure of over 200 American cities. Stafford (1966), in a study of the industrial structure of Illinois, has shown that the probability of finding a given type of industry in an area is directly related to the population of the area; the manufacture of cigars, optical instruments, and jewelry is more likely to be found in Chicago than in a small town in southern Illinois.

Economic-base theory and related research has thus been able to establish that there is some degree of regularity in the relationship between the size of a city and certain aspects of its industrial structure. The basic-nonbasic distinction and the notion of a minimum requirement provide a conceptual framework within which these observations can be interpreted. But as the basis of a general theory of industrial location, these concepts are clearly inadequate. In stressing the relationship between industrial location and city size, undue weight is attached to one causal factor, which is in any case largely a surrogate for the market. Nevertheless, economic-base theory has been used quite extensively in research, particularly as a device for predicting the impact of new industrial development—an application which is discussed in Chapter 23.

7.3 RAWSTRON'S THREE PRINCIPLES

One of the most important geographical contributions to the general understanding of industrial location is to be found in a short paper by E. M. Rawston (1958b). His approach is directed toward finding to what extent choice of location is restricted if economic viability is to be achieved, and how this restriction is imposed. Three principles of industrial location are offered: *physical restriction, economic restriction,* and *technical restriction.* They are all economic in application, but only the second is dominantly economic in its formulation.

The physical restriction applies if some natural resource is to be produced. But it only applies insofar as it decides where, for example, one cannot mine or quarry; which deposit should be worked, what the level of output should be, and where the mines should be located, is determined by the economic factors embodied in the second principle.

It is the formulation of the principle of economic restriction that makes Rawstron's contribution such a valuable one. The approach involves knowledge of the cost structure of industries, and embodies the concept of *spatial margins to profitability* where costs become too great for industries to be economically viable. Rawstron lists expenditure on labor, materials, land, marketing, and capital as the components of a firm's cost structure; unlike most writers he does not identify transport as a separate cost factor, but views it as contributing to spatial variations in the cost of other items. Expenditure on each component will vary from place to place, and the sum of the costs arising solely from choice of location is termed the *locational cost*.

The locational element in cost structures is illustrated in Figure 7.1. Three plants (A, B, and C) at three different locations require equal quantities by value of labor, materials, land, marketing and capital, but the cost of these inputs varies with location. For example, it costs more to get the necessary amount of labor at B than A, and materials are more expensive at C than at the other two plants. Figure 7.1a shows locational costs (the shaded portions) allocated to each component,

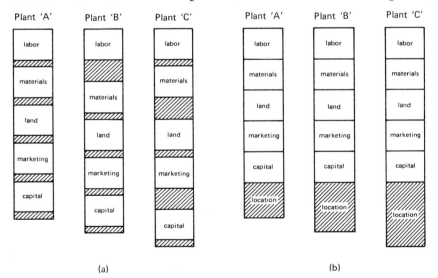

Figure 7.1. The effect of location on the cost structures of three imaginary plants. (*Source.* Rawstron, 1958b, 136–137, Figures 1 and 2.)

and Figure 7.1b indicates total locational costs. Clearly, operation at A will be cheapest, and operation at C will be most expensive. The importance of any one component of the cost structure as a locational influence is determined by how large a share its basic cost (that is, without locational cost) is of total cost, and the extent to which its locational cost varies from place to place.

Spatial variations in production costs lead to the imposition of limits, or margins, to the areas within which viable operation is possible. These margins arise from variations in total costs, but in certain circumstances they may, in effect, be a reflection of the cost of one component. This would be the case if only one component showed significant cost variation from place to place.

The third principle—that of technical restrictions—encompasses the effect of the level of technology on location. If an industrialist knows that his plant will need frequent modification to keep up with technical progress he may not pay great attention to his location, but as technical improvements become less frequent, locational economies may become more important. In most cases the effect of technical change is felt through some change in the nature or cost of the inputs required, and this can be analyzed in the framework of the second principle.

Implicit in Rawstron's idea of spatial restrictions on plant location is the concept of narrowing down of locational choice. A series of location factors, or components of the cost structure, may impose a gradual narrowing of choice, as successively more restrictive factors eliminate sites or areas which more permissive factors had suggested as possibilities. The location of electricity-generating stations in the Trent Valley of midland England illustrates this (Rawstron, 1951, 1954, 1966). The basic requirements of this industry are a market, cheap coal, an extensive level site, land for waste disposal, water for cooling, and rail access. The market is the least restrictive factor, since the national electricity grid enables plants to be located virtually anywhere other things being equal. The next restriction is imposed by the need for coal, which means that power stations must be on or near a coalfield; as part of the lowest-cost coalfield in Britain, the Nottinghamshire field has a special advantage for the location of this industry. Three more factors narrow down the choice still further: the need for large quantities of water for cooling suggests a site beside the river Trent; the flood plain provides extensive level sites and, in some places, old gravel pits that can be used for waste disposal; and the rail routes act as the final restrictive factor. As Figure 7.2 shows, all the power stations actually occupy riverside sites in the Trent valley, at points of rail access to coal supplies.

This idea of a successive narrowing down of choice cannot be applied

INDUSTRIAL LOCATION THEORY 105

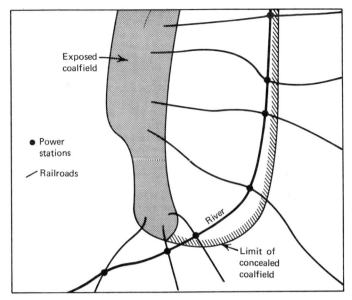

Figure 7.2. The principle of narrowing down of locational choice by successively more stringent restrictive factors, as illustrated by the location of electricity generating stations in the East Midlands of England. (*Source.* Simplified from Rawstron, 1966, 311, Figure 54.)

to every industry in a useful way. But it can help to sort out the importance of different causal factors, and the restrictions they impose. And in some instances, where cost data are unavailable or imprecise, this approach may be as near as one can get to a sensible evaluation of the effect of different variables.

Rawstron's contribution to the geographical literature on industrial location is thus a very valuable one. In stressing the importance of cost structure he got to the root of matters which Renner and others had been able to approach much less directly, and by introducing the concept of spatial margins to viability he was able to avoid couching his theory in terms of profit maximization. There is much in Rawstron's 1958 paper that is worth elaborating, and some of its ideas figure prominently in the theoretical synthesis attempted in Part Three of this book.

7.4 THE BEHAVIORAL APPROACH

One of the reasons why geographers have been reluctant to generalize or theorize about industrial location is the apparently fortuitous nature of many real-world locational decisions. The classic case of the manufacturer located near his favorite golf course, and similar circumstances mentioned in Chapter 6, have often been put forward as preventing the development of any kind of theory which can accord with empirical observation. The perfectly informed, rational, and optimizing "economic man" assumed in much economic analysis, including location theory, does not exist in practice; instead, men act with imperfect knowledge, and often in pursuit of partially nonmaterial ends.

In recent years a behavioral view of location that stresses the suboptimal nature of man's decisions has been gaining ground, the most thorough statement to date being by Allen Pred (1967, 1969). Man is seen as possessing both limited knowledge and limited power to use it: "Every locational decision is viewed as occurring under conditions of varying information and ability, ranging, at least theoretically, from null to perfect knowledge of all alternatives, and as being governed by the varying abilities (as well as objectives) of the decision-maker(s)" (Pred, 1967, 24). Any entrepreneur thus has a place in what Pred terms the *behavioral matrix* (Figure 7.3). A position toward the bottom right of the matrix indicates a good level of knowledge as well as good ability to use it, and there would be a high degree of probability of a good choice of location, perhaps one near the economic optimum. As knowledge and ability decrease, toward the top left of the matrix, the probability of a good locational choice is reduced. The emphasis is on probability because good knowledge and ability are not a guarantee of a good choice of

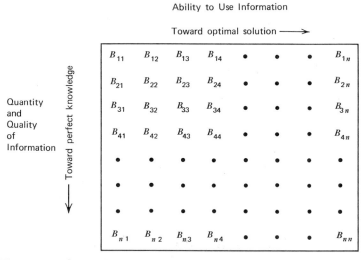

Figure 7.3. The behavioral matrix. (*Source.* Pred, 1967, 25, Figure 1.)

location (though they make it very likely), just as there is an outside chance that a firm with little knowledge of the alternatives and a poor management could be lucky enough to make a good decision.

The behavioral matrix is put forward as an interpretive device to assist in the understanding of real-world deviations from location patterns produced by deterministic models based on the assumption of economic man. Variations in the information available to individual decision makers and in their ability to use it helps to explain the simultaneous presence of random and nonrandom elements in spatial distributions. The argument is that the regular elements are the result of locational decisions in general but perhaps not perfect accord with theory of the deterministic kind (that is, near-optimal decisions made from a position toward the bottom right of the matrix). The random elements reflect choices made from a position of more limited information or ability to use it, which would tend to depart significantly from the economic optimum.

Pred applies the behavioral matrix concept to the interpretation of patterns of agricultural land use and the distribution of central places as well as to industrial location, but it is the latter which is the present concern. His approach is illustrated simply in a diagram which relates specific locations in an imaginary situation to the position of firms in the matrix (Figure 7.4). In this illustration three areas exist in which the profitable operation of some industrial activity is possible. These areas are bounded by the spatial margins introduced in Section 7.3 (Rawstron, 1958b; Smith, 1966), and each contains an optimum location designated 0. The location of thirteen imaginary firms is indicated by dots, each of which is connected by a line to that cell in the behavioral matrix which best summarizes the firm's hypothetical information and ability-to-use characteristics. Those toward the bottom right of the matrix in general have chosen locations near one of the optima, while of the four firms with very limited information and ability three are in extramarginal (unprofitable) locations and the other is within a margin but well away from the optimum. The choice of satisfactory locations by some firms with information or ability-to-use handicaps emphasizes the failure of the matrix position to predict exactly how good a choice will be made. The general message conveyed by this illustration is that "the apparently chaotic qualities of the spatial distribution of most manufacturing production at any one date is ascribable to the fact that the real-world is populated by a broad spectrum of bounded rational, satisficing locational actors and not by undifferentiated profit maximizers" (Pred, 1967, 91–93).

As Pred concedes, the behavioral-matrix interpretation of location decisions is "only a verbal formalization of the fairly obvious" (Pred, 1967, 121). But it is a useful way of conceptualizing the effect of imperfections

108   APPROACHES TO THEORY

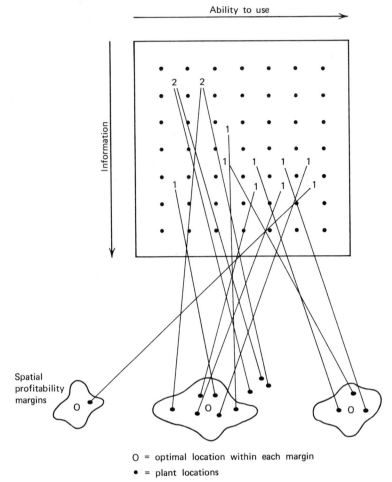

Figure 7.4. The behavioral matrix and locational choice in an industrial situation. The numbers 1 and 2 in the diagram indicate the number of firms occupying specific positions in the matrix. (*Source.* Pred, 1967, 92, Figure 11).

in the ability of the entrepreneur and the information available to him. As an operational model that could be used in the explanation of a specific location pattern its value at present is clearly very restricted, because even if numerical scales could be attached to the matrix for the positioning of a set of real-world firms, their actual locations could still not be predicted exactly.

The behavioral approach is becoming increasingly popular in human geography as a whole, and this is now influencing research in industrial location analysis. Growing interest is being shown in the way business decisions are actually made by the individual private entrepreneur and the large corporation, and in how this affects choice of plant location (for example Krümme, 1969; Stafford, 1969; Townroe, 1969; Wood, 1969; and Taylor, 1970). It is too early yet to judge how far this kind of work may eventually produce useful empirical generalizations relating to locational behavior. And it is certainly premature to see the behavioral approach as offering a major alternative conceptual framework to classical industrial location theory, as elaborated in Chapter 8 and Part Three of this book. However, the increasing emphasis on observed locational behavior is already leading to some modification of existing theory, with its bias toward economic determinism.

7.5 OTHER RECENT DEVELOPMENTS

During the past two decades geographical inquiry has undergone considerable changes, with the increasing use of quantitative methods and a growing preoccupation with research design. But little progress has been made specifically in the field of industrial location theory. Hamilton, writing on industrial location in *Models in Geography* (Chorley and Haggett, 1967), includes in his geographical references only one paper (Smith, 1966) of an exclusively theoretical nature published since the end of the 1950s. And the detailed bibliography of more than 800 entries compiled by Stevens and Brackett (1967) is similarly devoid of recent theoretical contributions by geographers.

This does not suggest that no progress at all has been made. The development of new structures for knowledge in human geography, as exemplified by the work of Bunge (1962), Haggett (1965) and Morrill (1970), is helpful in suggesting ways in which industrial location can be viewed in the broader framework of man's overall spatial behavior. Some of Warntz's work in what he terms macroeconomic geography may ultimately have important implications for industrial location analysis (Warntz, 1959, 1965); his concept of potential surfaces will be referred to later, in Part Four. Hamilton (1967) offers some interesting views on a number of matters, including an application to the formation of industrial location patterns of the evolutionary approach used by Taaffe, Morrill, and Gould (1963) to show the development of transportation systems.

Mention might also be made of the systems approach, since in recent years it has been fashionable and, on occasions, quite useful to apply the concepts of *general systems theory* to the organization of geographical knowledge. Stated very simply, systems theory proposes that all things have connections with many other things, and that the significance of any one thing depends on its relationship with others (von Bertalanffy, 1950, 1963). Thus the unit of investigation should not be a single thing but a group or system of interrelated things, within which a change in one will effect the nature and operation of others. General systems theory therefore helps to emphasize the interconnectedness of the space economy—for example, the relationship between industrial location, the transportation system and the resource base, or the relationships between different areas in the national or world economy. Some geographers consider the systems approach to be a means of integrating the disparate subject matter of economic geography, providing a new way of organizing knowledge in this very diverse field (McDaniel and Hurst, 1968). But others view it as just a monumental statement of the obvious or, as Chisholm (1967) has put it, an irrelevant distraction.

Despite the current emphasis on new conceptual frameworks, the geographer still has an important contribution to make through attempts to establish and set down some kind of generalizations based on observation of the real industrial world. One example is a paper by John Thompson (1966), in which a number of "theories" relating to manufacturing geography are offered, derived largely from empirical investigation of New England. The first is the *Cycle Theory,* which stipulates that a manufacturing area, once established, goes through a predictable sequence of change. The *Differential Growth Theory* holds that as an industrial society advances and the population becomes more affluent, the growth in demand for certain products greatly exceeds that for others. The *Concentration Theory* maintains that strong locational affinities lead manufacturing activities to group themselves in such a way as to form a hierarchy of concentrations. The *Agglomeration Theory* stipulates that the advantages which large urban areas offer to manufacturing industry increase as the stage of economic development advances. Finally, the *Changing Role Theory* states that the importance of manufacturing to the overall economy of an area changes as economic development advances. Thompson claims that these generalizations help to explain a good deal about the evolving manufacturing geography of many areas, and shed light on their industrial problems. These notions, even though they may not yet justify the term theories, provide a useful summary of observed tendencies.

In conclusion, it is important to emphasize the improvement of empirical geographical research as a contributor to the development of theory. The geographer's growing theoretical awareness, together with the sharper descriptive and analytical tools provided by the quantitative revolution, are leading the empirical investigator toward more fundamental explanatory problems than many of the problems previously tackled, and more research is being designed with a view to revealing something of general validity. The attempt by Lewis (1969) to establish lawlike statements relating to the location of the English paper industry, based on a careful statistical analysis, exemplifies this more sophisticated approach to the study of specific industries. Discussion of some of the more important empirical work is reserved for Part Four, where its relationship to the theoretical framework toward which this discussion is moving can more conveniently be considered.

8

Industrial Location Theory: The Economist's Contribution

For a long time economic theory was based largely on assumptions that eliminate the space dimension and the effect of distance. Some economists were well aware of the importance of location, but few attempted to introduce it as a variable in their theoretical models. And few regarded the explanation of locational decisions as requiring the rigorous analytical procedures that were applied to the understanding of other major aspects of business behavior. However, recent years have seen an increasing interest in spatial aspects of the economy in general, and in industrial location in particular.

This chapter contains a summary of the approaches of the main economic contributors to industrial location theory. The writers considered are discussed in chronological order, to trace the gradual emergence of the subject through time. As each successive work is examined its major contributions to the growing body of theory is extracted for discussion, the aim being to emphasize the continuity of development which tends to distinguish the economist's work in this field from that of the geographer.

Four comments are necessary to explain the subject matter of this chapter. (1) The concern is with industrial location rather than with the entire space economy, which means that some important contributions to general location theory are omitted or mentioned only briefly, and that related matters such as land-use theory and many aspects of regional economics have also been left out. (2) Limitations of space restrict the number of contributions to which anything approaching full justice can be done, and treatment has thus been generally confined to those writers whose work has been substantial enough to be published in book form. (3) Few of the writers dealt with limited their views to manufacturing industry, and to explain their ideas fully occasional reference has to be made to the place of primary and tertiary activities in their theoretical frameworks. (4) It must be emphasized that the evaluation of the approaches considered here is made from the standpoint of the objectives outlined in Chapter 1; in other words, the view is largely that of the geographer looking for theoretical frameworks which not only help to explain industrial location in general, but are also capable of application in empirical inquiry. What each of the writers examined may have contributed to the general field of economic theory is another question entirely.

8.1 ALFRED WEBER

The birth of modern industrial location theory is generally dated at 1909, when the German economist Alfred Weber published his book entitled *Über den Standort der Industrien.* Weber was certainly not the first to turn his attention to industrial location however, for by the end of the nineteenth century a number of other Germans had written on this subject. The most important of Weber's predecessors was probably Wilhelm Launhardt (1882, 1885), who attempted to show how the optimum location could be found in a simple situation with two sources of material and a market represented by the corners of a triangle. He also developed another approach based on the concept of market areas, showing how these might be delimited in a very simple situation. The influence of Launhardt and his contemporaries extended little beyond Germany but the translation of Weber's book into English in 1929 insured it of a much wider reading and, in any case, Weber's theory was a fuller and more rigorous exposition than anything that had been done before.

Weber limited his inquiry to the location of manufacturing, although Isard (1956, 27–28) has described his last chapter as the first attempt to construct a general theory of the location of all economic activity. His initial approach was entirely deductive, aimed at deriving "pure" rules of location which might then be tested out in the real world. The second major part of his work, in which he intended to use empirical material to produce what he called a "realistic" theory, was published in brief outline only.

Weber approached his problem by making three basic assumptions, in order to eliminate many of the complexities of the real world. The first is that the geographical basis of materials is given (that is, fuels and other raw materials are found in some localities only). The second is that the situation and size of places of consumption are given, with the market comprising a number of separate points. Conditions of perfect competition are implied, with each producer having an unlimited market with no possibility of deriving monopolistic advantages from choice of location. The third assumption is that there are several fixed labor locations, with labor immobile and in unlimited supply at a given wage rate. Other assumptions and simplifications are made as the need arises, such as disregarding certain institutional factors like interest rates, insurance, and the level of taxation; and a uniformity of culture and of economic and political systems is also assumed implicitly.

In Weber's simplified world three factors influence industrial location. These are the two *general regional factors* of transport and labor costs, and the *local factor* of agglomerative or deglomerative forces. He first examines the manner in which the point of minimum transport costs can be found, and then he examines the circumstances in which labor or agglomeration advantages will operate.

Transport costs are viewed as the primary determinant of plant location. Costs are not considered directly, however, but as a function of weight to be carried and distance to be covered. Weber demonstrates the derivation of the least-transport-cost location by using the same framework as Launhardt—the now familiar *locational triangle*. He takes from his simplified space economy one point of consumption (C) and the most advantageous deposits of the two necessary materials (M_1 and M_2) as a framework within which to examine the way any factory will be located (Figure 8.1). The least-transport-cost location is the point at which the total ton-miles involved in getting materials to a place of production and the finished product to the market is at a minimum; each corner of the triangle exerts a pull on the point, measured by the weight to be transported from or (in the case of the market) to that corner. In Figure 8.1 the manufacture of one unit of production requires x tons of material M_1 and y tons of material M_2, with the finished product weighing z tons to be transported to the market at C. If P is the point of production and a, b, and c the distances PM_1, PM_2, and PC respectively (the unknown distances from P to the corners of the triangle), the problem is to find that location of P which minimizes $xa + yb + zc$. The point can be found by geometry; for example, by a simple application of the theorem of the parallelogram of forces. It can also be discovered by the use of Varignon's mechanical model, in which weights of appropriate size attached to the pieces of string passing over pulleys are suspended from the corners of the triangle; the three pieces of string are tied together, and the position within the triangle where the knot comes to rest

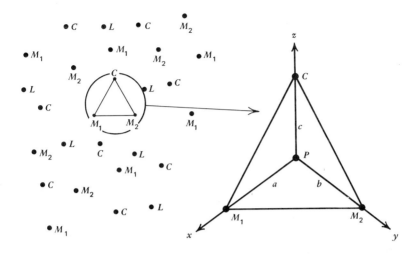

C = point of consumption
M_1 = source of material 1
M_2 = source of material 2
L = a cheap-labor location

Figure 8.1. **A locational triangle in Weber's space economy.** The symbols *x*, *y*, and *z* represent the pulls exerted by the respective corners of the locational figure.

indicates the point of compromise between the three forces. If the pull of any one corner is greater than the sum of the pulls of the other corner, production will be located at the point or corner of origin of the dominant force (Pick, in Weber, 1909, 227–239). Computer algorithms can also be used to find Weber's optimum production point (for example, Kuhn and Kuenne, 1962; Cooper, 1967), which is in practice very much more elusive than the discussion here might suggest.

Weber explains the circumstances in which an industry will be material oriented or market oriented. He introduces the *material index* of an industry, which is the proportion of the weight of localized material used to the weight of the product. A material index of greater than one indicates material orientation for the weight of localized materials used exceeds the weight of the finished product, but if ubiquitous materials enter significantly into the manufacturing process, to give the finished product a weight greater than that of the localized materials (that is, a material index of less than one), the industry should locate at the market. If ubiquities only are used, the locational figure reduces to a single point at the market.

Up to this stage uniform transport rates in all directions are implicit in Weber's analysis. But he then considers the effects of relaxing this assumption, by transforming the weight to be transported into an *ideal weight*, which is a function of actual weight and transport rates. This attempt to bring more reality into his transport system is a recognition of the fact that it is cost per unit of distance transported and not ton-miles that really matters.

Turning to labor costs (the second of Weber's general regional factors), he construes a place at which labor is relatively cheap as something that could divert the factory from the least-transport-cost location. This takes place if the saving in labor costs exceeds the additional transport costs incurred, the analysis of this situation requiring the use of *isodapanes*, or lines which can be drawn around the least-transport-cost location joining places of equal additional transport costs. In Figure 8.2, P_1 is the least-cost location in relation to the market at C and material deposits at M_1 and M_2. The circles centered on P_1 are isodapanes, indicating how transport costs rise away from P_1 (say, in dollars per unit of production). At L_1 there is a source of cheap labor, the use of which would reduce labor costs by $3 per unit of production. Since L_1 is nearer to P_1 than is the $3 isodapane, a movement from P_1 to L_1 would incur less than $3 of additional transport costs, so total costs will be lower at L_1. Weber terms the isodapane which has the same value as the savings in labor cost the *critical isodapane*. If the cheap labor location is within the critical isodapane it is a more profitable location than the least-transport-cost site (as in L_1 in Figure 8.2), but if it is outside (like L_2, where the labor cost saving is still $3), P_1 will remain the best location.

But movement to a cheap-labor location may introduce further complications. Deposits of materials previously too far from the point of production may now be brought into use. In Figure 8.2, M_3 is a deposit of the same material as is found at M_1, and it is obvious that a factory at L_1 will prefer to use M_3. A new locational triangle will be set up (M_2M_3C) and a new transport-cost situation will arise, including a new set of isodapanes. A new least-transport-cost point (perhaps at P_2) will emerge, which could conceivably be a better location than L_1.

As Weber broadens his analysis to consider the orientation of an entire industry, he says, in effect, that the more important labor is as a factor of production in any particular industry, the greater the likelihood of a cheap-labor location. To measure the importance of labor he uses an *index of labor cost*, which for any industry is the average cost of labor needed to produce one unit weight of output. The higher the index, the greater the industry's susceptibility to diversion from the least-transport-cost location. But Weber feels that it is more satisfactory to evaluate the pull of labor by finding the ratio of labor cost per unit of product weight

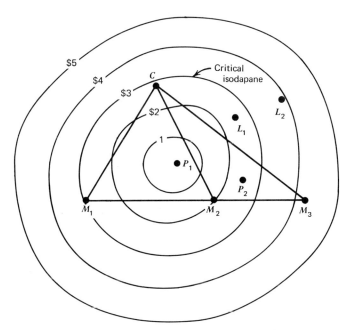

Figure 8.2. The effect of a cheap-labor location, illustrated in Weber's isodapane framework.

to the total weight of material and product to be moved. This ratio is the industry's *labor coefficient*.

Agglomeration tendencies are treated in much the same way as cheap labor—as something that may divert a factory from the least-transport-cost point. This is illustrated in Figure 8.3 where five firms (A, B, C, D and E) are in business, each occupying a separate location inside its own locational triangle. The firms find that they could cut their production costs by $20 per unit if at least three of them operated in the same location, taking advantage of economies of agglomeration, but in order to gain from this a firm must not incur more than $20 of additional transport costs. In Figure 8.3 the circles represent the critical ($20) isodapanes for each firm. The shaded area is the only place where three firms (C, D and E) can locate together and still each incur less than $20 of extra transport costs. Agglomeration is thus possible here, but neither A nor B will join the agglomeration as it is beyond their critical isodapanes, unless they can reduce transport costs by using new material sources or supplying a different market. The stippled areas, where only two isodapanes intersect, cannot act as agglomeration locations because they cannot attract the minimum requirement of three firms. Weber

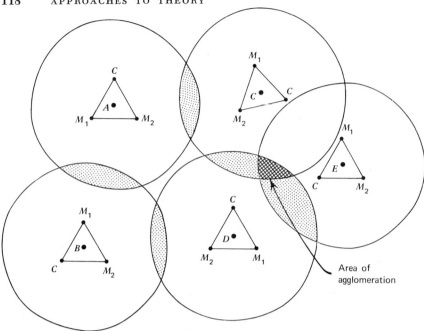

Figure 8.3. Weber's analysis of the operation of agglomeration tendencies. (*Source.* based on Weber, 1929, 139, Figures 20 and 21, by permission of the University of Chicago Press.)

stresses that in practice the point of agglomeration may also be a cheap-labor location.

In considering the total orientation, Weber takes into account industries splitting into separate processes, and the fact that there may be connections between different industries. But the analytical framework is basically that already discussed.

Since its publication sixty years ago, Alfred Weber's theory has been subjected to a considerable amount of penetrating review. Some of his assumptions have been attacked by later theoreticians, particularly those relating to transportation rates, agglomeration, and the spatial uniformity of demand conditions, and there has also been criticism of the high degree of abstraction from the real world. Other criticisms concern the indirect nature of his approach. The initial search for the least-transport-cost location and the interpretation of other factors as possible diversions is inferior to the approach based on the direct search for the point of least total cost, and concepts such as the material index and labor coefficient, though clearly not without interest, are of value only in the absence of cost data.

But despite these and other criticisms, Weber's approach has much to commend it. As Weber said, his book was expected to be a beginning and not an end, and as a beginning to modern industrial location theory it has proved very valuable indeed. Most later writers have gained something from Weber, and a number of his concepts and analytical devices have been greatly extended—in particular, his isodapanes. Despite Weber's preoccupation with transport costs, his model can be fairly easily modified to provide a much more general variable-cost theory, as will be shown in Part Three.

The direct value of Weber's theory as a framework for empirical inquiry must also not be overlooked. Isard (1956, 37) has claimed that it was only by utilizing chiefly the Weberian approach that he could meaningfully analyze the location of the iron and steel industry in the United States. And in some other cases the Weber framework has been applied successfully to the explanation of real-world patterns, as is demonstrated in Part Four. To have provided such a useful starting point for theory and also some kind of operational model for empirical investigation was no mean achievement.

8.2 TORD PALANDER

The next major contribution came from the Swedish economist, Tord Palander, whose thesis was published as *Beitrage zur Standortstheorie* in 1935. Palander was concerned about the difficulty of adequately considering industrial location within conventional general equilibrium theory, in which everything was assumed to happen at one point in space. After giving a general introduction to the problem of location theory, Palander reviews previous work in this field, and then sketches his own location theory.

Palander distinguishes two fundamental questions in attempting to develop a theoretical approach to industrial location. First, given the price and location of materials and the position of the market, where will production take place? This was basically the question Weber tried to answer. Second, given the place of production, the competitive conditions, factory costs, and transportation rates, how does price affect the extent of the area in which a certain producer can sell his goods?

Palander first deals with the problem of market areas (*Marktbereichs*). He takes the simple case of two firms making the same product for a linear market, and uses this to demonstrate how the boundary between the two market areas will be arrived at. This is illustrated in Figure 8.4, where A and B are two firms serving a market distributed along the

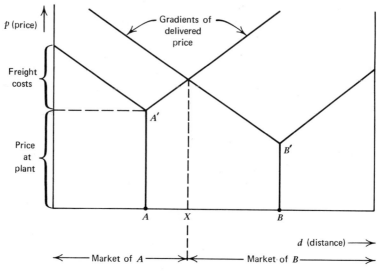

Figure 8.4. The derivation of a boundary between the market areas of two competing firms. (*Source.* Palander, 1935, 224, Figure 39.)

horizontal axis of the diagram. The plant cost, or price changed for the product at source, is given by the vertical distance AA' for firm A, and firm B's cost is slightly lower at BB'. Away from the plant the price the consumer has to pay is raised by the necessary cost of transportation, as shown by the lines rising in both directions from A' and B'. Thus, at any point, the price charged includes a fixed plant cost and a variable cost of transportation. The boundary between the market areas of the two firms will be at X, where the delivered price from both producers is equal and customers will be indifferent as to which firm they buy from.

Palander illustrates a number of variations on the situation depicted in Figure 8.4, changing the relative values of the plant price (p) and the freight charges (f). These are shown in Figure 8.5. In case *a* the two firms have equal plant price and the same freight costs per unit of distance, and so the market area boundary is midway between A and B. Case *b* shows equal freight rates but lower plant price at one location (B) enabling it to control more of the area between the two firms than can A. In case *c*, firm B has both a higher plant price and higher transport costs per unit of distance than has A, but it is still able to control a small market area by virtue of the higher delivered price from A near B. Case *d* shows that where one firm has a lower plant price but higher transport costs than the other it is able to control a fairly extensive section of the market, but there comes a point to the left of A where B

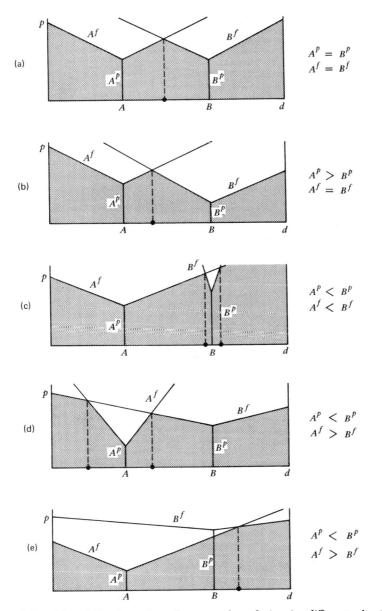

Figure 8.5. The derivation of market area boundaries in different situations. (*Source.* Palander, 1935, 228, Figure 40.)

regains control by virtue of its lower freight cost, Finally, case *e* shows the same situation as case *d,* except here firm B cannot serve the market immediately adjoining its factory because the price at the plant is so high; it is only at some distance to the right that the relatively low freight rate from B allows the firm to sell at a lower price than A.

When the assumption of a linear market is relaxed these situations can be seen in three-dimensional terms. Now the market area boundary becomes a line (termed an *isotante*), which is a locus of points where the delivered prices from both producers are equal, and the gradients of delivered price can be seen as inverted conical surfaces with an apex directly above the point representing the factory. Certain generalizations can be made concerning the form of the isotante, or market area boundary, in different circumstances. If for the two firms, both plant price and transport rates are equal, the boundary will be a line perpendicular to the line joining the firms and midway between them. If prices are equal but costs of delivery vary, the isotante will be a circle round the factory with the higher freight rate. If transport rates only are equal the isotante will be a hyperbole concave toward the factory with the highest price. Palander demonstrates mathematically the effect of differences and changes in transport rates on market area boundaries.

The size of the market area that a firm controls will influence the profit that it makes. With the cost of production and profit per unit of output given, and sales related in volume to the size of the market area, total profits become a function of the distance from the plant that a firm can extend its market. The sales area and hence the profits of any one firm will be influenced by the locational decisions and other actions of competitors, and Palander, in his two producer cases, develops a simple theory of spatial duopolistic competition. He considers the pricing strategy of two competing firms, showing how far they can influence profits, and how a state of equilibrium will be arrived at in which the firms have nothing to gain from further competitive action.

After his analysis of market areas in a context of spatial competition, Palander turns to his other major question: given the price and location of materials and market, where will production be located? The point of departure is Weber's analysis of transport orientation, which Palander reviews and develops considerably. He looks at transport in terms of costs of movement rather than weight to be shipped, and introduces various complicating factors which Weber mentioned only in passing.

Palander uses Weber's isodapane technique to demonstrate the effect of transport costs on location. As well as isodapanes and isotantes, Palander makes reference to the following: *isodistantes*—lines joining places of equal distance from one point; *isochrones*—lines joining places of equal transport time; *isotims*—lines joining points where a commodity costs the same; and *isovectors*—lines joining points where the transport costs of a given commodity are equal. Palander saw transportation in terms of surfaces, lines, and points. A *transport surface* (*Transportfläche*) is a region in which all points are connected up by a given means of transport, a *transport line* connects together groups of points, and a *transport point* is a point of access, like a railway station or transshipment point, on a transport line (Palander, 1935, 304–307).

Palander was particularly concerned with the effect of freight rates on isodapane patterns. He makes an important distinction between rates that rise evenly with distance (*Entfernungstarif*) and the more realistic arrangement under which the rate tends to fall off with distance traveled (*Staffeltarif*). The uniform rate will produce a series of isovectors around a given point taking the form of concentric circles spaced at regular intervals, whereas the variable rate makes the isovectors successively further apart as cost per unit of distance falls. Palander uses a simple case of one material source and a single point of consumption to show that with the uniform rates, total transport costs will be the same at any place on the line between the two points, whereas with variable rates both the material source and the market have lower costs than any intermediate location (Palander, 1935, 311, 313–314). When a third point is introduced to form the locational triangle used by Weber and Launhardt (Figure 8.6a), the effect is similar. A uniform increase in transport costs in relation to distance from each point makes isodapanes interpolated from the three sets of isovectors reveal a least-transport-cost point within the triangle (Figure 8.6b), whereas with variable freight rates locations at the corners are more attractive (Figure 8.6c). This leads to the general conclusion that a least-transport-cost point within the locational triangle is much less likely than Weber suggested; the kind of freight rates found in the real world make an optimum location at the market or at a material source much more of a possibility. The isodapane technique is used to examine other complications such as alternative sources of materials and different means of transportation.

In attempting to introduce market areas into the analysis of transport orientation, Palander demonstrates that different sections of the market will be served by different least-transport-cost points. Isotantes are used to show how market areas for different production points are delimited, and there are also diagrams that show how the size and shape of the various orientation zones of the market will depend on the weights in the locational figure (Palander, 1935, 148–165). Further discussion of this aspect of Palander's theory is reserved for section 8.7.

The approach to industrial location developed by Tord Palander was

124 APPROACHES TO THEORY

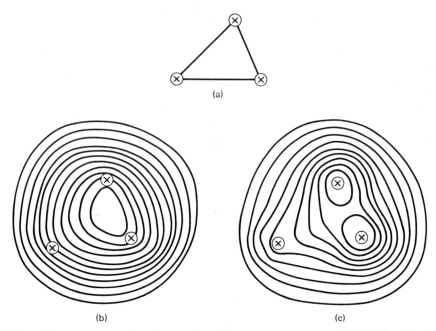

Figure 8.6. Patterns of isodapanes for different transport rates: (a) The locational triangle; (b) tariff uniform with distance; and (c) tariff varies with distance. (*Source.* Palander, 1935, 318, Figures 60 and 61.)

clearly influenced by Alfred Weber's work, but there were things in Weber that Palander could not accept. Weber's analysis of agglomeration is criticized on the grounds that no firm would move away from the least-transport-cost location to a potential agglomeration point unless it was sure that others would do the same. Another thing that Palander stressed was the importance of a dynamic view of location, taking into account changes in causal factors through time. Weber was aware of the time factor and brought it into some of his illustrations, but it was not built into his basic analytical framework.

Palander's work is, of course, much more than a refinement and extension of Weber. The introduction of market area analysis in the context of spatial competition between firms added a new dimension to the Weberian framework, based as it was on a variable-cost situation with demand held constant. Unfortunately, *Beiträge zur Standortstheorie* has never been translated from the German, and the only extensive summary is in French (Ponsard, 1958). Palander has thus had somewhat less impact on later writers, and on the general development of location theory, than might otherwise have been the case.

8.3 EDGAR HOOVER

Hoover's early work on industrial location is still among the most useful in this field, particularly for those who seek a clue to the general nature of the location problem without a high degree of abstraction and complex microeconomic theory. In 1937 he published a study of the shoe and leather industries and, in 1948, a more general work, *The Location of Economic Activity*. Hoover's first theoretical statement (1937) was greatly influenced by Palander, and helped to give wider exposure to some of the ideas in *Beiträge zur Standortstheorie*.

Location Theory and the Shoe and Leather Industries contains both a theoretical statement and two major case studies. This discussion is confined to the theoretical work. Hoover starts with the assumption of perfect competition between producers or sellers at any one location and perfect mobility of factors of production, and takes transportation costs and production or extraction costs as the determinants of location. He considers extractive industries first, with the location of deposits as given, and attempts to determine the area that each producing point will serve. The delivered price to any buyer will be the cost of extraction plus transport costs, as in the Palander cases (Figures 8.4 and 8.5), and this can be represented by a system of *isotims* radiating from the point of production and joining places of equal delivered price. Buyers will obtain the commodity from the source that offers the lowest delivered price, as in Palander's analysis, and the boundary between the market area of two producers will be a line joining points at which delivered price is the same from both sources.

As long as the cost of extraction does not vary with output, transport costs are the only variable affecting price, but Hoover extends his analysis to include the influence of diminishing returns. He argues that extractive industries characteristically operate in a situation where average cost rises with increased production as the market area gets bigger. The effect of this on market area boundaries is illustrated in Figure 8.7, where cost or price is plotted on the ordinate and distance on the abscissa. A mineral is extracted at point X, and A, B, and C indicate possible edges to its market area in one direction. If the area XA is supplied, production costs are represented by the distance Xa on the ordinate, and the line aa' shows how delivered price increases away from X as transport costs are added. This line, which Hoover terms the *transport gradient*, is simply a cross-section through an isotim map (Hoover 1937, 9). If the market is extended to B the cost of extraction rises to b,

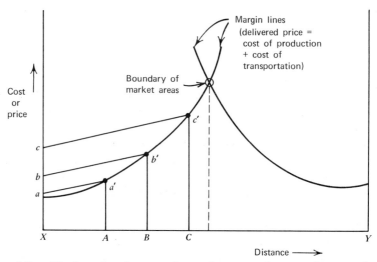

Figure 8.7. The boundary between the market areas of two producers under conditions of diminishing returns to scale. (*Source.* Hoover, 1937, 17 Figure 7. Reprinted by permission of the publishers from Edgar M. Hoover, Jr., *Location Theory and the Shoe and Leather Industries,* Cambridge, Mass.: Harvard University Press, Copyright, 1937, by the President and Fellows of Harvard College; 1965 by Edgar Malone Hoover, Jr.)

and a new transport gradient (bb') is introduced. Extension to C has a similar effect. Joining together points a', b', and c' with the delivered price at all other possible edges of the market area produces what Hoover terms the *margin line*. The introduction of a margin line relating to a second source of the mineral (Y) reveals a point of intersection, which represents the boundary between the two market areas. At the intersection delivered price is the same from X and Y; elsewhere one source offers the product at a lower price than the other.

Although illustrated in the context of an extractive activity, this analysis is applicable with only slight modification to the formation of market areas for a manufactured product. In a situation where the cost of production decreases with rising output, as might be expected in most manufacturing industries, the margin line will fall with increasing distance from the producing point. This is because output rises as the market area is enlarged to create economies of scale. When the point of diminishing returns is eventually reached the margin line will turn upwards (Figure 8.7).

Hoover further considers the slope of the margin line and its implications for plant locations. A situation in which margin lines rise steeply away from the point of extraction will encourage other producers to set up in intermediate locations to serve areas with relatively high delivered price, but if delivered price differs little with distance from the point of production a small number of producers will tend to supply large market areas. Hoover thus develops a theoretical framework in which the locational effect of market areas and their spatial extent can be examined.

After introducing his analytical procedures in the context of extractive industries, Hoover turns to manufacturing. He follows Weber fairly closely at first, pointing out that in the absence of production cost differences the best location will be at the point of minimum transport costs, which may be at a material source, at the market, or at an intermediate point. The least-transport-cost location is found by constructing isotims around given material and market points, from which lines of equal total transport cost (isodapanes) can be constructed (Hoover, 1937, 43). But Hoover goes further than Weber by showing graphically how different sections of the market will be served by different producing points, a matter that Palander also considered. This is illustrated in Figure 8.8 where there are three points of production (*A*, *B*, and *C*), each having

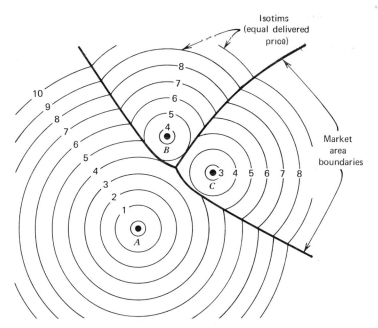

Figure 8.8. Market area boundaries between different producers, arising from areal variations in production costs and delivered prices. (*Source.* Hoover, 1937, 48, Figure 18. Reprinted by permission of the publishers from Edgar M. Hoover, Jr., *Location Theory and the Shoe and Leather Industries*, Cambridge, Mass.: Harvard University Press, Copyright, 1937, by the President and Fellows of Harvard College; 1965 by Edgar Malone Hoover, Jr.)

a different cost. Systems of isotims are drawn around them, and the boundaries of their respective market areas are at the delivered price watersheds.

Following Palander, Hoover takes issue with Weber's emphasis on least-transport-cost points within locational triangles. Even with the assumption of uniform transport costs, the possibility of a separate minimum point not at one corner of the triangle is much less than might be thought at first glance. It is far more likely than Weber suggested that a material source or the market will have a pull exceeding that of the other corners, and when the fact that transfer costs are actually less than proportional to distance is also considered, the chance of a location not at one corner is even less likely. In addition loading costs and other terminal charges operate against least-cost location inside the triangle. If a separate point away from material sources and the market does occur, Hoover suggests that perhaps this is a sign that the industry is not primarily transport-oriented at all, and that possibly a low-labor-cost location enters into the picture. Hoover concludes his transportation section by claiming that in practice the influence of transfer costs tends to locate production at markets, at sources of materials, or at junction breakpoints in the transport network.

Hoover considers the effect of transport rates further in his second book (1948), demonstrating the influence of convex gradients and transshipment points. In Figure 8.9 an industry uses a single material

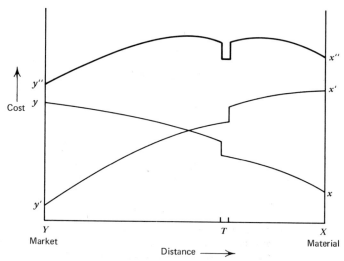

Figure 8.9. The effect of convex transfer-cost gradients and a transshipment point on costs at alternative locations. (*Source.* Hoover, 1948, 39, Figure 3.8.)

at X and sells its product at the market Y. The transfer-cost gradients xy and $x'y'$ indicate, respectively, the cost of moving material away from X and the cost of distributing to the market at Y. The vertical distance X to x is the terminal or loading charge at the material source, and Yy' is the cost incurred in distributing if the factory is at the market. The curve $x''y''$ is the total transfer cost (the sum of xy and $x'y'$), and shows the least-cost location at Y. With convex gradients, the total cost is bound to be more between Y and X than at these points. The effect of a transshipment point is illustrated by assuming a town, T, at which additional transfer costs are incurred through, perhaps, unloading from railroad to canal. Both curves xy and $x'y'$ take a jump here. A location in this town avoids these transshipment charges and is in fact as advantageous as being at the source of material (X).

In considering production costs, as opposed to transfer costs, Hoover follows Weber's analysis of a cheap-labor location fairly closely. He views it as a possible production point if the saving in labor cost compensates for increasing transfer charges, and illustrates different situations by using isodapane or isotim maps (Hoover, 1937, 79–84). Inherent in this approach is the concept of plants producing for particular market areas; he illustrates situations similar to that shown in Figure 8.7, but with one area served by a cheap-labor location and others by least transport-cost points. Hoover sees economies of concentration as part of production costs, and repeats Palander's criticism of Weber's theoretical approach to agglomeration.

Hoover's second book is of less strictly theoretical interest than is *Location Theory and the Shoe and Leather Industries*. As Greenhut (1956, 17) remarks, his main contribution here lies not in theoretical originality but in the penetrating discussion of the influences of various location factors. As well as containing detailed consideration of transfer costs, *The Location of Economic Activity* offers valuable discussions of land-use competition, locational change and adjustment, and the locational significance of boundaries. Of particular interest are sections on economic development problems and the role of public policy in relation to the location of economic activity.

Hoover's contribution to the understanding of plant location is considerable, and by no means confined to the two books reviewed here. His theoretical framework is broader than Weber's, and in both books examples from the real work support deductive theory. His investigations of the shoe and leather industries, published as Parts II and III of his first book, are classics among industrial location case studies. Hoover's approach has its limitations, of course; like Weber he viewed transport orientation as something that could be analyzed separately and did not integrate other causal factors into his theory as fully as he might have done, and despite his references to market areas he was much more concerned with cost than with the demand factor. Nevertheless, Hoover's early work remains of great interest, and one of his later models is featured in the next chapter.

8.4 AUGUST LÖSCH

A major criticism of early location theory is its abstraction from demand. Location is seen largely as a product of spatial cost differences, with variations from place to place in sales potential virtually ignored. Hoover's two books do not escape this criticism, for his analysis of the demand factor was confined to showing what market area a given location would serve, with the effect of the volume of demand on location not being considered. In the 1920s and 1930s some economists began to turn their attention to the locational implications of competition between firms, and Palander (1935) went a considerable way in this direction, but it was 1940 before the German economist August Lösch produced the first general theory of location with demand as the major spatial variable.

Lösch's *Die räumliche Ordnung der Wirtschaft* has been available in an English translation since 1954, and has probably aroused more interest than any other single contribution to location theory. This is partly because Lösch was the first to describe general spatial relations in a set of simple equations (Richardson, 1969, 107), and to present what Wolfgang Stopler, in his introduction to the translation, portrays as "a full general equilibrium system describing in abstract the interrelationship of all locations." But it is also a reflection of the great originality of approach and profundity of thought that Lösch brought to spatial economics.

It is clear from the outset that it is not Lösch's intention to explain the location of economic activity in the real world. As he puts it, "The real duty of the economist is not to explain our sorry reality, but to improve it. The question of the best location is far more dignified than determination of the actual one" (Lösch, 1954, 4). Briefly, what he tries to do is to show what pattern of location will, in a given simplified situation, fulfill certain conditions which define a state of equilibrium. His basic philosophy is that there is order and reason behind the apparent chaos of the economic world.

Lösch rejects the least-cost location approach of Weber and his followers, and the alternative of seeking the location at which revenue is greatest. The right approach, he says, is to find the place of maximum profits, where total revenue exceeds total cost by the greatest amount. But in attempting to introduce more reality to location theory than his predecessors, with spatial variations in demand as well as in costs, Lösch finds the problem of optimum location for the individual firm insoluble. As soon as the interdependence of firms is accepted, with the possibility that the action of one firm in locating itself can require the relocation of existing firms, the problem becomes too complex for mathematical formulation (Lösch, 1954, 8):

> If we wish to be precise and to consider the influence of the selection of a particular location on all other locations . . . then we enter upon the general theory of location. The repercussions, strictly speaking, are transformed into mutual relations, and it ceases to be meaningful to pick out one location and examine its relation to its neighbors in isolation. We are faced with the interdependence of all locations. Equilibrium of the location system can therefore no longer be charted, but can be represented only by a system of equations that are insoluble in practice.

And later (Lösch, 1954, 29) he remarks:

> A geometrical solution becomes impossible as soon as price and quantity are added to the two spatial variables, for it can be applied to three variables at most. Yet algebraic treatment leads to equations of an insoluble degree. This complexity stems from the facts that, as already explained, there is more than one geographical point where the total demand of a surrounding district is at a maximum, and that from these points outward total demand does not decrease according to a simple function. We are thus reduced to determine separately for every one of a number of virtual factory locations the total attainable demand, and for similar reasons the best volume of production as a function of factory price (market and cost analysis). The greatest profit attainable at each of these points can be determined from the cost and demand curves, and from this place of greatest money profits, the optimum location can be found. Now the procedure is no longer theoretical, however, but simply empirical testing, since the result holds only for the locations actually examined and cannot be interpolated. As all points in an area can never be analyzed in this manner, we cannot exclude the possibility that among the locations not examined there may be one that would yield a higher return than the most advantageous of those investigated. There is no scientific and unequivocal solution for the location of the individual firm; but only a practical one: the test of trial and error. Hence Weber's and all the other attempts at a systematic and valid location theory for the individual firm were doomed to failure.

This does not mean that theorizing is a waste of time, but those who work toward a theory of industrial location must be aware of the degree of simplification involved and avoid a one-sided approach to such a complex multivariate problem.

Lösch's general theory is an attempt to show how, in given circumstances, all economic activity should be arranged in space. He assumes a broad homogeneous plain with an even distribution of raw materials and uniform transport rates in all directions. The agricultural population is evenly distributed, and all individuals have identical tastes, technical knowledge, and economic opportunities. The settlement pattern is one of evenly distributed self-sufficient farmsteads. In considering industry, the question posed is: if farmers start producing a surplus of some commodity, what spatial economic pattern will eventually constitute a state of equilibrium? To achieve equilibrium, Lösch's space economy must satisfy the following conditions (Lösch, 1954, 94–97).

1. The location of every individual must be as advantageous as possible, in terms of profits for the producers and gains for the consumers.

2. The production locations must be so numerous that the entire space is occupied (that is, there are no areas where the absence of a source of supply might attract a new firm).

3. In activities open to everyone there are not abnormal profits, for they will be competed away by the entry of new firms.

4. The areas of supply, production, and sales must be as small as possible, since only then has the number of enterprises that can survive reached its maximum.

5. At the boundaries of market areas consumers are indifferent as to which of two neighboring producing locations they get their supply from.

These conditions must be fulfilled if the spatial order of the economy is to have, as Lösch puts it, meaning and permanence.

Lösch described his equilibrium conditions in five equations, from which the form of the space economy can be worked out (Lösch, 1954, 92–100; Richardson, 1969, 105–108). How equilibrium is reached may be demonstrated as follows. If a single farmer decides to produce a surplus of, say, beer for sale, then his sales area will be circular, bounded by a locus of points at which his price becomes too high to sell any beer at all. But if one farmer can produce a surplus, so can the others; therefore, others enter the beer trade. Competition gradually reduces the size of sales areas until ultimately they become hexagonal in shape as all space is filled. Of the geometrical forms that could fill all space (hexagons, triangles, and squares), the hexagon most nearly resembles a circle. It has the highest demand per unit of area, and minimizes the total distance from its center to all points within the market area, as Christaller (1933) had already demonstrated.

Figure 8.10 illustrates three stages in the development of a system of hexagonal market areas for one industry. In stage 1 a single producer

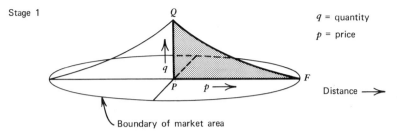

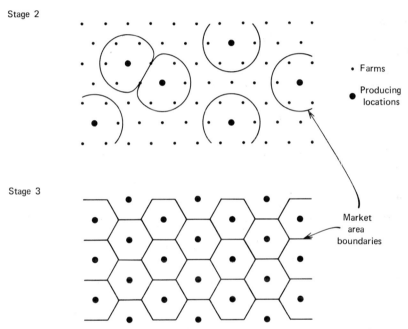

Figure 8.10. Stages in the derivation of Lösch's system of hexagonal market areas. (*Source.* Based on Lösch, 1954, 106 and 110, Figures 21 and 23.)

at P operates with a demand curve QF. Price (p) is a function of distance and rises with transport costs along PF, and the vertical distance between PF and QF shows the quantity (q) demanded at any price. When PF is taken as a measure of distance and is rotated about P, the circular market area is formed, bounded by the locus of points F, where the price becomes too high. The total sales are given by the volume of the cone produced by the rotation of PQF (Lösch, 1954, 10). In the second stage a number of firms operate within circular market areas, but they are unable to supply all the potential market. The space between them attracts in other producers, and the market areas decrease in size as abnormal profits are competed away, until finally the regular hexagonal grid is formed (stage 3).

As different goods are produced, a system of hexagons will arise for each industry, with the size of market area varying from industry to industry according to the nature of the product. Lösch then superimposes all the individual systems so that all have at least one production center in common. At this center, where every product is made, there will be a metropolis, and at other places where two or more production points coincide there will be towns or cities.

Thus far Lösch's pattern of locations and market areas resembles that developed by Walter Christaller (1933) a few years earlier, although their mathematical specifications are not identical (Berry, 1967, 59–73). But Lösch then shows how concentrations of towns will occur in certain parts of the uniform plain. If the individual systems of hexagons are all rotated about the common center of the metropolis, it is found that a pattern can be formed in which there are six sectors with many production sites coinciding, and six intervening sectors in which there are few. In this situation, where the greatest coincidence of production sites exist, the maximum number of purchases can be made locally, and transport costs are minimized. This is the spatial arrangement of economic activity which fulfills the original equilibrium conditions. Such *economic landscapes,* as Lösch terms them, are distributed throughout the world like a network, and in accordance with definite laws (Lösch, 1954, 137). In the first brief exposition of these ideas in English (Lösch, 1938), the area within one hundred miles of Indianapolis was used as empirical evidence supporting the city-rich and city-poor sectoral arrangement which Lösch had deduced, and in the book (1954, 125), Toledo and its environs up to a radius of sixty miles is used as another demonstration.

In practice the regularity of Lösch's ideal economic landscape is disturbed by factors thus far assumed away. Of particular importance is the effect of pricing policies on the market area, and Lösch argues that spatial price differentiation, reinforced by the tendency toward the maximization of the number of separate enterprises, makes for further reductions in the size of market areas. The implications of various alternative geographical pricing policies are examined, and Lösch also considers the effect of the irregular distribution of resources and population, local differences in accessibility, human differences, and political factors such as boundaries.

Lösch (1954, 129) fervently rejects a chaotic interpretation of the space economy, no matter how much the real world may depart from the ordered regularity of his theory:

THE ECONOMIST'S CONTRIBUTION   135

No doubt the spatial economic pattern about us contains enough illogical, irregular, lawless features. But I refuse to put the whole emphasis on this lack of order. No matter how widely a chaotic interpretation may be confirmed by the facts, it is not only unworthy but dangerous. Unworthy because there is also a reality of reason, upon which incomparably more depends in the long run than upon the reality of the factual. Dangerous because our idea of reality is one of the factors that shape the future.

Lösch next turns his attention to trade. Much of this is of less direct relevance to industrial location theory than what has gone before, but there are some sections of great interest. For example, the effect of a local price change on the size of a firm's market area is illustrated in a simple but effective diagram (Figure 8.11). Plants are located at B_1 and

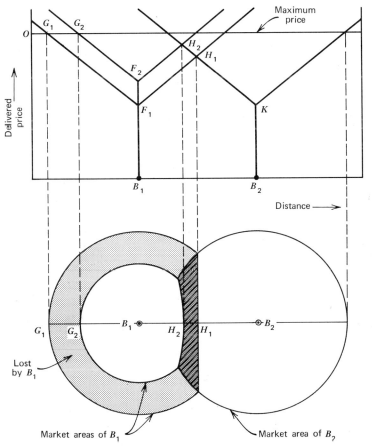

Figure 8.11. The effect of price inflation on the size of market areas. (*Source.* Lösch, 1954, 268, Figure 56.)

B_2, with operating costs of F_1 and K, respectively, and V-shaped delivered price gradients. The market areas of the two plants intersect at H_1 in the cross-section, and their spatial forms are shown below. Notice that except where the two market areas intersect, their limits are determined by a critical price (0) at which sales cease. An increase in the price at B_1 to F_2 has the effect of narrowing the market area, as the limit moves in from G_1 to G_2 on the left and from H_1 to H_2 on the right. The plant at B_2 thus gains customers at the expense of B_1. Lösch's discussion of this situation adds a dynamic element to market area analysis, and elsewhere he considers the effect of international trading conditions such as tariff walls on the form of market areas.

The final part of the book contains examples. These illustrate the distribution of towns, the shape of market areas, and how prices vary in the real world. Of particular interest is a discussion of spatial variations in the prices of factors of production, including comments on the cost of land, wage rates and the money market, and some maps of the price of a number of goods and services as they vary within the United States (Lösch, 1954, Chapter 26). Lösch introduced examples from the real-world not as a verification of theory but as an indication of how far reality is rational; his theory was an attempt to construct what is rational rather than to explain what actually is.

Like any other attempt to theorize about the location of economic activity, Lösch's work has its weaknesses. Perhaps the most serious is his failure to consider spatial cost variations, which were eliminated in his assumption of a uniform plain with evenly distributed materials and population. After criticizing the one-sidedness of the least-cost approach, Lösch goes to the other extreme and creates an idealized space economy in which demand in effect determined the location of producers. In the equilibrium situation the viable location is one that commands a sales area of a certain size. Cost factors enter the analysis only through transport costs limiting the size of market areas (that is, by their effect on demand) and through the agglomeration advantages implicit in the emergence of Lösch's six sectors of many towns—the pattern that maximizes effective demand. Lösch has also been criticized on the grounds that his ideal system of location could be brought about only by state direction; in other words, it is irrelevant to a competitive capitalist economy (Greenhut, 1956, 269–272).

The validity of certain aspects of Lösch's space economy has been questioned on other grounds (Beckman, 1955; Valavanis, 1955; Robertson, 1956; Isard, 1956, 48 and Chapter 11; Greenhut, 1963, 174–175, 183–185; and Richardson, 1969, 72–77, 107–108). It is a particular type of economy, characterized by agriculture spatially distributed but producing for a punctiform market, and industry punctiform in location but producing for a market of areal extent. This contains elements of the real world, but such a rigid distinction between the spatial expression of agriculture and industry is seldom found in practice. Lösch's examples show that the regularity of his economic landscape approaches nearest to reality in large agricultural areas of fairly uniform relief, like the American Midwest, where there are no major industrial belts.

The highly abstract nature of Lösch's location theory, and the assumptions on which it rests, restricts its usefulness as an aid to interpreting the real world, but to criticize it on these grounds is to misunderstand the basic philosophy behind the work. Lösch viewed economics as a creative science, with a duty to improve the world rather than to describe and explain it. He thus sought through location theory the spatial pattern of economic activity which would be the best in given circumstances: "whenever something new is being created, and thus in settlement and spatial planning also, the laws revealed through theory are the sole economic guide to what *should* take place" (Lösch, 1954, 359).

8.5 LOCATIONAL INTERDEPENDENCE

At this point, a brief digression from the author-by-author review is required. By the 1950s it was clear that two largely independent schools of thought on industrial location theory had emerged, embracing respectively the traditional "least-cost" approach and a view that emphasized the locational interdependence of firms. It is now necessary to examine this situation, and outline certain features of the locational interdependence approach which it would be incorrect to ascribe to one specific author.

Classical least-cost location theory has its roots in the work of Alfred Weber, and includes much of Palander and Hoover. This school emphasizes the search for the least-cost location in conditions where the demand factor is held constant, and where the locational interdependence of firms is disregarded. Implicit in this approach is the assumption of perfect competition, with no monopoly advantages with respect to the market arising from specific locations. The weakness of the approach is that as soon as demand is allowed to vary in space the least (average) cost location does not necessarily yield maximum profits, since it may be preferable to move to a new location with higher unit costs but where greater sales will increase total profits. Least total cost is a meaningful concept in industrial location only in conditions where demand is a spatial constant; otherwise, a low total cost may simply indicate a low volume of output in a location badly situated in relation to the market.

To overcome some of these weaknesses in traditional least-cost theory the "locational-interdependence" or "market-area" school of thought developed. To this school belongs some of Palander and Hoover, much of Lösch, and the work of certain economists interested in aspects of the theory of imperfect or monopolistic competition (Fetter, 1924; Hotelling, 1929; Robinson, 1934; Chamberlin, 1936; Lerner and Singer, 1939; Smithies, 1941; and Ackley, 1942). This approach generally assumes that all firms have identical production costs, and sell to a spatially distributed market instead of the punctiform market assumed by Weber. The delivered price to consumers varies with the cost of overcoming distance from the factory. Each seller, in choosing his location, seeks to control the largest possible market area, the position and extent of which will be influenced by consumer behavior and by the locational decisions of other firms. The manufacturer exercises monopoly control over that section of the market which he can supply at a lower price than his rivals. The spatial pattern of plant location and market areas is thus a product of variations from place to place in demand and of the locational interdependence of firms. The basic weakness of this approach is its disregard of spatial cost variations, which is just as unrealistic as the least-cost school's abstraction from demand.

The locational-interdependence approach arose out of the theoretical discussion of how a situation of equilibrium would be achieved under conditions of imperfect competition. It has been largely worked out in the highly simplified context of two firms, or *duopolists,* competing along a linear market. The first major contribution was by Fetter (1924), who considered some of the ways in which firms might compete to control as much of the market as possible, and how this could effect the shape of the market area. Some of Fetter's ideas found their way into the work of the major location theorists of the 1930s, but somewhat more influential was a later paper by Hotelling (1929). In the simplified situation of two ice cream sellers competing to supply an identical product to customers evenly distributed along a seaside beach, with each purchasing one ice cream in one unit of time, Hotelling deduced the seemingly improbable conclusion that the two sellers would end up standing back-to-back in the center of the beach, each serving one half of the market. He developed this into a generalization relating to industrial agglomeration under certain demand conditions.

The rationale behind Hotelling's argument, and some of its implications, can be explored in a series of simple diagrams of the kind which have already been used to demonstrate certain aspects of the theories

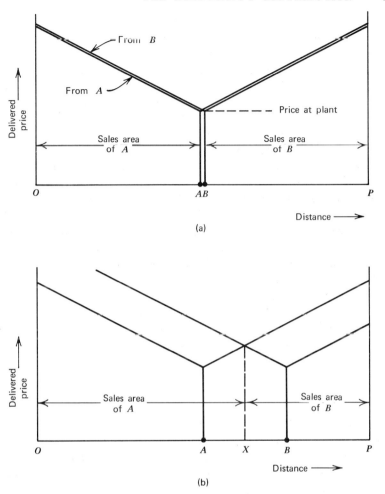

Figure 8.12. The location of duopolists competing for a linear market in conditions of infinitely inelastic demand, according to Hotelling.

of Palander and Lösch. In Figure 8.12, two producers are competing to serve customers uniformly distributed along the linear market *OP*. The assumption of a linear market is made simply for ease of graphic presentation, and greater reality can be introduced merely by thinking of *OP* as a section through a three-dimensional situation as in Figure 8.11. It is assumed that production costs are the same everywhere, that freight rates are the same per unit of distance throughout the market, and that producers sell on an f.o.b. price system so that the cost of transport from the factory is paid by the consumer. Demand for the product is infinitely inelastic; each consumer buys one unit of the product in one unit of time irrespective of price. Firm A enters the scene first and locates in the center of the market, although under the assumptions made any location will give him the entire market. A second firm (B), free to locate anywhere and prepared to compete with A, will find that a location at the center of the market as close as possible to A is the most advantageous. This is shown in Figure 8.12a where firm A serves the left hand side of the market and B the right hand side. If B had chosen another location (Figure 8.12b), he could have served the right-hand extremity of the market cheaper than from a central location, as indicated by the height of the two delivered price lines, but as demand is infinitely inelastic buyers here will purchase whatever the price is, so B derives no advantage from this. And the location away from A means that firm A can compete with B in part of the area between the two firms, where A's delivered price is lower, which deprives B of some of the market he had in Figure 8.12a. Thus a location at the center of the market as close as possible to A is the only position that enables B to control as much as half of the market. Each firm has a monopolistic control over its share of the market, and Hotelling argues that this factor puts stability into the otherwise indeterminate solution of equilibrium under conditions of duopoly. He claims that in the situation described above a third firm entering the industry would try to take up a position close to A and B but not between them, and that subsequent entries would also join the cluster.

The situation generally referred to as "Hotelling's case" has stimulated much discussion. Chamberlin (1936, 194–199) and Lösch (1954, 72–75) revealed certain inconsistencies in Hotelling's argument, both with respect to the necessity of a back-to-back location for the duopolists and the agglomeration implications. It is not difficult to see that, under Hotelling's own assumptions, duopolists do not have to occupy the central location, for as long as they are located symetrically along the line, they will share the market. For example, locations at the quartile positions in Figure 8.12 would do this. Even if the two did occupy the center, the entry of a third firm will tend to make for dispersal, for in the linear market one firm has to be between the other two thus getting virtually no sales, and there will be constant shifting around to avoid becoming "piggy-in-the-middle". Chamberlin (1936, 195) suggested that with three competitors A and B would be at the quartiles and C in any position between them, and that as the number of firms increases they will tend to spread out in groups of two along the line. The outcome of all this is to discredit Hotelling's deduction of an agglomeration in the center of the market under conditions of infinitely inelastic demand.

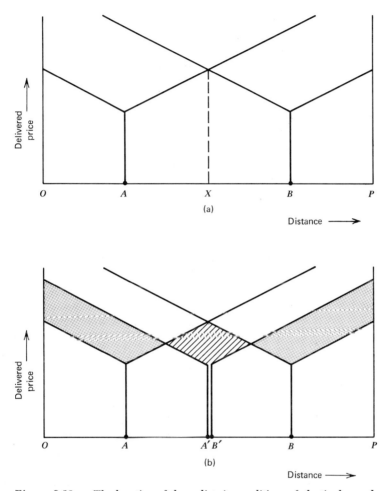

Figure 8.13. The location of duopolists in conditions of elastic demand.

What are the implications of relaxing the assumption of inelastic demand? If price is allowed to affect sales, it becomes important to reduce delivered price at the extremities of the market, where it is highest. In this situation two firms working in collusion, like a two-plant monopolist, would locate at the quartile positions in a linear market (Figure 8.13a), since this minimizes transfer costs and thus maximizes sales. These locations would also be most advantageous for two competing firms, who would each be able to take half of the market. A comparison with the central back-to-back location (Figure 8.13b) shows that the transfer cost saving at the quartile locations (stippled) is greater than the saving near the center of the market which the central locations would offer (shaded), and the advantage of the quartiles over any other possible alternatives can be demonstrated graphically in a similar way.

In recent years the major contributions to the development of the locational-interdependence view of industrial location have been made by Melvin Greenhut, whose work is discussed in the next section. Another recent contribution is a paper by Devletoglou (1965), in which issue is taken with certain aspects of the conventional approach to spatial competition in the duopolistic situation. He adds his weight to the criticism of Hotelling's analysis, as well as questioning the variations of Smithies (1941) on the same argument. Devletoglou feels that it is unrealistic to think of market areas separated by some rigid indifference line as in conventional market-area theory, preferring the notion that there will be a *doubtful area* within which proximity to one producer as compared with his competitor is not a strong enough factor to determine a consumer's source of supply. Within this doubtful area, or region of uncertainty, consumers are subject to a "fashion effect," and are as likely to purchase from one of the producers because they prefer his product as because his distance (price) is lower. Under such an assumption, "if the duopolists converge unduly toward the center, each would be able at best, to count on the possible patronage of everyone in general, and hence no one in particular" (Devletoglou, 1965, 158). In other words, if one of Hotelling's ice cream sellers could successfully differentiate his product from that of his competitor he might capture much more than his own half of the market; if they move apart, distance alone might insure the vendor of the inferior product some sales from near customers who will not make the effort to travel the distance to his competitor.

As a final illustration of locational interdependence, differences in cost and price can be introduced into the simple graphic models to demonstrate some additional matters relating to competitive strategy as it affects location. In Figure 8.14, firm A sets up in the center of the linear market OP in a situation where all consumers will buy from him at the delivered prices shown. His factory cost per unit of production is AA'. A second firm enters the industry and considers a location at B, but here the cost of production (BB') is so high that no part of the market could be served cheaper than from A. B is thus an unprofitable location unless some way can be found to reduce the delivered price to a level below that from A over some part of the market. At C costs are again higher than at A, but low enough to enable firm C to undercut A in the section of the market from O to X. A firm can attempt to extend its market against a competitor by geographical price discrimination, and this can be demonstrated with respect to firm C. If inelastic demand is assumed

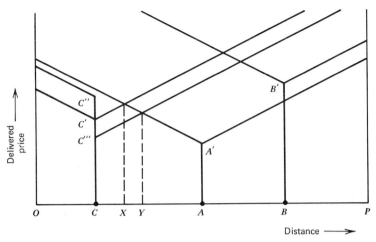

Figure 8.14. Market-area competition between firms with different plant costs.

so that a rise in price will not adversely affect sales, C can raise his price slightly to the left of the plant (as long as it is kept below A's price gradient) to give a new gradient for C rising to the left from C″. The extra revenue obtained in this way could be used to lower the price to the right of firm C, as shown by the gradient rising from C‴, which could enable C to extend its market area to Y, at the expense of firm A, thus increasing total sales. But, in practice, A would no doubt react to this, and further price competition would result in the area between A and C until some kind of equilibrium position had been reached.

This discussion of locational interdependence has been brief and at a fairly elementary level. So many abstractions from the real world have been made that the analysis of competition along a linear market often looks more like simple geometry than the study of plant location. However, enough of the main issues have been introduced to show that the concept of locational interdependence adds a new dimension to classical theory based on the search for the least-cost location. How the two approaches can be reconciled in a comprehensive theory of industrial location is a matter of major concern, which has yet to be resolved satisfactorily.

8.6 MELVIN GREENHUT

The first major attempt to integrate the least-cost and locational-interdependence theories was made by Melvin Greenhut. In 1956 his *Plant Location in Theory and in Practice* brought together ideas that he had already expressed in a number of published papers (1952a, 1952b, 1955), and in a second book—*Microeconomics and the Space Economy* (1963) —he took a further look at the effect of space on conventional economic theory. This work, together with a number of other papers in the field of spatial economics (1957, 1959, 1960, 1964, 1967), makes Greenhut's contribution to industrial location analysis very important.

In Greenhut's first book he states at the outset that the purpose of location theory is to explain why a particular causal factor is important to one industry and not to another (Greenhut, 1956, 4). He begins with a look at the approaches of the least-cost and locational-interdependence schools, and then attempts to integrate the two in a theory that includes both cost and demand factors. Next he breaks down his theory, examining the various cost and demand forces which influence plant location. Then he tests his theory in a study of the site selection of a number of small firms, which enables him to refine it in the light of practical experience.

Of particular value is Greenhut's discussion of the location factors. He lists these as transportation, processing costs, the demand factor, and what he describes as "cost-reducing" and "revenue-increasing" factors. Generally one factor is of particular importance, with secondary factors coming into play when the governing factor gives alternative sites.

Transportation is regarded as a major determinant of plant location, and Greenhut feels that it should be distinguished from other factors, not confused with them. An entrepreneur will tend to economize on transportation if freight costs comprise a large part of total costs, but this will be possible only if transfer costs vary significantly at different locations. Material orientation as a product of transport costs is considered, and it is concluded that today this occurs in two special cases: (1) where the materials are perishable, and (2) where transport cost on the material is much greater than on the finished product. Otherwise, the transport factor may be expected to favor a location near the market.

Under processing costs, Greenhut considers labor, capital, and taxation. They can be expected to have great influence on location where transport costs or the demand factor do not require material or market orientation.

Greenhut gives special attention to the demand factor, and the effect on location of the interdependence of firms. The discussion of how firms will locate in various competitive and pricing situations (which draws on the work of Hotelling, Smithies, and others) occupies a considerable part of his first book and is taken up again in *Microeconomics and the Space Economy*. The discussions of how the interdependence between firms influences location under various conditions leads to some important general conclusions about the tendency of industries to concentrate or disperse. Greenhut considers the Hotelling case where infinitely inelastic demand makes for concentration of two producers at one point, and reviews the alternative interpretations. He points out that the reverse of the Hotelling case, with infinitely elastic demand, would be all production taking place at the point of consumption, since any rise in price with freight costs would eliminate demand. As a general rule, the more elastic the demand for a firm's product, the more dispersed production will be. But the tendency to disperse also depends on the height of freight rates (high transport costs to the consumer will make for dispersal), and the characteristics of marginal costs (decreasing marginal costs make for dispersal) (Greenhut, 1963, 192–193). Also, the larger the number of firms, the greater the force for dispersal increases, since small firms seeking a relatively small market area will move to a distant point of the market more readily than a large firm, who may want a location from which he can serve a major part of the market. In comparing various system of oligopoly (that is, a situation in which a small number of firms exist, each aware of the activities of the others), Greenhut makes an important distinction between an organized and an unorganized market situation. Unorganized oligopoly, where firms compete freely in price, leads more readily to dispersal than organized oligopoly, in which a basing-point system or similar practices encourages undue localization: "organized oligopoly just does not promote an efficient distribution in space" (Greenhut, 1963, 158).

In addition to transportation, processing costs, and the demand factor, Greenhut considers the effect of cost-reducing and revenue-increasing factors. Cost-reducing factors refer to certain gains that arise essentially from agglomerating or deglomerating; for example, the external economies that a firm may derive from a location in a city familiar with the firm's type of business. Revenue-increasing factors cover similar considerations that affect sales. Also distinguished are personal cost-reducing and personal revenue-increasing factors, which refer to advantages gained from personal contacts between individuals. Greenhut (1956, 175–176, 277–279, 282–283) also mentions the purely personal considerations that may influence the precise choice of location, providing the entrepreneur with psychic income. But the inclusion of nonprofit motives in economic theory raises problems, leading as it does to the possibility of substituting the maximization of total (pecuniary and psychic) satisfaction as the guiding principle for the understanding of business behavior in place of the conventional profit maximization.

In an early paper (1951) based on empirical inquiry, Greenhut had suggested a theoretical reorientation to accommodate suboptimal behavior. This was that the definition of the locator's objective in plant locations must be broader than the simple claim that the individual seeks maximum profits; that the free choice of location by a rational individual can be explained under the postulate that maximum satisfactions are sought in plant-site selection; and that the personal considerations which should be included in the location factors react upon price by way of imputed cost, since the entrepreneur may charge his firm a lower implicit wage in a locality that offers him psychic income. This kind of argument is very much in line with the contemporary behavioral view of locational analysis (for example, Pred, 1967), and with the interpretation of Galbraith (1967) and others interested in the suboptimal nature of economic decision making. Greenhut considers these matters further in Chapter 1 of his *Microeconomics and the Space Economy*, where he points out that the choice of a maximum-profit course of action implies perfect knowledge and certainty as to what will follow. Under the conditions of uncertainty in which business decisions are made in practice, profit potential and the risk of making a loss may vary with location, since one place may offer a range of possibilities from a big profit to a big loss, depending on how market conditions turn out, while another place may give a narrower range between a small profit and a small loss. In these circumstances, the choice of location will depend on the financial status of the company (for example, whether they have enough reserves to risk a big loss) and on the attitudes and character of the entrepreneur (for example, whether he is conservative, optimistic, or has a gambling instinct).

Greenhut's theory of industrial location (1956) thus requires the inclusion of the following:

1. Cost factors of location (transportation, labor, and processing costs).
2. Demand factors of location (locational interdependence of firms, or attempts to monopolize certain market segments).
3. Cost-reducing factors.
4. Revenue-increasing factors.
5. Personal cost-reducing factors.
6. Personal revenue-increasing factors.
7. Purely personal considerations (perhaps).

These are the causal factors suggested by a priori reasoning, and supported by the findings of empirical research.

He achieves his avowed intention of integrating the least-cost and locational-interdependence approaches by taking maximization of total profits rather than minimization of costs or maximization of revenue as the criterion of optimum location. Lösch, of course, also couched his theory in terms of profit maximization, but as Greenhut stresses, he paid only lip service to cost factors. The core of his theory is summarized as follows (Greenhut, 1956, 285):

... each firm entering the competitive scene will seek that site from which its sales to a given number of buyers (whose purchases are required for the greatest possible profits) can be served at the lowest total cost. ... In time, the successful attempts of competitors to locate at the profit-maximizing site will so shrink the relative demand as to cut profits, thereby leading eventually the state of locational equilibrium. Such equilibrium would find (1) marginal revenues equated with marginal costs, (2) average revenue (or better yet, let us use the words net-mill price) tangent to average costs, and (3) concentrations and scatterings of plants in such order that relocation of any one plant would occasion losses.

Any change in the cost or demand factors would, of course, upset this equilibrium and result in locational readjustment. In the end, Greenhut resists the temptation to rest his general theory on a postulate other than economic man by introducing nonpecuniary satisfaction, but he states firmly that purely personal factors are forces to be reckoned with not only from the standpoint of particular site selection but for general equilibrium in space.

The comprehensive nature of Greenhut's theory makes it one of the most useful general statements on industrial location yet to be offered. If any major reservation has to be made, it is that the analytical sections of the two books are almost entirely confined to the demand factor, and that the integration of existing theory is achieved rather from the locational-interdependence side. The empirical investigator looking for an operational model in which there is a real fusion of the least-cost and locational-interdependence approaches will still have difficulty finding it here, but this may always be too much to ask of any theory.

Despite Greenhut's emphasis on the demand factor, both theoretical and empirical inquiry have subsequently remained preoccupied with the cost approach. When the demand factor is included, it is generally in the context of the transport cost involved in supplying a given market as in the Weber model. In a more recent paper, Greenhut (1964) has taken issue with this, urging that more attention be given to the demand factor. He points out that demand is dependent on the choice of location and also influences it, and may actually be more variable than cost from place to place. He makes a useful distinction between demand as an *area-determining* factor of location, selecting one area for location instead of others because of the greater size of the market in the one, and demand as the *site-determining* factor of location, which involves choice in relation to the location of competitors, or locational interdependence. It is the site-determining effect of demand that the empiricists have failed to take account of (Greenhut, 1964, 178). The full integration of locational interdependence into operational explanatory models thus remains a major task for industrial location analysis.

8.7 WALTER ISARD

Isard's major work on location theory is *Location and Space Economy*, published in 1956. This was followed by *Methods of Regional Analysis* (1960) and he has made many other contributions to the fields of spatial economics and regional science. *Location and Space Economy* must be viewed in relation to Isard's other work, for although the general theory that he evolves is of little direct utility for handling specific problems of reality, he viewed it as a first step toward the building up of a body of theory and analytical tools to assist the understanding of the operation of economic processes in the real world. In *Location and Space Economy* the stated aim is to develop principles for a general theory of location, drawing upon various elements of the work of others. Isard embraces all aspects of the space economy, but his emphasis is mainly on manufacturing.

Initially, Isard sees a combination of the frameworks of von Thünen, Lösch and Weber as a possible approach to a general theory. Von Thünen's pattern of concentric agricultural zones around a central city (see Chisholm, 1962; Hall, 1966) combines readily with Lösch's hexagonal pattern of settlements and market areas centered on a major metropolis. The assumption of uniform and equal distribution of resources in the level plain of von Thünen and Lösch is relaxed by the introduction of a Weberian type of analysis, in which plant location in conditions of material localization is considered. Thus, new production sites and cities may emerge from a Weberian mechanism, to be added to the Thünen-Lösch hierarchy.

Isard attaches great importance to the fusion of location theory with other branches of economic theory, which he attempts through the well-known substitution principle. Andreas Predöhl (1928; Isard, 1956, 32–36) appears to have been the first to claim that this principle could be applied to location analysis. The basic idea is that general location theory can be developed in a similar manner to other aspects of economic theory by applying the principle of substitution to the way an entrepreneur combines expenditure on the various factors of production in making his choice of location. The substitution approach to location theory is summarized by Greenhut (1956, 4) as follows:

> The theory of plant location is one segment of economic theory. It, too, rests on the principle of substitution. The extent to which labor can be substituted for capital or land and vice versa is basically the same problem as the selection of a plant site from among alternative locations. Both decisions attempt to maximize the ends. The objective is accomplished when the scarce means are allocated among competing ends in the optimum manner.

Like most earlier location theorists, Isard gives much attention to the transport factor. He puts *transport inputs,* previously referred to as distance inputs (Isard, 1951), on the same level as the four conventionally recognized factors of production (land, labor, capital, and enterprise) as a requirement of the productive process. He does this not necessarily so that transport is regarded as another factor of production, but simply to emphasize the important role transport inputs play in production and consumption processes (Isard, 1956, 90).

Isard's analysis of the locational equilibrium of the firm under transport orientation illustrates how the substitution approach is applied. The framework is the familiar locational triangle, with the market at one corner (C), sources of two materials at the other corners (M_1 and M_2), and distances as shown in Figure 8.15a. The initial problem is to find the optimum location, given certain assumptions regarding freight rates and quantity of material needed, for a plant at some set distance from one corner of the triangle, say, three miles from C. The arc TS represents a locus of possible points. The next step is to transpose this arc into what is termed a *transformation line* on a graph in which distance from M_1 is plotted against distance from M_2 (Figure 8.15b). Moving along the transformation line from S to T distance from M_1 decreases and from M_2 increases; in other words, transport inputs from one point are being substituted for transport inputs from another. To illustrate this, simply assume one unit of transport inputs (costing $\$x$) for every mile of distance; a factory located at S, which is $4\frac{1}{4}$ miles from M_1 and five miles from M_2 would incur a cost of $\$4\frac{1}{4}x$ in transport inputs from M_1 and $\$5x$ from M_2. Located at T the expenditure would be greater on inputs from M_2 ($\$7x$) and less from M_1 ($\$2x$), transport inputs from M_2 having been substituted for those from M_1.

But where will the optimum or least-cost location be along the curve ST? To find this, it is necessary to add *equal outlay lines* to Figure 8.15b. Assume that production requires one ton of material from M_1 and one ton from M_2, and that transport rates are the same and proportional to distance. Lines can now be constructed showing what it will cost to move these materials to places at various combinations of distances from M_1 and M_2. Because of the assumption made, these lines will be straight and have a negative slope of 1.0. This is shown in Figure 8.15c, in which the three equal outlay lines show respectively the various combinations of distances from M_1 and M_2 which will require expenditure on transport to the extent of the outlays given. The optimum location, or equilibrium position, along the curve ST is the point at which it is tangential to the lowest value equal outlay line (that is, at X), for any movement along the curve away from X approaches the next highest equal outlay line. This analysis is almost identical to the procedure for determining input com-

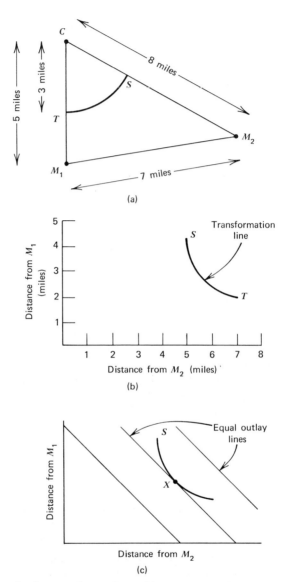

Figure 8.15. The locational triangle problem, interpreted in a substitution framework. (*Source.* Isard, 1956, 98 and 102, Figures 17, 18, and 21. Reprinted from *Location and Space Economy* by permission of The MIT Press, Cambridge, Mass. © 1956 by The Massachusetts Institute of Technology.)

bination, as described in Chapter 3, where the optimum, as in Isard's analysis, is where nothing is to be gained by substituting one input for the other. But this exercise indicates only the optimum location at an arbitrarily chosen distance (3 miles) from C, and to find the true optimum or "full" equilibrium position requires repetition of the process outlined above, but with distances from M_1 and then M_2 held constant (Isard, 1956, 95–104, 113–119).

Isard claims that by using the concept of transport inputs in a substitution framework, Weberian transport orientation can be integrated into production theory, dependent as it is on the principle of substitution between factors. But he concedes that Weber's weight triangle solution, Launhardt and Palander's geometric constructions, Varignon's mechanical model, and isodapane or contour-line techniques shortcut the process of finding the site of locational equilibrium in practice (Isard, 1956, 121–124). All are more direct than his method involving transformation curves and equal outlay lines, the only advantage of which is the conceptual one of analyzing locational choice in substitution terms.

After dealing with transport, Isard examines labor orientation, and shows how cheap-labor sites can be introduced (1956, 127–131). Again his framework is based on the substitution principle. He considers market and supply areas, following Hoover fairly closely. He reproduces Hoover's illustration of market area boundaries at the intersection of margin lines (see Figure 8.7), but interprets the situation in substitution terms; by choosing to purchase from the producer at X rather than Y, consumers are substituting transport inputs from Y, or alternatively they are substituting lower production outlays by the firm at X for higher ones by the firm at Y. Lösch's hexagonal net is found to be an acceptable spatial market pattern, which can be described in simple substitution terms. In considering agglomeration, Isard brings Weber's approach into his framework, showing that a move from the least-transport-cost location to an area of agglomeration involves substituting transport outlays for production outlays.

The formal mathematical statement of Isard's general theory in his Chapter 10 follows an earlier paper (Isard, 1952) fairly closely. First, Weber's theory is restated and generalized to incorporate many shipments of materials to production points and of products to many consuming points, and also market and supply areas. Then the possibility of more than one production site is allowed. Finally the Löschian market area analysis and agricultural location theory based on von Thünen is embraced, to complete the space economy. The equilibrium conditions are stated formally in substitution terms, which are summarized in the basic principle that "the marginal rate of substitution between any two transport inputs or group of transport inputs . . . must equal the reciprocal of the ratio of their transport rates, social surplus (however defined) less transport costs on all other transport inputs being held constant" (Isard, 1956, 252). This principle implies a large part of preexisting location theory, and Isard views it as a means of allowing location theory to be stated in a form comparable to that of most production theory. Isard's synthesis, no matter how abstract it may be, thus advanced both industrial and general location theory, and also achieved some kind of integration with other aspects of economic theory.

What kind of industrial location patterns are implied by Isard's theory, and what would be the general form of the space economy in its state of equilibrium? The starting point is an analysis originally proposed by Launhardt and later adopted by Palander, in which the implications of numerous points of consumption in a Weber-type situation are worked out. This involves a geometrical construction described more fully in Palander (1935) and Isard (1956) whereby the locations serving different sections of the market can be established. In Figure 8.16a M_1 and M_2 are sources of two materials and the points $C, C_1, \ldots, C_7$ are points of consumption. For any point C_i a locational triangle $M_1M_2C_i$ can be drawn, together with a *weight triangle* M_1M_2O which reflects the pulls of the corners of the locational triangle. If a circle is circumscribed about the weight triangle and a straight line drawn from the *pole O* to C_i, the point at which it intersects the circle within the locational triangle is the production point from which C_i should be served to minimize transport costs. In the generalization of this situation, with a spatially continuous market represented by an infinite number of points C, it can be shown that part of the market will be served from a location at M_1, part from M_2, and the remainder from various points along the relevant circumscribed circle (that is, the two arcs M_1M_2 in Figure 8.16a). Any point of consumption within the two arcs, like C_7 in Figure 8.16a, would be served from a factory at that point.

Isard extends this framework to incorporate a cheap-labor location or some similar kind of orientation and, following Palander, adds additional sources of the materials. As a result, the subdivision of the market becomes complex, but still amenable to solution by geometry. Figure 8.16b indicates a system of market zones in a situation where there are two sources each of M_1 and M_2, and cheap labor at L. Some parts of the market are served from the material sources, some from locations on arcs of the relevant weight-triangle circles, some from market-oriented plants within the arcs, and part is served from the cheap-labor location. In different parts of the markets the production points will obtain their materials from different combinations of M_1, M_2, M'_1, and M'_2. Details

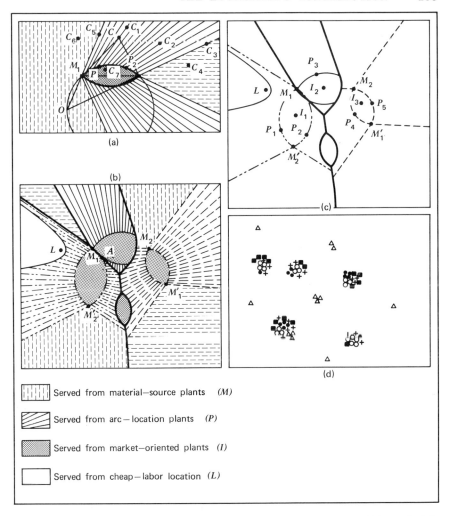

Figure 8.16. Isard's graphic synthesis of the generalized Weber model, partly following Palander. (*Source.* Based on Isard, 1956, 256, 262, and 269, Figures 44, 47, 48, and 50. Reprinted from *Location and Space Economy* by permission of The MIT Press, Cambridge, Mass. © 1956 by The Massachusetts Institute of Technology.)

of the derivation of this pattern, and the assumptions involved, will be found in Palander (1935), where a number of variations on this theme are considered, and in Isard (1956, 262–265). Isard then introduces scale economies, arguing that in the kind of situation depicted in Figure 8.16b material-source plants will serve a bigger market than other plants and will therefore be larger than arc-located plants, which in their turn will be larger than the market-oriented plants serving single consumption points. But because only a relatively small number of plants is realistic, Isard eliminates most of the arc and market-oriented locations to produce the pattern shown in Figure 8.16c. Finally, economies of localization and urbanization are introduced, to bring about agglomerations of the kind shown in Figure 8.16d.

Having deduced a pattern of industrial location characterized by a number of agglomerations, it is then a simple matter to graft onto this Lösch's systems of market areas and the concentric zones of agricultural land use by von Thünen. A graphic synthesis is thus achieved which incorporates classical Weberian theory, Palander's extensions, the central-place and market-area frameworks, and agricultural land-use theory. The combination of all this in Isard's final diagrams probably represents the nearest thing to the spatial arrangement of economic phenomena in the real world that deductive theory has yet produced. As an ideal space economy or economic landscape it provides the empiricist with a useful model against which to test reality.

Among Isard's more recent contributions, his approach to certain problems of classical location theory via *game theory* is of some interest in the present context (Isard, 1967; Isard and Smith, 1967, 1968, and Isard, 1969). The question of the interdependence of locations has been a particularly difficult one for the industrial location theorist to resolve, not only in demand situations involving spatial competition but also in the analysis of agglomeration. The development of locational games, in which each participant wishes to locate some activity and in which his decision depends on where others locate, provides a possible approach to the understanding of these problems.

In the main development of this approach (Isard and Smith, 1967) it is first applied to an agglomeration situation of the type originally suggested by Weber. It is assumed that there is an island with a deposit of iron ore, and that three countries (1, 2, 3) are interested in building a refinery to process this ore for export. There are three ports (P_1, P_2, P_3), and a comparative-cost analysis shows that R_1, R_2, and R_3 are the best locations at which the three countries can each run an independent refinery. The locations chosen are where the ore deposit comes closest to the three ports (Figure 8.17). Following Weber, an area within which agglomeration of the three plants would be possible is found in the center of the island by the intersection of the relevant isodapanes. The area thus defined (shaded in Figure 8.17) offers a lower unit delivered price of refined ore at the ports, providing all three countries will locate their facility there, because here economies of agglomeration are sufficient to overcome increased transport costs. The area within which agglomera-

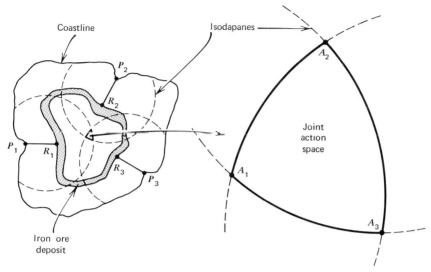

Figure 8.17. The framework for a locational game interpretation of the Weber agglomeration problem. (*Source.* Based on Isard and Smith, 1967, 49 and 51, Figures 2 and 3.)

tion is possible is termed the *joint action space*. Within this space the best location for each country would be at the point closest to their original least-cost location and their port (that is A_1, A_2, and A_3), but in order to take advantage of economies of agglomeration all must be in the same place. Isard and Smith develop a *Weberian Locational Game,* in which the conflict between the interests of the three nations are resolved under alternative assumptions regarding the way the participants will behave. Successive concessions on the part of the three participants tend to lead them (not unexpectedly) from their preferred locations at A_1, A_2, and A_3 toward a point of compromise in the middle of the joint action space.

Game theory is subsequently applied to the problem of locational choice where firms are competing for an areally distributed market. The basic frame of reference is the Hotelling case referred to earlier in this chapter. Isard and Smith claim that game theory helps to clarify many of the structural properties of these interdependent locational problems, indicating certain common elements within them. In addition, some cooperative procedures for the resolution of locational conflict are suggested, which may have practical applications. Perhaps the time is not far away when industrial competitors will meet in some consultant's office and play games under the supervision of a regional scientist, before they make their choice of location.

8.9 SOME OTHER RECENT CONTRIBUTIONS

As was stated at the outset, this survey of the economist's contribution to industrial location theory could at best be highly selective. In concluding this chapter, summary remarks on a few other contributions may help to fill in the gaps. The comments made here must be very brief, but elements from some of the work referred to will reappear in subsequent chapters.

It will be clear from what has already been said that much attention has been given to the extension of classical location theory, with its roots in Weber, since all of the major theorists who followed him incorporated something from Weber. In addition, Moses (1958) has taken the important step of introducing a variable production function, thus allowing variations in scale and combination of factors for the locating firm, and others, such as Sakashita (1968), have contributed to this kind of extension. Alonso (1967) has attempted to reformulate classical theory, incorporating such complications as economies of scale, factor substitution and elastic demand into an expanded and generalized Weber-type model.

Work has also continued in the field of spatial competition, with the Hotelling case often acting as a starting point for a discussion of how firms will share a market. Hotelling's original analysis, modified by later writers, has been expanded to encompass more than two participants, and Teitz (1968) has examined some of the implications of the existence of competing systems, that is, firms with branches who may locate them in order to gain competitive advantages with respect to the market. The analysis of competition along a linear market has been extended into two-dimensional space by Hyson and Hyson (1950), who refined the original law of market areas proposed by Fetter (1924), to define the line of consumer indifference between the territory controlled by competing suppliers. Further comments on the geometry of market areas have been provided more recently, including a paper by Gambini, Huff, and Jenks (1968). In attempting to confront the difficult problem of locational interdependence, the game theory approach has been tried by Stevens (1961b), as well as by Isard and Smith in the papers cited previously.

The question of a general equilibrium theory applied to the location of economic activity has continued to occupy the attention of a number of economists. Models such as that of Lefeber (1958) represent attempts to combine classical location theory with the more general economic theory of equilibrium, along lines suggested by Isard (1957). One of the major problems in formulating a general equilibrium approach to the space economy is how to tackle in the same framework the punctiform location of some economic activities and the areal extent of others. This was one of the difficulties encountered by both Lösch and Isard, culminating in Isard's graphic synthesis referred to earlier in this chapter. Von Böventer (1962a, 1962b) has made a significant contribution in this context, following on from Lefeber, and Stevens and Brackett (1967, 6) feel that von Böventer has perhaps come closest to creating a general system incorporating both distance between discrete locations and spatial extent of activities at locations. Further useful comments on the development of general location theory will be found in Bramhall (1969) and Richardson (1969, 101–116).

The work in general locational equilibrium theory is of a highly abstract nature, and at the moment is of little utility as a means of tackling empirical inquiry in industrial location. But the past few years have seen an increasing number of economists turning their attention toward more practical problems in such fields as development planning. Of special theoretical interest is the work of a group of Dutch economists, including Tinbergen and Bos, who are concerned about the absence of an appropriate methodology for solving planning problems relating to the location of industry. The critical question as they see it is the identification of an optimum pattern of spatial dispersion. This problem was first considered by Tinbergen (1961, 1964), who set up a simple situation in which there were different industries with varying numbers of plants and posed the problem of how the productive units could be combined into industrial centers so as to minimize production and transport costs. He was able to deduce some kind of hierarchy of centers not unlike that proposed in central place theory, including the number of centers in each category and their industrial composition, but he was unable to determine their location. This work has been extended by Bos (1965), who found that the optimum spatial arrangement in one-dimensional space (a linear market) is firms equidistant along the line and separated by distances equal to twice the optimum trade area radius. The analysis is then extended into the second space dimension, to consider the effect of circular and irregularly shaped market areas. Finally, a linear programming model is formulated to determine the optimum pattern of dispersion, but unfortunately there is no known mathematical solution to this. Some simple numerical examples enable a few generalizations to be made regarding the likely pattern under alternative assumptions (Bos, 1965, 70–78), but it will be some time before this kind of research will yield results capable of practical application.

Although not available in English, the work of the French economist Claude Ponsard also deserves notice. His first book—*Economie et Espace*

(1955)—was an attempt to integrate spatial factors into conventional economic theory, while his *Histoire des Theories Economique Spatiales* (1958) is a historical account of the development of location theory. The forthcoming translation of this second book in the Regional Science Research Institute's Monograph Series should provide a very useful additional text in this field.

Finally, brief reference should be made to four useful short summary statements on location theory. The first is by Tiebout (1957), which is a succinct review of the state of theory toward the end of the 1950s and contains the suggestion that the behavioral concepts of adaptation and adoption proposed by Alchian may be usefully applied to industrial location. The others are summaries of industrial location theory, with graphic illustrations of both the least-cost and market-area approaches, by Alonso (1964), Richardson (1969, 42–116), and Karaska (1969a). These papers, taken together, make an excellent supplement to the subject matter of this chapter.

9

Operational Models of Industrial Location

Thus far, Part Two has summarized the development of theoretical thinking on industrial location. The emphasis now shifts from theory to models. Few of the major contributors considered in the previous chapters attempted to generate operational models from their theories; some of the space economists—in particular Lösch (1954) and Isard (1956)—formalized their theories in mathematical terms, but the data requirements are such that it is unlikely that they could be run operationally to solve practical problems. Although all theory, no matter how abstract or loosely formulated, should offer some guide to the empirical investigator, the development of fully operational models is particularly important. A discussion of this question, together with a detailed illustration, provides a link between the contents of Part Two and the chapters that follow.

9.1 THE DEVELOPMENT OF OPERATIONAL MODELS

The nature of models, and their relationship to theory, was considered briefly in Chapter 1. A model is a device that in some way replicates a situation in the real world, and assists in its understanding. In industrial location analysis, a model might be constructed largely on the basis of observed conditions in a particular industry, in an attempt to shed light on that specific case; for example, it might be built to test some locational hypothesis arrived at inductively. But far more useful and important are general models that can be fitted to any industry. These models form a logical extension of industrial location theory.

The distinction between theory and models has been usefully summarized by Lowry (1965):

In formulating his constructs, the theorist's overriding aims are logical coherence and generality; he is ordinarily content to specify only the conceptual significance of his variables and the general form of their functional interrelationships. The virtuosity of the theorist lies in rigorous logical derivations of interesting and empirically relevant propositions from the most parsimonious set of postulates.

The model builder, on the other hand, is concerned with the application of theories to concrete cases, with the aim of generating empirically relevant output from empirically based input. He is constrained, as the theorist is not, by considerations of cost, of data availability and accuracy, of timeliness, and of the client's convenience. Above all, he is required to be specific, where the theorist is vague. The exigencies of his trade are such that, even given his high appreciation of "theory," his model is likely to reflect its theoretical origins only in oblique and approximate ways. Mechanisms that "work," however mysteriously, get substituted for those whose virtue lies in theoretical elegance.

The art of the model builder is in establishing a compromise between theoretical perfection and practical necessity. It is models that help to bring theories out into the open, being offered when the theoretician is asked to "put up or shut up" (Kaplan, 1964, 269).

A model generally consists of three elements: (1) *variables* embedded in mathematical formulas indicating relationships; (2) *parameters* or numerical constants; and (3) an *algorithm* or computational method required to find a solution. Any such structure comprises an operational model if it can be *calibrated,* or fit to real-world situations. The process of calibration includes defining the variables empirically and assigning values to the parameters. Defining the variables involves getting the best approximation to what the model needs (or what theory suggests) if the available data are not perfect (for example, using average wage rates as a surrogate for labor costs in a particular industry). Parameter fitting involves the estimation of certain conditions empirically if there is no a priori basis for specific figures; for example, a transport-cost/distance function might be established by regression analysis. Questions of calibration are dealt with further in specialist texts such as Beach (1957).

When loaded with the necessary data, the solution of the model indicates the outcome of the circumstances specified. In industrial location analysis these results can be used in two ways. First, a model offers something against which reality can be judged (that is, it provides a basis for determining how far reality accords with what the theory expressed in the model suggests should be the case). Second, industrial location models can be used to determine the best locations for new development or the impact of changes in some of the conditions under which industry operates.

A simple illustration will clarify the nature of operational models of industrial location. Consider this statement of the classical least-cost location theory: a new entry to any industry will, other things being equal, locate where the total cost of producing a given output is minimized, subject to the entrepreneur acting rationally, total cost being determined by the cost of the required quantity of the necessary inputs. Suppose that there is a firm in a certain industry, with two alternative locations (1 and 2) and needing the two inputs of capital (C) and labor (L) in the quantities Q_C and Q_L. The unit costs of the two inputs are U_{C1} and U_{L1} at location 1 and U_{C2} and U_{L2} at location 2. Total costs in alternative location could be represented by the following equations, which simply sum the products of the input coefficients and unit costs:

$$TC_1 = Q_C U_{C1} + Q_L U_{L1}$$
$$TC_2 = Q_C U_{C2} + Q_{L2} U_{L2}$$

(9.1)

The chosen location would, of course, be where TC is minimized, as determined by the actual values for Q and U in each case.

The two equations (9.1) comprise an elementary model of the conditions determining the optimum location. Its structure is illustrated in Figure 9.1. The values for the parameters (Q) and variables (U) can be thought of as inputs to a system closed about a certain simplified mechanism which determine TC, with all other consideration excluded. The output of the system is the optimum of least-cost location. This model

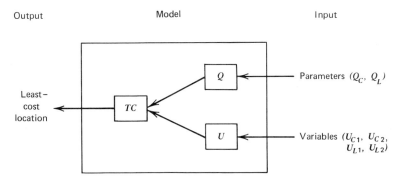

Figure 9.1. A simple industrial location model.

may easily be generalized as follows: Let

TC_i = total cost at plant location i ($i = 1, 2, \ldots, m$)
U_{ij} = unit cost of input j ($j = 1, 2, \ldots, n$) at location i
Q_j = required quantity (input coefficient) of input j for the given output

Then the desired or optimum location will be where

$$TC_i = \sum_{j=1}^{n} Q_j U_{ij} = \min \quad (9.2)$$

This is now a simple general mathematical model of the determination of optimum plant location, as indicated by the theoretical statement made at the outset. The variables are the costs of the n inputs at the m plant location. The parameters are the input coefficients, varying as between the n inputs but assumed constant as between locations. The relational statements between the variables and parameters are simply the summations and multiplications indicated in the equation. An appropriate algorithm would be any device or calculus capable of providing a solution to the question of which plant location satisfies equation 9.2.

As a second illustration, consider the theoretical statement that the magnitude of an industry in any area will be proportional to the availability of labor and to the size of the local market. This might be modelled by the multiple linear equation:

$$X = a + bL + cM \quad (9.3)$$

where

X = the magnitude of the industry in a given area
L = some measure of labor availability in that area
M = some measure of the size of the local market

and a, b, and c are constants. In this case, L and M are the variables, with different values for different areas. The constants a, b, and c are parameters, the empirical identification of which can produce an equation of best fit for a given areal distribution. The use of such a *multiple regression model* in industrial location analysis will be reviewed more fully in Part Five, Chapter 19.

9.2 SOME MODELS IN CURRENT USE

Various kinds of operational models of industrial location have been developed. Some produce an optimal solution to a particular problem by specifying the location or pattern which satisfies some objective function such as the maximization of profits or the minimization of costs. Others replicate a process, or a sequence of decisions, and simulate the way things are supposed to happen. There are also a few analogue models, such as the Varignon frame for solving the Weber locational figure (Section 8.1) and an electrical analogue for determining commodity flows and prices (Enke, 1951; Morgan, 1967).

The basic problems of classical location theory have perhaps attracted the greatest attention in operational research. Many attempts have been made to develop algorithms to find the optimum point in the locational triangle and its more general form as a locational polygon. The problem is that of identifying a single point in two-dimensional Euclidian space from which a number of destinations can be served with the minimum overall coverage of distance (cost). Stated more formally, it is required to find the coordinates x and y such that

$$\sum_{j=1}^{n} w_j [(x_j - x)^2 + (y_j - y)^2]^{1/2} = \min \qquad (9.4)$$

where the locations of destinations is given by the coordinates x_j, y_j ($j = 1, \ldots, n$), and the weights relating to the amount to be shipped are w_j. In this expression (9.4) the distances are calculated within a system of Cartesian coordinates by the familiar Pythagorean theorem concerning the length of the sides of a right-angle triangle, which has it that the required distance from the source (x, y) to any destination j (that is, the hypotenuse) will be the square root of the sum of the squares of the other two sides $(x_j - x$ and $y_j - y)$. Several writers have independently presented solutions based on iterative computer techniques (for example, Meihle, 1958; Kuhn and Kuenne, 1962; and Cooper, 1963, 1964). Leon Cooper has considered the problem extended to more than one source, for which no exact method of solution exists at present, and has proposed an approach using approximate or heuristic methods (Cooper, 1964, 1967). He has also shown that the technique designed to solve the problem where costs of movement are assumed to be proportional to distance can be applied if distance is raised to some power, to conform to the more realistic condition of tapering freight rates (Cooper, 1968).

One very important fact revealed by this kind of work is the extreme difficulty of formulating even very simple locational problems in a way that is capable of mathematical solution. Thus there appears to be a growing feeling that the search for the illusionary optimum location, no matter how satisfying it may be from an intellectual point of view, may not be worth the expenditure of effort and computer time that is required. As Kuenne (1968, 179) has remarked, "Mathematical purism frequently leads economists to seek the very best where very good will suffice for all practical purposes." Therefore, there is an increasing tendency to develop algorithms that may not yield the optimum solution to any specific case, but that offer a high degree of probability of finding a solution close to the optimum (for example Maranzana, 1964; Vergin and Rogers, 1967; and Kuenne, 1968).

A particularly favored approach to certain operational problems of the kind outlined above has been linear programming. This method of seeking an optimum solution has been applied to a number of different situations, including the allocation of resources and output between alternative locations or regions, and distribution problems like the location of warehouses and the distance-minimizing route of the travelling salesman. Discussion of these matters is reserved for Part Five, where the application of linear programming to industrial location problems is illustrated. Linear programming formulations can only be solved for greatly simplified situations, in which very many of the complications of the real world are assumed away, and Greenhut (1967) has criticized these models for their failure to incorporate the demand factor other than through its effect on the transport cost of distribution.

These are just a few of the applications of operational model building in industrial location analysis. There is a need for much more progress in this field if location theory is to have a greater impact on empirical research and on the solution of practical industrial development problems. More specific aspects of the use of models in industrial location analysis are considered in later chapters.

9.3 AN INDUSTRIAL LOCATION MODEL ILLUSTRATED[*]

The structure and operation of an industrial location model can be considered further by means of an illustration. One of a set of programmed models developed by E. M. Hoover (1966, 1967a) has been selected for this purpose. It has the advantage of simplicity of construction and ease of operation, and should help to clarify the relationship between many of the variables introduced in Part One. Some demonstrations based on imaginary data are offered; an application to a real-world situation will be found in Part Four, Chapter 18.

---

[*] The author is grateful for the assistance of Tso-Hwa Lee, formerly of the Cartographic Laboratory at Southern Illinois University and now in the Department of Geography at Fullerton College, California, in the development of this illustration. It is taken from Smith and Lee (1970) which contains full instructions for the classroom application of this model. Professor E. M. Hoover, Department of Economics at the University of Pittsburgh, kindly provided copies of his original computer programs.

The model described here derives logically from some of the theoretical frameworks summarized above in Chapter 8, containing elements of both the variable-cost and the market-area or locational-interdependence approaches. The cost of materials and other inputs can vary between alternative location, while the inclusion of demand parameters and market competition between firms makes volume of sales a spatial variable. Transport costs figure prominently in the resolution of the model, which is primarily applicable to transport-oriented industry.

Although most current operational procedures for solving industrial location/allocation problems are based on linear programming, the set of models from which the one under discussion is taken deliberately avoids this approach. The intention is to provide something "both simpler and more capable of incorporating more realistic conditions such as elastic demands at markets and a variety of cost functions at sources of materials and processing locations" (Hoover, 1967a, 303). The models thus lose some of the elegance and generality of the linear programming format, but gain a little in simplicity and realism. The model under review involves a sequence of calculations on the basis of which material sources are assigned to plant locations and plants to markets, in a way which generates the most "efficient" pattern of production and flow. The criterion of efficiency is that "the final product is made available in the largest quantity and at the lowest delivered price consistent with covering the specified costs of material extraction, processing, and transportation" (Hoover, 1966, 2). The initial selection of the least-cost material sources for each plant location insures that all consumers are supplied at the lowest delivered price consistent with profitable plant operation. Since sales are a function of delivered price and are determined by the appropriate demand curve, the quantity of the product consumed at any market is maximized, which leads to the maximization of aggregate sales and volume of production. The average delivered price is minimized because every customer is supplied at the lowest possible delivered price. If profits are assumed to be proportional to the volume of sales, the model generates a profit-maximizing solution for the entire system. On the same assumption, the optimum (profit-maximizing) individual plant location is the one from which the largest volume of sales can be achieved.

The criteria of efficiency and optimality involved in this model are not, of course, suitable for the analysis of every industrial location problem. Indeed, there are many situations in which they would be quite unreasonable for predicting or explaining actual patterns of plant location, and this should be borne in mind in the discussions that follow. In situations where the application of the model under review is appropriate, it can be used to find the optimum location and market area for a single firm in a competitive situation. It can generate an optimum arrangement of branch plants or warehouses and the territories they serve. It can also find the optimum location pattern for an entire industry of competing firms. The main obligation on the part of the user is to insure that the situation under investigation conforms to the assumptions on which the model and its resolution rests. The only constraints on the complexity of the problem which can be tackled other than the assumptions involved are the need for precise cost and demand data, and the storage capacity of the computer.

a. The Structure of the Model

The basic assumptions underlying the set of models from which the one under review is derived are as follows:

1. There is one homogenous product, for which there are a limited number of possible production locations. At each location there is a certain production cost, which includes the cost of assembling all inputs other than materials.
2. The industry uses one or more transportable materials, for each of which there is a limited number of sources. The cost of the material may vary between alternative sources. The proportions of materials used (input coefficients) are fixed irrespective of the volume of production.
3. The industry ships its product to a limited number of markets which can be designated as points. The demand curve may vary between different markets.
4. The cost of transporting the materials or finished product is the same in all directions, and can be described by a fixed terminal charge and linear cost/distance function.
5. Materials and products are completely standardized. Each production location gets it materials from the sources which can supply them at the lowest delivered price, and each market is supplied by the production point which can deliver at the lowest unit cost.
6. The solution sought to any specific situation is the optimum in terms of minimizing the average delivered price of the product, and economic rationality and perfect knowledge on the part of producers and consumers is assumed.

The version of the model used here requires the following additional assumptions:

1. The unit cost of materials at any source is constant irrespective of output, and the supply at any source is unlimited.

2. Unit production costs at any plant location are constant irrespective of scale, and the capacity of any plant is unlimited.

These two assumptions can be relaxed fairly easily, as Hoover (1967a) shows. The model can easily be modified to allow the use of some approximation to the U-shaped cost curve of conventional production theory, thus accommodating the condition of costs falling and then rising with increasing scale of output. Restrictions on production capacity can also be introduced. However, these complications are not considered here.

The variables and parameters of the model may be listed as follows (Hoover's original notation is preserved, with some minor modifications).

I $(1, \ldots, i, \ldots, m)$ represents the material input sources, identified by locational coordinates. Although the model is designed specifically to take "materials," any input subject to regular spatial variations in locational cost could be inserted.

S_i is the unit cost at source i of the input or material in question.

R is the input coefficient, or the constant amount of material required per unit of product.

J $(1, \ldots, j, \ldots, n)$ represents the possible plant locations.

C_j is the unit cost of production at location j, which in this model comprises the cost of assembling all inputs other than those represented by I, together with processing costs and an item to cover the profit markup.

K $(1, \ldots, k, \ldots, o)$ represents the market points.

A_k, B_k are the demand parameters at market k, indicating respectively the intercept and slope of the demand curve, which is linear.

T_{ij} is the unit cost of transporting material from source i to location j, which is the sum of a given (constant) terminal charge (TERM) and line haul charge (TLM) per unit of distance. The units of distance (for example, miles) should be the same as the units in the coordinates which identify the locations of I, J, and K.

T_{jk} is the unit cost of transporting the finished product from location j to market k, which is the sum of a given (constant) terminal charge (TERP) and line haul charge (TLP) per unit of distance.

A_{ij} is the unit cost of assembly for material from i at location j (that is, $S_i + T_{ij}$).

P_{jk} is the unit cost of delivering the product to market k from location i (that is, $RA_{ij} + C_j + T_{jk}$, where the source i in question is the one from which the input can be supplied to j at the lowest delivered price).

This notation allows only one transported material input, which is the situation postulated in the first illustration described in the succeeding pages. The use of more than one material requires as many sets of values for I, S_i, R, T_{ij} and A_{ij} as there are materials.

When fed with the required data, the model selects the cheapest source of input for any location by finding where A_{ij} is minimized (A_{*j}). AC_j is the average cost per unit at a plant location j, assuming that it is supplied by the cheapest material source (that is, $AC_j = A_{*j} + C_j$). The model then selects the lowest-cost location for delivery of the product to each market, by minimizing P_{jk} (that is, P_{*k}). Then the model computes the following sets of values.

Q where $Q_k = A_k - B_k P_{*k}$, that is, the total sales at market k given the most favorable source of supply (J_*) and the specified demand curve.

W where $W_{jk} = Q_k$ if $P_{jk} = P_{*k}$ as previously determined, otherwise $W_{jk} = 0$, meaning that no location can supply the market at a delivered price acceptable to the customers. W_{jk} is thus the quantity of the product shipped from j to k.

G where $G_j = \sum_k W_{jk}$, that is, the total output at location j, comprising sales at all markets where j is the cheapest source of supply.

M where $M_{ij} = G_j R$ if $A_{ij} = A_{*j}$ as previously determined, otherwise $M_{ij} = 0$, meaning that i is not the cheapest input source for location j. M_{ij} is thus the quantity of the material shipped from i to j.

L where $L_i = \sum_j M_{ij}$, that is, the total output at each material source, comprising supplies to all locations where i is the cheapest input source.

In addition, the total cost of supplying the product in the required quantity to all consumers is calculated and also the average delivered price (which is the value minimized in the solution generated by the model).

The structure of the model is illustrated in Figure 9.2. This shows that there are three main sets of data inputs to the system, relating to material sources, production points, and markets, respectively. The relationships between the variables with the model are indicated, and the outputs or results are shown. The solution is achieved by a computer algorithm, the particulars of which are set down in Smith and Lee (1970).

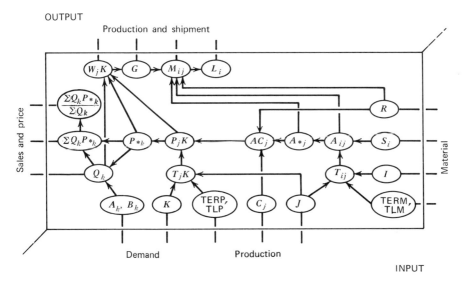

Figure 9.2. The structure of a model designed to solve industrial location problems with a number of material sources, production points and markets.

b. Applications

Two simple illustrations are now provided to show the kind of data that the model requires and the kind of results that it gives. The first case is described fully; the second case merely introduces a little more complexity and realism, and is covered by summary comments only.

Assume an area 120 miles square. There are eight possible production locations ($J_1, J_2, \ldots, J_8$) for a certain industry, with varying costs of production (C). One material is required in addition to the inputs the costs of which are included in C, and there are nine alternative sources ($I_1, I_2, \ldots, I_9$) with varying material costs (S). The input coeffcient (R) is two tons of material per unit of product. There are ten markets ($K_1, K_2, \ldots, K_{10}$), at each of which there is a different downward-sloping linear demand curve. The locations of all points I, J, and K have been generated at random, the coordinates required as input for the program having been drawn from a table of random numbers. The material sources, possible plant locations and market points are mapped in Figure 9.3, along with relevant cost and demand data. The situation set up provides a representation of typical real-world conditions, with some concentration of material sources and markets, and the possible production sites scattered spasmodically between them.

This problem is posed: given the general assumption stated in Section

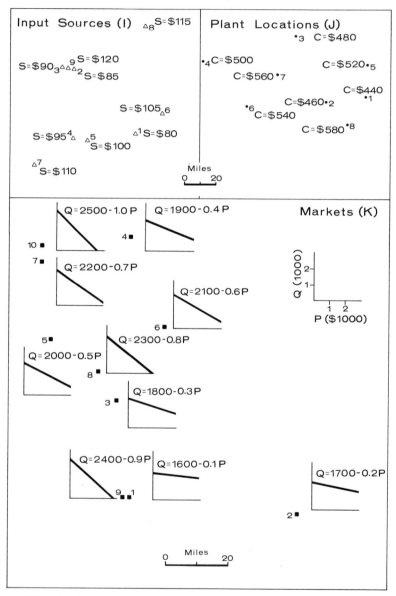

Figure 9.3. An imaginary industrial location problem with eight material sources, nine possible plant locations and ten market points.

9.3a, what pattern of plant location will satisfy the criterion of minimum average delivered price? Furthermore, which material sources will serve which plant locations, and which plants will supply which markets? And, within the whole area, which is the optimum location, assuming that total profits are directly proportional to sales?

The first stage in the working of the model is to compute the matrices of unit transport cost of the material as between pairs of I and J, and the unit transport cost for the product as between pairs of J and K once the best I has been found for each J. To do this, transportation rates are needed. It is assumed that for the material there is a terminal charge of $10 per ton and a line haul charge of $1 per ton-mile irrespective of the length of the haul, and that for the finished products the figures are $20 and $2 respectively.

The matrices of material and product transport costs are reproduced in Tables 9.1 and 9.2. The closest material source for each plant loca-

Table 9.1 Material Transport Costs per Ton (Dollars) between Each of Nine Material Sources (I) and Eight Possible Production Locations (J)

	J_1	J_2	J_3	J_4	J_5	J_6	J_7	J_8
I_1	43.97	30.00	73.89	100.05	60.25	62.81	58.27	24.32
I_2	75.25	52.94	38.32	50.31	74.07	35.94	**17.62**	71.29
I_3	83.25	60.57	43.60	**42.25**	82.03	34.33	25.52	78.60
I_4	79.08	55.28	77.05	71.85	89.63	**32.83**	50.79	62.77
I_5	71.27	48.42	75.92	78.59	83.11	39.00	51.01	54.15
I_6	**23.60**	**28.79**	70.80	110.57	42.28	77.19	64.12	**17.21**
I_7	107.94	84.63	102.18	76.71	119.04	49.22	75.37	90.32
I_8	57.01	56.39	**35.50**	96.59	**40.48**	84.41	57.01	70.41
I_9	79.12	56.52	41.14	46.35	78.07	34.35	21.40	74.66

tion and the best location to serve each market, as indicated by the lowest transport cost, are shown in bold type. Source I_6 is the one which has the lowest transport cost to most locations. T_{ij} is lowest between I_6 and J_8, and an examination of their locations in Figure 9.3 confirms that they are indeed the closest material source and location. With respect to the cost of transporting the product, location J_6 is particulary well placed, with the lowest transport costs to four of the markets. The lowest cost is between J_7 and K_6, which practically adjoin one another.

If the cost of production and the cost of materials did not vary at alternative locations, the answers to the locational problem could be deduced from these tables. Each location would be served by the source closest to it because this minimizes transport costs, and each market would be supplied from the nearest (or least-transport-cost) pro-

Table 9.2 Product Transport Costs per Unit (Dollars) between Each of Eight Possible Production Locations (J) and Ten Markets (K)

	K_1	K_2	K_3	K_4	K_5	K_6	K_7	K_8	K_9	K_{10}
J_1	172.32	109.84	160.91	177.54	203.32	134.02	220.61	172.01	175.79	224.31
J_2	127.81	103.52	110.55	143.24	154.94	89.97	177.54	122.31	130.89	182.60
J_3	178.24	193.46	125.68	**65.12**	128.41	70.99	120.18	117.84	179.40	120.08
J_4	160.98	242.04	109.20	105.09	**52.56**	117.02	**51.62**	88.41	158.92	**60.25**
J_5	197.23	149.07	172.64	161.68	204.88	132.45	212.35	178.62	200.28	214.16
J_6	**86.48**	164.40	**30.77**	119.64	66.69	78.00	110.38	**34.14**	**85.51**	119.54
J_7	125.91	162.80	72.15	81.35	90.26	**22.83**	106.83	67.71	126.73	112.09
J_8	135.88	**72.04**	137.39	181.44	187.63	127.20	214.20	152.97	139.62	219.73

duction location. But material and production costs are not spatial constants. This means that when the lowest assembly cost (A_{*j}) is found for any location the material source in question may not be the one with the lowest transport costs to j. And when the lowest delivered price (P_{*k}) is found for each market the production point which gives this will not necessarily be the one from which the product can be transported at lowest cost to k.

The solution generated by the model is illustrated in Figure 9.4. The location which serves most market points is J_2, where there is a total production of 9592 units. This exceeds the production at any other location, so on the assumption that profits are proportional to sales J_2 is the optimum location. Location J_6, which looked to be in a good position from the data in Table 9.2, serves no market, for it is a relatively high-cost location because of its high production costs. The best alternative to J_2 is J_4, which sells 4895 units to three markets in the top left corner of the area, and this is followed by J_3 with sales of 1583 to K_4. All other locations produce nothing, because they are unable to deliver the product to any market at a lower price than a competitor. The figures for average cost per unit (AC), on the basis of material from the lowest-cost source (A_{*j}) are included in Figure 9.4, and indicate that most of the unoccupied locations have costs considerably higher than J_2. One of them (J_7) has a lower average cost than both J_3 and J_4, but is too far away to compete for their markets. J_7 is very close to one market, but the cost of production is too high to compete with J_2. The locations with no output could enter production, but their costs would not be covered by the revenue which could be earned by selling to some market at a price no higher than that charged by the existing supplier.

Figure 9.4 also shows the direction and volume of material and product flows. Not all material sources are exploited, because the three viable plant locations require only one source each. The numbers attached to the product flows indicate the volume of sales to each market, which are the outcome of the delivered price from the most favorable supplier and the local demand function. The highest sales are to K_7, where the intercept of the demand curve is relatively high and the delivered price from J_4 is fairly low. Demand does not vary much between the markets, and because of the demand parameters chosen there are none where nothing is purchased. (A rerun of this illustration with the A parameter as shown in Figure 9.3 divided by ten in each market but with the B parameter and all other data remaining the same produced the result of no demand at any market.)

A second situation may be examined briefly to show how further complications may be built into this kind of model. The number of possible

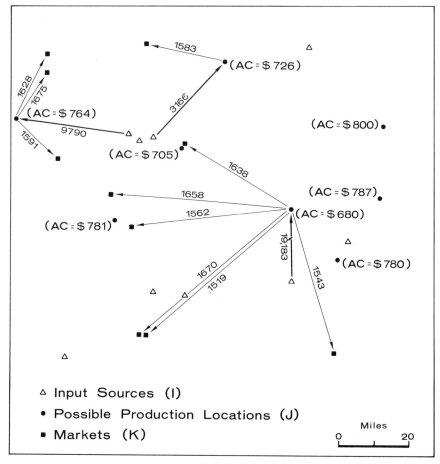

Figure 9.4. The optimum solution to the situation depicted in Figure 9.3.

production points and markets are both increased to eighteen, and the number of materials is increased from one to five (*A, B, C, D,* and *E*). The number of different sources of the same material vary from two to five, and each material has a different cost at source and its own input coefficient. The location of the market points and material sources have been generated randomly, but the possible plant locations are arranged in a regular pattern.

The solution to this situation is illustrated in Figure 9.5. This shows which locations are selected for plants, the total output (*G*) at each, and the direction and volume of the product flows. The pattern of material flows is now too complicated to be included on the map, although these data do form part of the computer output. Of the original eighteen

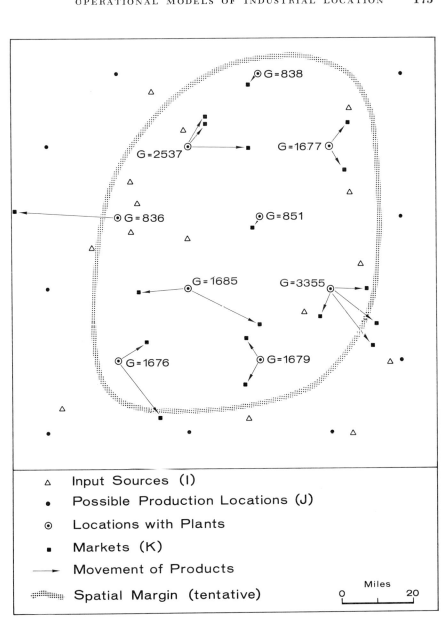

Figure 9.5. Production points and a tentative spatial margin in a situation with alternative sources of five materials, eighteen regularly spaced possible production points, and eighteen randomly located markets.

locations exactly one half have proved viable, the optimum by the criteria of maximum sales being J_{12} by virtue of proximity to four market points. All the locations where there is no production are on the periphery of the area, and it is tempting to draw a line around the viable locations and interpret it as the spatial margin to profitability. Within this line all *possible* locations offer some sale and hence some profit, but beyond it, production can only be undertaken at a loss. The introduction of the concept of spatial margins is of limited value in a case with so few possible production locations, but if all places were to be considered possible locations, and the ones fed into the model simply sample points, the notion becomes more meaningful. In this model the spatial margin is a locus of points where the volume of sales becomes zero.

PART THREE

Industrial Location Theory: A Synthesis

This discussion has now reached the stage where an attempt at synthesis can be made. In Part One the various factors influencing industrial location were identified, and the way in which certain geographers and economists have tried to integrate some of them into a theoretical framework has been demonstrated in Part Two. A number of these concepts and approaches may now be brought together, in a partial reformulation of industrial location theory.

The purpose here is to try to construct a theoretical framework that might be able to meet certain objectives set down in Chapter 1. In the initial discussion of the approach to industrial location analysis, great emphasis was placed on the interaction between theory and empirical inquiry. A major theme was the need for a body of theory capable of application in the interpretation of real-world situations, and incorporating the more significant findings of empirical investigations. Some of the approaches outlined in Part Two make a very important contribution in this direction, and elements of them will figure prominently in the framework to be developed here. But some of the major theoretical statements, interesting and instructive as they are, offer very limited scope for practical application. There are many reasons for this, one being the fact that the primary objective of most of the writers considered in Part Two was not to provide a guide for empirical research. Many of the economists who have been drawn into location analysis have been preoccupied with the problem of integrating space into general economic theory, with its emphasis on profit maximization and on the conditions which constitute a state of equilibrium. And most of the geographers contributing to this field have simply offered restricted empirical generalization or observations on the operation of a limited range of causal factors in specific cases, which does not go very far in the direction of a general theory of industrial location.

In the framework to be set up in this chapter the aim is to strike some kind of balance between the abstract theory which typifies the approach of the economist and the traditionally more empirical orientation of the geographer. The approach is very largely deductive, and at times far removed from the real world, but the ultimate need to generate something capable of empirical application acts as a constant restraint on the level of abstraction. This does not mean that all elements of this theoretical framework can necessarily be tested directly in empirical research, since this is seldom if ever the purpose of theory. What is attempted is the construction of an approach to the understanding of industrial location that should be sufficiently relevant to the actual circumstances in which locational decisions are made to be of direct assistance in the development of hypotheses concerning real-world situations. With this in mind, a number of major concessions to the observed facts of locational behavior have been made. The most important is the abandonment of the traditional practice of couching theory in terms of the search for some optimum course of action based on the maximization of financial profits, in favor of an approach which stresses the economic limitations imposed on the freedom of locational choice.

The emphasis of Part Three is mainly on the location of the individual entrepreneur or corporation. No attempt is made to deduce the precise form of industrial location patterns which satisfy some equilibrium conditions, or optimize some economic or social objectives. The argument is that the understanding of industrial location patterns, as they are observed in the real world, can best be advanced at the present time by the analysis of the circumstances in which the individual decision maker selects his location. The location patterns of entire industries are, after all, the product of a large number of individual decisions; if there is any order or regularity in the behavior of these individuals, it can be expected to appear in the pattern that emerges from their collective action.

Most of the contents of Part Three are derived directly or indirectly from existing theoretical contributions. However, certain concepts that are fundamental to the approach adopted here represent something of a departure from conventional location theory, as do some of the devices used for exposition. The theoretical framework is demonstrated largely through a series of simple graphic models, a method familiar to the economist but much less frequently found in geographical literature. These models are preferred to more formal mathematical statements because geometrical constructions are particularly convenient as a medium through which to analyze spatial problems requiring the introduction of a third dimension, and in which the concern may be more with areas than with points. Graphics are also easier than algebra for many people to understand; therefore, the kind of models used here may compensate in simplicity and clarity for what they lack in mathematical rigor. No matter how elegant some of the mathematical formulations of the economist might be, most of them have had very little impact on empirical research, and it seems necessary to attribute this to difficulty of comprehension as well as to the generally high level of abstraction. The use of mathematics in this chapter is limited to the formal statement of a model and to places where the development of an argument is facilitated by the use of symbols and elementary algebra.

The discussion begins with a presentation of certain principles fundamental to the framework that is being set up (Chapter 10). Then an initial variable-cost model is constructed (Chapter 11), and subsequently extended to incorporate various complications (Chapter 12). The demand factor is considered next (Chapter 13), first in a very simple context and then in conjunction with variable-cost situations. Finally, the time dimension is introduced, and some ideas are expressed relating to the evolutionary process by which industrial location patterns come about (Chapter 14).

10

Basic Principles

The mutual interdependence of the location decision, scale, and input-combination, makes the theoretical analysis of industrial location a very difficult matter indeed. The only way this complexity can be reduced is by simplifying the conditions found in the real world, so that certain causal factors are held constant in order to facilitate an examination of how the others operate. This is, of course, the approach adopted by the space economists whose work was considered in Chapter 8. It is the normal procedure in any form of economic analysis (and, indeed, in most fields of social inquiry), since it is only by simplifying reality that science has ever made any great progress in dealing with the complex. This raises the question of how far it is possible to abstract from reality before theory becomes too much of a simplification. Some simplification is always necessary but, as Lösch (1954, 338) remarked, "Theory is not useless because it simplifies; it is useless only when it does not simplify down to essentials, or simplifies more than necesary." The important thing is that the assumptions that have to be made must be chosen carefully, in relation to the ultimate purpose for which the theory is being set up, and they must be clearly stated so that the limitations of the theory are apparent.

A start can be made with the simple assumption that the motive of an individual or group who set up in business is to make money, and (as a temporary expedient only) that they wish to make as much money as possible. In these circumstances factories will be located at the place that offers maximum profits, assuming of course that the decision maker or makers have the perfect knowledge and ability necessary to find this place. In any industry the cost of production varies from place to place in accordance with the cost of assembling the necessary inputs, combining them in the production process, and distributing the finished product to the market. The revenue obtainable also varies from place to place according to spatial variations in demand, as partially determined by the location and strategy of competitors. Therefore, *the most profitable location will clearly be where total revenue exceeds total costs by the greatest amount.* This simple statement is the most elementary general principle concerning industrial location that can be formulated. However, its usefulness is greatly restricted by the stringency of the assumptions on which it rests, and in order to penetrate the problem with greater depth it is necessary to examine the conditions that determine business success in a little more detail.

The spatial interaction of cost and revenue is clearly of critical importance to the viability of the firm in alternative locations. This is illustrated in Figure 10.1, which constitutes an initial statement of some relationships that are fundamental to the theoretical framework to be developed. The situations depicted are very much a simplification of reality, and are based on the assumption that cost and price at any place are fixed and cannot be altered by the individual firm by large-scale production, changes of manufacturing techniques or input combination, or entrepreneurial skill. For simplicity of presentation it is also assumed that the output any firm can attain is constant in space, and that variations in demand, if they exist, are reflected in variations from place to place in price. In fact, location is determined solely by the interaction of unit cost and price (or revenue), all other influences having been assumed away.

The effect of spatial variations in cost and revenue can best be illustrated by holding one constant and allowing the other to vary. In Figure 10.1a, costs are variable in space while demand is constant and the price obtainable (p) is the same everywhere. Cost and price (dollars) are plotted on the vertical axis, and distance along the horizontal axis which may be taken as representing linear or one-dimensional space in the same way as in some of the diagrams used in Part Two. The average cost per unit of production at any point in space is indicated by the appropriate value on the line AC, which rises in both directions from a point O. This line has been termed a *space cost curve* (Smith, 1966), not to be confused with the conventional cost curve of production theory where the horizontal axis measures quantity instead of distance. The space cost curve will be employed extensively as an analytical device in the more detailed discussions which follow. The point of minimum unit cost is represented by O, and M_a and M_b show where the average cost is just equal to the price obtainable. The vertical distance between p and AC, where price exceeds average cost (that is, between

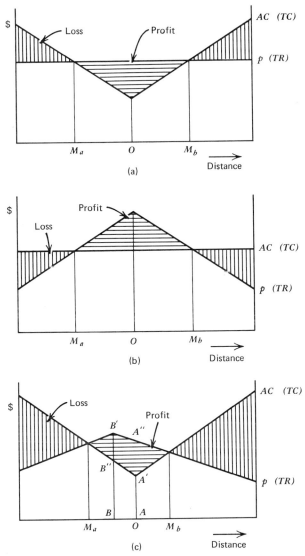

Figure 10.1. Optimum location and spatial margins to profitability in different spatial cost/revenue situations. (*Source.* Smith, 1966, 96, Figure 1.)

M_a and M_b), indicates the average profit on each unit of production. Because of the assumption that output does not vary from place to place or firm to firm, the spatial average cost/revenue situation can be taken as representing total cost and total revenue, with the appropriate adjustment of values on the vertical axis. If the assumption of constant demand had not been made, the point of least average cost need not have become the point of least total cost ($TC = AC \times$ output), and the line of total revenue need not have remained horizontal. Average cost now becomes total cost (TC) and the price line shows total revenue (TR), all values on the vertical axis simply having been multiplied by a constant representing total output. The vertical distance between TR and TC, where TR exceeds TC, now represents total profit, so O becomes the optimum location, where the profit-maximizing entrepreneur will build his factory.

But Figure 10.1a shows more than just the derivation of the optimum location in a given cost/revenue situation. It also indicates limits to the area in which profitable operation is possible. These spatial limits, or *margins* as Rawstron (1958b) termed them, are indicated by M_a and M_b, which are the points where $TC = TR$, that is, where firms can just break even. Beyond the margin, where costs exceed revenue, plants can operate only at a loss, the size of the loss being indicatd by the vertical distance between TC and TR. The importance to industrial location theory of the concept of spatial limits to profitability will be emphasized throughout Part Three.

Figure 10.1b represents the reverse of the situation illustrated in Figure 10.1a, with cost assumed to be the same everywhere, but with spatial variations in price as indicated by the form of the *space revenue curve*. These price variations are taken to reflect variations in demand, p being highest where demand is greatest. Again O is the location where average profit per unit of output is greatest and M_a and M_b are the spatial breakeven points. As with Figure 10.1a, this diagram can also represent the total situation, as output is assumed constant and cannot respond to spatial variations in demand, so AC becomes TC, and p becomes TR. The point of maximum total profits is O, where TR exceeds TC by the greatest possible amount and M_a and M_b represent the margin to profitability. This is only one way of representing a situation with demand as a spatial variable; alternatively, price could have been held constant and output allowed to vary in response to spatial variations in the volume of demand, in which case the TR line would have been a product of constant price and variable output instead of variable price and constant output. But the situation illustrated in Figure 10.1b is sufficient at this stage to show that the concepts of optimum location and spatial margins to profitability apply in just the same way as in a situation where demand is assumed constant.

In reality both cost and demand (or revenue) are likely to vary from place to place. This situation is shown in Figure 10.1c, where costs rise away from point A and revenue is reduced away from B as demand falls off. The vertical distance between TR and TC now shows that the maximum profit point is at A, where costs are lowest. Profit here (A'–A") is greater than at the point of highest price, or greatest demand (B'–B"), and the manufacturer seeking maximum profits will therefore choose the least-cost location despite the lower total revenue obtainable there. The reverse situation, with maximum profits at the high price (that is, high demand) location, could be illustrated simply by altering the slopes of the space cost and revenue curves. In these simple conditions the item with the steepest gradient will determine the position of the optimum location, although both will contribute to the position of the spatial margins to profitability.

It is now possible to state the basic principle underlying industrial location in any cost/revenue situation. *Spatial variations in total cost and total revenue create an optimum location at which profits may be maximized, and also spatial margins beyond which profitable operation is not possible; within the margin the firm is free to locate anywhere, providing profit maximization is not required.* This principal provides a means of incorporating suboptimal behavior into location theory, and thus enables the traditional assumption of economic rationality to be relaxed. It represents a very significant refinement of the profit-maximizing principle stated earlier in this chapter.

A position within the relevant spatial profitability margin is the most general necessary locational condition for plant viability that can be formulated. By definition some profit can be made anywhere within these limits, so an intramarginal location is also a sufficient condition for viability, assuming that location is the only determinant of the level of profits. How these margins arise in practice, which locations are occupied within them, and what kind of form is adopted by complete industrial location patterns, are much more difficult matters to analyze theoretically.

Only a very broad generalization can be offered at this stage regarding the likely form of industrial location patterns in different spatial cost/revenue situations. *The steeper the slope of the cost or revenue curves (that is, the greater the spatial variations in cost or demand), the more localized the industry is likely to be.* Shallow cost or revenue curves will tend to produce a more dispersed distribution pattern. This is a very simple statement, but once the assumption of profit maximization is dropped it is difficult to arrive deductively at any more precise general conception of spatial form in industrial location.

It must be repeated that the situations depicted in Figure 10.1 are very much simplifications of reality. In the real world the profitable area for a given industry might well be discontinuous, with a number of intramarginal regions each having a local optimum for the profit-maximizing entrepreneur. This is perfectly consistent with the framework introduced above,

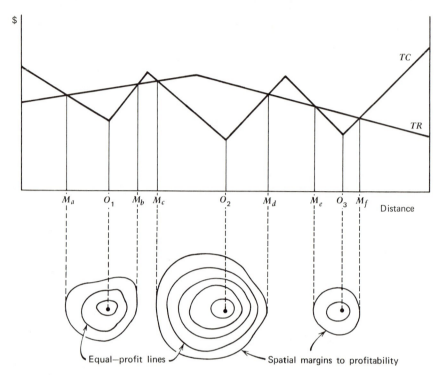

Figure 10.2. Local optima within intramarginal regions, with both cost and revenue as spatial variables.

as is illustrated in Figure 10.2 where the interaction of total cost and total revenue produces three areas within which profitable operation is possible. Each has its own maximum-profit location (O_1, O_2 and O_3), but only O_2 can be regarded as the true optimum location in the sense of offering more profit than any possible alternative location. The position of the margins, and the equal-profit lines drawn within them, reflects the slope of the cost and revenue curves in the upper part of the diagram.

Having introduced the conceptual framework that forms the basis of Part Three, more complex models may now be considered. Each of the three situations illustrated in Figure 10.1 could be used for this purpose, but the model to be developed in the next chapter will actually be built around the variable-cost approach, as summarized in Figure 10.1a. This has been chosen as a starting point for two reasons: (1) it is technically easier to develop a variable-cost model and then bring demand factors into it than to start with variable demand; and (2) a variable-cost approach, adapted as necessary to include demand factors, seems to be a more useful device for helping to understand patterns of industrial location in most advanced industrial regions and nations than an approach based on market-area analysis and the locational interdependence of firms. This does not minimize the importance of locational interdependence, but it should be recognized that much of the attention given to this factor in the theoretical literature has been prompted more by interest in extending the theory of imperfect competition than by a belief that such considerations necessarily determine the locational choices of a vast number of real-world entrepreneurs. Thus the procedure in succeeding chapters is to develop a variable-cost model capable of encompassing a number of complicating factors assumed away in this initial presentation, but with demand as a spatial constant throughout. Only when the variable-cost model has been fully explored will the integration of the demand factor be attempted.

11

The Variable-Cost Model

The most appropriate starting point for the development of a variable-cost model of industrial location is Weber's treatment of the determination of the point of least transport cost. As was shown in Chapter 8, later writers have demonstrated that the classical framework can be adapted with no great difficulty to encompass a number of the circumstances which Weber assumed away, and the generality of the model has thus been greatly extended. Yet as it is usually formulated, classical theory still suffers from an undue preoccupation with transport costs and with the determination of some optimum or least-cost location. The reformulation offered here is intended to overcome these two problems. It will be shown that a Weber-type model can be easily converted into one in which the focus is on total costs and not just the cost of transportation, with the cost of all inputs regarded as continuous spatial variables. The introduction of the concept of spatial margins to profitability gives the model enough flexibility to encompass suboptimal decisions, in line with the basic principles set down in the previous chapter.

11.1 EXTENDING THE CLASSICAL VARIABLE-COST FRAMEWORK

The main conceptual difficulty in extending classical theory has been the inability to see spatial variations in other costs in the same way as transportation. The effect of transport charges on what is paid for materials and what it costs to serve a market is easy to grasp, and the fact that transport costs can often be viewed as a simple (even linear) function of distance in theoretical work without unduly distorting reality makes mathematical treatment relatively easy. It has proved more difficult to conceive of other cost items as having the same readily identified and fairly regular spatial variations. Isard (1956, 138–139) recognized this difficulty when he suggested that location factors may be divided into three groups according to the nature of their geographical occurence. In the first group he included transport costs and other transfer charges, distinguished by the fact that they vary regularly with distance from any given point of reference. Although there are exceptions, these costs tend to vary in a systematic and predictable manner from place to place. A second group of factors comprises the various costs associated with such inputs as labor, power, water, taxes, and interest on capital. The geographical cost pattern of many such items may be relatively stable but, in contrast with the first group, it seems unlikely that the cost of any of these inputs will vary systematically with distance from any reference point. For example, there is no reason to anticipate that, given any set of spatial coordinates, cheap-labor points will be some function of distance and direction from a defined position. The third group of factors comprise the diverse elements which give rise to agglomeration and deglomeration economies, which Isard viewed as operating independent of geographic position.

Location theorists have always found it more difficult to deal with inputs the cost of which appears to vary haphazardly in space, independent of distance or direction. As Alonso (1967, 23) has remarked, most classical location theory "considers those factors that are continuous differentiable functions of geographic territory. It neglects discontinuities, such as steps in transport cost functions, actual transport networks, terminal costs, cheap labor, power, and other facts that exist at actual locations."

But these difficulties are certainly not as forbidding as might be imagined. Alonso (1967, 40) makes this perfectly clear in his discussion of the complimentarity of rent and location theories, where he sees rent gradients or surfaces as representing spatial variations in the cost of land. As soon as the cost of land, or any other input, can be thought of conceptually (if not practically) as varying over distance in terms of dollars per mile, its pull on plant location can be expressed in a comparable manner to that of material sources and the market in the Weber model. And then it is only a short step to seeing each input as a spatially continuous cost variable, with a set of single-input cost surfaces adding up to give the spatial topography of total costs. Alonso remarks that the rent surface would have many peaks and pits, and the same would doubtless be true of surfaces of labor cost, power cost, the level of taxation, and so on. However, in practice it could well be that the cost topography of these other items is often no more complex and no less regular than some real-world transport-cost surfaces.

Weber's graphical presentation involved designating material sources and the market as corners of a locational triangle. Thinking in terms of continuous cost surfaces it is not strictly necessary to identify "sources" of other inputs in the same way, but doing so helps to stress the generality of Weber's original model. The material points in his locational figure are the most advantageous sources with respect to a firm setting up to serve a particular market point (Weber, 1929, 48-49); that is, they represent the least-cost sources, away from which the cost of materials rises with transportation charges. Similarly the market corner of the triangle is the point from which the market can be served at lowest cost, because there transport cost is nil. Conceptually there is a cheapest source for labor, land, power, or any input, and these can be identified as corners in a locational figure. Thus to Weber's original triangle could be added corner-points representing the cheapest sources of all other inputs, each point exerting its own pull on plant location in accordance with the quantity of input needed and the extent to which its cost increases away from the cheapest source. The relative strength of all these pulls would determine the position of the least-total-cost location.

In this context it is useful to make a distinction between what have been termed the basic cost and locational cost of an input. The *basic cost* is the minimum that must be paid anywhere, irrespective of location (that is, the cost at the cheapest source represented in the locational figure). The *locational cost* is the additional cost incurred in overcoming distance, in order to obtain an input at some point away from its cheapest source. The cost of transporting materials, including terminal charges and things like loss of value in transit through perishability, would fall into the category of locational cost, as would additions to the minimum wage paid in order to attract labor to a particular place, or the higher than normal interest rates which might have to be met in order to get capital. Additional costs of marketing incurred in locations other than the one from which customers can be served at the lowest cost can also be regarded as locational costs.

Just as each input has its basic and locational cost, so these two elements can be distinguished in the total costs for any firm or industry (Figure 11.1). The least-cost location will obviously be where total locational costs are at a minimum, since each input's basic cost (and hence the total basic cost) is by definition constant in space. To evaluate the influence of individual inputs in any specific locational study, it is necessary to know not only how their costs vary from place to place but also their relative importance in the basic cost structure of the industry in question. As a general rule, the input or inputs making up a relatively large share of total basic cost and showing relatively large spatial cost

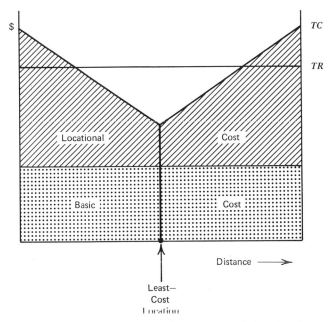

Figure 11.1. The distinction between basic cost and locational cost. (*Source.* Smith, 1966, 100, Figure 2.)

variations (locational costs) are likely to have the greatest influence on variations in total costs and thus on comparative locational advantage. A small component of total basic cost may have an important influence on location if its locational cost varies from place to place to a much greater extent than that of other inputs. An input that is ubiquitous in space, and therefore has no locational cost, should not influence plant location, no matter how high a proportion of total basic cost it comprises.

11.2 THE INITIAL VARIABLE-COST MODEL

In order to develop an elementary initial variable-cost model it is necessary to make a number of assumptions and simplifications. The following five general assumptions hold true throughout.

1. Firms are in business to make a profit (but not necessarily maximum profit) and choose their locations with this objective in mind. Firms are generally aware of spatial variations in costs and profit potential, but it is not necessary to assume perfect knowledge.
2. There are no restrictions on freedom of entry into the industry, and

the locational choice of a new firm is not influenced by the location of others except insofar as this might be reflected in the prevailing costs of inputs.
3. Sources of inputs are fixed and their supply is unlimited, so that any firm can obtain the quantity it needs at the same basic cost as any other firm. Inputs are mobile, and can be obtained anywhere for a basic cost plus a certain expenditure (locational cost) per unit of distance from the source.
4. Demand conditions are constant in space, so that all firms will produce the same output irrespective of location, and sell it at a uniform fixed price. No locations provide monopolistic control over any section of the market, and the complexities of competitive locational strategies are ignored.
5. The situation being examined takes place at one point in time, so that price and input costs cannot be changed. No new sources of materials, labor, and the like can be introduced, and technology cannot change.

In presenting the initial version of the model the following additional assumptions are made.

1. All entrepreneurs are equally skillful, so that exactly the same cost/revenue situation applies to them all.
2. No locations or firms are subsidized, or derive any other advantages or disadvantages from public policy measures.
3. No economies can be obtained from agglomeration.
4. There is no substitution between factors of production (that is, there are fixed input coefficients).
5. Volume of output is fixed, so there can be no economies of scale.
6. Chance and purely personal considerations do not affect choice of location.

These six assumptions will be relaxed in turn (Chapter 12) after the initial model has been developed, to introduce greater reality. The assumptions regarding the demand situation and the static temporal analysis (that is, the last two of the five assumptions previously listed), will be relaxed in Chapters 13 and 14.

The general model which is being set up, with its distinction between basic and locational costs, may be stated formally as follows.

$I\ (1, \ldots, i, \ldots, n)$ are the sources, or least-basic-cost points, of the inputs $1, \ldots, i, \ldots, n$, one of which is marketing.

$B\ (1, \ldots, i, \ldots, n)$ are the basic costs of one unit of the inputs.

$L\ (1, \ldots, i, \ldots, n)$ are functions (linear or otherwise) which express the locational costs per unit of the inputs, per unit of distance from source.

$Q\ (1, \ldots, i, \ldots, n)$ are the quantities of the inputs required for a given output (that is, the input coefficients).

$J\ (1, \ldots, j, \ldots, m)$ are possible plant locations, which may be thought of as infinite in number.

At any location (j) the total cost (TC) will be

$$TC_j = \sum_{i=1}^{n} Q_i(B_i + L_i d_{ij}), \qquad (11.1)$$

where d_{ij} is the distance between the source of input i and location j. The least-cost location is, of course, where (11.1) is minimized, and the maximum-profit location is where

$$TR_j - TC_j = \max, \qquad (11.2)$$

TR_j referring to the total revenue obtainable at j, which in this variable-cost model is held constant in space so that the least-cost location gives maximum profits. The spatial margins to profitability are defined by a locus of points where

$$TR_j = TC_j \qquad (11.3)$$

which, with TR constant, will be given by a constant value for TC.

It should be pointed out that the model as specified above assumes that there is only one relevant source or least-basic-cost point for any input. It does not take into account the possibility of there being alternative sources for certain inputs, and that a source with a relatively high basic cost may be the best for certain production points if it is very much closer than the one with the least basic cost. The introduction of alternative sources of inputs serves no useful purpose at this stage, since it greatly complicates graphical presentation. Some of the later developments of the isodapane technique were directed toward this problem, which can also be approached by linear programming and by some models of the kind described in Chapter 9, Section 9.3.

In order to use this model to demonstrate how spatial cost variations influence choice of location, it may be loaded with imaginary numerical data. Assume that there is a firm entering business to manufacture a certain product, with cost data as set out in Table 11.1 It uses one

Table 11.1 Imaginary Cost Data Used to Demonstrate the Variable-Cost Model

Input	Cheapest Source	Basic Cost of Required Quantity (Q) (Dollars) (B)	Locational Cost per Dollar Unit per Mile (Dollars) (L)	Locational Pull (Slope of Space Cost Gradient) (Dollars per Mile) (BL)	Distance between Cost Isolines at $5 Intervals (Miles) $\left(\dfrac{5}{BL}\right)$
Material	A	30.00	0.0333	1.00	5.0
Labor	B	30.00	0.0333	1.00	5.0
Power	C	30.00	0.0333	1.00	5.0
Land	None	5.00	Nil	Nil	—
Marketing	None	5.00	Nil	Nil	—

material the source of which is point A, labor which costs least at B, and power found cheapest at C. The costs of marketing and land are included as spatial constants, or ubiquities, although they could easily be made variable by adding more corners to the locational figure. For example, a fourth point might be the center of the market, a fifth could be the place with the lowest land cost or rent, a sixth could be the source of another material or component, and so on. Ease of graphical presentation alone restricts the location figure here to a three-cornered one. The basic cost of the necessary amount (Q) of material, labor, and power is $30 in each case, and land and marketing both cost $5. It costs 3.33 cents to move $1 worth of the material one mile from its source at point A, the same to transport the power from point C, and it will cost an additional 3.33 cents above the basic cost of labor for every mile from town B. These additional costs represent locational costs. The amounts specified are assumed to hold true irrespective of the distance and direction of movement (that is, transportation and other locational costs vary as a linear function of distance and are uniform in all directions). In this simplified situation the cost of a given quantity of any input at any point can be found from the equation $Y = a + bX$, where Y is the cost, X is the distance from the origin or least-cost source of the input, and the parameters a and b are respectively the basic cost and the locational cost per unit of distance for the quantity required.

If it is now assumed that points A, B, and C are equidistant from each other and 30 miles apart, then the spatial cost situation can be constructed graphically (Figure 11.2a). A series of concentric circles (the

THE VARIABLE-COST MODEL 195

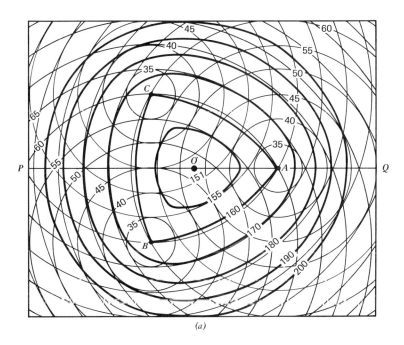

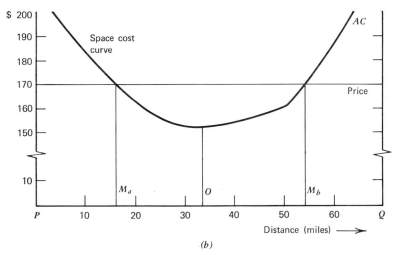

Figure 11.2. The derivation of cost isolines (a) and a space cost curve (b) in the variable-cost model. (*Source.* Smith, 1966, 103, Figure 3.)

thin lines) five miles apart have been drawn round points A, B, and C, representing isolines of the cost of material, labor, and power respectively as it rises from their cheapest sources. The isolines are at intervals of $5, and they are the same distance apart for each input because both their basic costs and locational costs are the same. From this the total unit cost of production at any one point can be calculated, by adding to the cost of the three spatially variable inputs the $10 spent on land and marketing. The total cost isolines can be interpolated (the thick lines), and the point of minimum unit cost identified. The least-cost location is shown to be at a central point O within the triangle ABC; away from this point cost rises from the minimum of $151 per unit of output.

An important omission from the costs considered in Figure 11.2 is the terminal charge in transportation. As has been pointed out elsewhere (Alonso, 1964, 89–92; Pred, 1967, 88), terminal charges mean that the minimum-cost point found in a diagram of this sort need not necessarily be a better location than one of the corners of the triangle where some terminal charges could be avoided. To incorporate terminal charges into the diagram means puncturing the cost surface at the appropriate points, to reduce the total cost by the amount of terminal charge saved by a corner location. Since this complicates graphic presentation, purely for the sake of convenience terminal charges are assumed away in this analysis. However, in reality this consideration makes a location at the source of a material or at the market somewhat more likely than in the simplified situations depicted in this section.

In his original analysis of the locational triangle, Weber saw each corner exerting a pull on the least (transport) cost location in proportion to the weight of the goods which has to be taken from or to that corner. If transport rates vary, then the weight has to be modified by a value representing the cost of movement (Weber, 1929, 43–46). The version of the variable-cost model presented here closely resembles that of Weber, except that input coefficients are substituted for weight and all costs of overcoming distance are substituted for transport cost. The model thus identifies the point of minimum total cost per unit instead of merely the least-transport-cost point. In the terms of the present model the locational pull of any corner, or input source (I), is measured by $Q_i \times L_i$, where Q_i is the required quantity of input i and L_i is the locational cost per unit of distance. An important additional property of this value is that it also measures the slope of the space cost gradient for the input in question. As Table 11.1 shows, the pulls of A, B, and C are the same, so the minimum-cost point is equidistant from the three corners. The inputs with no locational cost (land and marketing) exert no locational pull in any direction, and therefore do not influence the location of the factory.

Weber demonstrated how the minimum-cost point could be found by geometry, or by an application of Varignon's mechanical model (Weber, 1929, 227–239). But the derivation of cost isolines, which Weber introduced only when he wanted to look at a low-labor-cost location, is a more direct and realistic method, and has the important additional advantage of revealing the spatial margin to profitability when price is introduced into the model. This is illustrated in Figure 11.2b, where it is assumed that for each unit of production a price of $170 is obtainable irrespective of location. The $170 cost isoline thus becomes the margin; inside it a profit can be made anywhere, but outside firms will operate at a loss.

In Figure 11.2b a space cost curve for total unit cost has been constructed by simply taking a cross-section through the isoline map along the line PQ. The introduction of the price line shows the area of profitability between M_a and M_b, as was demonstrated in Figure 10.1. At the optimum location (O), where cost is minimized at $151 per unit, there is a (maximum) unit profit of $19. At O basic cost is, as everywhere, $100 per unit, while the locational cost is $51. As in the analysis in Chapter 10, the total cost situation is obtained simply by multiplying all values by a constant representing the fixed volume of sales.

11.3 SOME VARIATIONS ON THE INITIAL MODEL

The data used above are clearly unrealistic. It is highly unlikely in the real world that both basic cost and locational cost for all spatially variable inputs would be the same, and that locational cost would increase evenly in all directions as a linear function of distance. These simplifications were adopted solely to facilitate the geometrical construction, and each one can be relaxed in turn to show that the operation of the model is in no way dependent on them. The introduction of conditions more closely resembling reality at this stage will help to show how the optimum location and spatial margins to profitability may change under different circumstances.

Four cases will be discussed briefly.

Case 1. The locational cost is allowed to vary between the three inputs. Assume that the material is rather heavy, and costs 4.00 cents to carry $1 worth over a distance of one mile instead of the 3.33 cents in the previous illustration. Labor still costs an additional 3.33 cents per dollar of wages for every mile from B. As a third input, power has been replaced by marketing, with costs rising by 2.50 cents per mile for each unit of production, from a basic marketing cost of $30 at the location ($C$) from which spatially distributed consumers can be served cheapest. The assumption that C is the point of lowest distribution costs is a simple way to introduce the market into the locational figure without having to use punctiform markets as Weber did (Smith, 1966, 121).

Varying the locational costs per unit of distance now means that the pull of each corner on the least-cost location will be different (Table 11.2).

Table 11.2   Case 1: Cost Data

Input	Cheapest Source	Basic Cost of Required Quantity (Q) (Dollars) (B)	Locational Cost per Dollar Unit per Mile (Dollars) (L)	Locational Pull (Slope of Space Cost Gradient) (Dollars per Mile) (BL)	Distance between Cost Isolines at $5 Intervals (Miles) $\left(\dfrac{5}{BL}\right)$
Material	A	30.00	0.0400	1.20	4.2
Labor	B	30.00	0.0333	1.00	5.0
Marketing	C	30.00	0.0250	0.75	6.7
Power	None	5.00	Nil	—	—
Land	None	5.00	Nil	—	—

This is reflected in the isoline map constructed from this new data (Figure 11.3), which shows that O has been attracted closer to A than in Figure 11.2. The different locational costs per unit of distance are indicated in the spacing of the $5 isolines for each input, which are closest together for the heavy material from A and widest apart for distribution costs away from C. The isoline map, when compared with that in Figure 11.2, shows that the area within the margin has shifted in the direction of A, just as the optimum location has done. Point C is now only just a profitable location, and B has become a better location than C but inferior to A. In Figure 11.3b a space cost curve has been constructed along the line PQ which goes through A and O, and this has been superimposed on the curve from Figure 11.2. This further emphasizes the spatial shift in locational advantage resulting from the alteration of the cost data.

Case 2. The locational costs per unit of distance are equalized again but the input coefficients are altered. Instead of requiring the same number of dollar units of each of the three spatially variable inputs, these are now needed in different quantities. The largest requirement is for the material from A, the basic cost of which represents half the

THE VARIABLE-COST MODEL 199

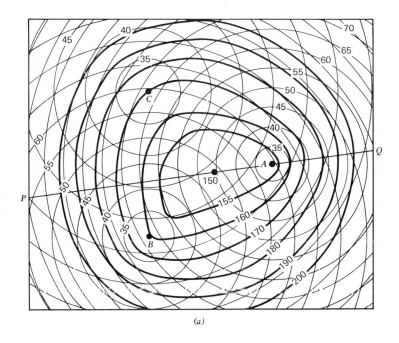

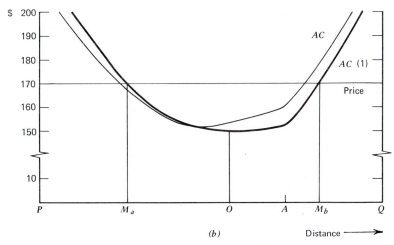

Figure 11.3. Cost isolines and a space cost curve with varying input locational costs.

total basic cost. Labor from B is needed to the value of $25 per unit of product. Land costs are introduced into this illustration, the assumption being that the cost of land is lowest at point C, where $15 can buy or rent what is needed for one unit of production, with cost rising with distance from this point. The cost data are listed in Table 11.3.

Table 11.3   Case 2: Cost Data

Input	Cheapest Source	Basic Cost of Required Quantity (Q) (Dollars) (B)	Locational Cost per Dollar Unit per Mile (Dollars) (L)	Locational Pull (Slope of Space Cost Gradient) (Dollars per Mile) (BL)	Distance between Cost Isolines at $5 Intervals (Miles) $\left(\dfrac{5}{BL}\right)$
Material	A	50.00	0.0333	1.65	3.0
Labor	B	25.00	0.0333	0.82	6.0
Land	C	15.00	0.0333	0.50	10.0
Power	None	5.00	Nil	—	—
Marketing	None	5.00	Nil	—	—

The variations in basic cost which have been introduced give different space cost gradients for each input, as in Case 1. The isolines of total cost differ from those derived in Case 1 and in the original demonstration of the model, as Figure 11.4 shows. The least-cost location is now at A (the material source), and the attraction of this point can be seen in the way it has distorted the pattern of isolines and the space AC curve as compared with the previous illustrations. The position of the margin on the isoline map shows that B is still just a profitable location but C is not; land makes up a relatively small share of basic cost and cheap land thus exerts little attraction on plant location.

Recall that Weber, in looking at the locational triangle problem, showed that if any one corner exerts a pull of a value equal to or greater than the sum of the pulls of the other corners, this would be optimum location. This is what has happened in Case 2. As Table 11.3 shows, the slope of the space cost gradient of material originating at A is $1.65 per mile, while the sum of the pulls of B and C is only $0.82 + 0.50 = 1.32$. The pull of the material source is therefore dominant.

For the next illustration, the basic costs of each input and the locational costs per unit of distance could both be allowed to vary, but this would show little that has not already been demonstrated in Cases 1 and 2. For the other two variations on the basic model it will be more

THE VARIABLE-COST MODEL 201

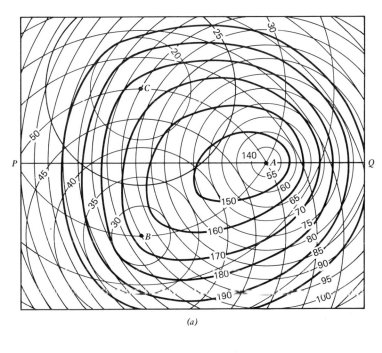

(a)

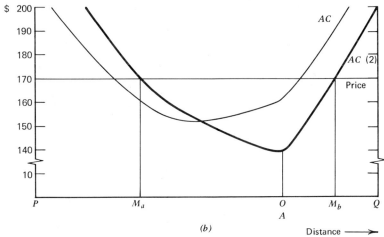

(b)

Figure 11.4. Cost isolines and a space cost curve with varying input basic costs.

useful to introduce some realism concerning transfer costs, by relaxing the assumption that costs rise in some linear relationship to distance and that movement is possible at the same cost in all directions.

Case 3. Transport-cost gradients are typically convex upward, as was shown in Chapter 5, and this situation can easily be encompassed in the model. Take the original data presented in Figure 11.2, and assume that although the cost of labor continues to vary evenly with distance the costs of materials and power tend to fall off with distance from A and C, respectively, according to two different curvilinear functions. Cost isolines based on this data are plotted around A, B, and C in Figure 11.5. The isoline interval for the material and power inputs gradually gets larger with increasing distance from the sources, with materials clearly having a steeper gradient than power. The isolines of total unit cost show that the relatively high cost of moving the material short distances from A is enough to give this point the dominant pull, and it becomes the optimum location with a total unit cost of \$150. But production at B costs only \$152, indicating that the labor location exerts a considerable attraction. An important effect of the decrease of transport costs with distance is to widen the intervals between the isolines of total cost, as a comparison with previous illustrations shown. This makes the area within the spatial margin to profitability in Case 3 more extensive than in any previous case.

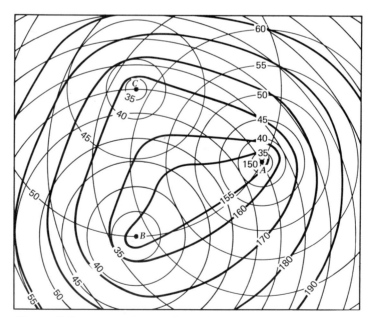

Figure 11.5. Cost isolines with curvilinear locational-cost functions.

THE VARIABLE-COST MODEL 203

Case 4. Here the assumption of free movement in all directions is relaxed by postulating a specific transport system. The basic costs of the spatially variable inputs are material A from point A $30, material B from point B $30, and components from point C $30. Assume that in the imaginary region the only means of transport are railroads and roads. The only railroads are continuous straight lines from the edge of the diagram (or region) through A and B, through A and C, through B and C, and through A and X (midway between B and C). For simplicity of construction the cost of movement along all railroads is taken to be the same, and the locational cost per unit of distance is 3.33 cents per dollar unit for each of the three inputs irrespective of distance moved. Assume that there are so many roads that road transport is in effect free in all directions from the railroads, but that it costs twice as much per unit of distance as rail transport.

Figure 11.6a shows the set of input cost isolines for material A. The patterns for material B and for components are not illustrated, though they do of course contribute to the total cost pattern. Isolines of total unit cost are drawn in Figure 11.6b, showing that the least-cost location is X, which happens to be a rail junction and is a more accessible point than any of the corners of the triangle. Away from the rail routes the total cost rises very sharply, and the $200 isoline (the highest one plotted in all the previous illustrations) is reached much sooner than in any of the other cases. The position of the margin (the $170 isoline) shows that the area in which a profit is possible is thus relatively smaller.

It would be possible to combine the various complicating factors considered in these four cases into a single illustration. The basic cost of the spatially variable inputs and their locational cost per unit of distance could be allowed to differ from one to another and realistic transport gradients could be added to a transport system of the kind used in Case 4. Many other complications could be introduced, such as terminal charges, transshipment costs, differential transport rates along different routes, and barriers to movement. The number of spatially variable inputs could be increased from three, with a locational polygon replacing the triangle. There is no limit to the increasing realism which can be introduced other than the technical difficulty of constructing the model geometrically, and even this can be overcome by the use of computer graphics. However, no useful purpose will be achieved by considering more of these kinds of variations on the initial model here. It has been shown that despite the simplifications made to facilitate the mechanics of its original presentation, the model is capable of adaptation to encompass many of the more complicated circumstances of the real world.

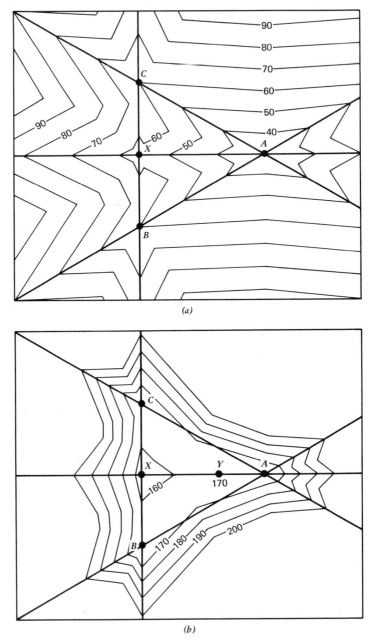

Figure 11.6. Input cost isolines (a) and total cost isolines (b) with a specified transport system.

11.4 COST SURFACES AND SPATIAL MARGINS IN INDUSTRIAL LOCATION THEORY

Central to the theoretical approach developed thus far is the concept of the *cost surface*. Isoline* diagrams are, of course, a well-established analytical device in location theory, as the discussion of the work of certain economists in Chapter 8 has made clear. George Pick, in his Mathematical Appendix to Weber's book (1929, 240–245) referred to "surfaces of transport costs" and made some useful generalizations about the properties of isodapanes. Weber used the analogy between spatial cost variations and topography, suggesting that the wages for skilled labor at the time he wrote formed "a rather mountainous terrain with deep gorges and relatively high peaks" (Weber, 1929, 49). Tord Palander took up Weber's isodapanes with enthusiasm, and illustrated the kind of surfaces that arise in different circumstances in an extensive series of diagrams (Palander, 1935, Chapter XII, Figures 52–78). Hoover also used isolines, and introduced the idea of rent surfaces, illustrating cross-sections through surfaces to reveal the troughs and peaks which would be expected to occur in any kind of space cost gradient (Hoover, 1937, 26–30, Figure 11). Lösch also reviewed Weber's isodapanes and suggested that occasionally the spatial pattern of wages will be so regular that isolines of labor cost can be drawn (Lösch, 1954, 24).

The development of the variable-cost model in this chapter has emphasized the derivation of the total cost surface from those of single inputs, rather than the traditional approach which concentrates on the pattern of transport costs. The great advantage of the total-cost view is that only in this kind of model can revenue be inserted, to show spatial margins to profitability as well as an optimum location. This is impossible in an isodapane model where the locational costs of some inputs, such as labor, are not included. Most location theorists have been aware of the technical and conceptual problems attached to the search for a single optimum location; for example, Lösch (1954, 30) recognized that theory might indicate not at what spot but in what neighborhood a new location might be sought. But the insistence on including profit maximization as a basic assumption has meant that most abstract approaches have been

---

* The hybrid term *isoline*, used throughout this and subsequent chapters to denote lines joining points of equal cost, revenue or profit, is frowned upon in some geographical circles. Although its meaning here is clear, readers may freely substitute isopleth, contour, isodapane, or any other term which seems less offensive to etymological convention.

concerned with identifying an optimum point alone. By revealing not only the optimum but also the general area within which some kind of profit is possible, the model developed here can encompass behavior which does not conform to profit maximization, and seems more relevant to the interpretation of a world of regional industrial clusters than an approach based on the search for an illusionary single best location.

The notion of an area of production bounded by a line where cost equals price need not be confined to industrial activity. The idea of margins in a spatial sense has been used in agricultural geography for some time, and McCarty and Lindberg (1966, 61–62) provide a useful graphic illustration of how a region of production is arrived at in an agricultural situation. The yield of a certain crop and hence the unit cost of production is shown to fall off with deteriorating physical conditions away from some optimum area, a price line is introduced to show how the limits to the area of production arise, and the difference between price and cost within the margin is seen as rent. The same concept has been applied in land economies; for example, Barlowe (1958, 156–159) illustrates a cost gradient rising from a point of production to intersect with a horizontal market price line, in a similar manner to Figure 11.1a. The point at which cost equals price, and economic rent ceases, is termed the *no-rent margin*.

Cost surfaces, and space cost curves drawn through them, promise to be valuable analytical devices in the study of industrial location. Obviously, surfaces in the real world will be far more complex than those illustrated through the model developed here. Different industries will reveal different types of cost patterns, ranging from the steep mountain and valley topography of an industry with large spatial cost variations to the almost level plain of the industry which is free to locate over a relatively large area. The shape and slope of space cost curves will vary with the cost topography; a gradient showing a number of V-shaped depressions separated by more elevated areas would indicate a series of separate low-cost locations, perhaps coinciding with isolated towns in a rural area, while a single broad depression bounded by areas of higher costs might represent a more extensive area with cost advantages, coinciding with a regional concentration of industry. Information on the likely form of cost surfaces and the slope of space cost curves is of fundamental importance in both the interpretation of existing industrial location patterns and the planning of industrial development. Some of the problems of identifying cost surfaces empirically are considered in Part Four, where a number of illustrations are presented.

12

Relaxing Some Assumptions in the Variable-Cost Model

The previous chapter showed that the variable-cost model is capable of adaptation to encompass different combinations of inputs, variations in locational cost, and realistic transport conditions. Now, some of the more fundamental assumptions made when the model was first presented are relaxed, to introduce further reality. The approach is to take the initial model and use it to demonstrate the operation of each additional variable in turn, with the others held constant. All the new variables could be brought together in one illustration, but this would be far more complicated and difficult to explain than taking each one separately. In some cases a cost surface depicting a three-dimensional situation is necessary to demonstrate the effects of the new variables, but generally this can be done more simply and just as effectively by using a two-dimensional situation represented by a space cost curve.

12.1 ENTREPRENEURIAL SKILL

The previous analysis was based on the assumption that all businessmen are equally skillful. It is only in these circumstances that a particular spatial cost/revenue situation can be regarded as applying to an entire industry, as was the case in the initial model. But in practice the skill with which a factory is run will vary from one firm to another, and this will have a bearing on the freedom of locational choice. With entrepreneurial skill as a variable there can in effect be a different spatial cost situation for every firm, with relatively low costs and wide margins for the highly efficient entrepreneur and perhaps only a narrow range of choice around the most profitable location for the less efficient firm.

This can be illustrated simply, by using the original space cost curve illustrated in Figure 11.2b. Assume that the curve AC in Figure 12.1 represents the average situation in the whole industry, from which individual firms may deviate in accordance with how skillfully they are run. A firm S has a management which, through its greater than average knowledge, skill and efficiency, can produce in any location at a cost that is 10 percent below the average. The space cost curve for this firm (ACS) shows that a profit is possible anywhere between MS_a and MS_b, wider limits than for the average firm (M_a to M_b). Similarly, if a firm T has a less efficient management, and operates at 5 percent above the industry's average cost, its cost curve (ACT) will indicate a relatively small area where a profit can be made (MT_a to MT_b).

The limiting cases would be where management is so efficient that a profit could be made in any location, or where a firm is so inefficient that it could not remain in business anywhere, even in the most profitable location. It is easy to envisage the latter case occurring in practice, but much harder to believe that some firms could stay in business anywhere. Although the most skillful entrepreneurs may have a very wide range of

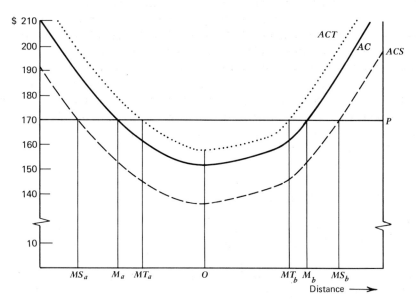

Figure 12.1. The effect of variations in entrepreneurial skill. (*Source.* Smith, 1966, 105, Figure 4.)

locational choice, there are spatial limits to the area in which even these firms can make a profit.

The highly skillful entrepreneur is thus seen as having relatively wide spatial margins. This helps to explain why the location of factories set up by industrial innovators or pioneers of new processes often seems to have been determined by fortuitous circumstances; such men operated within wide margins created by their personal enterprise, and freedom of choice as to precise location was therefore relatively great. An observation by Lösch (1954, 16) is relevant in this context: "Imitating entrepreneurs easily forget that this range [of locational choice] is more restricted for them than for their abler pioneers. A location that may yield the latter some profit, though not the greatest possible, may result in losses to the former." Pioneer firms or those that exercise technical leadership may act as location leaders, attracting other firms to their location. In these circumstances an industrial concentration might grow up in a location determined by the leader, which may originally have had a much greater range of locational choice than the firms who joined them.

The interpretation illustrated in Figure 12.1 is not the only way of looking at the effect of entrepreneurial skill on locational choice. Pred (1967, 87–88) has questioned an earlier presentation of these ideas (Smith, 1966, 105–106) on the grounds that they do not allow more efficient firms to narrow down their alternatives to a greater extent than their less efficient counterparts. It is certainly true that the entrepreneur with good information at his disposal and good ability to use it (that is, well-placed in Pred's behavioral matrix, as illustrated in Chapter 7) should in reality be more likely to be able to identify the optimum location than will a less skillful entrepreneur. And he will also be in a better position to judge the spatial limits within which he can exercise freedom of choice while remaining profitable. But this does not make the argument that the more skillful entrepreneur has wider spatial margins illogical. In practice the able businessman may generally identify a good location and disregard the relatively large number of alternative but less profitable locations open to him, but he may be no more interested in finding the optimum than his less skillful counterparts. If a firm locates without a careful comparative-cost analysis, as is generally the case in the real world, it matters greatly whether the spatial range of choice, if viability is to be achieved, is wide or narrow. Entrepreneurial skill alone can build a successful business in a poor location chosen in ignorance of the prevailing spatial cost/revenue situation. The relationship between the skill of the entrepreneur and freedom of locational choice is clearly a complex

12.2 LOCATIONAL SUBSIDY

Firms can operate in relatively high-cost locations if they are subsidized. A subsidy reduces costs, thus increasing the profit obtainable at the point in question if it is within the margin, or possibly changing a loss to a profit if the location is beyond the margin. This can be integrated into the general model by using the space cost curve from the original presentation again. If for social reasons, perhaps high unemployment, it was felt necessary to attract industry to the area E to F outside the existing margin (Figure 12.2), this could be made a profitable location by providing a subsidy sufficient to bring the cost curve below the price line between E and F. For example, a subsidy of $25 per unit of production would produce a new section of the cost curve ($E''F''$) between E and F, offering an average profit ranging from about $4 at E to $14 at F. This artificially created situation could, then, attract new industrial development.

Sometimes it is argued that certain metropolitan regions are attracting too much industrial development, and that this should be restricted by the imposition of a financial penalty such as payroll tax or some kind of congestion tax. The effect of increased taxation in a certain area, perhaps imposed to restrict industrial growth in the area G to H around the

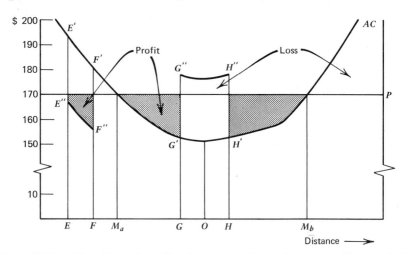

Figure 12.2. The effect of areally selective subsidy and taxation. (*Source.* Smith, 1966, 106, Figure 5.)

optimum location, can be illustrated in Figure 12.1. The imposition of a tax which had the effect of increasing cost per unit of output by $25 would raise the cost curve from $G'H'$ to $G''H''$. This would make the area no longer a profitable location for new firms or branch factories, and would make existing firms seek a location elsewhere if the tax also applied to them.

These illustrations help to emphasize that the attraction of industry into a relatively high-cost location by offering a subsidy, or the possible alternative of restricting industrial growth by taxation, is not a simple matter. In the case of a subsidy, the desired end will not necessarily be achieved by offering all firms and all industries the same arbitrarily chosen grant relating to, for example, the cost of their factory or machines. Each industry, and indeed each firm, has its own spatial cost/revenue situation within which locational decisions are made. If plans for industrial relocation are to succeed in a predictable way the appropriate subsidy must be worked out carefully for each industry in relation to the prevailing spatial cost situation. And it may even be necessary to consider a different incentive for a large plant compared with a small one, or a highly efficient firm as compared with the entrepreneur of average skill. Only if the subsidy is large enough to make the location not only intramarginal but also competitive with the profit potential other possible sites offer will the subsidized area be attractive to a firm.

12.3 EXTERNAL ECONOMIES

Like entrepreneurial skill and financial subsidy, external economies arising from some form of agglomeration act as cost-reducing factors. This matter was introduced in a general way in Chapter 6, and all that is necessary here is to attempt to integrate external economies into the variable-cost model. Assume that in the initial presentation of the model (Figure 11.2) economies exist in one city, arising from the fact that an agglomeration of firms has grown up there, but that these economies are not reflected in the general cost data from which the cost surface and curve have been derived. Let this town be point A, and assume that the agglomeration here has stimulated the development of a technical college, collective marketing and research facilities, and other specialized services. The economies derived in this situation are enough to reduce the cost of producing one unit by $15 at A. Away from A the economies decrease, so that five miles from A in any direction the saving is only $7.50, and the external economies cease to operate at locations ten miles away.

This situation can be represented on the original space cost curve

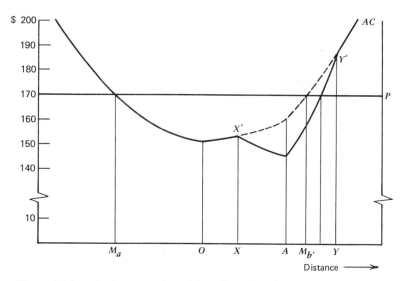

Figure 12.3. An interpretation of the effect of agglomeration economies.

by constructing a new section for the area within ten miles of A. Here the total unit cost worked out on the basis of input costs alone is reduced by the appropriate amount. This is shown in Figure 12.3, where the new section of the cost curve (between X' and Y') replacing the dotted section shows the cost-reducing effect of agglomeration between X and Y. This is enough to allow A to replace O as the least-cost location, and to extend the margin outward from M_b to M_b'.

In practice, of course, it is very difficult if not impossible to measure the reduction in cost that can be attributed to external economies in a particular area. But in investigating specific industries the possible operation of such economies must always be considered. They can be expected to distort the general cost/revenue situation in space in a similar way to that shown in Figure 12.3, and may be significant in explaining why one place is preferred as a location to another which, at first sight, appears to have the advantage from the point of view of low-cost assembly of inputs.

12.4 SUBSTITUTION BETWEEN INPUTS

Thus far it has been assumed that the combination of inputs is fixed, and that one cannot be substituted for another. But in reality this is seldom the case, as was explained at the beginning of Chapter 2. For example, it is often possible to substitute labor for capital in an area where labor is relatively cheap, economizing on the factor that is more expensive. A given output can generally be achieved with different combinations of inputs, although one particular combination may permit a lower unit cost than others. The spatial implications of substitution between inputs must now be considered, using the variable-cost model to show how the optimum combination at any one point is arrived at, and how this affects plant location. The effect of input substitution in a Weber-type locational model has already been examined by Moses (1958) and Alonso (1967), but a slightly different approach is necessary here if this consideration is to be integrated into the framework as it has been constructed in Chapter 11.

The implications of input substitution will be worked out in the context of Case 1 in Section 11.3 (Table 11.2), where there were three spatially variable inputs (labor, material, and marketing costs) required in equal proportions of $30 worth basic cost, but with locational cost per unit of distance varying between them (4 cents, 3.33 cents, and 2.50 cents respectively). For the purpose of this illustration, marketing is replaced by power. It is required to examine the effect which the possibility of substitution between inputs will have on the position of the optimum location and on the form of the spatial margins to profitable operation. This is a somewhat more complex question than those considered so far, and is best worked out initially in the simplest possible circumstances, involving only two inputs and a locational line rather than a triangle. The findings can then be applied to the triangle case and, by implication, to any locational polygon.

Consider the two inputs, material (a) and labor (b), with cheapest sources at A and B respectively, as in Figure 11.3a. Assume that in order to produce one unit of output the firm expects its outlay on a and b together to be $60, this figure referring to *basic* cost at source, on top of which will be locational cost. A minimum of $20 worth of labor and $20 worth of material (basic costs) is needed, after which the two inputs can be substituted for each other at a unit-for-unit rate, that is, $1 worth of labor is a perfect substitute for $1 worth of material and vice versa. This assumption of a uniform rate of substitution and a uniform basic cost irrespective of the combination of inputs is made simply to insure that the optimum combination is determined by locational cost alone, in other words by the distance factor.

The first step is a graphic analysis, following essentially the same procedure as Moses (1958, 261–263). Let P_{aj} and P_{bj} be the delivered prices of one unit of the inputs a and b at a plant location j. P will be the sum of the basic cost (B) of the input and the cost of moving it (L)

over the distance (d) to the plant, that is, $P_{ij} = B_i + L_i d_{ij}$. For any two inputs a and b the ratio P_{aj}/P_{bj} defines the constant slope of a system of equal outlay lines relating to production at location J (equal outlay lines were explained at the beginning of Chapter 2). Evaluating P for a and b at the end point of the line AB gives 1.00/2.00 at A and 2.25/1.00 at B, with respect to one unit of a and b (that is, $1.00 worth at basic cost). Equal outlay lines may now be drawn to show the various combinations of a and b which can be purchased with the same amount of expenditure. In Figure 12.4 equal outlay lines representing expenditures of $40, $60, and $80 are constructed for locations at A and B respectively, these lines being only six of an infinite number which could be drawn to indicate input combinations at all possible locations between A and B and for all possible levels of expenditure. An equal product curve must now be added, to show the various combinations of a and b capable of producing the given volume of output. This is drawn by plotting the

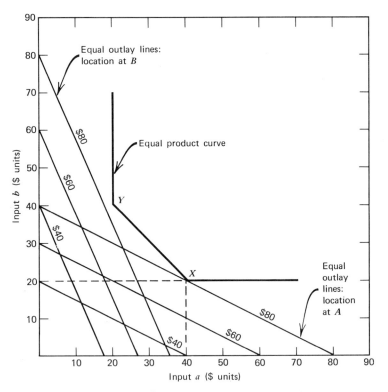

Figure 12.4.   Substitution in a two-input situation.

two limiting combinations stipulated in the previous paragraph, point X indicating $40 worth (basic cost) of material (a) and $20 worth of labor ($b$), and Y indicating $20 material and $40 labor. Because of the assumption of a uniform rate of substitution between these limits, the "curve" between X and Y is a straight line. The lines rising vertically above Y and extending horizontally to the right of X indicate that with $a = 20$ and $b = 20$ the unlimited addition of quantities of the other input are unable to raise production. The equal product curve depicted here is thus simpler than that used in conventional economic theory (see Figure 2.2) and in the diagrams in Moses (1958), where it is shown as a true curve to take into account variations in the rate of substitution. The simplification adopted here is purely for ease of graphic presentation, and is unlikely to affect the general findings to any significant degree.

Figure 12.4 can now be used to determine which of the two ends of the line AB would be the least-cost location. As in similar analyses in production theory, the optimum is found at the point of tangency of the appropriate equal product curve and the lowest equal outlay line. This is at X, where the equal product curve for the given output just touches the $80 equal outlay line for location A. A is thus preferred to B, where it would cost $88 to assemble the necessary inputs. The optimum combination of inputs at A can be read from the position of tangency: $40a$ and $20b$. This result conforms to that which is suggested intuitively, for the optimum location is at the source of the input with the highest unit locational cost, and at this point the best combination is as much as possible of the local input and as little as possible of the other.

This analysis introduces the basic principles involved in a spatial situation with variable input combinations. But it has only distinguished between two points, and it is of interest to find what would be the optimum combination of inputs at any point on the line. This question was discussed in Moses (1958), where it was found that there will be one combination of inputs for each location. More recently Sakashita (1967) has examined the question of substitution in a line situation under alternative assumptions regarding the production function and input coefficients. The approach adopted here is based on the simpler framework required for the eventual extension of the analysis to the case of the three-cornered figure.

The solution to the question of the best combination of a and b at any point between A and B is already suggested in Figure 12.4, but it may help to approach the problem from a different direction. The task is to find what combination costs least to assemble at any location j.

Stated formally, the objective function to be minimized in this illustration is the following version of expression (11.1) from the initial presentation of the model:

$$\min TC_j = Q_a(B_a + L_a d_{Aj}) + Q_b(B_b + L_b d_{Bj}), \quad (12.1)$$

subject to

$$Q_a \geqslant 20$$
$$Q_b \geqslant 20$$
$$Q_a + Q_b = 60$$

Notice that B refers to basic cost, whereas the subscript $_B$ refers to point B, source of input b. The rest of the notation follows that set down in the original formalization of the model in Chapter 11, Section 11.2.

What has now been presented is a simple linear programming problem. But in this case the solution requires no great effort, because (12.1) can be minimized by using as much as possible of a (that is, $40 worth) where its unit locational cost is lower than that of b, and vice versa. So there are only two alternative input combinations:

$$40a + 20b, \quad \text{where} \quad L_a d_{Aj} < L_b d_{Bj} \quad (12.2)$$
$$20a + 40b, \quad \text{where} \quad L_a d_{Aj} > L_b d_{Bj} \quad (12.3)$$

Somewhere between A and B is a point at which the unit costs of a and b are the same, and here the firm will be indifferent as to how it combines the two inputs. This *combination indifference point* is found from the two equations:

$$\left. \begin{array}{l} L_a d_{Aj} = L_b d_{Bj} \\ d_{Aj} + d_{Bj} = d_{AB} \end{array} \right\} \quad \begin{array}{l} (12.4) \\ (12.5) \end{array}$$

Substituting the locational costs from Table 11.2 and the known distance between A and B gives:

$$\left. \begin{array}{l} 0.0400 d_{Aj} = 0.0333 d_{Bj} \\ d_{Aj} + d_{Bj} = 30 \end{array} \right\}$$

the solution of which is $d_{Aj} = 13.6$ (miles) and $d_{Bj} = 16.4$. Any move from this indifference point in the direction of A will decrease the first half of (12.4) and increase the second half to make $L_a d_{Aj} < L_b d_{Bj}$, and (12.2) shows that then the combination of inputs has to be $40a + 20b$. A move toward B has the opposite effect.

Returning to Figure 12.4, it will be clear that the assumptions expressed in the shape of the equal product curve in this illustration allow only two alternative combinations to satisfy $TC_j = \min$, except at some point of indifference. Because the curve is made up of three straight lines no equal outlay line can just touch it and not also just touch point X or Y. Thus even in the case of the equal outlay line with the same slope as the line XY, which would in fact be the equal outlay line for the point of indifference between A and B (where the ratio of P_a to P_b is 1/1), no combination would be preferred to $20a$ and $40b$ or $40a$ and $20b$, even though the equal outlay line would just touch the equal product curve at every point (or combination) between X and Y. If the curve had been a true curve, as it is in production theory, then each set of equal outlay lines could have had their own point of tangency, and hence each location its own distinctive input combination. But if this is true, an analytical solution to the case of the three-cornered figure becomes quite impossible, as Alonso (1967, 29) and Sakashita (1968, 121) have both recognized in their approaches to the substitution problem. By retaining the simpler assumptions of this illustration, which may be regarded as representing a special case of real-world substitution conditions, some kind of analytical approach to the locational triangle is possible, using the framework already established in this chapter. This enables some quite useful conclusions to be drawn, but the limitations imposed on generality by the assumptions which have been made should be borne in mind throughout.

The findings arrived at in the case of the line AB can now be applied to the three-cornered figure ABC in Case 1 as described in Section 11.3 (see Table 11.2 for cost data). For material and labor points of indifference can be identified in the space above and below the line AB, simply by solving (12.1) for different values of d_{Aj} and d_{Bj}. These can then be joined to produce a *combination indifference line*, which is actually a curve concave to the source of the input with the greatest locational cost or pull and splits the area into two zones with two different input combinations (Figure 12.5). Similar lines of indifference can be drawn between the points of origin of all pairs of inputs (Figure 12.6), based on the cost data listed in Table 11.2 but with substitution allowed subject to $a \geqslant 20, b \geqslant 20, c \geqslant 20, a + b + c = 90$. The previous assumption of a uniform rate of substitution is retained for any pair of inputs. The firm is now free to substitute labor for material and power where labor is relatively cheap, materials for the other two where materials are cheap, and power for the two more expensive inputs where the unit cost of power is low. Thus at any point except on an indifference line the cost-minimizing combination of inputs will be $50 worth (basic cost) of the input with the lowest unit locational cost and $20 worth of the other two. The indifference lines where two inputs cost the same (which can be interpolated from the intersection of the appropriate input-cost isolines in Figure

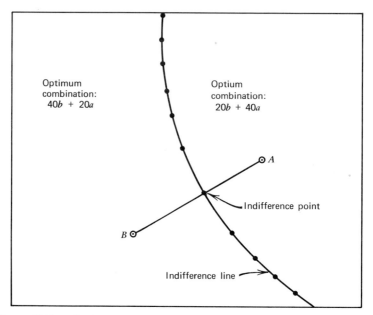

Figure 12.5. Optimum combinations in a substitution case with two inputs.

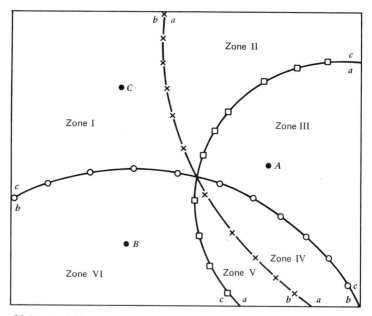

Figure 12.6. Indifference lines, and zones with the same input combinations, in a case with three inputs.

Table 12.1 Optimum Combination of Inputs in Different Zones of Figure 12.6

Zone	Quantity of Inputs (Dollar Units)			
	a	b	c	Total
I	20	20	50	90
II	20	20	50	90
III	50	20	20	90
IV	50	20	20	90
V	20	50	20	90
VI	20	50	20	90

11.3a) split the area into six zones, with optimum input combinations as listed in Table 12.1.

The final stage in this analysis is to feed this information into the graphic model to obtain the cost surface, least-cost location, and the spatial limits to profitability. The necessary data are set out in Table 12.2. Substitution under the assumptions made has produced three areas, centered on A, B, and C respectively, with different input combinations and hence different input-cost isoline intervals. The individual input

Table 12.2 Cost Data for Different Zones in Figure 12.6 with Different Combinations of Inputs

Zone	Input	Cheapest Source	Basic Cost of Quantity Used (Dollars) (B)	Locational Cost per Dollar Unit per Mile (Dollars) (L)	Distance between Cost Isolines at Five Dollar intervals (Miles) $\left(\dfrac{5}{BL}\right)$
I	Material (a)	A	20.00	0.0400	6.0
II	Labor (b)	B	20.00	0.0333	7.5
	Power (c)	C	50.00	0.0250	4.0
III	Material (a)	A	50.00	0.0400	2.5
IV	Labor (b)	B	20.00	0.0333	7.5
	Power (c)	C	20.00	0.0250	10.0
V	Material (a)	A	20.00	0.0400	6.0
VI	Labor (b)	B	50.00	0.0333	3.0
	Power (c)	C	20.00	0.0250	10.0
All Zones	Land	None	5.00	Nil	—
	Marketing	None	5.00	Nil	—

cost isolines are shown in the upper part of Figure 12.7a and in Figure 12.7b are the total cost isolines interpolated from them.

The least-cost location and the profitable area in this substitution case can now be compared with those arising in exactly the same cost and revenue situations but with a fixed input combination (Figure 11.3). Apart from the different form of the cost surfaces, three significant changes have been produced by the freedom to substitute a cheap input for expensive ones. (1) With the same unit revenue ($170) the area within the spatial limits to profitability is more extensive in Figure 12.7 than originally; substitution has widened the entrepreneur's locational choice. (2) The least-cost location (now $135 instead of $150) gives more profit than was the case before substitution. (3) The optimum location (O) has shifted from a point within the triangle to A, which is the source of the input with the greatest locational cost or pull. This last observation supports Alonso's contention that with a variable production function it is far more likely that one of the materials will have a dominant pull than is the case with fixed input coefficients (Alonso, 1967, 31).

The limitations imposed by the assumptions upon which this analysis has been based must be stressed once again. With the variable rates of substitution embodied in the conventional form of the equal product curve, there can be a different optimum combination of inputs in every location. The system of zones with the same combination which has been arrived at here will thus break down into an infinite number of points each with its own combination. Graphic analysis using the isoline method thus becomes impossible, because each location has its own set of input cost isolines. However, the present approach has something to commend it in that it does enable a simplified substitution situation to be integrated into the variable-cost model. Some reality has been lost in the process, but the idea of zones within which the optimum combinations of inputs is the same may not be as far removed from the real world as appears at first sight. After all, the cost of inputs in the real world is stable over distance to some degree, as for example with uniform wage rates for certain occupations, with the adoption of a c.i.f. pricing system for materials, and where a blanket system of freight rates applies, and such conditions might well lead to a spatially stable production function. But whatever its weaknesses, this analysis has generated a conclusion which can be expected to apply universally, namely that *input substitution will tend to strengthen the influence of certain input sources on the position of the optimum location, and widen the spatial margins and hence increase freedom of locational choice for the entrepreneur not seeking maximum profits.*

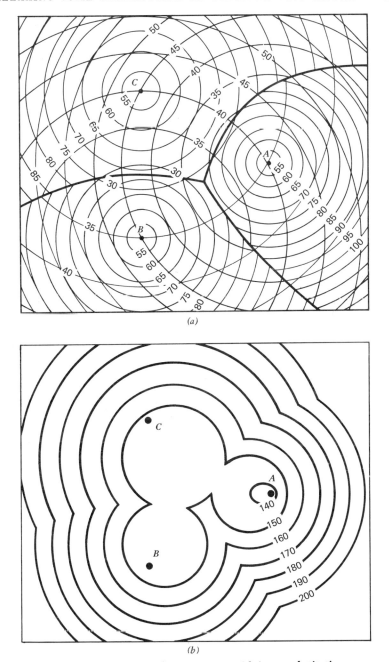

Figure 12.7. Cost isolines in a case with input substitution.

12.5 SCALE OF PRODUCTION

At the beginning of Part Three reference was made to the complexity of the interrelationships between location, combination of inputs, and scale of operations. Up to the discussion of substitution in the previous section the last two of these considerations had been held constant in the development of the variable-cost model, to enable the locational decision to be analyzed in isolation from such major complications. The possibility of varying the combination of inputs has now been taken into account, and it remains to integrate the effects of differences in the volume of output into the model.

The relationship between location and scale operates in both directions. Choice of location can affect scale through the volume of sales that can be achieved from a particular point which is of course a major determinant of the level of profit. And scale can affect location because different levels of output may require different locations if maximum profits are to be achieved. The discussion here is confined to the latter question, the intention being to examine the way in which scale can influence locational choice through its effect on the combination of inputs, which is a logical extension of the argument of Section 12.4. The next chapter considers how location influences volume of output, in the context of the operation of the demand factor.

The analysis here follows closely that of Moses (1958), although the simplified substitution relationship from the previous discussion is retained. Moses stressed the inseparability of optimum location, optimum combination of inputs, and optimum output in his attempt to integrate location into production theory. He pointed out that there can be different optimum locations for every level of output, because different scales may require different input combinations.

Some of the implications of relaxing the assumption of a fixed volume of output can be worked out in the same framework that was used in the initial analysis of substitution between inputs, as demonstrated in Figure 12.4. Assume the same situation as before, with a firm using two inputs a and b with sources at A and B and unit locational costs per mile of 4.00 cents and 3.33 cents, respectively. Imagine that in the case examined in Figure 12.4 the output of finished product is 10 units but that this is not fixed, and the firm is free to produce more if it seems advantageous to do so. If scale did not affect the combination of inputs there would be no problem to discuss with regard to the optimum location, as this would not change, although the spatial margins to profitability may widen if economies of scale reduce unit costs while price remains steady. However, the assumption here is that a change in output changes the input coefficients.

Table 12.3 contains imaginary data relating to input combinations at

Table 12.3 The Relationship between Scale and Input Combination in an Imaginary Case

Output (Units)	Min Q_a	Min Q_b	$Q_a + Q_b$	Optimum Combination
10	20	20	60	$40a + 20b$
20	30	37	100	$\{\begin{array}{l} 63a + 37b \\ 30a + 70b \end{array}$
30	35	55	135	$35a + 100b$
40	45	90	200	$45a + 155b$
50	60	140	300	$60a + 240b$

five different levels of output. The form of the data is the same as was used in the substitution problem, with minimum requirements of a and b specified and a fixed basic expenditure on the two inputs together. The simple assumption about the rate of substitution is retained. The figures show that at an output of 10 units equal minimum quantities of the two inputs are needed, but that as production rises the proportion of b increases as compared to a. This might be the case if, for example, a was labor and b capital and larger scale production required a more mechanized and capital-intensive operation.

The problem is to find the best location at any given scale, the criterion being least-cost assembly of inputs. As before, attention will be confined to points A and B. In Figure 12.8 equal product curves for the five levels of outputs are shown, specifying the values for min Q_a, min Q_b and $Q_a + Q_b$ as set down in Table 12.3. Equal outlay lines for locations at A and B are added; for simplicity only those which touch one of the equal product curves at its lowest point are included. It has already been determined (in Figure 12.4) that the optimum location at an output of 10 is at A, where input a will be substituted for input b to the limit of the technical constraint which has been imposed. But at an output of 20 the equal product curve is tangential to the same line for both locations; the firm will be indifferent as to whether it locates at A or B, for the substitution of b for a with increasing scale has just equalized the cost of assembling inputs ($137) at the two locations. As scale increases and substitution continues, B becomes the best location, because a greater proportion of input b is used and the importance of the relatively high locational cost on input a is consequently reduced. A scale line, or

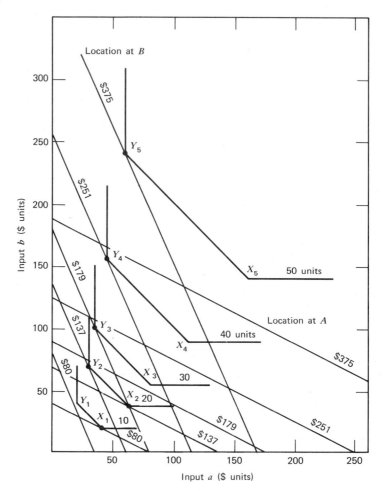

Figure 12.8. The relationship between scale and input combination.

expansion path, drawn in Figure 12.8 would run from X_1 to X_2 and then jump over to Y_2 and hence through Y_3, Y_4, and Y_5, as is shown in a similar diagram in Moses (1958, 267). Thus, for an output of up to 19 units, A is the optimum location, for 21 units and more B is preferred, while at 20 units there is locational indifference. The optimum combination of inputs at each level of output involves the use of as much as possible of the local and hence cheaper input and as little as possible of the other (Table 12.3) as in the analysis of substitution in Section 12.4.

If every point between A and B is a possible location, and if the equal product curves are true curves representing variations in the rate of substitution, the situation becomes more complex. As Moses (1958) showed, each change in scale would take the point of tangency onto one of another set of equal outlay lines and hence to another location. Thus the optimum location would move steadily along the line AB, as increasing output leads to input substitution. In the case of the locational triangle, the optimum location will trace a geographical expansion path across the map, as the point of least-cost assembly moves towards the source of the most expensive input (Alonso, 1967, 32; Moses, 1958, 265). The only circumstances in which optimum location would not shift with scale would be if the low-output location was at the source of the input which is used in larger quantities with increasing scale, for in these circumstances there would clearly be no advantage to moving.

The situation analyzed in Figure 12.8 is thus an extreme case, arising out of the simplifying assumptions which have been made. As in the substitution problem in the previous section, it does not allow for the continuous shift of the optimum location with changes in the relevant variables. But again the very simplicity of this analysis has its value. The circumstances in which plant location remains unchanged at the source of one input with increasing scale up to a critical point, beyond which a move directly to the source of another input is the optimum course of action, may well more closely resemble real-world conditions than the idea of a spatially continuous expansion path.

The analysis of Figure 12.8 could be extended into the case of the three-cornered figure, in a similar manner to the approach in the substitution problem. The principle involved is much the same, except that in the present case there would have to be a separate isoline pattern for each level of production as a different input combination is involved. Conceptually, it is necessary to think of there being a distinctive cost surface for every possible output, with different optimum points and spatial margins to profitability. However, the main conclusion regarding the effect of scale on the optimum location can be drawn without recourse to the construction of more isoline maps. *Insofar as increasing output leads to input substitution, its effect will be the same as a change in the combination of inputs for any other reason: it will tend to increase the attraction of certain input sources as plant locations, because expanding output will increase the importance of some inputs in relation to others.* If increasing scale brings greater efficiency in the use of materials it might well increase the pull of the market, with the importance of materials reasserting itself when diseconomies of scale arise (Alonso, 1967, 31).

But these conclusions do not exhaust what can be gained from the analysis of the relationship between location and scale. The best location for any given volume of output has been determined, but there remains the question of which scale and hence which location an incoming firm will choose. And the effect of all this on the position of the spatial margins to profitability and on the size of the area within them has yet to be discussed. Consideration of these issues requires the introduction of the demand factor in a very simple way, in order to look more closely at the interaction of cost and revenue. The main treatment of the effect of the demand factor on plant location is reserved for the next chapter, but there are aspects of this which belong logically with the study of scale as it influences locational choice.

In the situation discussed above, involving different scales and different input combinations, the implication was that a certain volume of output would be selected by the firm and that this would determine the locational decision and the combination of inputs. But how will the scale decision be made? Assuming the motive of profit maximization for the moment, the firm will attempt to find the volume of output at which total revenue will exceed total costs by the greatest amount. What scale this will be in the imaginary case analyzed in Figure 12.8 can be determined with the help of some additional cost data and some information regarding the price at which the product can be sold. This is given in Table 12.4, which lists the total and average costs for the five different levels of output used in constructing Figure 12.8. The figures refer to production at the optimum location for each specified level of output, and using the optimum combination of inputs as shown in Table 12.3. It is assumed that no expenditure is necessary to undertake production other than

Table 12.4   The Relationship between Scale, Costs, and Revenue in an Imaginary Case

Output	TBC	ABC	TLC	ALC	TC	AC	AR	TR
10	60	6.00	20	2.00	80	8.00	10.00	100
20	100	5.00	37	1.85	137	6.85	9.00	180
30	135	4.50	44	1.47	179	5.97	8.00	240
40	200	5.00	51	1.28	251	6.28	7.00	280
50	300	6.00	75	1.50	375	7.50	6.00	300

TBC	Total basic cost.
ABC	Average basic cost per unit produced.
TLC	Total locational cost.
ALC	Average locational cost.
TC	TBC + TLC = total cost.
AC	ABC + ALC = average cost.
AR	Average revenue per unit sold.
TR	Total revenue.

Note. All figures except those in the output column may be read as dollars.

RELAXING SOME ASSUMPTIONS IN VARIABLE-COST MODEL   227

what it costs to assemble inputs a and b. Also shown in the table is the price (average revenue) that prevails at different levels of output, and the total revenue that selling the product at this price will bring. It is necessary to assume that these prices are beyond the control of the individual firm, as was stated in the initial presentation of the variable-cost model.

The relationship between cost and revenue may first be examined by the construction of average cost and average revenue curves of the kind introduced in Chapter 2. Figure 12.9 shows the U-shaped average cost curve, indicating that the average unit cost falls with economies of scale until a certain point, beyond which diseconomies lead to increasing costs. The average *basic* cost curve is also included, the distance between *AC* and *ABC* being the average *locational* cost. The average revenue (demand) curve is of the down-sloping kind, indicating a fall in price as the supply of the produce increases. The vertical distance between *AR* and *AC* indicates the average profit per unit, which reaches a max-

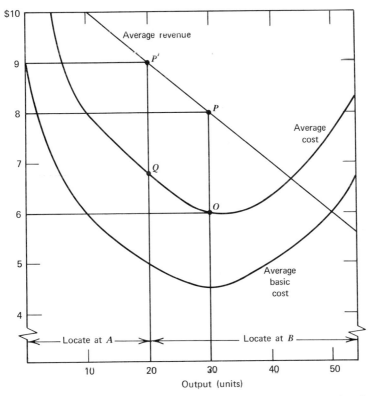

Figure 12.9. Average cost and revenue at different levels of output, related to the location decision.

imum at an output of 20 with unit profit measured by the distance QP'. However, this does not necessarily have to be the optimum scale with respect to total profits; in fact, the optimum is with an output of 30 units, because in the diagram $OP \times 30$ is greater than $QP' \times 20$.

The derivation of the optimum is clearer when total cost and total revenue are related to each other. In Figure 12.10 (based on data from Table 12.4) the vertical distance between the total revenue curve and the total cost curve represents total profit at any given output. Maximum profits of $61 are obtainable at an output of 30, and this is the scale at which the optimizing firm will choose to operate. But in making the scale decision two other decisions are also made, since if profits are to be

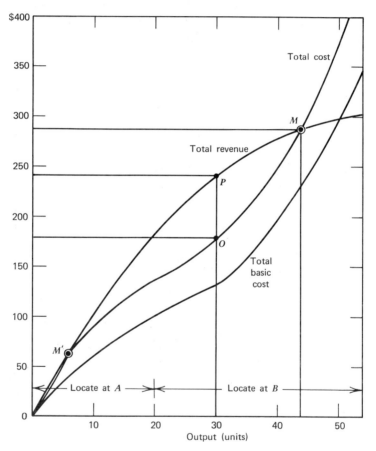

Figure 12.10. Total cost and revenue at different levels of output, related to the location decision.

maximized production must be at point B as this is the optimum location at the scale selected, and the combination of inputs must be $35a + 100b$ because this is the combination of inputs giving the lowest assembly costs at the selected location and scale. The significance of the interrelationship between plant location and the scale and input-combination decisions should now be apparent.

Further examination of Figure 12.10 reveals that although the maximum profit obtainable is at an output of 30 units, many alternative scales offer some profit. As long as the total revenue curve is above the total cost curve, profitable operation is possible. In the case under review TR dips under TC at the point M, where the output is 43 units, beyond which profitable operation is impossible because of the rapidly rising unit cost and the continuing fall in the price the consumer is prepared to pay. A similar point occurs at the lower end of the curves (M'), representing the minimum output consistent with profitable operation. These breakeven points are the equivalents in production theory to the spatial margins to profitability in location theory.

How does the introduction of variations in the volume of output affect the margins? It will be apparent from Figure 12.10 that although point B is the location of maximum profits, some profit could also be made at point A, because for any output up to 20 units A is the best location and outputs from 6 to 20 units are profitable in that $TR > TC$. But more can be learned about the affect of scale on the margin from some space cost and revenue curves of the kind used earlier. In Figure 12.11, curves through A and B have been drawn for three different volumes of output. They are simplified in that the total cost at A and B at each output is plotted using the actual values derived from the earlier analysis, but elsewhere areal variations in TC are taken to be a linear function of distance. The figures for TR are as used before (Table 12.4). At an output of 10 both A and B are within the margin, represented by M_1 and M_2, but A is the optimum location. At 20 units (not shown in Figure 12.11) there are two optima, but by output 30 the advantage has shifted to B. At the optimum scale the spatial margins have widened when compared with their position in the first diagram, but beyond the output of 30 they get closer again. By the time an output of 40 has been reached the margin has contracted to the extent that A is no longer a viable location, and the profile for 50 units of output, if it had been drawn, would have shown no margins, because all locations would have been unprofitable. The last profitable location disappears at the scale indicated by the point M in Figure 12.10 where TR dips beneath TC (that is, at 43 units). The cost and revenue curves of production theory and the space cost and revenue profiles of location theory can now be seen as

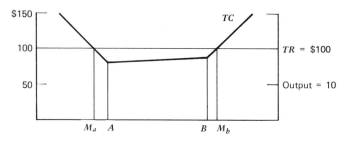

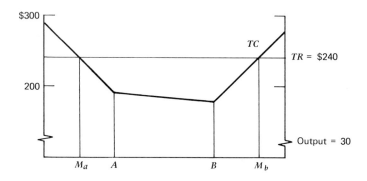

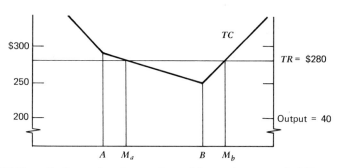

Figure 12.11. Optimum locations and spatial margins to profitability at different levels of output.

complimentary, the nature of the one being dependent on conditions in the other.

If the assumption of profit maximization is dropped, the individual firm may deviate from the optimum course of action. It will be apparent that in the case under review he can deviate from any or all of three optima: the optimum scale, the optimum combination of inputs, and the optimum location. The limits within which divergence from optimum scale is possible are shown by the breakeven points in Figure 12.10. The limits within which a firm may depart from the optimum input combination depends on the input coefficients and delivered prices, and the nature of the substitution relationship between them. And the limits to locational choice are, of course, the spatial margins. Thus the entrepreneur who, in the absence of perfect knowledge, is able to find a close approximation to the optimum scale and input combination, but not the best location, will be able to survive as long as he is within the spatial margins which are associated with the scale and input mix he has chosen. Conversely there will be an optimum location at which to conduct a business at a scale and with an input mix which depart from their respective optima, although if the departures are very large it is possible that no location will be intramarginal in the spatial sense. *But there is only one optimum location, and this requires both the optimum level of output and the optimum combination of inputs.*

The main conclusions from this analysis may be summarized very briefly. With volume of output as a variable, the optimum location will be at that point where the optimum output can be produced for the highest total profit. At optimum scale the spread between total cost and total revenue will be such as to create relatively wide spatial margins to profitability, and the entrepreneur not seeking maximum profits is likely to have a wider range of locational choice than those operating at other scales. *Optimum scale creates an optimum location, and the production limits to viability are at the same time limits to locational choice.*

12.6 PERSONAL CONSIDERATIONS

It now remains to integrate certain personal factors into the variable-cost model of industrial location which has been built up. The fact that chance, historical accident, and personal noneconomic considerations have a bearing on the choice of factory sites in no way inhibits the theoretical analysis of industrial location, as has already been stressed in this book. A casual remark by Lösch (1954, 16) provides an initial clue to the way these matters can be reconciled with theory: "as long as such a capricious choice costs no more than the entrepreneural profit, it is still consistent with theory." Lösch (1954, 260) also recognized that an individual entrepreneur may choose a location other than the economic optimum because he is concerned with the greatest total utility rather than with money profits alone.

Melvin Greenhut has developed a more detailed argument along similar lines (see Chapter 8). He has suggested that the nonpecuniary satisfaction which an entrepreneur may derive from setting up in a particular location can be regarded as psychic income, and that each entrepreneur will choose the location at which his total satisfaction in terms of both financial and psychic income is maximized (Greenhut, 1956, 175–176). The logical extension of this argument is that the location theorist should regard the maximization of personal satisfaction as the entrepreneur's goal rather than the maximization of financial profit. But as Greenhut points out, this creates logical difficulties. To say, in effect, that man puts his factories where it pleases him is clearly an inadequate basis for a theoretical framework aimed at assisting both the interpretation of actual industrial location patterns and the solution of practical industrial development problems. Useful though the concept of the maximization of total utility or total satisfaction may be in the explanation of particular cases, it is with the economic forces influencing location and restricting freedom of choice that this book is primarily concerned.

The intention here is simply to integrate the operation of personal factors into the theoretical framework developed above. One way this can be done involves a combination of the notion of psychic income and Weber's concept of forces diverting factories from the least (transport) cost location. Figure 12.12 shows a map of isolines of average

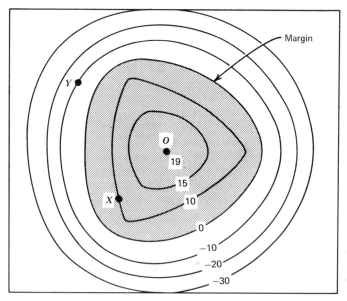

Figure 12.12. An interpretation of the effect of the personal factor in industrial location. (*Source.* Smith, 1966, 108, Figure 6.)

profit per unit of output derived from the original presentation of the variable-cost model in Figure 11.2. The maximum-profit (least-cost) location is in the center (O), the margin is where profit is nil, and the negative figures beyond the margin indicate a loss. Let X be a point within the margin which has certain personal attraction for one manufacturer, perhaps a golf course or an attractive house available. If the numbers on the isolines in Figure 12.12 are now taken to refer to some kind of units of satisfaction and not to money (for example, $5 profit gives 5 units of satisfaction), the situation can be analyzed in terms of psychic income. The manufacturer will site his factory at X if the psychic income obtainable there, measured in units of satisfaction, exceeds the loss of satisfaction (that is, 9 units) resulting from earning a profit of $10 on each of his products instead of the $19 possible at O. The plant is thus diverted from the maximum-profit location by personal factors offering higher total satisfaction. If the psychic income at X is 9, then, in Weberian parlance, X would be exactly on the critical isodapane, for the 10 isoline indicates a loss of 9 units of satisfaction by moving from the maximum profit location. In these circumstances the businessman would be indifferent as to whether he locates at O or X. If X (= 9) had been beyond the critical cost isoline, then the least-cost location would still have been preferred despite the noneconomic attraction of the alternative site.

An extension of this argument is that a manufacturer may operate outside the margin, at a loss, if he maximizes his satisfaction by so doing. A firm at Y in Figure 12.12 might be in this position, if his psychic income was, say, 35 units, or greater than the sum of the pecuniary satisfaction he is foregoing by not being at O (19 units) and the loss of satisfaction incurred by producing at a loss of $10 (10 units). It could be argued that a philanthropist running a factory to provide work in an isolated location is in this position, but this kind of situation can perhaps best be explained as subsidizing an extramarginal location. It is conceivable that an individual might derive satisfaction in certain other circumstances from operating a factory at a loss, but the interpretation of such eccentric behavior would hardly come within the sphere of the present discussion.

Pred (1967, 87–88) has taken issue with the original versions of the interpretation of the personal factor shown in Figure 12.12 (Smith, 1966, 107–109). His point is that the argument is dependent on the entrepreneur being able to identify the economic optimum, which requires perfect knowledge and is highly unlikely if not impossible in practice. This is of course true, just as it is true that without a high quality of knowledge he will not be able to judge accurately whether a suboptimal locational decision is within his own margins to profitability. But the argument does not necessarily depend on perfect knowledge. If the entrepreneur has an inaccurate perception of the best location from an economic point of view, he should still proceed as described above, weighing what he thinks he will gain personally from an alternative location against what he thinks he will lose financially by not being at what he believes to be the economic optimum, and making his decision on the basis of the results of this psychic arithmetic. If he is a skillful entrepreneur, with good perception of economic advantage, he will be in a better position to judge the psychic and pecuniary payoffs of alternative locations than will be his less skilled counterpart. In addition he will have wider spatial margins within which to indulge his personal whims, as was indicated earlier in Section 12.1. Much of this is implied in Pred's concept of the behavioral matrix, within which entrepreneurs may be differentiated in accordance with the information at their disposal and their ability to use it. The behavioral matrix and the concept of spatial margins to profitable business operation fit logically together, as Pred (1967, 90–95) has shown, and as was indicated in Chapter 7.

If entrepreneurial skill can increase the range of locational choice, then so should the scale of operations, for it has been shown that the spatial limits to profitability are likely to broaden as optimum scale is approached. Tiebout (1957) has made some interesting observations on the relationship between scale and the personal factor. He points out that there is empirical evidence to suggest that the personal element plays the biggest role in locational choice in the small firm and the new entry to an industry. He argues that the officers of the Ford Motor Company would not be expected to allow personal considerations to enter into the decision, which would be based in all probability on revenue and cost considerations. The clever small businessman, operating in a situation where he enjoys relatively large returns to capital invested, may be able to get away with a bad location. Although these observations may appear to conflict with some of the relationships between freedom of locational choice and the factors of scale and entrepreneurial skill suggested in this chapter, they are not inconsistent with the theory. The skillful, large-scale producer may not wish to exercise the freedom he has to choose between a relatively wide range of alternative locations, while the small firm run with indifferent skill may exercise the more restricted freedom it has to the limit. In any case, the economic objectivity of the decision-making process in the large corporation can easily be exaggerated, as Galbraith (1967) and others have argued, with the modern executive behaving less as a strict profit maximizer than the classic entrepreneur of the last century perpetuated in economic theory. With the control over consumer behavior exercised through advertising, and with the degree of control which such a corporation may have over the sources of its inputs, the choice of location within wide spatial limits seems very largely irrelevant to the long-run security of the corporation. And, as Galbraith argues, it is this security that the modern corporation may seek rather than the short-run maximization of financial profits.

There is obviously a close connection between the personal nature of the entrepreneur, or the decision-making group, and the locational decision. This involves not only the level of business skill that they possess but also the goals that motivate the individual or corporation and the presence or absence of such traits as a gambling instinct, a need for security or the wish to create some particular public image. These matters, which are receiving increasing attention in the study of industrial location, are very difficult to deal with theoretically. An inductive approach based on the search for empirical regularities in actual locational behavior may be a better way to attempt to understand the personal factor than further extension of the essentially deductive framework constructed here.

Nevertheless the concept of spatial margins to profitability, which is one of the central tenets of the theoretical framework offered here, greatly assists in the general interpretation of chance, personal considerations, and limitations of knowledge and skill as factors affecting locational choice. It provides an obvious means by which any kind of locational behavior which does not conform to profit maximization can be integrated into economic theory, even if the reasons behind this behavior are not fully understood. It may be stated as a general principle that within the margin freedom of choice exists, and the exact location of any plant may be determined by noneconomic considerations. Just how the exact locations are arrived at will remain a major challenge to both the theorist and the empiricist for a long time to come.

A further perceptive comment by Lösch (1954, 224) is offered as a fitting conclusion to this discussion:

The mathematical determination of the optimum transport point, for example, is infinitely more impressive as a solution of the location problem but also incomparably less accurate than the statement that an entrepreneur, all things considered, will establish his enterprise at a place that he likes best. We shall do well to recall from time to time the limited validity of our precise formulas, in order not to overlook the fact that they merely help us in arriving at a decision; in themselves they do not provide one.

13

Introducing the Demand Factor

In the previous two chapters a theory of industrial location has been built up based on the variable-cost approach. The models used to demonstrate the theory were very simple at first, but have become steadily more complicated as greater reality has been introduced. In the discussion of the substitution and scale problems a level of complexity was reached which made the earlier graphic approach difficult and in certain respects impossible to maintain, but it has nevertheless been shown that these factors can be accommodated within the theoretical framework that has been developed. Although it was not the intention to offer a fusion of location theory and production theory, the analysis has been able to indicate certain connecting threads between the two, in particular the inseparability of the decisions relating to input combination, scale, and location.

The next task is to see how far the variable-cost framework can be adapted to incorporate the demand factor. Some aspects of demand as it affects plant location have already been considered in Section 12.5 and in the more general discussion in Chapter 4. From the beginning of Part Three the location of the market and the cost of distributing the finished product to it has been included as a variable, just as it was in the original Weber theory, and the discussion of scale necessitated the introduction of the demand curve for the product and variations in average and total revenue. But this represents only slight progress toward the full integration of the demand factor, the difficulty of which was indicated in the discussion of the work of Hoover, Lösch, Greenhut, and others in Chapter 8.

What is now needed can best be explained with reference to Figure 10.1 at the beginning of Part Three. Three different situations are depicted, the first with cost as a spatial variable and demand (as reflected in price) as a spatial constant, the second with cost constant and demand variable, and the third with both cost and demand varying from place to place. The previous discussions have concentrated on the first of these situations, and the requirement now is to consider the implications of relaxing the assumption that the volume of demand and the revenue obtainable are spatial constants. Stated another way, it is required to add to the variable-cost model a demand or revenue surface which is not the horizontal plane assumed up to this point. The approach will be similar to that used in developing the earlier model: first the derivation of variations in demand and revenue will be considered in highly simplified circumstances, with most of the complications of the real world assumed away, and then greater complexity can be introduced when certain basic principles have been established.

But before proceeding, it is important to stress that this discussion is concerned with the demand a firm can expect to supply, and the revenue it can expect to earn, given a certain plant location. This is not the same as the identification of spatial variations in the level of demand, since the volume of consumption of a product can vary between different parts of the market without affecting the total revenue the firm could gain in alternative locations. Areal variations in the volume of demand will affect total revenue only if plant location affects the volume of sales and the price obtainable, for it is only in these circumstances that the demand factor has a bearing on locational choice.

13.1 FACTORS AFFECTING DEMAND AND REVENUE

If a specific location for a plant is being considered, what factors will affect the total revenue obtainable from production there compared with alternative locations? The first determinants are the volume of sales that can be achieved and the price that can be charged, because total revenue is by definition a function of these two variables. The sales that can be achieved in any area will depend on the nature of the market—on certain characteristics such as the number of possible consumers, their tastes, incomes and expenditure patterns, and hence their propensity to consume the product in question. Demand is also dependent on price, a relationship expressed in the form of the demand curve and its price elasticity. Price itself will be partially a response to the level of demand, but will also be influenced by other considerations such as the geographical pricing policy adopted, the competitive situation in which the firm finds itself, and the cost of production.

How these variables interact is the subject of extensive discussion in some of the writings reported in Chapter 8. Especially relevant is the work of Greenhut (1956, 1963), and of the locational-interdependence school in general. Although the methods of presentation to be used in this chapter differ in certain respects from those adopted in conventional locational analysis, the discussion leans heavily on the work of some of these earlier theorists.

The starting point is an extremely simple and highly unrealistic situation. Assume the following conditions: a firm proposes to set up in business to serve a spatially distributed market, and seeks the location at which total revenue will be maximized; customers are evenly spaced throughout the market and have identical tastes and expenditure patterns, or the same propensity to consume the product; demand for the product is at the extreme of inelasticity, which means that each consumer will purchase one unit at one point in time irrespective of price; no other firms exist to compete for the market. In these circumstances where the plant is situated is irrelevant as far as the entering firm is concerned, since the same total revenue can be earned from any location. Whatever price the firm charges and whatever the production costs, returns will be the same, for whatever location is chosen all demand will be satisfied. However, this is not to say that the total profit obtainable will be the same everywhere, unless it is assumed that the total cost of production is not a spatial variable. The situation outlined in this paragraph essentially represents the demand conditions assumed in the presentation of the variable-cost model, and the result is a revenue surface in the form of a horizontal plane.

But what happens if some of these assumptions are removed? Dropping the assumption that consumers are evenly distributed while retaining the others simply means that some of the territory may offer a larger volume of sales than other areas of comparable size. This might suggest that the firm would gain total revenue by locating in an area with a high level of demand, but this is not true while demand is insensitive to price and while there is no competition. Wherever production takes place the whole of the market will be served. The total *cost* of distributing the product to consumers will differ between locations, thus affecting total profit, but this is a component of the variable-cost model and will not affect sales while demand remains inelastic.

But infinitely inelastic demand, like the concept of perfect competition, is an assumption poorly suited to the analysis of spatial economics (Alonso, 1967, 33), as well as being patently unrealistic. If demand is allowed to vary as a function of price, then choice of location can have a direct effect on the volume of sales as long as demand does not go to the other extreme of infinite elasticity, where all production would be at the point of consumption. With some elasticity of demand, and c.i.f. pricing, the firm will be able to offer goods to all parts of the market at a uniform delivered price, but local sales will be influenced by whether this price is high or low compared with that of alternative suppliers, and this will depend on plant location. A plant located some distance away from the center of the market and with high distribution costs, or at a place where the cost of production is relatively high, will have to change a relatively high delivered price to cover expenditures, and this will have an adverse effect on sales. But in the theoretical analysis of the demand factor it is more usual to assume that the customer pays the factory price plus the cost of transportation to wherever he happens to be. With f.o.b. pricing, sales will tend to fall away with distance from the plant, until a point is reached at which the delivered price becomes so high that demand ceases. This reintroduces the concept of market areas, as outlined in the earlier discussion of the work of Palander, Hoover, and Lösch.

Some of the relationships between demand, market area, volume of sales, and revenue obtainable may now be stated in a more formal manner. The way in which the quantity of the product sold (q) at any market point is related to the delivered price is expressed by the *demand function*, which takes the form $f(p + t)$ where p is the price at the plant (that is, production cost plus profit markup) and t is the cost of transportation per unit of distance from the plant. The *market area* of a firm is the territory over which it is the sole supplier of the product by virtue of its delivered price, and is bounded by a locus of points where $f(p + t) = 0$, or where the delivered price for the firm in question exceeds that of a competitor. The *total volume of sales* (D) is the total output which the firm can sell in its market area within a given time period.

How the volume of sales is arrived at can be illustrated with the help of a simple diagram. Suppose that a firm sets up in business at a certain point to manufacture a product for which demand is price elastic. The demand curve is as shown in Figure 13.1, which indicates how the quantity decreases as delivered price ($p + t$) rises. The delivered price is a function of distance from the plant, and when the point F is reached demand ceases entirely as $p + t$ begins to exceed the maximum price the consumer is prepared to pay. The greatest possible shipping cost (t') is what it costs to send the product to the most distant consumers, at the edge of the market area, and its value is such that $f(p + t') = 0$. PQ indicated the sales that can be expected at the factory site, where no transport charges have to be added to the delivered price.

The sales to any point within the market area can be read from the

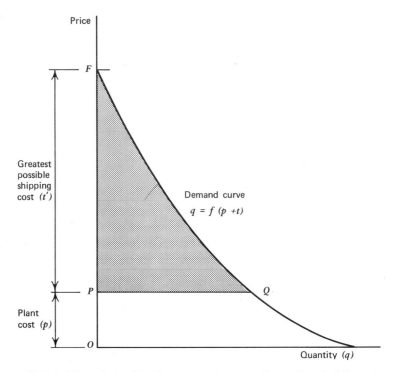

Figure 13.1. The relationship between volume of demand and delivered price. (*Source.* Based on Lösch, 1954, 106, Figure 20.)

demand curve, and expressed by $q = f(p + t_i)$ where t_i is the transport cost for serving point i. The total sales (D) can thus be written:

$$D = \sum_{i=1}^{n} f(p + t_i) \qquad (13.1)$$

where n is the number of separate market points. As Lösch (1954, 105–108) showed, this can be represented by the volume of the cone formed when FPQ in Figure 13.1 is revolved about the axis PQ. The height of this *demand cone* at the center is thus sales to customers adjoining the factory, and the radius of its base can be taken to be the radius (r) of the market area, as transport costs are proportional to distance and F is where $t_i = t'$. The relationship between the demand cone and the size and eventual shape of market areas was mentioned briefly in Chapter 8 (Figure 8.10). Following Lösch (1954, 106), but changing his notation slightly, the volume of the demand cone, and hence total sales (D) can be found from:

$$D = b \cdot 2\pi \int_0^r f(p+t) t \cdot dt \qquad (13.2)$$

where b is a constant representing the density of consumers per unit area. The demand function $q = f(p+t)$, which gives the height of the cone for any distance t from the center of the market area, is thus integrated out as far as the radius r shows that sales extend, the index of integration being given by dt. If a linear demand function is assumed the demand cone becomes straight-sided (see Nourse, 1968, 21, Figure 2–7), and the integral calculus is not required to evaluate its volume.

The total revenue obtainable in situations such as that depicted in Figure 13.1 is simply sales at every market point multiplied by the prevailing delivered price, or:

$$TR = \sum_{i=1}^{n} f(p+t_i)(p+t_i) \qquad (13.3)$$

This can also be represented by a conical figure, this time with the height at the center being the product of sales and price. The volume of the *revenue cone* would be given by:

$$TR = b \cdot 2\pi \int_0^r f(p+t)(p+t) t \cdot dt \qquad (13.4)$$

Whether the profile of such a cone is concave, as in the case of the Lösch demand cone (Lösch, 1954, 109, Figure 21), or whether it adopts more of a dome shape, depends on the nature of the demand function and the structure of transportation costs. A numerical demonstration of the derivation of total sales and total revenue according to the principles developed above will be found in Greenhut (1963, 154–155).

A useful review of Lösch's demand cone as an approach to the identification of the volume of demand is provided by Richardson (1969, 69–81). He points out that Lösch assumed away many of the conditions that cause demand to vary from place to place (for example, differences in population density, consumer demand schedules, and transportation rates), and suggests some modifications of the traditional approach. Richardson's general discussion of the demand factor, and its integration with the cost factor in industrial location theory, makes a valuable supplement to this chapter.

13.2 SPATIAL VARIATIONS IN DEMAND AND REVENUE

The analysis just completed was confined to the derivation of total sales and revenue for a single firm at a given location. But the volume of the demand cone and hence the total revenue obtainable can vary between possible locations, in accordance with variations in any of the cost and demand parameters involved. In the real world it is unlikely that population density, production costs, transportation rates, demand functions, and the like will remain fixed over anything other than a very small area, as Richardson (1969) has emphasized in his review of the Löschian approach.

If the density of population or consumers is higher in some parts of the market, sales will increase, for the value of b in expression (13.2) above will increase while the other values remain the same. Thus total revenue will be higher in some plant locations than in others. Conceptually this means that the flat horizontal revenue surface assumed in the development of the variable-cost model will be replaced by one that reflects in its undulating form the density of consumers per unit of area. In other words, the volume of the total demand cone will vary from place to place (Nourse, 1968, 22–24), and cities will be represented by peaks (Richardson, 1969, 72–73, 78–81).

The effect of areal changes in the other parameters may be less immediately obvious, but this can be illustrated very simply by some graphic models. The framework is again a linear market, as this facilitates graphic presentation yet produces conclusions that can be expected to apply with a two-dimensional market. There are three variable factors to be considered, as indicated in the previous section: (1) price at source (p), which can be expected to reflect factory costs; (2) shipping costs to the consumer (t); and (3) the maximum possible shipping cost (t'), reflecting the maximum delivered price which the consumer is prepared to pay. Individual consumer demand (q) as a spatial variable is covered by (1) and (2) as $q = f(p + t)$. In addition it is necessary to consider the effect of the location of competitors, so as to take into account the question of locational interdependence.

Assume a market extended along the line 0 to $0'$. Assume also that consumers are evenly scattered along the line and have identical personal demand schedules, that firms charge a price at the factory which is marked up by a fixed amount above the cost of production (that is, there is a uniform unit profit regardless of output), that the product is sold on an f.o.b. plant basis, and that freight rates per unit of distance are the same in all locations. Under these assumptions demand, and hence revenue and profit, will be a function of the size of the market area that a firm can control. These are the conditions generally assumed in the literature on locational interdependence, spatial competition, and market area analysis (for example, Greenhut, 1956, 26).

In the first case (Figure 13.2), production costs and hence the price charged at the factory vary from place to place. This represents the first step toward the fusion of the variable-cost model with the kind of situation in which demand and revenue are spatial variables. The assumption that there is a fixed unit production cost is necessary, for if AC is allowed to fall as increasing output brings economies of scale the problem under review becomes insoluble, since cost is dependent on the level of demand and sales which is itself a function of cost. There are three firms,

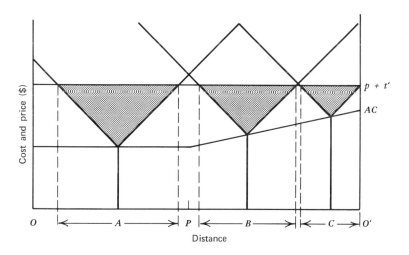

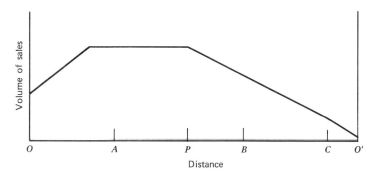

Figure 13.2. Demand in a situation with spatial variations in production costs.

A, B, and C, occupying separate locations along the linear market. Over the left-hand half of the area the unit cost of production (AC) is the same, but to the right of a point P costs rise because of the increasing cost of the assembly of inputs. The construction of delivered price gradients for the three firms, rising from the appropriate level for AC, indicates clearly that the size of the market and hence the total revenue falls as the unit costs increase. The edges of the respective market areas, indicated by the arrows along the distance axis, are where p ($=AC$) plus the maximum shipping cost (t') is intersected by the delivered price gradient.

For reasons that should be clear from the previous section, the total volume of demand at any location is proportional to the area in the diagram bounded by the delivered price gradients and the line of $p + t'$, that is, the shaded portions of the top part of Figure 13.2. In the bottom half of the illustration these volumes are plotted against the distance axis, and a *space demand profile* is interpolated. This shows the plateau of relatively high demand where AC is low, with demand falling off to the right. (The down slope of the demand profile toward the left-hand end of the market is explained by the fact that a firm locating too close to the end of the line will, in this simple illustration, have part of its market area to the left of 0, where demand ceases). Since total revenue will be proportional to the volume of sales, the profile can also be read as a space revenue curve, with the appropriate adjustment of units up the vertical axis of the graph. The optimum or revenue-maximizing location in this model is where the sales or revenue curve reaches its highest point that is, anywhere on the plateau.

The second case (Figure 13.3) illustrates the effect of variations in transport costs. Average cost is made uniform here, but the freight rate on the product per unit of distance increases in a regular manner from left to right. The effect of this on the size of the market area and on the volume of sales is shown clearly. The demand profile slopes steadily down to the right, to almost intersect the horizontal axis. Such an intersection would indicate that demand had ceased and that no revenue could be earned at a location beyond that point, which would be the spatial margin to profitability in this model. For the sake of simplicity, none of the diagrams in the present series have been drawn to include spatial margins, although their incorporation in the variable-demand model creates no technical or conceptual difficulty as will be shown in the next section.

The third case (Figure 13.4) is one in which the maximum price the consumer is prepared to pay for the product (t') is a spatial variable, increasing from left to right. The size of the market area thus increases from left to right, and the demand profile rises steadily to the right, to

INTRODUCING THE DEMAND FACTOR   245

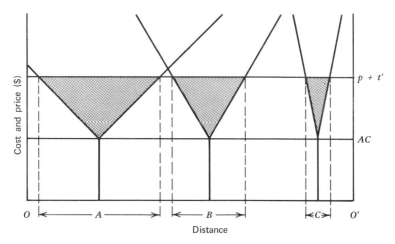

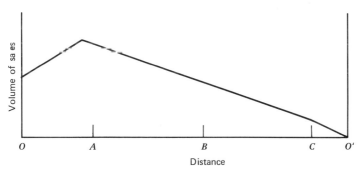

Figure 13.3. Demand in a situation with variations in transport costs to the market.

turn down again only when the market areas begin to extend to the right of O' where the imaginary linear market ends.

The final illustration in this series introduces the effect of competition on locational decisions. In Figure 13.5 the two firms A and B are located roughly at the quartile positions in the linear market OO', with uniform values for AC and t' irrespective of the location which might have been chosen. The heavy lines indicate the delivered price gradient of these firms, and their market areas are indicated by the sections of the line from a to a' and b to b'. As the diagram shows, there is a fairly substantial area of the market between the two existing firms, extending from a' to b', which is not served with the product in question because the delivered price from both A and B is too high. This potential market attracts a third firm into the industry, and the critical question for this new entry is where it should locate in order to maximize sales. Intuitively a location midway between the two existing firms would seem preferable, and this is in fact the revenue- and profit-maximizing location under the assumptions that have been made. The location of C shown in the diagram enables it to

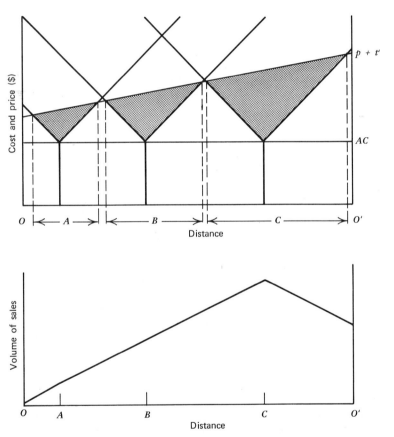

Figure 13.4. Demand in a situation where the maximum price the consumer is prepared to pay is a spatial variable.

control a market area from c to c', a small portion of which has been captured from A and B by virtue of C's lower delivered price. The volume of demand accessible from C (the shaded area in the diagram) is not much smaller than the sales achieved by A and B.

The profile of spatial variations in volume of sales in the bottom half of Figure 13.5 indicates the expectation for the new entry given the existing location of competitors. It shows the volume of sales falling as the location is moved from point C toward either competitor, for example to points a' or b', with the locations at which revenue for the newcomer is least coinciding with the locations of A and B. Firm C could not of course

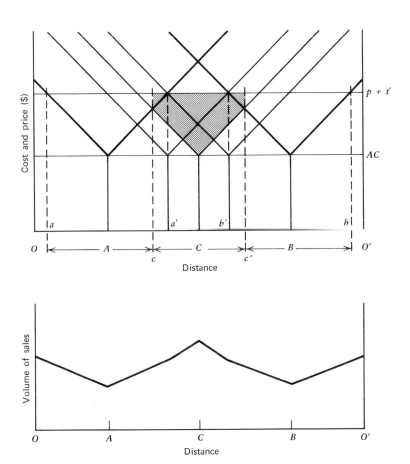

Figure 13.5. Demand in a competitive situation with locational interdependence between firms.

occupy physically the same spot as one of the others, but the two could operate "back to back" sharing the market now supplied by one (A or B) in a similar manner to Hotelling's ice cream sellers discussed in Chapter 8. Firm C could also have located at the far side of A or B, but the sales which could be achieved there are restricted by the termination of the market at 0 and $0'$. The success of C at the maximum sales location as revealed in the diagram is ultimately dependent on what kind of competitive reaction the existing firms might take in order to recapture some of the sales area lost to the newcomer, but this is beyond the scope of the present discussion.

13.3 A MORE COMPLEX SITUATION

Now that the major factors determining the revenue obtainable in alternative locations have been examined in a very simple situation, a little more reality may be introduced. The previous illustrations have demonstrated the derivation of space demand and revenue curves with respect to a linear market, and it is now necessary to demonstrate how a full total revenue surface may arise in a two-dimensional spatial situation. The method of analysis is as close as possible to that adopted in the development of the variable-cost model, so that a further step can be taken toward the fusion of these two approaches.

It would not be difficult to construct a situation in which all the factors influencing total revenue were spatially variable, but the graphic presentation would be very complicated. Instead, an imaginary case will be examined in which the cost of production varies between alternative locations, all other considerations being held constant except for the introduction of competition between firms at a later stage in the analysis. Simplified though it may be, this situation incorporates sufficient reality to bring together the concepts of cost surfaces, revenue surfaces, market areas, and the locational interdependence of firms. The major components of a variable-demand model are thus added to a situation of spatially variable costs.

Imagine an area within which there is a demand for a certain product, and in which potential consumers are evenly distributed and have identical tastes and preferences. The area measures seventy miles from east to west and sixty miles north to south, and can be regarded as part of continuous space (to avoid demand ceasing abruptly at the edge as in the diagrammatic representation of the linear market in the previous section). In this area the cost of assembling the necessary inputs varies from place to place, giving rise to variations in the average cost of production. At the least-cost location AC is \$7, and away from this point it rises in a regular fashion as indicated by the average cost surface in Figure 13.6. The addition of an average profit (AP) markup of \$3 per unit at any location enables the figure to be read as the prevailing surface of factory price ($p = AC + AP$) with the appropriate adjustment of the isoline values. The regularity of the cost surface thus identified is

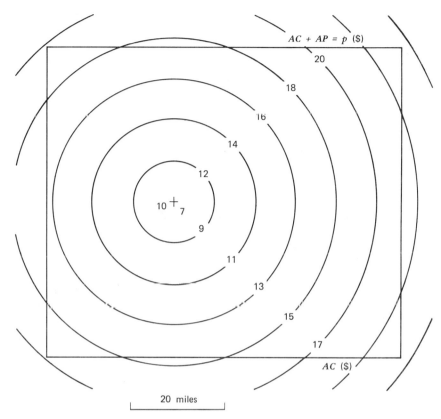

Figure 13.6. A surface of average cost and factory price in a variable-demand situation. The area under consideration is indicated by the border lines in this and subsequent diagrams.

highly unlikely to occur in the real world, having been adopted purely for the sake of ease of presentation. However, the cost surfaces derived from locational triangle situations during the presentation of the variable-cost model showed a distinct tendency towards this kind of regularity with increasing distance from the least-cost location, a fact also recognized by Weber (1929, 240–245).

The demand situation for the product is as follows: the density of consumers (b) is one per square mile, and they all have identical demand functions of $q = 20 - (p + t)$. The product is to be sold at an f.o.b. price, and the prevailing transportation rate is one dollar per unit per mile irrespective of distance, direction and quantity shipped. Holding b, q, and t constant throughout this analysis is purely a matter of convenience for the graphic presentation; the reader interested in greater reality is invited to rework the illustration relaxing any or all of these assumptions.

Given the demand function, the total sales a firm could expect anywhere within the area under review can be found by calculating the volume of the demand cone, and from these values a demand surface could be constructed. But the intention here is to proceed directly to the derivation of the total revenue surface. How the total revenue obtainable in any given location can be arrived at may be illustrated with respect to the point of minimum average cost, as identified in Figure 13.6. Using the demand function, a curve can be constructed to show the revenue (R) from any consumer (i) at any position between the plant location and the edge of the market area simply by evaluating $R_i = q_i(p + t_i)$. This is shown in Figure 13.7. The revolution of the area below the curve about the plant location produces a *total revenue dome*, in just the same

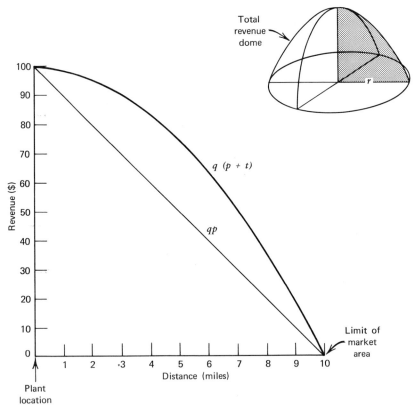

Figure 13.7. The relationship between demand and distance from the plant.

way as Lösch obtained his demand cone. Total revenue is equivalent to the volume of the dome. The method for calculating the volume of total revenue was given above in expression (13.4), but because of the assumptions adopted in this illustration it is possible to obtain a close approximation to the volume of the dome without the integral calculus.

The total revenue that can be earned by a plant at the least-cost location works out to just over $13,000. When TR has been evaluated for a selection of alternative locations the total revenue surface can be constructed, taking the form indicated in Figure 13.8a. As production cost is the only spatial variable affecting revenue, the revenue surface adopts a similar concentric circle pattern to that of the cost surface, but with the important difference that total revenue falls steeply away from the least-cost location at first and then evens out with increasing distance. This is shown in the space revenue curve drawn through the surface along PQ (Figure 13.8b). The reason for this form is that operating from a relatively high-cost location reduces the radius of the market area, which results in the loss of the most distant customers from whom the highest delivered price is exacted, as well as a reduction in demand from nearer customers. A rise in production cost is equivalent to taking a layer off the bottom of the revenue dome illustrated in Figure 13.7, so given the assumption of evenly distributed customers a rise in cost will take away a disproportionately large share of total revenue.

A firm setting up in business in the area under review, and in the conditions assumed, can maximize total revenue at the point at which average unit costs are lowest. But over most of the area some revenue is obtainable, even if it is generally much less than at the optimum location. Where $TR = 0$ the cost of production is so high that even at the lowest possible price there will be no demand, so a locus of such points becomes the spatial margin in this kind of situation (Figure 13.8a).

Thus far in this illustration consideration of cost has been confined to the average cost of production, and its effect on the volume of demand and revenue. But now that the sales which can be attained at any plant location are known, it is possible to identify the surface of total cost and couple it with the total revenue surface. The total cost surface is shown in Figure 13.9a; it adopts the same kind of geometrical form as the revenue surface, with a gradient concave upwards, because the volume of total demand falls more rapidly with distance from the least-cost location than does the average cost of production. In the bottom part of Figure 13.9 the space cost curve is shown with the space revenue curve from Figure 13.8. The vertical distance between the two curves at any point is the total profit (TP) which may be earned at such a location, which is at a maximum at the least-average-cost location where just over $3000

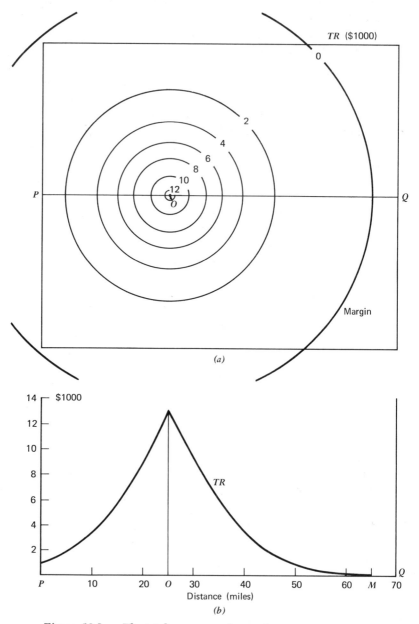

Figure 13.8. The total revenue surface and space revenue curve.

INTRODUCING THE DEMAND FACTOR 253

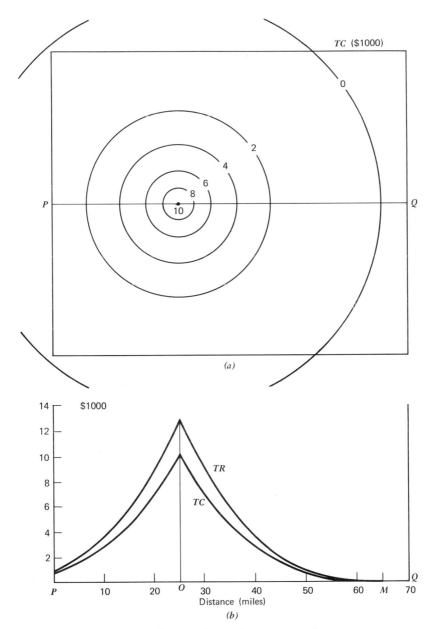

Figure 13.9. The total cost surface and space cost and revenue curves.

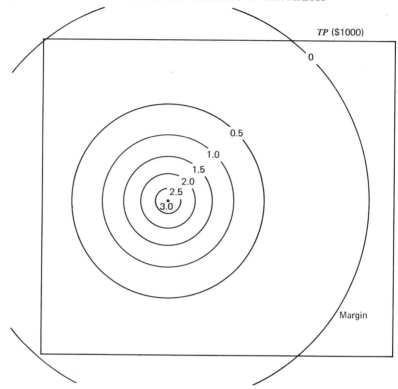

Figure 13.10. The total profit surface.

profit can be made. The two curves converge on the point where $TC = TR = 0 = TP$, which is the spatial margin to profitability. The total profit surface is illustrated in Figure 13.10. The incoming entrepreneur clearly has the freedom to locate almost anywhere within the area under review and make some kind of profit, but he must be at or near the least-average-cost location if he is to avoid a level of profit substantially less than the maximum which can be earned.

Now that the prevailing cost, revenue, and profit situation has been identified, attention may be directed toward the manner in which locational choice is made. Suppose that the first firm to enter the area (firm F_1) is possessed with perfect knowledge or extreme good fortune and choses to locate at the point of maximum profits (the least-average-cost or revenue-maximizing location). He is able to extend his market area out to a radius of ten miles, and sells 1047 units for a total profit of $3141. But as soon as there is one firm operating in the area the original revenue and profit surfaces have to be modified, since the existence of this competitor will clearly influence how much a newcomer can sell from certain locations. At any location where the market area intersects with that of the established firm, sales and hence total revenue will be less than if the first firm did not exist.

Suppose that the strategy adopted by all new entries is to avoid the competition for part of the first firm's market implicit in a market area overlap. Four firms (F_2, F_3, F_4, and F_5) enter the area, and choose locations as close as possible to F_1 without entering into competition (Figure 13.11). They locate where the unit cost of production is $14, compared with $10 where the first firm located, and consequently have smaller market areas and much smaller sales than F_1. A further fifteen firms (F_6, F_7, ..., F_{20}) set up in business, all carefully avoiding any market area overlaps. As the locations that can command relatively high sales are occupied, later entrants are forced out to the less profitable locations near the spatial margin. Figure 13.11a illustrates the kind of pattern of locations and market areas that might arise in these circumstances, with the exact location of plants and the failure of some of the later entrants to occupy the innermost remaining locations reflecting imperfect knowledge or the random element in site selection. In Table 13.1, cost, revenue, and

Table 13.1   Cost and Revenue Data for Selected Firms, as Identified in Figure 13.10a

Firm	p (Dollars)	t' (Dollars)	D (Units)	TR (Dollars)	TC (Dollars)	TP (Dollars)	r (Miles)
F_1	10	10	1,047	13,076	9,935	3,141	10
F_2	14	6	226	3,503	2,559	618	6
F_{10}	16	4	67	1,139	881	191	4
F_{16}	18	2	8	128	96	24	2
F_{21}	12	8	535	7,491	5,351	1,605	8

profit data are listed for four of the first twenty firms (F_1, F_2, F_{10} and F_{16}) to indicate how the economic attraction of a location is reduced rapidly with increasing distance from the optimum location.

As long as customers remain to be served, new firms will be attracted into the industry. But a point will eventually come at which a new entrant will be dissatisfied with a small market area toward the periphery of the profitable area, and will attempt to compete with an existing firm. Suppose that the twenty-first entrant (F_{21}) is attracted by vacant market territory to the north and northwest of the area served by F_1, but finds that it is impossible to locate anywhere here without overlapping with the market area of at least one existing firm (Figure 13.11a). Possessed with more entrepreneurial skill than the previous nineteen entrants, or with a more enterprising and aggressive management, firm F_{21} decides to locate only eight miles from the original optimum location at a point from which a substantial proportion of the vacant territory can be served by virtue of a relatively low production cost ($12). However,

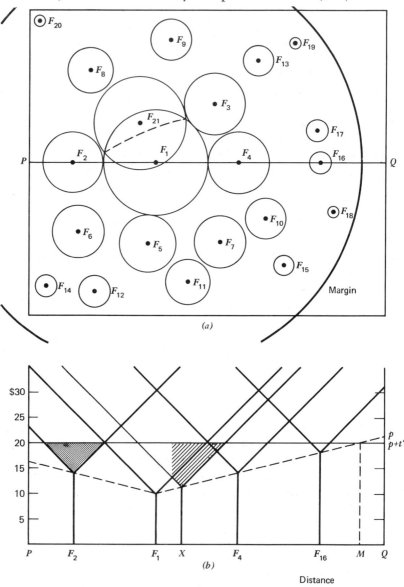

Figure 13.11. Market areas in a variable-cost and variable-demand situation, illustrating some aspects of spatial competition.

this location results in a large overlap with F_1's market area. In most of the area that both firms could serve, the delivered price from F_1 is lower than from F_{21}, but the newcomer is able to capture a little of the market area of the first entrant (as is indicated by the dashed line in Figure 13.11a showing where the two market areas would divide). The demand and revenue that the newcomer could claim if it could serve the whole of its circular market area is indicated in the last line of Table 13.1. The loss of less than half of its market area to F_1 still leaves a total revenue of about $4000, which is more than could be obtained by taking a location further away from F_1, such as that occupied by F_2. In fact, the closer the new firm moves toward the location of F_1 the more revenue it will get, because in this illustration the increase in sales as average cost falls is greater than the additional sales lost to the competitor as F_{21} moves toward F_1.

As a further illustration of this fact, the choices facing the second entry into the area may be considered with the help of a section through the diagram in the upper part of Figure 13.11. This shows the gradients of delivered price from four alternative locations, which coincide with those subsequently chosen by firms F_1, F_2, F_4, and F_{16} and also indicates the way in which price at the factory (p) rises with AC from the least-cost location occupied by the first firm. Firms F_2 and F_4 occupy two of the closest locations to the original optimum without overlap of market areas, but if a location closer to that of F_1 is chosen, for example point X in Figure 13.11, more revenue could have been earned. The revenue will be proportional to the area above the delivered price gradients in Figure 13.11b, and a comparison between this area at the location of F_2 (stippled) and at X (shaded) confirms the superiority of the location closer to F_1. This is the situation which arose in the previous section in the analysis centered on Figure 13.5.

The implication of all this with respect to the decision of the second entrant is now clear. Instead of avoiding market-area competition with the existing firm, as F_2 did in the original development described above, the second firm could have maximized its total revenue by locating as close as possible to F_1. In such a situation the second firm would have taken half the market area of the first firm and hence half the revenue, which amounts to just over $7500. This is more than twice as much as F_2 could earn in its original noncompeting location.

Knowing the advantages of competing with existing firms in relatively low-cost locations, subsequent entries would now adopt an entirely different locational strategy than that which produced the dispersed pattern with no market-area overlaps illustrated in Figure 13.11a. Each new firm would tend to locate near the least-cost location, competing with the existing firms for high-revenue market in that area, until the revenue available to the next entrant was no better than could be obtained by moving away from the emerging agglomeration. As all the market space is eventually occupied, and excessive profits competed away, the pattern becomes one of a number of firms close together round the original optimum location and having small market territories of relatively high sales per unit area, with firms getting steadily further apart and having larger market areas with increasing distance from the least-cost location.

This conclusion is consistent with certain elements of the modification of the Löschian economic landscape proposed by Isard (1956). It will be recalled that Lösch (1954) argued that as new firms enter an industry a regular pattern of market areas occupying all space eventually emerges, with the competitive process leading to the elimination of supernormal profits as the system approached its final state of equilibrium. Isard (1956, 272) proposed that spatial variations in population (that is, consumer) density would result in firms closer together in the areas of dense population, and with small market areas, while production would be more dispersed as population density was reduced away from the metropolitan area. The density of consumers is but one of a number of variables affecting revenue in alternative locations; another is production cost, and the analysis above has shown that spatial cost variations may be expected to have a similar affect on industrial location patterns as Isard argued would result from variations in population density.

The precise form any particular industrial location pattern adopts will depend on the degree of spatial variation displayed by whatever the critical causal factors happen to be. In the imaginary case under consideration here the determinant is the cost of production as it influences the volume of demand and hence total revenue, and it should be clear from what has already been said that the tendency to agglomerate around the least-cost location will be greatest in situations where the spatial cost variations are relatively large. In the case analyzed in Figure 13.11 the advantage that the second entrant derives from getting close to the least-cost location and competing with the existing firm arises from the extent of the loss of revenue in a high-cost location further out. But if the spatial cost variations had been less marked it might have been to the advantage of the second firm to keep away from the first, as would have been the case if the unit cost of production in some peripheral area had been low enough to enable a firm to gain more than half the revenue at the original optimum location (that is, more than could be obtained by moving in toward the location of the existing firm and competing with it). This tends to support one of the generalizations put forward in the statement of basic principles in Chapter 10, namely that the greater the spatial variations in cost and/or revenue, the greater the tendency for industrial agglomeration.

13.4 REVENUE, COST, AND THE PROFIT SURFACE

By the use of some simple graphic models, it has been possible to demonstrate the operation of various considerations affecting the total revenue a firm can expect to earn in alternative locations. The introduction of spatial variations in the cost of production into these models has permitted some kind of integration of the variable-cost approach with one that stresses demand and the locational interdependence of firms. Conceptually, a spatially variable total revenue surface has been added to the cost surface derived in the earlier model, to produce a third surface representing total profits. Throughout this analysis the important concept of the spatial margin to profitability has been retained, as a device that facilitates the incorporation of suboptimal behavior within the theoretical framework.

The concept of the cost surface, with respect to single inputs or total production outlays, has received much attention in the literature on industrial location theory, as was indicated in earlier chapters. But the idea that similar surfaces could be identified with respect to revenue has been given far less consideration. The main reason is probably that spatial variations in revenue are thought of as a more intangible phenomenon, subject as they are to the complex operation of the demand factor in location and on competition between firms. Certainly the empirical identification of total revenue surfaces, and the discovery of regularities capable of mathematical formulation, seems far less likely than is the case with cost surfaces. The same problems arise with respect to the profit surface, which is an even more nebulous concept than that of the revenue surface.

Nevertheless, the notion of revenue and profit surfaces is of considerable conceptual value in industrial location theory. An early demonstration that such devices may be usefully incorporated into the classical least-cost analysis derived from Weber appeared in a paper by Tiebout (1957). Tiebout takes a four-sided locational figure with corners represented by the sources of two materials and two markets, and shows profits measured up the vertical axis of a three-dimensional diagram (Tiebout, 1957, 77). A dome-shaped profit surface is illustrated, with its apex above what would be the least-cost site within the locational figure. As revenue is a spatial constant in the Weber model, this profit dome is simply a reflection of the fall in transport costs as a firm moves toward the center of the locational figure. Tiebout goes on to consider a case in which the dome could be viewed as a revenue surface, above a horizontal floor representing spatially-uniform production costs excluding transportation. In reality, he argues, the dome will be crinkled rather than perfectly regular in form as in his illustration, and the floor representing production costs will be bumpy to conform to spatial cost variations. The vertical distance between these two irregular surfaces is total profits, which, Tiebout claims, is unlikely to vary between alternative locations in an orderly manner. The concept of spatial margins to profitability can be introduced simply by allowing the total cost and total revenue surfaces to intersect.

Tiebout's model is, of course, somewhat different from those used in this chapter. Here the revenue obtainable in alternative locations is partially a function of spatial variations in the cost of production, with demand and revenue high where the unit cost is low, and with demand and revenue ceasing where costs become so high that customers could not be supplied at an acceptable delivered price. In Tiebout's illustration the surface of total revenue varies independently of the spatial variations in production cost. In these circumstances there may be some demand, and some revenue to be earned, in extramarginal locations, but insufficient for firms to cover the costs of producing such an output.

Whatever situation is postulated, the recognition of a specific revenue surface and profit surface as applying to a given industry is dependent on a number of important simplifying assumptions. In Chapter 12 it was shown that it is unrealistic to think of just one cost surface, as the spatial cost situation will vary between firms in relation to differences in entrepreneurial skill. The same is true of the revenue surface. A skilled businessman, using vigorous marketing methods, may be able to raise his total revenue surface above that of his less able competitors. And, like the skilled entrepreneur of the variable-cost model, he may be able to generate enough demand for his product to develop a profitable business in a location which would be beyond the margin for other producers.

The form of the revenue surface is also a function of scale, which raises some important considerations which have so far been disregarded in this chapter. Wherever the cost of production was introduced into the variable-demand model, it was assumed that there was a uniform average cost irrespective of output, ie a horizontal "curve" representing both average cost and marginal cost. But in production theory such curves are typically U-shaped, conforming to the tendency for unit costs to fall with rising output until economies of scale turn into diseconomies. The implications of this to the variable-cost model have already been considered, and it was concluded that there can be a different cost surface, with different optimum locations and different spatial margins, for each level of output. A similar situation arises with respect to the revenue surface in the variable-demand model. As a firm increases its output and its average unit costs fall it will be able to reduce its delivered price to consumers, and this can further increase the volume of demand and hence the scale of operations. Thus the firm operating at the least-cost location in the illustration of the previous section, and enjoying a high level of demand, would probably be able to produce at a lower unit cost than firms with smaller markets, quite irrespective of the spatial variations in production costs. This would enable the firm to take a greater profit markup while retaining the same number of customers, or alternatively lower the factory price, bring down the delivered price gradients, and raise profits by extending the market area and volume of sales.

Just as was demonstrated in the variable-cost model, there will be an optimum scale in a variable-demand locational situation. This will be at the output where total revenue exceeds total cost by the greatest possible amount, or, in terms of conventional production theory, where the marginal cost curve intersects the marginal revenue curve from below. To increase production beyond this level may increase total revenue, but as total cost will rise by a greater amount the total profits earned will fall. In the variable-demand approach to industrial location theory the firm will increase output and extend its market area up to that point where no further additions to total profits can be made. How large this profit will be can vary in space, with variations in the total cost of producing the optimum output and variations in the revenue obtainable from selling it. Thus the critical surfaces are those that identify in any location the cost, revenue, and profit relating to the optimum scale at that point, which further emphasizes the inseparability of location theory and production theory. At present the question of whether such surfaces could be identified empirically is less important than whether they are of theoretical value. But ultimately such concepts must be applied empirically if they are to become something more than textbook abstractions.

14

Introducing the Time Dimension

Up to now the analysis has been confined to a static temporal situation. The possibility of changes in the spatial patterns of cost, revenue, and profit has not been considered, except briefly in the context of the locational interdependence illustrations in Chapter 13. And it has been assumed implicitly that the time period under review has not been long enough for changes in technology or the emergence of alternative sources of inputs to take place. In other words, the analysis has been restricted to the short run, and it is now necessary to introduce the time dimension in order to incorporate some long-run conditions into the theoretical framework which has been built up. First, changes in price, costs, the combination of inputs, and the demand situation will be analyzed briefly. Then an approach to the understanding of the evolution of industrial location patterns will be suggested, bringing together in a more dynamic context certain of the principles that have emerged from earlier chapters.

14.1 CHANGES IN THE SPATIAL COST/REVENUE SITUATION*

In any industry, the optimum location and the spatial margins will be constantly changing their position, in response to changes in the spatial cost/revenue situation. This makes the best location for the profit-maximizing entrepreneur even more elusive than in a static temporal situation: as Lösch (1954, 16) put it: "Dynamically there is no best location,

---

* The discussion here follows closely a previously published version (Smith, 1966), and the illustrations are reproduced, together with a number in Chapters 11 and 12, by permission of *Economic Geography*.

because we cannot know the future." In practice a manufacturer is unlikely to go to great lengths to find the short-run optimum location, because he knows that there is no guarantee that it will remain in the same vicinity for long. He is far more likely to look for a location that he can be reasonably sure will remain within the spatial margins to profitability in the long run, relying on his entrepreneurial ability to achieve something approaching optimum scale and efficiency in order to build up profits. This further emphasizes the value of the concept of the spatial margin as a restriction on the firm's freedom of locational choice, as the search for the optimum becomes of even less practical and theoretical significance than in the previous static analysis. But it must be remembered that the spatial margin is just as liable to change as the optimum location. The circumstances in which a change in one or other or both may be expected can be examined very simply by the use of the same kind of graphic model that already has been employed extensively in Part Three.

The effect of a change in the price obtainable for a product is illustrated in Figure 14.1. Here the original space cost curve derived from the initial version of the variable-cost model (Figure 11.2) is shown, together with the price line (P) at $170. If the price is raised by $10, the new price line ($P'$) changes the position of the spatial margin, and the area in which a profit can be made is extended to M_a' and M_b'. A reduction in price would have the opposite effect, narrowing the area in which the industry can be undertaken successfully. But as long as the change

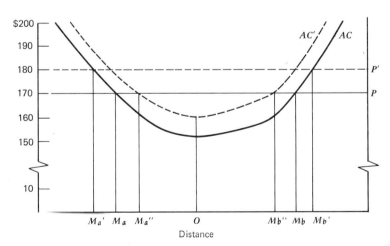

Figure 14.1. The effect of a uniform change in price or unit cost on the spatial margins to profitability. (*Source.* Smith, 1966, 110, Figures 7 and 8.)

in price is uniform in space, the position of the optimum location will remain unchanged under the assumptions on which this model rests.

A uniform change in production cost has exactly the same effect as a change in price (Figure 14.1). If, for example, $10 is added to the cost of each unit of production irrespective of location, the new cost gradient (AC') produces a contraction of the area in which a profit can be made, to M_a'' M_b''. A reduction in cost results in a widening of the margin. As in the case of a uniform change in price, the optimum location remains the same. The effect of changes in costs which are not uniform in space and of changes in the cost of individual inputs can best be examined in the context of changes in technique and in input combination, for this

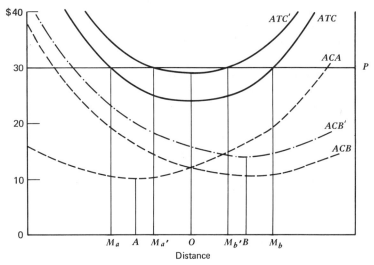

Figure 14.2. The effect of a change in the basic cost of a single input. (*Source.* Smith, 1966, 110, Figure 9.)

enables the reason for the changes in cost to be introduced into the analysis.

Changes through time in the cost of individual inputs, in production techniques, and in the combination of inputs influence industrial location through their effect on cost structure and on the spatial cost/revenue situation. This could be illustrated with further adaptations of the model which has been used already, but it is more convenient to use a slightly different framework. Assume that an industry exists using two inputs, the basic cost of each being $10 per unit of output. Let the source or least-cost point of these inputs be A and B respectively (Figure 14.2). The cost of the inputs rises away from A and B, the space cost curve having identical shallow U shapes. This assumption of a U-shaped space cost curve has been adopted simply as a device for insuring that optimum location lies initially between the sources of the two inputs so that their relative pull under different circumstances can be considered. A curve for total cost per unit (*ATC*) can be derived from the two input-cost curves (*ACA* and *ACB*), and when a price line at $30 is introduced the limits of the area of profitability can be indicated by M_a and M_b. Optimum or least-cost location is at *O*.

The first case to be examined is a change in cost structure resulting from a uniform increase in the basic cost of one input. Assume that the cost of input *B* at source is increased by 50 percent, resulting in an

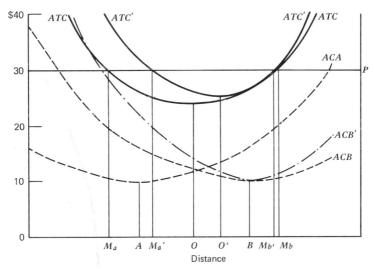

Figure 14.3. The effect of a change in the locational cost of a single input. (*Source.* Smith, 1966, 111, Figure 10.)

increase of $5 in the cost of each unit of output. The new cost curve for input *B* is *ACB'*, and the curve for average total cost curve becomes *ATC'*. The spatial margin contracts to M_aM_b', but the position of the optimum location remains where it is. The effect is thus the same as in the cases of the uniform change in price or cost considered above.

The effect of a change in the locational cost of one input is illustrated in Figure 14.3. Assume that the cost of moving input *B* from its source doubles as a result of a change in freight rates. The new cost gradient *ACB'* is drawn, and from it a new average total cost gradient *ATC'*. The result of this is not only a contraction of the margin (from $M_a M_b$ to $M_a' M_b'$) but also a shift in optimum location from *O* to *O'*. The least-cost point has moved toward the source of input B, in response to its increase in locational cost.

The two cases examined in Figures 14.2 and 14.3 reveal an important distinction between the effect on location of changes in basic costs and locational costs, which can be stated as a general principle. *A change in the basic cost of any input will, other things (including price) remaining the same, lead to a change in the spatial margin to profitability, but will leave optimum location unaltered, whereas a change in an input's locational cost is likely to affect the position of both the margins and the optimum location.* In other words, a change in locational cost alters the pull of one corner of the locational figure, while a change in basic cost does not unless it leads to the substitution and the alteration of the input combination.

In many instances in the real world a simultaneous change in both basic and locational cost takes place. In Figure 14.4 the quantity of input B required in the production process is halved, perhaps by an improvement in technique. As a result, basic and locational cost are both halved, giving a new cost curve (ACB') below the old one. ATC' becomes the new average total cost curve, which indicates a widening of the margin, and there is a shift in the optimum location toward the source of input A the locational pull of which has been strengthened.

A final example illustrates the result of the replacement of an input

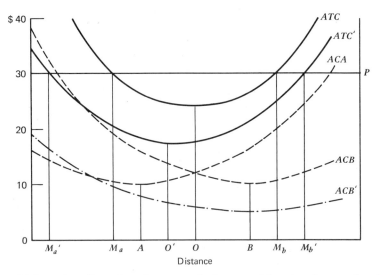

Figure 14.4. The effect of a change in the basic and locational cost of a single input. (*Source.* Smith, 1966, 111, Figure 11.)

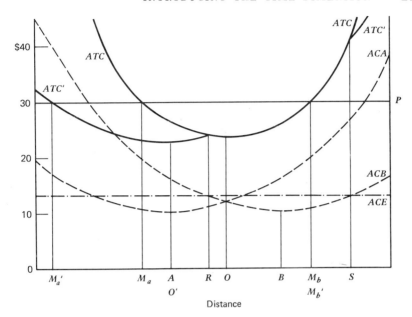

Figure 14.5. The effect of the replacement of an input with spatially variable costs by one which is ubiquitous. (*Source.* Smith, 1966, 111, Figure 12.)

with considerable locational cost by one which is ubiquitous. This may arise from technical innovation, such as the introduction of electricity as an alternative to steam power based on coal. In Figure 14.5 let input B be coal, the cost of which increases away from its source. The use of electricity is introduced, the cost involved being $13 per unit of output irrespective of location, which makes the cost gradient for electricity a horizontal line (ACE). The figure of $13 has been chosen to introduce a complication, namely that the cost of coal at source ($10) is cheaper than electricity, and that between the points R and S (perhaps representing the coalfield) it is in fact cheaper to continue to use coal than to change to electricity. The new space cost curve for power, from whatever source is cheapest, therefore follows electricity's horizontal line as far as R but then dips down to follow the coal curve to S. This is also reflected in the new total cost curve (ATC') which corresponds to the original curve (ATC) between R and S. The general effect of the introduction of electricity is, however, to reduce costs over a large area, resulting in a widening of the spatial margin. But the margin is extended in only one direction; on the coalfield the original cost situation still obtains, and the margin remains unaltered. The introduction of electricity results in a shift of the optimum location to the source of input A in this simple situation, for over most of the area under review it is now the only input with locational cost attached to it.

The situations considered thus far in this section have all related to the variable-cost model, but changes in demand and revenue, and in the variables affecting them, can be illustrated just as easily. To avoid further diagrams, some of those used in Chapter 13 may be referred to for this purpose. Figures 13.2 to 13.5 demonstrated the effect on demand and total revenue of four major variables—the cost of production, the cost of transporting the finished product, the upper limit to the price the consumer is prepared to pay, and some aspects of the locational interdependence of firms. The density of consumers per unit of area was also mentioned as a relevant consideration. A change through time in any of these variables will have an effect on the spatial demand and revenue situation, which may lead to a change in optimum location and in the position of the spatial margins.

The effect of a change in producton cost on the revenue situation is obvious, and has already been suggested by the analysis of a change in cost in Figure 14.1. If the AC gradient in Figure 13.2 is raised in any location it will reduce the size of the market area, the volume of demand, and the total revenue which can be earned. An irregular increase in cost may change both the optimum location and the margins, whereas a change which is uniform in space will leave the optimum where it is, while bringing in the margins if costs rise and relaxing them if costs fall.

A change in freight rates resulting in a change in the cost of distribution may be illustrated with reference to Figure 13.3. If rates from one location only change, this location will be made more or less attractive in terms of its revenue-earning capacity, depending on whether the rate per unit of distance is raised or lowered. This could have the effect of shifting a location from one side of the margin to the other, and it could change the maximum-revenue location. A uniform overall increase or decrease in transport cost should lead to a widening or contraction of the margins, while the optimum location remains unchanged, just as in the case of a spatially uniform increase in production costs.

If the maximum the consumer is prepared to pay for the product ($p + t'$ in Figure 13.4) is increased for some reason demand and total revenue will rise, while a fall in price has the opposite effect. Again a change that is uniform in space should affect the margins only, while a change which differentiates geographically might also alter the position of the optimum. A change in the geographical distribution of consumers and in their density will have obvious effects on areal variations in demand and revenue, with the same principle applying to changes in the optimum and margins as apply to other variables.

The main conclusion from this discussion is intuitively rather obvious, but it is important enough to add to the general locational principles which have emerged. *Changes in the variables affecting cost and revenue will bring about changes in the prevailing spatial cost/revenue situation, and thus changes in the comparative economic advantage of alternative locations. Changes which are uniform spatially can be expected to alter the position of the spatial margins to profitability while the optimum location remains the same, assuming that the initial change does not bring about a geographically selective change in another variable which can affect cost and revenue patterns. A change which is not uniform in space is likely to lead to a change in position of both the optimum and the spatial margins.*

14.2 THE EVOLUTION OF INDUSTRIAL LOCATION PATTERNS

The attention of Part Three has been focused largely on the locational decision of the individual firm, and on the economic circumstances which influence this and restrict freedom of choice. This was the stated intension at the outset, the justification being that it is through the analysis of the action of individual participants that understanding of complete location patterns can best be achieved. As in most other kinds of economic theory, it is the analysis of the single firm which permits the initial penetration of the complexity of the whole system.

Nevertheless, something has been implied during the course of this discussion about the form that industrial location patterns might adopt in certain circumstances. The degree of dispersal of production units has been related to the nature of the spatial cost/revenue situation and how steep the gradients on the cost or revenue surfaces are. The relationship between industrial dispersal and the nature of the market, including the price-elasticity of demand for the product, has also been referred to briefly. And the tendency for firms to group around favorable locations has been suggested a number of times, with economies of agglomeration not necessarily the only relevant causal factor.

It is now necessary to be a little more specific about the process by which complete industrial location patterns are formed, and how they change through time. Certain concepts used throughout this chapter provide a sensible framework for such a discussion, with the spatial margins to profitability providing a means of avoiding the deterministic theory implicit in the assumption of profit maximization. However, what is offered here must be regarded merely as a tentative suggestion of the kind of dynamic models that might be developed. It is too early to attempt a more formal presentation.

The central theme running through Part Three has been that spatial restrictions on locational choice exist if viability is to be achieved, but that within certain limits the firm has freedom of choice. Some profit can be earned anywhere within the spatial margins; the entrepreneur seeking to make as much money as possible will tend to locate himself as near to the optimum location as his knowledge and skill permits, while those who attach more importance to nonpecuniary matters can locate nearer the margins at the expense of some of their profits. Most firms may choose a reasonably good location from an economic point of view, though few may approach close to the optimum, but there is always some possibility of a relatively poor yet successful location being selected by personal whim or limited entrepreneur ability.

The development of industrial location patterns may thus be regarded as a random or *stochastic* process, played out within a certain spatial probability framework. A stochastic process is one that develops in time according to probabilistic rules, which means that its future behavior cannot be predicted with certainty. There are a number of stochastic models which might possibly be used to replicate the development of industrial location patterns for analytical purposes. One is the Monte Carlo model, which has been applied to other geographical problems including the diffusion of innovation and the evolution of settlement patterns. The Monte Carlo model is a device for simulating the development of spatial patterns, according to specified rules. A certain probability of an event taking place at a given point is established, on a priori grounds or on the basis of empirical observation, and the precise form or pattern adopted by the phenomena under investigation is then simulated by some random process operating within the probability framework which has been set up. A comparison between the simulated pattern and the observed pattern provides a basis for the evaluation of the reasoning which went into the construction of the model, and its adequacy as a possible explanation of the real-world pattern. A more complete summary of the main principles of Monte Carlo simulation procedures may be found elsewhere; for example, in Haggett (1965, 96–8, 305–309), Yeates (1968, 53–63), and Hägerstrand (1967).

One serious difficulty in applying something like the Monte Carlo model to the simulation of industrial location patterns is finding a suitable basis for establishing the spatial probability framework. Another is that in reality the occupation of any location by an industrial plant may alter the probability that other locations will be occupied; nearby locations may increase their attraction due to economies of agglomeration, or they may become less attractive if the new plant is a competitor for some local inputs or market. This condition might be accommodated in a

Markov Chain type of model, which allows for the probability of development at a particular time and place to be related to what has gone before. However, the application of stochastic models to geographical processes is still in its infancy, and it is too early to say how far this can assist in the understanding of industrial location patterns.

Any dynamic model of industrial location must be able to take into account changes in the prevailing cost/revenue situation. In the absence of a satisfactory formal model, all that can be offered here is a simple illustration of what seems intuitively to be a reasonable interpretation of the manner in which industrial location patterns actually evolve. Figure 14.6 shows three stages in the development of an imaginary pattern. During each stage short-run conditions of a fixed optimum location, profit surface and spatial margin are assumed, but between the stages the situation facing the industry may change. In stage 1 twenty firms enter the industry; all locate within the margin otherwise they could not remain in business, but while the majority gravitate towards the general vicinity of the optimum others, because of their limited skill, knowledge, or avarice, take up locations less endowed with profit potential. It is assumed that the same cost/revenue situation applies to all firms, otherwise the graphical presentation would be impossible, but the possibility that some of the firms might for a variety of reasons operate within wider or narrower margins than others should be borne in mind.

After the initial twenty firms have established themselves, the spatial cost and revenue surfaces change, and with them the position of the optimum location and the margins to profitability. Twenty new firms enter the industry, but they are faced with a new profit pattern and tend to cluster around a new optimum location. To most of the original firms their existing location is still satisfactory; the new situation has improved the locations of some while others make less profit. But for five of them the shift of the margin has made their location unprofitable, and they now go out of business.

This process is repeated in the next stage, following a further change in the spatial profit geography. More firms enter, and a few of the existing ones go out as their locations become extramarginal. Although the failures in this simple illustration are attributed to the movement of the industry's common margin, in reality they may be the result of lower sales or reduced managerial efficiency, which in turn reduces the firm's individual margin. As the process of change continues the area in which the largest concentration of the industry emerges will build up the advantages associated with economies of agglomeration, which will help maintain its attraction to new firms. This model thus has built into it an element of stability, involving the self-perpetuating tendency of the industry's core

272   INDUSTRIAL LOCATION THEORY: A SYNTHESIS

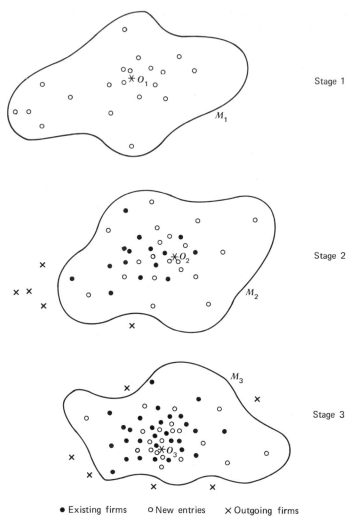

Figure 14.6.   **An interpretation of the evolution of industrial location patterns.**

area. It is at or near the spatial margins where the uncertainty is; the best way to insure long-run viability, given a necessary minimum of entrepreneurial ability, is to find that area which is unlikely ever to slip outside the margin.

This interpretation of the evolution of industrial location patterns is similar to one that has been put forward independently by Pred (1969, 103–115). It expresses specifically certain ideas which have existed in the literature for some time. More than twenty years ago, Hoover (1948, 10) drew an analogy between the locating of factories and the scattering of seeds: some fall in good places and get a quick and vigorous start, while some fall in areas with less suitable conditions. The survival of plants that happen to be well located (that is, intramarginal in the long run) results in the pattern from generation to generation following closely the distribution of favorable conditions. Tiebout (1957), following the terminology of Alchian (1950), interprets the economic system as a compromise between the tendency for activities to adapt themselves to the prevailing conditions and the tendency for the fortunate concerns to be adopted by the system. In industrial location, the successful adapters are those who have enough skill to find a good location and keep within the spatial margins of profitability in the long run. Those who are adopted by the system may have located in ignorance or with the exercise of meager skill, but were fortunate enough to be within the margin. Those who do not adapt successfully, and those who are not adopted by the system, end up beyond the margin sooner or later, and go out of business.

Both Hoover and Tiebout stress that no matter how random the process by which industrial location patterns evolve may appear to be, the end result has a certain economic rationality. As Hoover (1948, 10) stated: "Competition, insofar as it prevails, will reward the well-located enterprises and shorten the lives of poorly located ones. Even if new establishments were to be located purely by guesswork or whim or by sticking pins into a map at random, and if they were never relocated, some semblance of a reasonable pattern would still emerge as a result of competition." And Tiebout (1957, 84) remarked: "If enough firms set up and the economic system gets to pick and choose, it would not be surprising if reality yields results consistent with optimal conditions. And all of this, of course, can take place without assuming that the firm can find the path to (adapt to) the optimum location." Thus despite the apparently random or fortuitous nature of so many locational decisions, a process of economic Darwinism will eventually sort the weak from the strong, and leave a pattern which, if not conforming perfectly to some theoretical state of equilibrium, should at least display an element of order which is capable of rational interpretation.

PART FOUR

Some Empirical Applications

The development of theory of the kind discussed in Parts Two and Three has two main objectives: (1) to advance the understanding of industrial location by largely deductive means, arguing from a restricted set of postulates and assumptions the forms of behavior likely to be adopted; and (2) to provide a basis from which to embark on the explanatory side of empirical inquiry. As was pointed out in Chapter 1, these two objectives are closely interconnected, since abstract theory must be constantly related to reality if it is to be anything more than an exercise in applied logic or mathematics, and must ultimately be judged by its capacity to explain industrial location patterns in the real world. The empirical application of industrial location analysis is the subject of the next four chapters.

It must be conceded at the outset that very little progress has yet been made in the direct application of industrial location theory to real-world situations. As Stevens and Brackett (1967, 7) remark in their survey of the literature: "A large number of empirical studies have been carried out in the last twenty years, but most have been for the purpose of gaining general understanding of location factors and patterns rather than of testing theory. This is partly because it has been difficult to generate testable hypotheses from existing theory. More important, the goals of the theoreticians have been quite different from the goals of researchers interested in empirical work." As was shown in Chapter 8, the space economists have generally been more concerned with the construction of elegant theories of locational equilibrium, or with the fusion of location theory and production theory, than with providing a guide for empirical inquiry. And the empiricists have generally lacked both the knowledge of location theory and the technical capacity required to provide a strong conceptual basis for their case studies. Thus, to quote Stevens and Brackett (1967, 13) again, ". . . there is a distinct lack of definitive research. Many of the conclusions about cause and effect are intuitive and go well beyond the evidence presented by existing data."

Two main problems are encountered in applying location theory to empirical research. The first is the difficulty of obtaining the necessary data. Identifying, for example, the least-cost location for a particular industrial activity requires a large amount of accurate information, of a kind that can often be obtained only by direct inquiry of existing firms. Other important variables, such as the demand function for different sets of customers and psychic entrepreneurial income in alternative locations, may be incapable of measurement in a way that would allow their incorporation in an operational locational model. The second main problem is that conventional industrial location theory does not necessarily permit the formulation of the kind of explanatory hypotheses or models called for by real-world situations. Finding the optimum location for one firm at one point in time is often of little help in explaining the areal distribution of a whole industry, which may be the end product of a long process of evolution and which contains firms of different size, technology, and entrepreneurial skill. Even the theories that are concerned with the spatial arrangement of plants, such as Lösch's economic landscape and Isard's modification of this, have thus far proved incapable of application to the explanation of actual industrial location patterns.

The theoretical framework developed in Part Three suffers from the same problems. If it is to do anything more than strengthen intuitive judgement, its application requires a large volume of data, much of which is difficult to compile. Although the introduction of the concept of spatial margins to profitability appears to facilitate the general interpretation of real-world patterns and their evolution, the formulation of predictive models of industrial location is an entirely different matter. This theoretical approach implies patterns that have a certain general resemblance to some of those actually found, with a tendency toward agglomeration around favored localities but with random dispersal within certain spatial limits, but it is impossible to predict the precise spatial arrangement of plants within the margin. The truth is that industrial location, like many other forms of human behavior, is very difficult to understand, and no theory will ever produce models that can perfectly replicate and completely explain actual patterns of plant location.

A major purpose of Part Four is to explore the extent to which various elements of the theoretical synthesis of Part Three are capable of practical application. Emphasis is given to areal variations in cost and demand, identified as surfaces, as well as to the discovery of the optimum location. The general aim is to indicate ways in which theory may assist in the understanding of industrial location in the real world. First, the empirical identification of cost surfaces is considered (Chapter 15), followed by a demonstration of ways in which the variable-demand and market-area approaches may be applied (Chapter 16). Then a number of more complete analyses of comparative locational advantage are considered, drawing illustrations from the published research of the past quarter of a century (Chapter 17). These three chapters should be viewed not as a test of a theory of industrial location which is still far from complete, but merely as a set of suggestions as to what can be achieved in empirical inquiry, given this kind of theoretical framework. Chapter 18 extends the scope of these illustrations by presenting three major case studies incorporating further application of various theoretical concepts.

15

The Identification of Cost Surfaces

It is now obvious that the concept of the cost surface is central to the neoclassical approach to industrial location theory developed in Part Three. In the variable-cost model, comparative locational advantage is measured directly by areal variations in the total cost of producing a given output, and even when demand is introduced as a spatial variable the cost surface remains a major determinant of the position of the optimum location and the margins to profitability. The question of how far the abstract concept of the cost surface can be given empirical identity is thus of critical importance in the application of theory to practical situations. Only if the relevant cost surface can be found empirically can the neoclassical theory be translated into operational models.

Since total cost is made up of a variety of different items of expenditure, the identification of areal variations in the cost of single inputs is an essential prerequisite to the derivation of the total cost surface. And there are some industries where the cost of one or two inputs is so important that they effectively determine comparative locational advantage, as is the case in certain activities that are heavily dependent on bulky materials, and in some activities that are highly labor intensive. In these circumstances the form of the cost surface of the critical input or inputs may be able to provide an adequate explanation of locational choice, without the necessity for constructing the total cost surface or introducing other possible causal factors such as the demand situation.

But in many industries the identification of even one input cost surface with any precision may be a difficult matter. This chapter considers some of the problems involved, and gives illustrative examples of surfaces relating to the cost of land, construction, materials, labor, and taxes. Spatial variations in the cost of these inputs were considered in a very general way in Chapter 3; this chapter is a logical extension of that discussion, being concerning with cost surfaces relevant to specific industries and of a kind capable of incorporation within a locational model.

Most cost and demand data are of a sporadic nature in their areal occurence, generally being available for a set of discrete points with no information on intervening locations. The conversion of such data into spatially continuous variables is greatly facilitated by isoline mapping, and in certain instances by trend surface analysis. In Part Four extensive use is made of isoline maps, many of them having been prepared by computer using the SYMAP system developed at Harvard, as was the case in a number of the illustrations in Chapter 3. The advantage of the computer is its speed and objectivity, which permits the graphic representation of a surface interpolated from a large number of data points to be achieved in a matter of minutes, and with the elimination of much of the subjectivity which is a feature of isoline mapping. The importance of computer mapping as a practical aid in the identification of cost surfaces, and surfaces relating to demand or revenue, can hardly be overemphasized. As Alonso (1967, 24) has pointed out, the recent coupling of the calculating and graphic potentialities of the computer has made the isoline techniques of classical location theory much more accessible to the researcher than when they were originally proposed.

15.1 LAND-COST SURFACES

In Chapter 3 it was suggested that the cost of building land can vary in a fairly regular and predictable manner, both within major cities and at a national level. However, spatial variations in the cost of industrial land are somewhat more difficult to identify than the smooth curve of the classic urban land-cost profile might suggest. For many firms the precise location chosen will be determined by the quality, size, and situation of available sites, and these considerations can disturb the regularity of areal cost variations. For example, a level site with good access will often cost substantially more than a site that needs preparation and is some distance from the main highway, even though both sites are in the same part of town. Local cost variations reflecting the quality of individual sites may actually be greater than intracity or intraregional variations arising from general locational advantage.

Considerable generalization will thus be involved in any attempt to build up an industrial land-cost surface. The selling price of as many sites as possible must be determined, and supplemented by data relating to what a new firm could reasonably expect to pay in different areas from informed sources such as real-estate offices and local industrial development agencies. Then some kind of average figure has to be established for each locality, town, or city, taking into account the local variations resulting from the nature of specific sites.

Two surfaces derived in this way are illustrated in Figure 15.1. The map of variations in the cost of industrial land in Northwest England was built up from data for the actual price or anticipated cost of a sample of representative sites in all parts of the region. Costs were found to vary from as low as £1000 per acre for a poorly situated plot in one of the declining cotton-mill towns on the eastern fringe of the region, to thirty times this figure for one of the few remaining sites near the center of the cities of Manchester and Liverpool. The isolines are not continued beyond £15,000, because in the inner city areas the price of land fluctuates very considerably with variations in the quality of individual sites. In general,

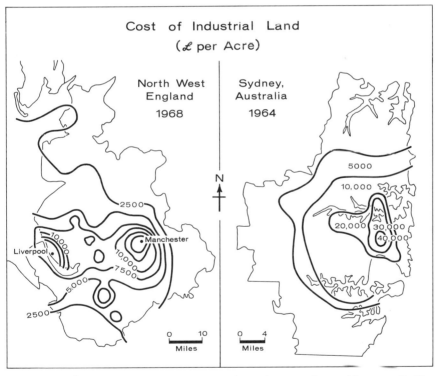

Figure 15.1. Two illustrations of industrial land-cost surfaces. (*Sources.* Smith, 1969a, 123, Figure 22, for Northwest England, and Logan, 1966, 456, Figure 3, for Sydney.)

this surface is a reasonably accurate representation of the state of the regional land market, and could be used fairly confidently in a model designed to measure the overall economic advantage of alternative locations. However, it does not take into account the fact that land is not available for industrial development everywhere. About 10 percent of the land is already developed, and there are also large areas that are designated green belt, national park, or some other protected category, or allocated on city plans for nonindustrial uses. In these areas the cost of land for industrial purposes has to be regarded as infinitely high, so in reality the cost surface should be discontinuous.

The second map in Figure 15.1 covers a smaller area and relates to the single city of Sydney, Australia. The highest costs, of around £(A) 45,000 in the central business district, are more than ten times what a manufacturer can expect to pay on the outer edge of the city. This map was prepared from data on actual land sales over a twelve month period, derived from the files of the three largest real-estate specialists in industrial property in Sydney.

Surfaces such as the two illustrated are clearly simplifications of the actual situation, with many local features of the cost topography generalized away. However, they are probably quite adequate as a means of introducing land costs as a spatially continuous variable into an explanatory or predictive model of industrial location, providing their limitations are not overlooked in the final interpretation.

15.2 BUILDING-COST SURFACES

The cost of factory construction is difficult to evaluate, since it must include the cost of building materials, different grades of labor, the services of the architect and other professional fees, and various additional incidental items. However, the task is simplified by the availability of sets of indexes, which enable the cost of construction in different localities to be estimated fairly accurately without having to identify the cost of each item separately.

One such index is provided by the *Dow Building Cost Calculator* (1969). This contains illustrations of a variety of different kinds of factory buildings and specifies a base cost per cubic foot for each. The base cost covers the construction costs irrespective of location, but not the cost of excavation, foundations and subfoundation work, design fees, and builders' overheads and profit. The base cost thus represents the most stable and comparable cost components of a building without regard to site problems, profit rates, and competition between builders, all of which can vary extensively from place to place.

In order to find the actual cost of construction of the type of factory selected at a given location it is necessary to apply a local cost modifier. This index varies from 1.027 in Montgomery, Alabama, to 1.674 in New York City. Indexes have been calculated for 181 cities within the United States and a further 37 in Canada, and generally apply to all sites within twenty-five miles of the city in question. Multiplying the base cost of the type of building required by the appropriate local cost modifier gives the local base cost per cubic foot, and to get the total building costs this is then multiplied by the total cubic footage needed.

If it is required to include the various items not accounted for in the base cost, then a general purpose multiplier is used in place of the local cost modifier. This simply adds 20 percent to the base cost. It is the general-purpose multiplier that would be used in attempting to arrive at an all-inclusive cost for factory construction, although local conditions are more likely to affect the 20 percent addition than the original base cost. This index, like all other similar devices, cannot possibly take into account all local circumstances, although there is every reason to believe that it can give a close approximation to the likely cost in alternative locations.

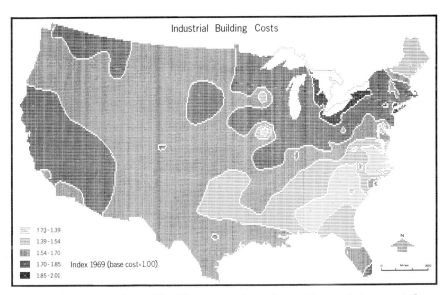

Figure 15.2. An industrial building-cost surface, derived from relative cost indexes for 181 metropolitan areas. (*Source of Data.* Dodge, 1969.)

The general-purpose multiplier for United States cities is mapped in Figure 15.2, to indicate the form that would be adopted by a cost surface identified for any specific type of factory building. The zone of lowest building cost is clearly defined, extending almost continuously from southern Alabama into North Carolina. The highest costs appear in the New York area and along the shores of Lake Huron, Lake Erie, and Lake Ontario. A comparison with Figures 3.3–3.6 in Chapter 3 will show that the surface of building costs is a fairly close reflection of the general pattern of labor costs, as might be expected.

15.3 MATERIAL-COST SURFACES

Materials are often the easiest inputs for which to identify accurate cost surfaces. Many materials are supplied at a uniform delivered price, in which case the cost surface will be a horizontal plane. When the price varies from place to place it is very often only a reflection of distance from the source of supply, since the cost of extraction or manufacture of a material is frequently much the same at alternative sources. In this case the identification of the cost surface involves finding the transport cost from the nearest source to alternative locations, using the appropriate freight-rate schedules.

If a very precise surface is required, it is necessary to work out the transport cost to a large number of different points. This is because of the complexity of some local freight-rate structures, which tend to disturb the geographical regularity of transport costs. However, it is often possible to construct a reasonably accurate surface from much more limited data, using the freight rate to a carefully selected sample of points to construct a representative cost/distance profile from which isoline intervals can be determined.

This method can be illustrated briefly by specific examples. In Chapter 17 there is a case study of the location of a firm manufacturing electrical appliances, the two major materials for which are motors and galvanized steel. Transport costs per hundredweight (cwt) of each of these commodities have been found for nine places in the eastern half of the United States, and from this it is possible to construct adequate if somewhat generalized locational cost surfaces.

The surface for motors is the easiest to derive, since there is only one source of supply for the particular type needed. Plotting the transport rate to each of the nine points against their distances from Tecumseh indicates that the cost/distance relationship is closely if not exactly linear. It can be described by the expression $Y = 40 + 0.22X$, where Y

is the cost in cents of transporting 1 cwt and X is the distance in miles. In other words, there is a fixed cost of 40¢ per cwt irrespective of the distance moved, plus 0.22¢ for each mile from Tecumseh. From this information, a series of concentric circles can be drawn about the material source, representing the first approximation to cost isolines. The form of the isolines can then be modified to take into account the deviation of some of the rates from the general linear relationship. For example, the regression line fitted to the data underpredicts the rate to Richmond, Virginia, so the isolines can be pulled in around this point. The rate to Montgomery, Alabama is overestimated, so the isoline interval in this part of the South is increased. The final result is illustrated in Figure 15.3a. This is clearly a simplification of the pattern which would be pro-

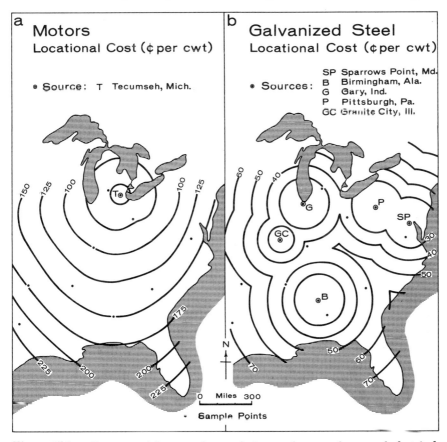

Figure 15.3. Two material-cost surfaces relating to the manufacture of electrical goods in the eastern United States, based on data for nine sample points. (*Source of Data*: The Fantus Company, Chicago.)

duced with data for a larger number of points, but it is quite adequate as a general indication of relative cost in alternative locations.

The derivation of a cost surface for galvanized steel is a little more involved. Instead of the single source for motors there are now five, as indicated in Figure 15.3b. Plotting rates against distance this time produces a curvilinear relationship of the kind frequently found when dealing with transport costs, with more distant places having a lower ton/mile rate than those closer to the material source. There is an additional complication, in that the cost at source is 10¢ per cwt higher at Granite City than at the other plants, and this has to be taken in account if the surface is to be a true reflection of the spatially variable (or locational) element in the cost of galvanized steel. Using the cost/distance profile to estimate the intervals, as in the previous illustration, isolines of freight cost per cwt can be constructed from series of concentric circles drawn about each of the steel sources. The final surface (Figure 15.3b) indicates the addition to basic cost at source which will be incurred at any point within the eastern United States. The isolines get further apart with distance from the steel plants, to conform to the curvilinear cost/distance relationship, and the slightly different pattern around Granite City reflects its higher factory price. No attempt has made to adjust the isolines to conform to known local departures from the general cost/distance relationship, as only one of the nine sample points shows any significant deviation from the curve.

The surfaces illustrated in Figure 15.3 refer only to transport or locational cost per unit of material. In order to find the total locational cost at any point the cost per cwt there must be multiplied by the total requirement in some relevant time period. Then the basic cost of the required quantity has to be added, to give a figure for the total outlay on the material in question. But as long as there is no input substitution between alternative locations the form of a surface of total locational cost or total outlay (basic and locational cost) will be identical to that of unit locational cost, for this has merely been multiplied by and added to spatial constants. Thus for many purposes in industrial locational studies, where the attention is focused on the influence of a single material, a surface of unit locational cost is quite adequate as an analytical device.

As a second illustration of material-cost surfaces, the cost of coal as a fuel for steam-powered electricity generating stations may be considered. The analysis is confined to the state of Illinois, where data are available for thirty-one generating stations, and the approach is one that might be used to provide a quick indication of the likely cost of coal in various parts of the state. This is an interesting case because it introduces the complication that there is more than one possible definition of the cost of coal. The first is the *cost per ton f.o.b. plant*, which simply consists of the price at the mine plus freight charges, or the cost of coal as delivered to the plant. Second, there is the *cost per ton as burned*, which refers to the cost at the bunker from which the coal goes into the boilers. This includes the f.o.b. plant cost plus the cost of labor involved in handling the coal between delivery and use, and also the cost (or revenue) arising from the disposal of the ashes remaining after burning (National Coal Association, 1968, 1). In Illinois the average per ton cost f.o.b. in 1967 was $4.92 compared with $5.07 as burned. The third definition is *cost per million BTU*, which is the cost of coal as burned related to the thermal units produced. This takes into account the interplant variations in BTU per pound of coal. These three definitions help to emphasize that the cost of an industrial material may have different meanings, which may lead to different forms of cost surface.

The surfaces that result in the present case are illustrated in Figure 15.4. All of the maps have certain features in common, the most obvious being the distinction between the low-cost zone extending northward from the Southern Illinois Coalfield, and the high-cost area in the northern part of the state. But the maps also show some important differences; for

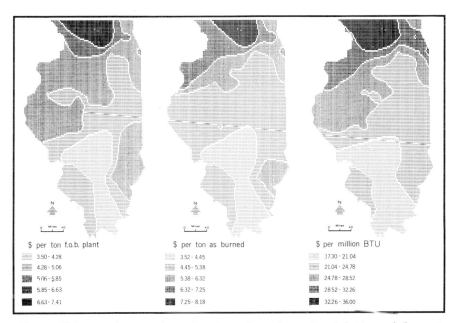

Figure 15.4. Fuel-cost surfaces, based on three alternative definitions of the cost of coal as used in steam-powered electricity generating stations in Illinois. (*Source of Data.* National Coal Association, *Steam-Electric Plant Factors*, 1968.)

example, the figures for cost per ton as burned enlarge the area within the lowest two cost categories when compared with the cost f.o.b. plant. The map of cost per million BTU more closely resembles the pattern for f.o.b. cost than cost as burned, except in the southeastern part of the state.

No significance should be attached to the minor local differences in the cost pattern shown on these three maps, since the interpolation is based on only thirty-one points which tend to be clustered in certain areas such as Chicago and Peoria. The cost surface in parts of the state with no electricity generating stations is based entirely on the data for existing plants. Therefore, although the maps provide a good general indication of areal variations in the cost of this one material, the costs that a new plant could expect to incur would be partially determined by the existing transport route and any local anomolies in the freight-rate structure— factors that will not necessarily be reflected in a map compiled from existing plant costs.

15.4 LABOR-COST SURFACES

The cost of labor in alternative locations may be more difficult to identify accurately than the cost of any other input. Surfaces of the kind illustrated in Chapter 3 provide a general indication of where the high-cost and low-cost areas are, and may be adequate as a means of introducing the labor factor into some locational models. But if anything approaching a precise picture of the labor-cost pattern facing an individual manufacturer or a narrowly defined industry is required, these kinds of surfaces are hardly suitable.

The labor force of any factory is made up of persons possessing a variety of different skills and performing different functions. Each occupational group may have its own wage rates, and the total labor cost is a product of these rates and the number of workers employed in each category. Thus the most accurate way of deriving a surface for total expenditure on labor is to build it up from data on areal variations in wage rates in specific occupations. Some figures of this kind are available in the *Occupational Wage Surveys* compiled by the U.S. Department of Labor. The Bureau of Labor Statistics conducts periodic surveys in eighty labor markets comprising the nation's major metropolitan areas, and prepares figures for average hourly earnings in selected occupations based on a sampling of local firms. The figures exclude premium pay for overtime and bonuses not related to production, but include cost-of-living bonuses and incentive payments.

Cost surfaces for two of these occupations are illustrated in Figures 15.5

and 15.6. Wages of power forklift truck operators range from $1.51 to $3.01, and for material handling laborers from $1.42 to $3.05. The two patterns are broadly similar in that they conform to the general tendency observed in Chapter 3 for wage rates to decrease from the northwest to the southeast, and certain more local features such as the three low areas in the south are also found on both maps. The main difference between them is the much greater variability in the wages of forklift truck operators in the eastern half of the country, as indicated by the number of local troughs and peaks. The greater detail shown in the east is partly the result of the larger number of control points there than in the areas west of the Mississippi.

As in the case of cost surfaces for other inputs, this method of producing isoline maps by computer from data for a limited number of points provides a means of estimating labor costs in intervening locations. However, there is one major difficulty involved here, and in the general interpretation of labor-cost surfaces: there is a tendency for them to be based on observations for the larger urban areas where earnings may be relatively high. The actual rate that a firm could expect to pay in some of the intervening nonurban areas could thus be somewhat less than the figures that would be read off the surfaces in Figures 15.5 and 15.6.

If it is impossible or impracticable to build up a total labor-cost surface for individual occupations, figures may be available for average earnings in the industry under investigation. In most cases these figures would be preferable to the averages for all industry or for different skill categories, as illustrated in Chapter 3. Again, figures published by the Department of Labor are helpful in this respect, identifying the average level of earnings by industries in selected cities. Another source is the *Census of Manufacturing*, where figures for man-hours of labor employed and the total wage bill enable figures for average cost per hour to be worked out. An illustration of the application of this latter technique can be found in Wonnacott (1963), where labor costs calculated on this basis are used as part of a general assessment of relative industrial costs by states.

As an illustration of industrial labor-cost surfaces, the average hourly earnings in food manufacturing are mapped from two different sets of data in Figures 15.7 and 15.8. The first map shows a surface derived from state data calculated by Wonnacott. The use of six intervals here instead of the five in the previous two illustrations helps to identify the steep gradient between the low-wage areas in the southeast and New England and the northern and western parts of the country where rates are higher. The second map is based on Department of Labor data for ninety-one cities, and picks out certain local features of the cost topo-

290   SOME EMPIRICAL APPLICATIONS

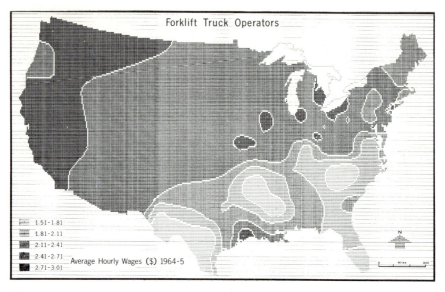

Figure 15.5.   Wage rates for power forklift truck operators, 1964-5. (*Source of Data.* U.S. Department of Labor, *Occupational Wage Surveys.*)

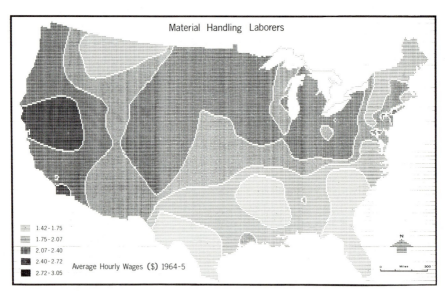

Figure 15.6.   Wage rates for material handling laborers, 1964-5. (*Source of Data.* U.S. Department of Labor, *Occupational Wage Surveys.*)

THE IDENTIFICATION OF COST SURFACES 291

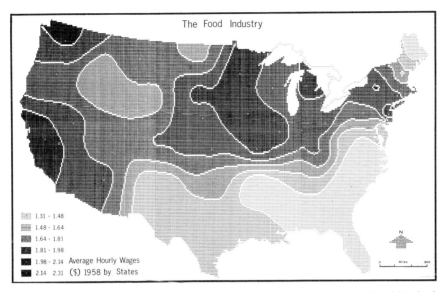

Figure 15.7. Wages of production workers in the manufacture of food and kindred products, by states, 1958. (*Source of Data.* Wonnacott, 1063, 6.)

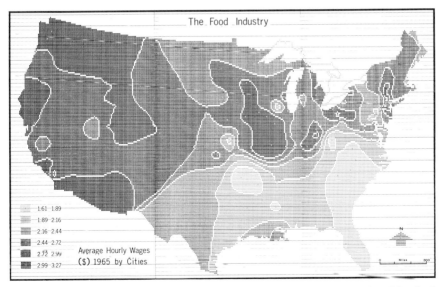

Figure 15.8. Wages of production workers in the manufacture of food and kindred products, by major cities, 1965. (*Source of Data.* U.S. Department of Labor, *Employment and Earnings Statistics for States and Areas.*)

graphy hidden in the state data. Despite the very broad similarity between the two patterns, there is enough difference to indicate that alternative approaches to the measurement of labor costs in specific industries need not give identical results—a point that must be borne in mind in selecting the data to represent the labor-cost variable in any locational analysis. Figure 15.7 would be suitable for indicating the comparative advantage of broad regions, while the map based on city data would be more useful in finding local areas with labor-cost advantages.

The problem of obtaining a precise estimate of the wage rates that a new entrant could expect to pay in any locality is virtually insoluble. As was indicated in Chapter 3, the fact that there is a certain prevailing level of pay in a city for a given occupation, or in a given industry, is no guarantee that a new firm can get the number of workers required for the same expenditure. Some researchers in this field are so doubtful about the value of published figures that they prefer on-the-spot inquiries, but this is a practicable approach only if a very limited number of alternative locations are involved. More sophisticated methods of overcoming this problem include the construction of an occupational profile of the firm or industry in question, identifying the relative wage levels in all significant occupations at one location. This is then used to estimate wage levels at locations where there is less complete information, on the assumption that the missing occupations will have rates of pay which bear the same relationship to those in the known occupations as in the location with the complete information (Reifler, 1957).

15.5 TAXATION SURFACES

The basis for taxation of industrial firms varies from state to state. It also varies between different communities, in a manner so difficult to predict that the exact tax bill that a firm could expect in a specific municipality can often be determined only by direct personal contact with local taxation officers. This makes the calculation of areal differences in state and local taxes, and the derivation of taxation surfaces, a complex and at times hazardous operation.

The best way to illustrate the procedures involved is through a specific illustration. Particularly suitable for this purpose is a study prepared by the Pennsylvania Economic League (1960), which attempted to determine the relative tax position for an imaginary corporation in Philadelphia and eighty-one other municipalities within a radius of about seventy-five miles of this city. The study covers state taxes, local taxes, and local charges for water and sewage-disposal services.

In any taxation study the nature of the firm involved must be specified precisely. In the present case it was assumed that the corporation was in the first year of its existence, employed about 1000 workers, and had gross sales of $13.9 million and net income before tax of $2,525,000. Sales were assumed to be distributed as follows: Philadelphia 25 percent, elsewhere in Pennsylvania 25 percent, New Jersey 20 percent, Delaware 15 percent, and Maryland 15 percent. In addition, an income statement and balance sheet were prepared to provide additional information needed to compute some of the taxes.

A complete tax bill was calculated for each of the eighty-two places covered by the study, at 1959 rates. The state taxes are easiest to work out, because there is some degree of uniformity within each state. The state taxes include a Selective Sales and Use Tax, Corporation Income Tax, a Net Worth Tax, an Annual Franchise Tax, and a Gross Receipts Tax. Not all of these apply to all of the four states under review, and where they do apply the rate at which the tax is levied differs from state to state. The calculation of the total state tax bill produced a range from almost $142,000 for the year down to about $86,700. The highest figures were in Pennsylvania with slight fluctuations about $140,000; the Maryland figures were roughly $125,000 to $130,000; those in Delaware were about $122,000; and in New Jersey they were all below $92,000.

The local taxes fall into two main categories: the Real Property Tax and the Tangible Personal Property Tax where applicable. The range of the total bill was found to be much greater than in the case of state taxes, the extremes being $201,200 and $7100. The higher figures were generally found in New Jersey and Maryland, with most municipalities within the range of $135,000 to $80,000. In Pennsylvania the range was generally $70,000 to $40,000, while most places in Delaware were below $40,000. An interesting feature of these figures is that high state taxes appear often to be offset by low municipal taxes.

For the purpose of estimating water charges, it was assumed that the corporation used almost 120 million gallons per year. The charge for this amount of water ranged from just over $40,000 down to $7400. In assessing the sewage charge it was found that ten of the municipalities did not impose separate rates for this but included it in the general tax levy. On the assumption that all the water used is discharged into the public sewage system, the charge for this service was found to vary from almost $58,000 to $15 in the municipalities quoting a separate figure for sewage. Taking both water and sewage charges together, the higher figures were found to be in Pennsylvania in and around Philadelphia, while the lowest were in some of the smaller peripheral municipalities.

The total tax bill at a location within a given municipality is the sum of state taxes, local taxes, and the water and sewage charge. When this was calculated for the eighty-two places under investigation the highest figure came to almost $311,000, in Baltimore City, which was approximately twice the size of the lowest tax bill. Figures for most of the places included in this study are mapped in Figure 15.9. Tentative isolines have been interpolated to give a general indication of the form of the taxation surface, but too much significance should not be attached to these. Each figure shown is in reality constant over the area of the municipality in question, and there is a certain random element in the pattern, with some isolated high or low figures in areas which otherwise show the opposite characteristic. The general impression is of relatively high tax bills in

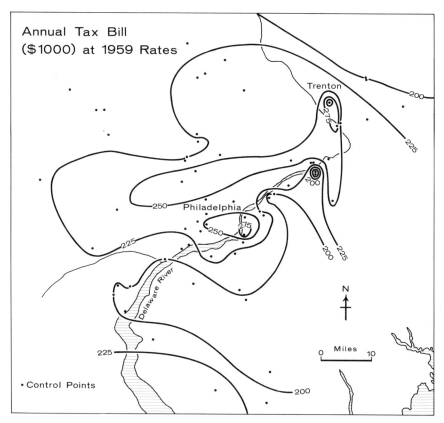

Figure 15.9. Areal variations in the level of taxation for an imaginary industrial corporation in the Philadelphia area. (*Source of Data.* Pennsylvania Economic League, 1960.)

Philadelphia and some of its fringe areas, and also in the general vicinity of Trenton, with the lower values in the peripheral areas.

Just how important would these areal differences in taxation be to the imaginary firm as it decided on its location within the area under review? According to the firm's income statement, the total annual cost of operating the plant without taxes would be $11,455,000. The highest tax bill, of $311,000, would thus add about 3 percent to the total cost and the lowest bill ($162,000) about 1.5 percent. This analysis thus tends to support the conclusion of the earlier discussion of the taxation factor (Chapter 3), namely that this will not significantly affect plant locational decisions unless it is reinforced by areal differences in the cost of other inputs. For most practical purposes it is therefore unlikely that the expenditure of time and effort on the scale needed to accurately identify local variations in tax levels is justified. If this item has to be introduced into a model as a continuous spatial variable, a highly generalized surface based on a few sample locations is probably adequate. However, care must be taken not to overlook places where a specially favorable tax situation might have been created for the purpose of attracting new industry, since these may on occasions offer a very significant cost saving when compared with alternative locations.

16

The Market, and Areal Variations in Demand

Variations in demand (sales or revenue) between alternative locations are very difficult to measure directly. To do this in a proper fashion would require the identification of demand curves for each set of consumers or each section of the market, and relating this to the cost of production and the geographical price policy which is in force. This may be fairly easy in certain circumstances—for example, if demand is extremely inelastic or if the firm or industry in question sells to a known and secure market at a uniform c.i.f. price. But if an f.o.b. plant pricing system is adopted, if there is market-area competition between firms, if demand is sensitive to price differences, and if the elasticity of demand varies from place to place, the definitive identification of the comparative advantage of alternative locations is virtually impossible.

The derivation of total revenue surfaces thus seems to be far more difficult from a practical point of view than the identification of cost surfaces. It appears that, no example of an empirically derived revenue surface has yet been published, and the first one may still be a long way off. Of course, this does not destroy the theoretical value of the concept of revenue surfaces, just as the difficulty of combining input cost surfaces to form a total cost surface does not invalidate this concept. However, it does pose the important problem of how the demand factor can be incorporated into operational industrial location models as a continuous spatial variable.

In attempting to assess the effect of the market and the demand factor on plant location there are a number of alternative procedures to the actual identification of revenue surfaces. Two are of special interest in the present context: the aggregate travel model and the potential model. Both were introduced into industrial location analysis in a classic paper by Chauncy Harris (1954), and are very useful devices for considering the effect of the spatial distribution of consumers on plant location under different assumptions about the demand situation. This chapter illustrates the application of both models, and then discusses the identification of market areas under conditions of spatial competition for sales.

16.1 THE AGGREGATE TRAVEL (TRANSPORT COST) MODEL

The aggregate travel model really belongs more logically to the variable-cost approach to industrial location than to the demand side. It is a means of finding the relative cost of distributing a product to a market of known spatial distribution, based on the measurement of the total cost or coverage of distance involved. The cost of serving consumers at any market point j from a plant location i is the unit cost of transportation over the distance from i to j multiplied by the number of units to be shipped. The total cost of distributing to a given market is thus the sum of this value for all j, and the aggregate travel model evalutes this for all possible plant locations.

The model may be expressed symbolically as

$$A_i = \sum_{j=1}^{n} Q_j T_{ij} \qquad (16.1)$$

where

A_i is the aggregate travel involved in serving the market from location i, which may be measured in terms of distance or cost depending on the data applied to T.

Q_j is the quantity of the product which is sold at the market j ($j = 1, \ldots, n$).

T_{ij} is the unit cost of transportation between i and j or, alternatively, the distance between the two points if suitable data on freight rates are not available.

If Q is an accurate expectation of sales, and if T is the actual transportation rates that will be paid, A_i will be the total cost of distributing the product to the market, and the evaluation of expression (16.1) for all i will provide the data from which a surface of actual marketing transport costs could be constructed. But the necessary information is seldom available to run the model in this way. More often it is necessary to use a surrogate like population, per capita income or retail sales to estimate Q at different points, and distance (perhaps raised to some power) may be used in the place of the cost of transportation. In this case, A does not give the actual cost of distribution but an indication of its likely relative magnitude, given the assumptions implicit in the way Q and T have been measured.

No matter how the model is calibrated, the optimum location will be where A is minimized, other things being equal. This is where total transportation cost or coverage of distance is least for the given areal distribution of the market. The technical problem of finding the elusive point of minimum aggregate travel, or the median center of the market, has already been referred to in Chapter 9 (Section 9.2); here the concern is less with finding the optimum point than with evaluating A for a suitable number of alternative locations and interpolating a surface of comparative advantage from these observations. This procedure seems to be of more theoretical and empirical value than the search for the single minimum point, which in practice may be unsuitable for an industrial plant for a variety of reasons.

Before illustrating the aggregate travel model, the assumptions about the demand situation which it implies must be clearly stated. As the same quantity is shipped to a given point j, whichever point i is being considered, the model does not allow for demand to vary with choice of plant location. In other words, Q is insensitive to the distance between j and i, which means either that there must be a uniform delivered price with no discrimination against distant consumers or that demand is infinitely inelastic. The possibility that the manufacturer's price might be related to his cost of distribution (that is, price will be higher the higher the value of A) can only be accommodated in this model if it is assumed that the demand curve is a vertical line and that the only difference between places is in the intercept, which is, of course, the Q value.

As an illustration of the application of the aggregate travel model, a case of a manufacturer setting up in business to serve the United States market may be considered briefly. Assume that the firm expects sales in any section of the market to be related to the local level of earnings, for which the median income is a suitable surrogate. Dividing the national market into the forty-eight contiguous states, and with sales in each one attributed arbitrarily to the center point of the state, the aggregate travel model can be used to determine the best location from which to serve this market. In applying the model, it is assumed that the volume sold in and shipped to each state is directly proportional to its median income, that sales are not influenced by distance from the point of origin of the product, and that the straight line distance between any pair of markets and production points is an adequate measure of the cost of moving goods from one to the other. In this application there are forty-eight alternative plant locations to be considered, namely the center points of the states.

To find the optimum location, expression (16.1) is evaluated for each of the alternatives. The median income data provide the figures for Q, and the values for T are derived from a 48×48 matrix of distances between the center points of the states. The results are mapped as a surface in Figure 16.1, to indicate the comparative advantage of different sections of the country. The optimum location, or point of minimum aggregate travel, is in the state of Indiana, and the figures rise steadily away from this point in a fairly symmetrical manner. The range in the values of A, or the total coverage of distance, is from 23.1M miles in Indiana to 57.9M in Washington. These figures are of purely relative significance, and can be interpreted as the actual miles of distance to be covered only if the volume of sales in each state is equivalent to the median income (that is, one unit for each dollar) rather than simply being proportional to it.

In the situation under review the profit-maximizing entrepreneur will locate his plant in the state of Indiana, other things being equal, since it is from this point that he can minimize his cost of distributing goods to the market. But there are other states nearby from which the market can be served with only a slight increase in the total coverage of distance, including Ohio with a figure of 23.2M and Illinois with 23.9M. Thus, within spatial limits that include all of the western part of the major manufacturing belt, the firm could diverge from the optimum location with relatively little addition to its distribution costs. The concept of the spatial margin can be introduced into the aggregate travel model here; if it is necessary to keep the cost of distribution below a certain sum to insure viability, the aggregate travel figure representing this critical level of expenditure gives the value for the spatial margin, which can be identified by the appropriate isoline on the aggregate travel surface. For example, if it was the case in the present illustration that to stay in business the total coverage of distance involved in distributing the product must be less than 30M miles, the relevant isoline can be drawn and read as the spatial margin to profitability in this situation, assuming no other considerations influence the level of profits. The entrepreneur not seeking the optimum location would thus have a wide range of locational choice within practically the whole of the eastern United States.

Other illustrations of the application of the aggregate travel model can be found in the original paper by Harris (1954). Using retail sales for his estimate of the market and generalized transportation costs derived empirically from sample freight rates, Harris mapped a surface of trans-

300 SOME EMPIRICAL APPLICATIONS

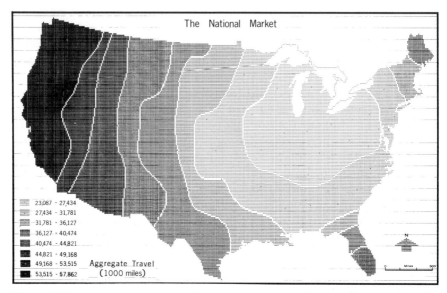

Figure 16.1. An aggregate travel or transport-cost surface, with respect to the national market. Sales in each state are assumed to be proportional to the median income in 1959. (*Source of Data. City and County Data Book,* 1965.)

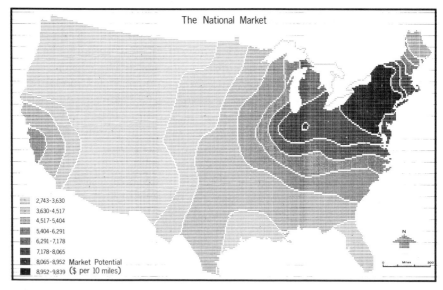

Figure 16.2. A market potential surface, with respect to the national market, based on data for median income by states in 1959. (*Source of Data. City and County Data Book,* 1965.)

port cost to the national market from about sixty cities. His minimum point was Fort Wayne, Indiana, and the aggregate travel or transport cost surface he produced closely resembles that drawn up from state data in Figure 16.1 (Harris, 1954, 324). He also prepared maps for particular states and regions, and surfaces of transport cost to the national mining, farming, and manufacturing market. Other applications will be found in the work of Dunn (1956), Kerr and Spelt (1960), Törnqvist (1962), and some other writers, to whom further reference is made later in Part Four.

16.2 THE MARKET POTENTIAL MODEL

The concept of *potential* as a measure of accessibility to some areally distributed phenomena is well established in location analysis. The potential exerted by any point j on a point i is found by dividing mass (P) at j by the distance (D) between i and j. If the mass is some measure of the demand for a particular product at j and the distance reflects the cost of getting the product from a plant at i to the market j, then the sum of $P \div D$ for all j gives an estimate of the market potential at i. Stated formally, the market potential (M) at any possible plant location i is

$$M_i = \sum_{j=1}^{n} \frac{Q_j}{T_{ij}} \qquad (16.2)$$

where Q and T are as defined above for expression (16.1). This formula is identical to that for the aggregate travel model except that division has been substituted for multiplication. The optimum location is now where $M_i = \max$, and not the minimum point as in the other model.

The assumptions about the demand situation implicit in the market potential model differ from those in the aggregate travel model in certain important respects. These must be considered carefully, because the potential model is sometimes used to assess the comparative advantage of different locations with respect to the market in situations where its assumptions are not necessarily fulfilled. The division of the measure of sales expectation (Q) at any market point j by the distance from the plant clearly expresses a progressive falling off of demand with increasing distance (or transport cost) from the point of production. This situation may arise if the product is sold on an f.o.b. plant basis to consumers with a downward-sloping demand curve, as considered above, in Chapter 13. Alternatively, it may be because the further away a customer is, the greater the probability that he will be served by another source of supply. Whichever situation is assumed, the market potential is more of a true demand model than the aggregate travel model because it makes allowance for the fact that sales at any market point may be a function of distance from the plant, and that plant location can affect the total volume sold and thus the total revenue earned.

If the market potential model is calibrated in an ideal manner, it can provide an estimate of the actual sales that can be anticipated in alternative locations. If Q measures the sales that could be achieved at any market j, if T_{ij} reflects the delivered price from a plant at i to the market j (delivered price being production cost plus the transport cost between i and j), and if the demand function Q/T accurately reflects the relationship between sales and delivered price in the situation under review, then expression (16.2) will measure the total sales that could be expected from a given plant location. It would then only be a short step to the derivation of a true demand surface, and then a surface for total revenue. But in practice it is seldom if ever possible to calibrate the market potential model exactly in this way. Either there is no basis for regarding Q as the intercept of a demand curve, or the appropriate transport cost data are not available, or there is no empirical support for a demand function of the form specified. Generally all three of these requirements are not fulfilled. The usual way of applying the model is to find some variable for Q which can be regarded as a reasonable estimate of the likely relative magnitude of sales, to use linear distance or some simple cost/distance function for T, and to assume that dividing Q by T provides some indication of the effect of plant location on the volume of demand at any point. The model thus provides an estimate of the relative attraction of alternative locations in the circumstances specified or, as Harris (1954, 321) expresses it, "an abstract index of the intensity of possible contact with markets."

An illustration of the application of the potential model is provided by reworking the case of the manufacturer setting up to serve the national market, as used to demonstrate the aggregate travel model. If it is assumed that median income remains a suitable predictor of the possible level of sales in any state but that the actual sales are now expected to be reduced with increasing distance from the point of production, the potential model becomes an appropriate means of determining the comparative advantage of different places as locations from which to serve this market. As before, the center points of the forty-eight states are taken to be the destinations of shipments of the product and also the possible plant locations. Expression (16.2) is thus evaluated for each state, with the income and distance data the same as used in the aggregate travel illustration.

The resulting market potential surface is mapped in Figure 16.2. The point of maximum potential, and hence the optimum location under the present assumptions, is in the state of Maryland, and it is here that the entrepreneur would locate his plant to maximize sales and profits other things being equal. Here the figure for market potential (M) is 9839, only a little higher than the 9651 in Pennsylvania and 9588 in the state of New York. Away from the zone of relatively high market potential, which corresponds closely with the major manufacturing belt, the figures decrease fairly steeply. The lowest values, of less than 3000, are in Washington, Oregon, Idaho, and Montana. It must be stressed once again that these figures provide only a *relative* indication of the likely volume of sales and revenue which can be achieved from a plant located in the state in question; as in the case of the aggregate travel model, it is only in special circumstances that this kind of model provides a figure for the actual volume of goods produced or the exact revenue earned.

A comparison between Figures 16.1 and 16.2 gives an interesting indication of the differences in comparative locational advantage arising from different assumptions regarding the market situation. Using identical data, the potential model identifies an optimum location at the eastern end of the major manufacturing belt, while the aggregate travel model puts it at the western end. The two surfaces adopt significantly different forms, with the one derived from the aggregate travel calculation tending toward the shape of a basin with a fairly flat bottom while the potential surface falls away steeply from the peak area. These differences become very important when the assumption of optimizing behavior in locational choice is dropped in favor of an approach that allows some freedom of locational choice, since it will be clear from the two maps that in the aggregate travel situation firms can diverge from the optimum within fairly wide spatial limits without greatly increasing their distribution costs, while under the conditions postulated in the potential illustration the volume of sales falls away steeply with relatively small distances from the optimum location. This suggests a narrower range of locational choice, or narrower spatial margins to profitability, in the situation where sales are sensitive to distance from the point of production than where the critical consideration is to minimize the total coverage of distance involved in distribution to the market. Much more of the United States falls within the lower half of the range of values in the aggregate travel surface than within the upper half of the range of the potential figures.

The differences in locational advantage suggested by mapping market potential and aggregate travel (transport cost) were emphasized by Harris (1954). His point of peak potential for the entire national market was found to be New York City, while the point of minimum transport cost was Fort Wayne, Indiana. The reason for this difference is that in the potential model the importance of a given market decreases with increasing distance, while in the aggregate travel model the same market increases its locational pull with increasing distance from the possible plant location. Stated another way, a large market at a considerable distance from a given point contributes little to the potential created at that point whereas it contributes substantially to the total transport cost involved in serving the entire market from that point. This explains the large pull exerted by the California market on the position of the point of minimum transport cost (or aggregate travel) compared with its pull on the location of the point of peak potential, and accounts for the slight rise of the potential surface in California shown on both Figure 16.2 and the map originally prepared by Harris (1954, 324).

Further illustrations of the application of the market potential concept can be found in the literature of economic geography and regional science. The most substantial application to date is William Warntz's *Towards a Geography of Price* (1959), which was an attempt to explain the spatial pattern of prices for certain agricultural commodities. As the approach could also be applied to the price of industrial products and the supply of inputs, the study is relevant in the present context. Warntz computed the *supply space potential* for a series of commodities by using production by states as the numerator in the potential formula and interstates distances as the denominator. The surfaces thus derived indicate accessibility to the supply of the commodity in question, and could suggest the most suitable locations for manufacturing plants for which the commodity was an input. Warntz then introduced the concept of *demand space potential,* using income potential as a measure of this. He then proposed that in any local area the price of a commodity varies inversely with the area's supply space potential and directly with the demand space potential. Testing this hypothesis by multiple regression analysis produced some quite convincing results.

Other applications can be found in a number of research papers, notably those by Dunn (1956), Kerr and Spelt (1960), and Ray (1965). Further discussion of these contributions is reserved for the next chapter, where the problem of combining the market potential model with variable-cost approaches is considered.

16.3 MARKET AREAS

The market area is an important concept in industrial location analysis. It is central to the determination of sales and revenue in alternative locations, and is critical to the understanding of the spatial arrangement of plants in many industries where control of sales over a certain territory is a major factor for the viability of the firm. It occupies a prominent place in theory, both in the work of Lösch and the locational-interdependence school and in the more cost-orientated approach of others such as Hoover. In view of this, there has been surprisingly little empirical research on the identification of market areas in an industrial context. A few illustrations can be found in the work of some of the major theorists, such as in Palander (1935, 366–367) and Lösch (1954, 418–419), and in some isolated empirical studies of industrial location, but most of the market-area analyses to date have been concerned with the service areas of cities in the context of central place theory (for example Berry, 1967).

Three simple examples of the identification of industrial market areas are offered here. They are based on actual cases, with real data on freight rates, the size of the market, and so on, but a few of the original facts have been altered for the sake of the illustration. They demonstrate the kind of market-area analysis that can be performed without any great technical or informational difficulties, and show some of the practical procedures involved.

1. The first case is concerned with the position of the textile industries in New England and the South with respect to supplying the national market. Competition between these two regions has been an important feature of the United States cotton industry since the first firms were attracted away from New England by the lower material and labor costs in the South, but for a long time it was believed that the structure of railroad freight rates tended to favor the New England manufacturers. In order to test this notion, the Committee of New England of the National Planning Association (1954) compiled comparative transport-cost data for a sample of destinations and a selection of New England and southern locations. The figures for finished cotton piece goods shipped from Lewiston, Maine, and from Greenville, South Carolina, are mapped in Figure 16.3. The freight-cost isolines are interpolated from data for the twenty-one sample points shown, and are generalized, but they give a fair indication of which of the two locations can serve different parts of the country at the lowest delivery cost.

If it is assumed that there are no significant differences in production cost (not necessarily true in this case), and that the cost of shipping the product is passed on to the consumer, then market areas can be defined from the freight-rate data. In Figure 16.3 the New England location controls a relatively small proportion of the market measured by its areal extent, although this includes most of the nation's major population centers. The position of Greenville gives it an advantage over New England

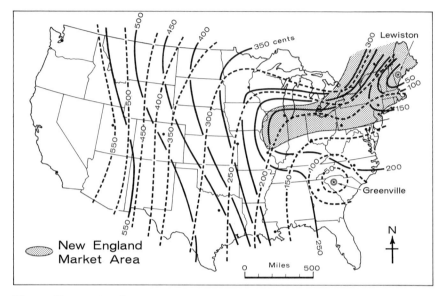

Figure 16.3. The division of the national market for cotton textiles between a New England location and one in the South, based on 1952 freight rates. (*Source of Data.* Committee of New England, National Planning Association, 1954, 453.) *Note.* The dots on the map indicate data sample points.

in the transcontinental rates, so that it can deliver cheaper than Lewiston to all markets west of the Mississippi, as well as to parts of the upper Mid-West. An interesting feature of the transport-cost surfaces is the steep rise from New England into the protected market of eastern Ontario and southern Quebec, where the South cannot hope to compete, compared with the relatively low rates to the highly competitive markets such as Chicago and St. Louis.

2. The second illustration introduces a little more complexity. The data are derived from an actual feasibility study for a firm seeking a site from which to distribute paper products to a specific market in the eastern half of the United States.* Four possible locations were identified on the basis of low production costs: Roanoke Rapids and Wilson in North Carolina, Bristol in Virginia, and a site in eastern Tennessee (Figure 16.4). The problem is to find out how plants at these locations would split up a market comprising about fifty cities, assuming that each city is served by the plant from which delivered price is lowest.

---

* The author is grateful to The Fantus Company, Chicago, for providing the data on which this illustration is based.

THE MARKET, AND AREAL VARIATIONS IN DEMAND 307

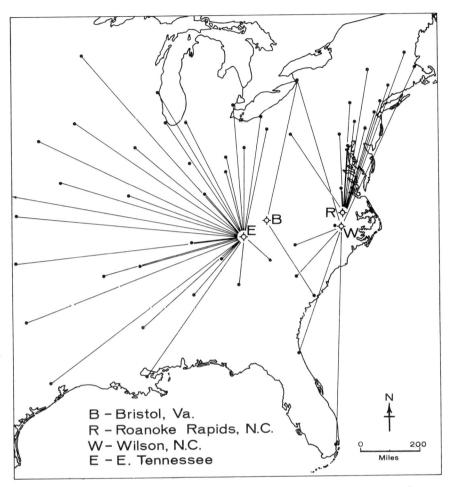

Figure 16.4. The division of a market for paper between four plants located in an area with low production costs. (*Source of Data.* The Fantus Company, Chicago.)

For the sake of simplicity it is assumed that there is no significant difference between the four locations with respect to production costs, so that if the cost of transport is added to production cost in determining the price quoted the consumer, each city can be allocated to one of the locations on the basis of the freight rate alone. In Figure 16.4, lines are drawn between locations and markets to connect each city with the location from which the cost of transport is lowest. The eastern Tennessee location clearly controls most of the market, with a well-defined sales area. Roanoke Rapids and Wilson serve a much smaller number of places, and Bristol is almost squeezed out of the market altogether by the position of competitors. Which locations would be viable and whether more than one plant would serve the market more efficiently than a single one in eastern Tennessee depends on what the minimum output consistent with profitable operation is, and on the relationship between output and scale economies.

The map is interesting for some of the anomalies that arise from the freight-rate structures along certain routes. For example, Bristol has a very low rate to Charleston, which enables it to take this market from the closer plant at Wilson, and both Bristol and Wilson, with equal rates to Buffalo, can serve this city cheaper than can Roanoke Rapids. These complications often make it difficult to draw the neat market-area boundaries shown in theoretical diagrams, and prevent the identification of market areas on the basis of distance alone.

3. The final illustration introduces the further complication of production costs varying between plants. Six Pennsylvania cities have been selected—Erie, Pittsburgh, Altoona, Harrisburgh, Scranton, and Philadelphia—and the problem is to find out how plants located in each city would split up the northeastern part of the United States into market areas on the basis of freight costs and possible differences in production costs. The industry is an imaginary one, but all of the other data are real.

Differences in production costs arise from intercity variations in the cost of labor and materials. Labor costs have been worked out on the basis of an output of 10,000 cwt per week requiring one hundred production workers, ten order clerks and ten stenographers, at the average rate of pay actually in force in the six cities or nearby places. The total weekly wage bill is divided by 10,000 to give the cost per cwt. The material costs are calculated on the basis of specific quantities of castings (which are transported at Class 70 rates), components (Class 100) and containers (Class 85), obtainable from specific sources and with the freight cost added to an assumed cost at source. Table 16.1 lists these figures for the individual cities. There is a range of almost 50¢ between the least-cost

Table 16.1 Production Costs (Dollars per Hundredweight of Output) for an Imaginary Industry in Six Pennsylvania Cities

City	Labor	Materials	Total
Altoona	0.86	1.57	2.43
Erie	1.13	1.52	2.65
Harrisburgh	0.92	1.54	2.46
Philadelphia	1.08	1.53	2.61
Pittsburgh	1.27	1.53	2.80
Scranton	0.78	1.51	2.29

Source. Freight-rate schedules and Department of Labor wage-rate figures.

location at Scranton and the high-cost location in Pittsburgh, due almost entirely to the considerable difference in the wages of production workers.

To divide the territory into market areas it is necessary to add the outgoing freight cost from the six cities to the production costs, and to find out where the delivered (f.o.b.) price would be lowest from which city. The procedure is similar to that employed in the previous chapter, in the illustration of spatial variations in the cost of galvanized steel. For each of the cities the actual freight rate is found for a sample of twenty cities within the area under review. Then a freight-cost/distance profile is interpolated. When the spatially constant production cost is added for each city the delivered price for any distance can be read from the graphs, and isoline intervals can then be worked out.

The cost/distance graphs and the final market-area map are shown in Figure 16.5. Each city has its own distinctive profile of freight rate against distance. The scatter of the dots shows that the curves give only an approximation to the actual situations, but they do take into account such local considerations as the relatively high cost of short distance hauls from Harrisburgh, and provide a result accurate enough for the present purpose. A more precise market-area delimitation would be possible only after the examination of freight rates from each location to a much larger number of places than the sample used here. As the production cost is included in each graph, the figures up the vertical axis can be taken to refer to delivered price.

Delivered price isolines are drawn as concentric circles about each of the cities, and market-area boundaries are defined on the conventional basis of identifying points of indifference (that is, the same delivered price) between two suppliers. Harrisburgh is a relatively low-cost location, but its steep freight-cost profile over the shorter distances deprives the city of this competitive advantage. Despite its low production costs, Scranton cannot extend its market area very far in the direction of its competitors, but has New England to itself. Altoona, which seems to be rather hemmed in by Pittsburgh and Harrisburgh, is able to widen its market area at the expense of both these neighbors in a southerly direction, by virtue of relatively low transport costs as distance increases. The high-cost location of Pittsburgh can sell only in the area to the southwest, and eventually (just beyond the left-hand border of the map) its market area is terminated completely. Philadelphia, with its relatively high costs and peripheral location, has the smallest market area, and is only just able to keep Harrisburgh from serving the city itself. Although this map is based on an imaginary industry and incomplete cost data, it probably gives a fairly accurate representation of the comparative advantage of the six cities with respect to serving the regional market.

310 SOME EMPIRICAL APPLICATIONS

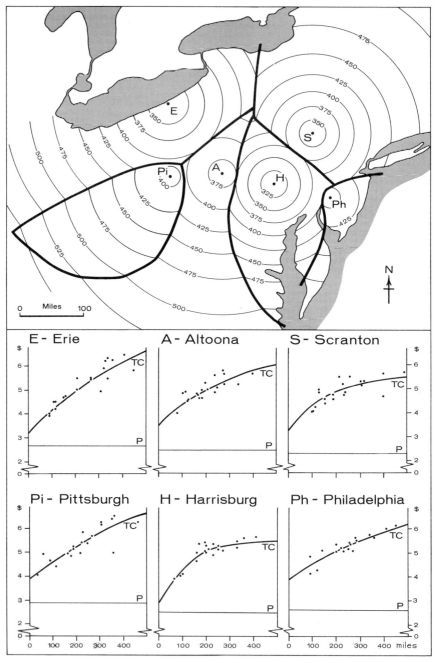

Figure 16.5. Market areas for six Pennsylvania cities for an imaginary industry, based on actual freight rates and production costs. Transport-cost/distance profiles and production-cost differentials for the cities are shown in the lower part of the illustration. P = production cost of the plant; TC = total cost (production cost plus transport cost).

In practice, of course, there is no guarantee that a given consumer will purchase from the plant within whose market area he appears to be on the basis of delivered price. All kinds of special arrangements and supplier/consumer deals can complicate market-area situations, and customers are no more prone to rational behavior than are businessmen. However, the procedures outlined here provide a basis from which the economically rational spatial allocation of the market can be worked out in any given circumstances, as a model against which to test reality.

17

More Complete Analyses of Comparative Locational Advantage

Thus far, in Part Four, the attention has been confined to single input cost surfaces and the identification of areal variations in comparative advantage with respect to demand. These are the basic building blocks from which more complete industrial location models can be constructed. This chapter illustrates some more comprehensive approaches, involving fuller comparative-cost analyses and the combination of cost and demand factors.

17.1 COMPARATIVE-COST STUDIES

The identification of areal variations in total cost for any plant or industry is a difficult matter, involving the analysis of a number of different input cost patterns. But the problems certainly are not insurmountable, and a number of fairly complete comparative-cost studies have been published during the past quarter of a century. They tend to be restricted to situations where there are a relatively small number of alternative locations to be evaluated, generally too few for the meaningful application of cost-surface techniques. And they have been mainly confined to industries in which the number of inputs is small.

Primary metal industries have been favorite subjects for studies of this kind. A reasonable approximation to total spatially variable costs in alternative locations can generally be derived from data for a single material and a source of fuel, which is largely a matter of finding the appropriate freight cost from the input source to the plant. A number of interesting comparative-cost analyses have been undertaken in *the iron and steel industry*, where the cost of two inputs (iron ore and coal) dominates all other locational considerations. This research will be reviewed in the next chapter, where the iron and steel industry is used for one of three major case studies.

An early comparative-cost study of another primary metal-manufacturing industry is one by Cotterill (1950) on *zinc smelting*. This is a weight-losing material-oriented process, with 1.858 tons of concentrate needed to produce one ton of slab zinc and material costs comprising 41.6 percent of the value of the product at the time of the study. The main materials used are zinc concentrates and coke, to which must be added less significant quantities of fire clay, chemicals, and water. The concentrate is mainly produced in Couer d'Alene, the southern Rockies, the Tri-State area occupying the contiguous corners of Kansas, Missouri, and Arkansas, and the New York-New Jersey area, while the major source of coke is the coalfield belt extending from Illinois to Pennsylvania. The market for slab zinc and the biproducts of the smelting process is largely within the major manufacturing belt.

Cotterill is primarily concerned with the comparative advantage of alternative smelter locations with respect to the major inward freight item (the transportation of concentrate) and the cost of shipping the slab zinc output to the consumer. The case of production for the Pittsburgh market is considered, examining four smelter locations near material sources (Anaconda, Dumas, Fort Smith, and East St. Louis) and one close to the market (Donora, Pennsylvania). Eight possible sources of concentrate are taken into account, and Table 17.1 summarizes the inward and

Table 17.1 Freight Costs (Dollars per Ton of Output) at Five Zinc-Smelting Locations Serving the Pittsburgh Market

Location	In-Freight (1.858 Tons of Concentrate)	Out-Freight (1.0 Ton of Slab Zinc)	Total Freight Cost
Donora, Pa.[a]	12.10	1.30	13.40
East St. Louis, Ill.[a]	6.32	5.60	11.92
Fort Smith, Ark.[a]	3.27	9.40	12.67
Dumas, Tex.[b]	6.85	11.40	18.25
Anaconda, Mont.[c]	2.78	11.99	14.77

Source. Cotterill (1950, 153-154). The figures refer to 1946.
[a] Concentrate from Tri-State (Kansas, Missouri, Oklahoma) area.
[b] Concentrate from Magdalena, New Mexico.
[c] Concentrate from Butte, Montana.

outward freight costs per ton of output for the five locations assuming that each uses the material source with the lowest freight costs. East St. Louis appears to be the best location from which to serve this particular market, although the Pennsylvania location can supply Pittsburgh cheaper than two of the material-oriented smelters when freight costs alone are considered. Generally the smelters near the material sources are at an advantage, however, as Table 17.2 shows. Here freight costs

Table 17.2 Total Freight Costs (Dollars per Ton of Output) at Five Zinc-Smelting Locations Serving the Pittsburgh Market, with Respect to Different Material Sources

Source of Zinc Concentrate	Smelting locations				
	Anaconda	Dumas	Fort Smith	East St. Louis	Donora
Butte, Mont.	14.77			27.45	28.90
Magdalena, N. Mex.		18.25	19.60	25.45	26.90
Miami, Ariz.		23.58	24.85	24.65	26.10
Murray, Utah		24.70	24.63	24.00	25.50
Sahuarita, Ariz.		22.77	24.04	23.85	25.30
Metaline Falls, Wash.	22.19			22.98	24.40
Hanover, N. Mex.		18.55	19.60	17.85	19.35
Tri-State District			12.67	11.92	13.40

Source. Cotterill (1950, 103). The figures are for 1946.

are compared for the same locations and market with respect to various sources of concentrate, showing that there is no source that would enable the market-located smelter at Donora to produce cheaper than a material-located plant using the same source. These figures emphasize again the freight-cost advantage of East St. Louis, which is strengthened by the fact that slab zinc is sold in the United States under a basing-point system with East St. Louis as the base (Cotterill, 1950, 106).

From the analysis of freight costs, Cotterill concludes that "If a zinc smelter lies along the line-of-haul to the market, the freight-rate structure tends to nullify any advantage to be gained by choice of geographical location, from the standpoint of raw material and market locative factors." To this rule he adds the following exception: "In the absence of a zinc smelter AT the market, freight-rate structure does not equalize the total freight cost between smelters but allows a more normal tendency to favour the raw material-orientated plant" (Cotterill, 1950, 102). In other words, a market-located plant has to be right at the point of consumption if it is to compete with the material-located smelter; being near the market, like the Donora plant, is not quite good enough.

After access to material, Cotterill designates supply of fuel and the labor situation as "controlling" factors in smelter location. Certain sites may gain considerable advantage from being able to use natural gas instead of coke as fuel, and the level of wages and the productivity of labor tend to favor some parts of the country over others. All the controlling factors were found to operate, in varying degrees, in favor of the southwestern region of the United States as a location for low-cost zinc production. Brief consideration was also given to certain "modifying" and "minor" factors, including the market, politics, transportation, and the supply of capital. Cotterill's study thus comprises one of the most thorough of the early comparative-cost analyses. In particular it provides an interesting practical illustration of something akin to the locational line situations (material source → production point → market) depicted in certain elementary theoretical statements (for example, Renner, 1947), and of how the relative importance of the various causal factors in location can be assessed from a farily limited amount of cost data.

Another interesting comparative-cost analysis in metal manufacturing is a study of *the aluminum industry* by Krutilla (1955). This activity involves three separate stages: the production of refined ore (alumina) from bauxite, the electrolytic reduction of refined ore to metallic aluminum, and the fabrication of aluminum products. The refining normally takes place at the source of material, since two tons of bauxite are required to produce one ton of alumina. The reduction of the refined ore to aluminum is undertaken in low-cost power areas because of the large quantity of electrical energy used. Fabrication is performed near the market, as the metal in its unfinished form moves at a lesser freight rate than the final product. The three stages in aluminum manufacturing are thus generally found to be spatially separated.

Krutilla is mainly interested in the second stage—the reduction of ore to aluminum. He attempts to assess the comparative advantage of three regions of the United States: the Tennessee Valley, the Texas Gulf Coast, and the Pacific Northwest. The approximate combination of inputs required for the production of one ton of aluminum is 18,000 kilowatt-hours of electric energy, two tons of refined ore, one-half ton of carbon, and sixteen man-hours of labor, and the market comprises the principal aluminum fabricating centers.

For electricity, the hydroelectric potential of the Columbia Basin gives the Pacific Northwest the advantage over the other two regions, with the natural gas sources putting the Gulf Coast in second place. The increasing dependence on imported ores makes the Gulf Coast the least-cost location for supplies of alumina, with the Tennessee Valley second. The regions come in the same order for carbon costs, although the differences between them are not very great. Average hourly wage rates tend to favor the Tennessee Valley in terms of labor costs, with the Gulf Coast second.

The precise regional cost comparisons for these four items are shown in Table 17.3. The relatively high cost of power in the Tennessee Valley

Table 17.3 Estimated Production Costs (Dollars per Ton) for the Manufacture of Aluminum in Three Regions

Input	Tennessee Valley	Texas Gulf Coast	Pacific Northwest
Alumina (2 tons)	97.00	94.00	106.36
Power (18,000 kwh)	88.20	72.00–78.90	49.50–58.60
Labor (16 man-hours)	21.60	23.20	27.52
Carbon (½ ton)	19.50	18.74	21.98
Total	226.40	207.94–212.84	205.36–214.36

Source. Krutilla (1955, 274–278).

is sufficient to more than offset the advantages of this region with respect to labor costs and access to material, making this the highest-cost region. The figures for the Gulf Coast and the Northwest are so close that the difference could be within the margin of error of the estimates.

A full evaluation of the regional cost position requires the addition of the cost of transport to the market. As a rough indication, the freight rate per ton of alumina from each region to eight principal rolling mills was determined (Table 17.4). The Tennessee Valley appears to have a defi-

Table 17.4 Estimated Transport Cost (Dollars per Ton) for Shipping Pig Aluminum to Rolling Mills from Three Regions

Rolling Mills	Tennessee Valley	Texas Gulf Coast	Pacific Northwest
Edgewater, N.J.	20.00	25.00	26.38
New Kensington, Pa.	18.20	22.00	23.11
Louisville, Ky.	8.00	19.00	21.58
Alcoa, Tenn.	5.00	18.00	23.11
Chicago, Ill.	19.20	17.50	17.44
Davenport, Iowa	19.40	16.00	17.44
Sheffield, Ala.	5.00	18.80	21.58
Spokane, Wash.	19.84	19.84	7.00
Average	14.33	19.62	19.70

Source. Krutilla (1955, 279).

nite advantage over the other regions, but not enough to compensate for its relatively high cost of input assembly as indicated in Table 17.3. Again, the figures for the Gulf Coast and the Pacific Northwest are so close that without further information it is not possible to say that one is clearly a better location for aluminum production than the other.

Despite the apparent similarity of the cost situation in these two regions, Krutilla found that the preponderant share of new capacity in the industry had been erected in Texas and Louisiana. Two possible reasons were offered for this; the first is that despite the Northwest's enormous hydroelectric potential, generating capacity has not been developed as rapidly as the aluminum industry's sharply increased demand, while the other is a regional advantage arising from a government tax amortization policy which favors Louisiana to an extent which represents a saving of between eight and nine dollars per ton of aluminum (Krutilla, 1955, 280). The Kaiser Aluminum Company's Port Chalmette location near New Orleans is attributed to unequal regional benefits accruing from tax amortization, an example of an occasion where such a factor can determine the choice between otherwise equally attractive locations. The alternative in this case was Spokane, where there are other Kaiser facilities, and which had a slight cost advantage over Port Chalmette under normal depreciation conditions (Krutilla, 1955, 281, Table 2).

Moving away from metal manufacturing, a good example of the comparative-cost approach applied to a different kind of activity is a study of *the synthetic fibers industry* by Airov (1956, 1959). The major location factors in this industry are regional differences in the cost of labor, fuel and power, transportation costs on the shipment of the major chemical inputs or the materials from which they are manufactured, transportation costs on the delivery of the finished product, and the regional availability of an abundant supply of water. Airov's approach is first to determine regions within which plant location is technically feasible, and then to evaluate the comparative cost advantage of hypothetical locations in each region. The two major attractive forces appeared to be the Gulf Coast petrochemical industry as the major source of materials for artificial fibers, and the main markets in the textile-manufacturing regions of New England and the South. However, within the textile regions the Middle Atlantic has substantial chemical industries that might provide materials, as well as its textile market.

One of the comparative cost tables prepared by Airov is reproduced in a simplified form in Table 17.5. The technical procedures and assumptions involved in the derivation of the figures can be found in the original source, and only summary comments are offered here. The manufacture of synthetic fibers is clearly labor oriented as far as the spatially variable

Table 17.5 Regionally Variable Costs at Hypothetical Locations for the Production of Nylon Staple Fiber (Dollars per 100 Pounds)

Plant Locations	Transport Cost of 250 Pounds Nylon Salt	(Difference Relative to Orange, Texas)			Total Labor Costs	Transport Cost of 100 Pounds of Fiber to National Market	Total Costs for Items Listed
		Fuel Cost	Power Cost				
Orange, Tex.	0.00	0.00	0.00		18.92	1.38–2.17	20.30–21.09
Institute, W. Va.	0.29[a]	0.00	0.00		17.36	0.98–1.51	18.63–19.16
Boston, Mass.	1.30–1.13[b]	1.56–2.04	0.26–0.34		17.27	1.10–1.72	21.22–22.70
Wilmington, N.C.	0.70–0.90[b]	1.03–1.35	0.17–0.23		17.27	0.96–1.34	20.13–21.09
Mobile, Ala.	0.15[b]	0.42–0.55	0.07–0.09		17.27	1.16–1.63	19.07–19.69
Chattanooga, Tenn.	0.58[b]	0.68–0.89	0.11–0.15		17.27	0.95–1.34	19.59–20.23
Memphis, Tenn.	0.30[b]	0.47–0.61	0.08–0.10		17.27	1.14–1.62	19.26–19.90
Puerto Rico	0.83–1.05	1.03–1.33	0.17–0.22		10.68–14.81	2.65–2.89	15.36–20.30

Source. Adapted from Airov (1956, 299, Table 3).
[a] Cost difference relative to Texas.
[b] Assumes that water transport is preferred to more expensive rail.

cost items are concerned, and by comparison the other inputs shown contribute relatively little to total costs. Airov concludes that there are unlikely to be any synthetic fiber plants located in two of the regions; the Texas Gulf Coast area represented in the table by Orange has a substantial labor-cost penalty, and New England (Boston) has the highest fuel and power costs of any region as well as a transport-cost disadvantage. The textile-manufacturing district of the South appears to be the most attractive general area, and the concentration of existing synthetic fiber plants in Virginia, North Carolina, and South Carolina provides a general confirmation that the recent locational behavior of this industry can be explained by the kind of cost differences identified in Table 17.5.

The most advantageous location, according to the Airov study, is Puerto Rico. Here the low wage rates more than offset the higher costs of the other inputs, but exactly how great the island's advantage is depends on which of a number of alternative assumptions about the likely level of wages is accepted (Airov, 1956, 298, 301). Further investigation of the possibility of production in Puerto Rico led to the conclusion that the labor-cost advantage could more than compensate for high transport costs if sufficient economies of agglomeration could be established through the development of an integrated petrochemical-synthetic fiber complex (Isard, Schooler, and Vietorisz, 1959; Isard, 1960).

These reviews of the zinc, aluminum, and synthetic fibers studies are sufficient to illustrate the kind of practical comparative-cost analyses that have been undertaken in recent years. Other studies of a similar kind include Lindsay (1956) on oil refining and Isard and Schooler (1956, 1959; Isard, 1960) on the petrochemicals industry. These are all related to the Puerto Rico situation outlined above, and represent an important attempt to introduce economies of scale and agglomeration into empirical comparative-cost analysis. There are some more limited studies of costs in alternative locations in Britain, mainly concerned with the possible effects of industrial relocation in accordance with government regional planning policy (Hague and Newman, 1952; Luttrell, 1952, 1962).

Virtually all the existing comparative-cost studies are confined to alternative locations within the same country or region. International comparisons are rare, but one example is provided by a study of manufacturing costs in the United States and Israel undertaken by Hirsch (1967). He considered the possibility of a plant located in Israel being able to compete in the United States market for crystals of the kind used in the manufacture of optical instruments and similar products. An output by value of $200,000 per year was assumed, and details of the costs in Israel as compared with the United States are listed in Table 17.6. Israel's main advantage is in labor costs, as might be expected, but there is also a

Table 17.6 A Comparison of the Cost (Dollars) of Producing and Marketing a Given Output of Crystals for the United States Market from Locations in the United States and Israel

Item	United States	Israel
Labor		
Production	59,400	23,200
Office and service	28,800	9,700
Total	88,200	32,900
Other Production Costs		
Raw material	2,600	2,700
Electricity	2,300	1,800
Rent and maintenance	12,000	5,000
Parts and supplies	8,000	10,000
Depreciation	15,000	15,000
Total	39,900	34,500
Shipping and Marketing		
Shipping and customs		9,300
Sales employees	19,200	40,800
Office and sales costs	18,100	25,200
Total	37,300	66,000
Total costs	147,200	142,700

Source. Hirsch (1967, 91–107).

slight overall saving in other production costs. The cost of shipping this high-value product to the United States is relatively small, but when the cost of maintaining overseas sales staff and office facilities is added the total shipping and marketing costs are almost twice as high from Israel as they would be from a site within the United States. Nevertheless, Israel appears to have a slight advantage over the domestic producer when all costs are taken into account. Careful international cost analyses like this one can be of assistance in determining what kind of goods certain developing countries might profitably manufacture for sale abroad.

17.2 THE ANATOMY OF A COMPARATIVE-COST ANALYSIS

The various illustrations just considered have concentrated on the results of comparative-cost studies rather than on the actual methods by which the figures are compiled. Previous discussions of areal variations in the cost of single inputs and the structure of freight rates will have indicated

Table 17.7 Specifications of a Plant in the Electronics Industry

Financial

Gross annual sales	$3,200,000
Cost of goods sold	2,528,000
Gross profit	672,000
Nonhourly payroll, sales, etc.	400,000
Income before taxes	272,000

Labor

Production (65 females, 32 males)	97
Toolmakers, machinists (males)	12
Maintenance	6
Miscellaneous	18
Office	7
Total	140

Raw Materials

Steel-strip (coils)	2,600 cwt
Brass and copper strip	3,600 cwt
Aluminum strip	26 cwt
Plastic laminated sheets (bakelite)	450 cwt
Screw machine parts	250 cwt

Power

300 kw, 120,000 kwh of electricity per month (power factor 0.81; 375 kva; 402 hp)

Fuel

1500 therms/month; 150,000 cubic ft/month of gas (1000 btu content)

Water

300,000 gallons/month

Investment

Real estate (land)	10 acres
Buildings	40,000 sq ft
Inventories	$400,000
Machinery and Equipment	$200,000

Outbound Shipments

6,200 cwt/year of small electronic devices shipped at LTL rates

Source. Fantus (1962).

some of the problems involved in compiling estimates for total costs in alternative locations. But a number of important matters of detail relating to just what has to be included in this kind of analysis, and how various figures are arrived at, remain to be discussed. The best way of doing this is by means of an example.

The case to be used for illustration is a comparison of costs in twelve Canadian locations, prepared by a prominent firm of industrial location consultants (Fantus, 1962). The number of locations and the number of cost items evaluated is greater than in any of the studies discussed above. The investigation is based on the characteristics of an imaginary firm in the electronics industry, manufacturing devices such as attachment plugs and caps, snap switches, connectors, and fittings. All of the data used are real.

Before any study of this kind can be undertaken it is necessary to compile certain information relating to the specification of the plant and its combination of inputs. This is listed in summary form in Table 17.7. For the purpose of this analysis the spatially variable cost items to be evaluated are divided into five categories—labor, freight, occupancy, taxes, and utilities—and each of these are examined in turn.

The analysis of labor costs is confined to wage earners, since it is assumed that the salaries of managerial personnel will be the same regardless of location. Three different approaches were used in the determination of realistic wage rates in the twelve different locations: inquiries were made of the local industrial promotion organizations, the published wage statistics were examined, and information was solicited from a sample of existing firms in each of the cities. Information from the local sources was important in determining the fringe benefits that should be added to the standard hourly wage rates. These additional payments for labor can be very significant cost items with substantial areal variations, as is shown in Table 17.8.

Freight costs can be subdivided into the inbound and outbound components. Five materials are involved in the inbound freight bill (Table 17.7), but the brass, copper, and aluminum strip are all sold on an equal delivered price basis and can thus be disregarded in the location analysis. Of the three remaining materials, the steel strip is sold on a modified basing point system whereby the purchaser pays the freight from the nearest mill, the plastic sheets come from Toronto and are sold f.o.b., and the small volume of screw parts was assumed to come in LCL quantities f.o.b. from Montreal or Toronto. The complete figures for the variable inbound freight costs are listed in Table 17.9.

In calculating outbound freight costs, estimates of the likely consumption of the product in different cities were made based on income figures. The calculation was confined to the seventeen most important cities, and

Table 17.8 The Components of Labor Costs (Dollars) in the Electronics Industry in Twelve Canadian Cities

City	Hourly Labor Cost		Fringe Benefits		Total Annual Labor Costs
	Average Hourly Rate	Annual Cost	Hourly Fringe Benefits	Annual Cost	
Winnipeg	1.80	525,000	0.38	110,700	635,700
Brandon	1.71	498,300	0.32	93,200	591,500
Portage la Prairie	1.62	473,100	0.30	87,400	560,500
Montreal	1.93	562,600	0.44	128,100	690,700
Toronto	2.07	602,200	0.54	157,200	759,400
Vancouver	2.14	623,700	0.60	174,700	798,400
Hamilton	2.28	663,500	0.66	192,200	855,700
Calgary	2.08	605,100	0.56	163,100	768,200
Edmonton	2.04	595,000	0.49	142,700	737,700
Windsor	2.31	672,800	0.69	200,900	873,700
Regina	2.06	599,300	0.52	151,400	750,700
Saskatoon	1.89	550,300	0.42	122,300	672,600

Source. Fantus (1962).

the cost of distributing the appropriate quantity of the product to each was worked out from the freight-rate schedules, to give the total outbound freight bill for each of the twelve locations.

The occupancy costs consist of the expenditures involved in the acquisition of land, construction of the premises, financing, and the mainte-

Table 17.9 Variable Inbound Freight Costs (Dollars per Year) for an Electronics Firm in Twelve Canadian Cities

City	Strip Steel	Laminated Sheets	Screw Machine Parts	Annual Variable Freight Cost
Winnipeg	5,096	180	148	5,424
Brandon	5,694	200	161	6,055
Portage la Prairie	5,330	186	153	5,669
Toronto	988	0	15	1,003
Hamilton	390	0	21	411
Windsor	2,106	0	72	2,178
Montreal	3,016	0	15	3,031
Regina	6,760	240	187	7,187
Saskatoon	7,644	256	197	8,097
Vancouver	11,986	401	292	12,679
Calgary	9,074	318	238	9,630
Edmonton	9,074	311	233	9,618

Source. Fantus (1962).

Table 17.10 Occupancy Costs (Dollars per Year) for an Electronics Firm in Twelve Canadian Cities

City	Land Cost (10 Acres of Improved Industrial Land)	Building Cost (40,000 sq ft)	Total Land and Building Cost	Annual Amortization Cost (Land and Building)	Annual Building Maintenance Cost	Estimated Total Annual Occupancy Cost
Winnipeg	45,000	332,000	377,000	35,500	6,600	43,100
Brandon	10,000	320,000	330,000	31,900	6,400	38,300
Portage la Prairie	10,000	316,000	326,000	31,500	6,300	37,800
Montreal	300,000	350,000	650,000	60,500	5,300	65,800
Toronto	200,000	396,000	596,000	55,500	5,000	60,500
Vancouver	60,000	406,000	466,000	45,100	5,100	50,200
Hamilton	100,000	396,000	496,000	46,200	5,000	51,200
Calgary	50,000	342,000	392,000	37,900	5,100	43,000
Edmonton	70,000	360,000	430,000	41,600	6,300	47,900
Windsor	50,000	396,000	446,000	41,500	5,000	46,500
Regina	35,000	316,000	351,000	33,900	6,300	40,200
Saskatoon	30,000	316,000	346,000	33,500	6,300	39,800

Source. Fantus (1962).

nance of the property (Table 17.10). Data on land costs were obtained by inquiry in the cities concerned, and building costs were worked out from estimates provided by local contractors. The amortization figure was based on the prevailing interest rate for a loan over 20 years, which was found to vary between 7 and 7½ percent per year. Maintenance costs vary from 1 to 2 percent per year, depending on local climatic conditions.

Municipal and provincial taxes could be estimated precisely only with the assistance of the local officials in each city under consideration. Six different items had to be evaluated: real property tax and business tax at the municipal level, and the provincial taxes on motor fuel, motor vehicle licenses, sales, and income. The relevant figures for income and sales on which the tax calculation was based were listed in Table 17.7.

The utilities bill includes the cost of power, water, sewerage (where applicable) and fuel. The data on which the estimates were made are again as shown in Table 17.7.

When all of these items have been evaluated, the estimates of total spatially variable costs can be compiled for each location. This is shown in Table 17.11, along with the figures for each of the five major items included. The least-cost location is Portage la Prairie, while the highest costs are in Windsor. In general the highest-cost locations are in Ontario, the main exception being Vancouver with its high freight bill. The differences in total costs are largely a reflection of the figures for labor, which are subject to very considerable areal variations. The industry in question is highly labor-intensive insofar as its spatially variable costs are concerned, and differences in the cost of the other items have little bearing on locational choice.

This represents the kind of investigation that locational consultants or individual firms might undertake in order to determine the best location for a new factory or branch plant. A very similar study of eleven Midwestern cities can be found in Haber, McKean, and Taylor (1959, 341–354), where the cost of operating a metal stamping plant was evaluated. Given the necessary time and resources, this approach can be applied to much larger numbers of locations, to provide comparative-cost data from which a surface of total spatially variable costs can be constructed. An illustration of such an application is included in the next chapter (Section 18.3).

17.3 COMBINING COST AND DEMAND FACTORS

The type of comparative-cost analyses outlined above suffer from one major deficiency which limits their value as general models for eval-

Table 17.11 Annual Spatially Variable Operating Costs (Dollars) for an Electronics Firm in Twelve Canadian Cities

City	Labor	Freight	Occupancy	Taxes	Utilities	Annual Operating Cost
Winnipeg	635,700	23,600	43,100	20,500	18,000	740,900
Brandon	591,500	29,600	38,300	15,300	20,600	695,300
Portage la Prairie	560,500	27,200	37,800	14,100	21,200	660,800
Montreal	690,700	21,600	65,800	37,200	14,700	830,000
Toronto	759,400	19,100	60,500	21,600	17,900	878,500
Vancouver	798,400	48,700	50,200	27,900	19,300	944,500
Hamilton	855,700	18,800	51,200	37,400	13,700	976,800
Calgary	768,200	30,400	43,000	20,700	18,500	880,800
Edmonton	737,700	30,600	47,900	20,700	20,000	856,900
Windsor	873,700	23,900	46,500	35,100	14,400	993,600
Regina	750,700	30,900	40,200	21,100	23,100	866,000
Saskatoon	672,600	38,000	39,800	20,700	19,100	790,200

Source. Fantus (1962).

uating spatial variations in locational advantage. This deficiency is that the market is considered only through its effect on the outbound freight bill, within the framework of the aggregate travel model. No attempt is made to incorporate the demand factor proper, by allowing for the complex reciprocal relationship between locational choice and the volume of demand or total revenue.

The construction of an operational location model to include both cost and demand factors is very difficult indeed. Some possible approaches were indicated in the theoretical analyses of Parts Two and Three, but the data used for demonstration purposes were all imaginary. It is the practical difficulty of adequately measuring the demand factor which is the major obstacle to the application of these more comprehensive industrial location models in empirical inquiry.

Most attempts to combine cost and demand factors to date have relied heavily on the market potential model to measure the effect of location on the volume of demand or revenue. Soon after the publication of the original paper by Harris (1954) referred to in the previous section, Dunn (1956) tried to combine the potential and aggregate travel (transport cost) models demonstrated by Harris in a study of the state of Florida. He produced surfaces of market potential and transport costs to the market, and then attempted to combine the two in a composite surface based on an *index of location*. Dunn's argument was that both market potential and transport costs are relevant to most firms, and that in any location an advantage with respect to one may be offset by a disadvantage with respect to the other. Dunn expresses potential and transport cost as indexes, with the maximum potential point and minimum transport-cost point equal to 100, and multiplies the two together for each of his data units (counties) to give what he terms a weighted transport-cost index. This figure is then re-indexed so that the county with the highest market potential is given a weighted transport-cost index of 100. Further manipulation of these indexes (Dunn, 1956, 187–189) produces the final index of location, which in effect measures the differential between market potential and transportation costs. Since it is advantageous for a location to have high market potential and low transport costs, the argument is: the smaller the difference between the two indexes, the better the location.

Unfortunately, Dunn's assumptions and procedures can be criticized on a number of counts (Isard, 1960, 518–527; Ray, 1965, 33–36). The market potential and aggregate travel models are attempts to measure the effect of the market on plant location under two different sets of assumptions, as was indicated in Chapter 16. To combine them in order to take into account both reduction of demand with distance from the plant and the cost of distribution thus raises both conceptual and practical difficulties. Conceptually, it cannot be assumed that the consumer has at the same time a fixed demand and one that is in some way sensitive to distance from the source of supply. It is possible in practice to find the geographical distribution of sales from a plant at the point of maximum potential and then use the aggregate travel model to find the point from which this market could be served for the lowest transport cost, but this would serve no useful purpose. Unless the points of maximum market potential and minimum aggregate travel coincide, a move from the former to reduce transport costs to the market will change the distribution of sales as worked out by the potential model, and hence upset the aggregate travel calculation.

A more profitable line of inquiry is to attempt a combination of the demand factor and spatial variations in the cost of inputs. The fusion of the comparative-cost approach and market potential is suggested by Isard (1960, 562), where he raises the possibility of adding, say, labor costs to Dunn's analysis. The interaction of a market potential surface and a total cost surface would come close conceptually to the model developed in Part Three, with potential acting as a surrogate for total revenue. But this raises the question of the interrelationship between cost and revenue. It would be quite possible to compute a market potential surface (calibrated to represent dollars of revenue rather than volume of sales) and then to identify a total cost surface by working out for a sample of locations the total cost of producing and distributing the required quantity of output. However, such a procedure would imply that the level of sales attainable at a given location was unrelated to production costs, whereas in reality scale might affect average cost, cost might affect price, and price might influence sales and revenue (which have already been determined by the potential model). And to start with a total cost surface and then proceed to a demand or revenue surface is equally tortuous, since both average cost and total cost can be a function of volume of sales.

Empirical research has not yet dealt with these very difficult problems. However, some attempts have been made to extend the market potential model by the addition of input costs, and two studies of industrial location in Ontario are of particular interest. In the first, Kerr and Spelt (1960) tried to explain the areal variations in industrial growth in southern Ontario during the postwar period. The observed facts are that the most rapid growth has been in the metropolitan area around Toronto, with moderate growth in the southwest along the northern shore of Lake Erie and only a small increase in the east. In attempting to account for this, the authors emphasize the two factors of market accessibility and the cost and stability of labor. The market potential and the aggregate travel model are both used to assess the advantage of different areas with respect to the market in southern Ontario and Quebec. The surfaces (Kerr and Spelt, 1960, 15–16, Figures 3 and 4) show Toronto and Montreal as the most attractive locations, and suggest that eastern Ontario is at no disadvantage when compared with the northern Erie shore. Labor costs are then introduced into the analysis. Wage rates for a variety of different occupations indicate that eastern Ontario and the Georgian Bay region have the advantage over the relatively high-cost locations in Toronto, Montreal, the Niagara-Hamilton area, and the southwestern corner of the Province. Labor stability, measured by the number of working days lost per worker, shows the lowest levels in eastern Ontario, the Georgian Bay region and the Middle Grand River area. Kerr and Spelt were thus unable to explain satisfactorily the fundamental contrast between the eastern and southwestern parts of southern Ontario.

This problem was followed up a few years later by Ray (1965, 1967). He developed the hypothesis that the major explanatory factor missing in the earlier study was the regional impact of United States capital and entrepreneurship operating through what he termed an *economic-shadow effect* on Ontario manufacturing and economic development. He suggested that manufacturing activity comprises two independent but overlapping spatial patterns, one controlled locally and the other externally. "Locally controlled industry is located in accordance with internal economic factors and hence with market potential; externally controlled industry is located in accordance with economic shadow, which takes into account external, or exogenous factors" (Ray, 1965, 25). By economic shadow, Ray simply means the attraction exercised by a region on external or foreign capital and entrepreneurship. Ray constructed a model that combined the concept of market potential with this economic shadow effect, which in the case of Ontario has the north Erie shore and the Niagara to Toronto belt particularly exposed to the influx of United States business. The test of the model showed that it adequately explains the accelerated industrial growth of southwestern Ontario as compared with the retarded growth of eastern Ontario.

Ray's thesis (1965) may be studied with great profit as an illustration of how a market potential model may be constructed, adapted, and tested. Whereas Kerr and Spelt attempted to add the labor-cost factor to demand as measured by market potential, Ray added access to external supplies of two other critical factors of production—capital and enterprise. Ray's isoline maps of the economic shadow effect (Ray, 1965, 135–136, Figures 41 and 42), which give a numerical rating to the possible contact with United States industrial centers, could almost be regarded as surrogates for cost surfaces with respect to capital and the entrepreneurial input. This kind of approach clearly represents a significant step toward the development of a flexible operational model that can accommodate both demand and cost factors.

But much more research remains to be done before a completely satisfactory comprehensive model can be developed for application to the interpretation of real-world situations. At present too much reliance is being placed in empirical research on the market potential model as a measure of the effect of the demand factor. As was indicated in Chapter 16, the market potential model represents rather special demand circumstances, in which sales at any point are predicted as a function of distance or cost of shipping from the plant and some initial measure of the size of the local market. The development and application of models based on more conventional demand functions, with production cost as a variable, could greatly assist in the formulation of an operational model in which there is a better fusion of the cost and demand factors.

17.4 THREE SELECTED EMPIRICAL STUDIES

As a conclusion to this chapter, three studies have been selected for more detailed review. They are particularly useful illustrations of the application of some of the concepts introduced in the theoretical sections of this book. They are of special interest from two points of view: the use of isoline techniques to identify cost surfaces, and the reliance placed on industrial location theory as a basis for the methods of analysis which are adopted.

a. Lindberg on the Swedish Paper Industry

Olof Lindberg's *Studier Over Pappersindustriens Lokalisering* (1951) is one of the most interesting extended empirical studies of industrial location yet to be published. The original (1951) is in Swedish, but contains an English summary (1951, 210–217) which was subsequently published separately (Lindberg, 1953). Lindberg's two major contributions are (1) the accumulation and interpretation of a mass of empirical material on the paper industry in a country where historical records of industrial location are probably better than anywhere else in the world, and (2) his extensive use of isoline techniques. It is the conceptual and technical aspects that are of special interest here, since Lindberg's approach is derived directly from classical variable-cost theory, as developed by Weber and extended by Palander.

Lindberg begins with a historical analysis. Since the first half of the nineteenth century, the paper industry has gone through a number of distinct phases, each characterized by different technical conditions. As technology and industrial organization changed, so did input requirements, and hence the geography of comparative locational advantage. Lindberg uses maps of hypothetical cost isolines (or isovectures) for an imaginary region to suggest how conditions changed between the 1830s and the 1930s. The region has two towns, A (a "central place" with a relatively large market for paper) and H (a seaport dealing with imports and exports). Both towns are located on a river (a); near to the river the land is agricultural, but farther away this is replaced by thinly populated forests. There are two tributary streams (b and c), and the rivers have a number of waterfalls (V) which are ranked in order of capacity by their subscripts (1, 2, ... , 6). Lindberg constructs maps for three points in time, representative of the handmill period, the groundwood period and the chemical pulp period, and these are reproduced in Figure 17.1.

The map for 1830 to 1839 shows conditions representative of the first half of the nineteenth century. Areal variations in the cost of materials and marketing are indicated by the sets of thin isolines, while the thicker ones relate to total costs. During this period the raw materials used in paper making were straw and rags, and these came from the more densely populated areas. Close to the river (a), materials can be regarded as a ubiquity (that is, available at a uniformly low cost), whereas farther away costs rise as is indicated by the increasing closeness of the isolines. The cost of transporting the finished product to the market increases rapidly away from the town A, but as only small amounts of paper are exported, the system of isolines around H is much less tight. The surface of total costs interpolated from the single-input surfaces shows a close correspondence with the pattern of transport costs to the market at A, and not until the distance from this town is quite large does the cost of materials have a significant effect on comparative advantage with respect to total costs. The optimum location thus appears to be at A. But during this period a waterfall was necessary to drive a paper mill, and this diverts the optimum location from A to V_4 which is the nearest water-power site. Although Lindberg did not include them, he implies the existence of a hole in the total-cost surface at the waterfall sites, representing a very steep or vertical rise in power costs with increasing distance from the waterfall.

The second map shows that by the end of the nineteenth century conditions had changed considerably. The raw material is now wood instead of straw and rags, and the cost isolines are close together in the more densely populated areas free of forest but farther apart as the wooded

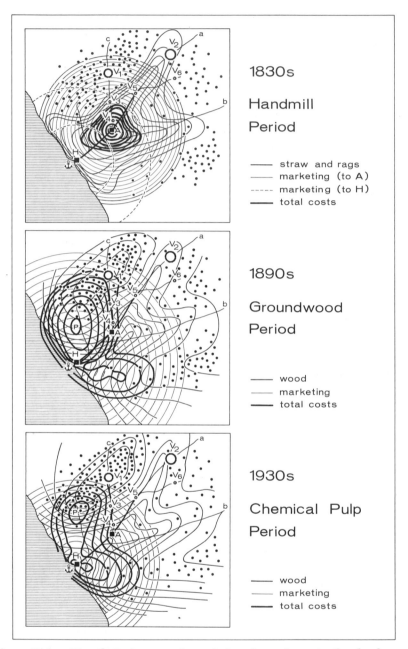

Figure 17.1. Hypothetical cost surfaces during three phases in the development of the Swedish paper industry. (*Source.* Lindberg, 1953, 31–2, Figures 5, 6 and 7.) *Note.* The dots indicate forest areas.

areas are reached. The low-cost areas for material are now well away from the major market for paper. The isolines relating to the cost of transportation to the market now indicate that the advantage appears to have shifted from A to H, by virtue of an increasing export trade. The total-cost surface, which as before includes transport costs only, now indicates an optimum location at P, between the port and one of the major areas of timber resources. But again the need for power to drive the mill is the dominant location factor. Water is still the main source of power, but because the plants are now larger than they were in the first period the amount of power required is much greater. Power cannot be transported from the waterfall, and the optimum is diverted from the least-transport-cost location to the nearest *large* waterfall (V_1).

Conditions during the 1930s are not much different from those prevailing during the second period, as the third map shows. The main difference is that the large waterfalls V_1 and V_2 now drive electric power stations, and technical developments have made it possible to transport this power over long distances at minimal cost. The very steep (or vertical) gradients of power costs in relation to distance have thus been replaced by gradients that are now in effect horizontal. Paper mills need no longer be at water-power sites, and are now free to locate where transport costs are lowest. The map suggests that the best location is actually on the edge of the forests closest to the main market.

Although the three maps in Figure 17.1 represent hypothetical situations and are not based on precise comparative-cost data, they suggest the likely locational characteristics of the paper industry at different time periods. Specifically, Lindberg proposed that the handmill phase would be one of small plants on streams near the main towns, that the groundwood phase would see a shift to the timber areas and the larger water-power sites, and that the chemical pulp period would be one of transport orientation. He attempted to discover how far the location patterns suggested on theoretical grounds actually were in accordance with reality. He found that during the first half of the nineteenth century some of the forest regions of southern Sweden had surprisingly large numbers of paper mills, which seems to be explained by the need to find outlets for the productive capacity of these poor and rather overpopulated districts. At the end of the nineteenth century the paper industry declined in southern Sweden, however, and the main center of activity shifted north to the outlying forest regions west of Lake Vänern, where there were the advantages of water power, timber, and good communications with the port of Götteborg to the west. This development corresponds closely with what is suggested on the second map in Figure 17.1. When the transmission of electric power freed the mills from the need for a water-power site the remoteness of the forest sites became a disadvantage, and many plants in these areas closed down. The location of paper mills during the chemical pulp period, although bearing traces of earlier location patterns, agreed well with the transport orientation suggested on a priori grounds. By constructing hypothetical cost surfaces, and by applying certain principles of Weber's location theory, Lindberg thus was able to offer a reasoned interpretation of locational changes in the Swedish paper industry.

The main part of Lindberg's study attempts to identify the transport-cost situation as it existed in the paper industry at the time in which he wrote. The first variable to be considered is the major material—the forest. In calculating the cost of transport an adaptation of the usual approach must be devised, since the material does not originate at a point as in conventional variable-cost analysis but is gathered from an area. A paper mill requiring a small quantity of timber will be able to obtain it from the surrounding territory at relatively low unit transport cost, but a larger supply requires a larger harvest area and hence higher average transport costs. Each mill thus has its own timber-supply *characteristics*, by which is meant the relationship between the quantity required and the transport cost per unit of volume. This depends on the distribution and density of the timber resources and on the spatial arrangement and freight-rate structure of the transport system.

In order to determine the timber-supply characteristics for a given mill, it is first necessary to construct a transport-cost surface. Lindberg uses actual freight-rate data for the railroads, and the existing pattern of routes. For road transport he assumes a uniform transport surface, that is, movement in any direction with the cost being the same linear function of distance. No great irregularities arise in the rail and road isovectures, but the use of waterways for floating timber may complicate the spatial cost pattern. An example of the timber transport-cost surface for one paper mill is illustrated in Figure 17.2. This shows how the concentric circles representing isovectures for road transport are interrupted by the rail lines, which can move timber further than trucks for the same expenditure. No waterways appear in this map, but examples of how this distorts the pattern of transport costs can be found in a number of the original illustrations (Lindberg, 1951, Figures 29, 31, 32, etc.).

To calculate the cost of timber at any mill the transport-cost surface is superimposed upon a map of the forest areas. Lindberg constructs a dot map on which each dot represents a certain lumber capacity, and adding the dots within a given isovecture produces a figure for the amount of wood which is at the disposal of the mill at a particular cost. Repeating the calculation for different volumes provides the figures from which

ANALYSES OF COMPARATIVE LOCATIONAL ADVANTAGE   335

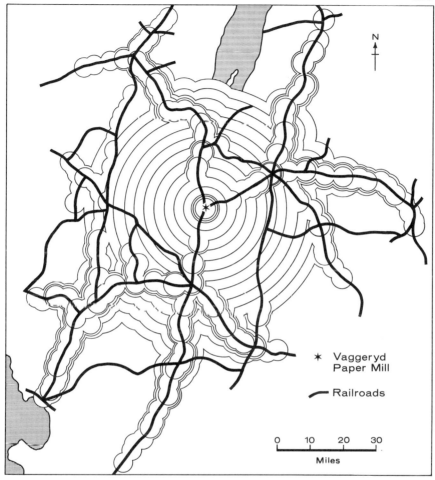

Figure 17.2. A surface of material transport costs for a paper mill at Vaggeryd, Sweden. The isovectures are at intervals of 20 öre per cubic metre of pine wood shipped. Road and rail transport are both included. (*Source.* Lindberg, 1953, 36, Figure 16.)

the mill's curve of unit transport cost against volume can be constructed. Lindberg performs this analysis for about fifty paper and pulp mills in southern Sweden, and all the surfaces and graphs are included in his original monograph (1951).

The next step is the construction of a cost surface for the timber input from the data for individual plants. Two different levels of consumption are established—12,000 and 120,000 cubic meters—and the transport cost for each quantity is obtained for each mill. Then the timber transport-cost surface is derived by isoline interpolation. The surface for a mill consumption of 120,000 cubic meters is illustrated in Figure 17.3, which shows relatively low costs inland and a steeply rising gradient along the coasts.

In addition to timber, quantities of coal, sulphur, and limestone are

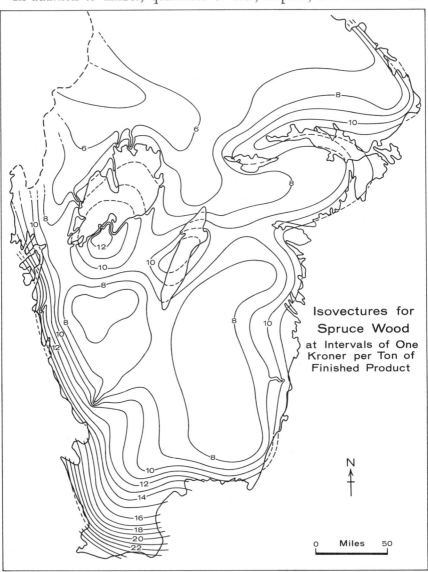

Figure 17.3. A transport-cost surface for spruce pulp-wood in southern Sweden. The figures are in kroner per ton of furnished paper, at a timber consumption of 120,000 cubic meters. (*Source.* Lindberg, 1953, 38, Figure 19.)

required for the process of production. Lindberg evaluates the transport costs on these inputs for each mill, and also the cost of shipping the paper to the market. When these figures are added to the transport cost for timber, a surface of total transport costs can be constructed. The surface for the 120,000 cubic meter level of timber consumption is illustrated in Figure 17.4. The pattern is a complex one, with no clear optimum or cost-minimising location but rather a number of local optima. The surface is punctured by points representing the ports, where costs tend to be somewhat lower than in the surrounding territory.

The timber-cost surface (Figure 17.3) clearly shows that the least-cost locations for the assembly of the main material are inland. But because most of the paper is exported, inland mills are often at a disadvantage when compared with those on or near the coast. Lindberg does not present separate surfaces relating to the cost of serving the market, but he does conclude that areal differences in the cost of materials are in general less significant than differences with regard to the ease and cheapness of communications to the export market (Lindberg, 1953, 40). Lindberg's analysis thus constituted a test of the generally accepted idea that the paper industry is material-oriented in its location, and he found this not to be true. Three tons of wood are required for one ton of the finished product, but as the material is virtually ubiquitous its locational influence is small. This conclusion stresses the important principle that no matter how large an input may be as an element of total costs, it will have a major bearing on locational choice only if the cost of getting it to the plant varies significantly from place to place.

b. Törnqvist on the Swedish Light Clothing Industry

This study closely resembles the one just considered: both are set in Sweden and both are concerned with transport costs. Like Lindberg, Törnqvist (1962) attempts to build up a total transport-cost surface from data for a relatively large number of locations.

The areal frame of reference on which the study is based comprises a subdivision of the country into 182 cells, each 50 by 50 kms. The center points of the cells constitute a regularly spaced system of control points, from which cost isolines can be interpolated with a greater degree of confidence than from points which occur more frequently in some parts of the area than in others.

This study is confined to the cost of transportation, the two components of which are the cost of shipping the one significant material (textile fabrics) and the cost of distributing the finished garments to the market. Since the cost of labor and other nonmaterial inputs is ignored, the results cannot be expected to provide a complete picture of comparative locational advantage. However, the method of analysis is one that can be

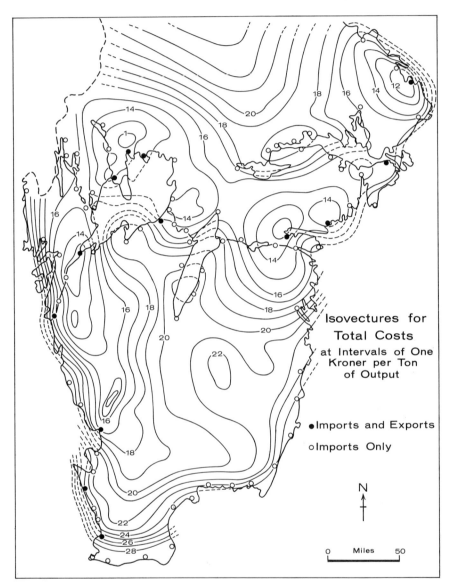

Figure 17.4. Total transport costs for paper manufacturing in southern Sweden. The figures include the cost of transporting spruce pulpwood, coal, sulphur, limestone, and the paper itself. They are expressed in kroner per ton of output, at a timber consumption of 120,000 cubic meters. The ports are indicated by circles, those open being import harbours and those filled in representing export and import harbours. (*Source.* Lindberg, 1953, 39, Figure 20.)

expected to provide a reliable guide to the areas which are the favored locations for an industry sensitive to variations from place to place in transport costs.

There are two sources of materials for the light clothing industry—domestic and foreign. Of the total material used, 58 percent comes from the town of Borås, the major textile-manufacturing center in Sweden. Virtually all the rest is imported; thus, for the purpose of calculating transport costs, it is assumed to originate at the ports of Götcborg, Trelleborg, Malmö, and Hälsingborg. The fabric generally travels by truck, and transport costs between each of the cells containing a material source and each of the rest of the 182 control points is calculated on the basis of existing freight rates.

Of the annual production of light clothing, 40 percent is exported through Göteborg, and for the cost calculation this port is taken to be the market for goods sold abroad. The rest of the output is allocated between the control points in proportion to a measure of the retail trade turnover in each cell, which is a fair indication of the areal distribution of the home market for this product. Transportation costs for each control point are calculated by the aggregate travel method (as in Section 16.1 of Chapter 16), with the estimate of sales as the Q value for each cell or market point and the distance from the assumed plant location measured by the cost of transporting a given volume of output. The T values are computed on the assumption of routes adopting the straight line distances between factories and markets, but using the actual freight rate.

Four transport-cost surfaces are presented in the Törnqvist study. Three of them are reproduced here in Figure 17.5, the one omitted being the cost of transport to the domestic market. The material transport-cost surface shows clearly the advantage of a small area in southwest Sweden which includes the main domestic source of fabric and the main importing port. About three-quarters of the total material used originates in this general area. This high degree of concentration of material supply makes the cost rise steeply away from the Borås area, so that within about 150 kms the figure has risen by 100 percent.

The finished product transport-cost surface with respect to all markets differs in some important respects from the first map. The isoline pattern is more complicated, because the market is much more dispersed spatially than the sources of materials. There appear to be two minima—one in the west reflecting the large share of output going to Göteborg for export and the other in the center of southern Sweden reflecting the pull of the Stockholm metropolitan market and the relatively heavily populated areas to the west and southwest. The variation from place to place in the cost of shipping to the market is much less than in the case of materials; over

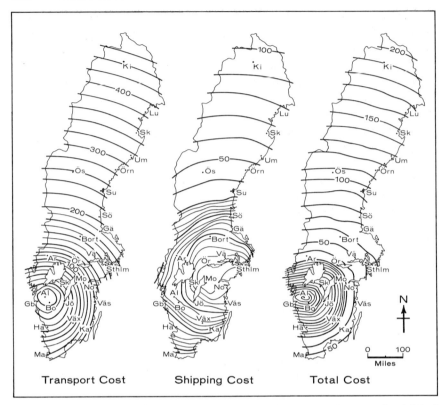

Figure 17.5. Surfaces of material transport cost, the cost of shipping the finished product, and total transport costs, in the Swedish light garment industry. The isolines are numbered according to percentages above the minimum point. (*Source.* Törnqvist, 1962, 51, 53 and 57, Figures 2, 4 and 5.)

almost the whole of Gotaland and Svealand the figure exceeds the minimum by less than 30 percent. The surface for the domestic market only (not reproduced here) shows the low-cost area pulled over to the east toward Stockholm.

The third map shows the two items combined, to give a surface of total transport costs. As might have been expected, the source of materials at Borås and the importance of Göteborg both for export of the product and import of fabrics is enough to assure this general area of the most favorable cost situation. The optimum location is in fact Alingsås, where the total transport costs make up a mere 0.66 percent of total production costs. On the assumption that other costs do not vary from place to place, a plant in Stockholm would incur an increase of 0.34 percent in total production costs compared with Alingsås, and the increase in Malmö would be 0.30. Investigations of actual plants showed transport costs varying between 0.7 and 1.8 percent of total production costs.

Törnqvist concluded that differences from place to place in the transport cost bill are so small in relation to total outlays that they are unlikely to have much influence on plant location in this particular industry. Since labor costs make up 30 to 40 percent of total production costs, their absolute effect on production costs can be very substantial, even if wage rates are not subject to anything like the same degree of areal variations as transport costs when measured in percentage terms. Despite the rather negative nature of these findings with respect to the explanation of the existing location of clothing factories, Törnqvist's study provides a model approach which could sensibly be applied to industries which appear likely to be transport oriented.

c. Kennelly on the Mexican Steel Industry

Like the previous two studies, this one emphasizes transport costs as a determinant of comparative locational advantage. The special interest of the Kennelly study (1954–1955) lies in the quality of the empirical data collected, and in the author's attempt to apply existing location theory. It can thus be offered as a guide to the way in which a real-world problem may be analyzed by a simple model derived from classical theory.

Kennelly has two major objectives: (1) to examine the existing transport-cost situation with respect to the two primary steel plants in Mexico, located at Monterrey (the Fundidora plant) and Monclova (the Altos Hornos plant); and (2) to determine the minimum transport-cost point for steel manufacturing in Mexico, using data relating to the existing plants. The study thus comprises a test of how far this two-plant industry is economically rational in its location, with respect to the cost of transportation.

The cost analysis of the two places is summarized in Table 17.12. Four major inputs are recognized; iron ore is the most important in terms of both cost and weight shipped. The ore is mainly from Durango, but small quantities are also obtained from six minor sources. The coke comes from Sabinas, which gives the Altos Hornos plant at Monclova a big cost advantage. The Fundidora plant is compensated for this by the availability of gas piped from Texas, which cuts down the quantity of oil used as fuel. The two sources of oil are Reynosa and Tampico. The scrap is assumed to come in equal shares from the United States and domestic sources, with the latter equally divided between Mexico City and Monterrey. The total output of 212,660 metric tons of steel from the two plants together goes to Monterrey and Mexico City, with the capital city taking

Table 17.12 Weight and Cost Data for Two Mexican Steel Plants (per Ton of Finished Product)

Item	Monterrey: Fundidora Plant		Monclova: Altos Hornos Plant	
	Weight (Kilograms)	Cost (Pesos)	Weight (Kilograms)	Cost (Pesos)
Inputs				
Iron ore	1940	24.15	1691	24.38
Coke	1400	31.57	1059	8.63
Oil	263	9.42	931	36.17
Scrap	200	5.65	323	10.09
Total cost		70.79		79.27
Markets				
Mexico City	500	39.15	800	68.92
Monterrey	500	0.00	200	4.64
Total cost		39.15		69.56
All transport costs		109.94		148.82

Source. Based on Kennelly (1954-5, Table XII).

the larger share. The Fundidora plant has a slight advantage with respect to the assembly of inputs, and a much more substantial one in terms of access to the market.

The determination of the least-cost point for transportation on materials and the finished product requires some modification of the actual situation facing the two existing plants. In the case of ore supply the minor sources are eliminated and it is assumed that Durango supplies all that is required. The other sources are so small that little error is introduced by this simplification. It is also necessary to make an assumption with respect to the supply of fuel, for the gas which helps to keep costs low at Monterrey can be expected to be available only in certain places near the border with the United States. Therefore, for the sake of the general cost analysis, Kennelly assumes that oil only is available and that the sources at Reynosa and Tampico are equally important. No simplifications are necessary in the case of coke and scrap supplies and the location of the market.

The quantity of the various commodities that enters into the calculation of transport costs in alternative locations is derived from weighted averages of data for the two existing plants, in the case of the four inputs. For the market, the actual division of 75 percent to Mexico City and 25 percent to Monterrey is used. The relative weights, or pulls, attributed to the material and market points are indicated by the symbols in Figure 17.6a, where the circles are proportional in size to the number of tons shipped.

Kennelly uses a number of different methods of determining the minimum-transport-cost point (MTP). The first is to consider the transport cost as a function of weight and distance, following Weber's original approach. Calculating the total ton-kilometers covered from various possible production points results in the identification of the point P_1 in Figure 17.6a as the minimum point. Excluding the market from the calculation shifts the optimum to P'_1, as the big pull of Mexico City in the South is eliminated. Next, the actual transport network is introduced, and an MTP is found at Paredon (P_2) on the basis of minimum ton-kilometers covered. Finally the use of actual freight rates produces yet another MTP (P), which is at Monterrey where the actual lowest-cost plant is operating; the advantage of this location arises largely from the local market for steel and the generally good accessibility in relation to material sources. Thus different assumptions have produced four possible optimum locations, and some theoretical framework is needed to interpret these findings.

The next stage in Kennelly's analysis is an attempt to apply models derived from existing industrial location theory to the understanding of this situation. His emphasis is on variable-cost theory, for which the steel industry, with its relatively simple input structure, is a good testing ground. The first model to be applied is Varignon's frame—the weight table that Weber used as a means of finding the point of balance between the attractive forces ($F_1, \ldots, F_7$) exerted by different material sources and market points. Using the weights indicated in Figure 17.6a, the model comes to rest with the point at P_1 (Figure 17.6b). This is the same P_1 as found by trial and error previously—the point where the total ton-kilometers of movement is at a minimum. Next, Kennelly attempts to apply some of the geometrical constructions of Launhardt and Palander, but the seven-cornered locational figure required to describe the situation in the Mexican steel industry is too complex for these models to generate any significant results.

Kennelly then returns to Weber's theory of industrial location. The steel industry conforms to Weber's concept of transport orientation, with other factors such as labor costs and agglomeration being of only minor importance. The test of Weber's principle relating to the location of MTP within the locational polygon by use of the Varignon model was found to give a fairly close approximation to the actual least-cost location, as a comparison between the positions of P_1 and P in Figure 17.6a indicates. An isodapane map was prepared on a weight/distance basis (Figure

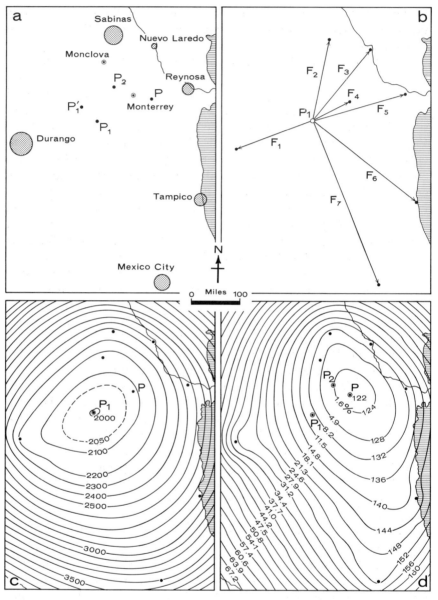

Figure 17.6. The Mexican steel industry: (a) major material sources and markets; (b) application of Varignon's mechanical model; (c) isodapanes based on weight and distance (values in ton-kms); (d) isodapanes based on weight, distance and freight rates (values in pesos). (*Source.* Kennelly, 1954–1955, Map 4 and Figures 7, 10 and 11.)

17.6c), and this shows that the total ton-kilometers covered from Monterrey (P) is only about 100 above the value at P_1 (that is, 5 percent above MTP), and the differential at Monclova where the other plant is situated is only 200.

However, Kennelly was unhappy about Weber's failure to build actual freight rates and transport routes into his model, and he argues that Palander's approach is preferable in this respect. The MTP calculated on the basis of the actual transport situation (P) accurately identifies Monterrey as the location of the least-cost plant in the Mexican primary steel industry, and the point found by using actual routes but weight instead of cost (P_2) is very close to the actual minimum. Figure 17.6d shows isodapanes drawn from the actual freight rates, and a comparison with those relating to ton-kilometers (Figure 17.6c) shows the shift of the least-cost area east to Monterrey, and the distortion of the regularity of the isolines in certain directions (in particular, southward towards Mexico City).

The Mexican steel industry thus proves to be an interesting case in which to test certain of the elementary principles of classical variable-cost theory. As a means of predicting the least-cost location the Weber weight/distance model is rejected in favor of the more realistic approach of Palander's modification, but the value of Weber's locational figure and the concept of cost surfaces is confirmed. The ability to predict a location and show that it is consistent with theory is probably the highest form of explanation to which the industrial location analyst can aspire. Kennelly explains the location of the Fundidora steel plant at Monterrey, as occupying the point of minimum transport costs in classical theory.

18

Three Case Studies

The previous three chapters presented a series of brief illustrations of the application of various concepts and techniques developed in the theoretical sections of this book. This chapter offers three more detailed case studies. The first looks at the United States iron and steel industry during the immediate postwar period; the second considers various aspects of the problem of determining the best location for a specific plant making electrical appliances; and the third uses a branch of the electronics industry to demonstrate a more comprehensive national view of comparative locational advantage. The purpose is not to offer factual information about these industries, but to provide fairly extensive illustrations of various approaches to empirical inquiry which derive logically from some of the contents of Parts Two and Three.

18.1 THE IRON AND STEEL INDUSTRY IN THE UNITED STATES

The high degree of localization of iron and steel manufacturing is one of the most important features of the economic geography of the United States. As was indicated in the previous chapter, the location of this industry is closely related to the transportation costs incurred with respect to a relatively small number of inputs, which creates almost ideal circumstances for the application of classical variable-cost theory. These facts, together with the importance of the iron and steel industry to the national economy, make it probably the most popular single subject for industrial location analysis. This was particularly true of the decade that followed the end of World War II, when the location of new capacity became a very important national economic issue.

The iron and steel industry has always been highly transport-oriented. The critical thing in selecting a location for a new plant is the cost of assembling the major materials and sending the finished product to the market. Although the cost of labor may be as high as 25 percent of total costs, areal variations in wage rates are of minor importance compared with differences in transport costs. Such considerations as water supply, the availability and quality of land, and the level of local and state taxes all enter into locational choice as factors that help to determine the selection of the exact site within a given region, but the general area of search is determined by the transportation factor.

Historically, there have been a number of important changes in the technology of the iron and steel industry, which have had a major bearing on plant location. In the eighteenth century, up to ten tons of coal were required to smelt one ton of pig iron, and the need for plants to be close to supplies of coal dominated all other locational considerations. Expressed in Weberian terms, the weight of the coal needed exceeded the combined weights of the other materials used and the finished product, so the pull of the coalfield was great enough to insure the location of plants there. As technology improved, the quantity of coal was reduced and, during the second half of the nineteenth century, coal supplies lost their dominant position. At first this had the effect of making iron ore deposits away from the coalfields viable locations for iron and steel plants, and the ease of access to sources of domestic or imported ore remains the major location factor in this industry in many parts of the world. But the reduction in the importance of coal also increased the pull of the market.

The growing importance of the market is suggested in Table 18.1, which shows how the percentage distribution of steel-making capacity changed in the forty years following 1920. The most important change is in the share of the industry concentrated in the Pittsburgh-Youngstown

Table 18.1 The Percentage Distribution of Steel-Making Capacity in the United States (1920-1959)[a]

District	1920	1930	1940	1950	1959
Eastern	18.3	16.1	19.8	20.0	21.8
Pittsburgh-Youngstown	51.4	46.4	42.2	39.4	33.7
Cleveland-Detroit	7.0	7.3	9.7	9.4	10.4
Chicago	17.8	24.6	21.8	20.9	22.4
Southern	2.6	3.0	3.8	4.6	5.9
Western	2.9	2.0	2.7	5.7	5.8

Source. Craig (1957, 261).
[a] The figures for 1959 were based on a projection.

district, which is the traditional coalfield location. The increases in the eastern district, Cleveland-Detroit, and Chicago can be interpreted as a response to the increasing relative pull of both the market and sources of ore, while the growth in the west is almost entirely geared to the rise of a substantial local market. The figures for the southern district are mainly a reflection of increased capacity in Birmingham.

An attempt to measure the pull of the market in relation to that of coal and ore supplies in the immediate postwar period was made by Rodgers (1952). He showed that on the basis of weight alone the finished product is of less significance than both the two major materials, but the situation is reversed when freight rates are introduced. Finished steel travels at a much higher rate than coal and ore, and this makes its transport cost greater than for both the materials together, as is indicated in the weighted cost figures in Table 18.2. Thus in the Weber model the market

Table 18.2 Some Transport Data for the United States Steel Industry: Weights and Cost Per Ton of Finished Steel[a]

Item	Weight (Tons)	Percentage of Total Weight	Transport Cost (Dollars) per Ton-Mile	Weighted Transport Cost (Dollars)	Percentage of Total Transport Cost
Coal	1.42	34	1.04	14,768	25.7
Iron ore	1.74	42	0.70	12,180	21.1
Finished steel	1.00	24	3.06	30,600	53.2
Total	4.16	100		57,548	100.0

Source. Rodgers (1952, 58).
[a] The weighted transport cost is weight × cost per ton-mile multiplied by 10,000. The figures relate to 1939.

would now have the dominant pull. The attraction of the market is also strengthened by the gradual increase in the use of scrap as a partial substitute for iron ore, since the industrial areas that make up the market for steel tend to be the main areas of supply of scrap metal.

In light of these figures, it might be expected that the location pattern of the iron and steel industry would tend to correspond broadly with that of the market. But Rodgers found that this certainly was not the case. His comparison of the patterns of production and consumption at the end of the 1940s showed the market to be much more dispersed than the industry itself (Rodgers, 1952, 58–60). This led him to suggest industrial inertia as one of the principal reasons for the existing location pattern, a factor also emphasised by Alexandersson (1961) and others as of particular importance in this industry. Iron and steel production require a very large investment in fixed capital equipment and this contributes toward locational stability. For a long time this tendency was also strengthened by the basing-point pricing system, which helped to preserve the comparative advantage of the Pittsburgh area with respect to the erection of new capacity. The natural trend toward market orientation thus appears to have been frustrated to a large extent by the immobility of fixed capital and the artificial protection of the old-established centers of production.

This discussion of locational trends in the iron and steel industry immediately before and after World War II sets the scene for a more detailed and precise comparative-cost analysis. The material in the remainder of this study can be regarded as contributing to a test of the hypothesis that the major markets had become the best locations for new capacity, and that economic rationality required a substantial shift in emphasis from material orientation to market orientation.

a. The Prewar Cost Situation

The comparative cost advantage of alternative locations at the end of the 1930s, and the future location pattern likely to come about, was the subject of a major paper by Isard and Capron (1949). At the time they wrote, it seemed that rather dramatic changes might be about to take place in the distribution of iron and steel production, for in addition to the increasing pull of the market the industry faced the imminent exhaustion of the better-grade iron ore of the Lake Superior deposits. The abolition of the old "Pittsburgh plus" pricing system, and the outlawing in 1948 of the multiple-basing-point system that replaced it, was being viewed as a further threat to the continuing viability of the Pittsburgh-Youngstown district.

Isard and Capron first attempted to work out the cost of assembling the three major inputs at thirteen different steel-producing centers (Table 18.3). In 1939 Birmingham had a considerable cost advantage, arising from the extremely low transport charges involved in the use of local ore and coal, and would doubtless have accounted for a much larger share of capacity if it had not been for the control of the industry from Pittsburgh and the South's relatively small market. The low cost of material assembly at two western locations—Provo in Utah and Pueblo in Colorado—made total costs comparable with those in the traditional centers in the major manufacturing belt, while the high cost of coal put the lakeside plants at Detroit, Buffalo, and Chicago-Gary at a slight disadvantage when compared with the Pennsylvania locations.

Isard and Capron next considered the effect of the cost of serving the

Table 18.3 Material Assembly Costs (Dollars) per Long Ton of Finished Steel at Different Production Centers, 1939

	Iron Ore	Coal	Limestone	Total
Birmingham	0.95	1.49	0.15	2.59
Provo	2.30	2.46	0.26	5.02
Duluth	1.15	3.79	0.37	5.31
Pueblo	2.89	1.95	0.79	5.63
Pittsburgh	4.67	0.36	0.62	5.65
Bethlehem	1.17	4.18	0.51	5.86
Cleveland	2.67	2.94	0.45	6.06
Youngstown	4.19	1.94	0.34	6.47
Detroit	2.66	3.52	0.31	6.49
Buffalo	2.67	3.43	0.45	6.55
Chicago-Gary	2.66	4.32	0.37	7.35
Sparrows Point	4.63	3.98	1.05	9.66
San Bernadino	2.51	7.44	Negligible	9.95

Source. Isard and Capron (1949, 121).

market. Table 18.4 shows how selected producing centers compared with respect to the market at New York, Detroit, and Seattle, and includes the cost of assembling the materials as well as freight charges on finished steel. The fact that Pittsburgh is at the bottom of the list for the first two markets strengthens the view that this area's competitive position was deteriorating, relative to both waterside locations well placed for cheap ore and locations at or near the markets (that is, Bethlehem and Detroit). The figures for the Seattle market show that the low cost of assembly at Provo and Pueblo is more than offset by high transport costs on the finished product.

The general assessment of the competitive positions of the major producing areas at the end of the 1940s, as offered by Isard and Capron, was as follows. The Pittsburgh-Youngstown-Cleveland area was the best location from which to produce for its own market, and Chicago-Gary was best placed to supply the market of the Chicago area. For serving the eastern seaboard the Bethlehem, Buffalo and Sparrows Point plants had the advantage over the western Pennsylvania-Ohio area. With respect to the Detroit market, including the motor industry, local production appeared likely to displace supply from plants in the Pittsburgh district. These observations support the hypothesis of market-oriented plants gaining competitive advantage at the expense of the traditional locations in and around Pittsburgh.

Looking to the future, Isard and Capron saw the depletion of the Lake Superior ores leading to a shift from the waterside locations on the Great Lakes to sites better placed with respect to access to other ores. Birming-

Table 18.4 Transportation Charges (Dollars) on Materials and Product per Ton of Finished Steel, for Selected Production Centers Serving Selected Markets[a]

	Assembly Costs of Ore, Coal, and Limestone	Freight Charges on Finished Steel	Total Transport Costs
New York City Market			
Bethlehem	5.86	3.81	9.67
Buffalo	6.55	3.64	10.19
Cleveland	6.06	4.87	10.93
Sparrows Point	9.66	1.68	11.34
Detroit	6.49	4.93	11.42
Pittsburgh	5.65	8.06	13.71
Detroit Market			
Detroit	6.49	0.00	6.49
Cleveland	6.06	1.06	7.12
Duluth	5.31	2.07	7.38
Buffalo	6.55	1.29	7.84
Chicago-Gary	7.35	1.68	9.03
Pittsburgh	5.65	5.54	11.19
Seattle Market			
Birmingham	2.59	15.46	18.05
San Bernadino	9.95	9.41	19.36
Sparrows Point	9.66	11.20	20.86
Provo	5.02	16.24	21.26
Pueblo	5.63	19.04	24.67

Source. Isard and Capron (1949, 122–3).

[a] The transport costs on the finished steel relate to rail or water routes, whichever is the cheapest.

ham's low-cost position for the assembly of materials seemed to favor expansion there, despite the restricted market for steel in the South. Further growth was anticipated in the major market areas in the east, and the Pacific coast was seen as reaching the position where the size of the market could justify a major integrated plant, despite the relatively high cost of materials. Again, all this seemed bound to reduce the relative importance of the Pittsburgh-Youngstown district, and bring about a more dispersed location pattern with the emphasis on market orientation. As Craig (1957, 259) was to confirm a few years later, both theoretical and empirical evidence indicated that the selection of the optimum location for steel production had become almost entirely a matter of market proximity.

b. New England as a Possible Location for an Integrated Iron and Steel Works

By the beginning of the 1950s considerable interest was being expressed in the north Atlantic seaboard as a possible location for new capacity. Isard and Cumberland (1950) undertook a feasibility study of two possible locations in New England, with a view to determining whether the northeastern market would best be served by a local plant. Their study can be considered as a specific test of the market-orientation hypothesis, in a region with a long established industrial market for iron and steel and the additional advantage of local supplies of scrap.

The two locations examined were Fall River in Massachusetts and New London in eastern Connecticut. Both had been proposed by their respective states as the best production point from which to serve the New England market. The approach adopted was to compare these places with other actual and possible locations outside the region. The existing major plants best located to serve New England were Sparrows Point, Buffalo, Bethlehem, Pittsburgh and Cleveland; the other point considered was Trenton (where the United States Steel Corporation had already announced plans to construct an integrated works beside the Delaware River), a strategically placed location both for importing Venezuelan ore and serving the eastern seaboard market.

A comparative-cost analysis was undertaken for all these locations, with respect to five selected market points in New England. The New York market was also considered, to see how far a New England location might be capable of competing with existing and potential suppliers there. Three cost items were evaluated—transportation of ore, coal, and the finished steel products—and the results are summarized in Table 18.5. Two sets of figures are shown for the New England locations, to indicate the difference between using ores from Venezuela as against Labrador. The table shows that three of the market points in New England could be served at lowest cost from Fall River and that for the other two New London would be best. In every case, ore could be obtained cheaper from Venezuela than from Labrador. Figures for the other locations considered indicate a very clear cost advantage for the New England locations, with the better of the two market-oriented plants often having a differential of $8 and more per ton below that of the outside plants. The nearest competitor is shown to be Trenton.

The addition of other cost items did not seem to alter the advantage of the New England locations. There is local limestone of excellent quality in the region, and although the deposits are not immediately adjacent to the New London and Fall River sites this would not impose a major

Table 18.5 Transport Costs (Dollars) on Ore and Coal per Ton of Steel, and on Finished Products, for Selected Production Locations Serving New England Markets and New York

Locations	Markets					
	Worcester	Boston	Providence	Hartford	New Haven	New York
Fall River						
Labrador ore	15.57	15.17	14.17	17.37	18.57	20.97
Venezuela ore	**14.31**	**13.91**	**12.91**	16.11	17.31	19.71
New London						
Labrador ore	16.15	17.15	15.35	15.35	15.15	19.15
Venezuela ore	14.90	15.90	14.10	**14.10**	**13.90**	17.90
Pittsburgh	22.11	22.31	22.31	21.11	20.71	19.51
Cleveland	22.01	22.21	22.21	21.41	21.41	21.01
Sparrows Point	20.59	21.39	21.19	19.55	19.19	17.39
Buffalo	19.83	20.03	20.83	19.63	19.63	19.03
Bethlehem	20.82	21.22	21.02	19.22	19.02	16.42
Trenton	17.93	18.73	17.93	16.73	15.73	**13.13**

Source. Isard and Cumberland (1950, 248–50, 255). Note. Figures in bold type indicate the least-cost supplier for each market.

problem. Variations in the cost of coal at the mine were considered to be of only minor importance, and the *effective* cost of ore (that is, transport charges and all other differentials) would be at least as low on Venezuela and Labrador supplies as on the Lake Superior ores. The degree of unionization and accepted minimum wage scales virtually removed labor costs from the category of spatial variable, and it was not anticipated that either of the New England locations would suffer any great disadvantage with respect to land availability and related factors, or from the size of the state and local tax bill.

The cost of the scrap input has always been difficult to estimate because it originates in an area and not from the single point which can reasonably be assumed when considering coal and ore supplies. Coming from a number of different places to one production point, it resembles in certain respects the timber input in Lindberg's study of the paper industry reported in the previous chapter. An examination of scrap prices in different cities (Isard and Capron, 1949) led to the conclusion that a New England plant might have an advantage of about $1 per ton of steel over points like Pittsburgh, with a small advantage over Buffalo, Cleveland, and similar locations, and an advantage over Sparrows Point and Trenton described as at best slight.

In general, then, cost factors were found to favor serving New England consumers from a New England plant. But the demand factor had not yet been considered. A critical question in this industry is whether the market that a new plant can reasonably expect to capture will be large enough to support the kind of major integrated facility necessary to achieve economies of scale. After an analysis of existing consumption, it seemed that the New England market was sufficient to support an integrated works with a capacity of 1.5 million tons of ingot. However, the degree of uncertainty surrounding whether a plant could get a viable market was such that Isard and Cumberland were finally unable to decide one way or the other. The main reasons for this uncertain (or marginal) market situation were the regional demand for specialized items which could not be produced in New England, the question of how far the agglomeration tendencies from which other iron and steel centers benefit could be expected to develop in New England, and how far the potential Trenton location would be able to cut into the regional market.

As a test of the market-orientation hypothesis in the iron and steel industry of the immediate postwar period, the Isard and Cumberland study is thus very interesting. It shows that there is strong support for this view with respect to New England, as long as the variable-cost approach only is adopted. But as soon as the demand factor is introduced, with the size of the market related to competition from other possible sources of supply, the validity of the hypothesis becomes much less certain. In an industry where scale is a vital factor and economies of agglomeration are also important, the simple variable-cost model based on classical Weberian theory is no longer adequate.

c. The National Cost Pattern in 1950

A more comprehensive national view of the relative cost advantage of alternative locations in the immediate postwar period is provided in a study by Barloon (1954). The analysis is narrower than those of Isard and Capron (1949) and Isard and Cumberland (1950), in that Barloon is concerned only with the assembly of materials and disregards the cost of serving the market and the effect of the demand factor. A major objective was to evaluate the cost situation in the west as it compared with that in the traditional locations.

Barloon concentrates his attention on the blast furnace phase of the industry. The cost structure, as indicated by figures for a representative plant in the Chicago area (Table 18.6), shows the dominant position of materials, the three principal inputs being, of course, iron ore, coal, and limestone.

The comparative-cost analysis is restricted to the cost of assembling

Table 18.6 Cost Structure in Pig Iron Production, as Indicated by Figures for a Representative Plant in the Chicago Area

Item	Percentage of Total Cost
Raw materials:	
Mining and preparation	54.0
Transportation to plant	41.6
Total cost of materials	95.6
Coke oven and blast furnace processing	22.2
Total cost before credits	117.8
By-product credits	17.8
Total cost of pig iron	100.0

Source. Barloon (1954, 5).

these three materials. Barloon selected thirteen blast furnace locations, and attempted to build up cost estimates which were generally representative of the areas within which the plants are situated. Published data on material costs were modified and supplemented by personal inquiry relating to the practices of individual firms. Every effort was made to eliminate cost variations which could not be attributed to geographical position, i.e. those arising from inter-plant differences in efficiency, furnace practices, and the particular institutional structure of individual establishments. Thus the figures produced are representative rather than particular, and provide a broad indication of interregional cost differences instead of precise information on the costs incurred at specific plants.

The thirteen locations considered, together with their cost data, are listed in Table 18.7. Separate figures are given for the cost of mining and beneficiation and the cost of transportation. Although compiled on a different basis, and for steel manufacturing instead of the blast furnace phase, the figures compiled by Isard and Capron (1949, 121) for 1939 (Table 18.3) can be usefully compared with those in Table 18.7. The most remarkable difference is in the position of Birmingham, where the gradual increase in assembly costs over the years had changed the city from the location with lowest material costs to one of the highest-cost locations. By 1950 the cost of mining and benefication of both ore and coal at Birmingham was the highest of all the locations considered, the only mitigating factor being the local occurrence of the materials and the consequent lowering of transport costs. The least-assembly-cost location in 1950 was Geneva in Utah, which appeared second to Provo in the Isard-Capron list. Second on Barloon's list is Baltimore (Sparrows Point),

Table 18.7 The Cost of Raw Materials (Dollars) per Net Ton of Pig Iron at Thirteen Blast Furnace Locations, 1950

	Iron Ore			Coal			Limestone			Total Raw Materials Cost per Net Ton of Pig Iron
	Pounds per Net Ton of Pig Iron	Cost of Mining and Beneficiation	Cost of Transportation	Pounds per Net Ton of Pig Iron	Cost of Mining and Preparation	Cost of Transportation	Pounds per Net Ton of Pig Iron	Cost of Quarrying and Preparation	Cost of Transportation	
Chicago	4032	4.46	4.55	2350	7.14	5.02	1000	.24	.37	21.78
Pittsburgh	4032	4.29	8.23	2485	7.16	.78	1000	.24	.68	21.38
Buffalo	4032	4.46	4.58	2485	7.40	3.98	1000	.25	.82	21.49
Duluth	4100	5.82	1.98	2460	6.82	4.55	1154	.28	.43	19.88
Ohio River	4032	5.27	8.60	2450	7.14	1.88	1000	.27	1.00	24.16
Granite City	4030	5.38	4.98	2515	6.43	3.76	1045	.26	2.04	22.85
Bethlehem	3790	6.66	5.69	2380	4.61	4.61	900	.15	.22	21.94
Baltimore	3580	3.39	6.90	2245	4.44	4.33	852	.21	.55	19.82
Birmingham	5400	8.97	.94	3700	12.43	.74	500	.13	.16	23.37
Houston	4160	5.30	4.98	2575	8.04	6.22	1555	.70	.83	26.07
Lone Star, Texas	3980	8.19	—	2710	8.85	2.68	1805	.93	1.07	21.72
Geneva, Utah	3780	3.41	3.46	2880	6.12	3.28	918	.23	.40	16.90
Fontana, Cal.	3670	3.52	3.60	2560	6.37	7.44	935	.23	.27	21.43

Source. Barloon (1954, 17).

where access to low-cost foreign ores had greatly improved the material-cost situation of 1939, as Isard and Capron predicted it would. Pittsburgh does not appear as badly placed as some contemporary observers were suggesting, but the Ohio River area, Granite City (St. Louis) and Bethlehem are well down the list. Fontana in California and Lone Star in northeast Texas look reasonably good locations from the point of view of material assembly, but Houston suffers from the very high cost of coal and a higher than average cost of iron ore.

Broad areal variations in the cost of each of the three inputs can be effectively portrayed by interpolating surfaces from the sum of the extraction and transportation costs. With only thirteen points, the derivation of cost surfaces may be asking a little too much of these data, but the fact that Barloon's figures were compiled specifically to indicate conditions representative of broad areas rather than single production points is some justification for this procedure. As in many previous illustrations of this kind, the surface has been interpolated by computer, which reduces the subjective judgment which can seriously influence the pattern derived from a small number of widely spaced points if the isolines are fitted by eye.

The three input-cost surfaces are illustrated in Figures 18.1, 18.2 and 18.3. The first map emphasizes the relatively high cost of ore in the east, except for the waterside locations at Sparrows Point and Buffalo, and the low costs in the west. The second map shows how the low cost of coal from the Appalachian field and the similar figure at the Utah location create two areas of apparent advantage with respect to this input, while costs rise rapidly in the direction of the Gulf Coast and California. The pattern of limestone costs, in the third map, is a simple one, with costs falling steadily from the peaks at the Granite City and Lone Star locations towards the locations better placed with respect to access to the stone deposits of the Rockies and Appalachians.

The surface of total assembly costs is illustrated in Figure 18.4. This is, of course, the sum on the three single-input surfaces just described, and confirms the growing impression of relatively high costs in the eastern parts of the country when compared with the west. The major exceptions to the general trend are the relatively low costs in the area in the east centered on Sparrows Point, and the high costs in California as indicated by the situation at the Fontana plant when compared with the other western location at Geneva, Utah. Although this map provides an adequate general indication of the comparative cost advantage at a broad regional level, it must be emphasized that the surface does ignore many local features of the iron industry's cost topography which could

358 SOME EMPIRICAL APPLICATIONS

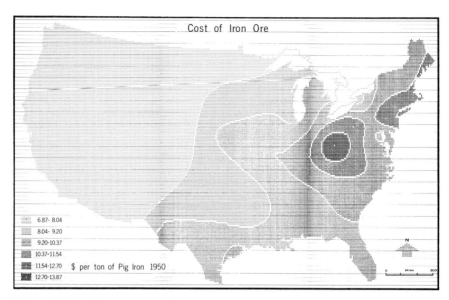

Figure 18.1. An ore-cost surface for the iron industry in 1950. (*Source of Data.* Barloon, 1954, 17.*)*

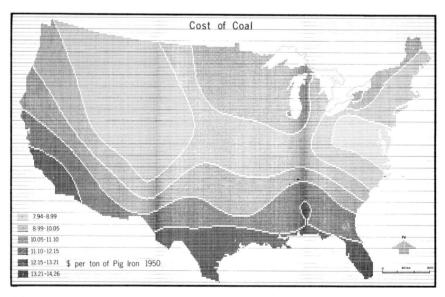

Figure 18.2. A coal-cost surface for the iron industry in 1950. (*Source of Data.* Barloon, 1954, 17.*)*

THREE CASE STUDIES 359

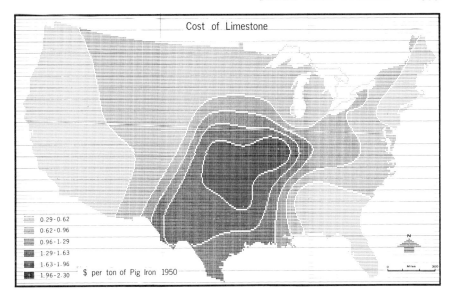

Figure 18.3. A limestone-cost surface for the iron industry in 1950. (*Source of Data.* Barloon, 1954, 17.)

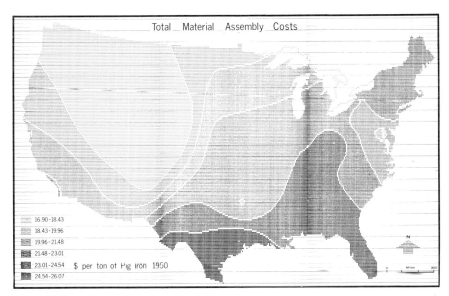

Figure 18.4. A surface of total material assembly costs (ore, coal and limestone) in the iron industry in 1950. (*Source of Data.* Barloon, 1954, 17.)

be identified only by the use of data for a much larger number of control points.

Barloon's general conclusion was that locations west of the Mississippi were somewhat better placed with respect to the cost of assembling materials than had been previously supposed. On balance, he considered the raw material situation of Texas and the West to be more economical than that of Pittsburgh, Chicago, and the other old-established northern centers. And he felt that the western locations enjoyed a cost position sufficiently favorable to absorb a degree of market disadvantage, if one should develop. However, he did not attempt to measure the cost of serving the market; if he had done this, as Isard and Capron did for the earlier period, he might have been less optimistic about the overall viability of expansion in the West, and less pessimistic about the future of some of the traditional centers of production.

d. Conclusions

The studies reviewed above comprise a loosely formulated test of the hypothesis that immediately after World War II the optimum location for iron and steel manufacturing had shifted from material sources to the point of consumption, and that this logically should lead to dispersal of production and to a substantial decline in the relative importance of the major existing concentration centered on Pittsburg. Simple comparative-cost analysis generally tends to support this hypothesis, for it appears that almost all the major national markets could be served cheaper from local plants than from those in other regions. However, when the demand factor is introduced in the form of the size of the market necessary to support a modern integrated facility, and when the additional factors of scale and agglomeration economies, the immobility of fixed capital (that is, industrial inertia), and corporation structure are taken into account, the argument is much less persuasive. In addition, those who predicted the large-scale movement of the industry to the market, and the demise of the Pittsburgh area, failed to anticipate certain changes in technology and transportation which can upset any predictions in location analysis. Of particular importance has been the successful exploitation of the taconite ores of the Lake Superior sources, and the construction of the St. Lawrence Seaway; both have worked to the advantage of the plants beside the Great Lakes, extending the life of the Superior ore supplies and making the Labrador ores not substantially more expensive in lake centers than Venezuelan ore on the east coast (Craig, 1957, 256). Thus the major manufacturing belt has lost little of its share of iron and steel capacity, and the degree of dispersal has been relatively slight.

18.2 THE LOCATION OF AN ELECTRICAL APPLIANCE PLANT

This second study is concerned with the locational decision of a single firm, and is based entirely on real-world data.* The firm in question manufactures electrical appliances at an existing plant in one of the Great Lakes states, for an established national market. The initial problem is whether it would be advantageous to relocate the existing facility, which involves a comparative-cost analysis of possible alternative locations. Then a different situation is examined, to provide a further illustration of market-area analysis, using one of the models discussed in Section 9.3 of Chapter 9 to find the best location under circumstances where spatial competition is a relevant consideration.

The plant specifications are as follows. A site of 20–30 acres is required, to hold a building with about 100,000 square feet of production space. A total of 450 production workers will be employed, 200 of whom are males, and 10 office workers are also required. Each month the plant will use 1200 kw and 232,000 kwh of electric power and 151,000 cubic feet of water.

The annual production for which the plant is being constructed is almost 100,000 units, with a total weight of approximately 144,000 cwt. The geographical distribution of the market is illustrated in Figure 18.5. There are 81 destinations for the product, with the volume to be shipped varying from less than 50 cwt to more than 15,000 cwt. The market is largely confined to the eastern half of the country, sales west of Denver, Colorado, being restricted to two west coast destinations. Within the eastern United States the market is widely distributed, the volume of sales at specific places being related partly to population and affluence and partly to a local factor which influences consumption of this particular kind of appliance.

Six materials or components are required to manufacture the product. Their sources are indicated in Figure 18.6, which shows that with one exception they originate in the major industrial belt extending from St. Louis to New England. The largest requirement in terms of weight is for motors with almost 206,000 cwt to be shipped annually from a single source in the Great Lakes area. Next comes galvanized steel, with

---

* The author is grateful to The Faulus Company, a subsidiary of Dun & Bradstreet, Inc., Chicago, for making available the data on which this study is based. To preserve the anonymity of the clients for whom the original data were compiled the precise nature of the product, the exact location of the existing plant, and certain other confidential information cannot be revealed here.

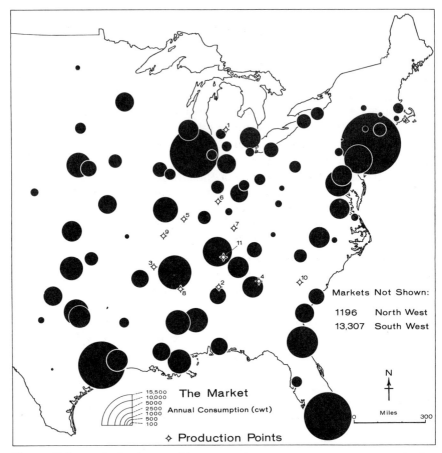

Figure 18.5. The location problem of an electrical goods manufacturer: the distribution of the market and possible production points. Production point 1 refers generally to the Great Lakes area and no significance should be attached to its exact location on the map.

50,000 cwt and a choice of five alternative sources. Third is metal tubes, with 15,000 cwt annually and sources of supply in central Indiana, and in Detroit. The remaining three components are capacitors, panels, and another part which, with a combined weight of only just over 5000 cwt to be shipped each year, have very little bearing on locational choice.

a. The Comparative-Cost Analysis

Deciding whether the plant might be profitably moved from its present location involves the costing of ten possible locations along with

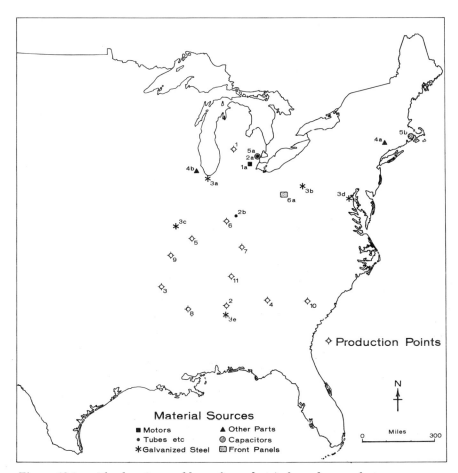

Figure 18.6. The location problem of an electrical goods manufacturer: sources of materials. Only those sources which could serve at least one possible production point on the basis of least delivered cost are included on the map.

the existing one. They are identified in Figure 18.5, which shows that the area of search is well to the south of the existing location, in parts of the eastern United States where the cost of labor is likely to be substantially less than in the Great Lakes area. The cost analysis of the possible new locations relates to general areas rather than specific sites; together the ten places provide a suitable sample from which the broad geographical pattern of spatial cost variation in the east-central United States can be built up.

The results of the comparative-cost analysis are summarized in Table 18.8. The least-cost location is identified as northern Mississippi, with an

364 SOME EMPIRICAL APPLICATIONS

Table 18.8 Annual Operating Costs ($1000) for an Electrical Appliance Plant in Selected Locations[a]

Item	1 Great Lakes	2 N. Ala.	3 N.E. Ark.	4 N. La.	5 S. Ill.	6 S. Ind.	7 C. Ky.	8 N. Miss.	9 S.E. Mo.	10 W. S.C.	11 C. Tenn.
Labor	1441	1179	1082	1092	1286	1249	1253	1057	1253	1085	1151
Materials (freight only)	180	355	352	360	270	261	271	361	328	366	315
Land and buildings	64	179	204	188	243	233	242	170	237	189	243
Utilities	112	56	76	62	95	89	83	58	101	74	64
Taxes	101	44	50	48	92	99	25	46	99	96	56
Interplant communication	8	24	24	24	18	15	18	24	21	24	21
Costs of relocation	0	153	153	153	153	153	153	153	153	153	153
Total factory costs	1905	1991	1940	1927	2156	2099	2046	1868	2192	1987	2013
Outbound freight	259	226	228	231	230	229	224	225	228	245	224
Total costs	2165	2217	2168	2158	2386	2327	2270	2093	2420	2231	2236
Difference from Great Lakes	0	+52	+4	−7	+221	+162	+106	−71	+256	+66	+72

Source. The Fantus Company.
[a] The figures are rounded to the nearest thousand, and may not add up exactly to the totals indicated.

annual advantage of $71,000 in spatially variable operating costs when compared with the existing location. Northern Georgia also has a small advantage over the Great Lakes. The fact that the other eight possible new locations all show higher costs than at the existing location is in most cases the result of the inclusion of the cost of relocation in the analysis, which adds $153,000 to the operating costs in any new location. This figure includes items relating to the cost of retaining the old buildings in the event of relocation, additional tool procurement costs in the new area, and the higher depreciation costs on the new equipment which would be acquired. The size of the total costs of relocation in relation to the differences in total costs between alternative areas stresses the importance of this item as a factor making for locational stability, or industrial inertia.

Brief comments are in order about the way the other figures in Table 18.8 were compiled. The labor costs include both wages and fringe benefits, the latter including vacations and other time off with pay, various insurance payments, and pensions. The land and building costs include both amortization and maintenance, and are substantially lower in the existing location than in other places where new buildings would have to be erected—a fact that adds to the general cost of relocation. The utilities item includes the cost of the fuel, power, water, and sewage services; taxes include those payable both locally and to the state; and the interplant communication item measures the cost of retaining connections between this and the company's other facilities. The figures for the cost of materials and shipping the finished product were derived from freight-rate schedules.

The cost analysis summarized in Table 18.8 suggests that the final figures for the total costs are largely determined by differences in expenditure on the labor input. The cost of labor is by far the largest item in total cost at all locations, and the low wages paid in the South is a major contributor to the attraction of the two locations with lower total costs than at the existing plant. In Table 18.9 the eleven locations are ranked according to total costs and the cost of the four most important inputs. The degree of correspondence between the ranking for individual items and total costs is indicated by the correlation coefficients (r_s). The ranking for labor costs follows closely that for total costs except in the case of the existing location, which has the highest labor costs but a relatively low total cost and makes the correlation much lower than it would have otherwise been. The greatest correspondence is between total costs and the cost of land and buildings, while the cost of the two freight items shows a negative rank correlation with total costs. In exercising its dominant influence on comparative locational advantage,

Table 18.9 The Ranking of Alternative Locations for an Electrical Appliance Plant, According to Total Production Costs and the Cost of the Four Major Inputs

Location	Total Costs	Labor	Materials (Freight)	Land and Buildings	Outbound Freight
1. Great Lakes	9	1	11	11	1
2. N. Alabama	7	6	4	9	8
3. N. Arkansas	8	10	5	6	6=
4. N. Georgia	10	8	3	8	3
5. S. Illinois	2	2	9	1	4
6. S. Indiana	3	5	10	5	5
7. C. Kentucky	4	3	8	3	10
8. N. Mississippi	11	11	2	10	9
9. S. Missouri	1	4	6	4	6=
10. W. South Carolina	6	9	1	7	2
11. C. Tennessee	5	7	7	2	11
Correlation with total costs (r_s) [a]		0.504	−0.595	0.791	−0.206

Source of Data. The Fantus Company.
[a] Spearman's rank correlation coefficient.

the labor input conforms to a principle that has been enunciated a number of times in previous chapters; it not only comprises a large element in total costs but also is subject to substantial spatial cost variations. Even if the cost of some other inputs, such as the land and buildings item, is subject to a greater relative fluctuation between alternative locations, their absolute contribution to total costs is very much smaller than that of labor.

The results of the comparative-cost analysis give the electrical appliance manufacturer only one sensible alternative to retaining its existing location. Only northern Mississippi offers a cost saving large enough to be taken as a convincing indication of a more profitable location, and the entrepreneur governed by economic rationality would relocate his plant. However, the cost calculation does not include the loss of psychic income which the entrepreneur or decision-making group might feel to be involved in leaving their familiar location in the north for the possibly less attractive economic and social environment of the South. In practice the $71,000 addition to annual profits might not be sufficient to lead a concern of this size to relocate in northern Mississippi, and in the actual case under review the firm did in fact choose to remain in the Great Lakes area.

The decision of a new entrant to the industry might have been different, however. With the important cost-of-relocation item in Table 18.8 removed, only southern Illinois and southeast Missouri have higher total costs than the existing location, and the advantage of northern Mississippi approaches $250,000. In pure cost terms the benefits from a location in the South are now considerable, and perhaps enough to outweigh any intangible or nonpecuniary disadvantages which a new entrant might detect there.

b. The Market-Area Analysis[*]

For the second part of this study the numerical data remain the same but the circumstances are altered. The firm still has its existing location in the Great Lakes area, but the other ten places are now seen as possible locations not only for this firm but also for competitors. A new firm might set up in any of these places and compete with the original firm for the market it has established, and the question arises as to which location would be the best from which to serve the given distribution of customers in a competitive situation. The problem is thus to identify the comparative advantage of eleven alternative locations with respect to a specific set of demand conditions, finding the one from which the largest volume of sales could be achieved.

This problem may be approached in a number of ways. The procedure adopted here is to use one of the programmed models developed by Hoover (1966, 1967a), and described in Section 9.3 of Chapter 9. Conducting the analysis in this manner enables the present case to be used as an illustration of the way in which an operational model may be calibrated for a real-world situation, as a supplement to the applications on imaginary data presented in Chapter 9.

The model in question uses a combination of cost and demand data, and allocates markets to specific production points on the basis of lowest delivered price. The delivered price from any plant location (J) to any market point (K) is determined by the cost of assembling the required materials at the plant, the cost of production, and the cost of shipping the finished product to the market. The following data are needed as input for the model:

1. The locational coordinates of the possible plant locations (J_1, J_2, ..., J_{11}), and the cost of production at each (not including the cost of materials).

---

[*] The author is grateful to Professor E. M. Hoover for making available the original version of the computer program used in this section, and to Tso-Hwa Lee for his assistance in modifying the program and running the final model used. This illustration originally appeared in Smith and Lee (1970).

2. The locational coordinates of possible source of the required materials ($I_1, I_2, \ldots, I_6$), and the cost of production or extraction at each.

3. The locational coordinates of each market point ($K_1, K_2, \ldots, K_{81}$) and their demand parameters A (intercept) and B (slope) relating quantity purchased to price charged.

4. The input coefficients, indicating the amount of each material needed per unit weight of output.

5. The terminal cost and line-haul cost of transport for each of the materials and for the finished product.

The location of the eleven possible production points is as shown in Figures 18.5 and 18.6 in the previous section, and the designation of coordinates for each is simply a matter of establishing a grid and reading off the required values in miles from some arbitrarily chosen origin. The cost of production at each location can be found from the results of the comparative-cost analysis summarized in Table 18.8. The figure required is an average per hundredweight of output, so the total annual operating costs less the materials item has to be divided by the total annual output of 143,800 cwt (Table 18.10).

Table 18.10 The Cost of Production (Operating Costs Less Freight Costs) at Alternative Locations for an Electrical Appliance Manufacturer

Location	Total Annual Production Costs (Dollars)	Average Cost per Hundredweight of Output (Dollars)
1. Great Lakes	1,725,700	11.99
2. Northern Alabama	1,635,800	11.32
3. Northeastern Arkansas	1,588,100	11.03
4. Northern Georgia	1,567,000	10.88
5. Southern Illinois	1,886,400	13.10
6. Southern Indiana	1,838,100	12.72
7. Central Kentucky	1,775,400	12.32
8. Northern Mississippi	1,507,200	10.46
9. Southeastern Missouri	1,864,100	12.94
10. Western South Carolina	1,620,600	11.26
11. Central Tennessee	1,697,900	11.79

Source. The Fantus Company.

The locational coordinates for the material sources are determined in the same way as for the production points. To simplify the analysis, only the three most important materials are included; the remaining three are required in such small quantities that their influence on material assembly costs is negligible. The only variation in the cost of materials at alternative sources is a ten-cent addition on steel from Granite City, so this source is given a cost of ten cents per hundredweight and the others a cost of zero.

The demand situation fed into the model comprises the coordinates of the market points and the demand function at each. As it is assumed in this case that the volume of sales at each destination is fixed, and insensitive to the delivered price, the weight of the product consumed (as mapped in Figure 18.5) is designated the intercept parameter *(A)* while the slope *(B)* is in every case zero.

The input coefficients are as listed in Table 18.11. They indicate the

Table 18.11   Input Coefficients for the Major Materials in the Manufacture of Electrical Appliances

Material	Quantity Required (cwt) for an Annual Output of 143,800 Hundredweight	Coefficient: Quantity of Material (cwt) per Hundredweight of Output
1. Motors	205,810	1.431
2. Tubes	14,955	0.104
3. Galvanized Steel	50,000	0.347

Source. The Fantus Company.

weight of each of the major materials or components required per hundredweight of output. The fact that the weight for motors is greater that the weight of the finished product is explained by the nature of the packaging, which of course enters into the weight shipped to the plant and helps to determine the freight cost.

Arriving at the transport-cost data required for the model is somewhat more complicated than in the case of the other information. The model does not use the actual cost of shipping between each pair of points, but calculates transport costs from a general cost/distance function. The required terminal and line-haul charges must be determined empirically, by regression analysis. In Figure 18.7 the freight rates for the shipping of electrical appliances from the location in the Great Lakes area (that is, point J_1) to all the markets except the two on the west coast are plotted against the straight-line distance from the plant location. Although there is a slight tapering off with distance, the relationship is very close to linear. The line of best fit, omitting the markets at distances of over 1000 miles, has the equation $X = 0.50 + 0.0015Y$, which can be interpreted as a terminal charge of 50¢ per cwt shipped and a line-haul charge of 0.15¢. Leaving out the more distant destinations in this calcula-

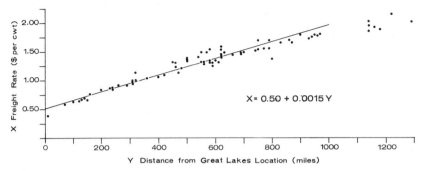

Figure 18.7. The calculation of a transport-cost function from data relating to the freight rate on electrical goods shipped from a location in the Great Lakes area to destinations in the eastern half of the United States. (*Sources of Data.* The Fantus Company.)

tion improves the fit of the line to the rest of the data, and the overestimate of the transport cost to such places when the model is run will have no effect on their market area allocation. On the assumption that the relationship between freight rates and distance from the other ten locations will not differ significantly from that identified for the Great Lakes plant, the function determined in Figure 18.7 can be used in the model for all shipments of the finished product.

The model also requires transport-cost functions for the three major materials. These have been determined in the same way as in Figure 18.7, with the freight rate between each destination and the appropriate material source plotted against distance. In the case of both motors and tubes the relationship is closely linear, and although the freight-rate structure for galvanized steel more closely resembles the conventional convex curve of transport-cost profiles, little error is introduced by adopting the simpler procedure of fitting a line instead of a curve. All four of the transport-cost functions used in this study are thus linear, and their parameters are given in Table 18.12.

Table 18.12 Transport-Cost Data for the Shipping of Materials and the Finished Product in the Manufacture of Electrical Appliances

Item	Terminal Cost (Dollars)	Line-Haul Cost (Dollars)
Motors	0.40	0.0022
Tubes	1.20	0.0023
Galvanized steel	0.12	0.0013
Finished product	0.50	0.0015

Source. The Fantus Company.

When given the data described above, the model finds the cheapest sources of each material for all the production points, calculates the total cost of assembling the materials (per hundredweight of output), and adds this to the cost of production to give total operating costs. The delivered price from each plant location to each market point is then computed by adding the shipping cost to the operating cost, and finally the markets are allocated to the plant from which they can be supplied cheapest. The results of the market-area analysis are displayed in Figure 18.8. This shows that only three of the eleven possible locations are viable in the kind of competitive situation postulated; none of the remaining eight can serve any market at a lower delivered price than another

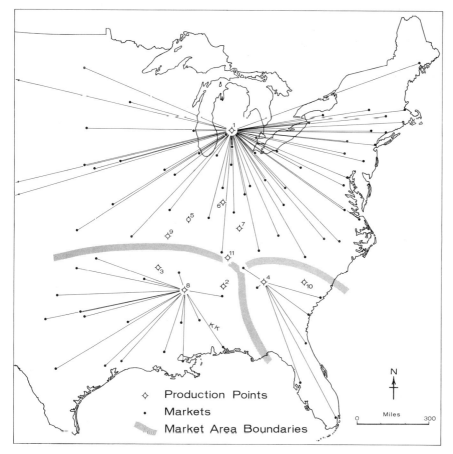

Figure 18.8. The allocation of the market for electrical goods between alternative production points.

Table 18.13 Average Costs (Dollars) per Hundredweight of Output, and Volume of Production, at Viable Plant Locations

Location	Cost of Production	Cost of Materials	Total Operating Costs	Volume of Output (cwt)
1. Great Lakes	11.99	1.12	13.11	86,403
4. Northern Alabama	10.88	2.94	13.82	19,821
8. Northern Mississippi	10.46	3.15	13.61	37,549

Source of Data. The Fantus Company.

location. The existing plant in the Great Lakes area is shown to be the optimum location, with a sales area taking in more than half the market, and the extent of its advantage over the other two viable locations is indicated in Table 18.13.

Two other parts of the model's output may be considered briefly—the flow of materials and the geographical pattern of delivered prices. Table 18.14 shows the weight of each material shipped from different sources to each of the three viable plant locations, on the assumption that all three are occupied and produce the level of output computed by the model. With only three locations occupied, three of the sources of steel have no production because either Gary or Birmingham is better placed to serve the plant locations in question.

The pattern of delivered prices is illustrated in Figure 18.9. The isolines take the form of concentric circles about the three plant locations, because

Table 18.14 Movements of Major Materials (Hundredweight) between Sources and Viable Plant Locations[a]

Material	Source	Plant Location		
		1 Great Lakes	4 Northern Georgia	8 Northern Mississippi
1. Motors	a. Great Lakes area	122,600	28,400	54,700
2. Tubes	a. Detroit	9,000		
	b. Indiana		2,100	3,900
3. Galvanized steel	a. Gary	30,000		
	b. Pittsburgh			
	c. Granite City			
	d. Sparrows Point			
	e. Birmingham		6,900	12,900

Source of Data. The Fantus Company.
[a] The figures have been rounded to the nearest 100.

THREE CASE STUDIES 373

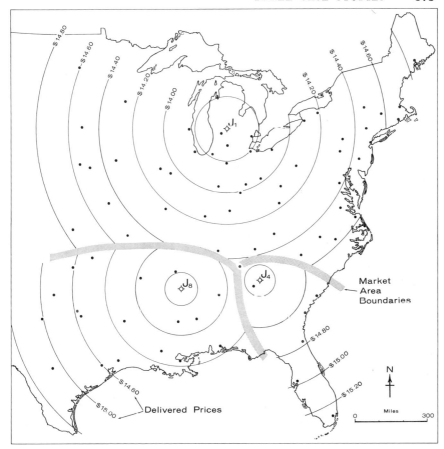

Figure 18.9. The delivered price of electrical goods from three competing plant locations.

the operating-cost component of delivered price from any plant is the same in all markets and the cost of shipping the product is in this case a linear function of distance. These delivered prices are, of course, based on the expectation that the manufacturer passes on the exact cost of delivery to the consumer.

The market-area analysis accomplished by this model clearly indicates that the manufacturer would be safe in retaining his existing location. None of the alternative locations offers as large a volume of sales as the Great Lakes location. However, the accuracy of this result is subject to a number of simplifying assumptions that have been made, both for the purposes of the illustration and because of the particular data requirements of the model used. In addition to the question of the pricing strategy that competitors might adopt, the possibility of a higher unit cost raising the delivered price from locations with a small volume of output has not been considered, the demand function is of the simplest possible form, and the linear transport-cost functions eliminate some features of the actual freight-rate structure. The introduction of further variables would add to the complexity of the analysis, but the model used here can be extended to accommodate many additional considerations (Hoover, 1966, 1967a). It is the shortage of empirical data on production functions and consumer demand curves, added to the general difficulty of compiling accurate geographical cost data, which restricts the application of this kind of location model in the real world, rather than lack of ingenuity on the part of the model builders.

18.3 THE LOCATION OF A BRANCH OF THE ELECTRONICS INDUSTRY

In the theoretical sections of this book great emphasis was placed on the cost-surface approach to industrial location analysis. The basic proposition is that in the absence of other factors operating on locational choice, the spatial variations in the cost of undertaking a given industrial activity should be capable of explaining the pattern of plant location (that is, there should be a correspondence between the form of the total cost surface and the areal distribution of the industry in question). As was suggested in Part Three, there are sound theoretical reasons for the expectation that such industries would tend toward concentration around the point or points of low costs, or maximum profits, with a random dispersal of plants in the peripheral intramarginal areas of higher costs and lower profit potential.

Testing such a proposition empirically is extremely difficult, and there is to date no single published attempt to show how far the location of a specific industry at a national level is consistent with this version of variable-cost theory. The two main problems are the technical difficulty of constructing a cost surface that provides a reasonable indication of comparative economic advantage for an entire industry, and the fact that there are always some variables other than input costs influencing locational decisions. The second of these problems is particularly serious, for even in a case where areal variations in costs can offer a reasonably good explanation of plant location, the incorporation of such factors as economies of scale, areal variations in the demand function, industrial inertia, and personal preference may be impossible in anything other than very indirect manner because of measurement difficulties. Nevertheless, attempting such a test is a useful exercise with which to conclude the sections of this book dealing with empirical applications. Doing this provides a final illustration of the identification of cost surfaces in the real world, based on much more detailed data than in any of the cases previously considered. It also provides another indication of the extreme difficulty involved in generating a precise explanation for an industrial location pattern directly from existing location theory.

The subject of this study is a branch of the electronics industry concerned with the manufacture of certain electronic equipment. Among the products included under this heading are telephone and telegraph apparatus, radio and television communications equipment, and some connected with government space and military projects. The 1963 *Census of Manufacturing* shows a total value of shipments of almost $9000 M, with the main contributors to the industry's costs being materials ($3527 M) and labor ($3380 M). About 475,000 workers were employed, in a total of 1222 establishments. The existing location pattern shows the main concentration in the major manufacturing belt, with the emphasis on the eastern end, and a secondary concentration in California.

In order to identify cost surfaces, information is required on the quantity of the various inputs needed and the volume and destination of shipments of finished products. There are two alternative ways of providing this; the first is to attempt to build up average figures for the entire industry, while the second is to base the analysis on actual data for a representative firm. The second approach is the one adopted here, the main reason being the availability of a particularly good set of data for one manufacturer of electronic equipment.*

The firm in question is a relatively large one, with a labor force of 3300. This puts it at the upper end of the plant size continuum, since only 55 of the industry's 1222 establishments in 1963 employed over 2500. However, it is the large firms that are responsible for the bulk of production in this industry, and it is the large establishments that mainly determine the geographical pattern of production.

The annual production is 59,000 cwt of goods, distributed to a national market. The volume of sales, allocated between fifty-seven territories, is mapped in Figure 18.10. Almost 40 percent of sales are in the major manufacturing belt while the rest are about equally divided between the Pacific coast, the southeastern region, and the rest of the nation—

---

* The author is grateful to The Fantus Company, Chicago, for access to the cost data on which this study was based. As in the previous illustration, some of the details have had to be obscured so as not to reveal the exact nature of the business in question.

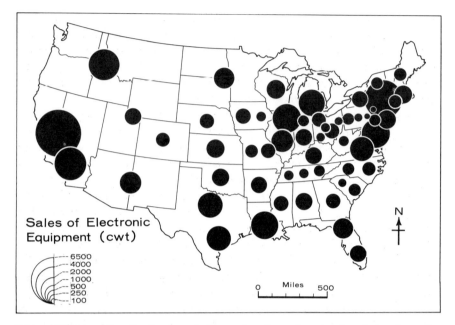

Figure 18.10. The distribution of the market for a firm in the electronic equipment industry in 1966. (*Source of Data.* The Fantus Company.)

a pattern that closely reflects the allocation of the national market for the entire industry.

The firm on which this study is based is, in most significant respects, representative of the major producers in the branch of the electronics industry which is under review. The geographical pattern of costs based on the characteristics of this firm should therefore provide a close indication of the general cost conditions under which this activity is conducted. However, no single firm can be truly representative of an entire industry in every respect, and in the analysis that follows it is important to keep in mind the possibility that certain distinctive features of the firm have some bearing on the results.

a. Constructing the Cost Surfaces

The first step in the identification of cost surfaces in this kind of analysis is to establish a suitable set of control points for compiling the necessary data. Ideally, a regular system of points would be used, as in the study of the Swedish clothing industry by Törnqvist (1962) summarized in the previous chapter, but it is impossible to prepare accurate cost figures on this basis in the present case. For this analysis, fifty-seven

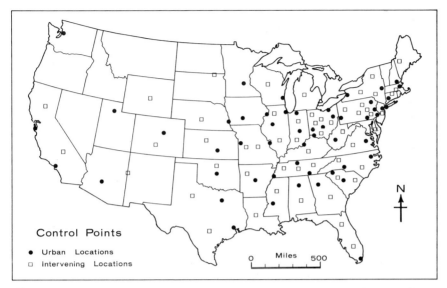

Figure 18.11. Control points used in compiling data for the identification of cost surfaces in the electronic equipment industry.

cities were selected, and to these were added an equal number of points considered to be representative of conditions in the intervening rural areas. The location of the control points is shown in Figure 18.11. The great advantage of the system used here is that the inclusion of both city and rural places avoids the emphasis on conditions in the major metropolitan areas, which is a serious source of bias in much official data on the cost of industrial inputs, in particular labor. The main disadvantage is the uneven distribution of points across the nation, which means that the surfaces will be identified in much more detail in the eastern half of the country than in the western half.

The major inputs contributing to areal variations in total costs in this industry may be summarized under five headings. These are listed in Table 18.15, together with summary figures relating to the extent of cost differences between the 114 control points. The industry is highly labor intensive, with expenditure on this input making up on average about 90 percent of the total spatially variable operating costs. State and local taxes are the item subject to the greatest relative variation, the bill at the location where it is highest being twelve times the figure where it is least, compared with a ratio of only about two for the cost of labor. How each item contributes to the pattern of total costs is indicated in a comparison between the forms of the respective surfaces. The five input cost surfaces are illustrated in Figures 18.12 to 18.16, and each of these

Table 18.15 Variations in the Cost of the Major Spatially Variable Inputs among 114 Alternative Locations for an Electronics Firm, 1966 ($1000)

Item	Median Cost	Highest Cost	Lowest Cost	Range	Highest ÷ Lowest
Labor	11,891	14,530	7,070	7,460	2.05
Freight	377	619	345	274	1.80
Occupancy	585	846	399	447	2.12
Utilities	226	343	128	215	2.68
Taxes	140	447	37	410	12.08
Total	13,139	16,147	8,203	7,944	1.97

Source of Data. The Fantus Company.

may be examined in turn along with an explanation of exactly how the figures were compiled.

Labor costs were calculated on the basis of 2100 production workers, 850 of them males, and 1200 salaried employees all but 300 of which are males. The big proportion of salaried employees is a typical feature of this industry, which needs large numbers of highly skilled technologists and scientific personnel; in the industry as a whole in 1963 the wages of production workers in fact made up only half the total payroll. The general features of the labor-cost surface (Figure 18.12) conform fairly closely to those shown on some of the maps in Chapters 3 and 15, with relatively low costs in the South and high costs in the north and west. The lowest-cost area for labor is in rural eastern South Carolina, while the maximum figure is in Detroit.

There are two elements in the calculation of the total freight bill, relating to outbound and inbound shipments, respectively. The outbound freight costs were computed on the basis of the distribution of sales indicated in Figure 18.10. Freight rates from each of the control points to each of the fifty-seven market territories were determined, and the cost per hundredweight was multiplied by the total weight to be shipped to the territory in question. Less than truckload Class 100 rates were assumed, and adjustment factors were applied to the figures to reflect the different rates on different sizes of shipments. The basic procedure is, of course, identical to that involved in the application of the aggregate travel model (see Chapter 16).

The five major materials are metal stampings, transformers, die castings, wire, and cables. However, most of these are of high value in relation to bulk, and the cost of transportation is in consequence very low. Although the cost at highest point was almost five times that at the lowest, the actual range was only just over $40,000, which is much

THREE CASE STUDIES 379

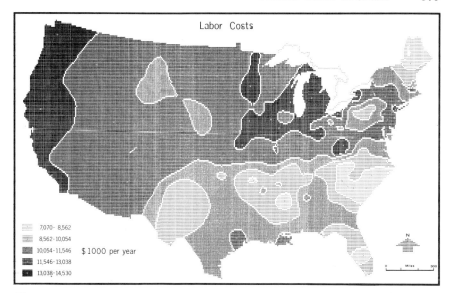

Figure 18.12. The manufacture of electronic equipment: the labor-cost surface. (*Source of Data.* The Fantus Company.)

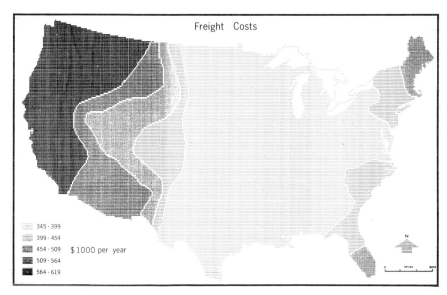

Figure 18.13. The manufacture of electronic equipment: the freight-cost surface. (*Source of Data.* The Fantus Company.)

smaller than the range in the cost of the other inputs considered (Table 18.15) and insignificant in relation to the figures for total costs. For this reason the transport costs involved in the assembly of materials were omitted from the cost-surface analysis.

The surface of freight costs (Figure 18.13) thus refers entirely to the outbound shipments of the finished product. As the distribution of the market broadly reflects the pattern of the national market as a whole, the general form of the surface bears a strong resemblance to the aggregate travel surface illustrated in Chapter 16 (Figure 16.1). The point of minimum freight costs, or optimum access to the market, is St. Louis, while the highest cost is from the Pacific northwest.

The occupancy costs were calculated on the basis of buildings with 500,000 square feet of floor space, including 360,000 square feet for manufacturing and the remainder occupied by offices and laboratories. The figures include the cost of both buildings and land, with amortization over a twenty-year period at current rates. The general form of the surface (Figure 18.14) is similar to that for labor costs in certain respects, with a zone of low costs in the South, relatively high costs in the major manufacturing belt, and peaks along the Pacific coast. The lowest figure is found in rural Mississippi, and the highest is in New York City.

The utilities requirements are gas for heating the 500,000 square feet of building space, 2,400,000 gallons of water per month for washroom facilities for the employees, and the same volume of sewage to be disposed of. Power is provided by electricity, consumption being at 5000 kw, 1,000,000 kwh per month. The surface of utility costs (Figure 18.15) is mainly a reflection of the electricity bill. The largest area of costs in the lowest category is in the Pacific northwest, where the cheap hydroelectric power gives this corner of the country the only major advantage for the electronics industry revealed by a comparative-cost analysis. The lowest utility costs are in Memphis, within a well-defined area of low costs in Tennessee which is largely explained by the relatively cheap power from TVA dams. The highest figure is in rural southern New York state, where the utilities bill slightly exceeds that in New York City.

The tax costs include local ad valorum and real property taxes. They are based on $3,200,000 worth of machinery and equipment, raw materials in the value of $5,200,000, and $3,000,000 of finished goods. The tax-cost surface (Figure 18.16) differs in certain important respects from the other surfaces. The South again shows up as an area of relatively low costs, but so does part of the northwest. The major manufacturing belt contains local areas of very high and very low figures, and the surface as a whole shows much greater relative spatial variation than in the case of any of the other inputs, as was suggested in Table 18.15. The highest figure is in Boston, while the lowest is in Atlanta.

THREE CASE STUDIES 381

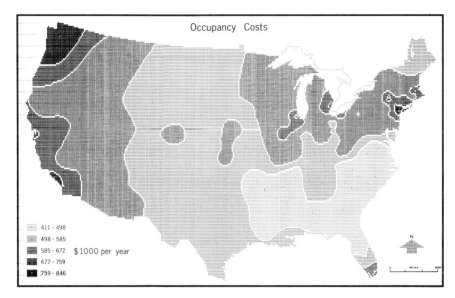

Figure 18.14. The manufacture of electronic equipment: the occupancy-cost surface. (*Source of Data.* The Fantus Company.)

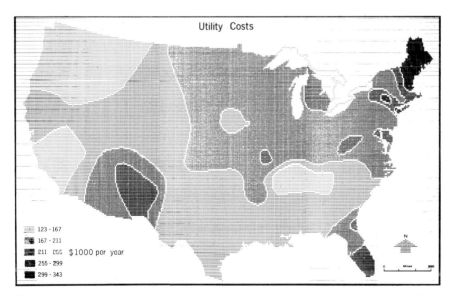

Figure 18.15. The manufacture of electronic equipment: the utilities-cost surface. (*Source of Data.* The Fantus Company.)

382   SOME EMPIRICAL APPLICATIONS

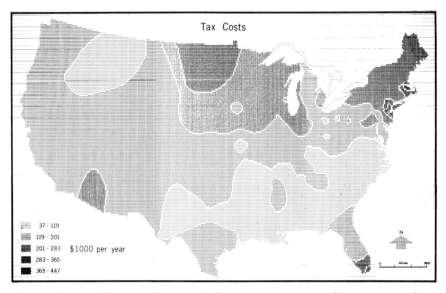

Figure 18.16. The manufacture of electronic equipment: the tax-cost surface. (*Source of Data.* The Fantus Company.)

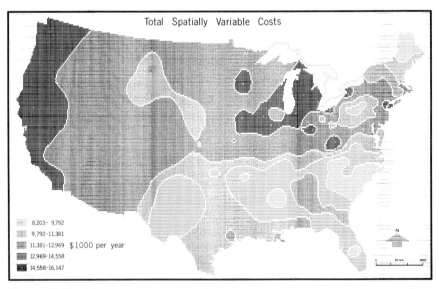

Figure 18.17. The manufacture of electronic equipment: the total-cost surface. (*Source of Data.* The Fantus Company.)

The sum of the five input cost surfaces gives the surface for total spatially variable operating costs. This is shown in Figure 18.17. The least-cost location is in rural eastern South Carolina, within the most extensive single area to fall in the lowest of the cost categories recognized on the map. The five locations with the lowest costs are all rural control points, the least-cost city site being Columbia, South Carolina. The highest costs (almost exactly twice the lowest figure) are in Detroit, followed by the San Francisco-Oakland area, Davenport in Iowa, and Seattle. The general form of the total-cost surface indicates that the most advantageous region for the manufacture of this kind of electronic equipment on the basis of comparative operating costs is the South, while the highest-cost regions are the mid-west and the Pacific coast.

It will be apparent from a comparison between Figures 18.17 and 18.12 that the form of the surface of total costs is very largely explained by the nature of the labor-cost surface. They are very similar to one another, and virtually identical in many areas. This is to be expected in view of the large contribution of labor costs to the total operating costs of this industry. The hypothesis that the location of the production of electronics equipment can be explained by spatial variations in operating costs can thus almost be restated as that the location pattern will be a reflection of the geography of labor costs.

b. Explaining the Location of the Electronic Equipment Industry

How far does the total-cost surface explain the existing location of the manufacture of electronic equipment? The state distribution of value added in this industry in 1963 is illustrated in Figure 18.18, and a comparison with the cost surface in Figure 18.17 shows very little correspondence. The main concentration of production, in a belt extending from Massachusetts southwestward through New York and New Jersey into Maryland, is revealed as an area of varying cost levels with the highest value added being in the central part where costs are higher. The two secondary concentrations, in the mid-west and on the west coast, both correspond with two of the areas of highest operating costs. In the low-cost zone which occupies much of the South there is very little electronic equipment manufacturing, and in South Carolina, which contains the optimum location determined by comparative-cost analysis, the industry is virtually nonexistent.

The hypothesis that the actual location of the electronics equipment industry can be adequately explained by areal variations in operating costs thus must be rejected. The failure of this test of the predictive capacity of variable-cost theory does not of course mean that the distribution of the industry in question is incapable of rational explanation.

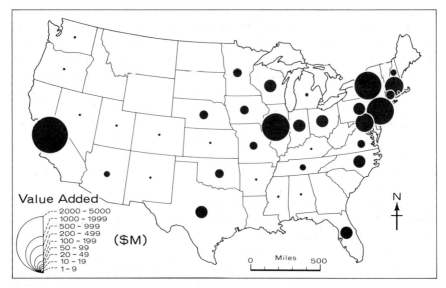

Figure 18.18. The location of the electronic equipment industry, 1963. (*Source. Census of Manufacturing*, 1963.)

Nor does it immediately invalidate the variable-cost approach to industrial location analysis. It simply means that in this case the prevailing geography of input costs, measured in a particular manner, is by itself incapable of providing an explanation, and that there are other causal factors yet to be identified.

There are two possible general reasons for the failure of a variable-cost model to explain the location of a specific industry. The first is that the cost data used in the construction of the surfaces might not accurately represent the comparative advantage of alternative locations with respect to access to certain of the inputs considered, because the figures are not a true measure of real cost per unit of output. The second is that low-cost access to the inputs included in the analysis is itself not the major determinant of plant location. A third possibility—that entrepreneurs in this particular industry make their locational decisions with almost complete disregard for the prevailing geographical pattern of economic advantage —must be rejected as being at variance with both theory and observation of business behavior, although the operation of personal noneconomic factors will have some bearing on the location of the manufacture of electronic equipment, as in any other industry.

The main factor which falls into the first of these categories is the possible failure of the data on labor costs to provide an accurate indication of the comparative advantage of different areas for this critical input. In a thorough study of the electronics industry in the state of Illinois, Nourse (1967, 52) stresses the difficulty of measuring the labor factor in an industry which is not particularly interested in cheap labor in the usual sense of the term. He emphasizes the importance of scientists, engineers, and skilled electronic technicians, and the fact that only half of the payroll is accounted for by the wages of production workers has already been mentioned. In addition, labor with high attainments of skill and education generally tends to be relatively mobile, and this can reduce its influence on plant location.

However, it cannot be argued that labor exercises no effect on the location of the electronic equipment industry. Areas that contain relatively large numbers of the right sort of skilled employees would exert some kind of attraction, which would tend to favor the existing concentrations of the industry. A firm setting up a new plant could probably be assured of an adequate choice of workers in the Boston or Los Angeles areas, but there could be no such expectation in rural eastern South Carolina. Thus a location which (in Figure 18.12) has high labor costs might well be prefered to one where costs appear to be substantially lower. Another reason for the apparent anomaly of an industry concentrated in areas of high labor costs is that wage rates there may be a reflection of greater skill and higher productivity. There are thus a number of reasons for not accepting the labor-cost figures presented above at face value, and it is these figures that very largely determine the form of the total-cost surface.

It is now necessary to consider the second possibility—that there are other important factors influencing plant location in this industry which tend to reduce the significance of areal variations in operating costs. These factors might be strong enough to counteract the apparent cost disadvantages in certain areas, making the high-cost locations far more attractive than they appear. In the manufacture of electronics equipment there is one factor of this kind that can be expected to have a very considerable influence on locational choice—the external economies arising in certain existing industrial agglomerations.

The industry under review, which includes the manufacture of highly sophisticated equipment for missile systems and space exploration, is in the forefront of scientific research. This research, both pure and applied, is a critical factor in the design of products and in the process of manufacture, and scientific information can perhaps be regarded as the most important single input in the production of electronic equipment. Although this input cannot be costed for alternative locations in the same way as the items studied in the previous section, there is no doubt that such information can be very expensive indeed. This factor will influence plant location if the cost or availability of scientific information varies significantly from place to place, and there is ample evidence that it does. Firms in this kind of industry have much to gain from close contact with universities and other technical institutes where there are people conducting relevant research, and in general from being part of a complex of plants engaged in a group of related activities. Any information that can be derived partly or entirely from an external source, such as a university, obviously will save a firm a considerable amount of money.

Nourse (1967, 54–57) has used the distribution of military prime contracts for research work as an indication of where the main research centers in this field are. In 1962, 34 percent by value of all contracts were awarded to institutions within the state of Massachusetts, with Maryland second (14 percent), California third (12 percent) and Illinois fourth (almost 8 percent). The twelve southeastern states accounted for only about 3 percent, and those of the plains and the Rockies had even less. Even though research and manufacturing do not have of necessity to be at the same location, these figures may go a long way toward explaining the attraction of certain areas, and the fact that their concentrations of electronics equipment manufacturing are at variance with their relative status with respect to operating costs. However, they do not explain the very large components of this industry in New York and New Jersey (together having only about 8 percent of military contracts), which must be attributed more to their general position in the core of the major agglomeration extending from Massachusetts to Maryland. Another related factor that helps to explain the concentration in the northeast is proximity to the centers of government decision making, which is of obvious importance in an industry where the national government is not only the major market for many products but also in effect an active partner in business planning.

The location of this electronic equipment industry is thus a case where the conventional variable-cost approach is incapable of providing a sound explanation, despite the quality of the input cost data which are available. The external economies which appear to exercise the dominant influence on locational choice are notoriously difficult to measure, which made it impossible to incorporate them into the original variable-cost model. If there were some way of accurately measuring areal differences in the cost advantages arising from access to an existing concentration of the electronics industry and related research activity, this could be added to the input cost data, and could be expected to have a dramatic effect on the form of the total-cost surface. Such a surface might well provide a reasonably good explanation of the existing location of production, although other factors such as industrial inertia and the personal element in locational choice would doubtless prevent the explanation from being anywhere near perfect. Unfortunately, this hypothesis cannot be tested. Another line of inquiry (beyond the scope of this illustration) would be to examine the location of new plants, to see how far this conforms to the comparative areal advantages suggested by input costs.

Although the comparative-cost analysis conducted here did not provide an explanation of the location pattern, something of importance was achieved by the identification of the cost surfaces, in addition to their value as an illustration of the technique itself. First, the failure of the surface of total cost to correspond with the distribution of production led the inquiry towards other causal factors, and a consequent alteration of the initial hypothesis. Second, the cost analysis does suggest a very considerable spatial variation in operating costs, against which a new firm might weigh its assessment of the more intangible advantages arising from external economies. Assuming for the sake of argument that the data on input costs, including the labor figures, provide an accurate indication of a manufacturer's likely operating costs, then the firm in question would be able to judge the size of the cost penalty in California or Massachusetts, for example, which external economies would have to compensate for. On the basis of the cost data, a firm for whom the external economies are not particularly important might well find a good location in South Carolina.

18.4 CONCLUDING REMARKS

The three case studies presented in this chapter, together with the briefer illustrations in Chapters 15, 16, and 17 give some indication of how far the theoretical approach to industrial location anaylsis developed in Part Three is capable of direct application in empirical research. Great emphasis has been placed on the use of cost surfaces as a means of identifying areal variations in economic advantage, in the general context of the variable-cost model. This approach has its roots in classical location theory originating with Weber, but its application to real-world situations has, to date, been rather limited. The study of the electronics equipment industry in this chapter, and those of the Swedish paper and clothing industries summarized in Chapter 17, show that the empirical identification of cost surfaces is much more of a practical possibility than is generally assumed. This greatly assists the use of the variable-cost model as an explanatory and predictive device.

Using cost surfaces as the basis for a model capable of explaining actual patterns of industrial location is a procedure fraught with difficulties, however. It has not proved possible to offer in this book a really convincing illustration of a single industrial location pattern displaying a form close to that predicted by areal variations in total operating costs. As previously emphasized, there is a strong theoretical basis for believing that the location of industries where the demand factor is not particularly important should reflect the prevailing cost geography, subject to random deviations expressing the process of historical evolution and the entrepreneur's freedom of locational choice within certain spatial limits. However, this general proposition has yet to be subjected to adequate empirical testing. There is enormous scope for research in this field, replicating the kind of analysis attempted above in the study of the electronic equipment industry in a wide range of other activities to see how far a surface relating to spatially variable operating costs can in fact explain actual location patterns. If the results were as unconvincing as in the electronics equipment case, serious doubt might be cast on the validity of the variable-cost model, and the body of theory on which it rests. No matter how sensible this theory may be on a priori grounds, its ultimate acceptance as a true guide to the way plant locations are arrived at is dependent on the results of the kind of testing advocated here. And this requires overcoming some serious problems involved in the accurate measurement of spatial variations in input costs and the effect of such other factors as external economies of agglomeration.

The development and application of models incorporating the demand factor, in the sense of areal variations in the volume of sales and total revenue, remains a most difficult matter. Despite limited success with the market potential model, market-area analysis, and models such as those developed by Hoover (1966, 1967a) and capable of incorporating demand functions, empirical applications are still very few indeed. The reciprocal relationship between supply and demand, and the locational interdependence of firms, makes the demand factor particularly difficult to handle in operational models, as well as in theory, as is readily apparent from previous sections of this book. The full incorporation of the demand factor within the conventional variable-cost model continues to be one of the major research problems facing industrial location analysis.

It is largely the failure to adequately integrate cost and demand within the same operational model which limits the practical application of the concept of the spatial margin to profitability. Such emphasis was placed on the value of this concept in the theoretical synthesis of Part Three that the failure to include specific examples in the subsequent case studies cannot pass without comment. With the sole exception of a brave attempt by Taylor (1970) there is as yet no published example of the actual identification of a spatial margin, though inferences based on their likely form have been made in a few empirical studies (for example, Smith, 1970b). The truth is that the empirical identification of spatial margins requires more data than the construction of a cost surface or the running of a market potential model, even when simplifying assumptions relating to such matters as scale, price, and entrepreneurial skill have been made. To find in practice a locus of points where total operating costs for a representative or average firm exactly equal the revenue obtainable at that location requires far more information than is normally available. Again there is a fruitful field of research here; cost surfaces are easier to identify than is often supposed, and so it may be with spatial margins to profitability when suitable operational procedures have been evolved. But even if they cannot yet be constructed for real-world situations, the spatial margin to profitability, as an abstract theoretical concept, remains an important aid to the interpretation of an industrial world governed by decisions which seldom conform to economic rationality.

Part Four has thus indicated many of the limitations of existing theory as a basis for explaining the real world, as well as illustrating some aspects of its useful application. Above all is the very great difficulty of generating sound hypotheses, or accurate explanations, of existing industrial location patterns. Successful attempts to do this by direct measurement of the cost and demand factors are restricted to cases with a very small number of firms, such as in Kennelly's study of the Mexican steel industry reported in Chapter 17. This is understandable, since many variables have to be held constant to develop any operational model of industrial location, and the ones that remain are often very hard to measure precisely.

Although these conclusions have stressed the limitations of classical or neoclassical location theory, this should not be interpreted as questioning the basic validity of this approach. The space devoted to the exposition and extension of classical theory in this book is, in fact, a personal testament of faith in this body of knowledge as the best general conceptual framework which human ingenuity has yet been able to devise in this field. As has been made clear, the problems arise more from difficulties of measurement than from the inadequacies of the theoretical structures and models themselves. The classical models certainly have their conceptual weaknesses, but they cannot be dismissed until they have been shown to be either entirely nonoperational or largely impotent as explanatory or predictive devices. The contents of Part Four, while revealing some of both the practical and the conceptual problems inherent in the classical approach, offer hope that this body of theory may yet be capable of providing an interpretation for much of the complexity of the real industrial world.

PART FIVE

Some Alternative Approaches

Part Five discusses some alternative approaches to industrial location analysis. They differ from those considered in Part Four in that they are less directly derived from the theoretical framework developed in Part Three. Taken together, they have a very considerable range of possible applications, for they can assist in practical matters of plant site selection and in the explanation and prediction of locational change, as well as in the interpretation of existing industrial locations.

First, correlation and regression analysis is examined, as a means of developing and testing specific hypotheses regarding the distribution of particular industries (Chapter 19). This is followed by a review of the application of linear programming to industrial location problems (Chapter 20). Finally, there is a short discussion of input-output analysis (Chapter 21). All three approaches involve the manipulation of matrixes of numerical data, but no knowledge of matrix algebra on the part of the reader is assumed.

The three chapters that follow are not exhaustive treatments of the topics in question. The reviews of the literature are somewhat more selective than in previous chapters, although an attempt has been made to refer to most of the major contributions under each heading. The examples presented in the text are offered as a general indication of some of the ways in which the approaches considered may usefully be applied to a variety of industrial location problems, rather than as model illustrations. It must also be stressed that none of the three approaches dealt with belong exclusively to the field of industrial location analysis, and that they have a much wider general range of application in spatial economic studies than is indicated here.

19

Correlation and Regression Analysis

There are many circumstances in industrial location analysis where it is necessary to conduct a statistical test of some explanatory hypothesis. An obvious case would be where a model derived from location theory (for example, the variable-cost model as used in Section 18.3 in the previous chapter) generates an expectation of the way some industry should be located, which it is required to compare with reality. Measuring the association between the expected and observed pattern by an appropriate statistical test would indicate how far the initial hypothesis constituted an adequate explanation of the location of the industry under review. There are also circumstances in which some standard statistical procedure, such as linear regression analysis, provides a reasonable method of modeling a situation where location theory itself cannot offer a suitable operational device to accommodate the relevant variables. In such a case the model would generate an expectation, and test it against the observed pattern.

The designing and constructing of statistical tests is a complex subject, and beyond the scope of this volume. Useful treatments will be found in a number of books on quantitative methods in geographical inquiry (for example, Gregory, 1963; Cole and King, 1969; and King, 1969), and there are more complete discussions in statistics texts (for instance, Hagood and Price, 1952; Siegel, 1956; Ezekiel and Fox, 1959; and Huntsberger, 1961). All that is attempted here is a brief introduction to some of the most commonly used methods of comparing a set of observations with other sets, together with some illustrations of the application of the multiple linear regression model as probably the most useful of these methods to industrial location analysis.

19.1 METHODS

The simplest numerical method for comparing one (observed) industrial location pattern with another (expected) pattern is by the use of the *coefficient of geographical association* (C_g). This is one of a set of similar measures, sometimes referred to as *Gini* coefficients, which are used frequently in economic geography. The coefficient of geographical association is found from:

$$C_g = \tfrac{1}{2} \sum_{i=1}^{n} \left| \frac{X_i}{X_t} - \frac{Y_i}{Y_t} \right| \qquad (19.1)$$

where

X_i = magnitude of industry X in area i
X_t = total magnitude of industry X in region or nation under study
Y_i = magnitude of industry Y in area i
Y_t = total magnitude of industry Y in region or nation.

The summation is over n areal units, and the vertical brackets indicate the modulus or absolute value of the expression within, ie the differences irrespective of sign. The values for C_g range from 0, indicating exact correspondence between the two patterns, to 1.0 indicating that the one is the exact reverse of the other. In some texts X_i and Y_i are multiplied by 100, in which case the calculation becomes a comparison between two percentage distributions with C_g being half the sum of the deviations between them, and the coefficient then ranges from 0 to 100. Examples of the calculation and use of this and similar coefficients can be found in such texts as Alexander (1963, 406–410, 594–600), Isard (1960, 249–279), and Nourse (1968, 65–68, 152–4), as well as in numerous research papers (for example, Rodgers, 1957; Conkling, 1963, 1964). The two sets of values for X and Y can represent two industries where a causal relationship is postulated, or one might be an observed distribution while the other is an expectation generated by some model.

Unfortunately this coefficient is subject to a number of serious reservations as a means of testing the association between two variables. Like other measures of a similar kind, C_g is highly sensitive to the size of the areal units for which the data have been compiled, and the result can change substantially with slight alterations of the areal or industrial classification (Duncan, Cuzzort, and Duncan, 1961, 82–90; Lloyd and Dicken, 1968). And C_g does not detect the degree to which systematic changes in one variable are accompanied by change in another, but simply measures what proportion of one variable would have to be moved over to the other to make the two distributions correspond. Thus there are few circumstances where this coefficient could legitimately be preferred to the more conventional correlation techniques if anything more than a very rough comparison between two distributions is required. As has been shown by McCarty, Hook, and Knos (1956, 30–44), C_g may give results which differ considerably from those of other correlation methods.

The most frequently used of all measures of correlation is undoubtedly the *product moment correlation coefficient* (r). With linear regression analysis, it is often used as a means of testing the association between an observed and an expected pattern. The value of r varies from 1.0, indicating a perfect positive relationship between the two variables, to -1.0 which represents a perfect negative relationship. If more than one causal factor is involved (that is, if it is required to predict the values for one variable from values for more than one other variable), then *multiple correlation and regression analysis* can be used. These methods will be examined in the next section, but it is necessary to point out here some of the problems that can arise in applying such standard statistical devices to areally distributed data. As Robinson (1956) has shown, varying the size of the areal units used to compile the data can substantially affect the result when calculating r, a general problem which has been reviewed by Duncan, Cuzzort, and Duncan (1960, 62–80). Robinson has suggested a method of weighting the values in correlation analysis involving areal data, and Thomas and Anderson (1965) have put forward an inferential approach to the problem based on knowledge of the probability of specific r values being attributable to random factors. It seems sensible to regard the system of areal units as one of an infinite number of possible alternatives, and if the actual system can be viewed in statistical terms as a chance occurrence (just as a random sample of observations would be) it is possible to regard calculated r values as correct within the margins of error usually calculated in any form of parametric statistical analysis. Another problem in spatial analysis is that of autocorrelation, arising from the contiguity of data collection units and the fact that the value in one area can be regarded as partially related to those in adjoining areas (Tobler, 1966; King, 1969, 157–62).

The technicalities of the calculation of the product moment correlation coefficient impose two major constraints on the kind of data that can be used: (1) the data should be normally distributed, or capable of transformation by the use of logarithms or any other appropriate function; and (2) the data should be on an interval or ratio scale. If these conditions are not met, another technique must be used to measure correlation.

If the best data available are on an ordinal scale (that is, the observations can be placed in rank order but individual values are not known), a rank correlation technique may be employed. The one generally used is *Spearman's rank correlation coefficient* (r_s), which is given by:

$$r_s = 1 - \frac{6 \sum_{i=1}^{n} d_i^2}{n^3 - n} \qquad (19.2)$$

where d_i is the difference between the rank scores on the two variables for observation i, and n is the total number of observations. The coefficient will vary between 1.0 and -1.0, and can give a fairly reliable estimate of the product moment coefficient (Siegel, 1956, 202–213; Gregory, 1963, 181–184; McCarty, Hook and Knoss, 1956, 26–30). An illustration of the use of r_s appeared in Section 18.2 of the previous chapter (Table 18.9). This coefficient may sometimes be used if data on a higher-order scale of measurement are available but are not considered reliable enough to give anything more than information on the ranking of individual observations.

There may be situations in which not even ranking is feasable. But some measure of association between the occurrence of two attributes is possible as long as areas can be classified on a nominal scale according to whether they have or have not the attributes in question. The *chi-square* (χ^2) *test* can indicate the probability that the observed association could have arisen by chance, and the contingency coefficient (C) can measure the degree of association between the occurrence of the two attributes. An example of a situation in which these methods could be used is where a number of factories are observed, with some occupying sites beside railroad stations and others not; χ^2 could show whether the factories are significantly concentrated in railroad station locations at a given level of probability, and the calculation of C could show how strong the association is. The formulas for the chi-square test and the contingency coefficient and the procedure for conducting the test are described in most statistics texts (for example, Walker and Lev, 1953, 95–106 and 186–187; Siegel, 1956, 104–111 and 196–202; Huntsberger, 1961, 180–185). Some illustrations of the use of χ^2 in industrial location analysis will be found in a study of the British paper industry by Lewis (1969).

One further coefficient that may be useful in special circumstances is the *point biserial correlation coefficient* (r_{pb}). This can be used when data on a ratio or interval scale exist for one variable but the other can only be scaled according to whether areas have or have not the attribute in question. The procedure is simply to assign arbitrary numbers to the nominal data, generally giving 1 to the "has" items or areas, and 0 to the "has not" items, and then calculate the product moment coefficient (Walker and Lev, 1953, 261–267).

19.2 MULTIPLE CORRELATION AND REGRESSION ANALYSIS

The simple linear regression model describing the relationship between two variables takes the form $Y = a + bX$, where Y is the dependent variable (that which is to be explained), X is the independent variable (the postulated causal factor), and a and b are constants. To be strictly correct, a random error variate (e) should also be added to the expression. Simple regression analysis may be used in an attempt to explain or predict an industrial location pattern in circumstances where it seems reasonable to propose just one significant causal factor, with the correlation coefficient (r) indicating the strength of the observed relationship between the sets of values for X and Y.

However, the location of an industry can seldom be adequately accounted for by only one causal factor. Usually a number of independent variables are involved, and a multiple correlation and regression analysis is then required. The general multiple regression model takes the form:

$$Y = a + b_1X_1 + b_2X_2 \ldots + b_nX_n + e \qquad (19.3)$$

where Y is the dependent variable, X (1, 2, . . . , n) the independent variables, a the intercept constant, b (1, 2, . . . , n) the regression coefficients, and e the error term. The coefficient of multiple correlation (R) measures the strength of the relationship between the dependent variable and the set of independent variables. Multiple regression analysis provides a model for predicting the magnitude of some variable according to a specific hypothesis. The examination and mapping of the residuals from regression (that is, the difference between the actual values and those predicted by the regression equation) can help to indicate the adequacy of the hypothesis which has been tested; if all the relevant independent variables have been included the geographical pattern of the residuals should be random, whereas a regularity of occurrence could suggest other possible causal factors not originally considered. The methods of calculation involved in simple and multiple correlation and regression analysis are fully described in statistics texts (for example, Ezikial and Fox, 1959), and a particularly useful summary with geographical illustrations will be found in King (1969, 135–152).

Before demonstrating the application of multiple correlation and regression analysis in the field of industrial location, some general comments on its use in this context are required. Although there are many circumstances in which this technique may be the best practical approach to explanation in an industrial location study, it must be regarded as a less than perfect alternative to the more direct methods outlined in previous chapters. The use of a multiple regression model is in fact generally a response to the type of numerical data available for the measurement of the independent variables. As will be clear from the examples presented in Part Four, the practical application of models generated directly from location theory requires a very high quality of cost and revenue data, and there are serious difficulties involved in adequately encompassing the more intangible factors in plant location because of measurement problems.

The multiple regression model is more flexible, since it can incorporate variables that are not direct measures of cost and revenue in alternative locations. Thus the effect of the occurrence of a certain mineral might be built in by the use of areal data relating to the volume of production, if figures for delivered price at alternative plant locations are not available. The effect of the market could be measured by areal variations in income or per capita sales, in the absence of figures on the cost of serving the market or on the total revenue obtainable from different locations. Even less easily measured factors such as external economies of agglomeration can be built into the model, for example by a variable relating to city size or the range of industrial employment. In addition, the presence or absence of some significant areal attribute (such as a port or a railroad station) can be included as a dichotomous variable. The use of such surrogates inevitably reduces the precision of the explanatory model, but the alternative may be the failure to include certain critical variables at all. Great care is needed to insure that the variables selected for a multiple regression model are adequate measures of the causal factors originally proposed, since the selection of poor surrogates can change the meaning of the hypothesis being tested.

Something of the rationale behind the use of multiple regression analysis, as it is generally applied to problems of industrial location, has been described by Spiegelman (1968, 4) as follows:

Multiple regression can explain location patterns that result from the location decisions of individual owners and managers when these decisions are economically "rational" and are based upon past experience and knowledge of existing area characteristics. Regression can also explain location patterns that are created by a process of differential economic success. For example, if economic success is awarded to electronics plants that locate near universities, a close correlation of growth in electronics employment with distribution of universities may result either from the actual decisions made by entrepreneurs to locate their plants near universities, or by a process of differential success in which plants so located expand while plants located elsewhere fail to expand.

Thus the location of an industry, or changes in its distribution, are generally explained as a function of a set of existing measurable areal characteristics.

This approach has its limitations, of course. It attempts to explain location patterns on the basis of conditions as they are at present or in the very recent past (for example, the date of the last census), whereas many plants were set up under circumstances which have subsequently changed considerably, and new ones may be a response to anticipated future conditions. Like most other approaches to industrial location analysis, it cannot readily accommodate such factors as industrial inertia, historical accident, and the personal preferences and character traits of the businessmen involved. In addition it must be stressed that the multiple linear regression model is concerned with a particular kind of statistical relationship between one dependent variable and a selected set of independent variables. As is true with all such techniques, a strong statistical relationship, as indicated by a high correlation coefficient, does not necessarily prove a strong cause-and-effect relationship. The results of a multiple regression analysis will have meaning in an explanatory context only if the research has been carefully designed and the independent variables selected on the basis of sound a priori reasoning. This is where the existing body of location theory enters the picture, assisting the investigator in erecting a sensible hypothesis for which multiple regression analysis is an appropriate test. For example, an examination of the cost structure of the industry in question and knowledge of the degree of areal variation in the cost of the major inputs can help the investigator to choose these variables that are most likely to have a bearing on locational choice. A sound theoretical basis helps to avoid the acceptance of spurious causal relationships suggested by high statistical correlations.

There are two basic approaches that can be used in applying multiple regression to industrial location analysis. The first involves starting with a relatively large number of independent variables and, by a process of elimination, finding the ones that most effectively account for the distribution of the industry in question. This so-called "shot-gun" approach may provide an efficient statistical prediction, but this must not be confused with an explanation, one variable may be able to predict another accurately without there being a causal relationship. There are a number of ways in which this kind of predictive model can be built, but usually a stepwise procedure is adopted. This involves starting with the

independent variable that has the highest simple correlation with the dependent variable, then adding the one that contributes most to the unexplained variation in the dependent variable, and then successively adding the other independent variables according to the same criterion. The procedure can be terminated at any stage when the addition of further variables brings no significant increase in the proportion of variance in the dependent variable that the model accounts for, thus eliminating the less important of the original variables. Stepwise regression analysis is explained and illustrated in more detail in texts on statistical methods (for example, in King, 1969, 145–148).

The second approach involves the testing of a specific explanatory hypothesis developed by deductive or inductive reasoning, and with a relatively small number of independent variables. The original hypothesis is accepted, rejected, or modified according to the results of the test. This approach is the one illustrated in the next section.

19.3 ILLUSTRATIONS OF MULTIPLE CORRELATION AND REGRESSION ANALYSIS

The multiple regression model can be used in the analysis of both existing location patterns and changes in industrial distribution. The illustrations that follow are concerned with explaining the existing location of two industries—machinery manufacturing and the production of paperboard containers—and represent two of the earliest applications of this approach. Examples of multiple regression analysis applied to the explanation or prediction of industrial changes can be found elsewhere (for example, in Thompson and Matilla, 1959; Spiegelman, 1968; and Smith, 1969b).

a. McCarty et al on the Location of the Machinery Industry

A useful illustration of the use of multiple correlation and regression analysis in the testing of specific locational hypotheses is provided in a well-known monograph by McCarty et al (1956). The industry under consideration is the manufacture of machinery other than electrical (SIC major industry group 35). There are strong a priori grounds for expecting this activity to be market oriented in its location, for there is very little loss of weight in the production process and a very considerable gain in bulk, which would make the finished product more costly to transport than the materials. However, the interconnection between the various branches of machinery manufacturing are so complex that it is difficult in practice to separate markets from material sources, for the customers of some firms may be the suppliers of others. Each activity forms a link in a production sequence, or "chain of production," and although firms in later stages of the sequence could be expected to locate near their markets those concerned with the earlier metal processing stages might well be material oriented. Any firm concerned with the manufacture of machinery can be expected to form part of a group of closely linked activities, and how it relates to other elements within the system will have an important bearing on locational choice.

The nature of the machinery industry and its place in the wider industrial system leads to the formulation of three hypotheses concerning the location of this activity. These are as follows:

1. *The area specialization hypothesis*, which proposes that the occurrence of the machinery industry will vary directly with the degree of specialization in manufacturing, in other words the greater the emphasis on manufacturing in an area's economy the greater the number of workers in machinery manufacturing. This hypothesis rests primarily on the assumption that machinery manufacturing is market oriented and that the markets consist of other manufacturing industries.

2. *The production sequence hypothesis*, which proposes that the occurrence of the machinery industry will vary directly with the occurrence of those industries which occupy the same or adjacent stages in the production sequence. Eleven industries, mainly concerned with the production of metal shapes and forms and fabricated metal products, are specified as falling into this category.

3. *The related industries hypothesis*, which proposes simply that the occurrence of machinery manufacturing will be more closely associated spatially with metal-using rather than nonmetal-using industries.

The first hypothesis was tested by simple regression analysis. The dependent variable is the number of workers employed in SIC group 35, and the independent variable the percentage of all workers engaged in manufacturing. The test was conducted by using four different sets of areal units, and it was found that the correlation at the state level in the United States ($r = 0.564$) and by prefectures in Japan ($r = 0.841$) was markedly higher than for United States counties ($r = 0.277$) and metropolitan areas ($r = 0.306$). Except in the case of the metropolitan areas, these coefficients are higher than the correlations between the specialization variable and employment in other selected industries (that is, food, tobacco, petroleum and coal products, and blast furnaces and steel mills) which would not be expected to be associated with the degree of specialization in manufacturing. The area specialization hypothesis is thus accepted as a partial but by no means complete explanation of variations in the spatial occurrence of machinery manufacturing.

The first step in testing the second hypothesis was to establish the degree of correlation between the distribution of machinery manufacturing and that of industries closely related to this activity in the production sequence. The results, at the state level in the United States, are given in Table 19.1. Most of the correlations are very high, with a tendency

Table 19.1 The Correlation between the Distribution of Employment in Machinery Manufacturing (SIC 35) and in Other Selected Metal-Consuming Industries in the United States, by States, 1950

Industry (SIC Number)	r	r^2
Later Stages		
Iron and steel foundries (332)	.879	.773
Nonferrous metal rolling and drawing (335)	.614	.377
Nonferrous foundries (336)	.959	.920
Miscellaneous primary metal industries (339)	.927	.859
Cutlery, hand tools, and hardware (342)	.741	.549
Heating and plumbing equipment (343)	.896	.803
Structural metal products (344)	.817	.668
Metal stamping and coating (346)	.954	.910
Fabricated wire products (348)	.842	.709
Electrical machinery (36)	.876	.767
Motor vehicles and equipment (371)	.514	.264
Earlier Stages		
Blast furnaces and steel mills (331)	.657	.432
Primary nonferrous metals (333)	.145	.021
Secondary nonferrous metals (334)	.802	.643

Source. McCarty et al (1956, 82).

toward a closer relationship between machinery manufacturing and later-stage activities than the earlier ones.

The next step is the multiple correlation and regression analysis. Eight of the original eleven later-stage industries were selected for this purpose, largely on the basis of their simple correlation coefficients with the machinery industry, those excluded being SIC groups 335, 342, and 343. The specialization variable from the first hypothesis was then added. These nine independent variables together were able to account for as much as 97.6 percent of the variance in state employment in machinery manufacturing, the coefficient of multiple correlation (R) being 0.988. However, when all of these variables are considered at the same time in the multiple regression model, five of them (SIC groups 332, 339, 348, 371 and the percentage of all workers in manufacturing) appear relatively unimportant in explaining the spatial occurrence of machinery manufacturing. This is because there is a high degree of intercorrelation between the independent variables, and the five referred to above can be adequately represented by the remaining four. The five can in fact be eliminated from the multiple regression analysis with very little reduction in the value of R. The final multiple regression equation is thus:

$$Y = 103.32 + 8.24X_1 - 1.08X_2 + 2.79X_3 + 0.05X_4 \tag{19.4}$$

where

X_1 = employment in nonferrous foundries
X_2 = employment in structural metal products
X_3 = employment in metal stamping and coating
X_4 = employment in electrical machinery manufacturing

and

Y = employment in machinery manufacturing (SIC group 35).

The coefficient of multiple correlation is now 0.986, and $R^2 = 0.972$. The production sequence hypothesis, formulated in this way, was thus found to provide a very accurate statistical explanation of the location of machinery manufacturing at the state level in 1950.

Repetition of the analysis at the county level for the same year produced almost as good a result. With seven independent variables (percentage of all workers in manufacturing together with employment in SIC groups 333, 336, 339, 346, 348, and 36), the coefficient of multiple correlation was 0.913, giving an explained variance of just over 83 percent. An analysis of the metropolitan areas gave $R = 0.942$ and $R^2 = 0.888$. These results further support the production sequence hypothesis as an explanation for the location of the machinery industry in the United States. A similar analysis at the prefecture level in Japan was able to account for almost 90 percent of the variance in machinery manufacturing with only three independent variables—percentage employed in manufacturing, employment in electrical machinery manufacturing, and employment in the production on transport equipment.

Testing the third (related industries) hypothesis produced a less positive result. The machinery industry was found to be generally more closely related in its distribution to that of the metal-using industries than the nonmetal-using industries, with a difference in the correlation coefficients large enough to accept the hypothesis tentatively in the United States.

But in Japan the reverse was found, with machinery manufacturing being more closely associated with the nonmetal-using industries.

b. Stafford on the Paperboard Container Industry

Another interesting study of a single industry is one by Stafford (1960) on the manufacture of paperboard containers (SIC group 267). As in the case of machinery, there are a priori reasons for proposing that the location of this activity will reflect the distribution of the market, since most of the material used is sold at a uniform delivered price throughout the United States and, in addition, proximity to the customer enables manufacturers to provide a faster and more personalized service. It is therefore hypothesized that the magnitude of the paperboard container industry will vary directly in relation to the magnitude of the market. The dependent variable is employment in SIC group 267 in 1953, by counties.

The size of the market in a given area cannot be measured directly, and the surrogate used by Stafford is employment in those industries which comprise the major markets for containers. These are food (SIC group 20), textiles (22), apparel (23), furniture (25), machinery (35), and electrical machinery (36). To these six independent variables is added the number of workers in manufacturing, in recognition of the fact that almost all industries use paperboard containers in one way or another.

The simple correlation coefficients between employment in the container industry and each of the independent variables, at the county level, are listed in Table 19.2. Multiple regression analysis indicated that the seven variables operating together could account for almost 89 percent of the variance in the dependent variable ($R = 0.941$). However, the least significant variables (the furniture industry, machinery manufactur-

Table 19.2 Correlation between the Distribution of Employment in the Manufacture of Paperboard Containers in the United States and Activities Taken to Measure the Market

Industry (SIC Number)	r	r^2
Food (20)	.900	.810
Textiles (22)	.473	.224
Apparel (23)	.748	.558
Furniture (25)	.814	.662
Machinery, except electrical (35)	.654	.427
Electrical machinery (36)	.820	.673
Total workers in manufacturing	.878	.771

Source. Stafford (1960, 264).

ing and total workers in manufacturing) could be dropped with almost no loss of explained variance ($R = 0.940$, $R^2 = 0.884$). The final multiple regression equation is:

$$Y = -0.0400 + 0.0601X_1 + 0.219X_2 + 0.0154X_3 + 0.0313X_4 \qquad (19.5)$$

where

X_1 = employment in the food industry
X_2 = employment in the textile industry
X_3 = employment in the apparel industry
X_4 = employment in the manufacture of electrical machinery

and

Y = employment in the manufacture of paperboard containers.

The market-orientation hypothesis can thus be accepted as a reasonably convincing general explanation of the location of the industry under review.

Like McCarty et al (1956), Stafford used the mapping of residuals from multiple regression to shed further light on the adequacy of the explanation provided by his final model. He found that the regression equation predicted well for counties with very few workers in the paperboard container industry, in other words absence of the industry is very closely related to the absence of a local market. Areas of extreme over or under prediction were found generally to be counties with moderate to heavy concentrations of workers in the industry, but employment in some of the major centers, such as Chicago and New York, was very well predicted. Although the residuals from regression indicated the possible operation of variables not incorporated in the market-orientation hypothesis, Stafford found that some of the discrepancies could be accounted for by the areal units used, since the product will not necessarily be consumed in the same county as it is produced.

20

Linear Programming

In Chapter 9 brief reference was made to the application of linear programming to problems of industrial location analysis. This approach has found particular favor with economists, and occupies a prominent place in the recent literature in regional science. It may now be examined more fully.

Linear programming provides a means of finding optimum solutions to practical problems. It can be used in a situation where it is required to maximize or minimize some quantity which is a function of a set of variables, subject to certain rules or constraints. The quantity to be maximized or minimized is known as the *objective function,* and takes the form of a linear equation. The *constraints* can be written as a series of linear equations or inequalites. Every linear programming problem has its original or *primal* solution and also a *dual;* if the primal problem is one of maximization the dual will be one of minimization and vice versa, so the dual can be thought of as the primal problem turned inside out.

A wide range of practical problems in industrial location can be stated in a linear programming format. The major operational advantage is that once the problem has been structured in this way it is capable of solution by one of the computer algorithms designed for solving the sets of equations in the general linear programming model. As well as offering the best course of action in a given set of circumstances, a linear programming solution can also be used as a model against which to test reality, thus providing a basis for judging how far actual locations or patterns are economically efficient, or predictable from the conditions incorporated into the program.

In addition to its value as an operational model, linear programming has a conceptual contribution to make to industrial location theory. The formulation of location problems in linear programming terms helps to reveal something of their general nature, stressing their common structural characteristics. Many aspects of classical location theory, including the basic Weber and von Thünen models, can be expressed as linear programming problems, and this approach has helped to show some of the complimentarity between location and other aspects of economic theory.

The treatment of linear programming here is confined to a simple exposition of general principles and a few highly selective practical illustrations. Many kinds of applications, including the more complex allocation and interregional linear programming models, are beyond the scope of this book, but summaries of these approaches and references to the relevant literature will be found elsewhere (for example, in Garrison, 1959b; Isard, 1960; and Massey, 1968). No attempt is made to explain the mathematical basis of the linear programming model and its solution, which is dealt with in specialist texts and in a number of papers to which reference is made below.

20.1 BASIC LINEAR PROGRAMMING FORMULATIONS

The best way to illustrate the structure of a linear programming problem is by a simple numerical example solved graphically. Imagine that in a given area it is required to find out how certain resources should be allocated between different industries in order to maximize the amount of production, income, or employment provided. Assume that there are two industries, manufacturing respectively textiles and metals, using different quantities of land, labor, and capital. The amount of each input available in the area is limited, and these figures, together with the input coefficients for the two industries, are listed in Table 20.1. The quantity to be maximized is in this case the total value of industrial production, that is,

Table 20.1 Input Coefficients and Resource Limitations in a Simple Linear Programming Problem

Inputs	Input Coefficients: Quantity (Dollars) Needed per Unit of Production		Maximum amount of Input Available (Dollars Units)
	Textiles	Metals	
Land	0.25	0.70	3,000,000
Labor	0.60	0.30	4,000,000
Capital	1.20	2.00	10,000,000

408   SOME ALTERNATIVE APPROACHES

the sum of $p_T X_T$ and $p_M X_M$, where X indicates the volume of production, p the value in dollars per unit of output, and the subscripts T and M refer to textiles and metals, respectively. For the sake of simplicity, it is assumed that $p_T = p_M = 1$. The total production that can be achieved is limited by the availability of resources and the particular quantities of each input required in each industry. These constraints can be expressed by inequalities developed from the figures in Table 20.1, which simply state that the total amount of each input used by the two industries (that is, the input coefficient multiplied by output) cannot exceed the total amount available in the area.

The resource constraints, read as linear equations, can be plotted as straight lines in a graph (Figure 20.1). The axes of the graph measure the value of production of the two industries, and the lines indicate the

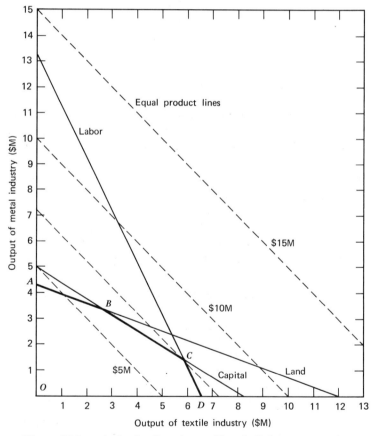

Figure 20.1.   A simple allocation problem in linear programming.

possible combinations of X_T and X_M if the total available amount of each of the three inputs is used. For example, the capital line shows that if all this input is used in textile manufacturing an output of $8.33M is possible, that is, the maximum amount available ($10M) divided by the input coefficient (1.20) per dollar of output; if it all goes to metal manufacturing the output is $5M, or $10M ÷ 2.00. Now consider the line $ABCD$, known in linear programming jargon as the *efficiency frontier*. Any combination of X_T and X_M above and to the right of this line is impossible, because it conflicts with one or more of the resource constraints by requiring more inputs than are available. However, any combination within the polygon $ABCDO$ is feasible, as all constraints are obeyed.

In order to find the optimum combination of textile and metals production it is now necessary to insert in the diagram a set of equal product lines. These have a negative slope of one (because $p_T = p_M$), and express the total value of production attainable from different combinations of the two industries. Thus the $10M equal product line indicates that this value of output can be achieved from 10M units of textile output and nothing from metals, from 10M units of metals production and none from textiles, from 5M units of each, and so on. The optimum combination is where the highest equal product line just touches a point on the efficiency frontier, that is, at C in Figure 20.1. The production figures for each industry at this point can be read off the graph, and are approximately $X_T = \$5.85M$ and $X_M = 1.45M$. The sum of these ($7.3M) represents the maximum possible value of industrial production in the circumstances specified. The amount of each input used and their allocation between the two industries can be calculated from the production figures and the input coefficients.

The problem that has just been solved may now be stated more formally. The objective function is the maximization of the sum of $p_T X_T$ and $p_M X_M$ ($= Z$), while the total amounts of resources available impose the constraints which have to be met. The problem is thus:

maximize
$$Z = 1X_T + 1X_M$$

subject to
$$0.25X_T + 0.70X_M \leq \$3,000,000$$
$$0.60X_T + 0.30X_M \leq \$4,000,000$$
$$1.20X_T + 2.00X_M \leq \$10,000,000$$
$$X_T \geq 0; \quad X_M \geq 0.$$

The fourth constraint is added to express the condition that the production figures cannot be negative.

This format may now be generalized into a model involving m industries and n inputs, as follows:

maximize
$$Z = p_1X_1 + p_2X_2 + \ldots + p_mX_m$$

subject to
$$a_{11}X_1 + a_{12}X_2 + \ldots + a_{1m}X_m \leqslant b_1$$
$$\vdots \qquad \vdots \qquad \qquad \vdots \qquad \vdots$$
$$a_{n1}X_1 + a_{n2}X_2 + \ldots + a_{nm}X_m \leqslant b_n$$
$$X_i \geqslant 0 \ (i = 1,2,\ldots,m),$$

where X_i $(i = 1,2,\ldots,m)$ is the output of industry i

p_i $(i = 1,2,\ldots,m)$ is the value or price obtainable for one unit of output

a_{ij} $\begin{pmatrix} (i = 1,2,\ldots,m) \\ (j = 1,2,\ldots,n) \end{pmatrix}$ is the input coefficient for industry i and input j

b_j $(j = 1,2,\ldots,n)$ is the maximum available amount of input j.

Although the very simple two-industry and three-input problem posed above could be solved graphically, this is not possible for the far more complex problems to which linear programming is generally applied. The mathematical solution normally used for this purpose is an iterative procedure which starts from any feasible solution and gradually approaches the optimum. Simple step-by-step illustrations of this method applied to elementary problems are presented elsewhere (for example, in Isard, 1960, 419–431; Slater, 1967, 109–124; and McDaniel and Hurst, 1968, 76–79). More detailed discussions will be found in the specialist texts, such as Vajda (1960), Dorfman, Samuelson, and Solow (1958) and Baumol (1965).

Closely related to the general formulation outlined above is *interregional linear programming*. This technique is designed to find the optimum allocation of different economic activities between a set of regions (areas or locations), subject to given constraints, in order to maximize income, employment or some other magnitude within the nation or system of regions. Pioneer work in this field includes that of Stevens (1958) who related patterns of industrial production to regional demands, resources, and interregional transport costs with the objective of maximizing GNP in a multiregional economy, Stevens and Coughlin (1959) who demonstrated an intrametropolitan approach, and Lefeber (1958) who

Table 20.2 The General Form of the Data Matrix in the Transportation Problem in Linear Programming

		Destinations 1 2 ... j ... n	Total Production Capacity
	1	$t_{11}\ t_{12}\ \ldots\ t_{1j}\ \ldots\ t_{1n}$	C_1
	2	$t_{21}\ t_{22}\ \ldots\ t_{2j}\ \ldots\ t_{2n}$	C_2
Origins	i	$t_{i1}\ t_{i2}\ \ldots\ t_{ij}\ \ldots\ t_{in}$	C_i
	m	$t_{m1}\ t_{m2}\ \ldots\ t_{mj}\ \ldots\ t_{mn}$	C_m
Total Demand		$D_1\ D_2\ \ldots\ D_j\ \ldots\ D_n$	$\sum_i C_i = \sum_j D_j$

used a linear programming framework to maximize the sum of the total value of different goods delivered to different markets. A detailed summary of interregional applications will be found in Isard (1960, 413–492).

The most frequent application of linear programming in industrial location analysis is in what is usually described as *the transportation problem*. This can take various forms, but it generally involves finding the optimum or least-cost flow of goods between a set of origins and a set of destinations, given data on the volumes of supply and demand and on the cost of transportation. The format of the data matrix in this kind of problem is indicated in Table 20.2. The four variables are as follows:

C_i is the production capacity at the plant, warehouse or area of origin i (1, 2, ..., m)

D_j is the total volume of demand by customers at the destination j (1, 2, ..., n)

t_{ij} is the cost of transporting one unit of the product from i to j

X_{ij} is the quantity shipped from i to j.

The problem is to find the flows which minimize the total cost of transportation, that is, the system of movement which represents the economic optimum. Formulated as a problem in linear programming, this becomes:

minimize

$$Z = \sum_{i=1}^{m} \sum_{j=1}^{n} t_{ij} X_{ij}$$

subject to

$$\sum_{i=1}^{m} X_{ij} \geqslant D_j$$

$$-\sum_{j=1}^{n} X_{ij} \geqslant -C_i$$

$$X_{ij} \geqslant 0$$

$$\sum_{i=1}^{m} C_i = \sum_{j=1}^{n} D_j.$$

The first constraint requires that all demands be fulfilled, the second that no plant capacities are exceeded, the third that there are no negative shipments, and the fourth that the total supply exactly equals total demand. The notation here is that adopted by Stevens (1961a); variations will be found in some sources; for example, the first two constraints may be stated as equalities.

Elementary problems of this kind, involving a very small number of origins and destinations, can be solved relatively simply, as is demonstrated by Cox (1965). But as m and n increase, the number of possible combinations of origins and destination becomes very large indeed and the application of a computer algorithm is necessary.

The transportation problem as formulated above is analogous to a range of allocation problems which occur in spatial economic analysis, and is closely related to the classical approach to industrial location theory. A number of important papers published in recent years have helped to extend the framework. For example, Goldman (1958) has discussed the question of backhauling along some routes, in the context of an imaginary steel industry with three locations, three materials, and a given program of consumption. Beckmann and Marschak (1955) have developed a model identifying optimum flows given several materials and a number of sources of each, several processing plants and a number of markets, given transport costs and limitations on material production and plant capacity. And Moses (1960) has combined input-output analysis with the transportation problem in linear programming in a three-industry and two-region model where an input-output matrix was specified for each region. Also related to the transportation problem are some of the contributions to the mathematical solution of the generalized Weber model, to which reference was made in Chapter 9.

The interpretation of the dual is a matter of considerable interest in linear programming. As was pointed out above, the dual is the primal problem turned inside out, and its formulation may help both in the interpretation and the solution of the original problem. Often the dual is an entirely artificial problem of no practical significance, but there are cases where it is of great conceptual interest. Of special importance is the interpretation of the dual in the transportation problem as relating to *location rent* in the classical economic sense of the term, that is, the comparative advantage accruing to a producer at a particular point because of geographical position alone, or more simply the profit arising from locational advantage.

This interpretation, which is explained fully in Stevens (1961a) and Böventer (1961), may be outlined briefly in the context of the general transportation problem as set out above. For the dual it is necessary to specify two new sets of variables:

u_i is the shadow price of the product, or the marginal value f.o.b. source, at plant i $(1, 2, \ldots, m)$

v_i is the shadow price, or marginal value delivered, at market j $(1, 2, \ldots, n)$.

The dual problem is:

maximize

$$Z' = \sum_{j=1}^{n} D_j v_j + \sum_{i=1}^{m} - C_i u_i$$

subject to

$$v_j - u_i \leq t_{ij}.$$

In other words, the dual maximizes the difference between the sum of the marginal value of all goods at the plant and as delivered to the market, subject to this difference for any pair of origins and destinations being no more than the transport costs involved.

It is not difficult to appreciate intuitively that the cost-minimizing solution to the transportation problem is an optimum solution from an economic point of view because it is at the same time the solution that maximizes the total returns which arise from the spatial relationship between producers and customers. But the more formal argument offered by Stevens (1961a) may help to explain this. A price p is introduced to express production costs (plus normal profits) or the base price of the commodity at all locations, and $u_i + p$ now represents the f.o.b. price at plant i while $v_j + p$ is the delivered price at market j. If there are a number of alternative sources which can supply this market, $v_j + p$ will in fact be the delivered price from the most distant plant (g) which can serve this market, v_j being just equal to the transport cost t_{gj}. Here $u_g =$

$v_j - t_{gj} = 0$, but at all plants closer to the market j, u will be positive because transport costs will be less than t_{gj} (assuming, of course, that transport costs are a direct reflection of distance). The variable u can thus be interpreted as location rent. The prevailing (equilibrium) price for the product at any market point is established by the furthest plant which can serve this market. This plant earns no location rent ($u_g = 0$), but all closer plants will earn some such rent. If a plant was located actually at the market j, then $u_j = v_j - t_{jj} = v_j - 0 = v_j$ (because no transport costs are involved), so v_j is simply location rent on marginal production capacity at the market.

Profit may now be introduced into this analysis. The unit profit (w) on a transaction between any pair of origins and destinations is given by:

$$w_{ij} = (v_j + p) - (u_i + p) - t_{ij},$$

that is, the delivered price, less the sum of f.o.b. plant price plus transport costs. This represents the increase in the value of the good between the production point and the market when the cost of transportation has been met. Total profits (W) in the entire system can thus be written:

$$W = \left(\sum_{j=1}^{n} D_j v_j - \sum_{i=1}^{m} C_i u_i \right) - \sum_{i=1}^{m} \sum_{j=1}^{n} X_{ij} t_{ij}$$

The two terms in parentheses are equal to Z', or the objective function of the dual, and the last term is equal to Z which is the primal objective function. The maximum total profit is achieved by maximizing the difference between Z' and Z, or simultaneously maximizing Z' and minimizing Z. Under the assumption of perfect competition, $Z' = \max$ will be equal to $Z = \min$, and no super-normal profits will be made.

The argument relating to location rent may be further clarified by a graphic illustration offered by Stevens. He depicts a situation in which five warehouses (or production points) designated S and three consumers R are located along a line, as shown in Figure 20.2. The vertical axis measures rent, and u and v are plotted for the plants and markets, respectively. Transport-cost gradients express the increase in rent moving toward the markets, indicating what the rent should be for new plants established at intervening locations.

The construction of this *rent gradient* leads logically to a *rent surface*, with the addition of the second distance dimension. Such a surface is closely related conceptually to the surfaces of production costs, revenue, and levels of profit discussed in Part Three. The rent surface measures the comparative advantage of alternative locations, in terms of their capacity to derive financial returns from their geographical position in

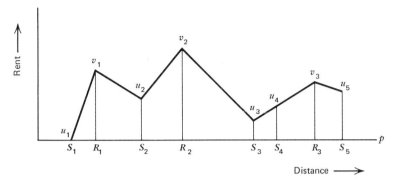

Figure 20.2. The dual of the transportation problem in linear programming, interpreted as a location-rent gradient. (*Source.* Stevens, 1961a, Figure 2.)

relation to the market, and with certain assumptions made it is the equivalent of a profit surface. Where the rent gradient or surface intersects the line or plane representing plant price (p), as at S_1 in Figure 20.2, the zero-rent point or margin arises, analogous to the spatial limits to profitable operation which figured prominently in the theoretical framework developed in Part Three. Demonstrating the complementarity of location theory and rent theory has been one of the most important outcomes of the application of linear programming in spatial economic analysis.

The linear programming model is thus a very versatile device, with both operational and conceptual contributions to make. But it has its limitations, including the inability to incorporate variables such as economies of agglomeration and others which are not easily measured. It also has difficulty encompassing the demand factor, as Greenhut (1967) has pointed out, for the effect of the market is generally included only through the cost of delivering the product. And if nonlinear relationships are involved, then a more advanced form of programming will be required. As one of the leading proponents of the linear programming approach has remarked, these models should not be regarded as a cure-all (Stevens, 1968, 23), but they do facilitate the formalization of some major problems in industrial location analysis.

20.2 SOME PRACTICAL APPLICATIONS

Three different applications of linear programming have been selected to show some of the ways in which this kind of approach can be used in the solution of practical problems.

a. The Location of a Single Firm

The first illustration relates to the location decision of a firm with two existing plants distributing a product to a widespread market within the United States (Johnson, 1958). These plants both have a capacity of just under 70,000 tons, and an estimate of the demand at forty-one market points indicates the need to increase the firm's total capacity by about 30,000 tons. Three possible new plant locations are selected, and the firm faces a choice between the alternatives of building at one of these places or adding new capacity at an existing location. The position of the existing facilities (S) and the possible new locations (P) in relation to the market are shown in Figure 20.3.

Data on transportation costs are given, and the objective function is the minimization of the total cost of movement. Two models were run, the first taking into consideration only the cost of distributing the finished product while the second also included the transportation of raw materials to the factories. The first model showed that new plants at either P_2 or P_3 would have a cost advantage over building new capacity at the existing plants, which were considered together for the purpose of this calculation (see Table 20.3). The difference between the total cost of distribution when P_2 and P_3 are compared is less than $25,000, however, and it would

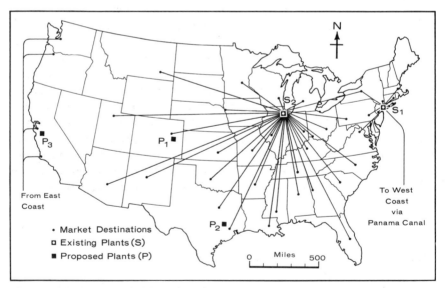

Figure 20.3. Factory locations, markets, and possible production sites for new branch plants, in a situation amenable to solution by linear programming. (*Source.* Johnson, 1958, 5, Chart 2.)

Table 20.3 Differences in Transport Costs between Alternative Plans for the Expansion of Production Capacity, as Determined by Linear Programming

Location of New Capacity	Total Transport Costs of Distribution (Dollars) a	Additional Transport Costs on Materials (Dollars) b	Total of All Transport Costs (Dollars) $a + b$	Cost Differences Compared with P_3 (Dollars)
Existing plants	1,646,789	0	1,646,789	87,836
New plant P_1	1,704,341	151,948	1,856,289	297,336
New plant P_2	1,460,708	345,279	1,805,986	247,033
New plant P_3	1,436,062	122,891	1,558,953	0

Source. Johnson (1958, 7).

be difficult to argue that expansion at P_3 is very clearly the best decision. But the introduction of transport costs on raw materials clarifies the situation, for although P_3 has only a slight edge over P_1 in this respect the advantage over P_2 is sufficient to give P_3 an overall cost advantage of $247,000 over P_2. The optimum course of action is thus to build a new plant at P_2, which gives a saving of almost $90,000 compared with expanding existing capacity. Under this plan the new factory would serve the four west coast markets and two in the Rockies, but otherwise the preexisting pattern of distribution would remain unchanged except for any adjustments between the market areas of the existing plants needed to equalize their production. It must be stressed that this kind of analysis provides an optimum solution on the basis of transport costs only, and does not evaluate the additional overhead costs which may arise from running a new plant on the west coast. However, these costs can be evaluated separately if necessary, and related to the results of the linear programming analysis. In the present case, the additional overhead costs would have to amount to at least $87,836 before a new plant at P_3 would not be worthwhile.

b. Interregional Commodity Flows and the Allocation of Production

The second illustration is concerned with the use of linear programming to compute the optimum interregional flow of a commodity for an entire industry in order to provide a model against which to measure the efficiency of the existing pattern of production and exchange. It is taken from a detailed study of the Indian cement industry, by Ghosh (1965). The areal framework is a set of nine regions, each of which is at the same time an origin of and destination for cement products. The basic data thus comprise 9 × 9 matrices of existing flows and estimates of interregional transport costs, together with information on regional production capacity and conditions of supply and demand for cement.

Ghosh uses a number of different models to find the optimum flows under alternative sets of assumptions, comparing the results with the actual flow for different years. The results from the simplest model, for 1957, are set out in Table 20.4. In this case the objective function is the minimization of total transport costs, subject to all outward shipments from a given region adding up to the actual total outward shipments, all inward shipments adding up to the total inward shipments, and not considering any intraregional movements. A comparison between the actual and optimum flows shows, among other things, that the cost-minimizing pattern cuts out a lot of very small interregional movements which may well be dependent on considerations other than economic rationality. But in general the existing pattern is not highly inefficient. The total cost of the optimum plan was found to be Rs 19,416.70 compared with Rs 20,553.70 for the actual flows (Rs = rupees). The average unit costs (per md, where 1 md = 37.3242 kg) were Rs 0.61 for the optimum and 0.65 for the actual, giving the optimum pattern an advantage of about six percent.

From this simple application Ghosh proceeds to develop more complex programming models. First, production costs are allowed to vary between regions, but as regional production is fixed (as it was in the first model) the flows remain the same as when the objective function is the minimization of transport costs alone (Ghosh, 1965, 56). Next, the production in any region is permitted to be different from capacity, to allow for the effects of production cost differentials on interregional movements while intraregional movements remain fixed. The result is a saving of Rs 0.08 per unit compared with Rs 0.04 in the transport-cost model, but in relative terms the difference between the cost of the actual and optimum patterns is now only three percent (unit transportation and production costs are Rs 2.27 for the optimum and 2.35 for the actual pattern in 1957). Finally, the model is further complicated to allow a region's capacity to serve its own market to be subject to competition from outside, so the diagonal of the matrix of interregional flows is now encompassed by the optimizing process. The result is a six percent saving for the optimum in 1957 compared with the actual pattern.

Of the various other results of the Ghosh study, one more may be illustrated—the optimum regional allocation of cement production compared with the actual distribution (Table 20.5). These figures show a tendency for the two leading regions (Bihar and Madras) to produce at above the optimum level, while most of the less important regions underproduce. Although the overall efficiency of the industry's location might

Table 20.4 Interregional Flows of Cement in India for a Nine-Month Period in 1957 (1000 md)

Region of Origin	\multicolumn{9}{c	}{Region of Destination}	
	1	2	3	4	5	6	7	8	9	Total
1. West Bengal		146 (118)[a]	(19)	(0.8)	(0.1)	(0.5)		(6)	(0.9)	146
2. Bihar	6394 (6880)		(715)	1717 (506)	(6)	(1)		(3)		8111
3. Orissa	1159 (667)	580 (569)			(499)			(2)		1739
4. Utter Pradesh	(3)	(26)			(11)	(2)	(2)	108 (66)		108
5. Punjab, Delhi, etc.		(5)		(367)				(871) (479)	(6)	871
6. Bombay	1)	(0.5)		784 (28)	(66)	(14)	(14)	77 (668)	(83)	861
7. Madras			14 (12)	(7)	(0.6)	(86)			1486 (1394)	1500
8. Rajasthan, etc.	(2)	(7)	(0.6)	2836 (4428)	11286 (9635)	(47)			(2)	14122
9. Hyderabad, etc.			733		(1068)	3042 (2891)	414 (398)	170 (2)		4359
Total	7553	726	747	5337	11286	3042	414	1226	1486	31817

Source. Ghosh (1965, 49).

[a] The figures in parentheses are the actual flows, the others are optimum flows based on a linear programming solution minimizing transport costs. One md = 37.3242 kg.

Table 20.5 **The Actual Regional Production of Cement (1000 md)[a] in 1957, Compared with the Optimum Regional Allocation as Determined by Linear Programming**

Region	Actual Production a	Optimum Production b	Deviation $a - b$
West Bengal	146	0	+ 146
Bihar	21,172	18,863	+2309
Orissa	5,855	7,406	−1551
Utter Pradesh	4,539	4,712	− 173
Punjab, Delhi, etc.	17,215	18,401	−1186
Bombay	19,470	20,237	− 767
Madras	22,039	20,953	+1086
Rajasthan, etc.	14,449	15,772	−1323
Hyderabad, etc.	9,736	8,277	+1459

Source. Ghosh (1965, 77).
[a] One md = 37.3242 kg.

be improved by some dispersal of production, the actual pattern is not greatly different from the optimum one.

Other similar applications of linear programming include a comparison between the optimum and actual supply pattern and delivered prices in the United States coal industry by Henderson (1958), an examination of location and flow of production in the tomato processing industry by Koch and Snodgrass (1959), the development of a model to determine the optimum pattern of investment in the fishing and fish processing industry in northern Norway by Serck-Hanssen (1963), major study of domestic airline routes by Miller (1963), and a series of papers on the spatial structure of the livestock economy in the United States (Judge, Havlicek, and Rizek, 1964; Havlicek, Rizek, and Judge, 1965; Rizek, Judge, and Havlicek, 1965; and Crum, 1967).

c. The Dual and Location Rent

The final illustration is a practical application of the interpretation of the dual as relating to location rent. It is taken from a study of the marketing of wheat in the United States, by Maxfield (1969). Although not strictly an industrial illustration, this draws attention to an application of linear programming which may prove to be very useful in industrial location analysis.

The problem posed is to determine the least-cost method of satisfying overseas demand for United States hard red wheat in 1964. This involves finding the optimum pattern of movement from growing areas to the markets via transshipment points, which is a version of the transportation problem and capable of solution by linear programming. The world market is divided up into ten broad sections comprising the destinations in the problem, and the wheat producing states of Idaho, Montana, North Dakota, South Dakota, and Minnesota are divided into fifty growing areas or origins. Four different models were used, the first having transport cost as the only variable, the second including differences in the farm price of wheat, the third having variable transport costs, uniform prices and a restriction on the amount of wheat that could be produced in each area, while the fourth model included both transport costs and farm prices together with the supply restrictions.

Linear programming was used to find which markets would be served by which growing areas and to calculate the optimum pattern of flows for each model. But of special interest are maps based on the results from the solution of the dual problem. For each origin, or growing area, values for location rent are computed, to indicate the relative competitive strength of each area, and from these are constructed isoline maps of the location rent surfaces. The figures plotted are the differences between the lowest dual value in the solution and the dual value for each growing area.

Two of these location-rent maps are reproduced in Figure 20.4. The one at the top is the result from the first model, which shows that with no restriction on the amount of the product that each area can supply demand is satisfied from a relatively small number of growing areas in western Idaho and eastern Minnesota, i.e., the areas closest to the exporting ports on the Great Lakes and the Pacific Coast. Those areas with no production, and hence no location rent, are beyond the no-rent margin, in other words wheat cannot be produced for the overseas market at a profit under the conditions assumed. The second map shows the results from the fourth model, which takes account of differences in farm prices and imposes restrictions on the production of each area. Under these conditions production is much more evenly spread over the wheat belt, with only three growing areas left out. Although the area beyond the no-rent margin has now almost disappeared, the eastern and western parts of the wheat belt are still the most favorable areas in which to produce for the overseas market, as is indicated by the peaks in the rent surface.

The application of this kind of approach to an industrial situation should be fairly obvious. Given a set of plants and a set of market points, the necessary transport cost data, the demand at each market, and information on capacity, output and production costs at the factories, solving the dual of the transportation problem by linear programming can yield a set of values for the location rent at each plant. These values can then form the basis for the identification of a location-rent surface,

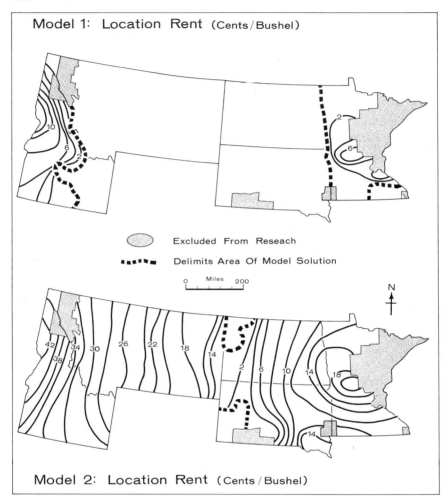

Figure 20.4. Location-rent surfaces in the United States hard red spring wheat industry 1964, identified from the solution of the dual in linear programming. (*Source.* Maxfield, 1969, 256 and 259, Figures 1 and 4.)

which represents the comparative advantage of alternative plant locations. The zero isoline, or the no-rent margin, can be interpreted as the spatial limits to profitable operation. Linear programming thus provides a means by which spatial margins as well as the optimum location may be identified in an empirical industrial location problem which fits the appropriate linear programming format.

21

Input-Output Analysis

During the past quarter of a century few methods of economic analysis have attracted greater interest than the input-output model. Pioneered by Wassily Leontief in the 1930s, and subsequently adopted with enthusiasm in regional science, the input-output table is now widely recognized as a valuable descriptive device for organizing data concerning the interrelationship of different sectors of the economy. To quote Leontief (1951, 6), "the input-output table thus reveals the fabric of our economy, woven together by the flow of trade which ultimately links each branch and industry with all others." Input-output analysis also provides a basis for predicting the outcome of certain changes in levels of production and consumption.

As with linear programming, it would require much more space than is available here to do full justice to the range of possible applications of input-output analysis, and the recent attempts to use the technique in empirical research. The treatment here is no more than a summary, introducing the input-output table as a descriptive and analytical device and offering one restricted illustration. A more detailed review can be found, for example, in Leontief (1951), Leontief et al (1953), Chenery and Clark (1959), Isard (1960), and Miernyk (1965).

21.1 INPUT-OUTPUT TABLES AND THEIR USES

The principle behind input-output analysis is very simple, and may be introduced by taking the case of an imaginary single industry. Suppose this industry is engaged in the manufacture of some kind of metal goods, which requires inputs in the form of materials, labor, capital, and so on.

Table 21.1 Input-Output Data for an Imaginary Metal Industry ($1000)

Source of Inputs	Markets				
	Metal Industry	Engineering Industry	Electronics Industry	Final Demand	Total
Metal Industry	100	600	250	50	1000
Engineering Industry	450				
Steel Industry	200				
Households	250				
Total	1000				

The market mainly comprises other industries, but also includes some direct sales to the final consumer. The sources of inputs and destinations of output can be set down as in Table 21.1. The column total includes expenditure on materials provided by two other industries, and also inputs from the metal industry itself. In addition the input sources include *households*. This item covers payments for labor, interest, rent, and profits and is equivalent to the value added in the process of manufacture. The row total is of course the same as the column total, for both indicate the value of the production of the industry. The row includes sales of metals to two other industries, and also some personal consumption representing *final demand*. In input-output analysis the final demand for a good includes personal or household consumption, purchases by other industries for investment purposes (that is, the extension of plant or equipment), sales to national and local government, and exports.

A table like the one illustrated can reveal important information about an industry, including factors likely to have a bearing on locational choice. For example, this imaginary metal industry is obviously closely linked with the engineering industry both as a supplier of inputs and as a market for its finished products, which might suggest a spatial association between the two activities.

A regional or national economy is made up of a large number of activities, and a table of exchange between all industries will thus be much more complicated than Table 21.1. Its general form is indicated in Table 21.2, where x represents the shipment from one industry to another, C is the final demand for the product of an industry, X is the total output of the industry, V is the household sector's contribution (or value added), and Y is the total value of the inputs used.

Table 21.2   The General Form of an Input-Output Table

		Consuming Sectors 1, 2 ... n	C	Total X
	1	$x_{11}\ x_{12}\ \ldots\ x_{1n}$	C_1	X_1
	2	$x_{21}\ x_{22}\ \ldots\ x_{2n}$	C_2	X_2
Producing	.	. . .	.	.
	.	. . .	.	.
sectors	.	. . .	.	.
	n	$x_{n1}\ x_{n2}\ \ldots\ x_{nn}$	C_n	X_n
	V	$V_1\ V_2\ \ldots\ V_n$	$\Sigma V = \Sigma C$	
Total		$Y_1\ Y_2\ \ldots\ Y_n$		
	Y			

This kind of input-output table has a number of important properties. Every sale for one industry is also a purchase for another (that is, every output shown is at the same time an input), so the figure x_{12} for example represents both a part of the total output of industry 1 and part of the inputs of industry 2. The sum of any row in the industry section of the table is equal to the sum of the same industry's column, e.g., $X_1 = Y_1$. Also, the total final demand for all industries is equal to the total value added, which is gross domestic product or the total activity of the economy in terms of the expenditures by which goods and services are acquired for final use. The bottom right cell (total output and total inputs) is left empty, for such a figure would compound all intermediate transactions through which goods and services reach the final consumer, and this would involve double counting.

Table 21.2 applies to a closed economic system. Allowing external trade requires the addition of another row (for imports) and another column (for exports). If imports are added to the households or value added item and exports are included in final demand, then ΣV is still equal to ΣC, but the value of imports must be subtracted from total final demand to give gross domestic product. Putting together a set of interconnected tables, with imports to one economic system being exports from another, is the basis of an *interregional input-output model*.

A dollar-flow table can reveal important differences between input and output characteristics of different industries. Some (such as the manufacture of clothing and food products) sell most of their output to the final consumer, while others (including iron and steel, leather, and other producers of basic commodities) send almost all of their output to other industries. Some activities draw their inputs from a wide range of different sources, as is the case with the manufacture of motor vehicles and aircraft, while others, such as the food and primary metals industries, have a small number of dominant input flows. And a large proportion of the input and output transactions may take place within a single industrial category, as is the case in many of the engineering and metal trades. By providing a detailed and systematic description of all these interindustry flows, the input-output table offers many clues as to the possible spatial associations between industries which may arise from close input-output linkages.

For many purposes in industrial location analysis another kind of input-output table is preferred to that showing actual dollar flows. This is a table of *input-output coefficients*. These figures express the ratio of the input from the industry in whose row the cell appears in the table to the total output of the industry in whose column the cell appears. The coefficient (a) where part of the output of industry i is supplied as an input to industry j is thus given by:

$$a_{ij} = \frac{x_{ij}}{X_j}$$

The larger the value of a_{ij}, the greater the importance of industry i as a source of inputs for industry j. In a table of these coefficients the sum of all the figures in any column plus the coefficient for value added or the household sector's input comes to a constant (for example, $1 or $1000), indicating how the various inputs are combined in different industries to produce the same given quantity of output.

The significance of a table of these coefficients has been summarized by Leontief (1963, 33), as follows:

For the economy as a whole the input-output [coefficient] table reveals the structure of the interlocking interdependencies that tie the highly differentiated and specialized parts of the system together as a whole. It represents, in effect, a working model of the system. As such it can be employed for the experimental study of a great many theoretical and practical questions about the economy. . . . Input-output analysis derives its conceptual framework from recognition of the fact that all the possible interconnections of the different sectors of a national economy can be regarded as special instances of the general solution of a single large system of equations in matrix algebra.

In each such table there will be n equations, each corresponding to an industry or sector and each involving n distinct but independent variables. The parameters of these variables, or the constants of the equations, are the input-output coefficients.

Two simple illustrations, using imaginary data, will demonstrate some of the versatility of the table of input-output coefficients. The first is con-

Table 21.3 Direct Inputs per Dollar of Output in an Imaginary Four-Sector Industrial Economy

		Consuming Sectors			
		Engineering	Machinery	Metals	Households
Producing sectors	Engineering	0.3	0.5	0.1	0.2
	Machinery	0.2	0.2	0.4	0.4
	Metals	0.1		0.3	
	Households	0.4	0.3	0.2	0.4
	Total	1.0	1.0	1.0	1.0

cerned with predicting the impact of an increase in production in one industry or sector on output in others. Table 21.3 lists the coefficients for a four-sector economy in which there are three industries and the household sector, each figure indicating the value of inputs required per dollar of output. Suppose that it was proposed to increase the value of production in the engineering industry by $1M. This would clearly create pressures on other sections of the economy, through the increased requirements for inputs. The increase needed to sustain expansion of this order in engineering can be found simply by multiplying each of the coefficients in the first (engineering) column of Table 21.3 by 1,000,000. These are known as the first-round inputs, and are listed under this heading in Table 21.4. But to produce these increased outputs will re-

Table 21.4 Round-by-Round Input Requirements ($1000) for an Increase of $1M Output in Engineering, in an Imaginary Four-Sector Industrial Economy

	Round 1	Round 2	Round 3	Round 4	Round 5	Total (1–5)
Engineering	300	230	213	174	134	1051
Machinery	200	220	168	125	90	803
Metals	100	60	24	9	4	197
Households	400	280	230	184	149	1243
Total	1000	790	635	492	377	3294

quire further inputs again: to produce the $300,000 worth of engineering goods shown under round 1 will require inputs representing $300,000 × 0.3 worth of further output from the engineering industry, inputs representing $200,000 × 0.2 worth of output from the machinery industry, and so on. The additional inputs needed for the expansion of the machinery and metals industries in round 1 are calculated in the same way, using the input-output coefficients for these activities. The household sector is treated in a different way, however, since it is not expected that all the additional payment of $400,000 will be spent. The arbitrary assumption in the present case is that only half of the additional wages etc. resulting from the initial expansion of the engineering industry are used for the acquisition of goods, so in establishing the quantity of inputs required to sustain the new demand from households the input coefficients in the last column of Table 21.3 are multiplied by $200,000. The sum of the inputs from each sector needed as a result of new production under round 1 is listed in Table 21.4 under round 2. Round 2 production in its turn requires further inputs, which leads to another round of production increases, and so on ad infinitum. Because of the assumption that not all the income received by households each round is spent, the total value of additional inputs needed in each round gets smaller, and the gradual convergence of this figure means that the round-by-round calculation can be stopped after a while and the remaining requirements found by extrapolation. In the imaginary case under review the initial increase of $1M in engineering output has multiplied itself by more than three by round 5, in terms of the total value of the additional inputs needed.

The results of this kind of analysis can assist in determinig the response that can be expected from one sector of the economy as a result of changes in another sector. The simple illustration offered above relates to a single economic system, and no spatial implications are considered, but an interregional model would indicate the impact of an increase in production or demand on different areas or regions as well as different industries. Expansion in one sector will stimulate related expansion in some industries more than in others; for example, the impact of growth in engineering in the case above was felt to a much greater extent in this industry itself and in the machinery industry than in the metals sector. Insofar as industries are unevenly distributed areally, or spatial variations exist in comparative advantage with respect to the location of new capacity, expansion in one sector will set off a chain reaction of differential regional industrial growth. An illustration of this kind of analysis in a three-region economic system will be found in Isard and Kavesh (1954), and Isard (1960, 327–335) conveniently summarizes some of the practical and conceptual problems involved in using input-output analysis for this kind of projection.

The second illustration is of a slightly different problem. It concerns a three-industry economy from which the household sector is omitted, where input-output coefficients are known, and it is required to calculate the quantity of production required from each industry to satisfy known

Table 21.5   Input-Output Coefficients for Three Imaginary Industries

		Consuming Industries		
		Food	Textiles	Engineering
Producing industries	Food (F)	0.4	0.1	0.3
	Textiles (T)	0.2	0.3	0.1
	Engineering (E)	0.2	0.3	0.5

levels of final demand. The coefficients are listed in Table 21.5, and the final demand figures are $5M for food products, $3M for textiles, and $10M for the engineering industry. From Table 21.2, it can be seen that input-output flows take the form of a series of linear equations, which are in general:

$$x_{i1} + x_{i2} + \ldots + x_{in} + C_i = X_i.$$

For any industry i the final demand (C_i) is thus given by:

$$X_i - x_{i1} - x_{i2} - \ldots - x_{in} = C_i.$$

Replacing each dollar flow by the appropriate input-output coefficient multiplied by total value of output, this becomes:

$$X_i - a_{i1}X_i - a_{i2}X_2 - \ldots - a_{in}X_n = C_i.$$

Inserting the known values for a and C in the problem outlined above allows the situation to be described by three equations:

$$X_F - 0.4X_F - 0.1X_T - 0.3X_E = \$5{,}000{,}000$$
$$X_T - 0.2X_F - 0.3X_T - 0.1X_E = \$2{,}000{,}000$$
$$X_E - 0.2X_F - 0.3X_T - 0.5X_E = \$10{,}000{,}000$$

The solution of the equations is achieved by matrix algebra. The mechanics of the calculation are of no interest here, since in all practical problems of this kind the size of the matrix would be such as to require the use of a computer. However, a step-by-step account of the method by which the three equations above are solved can be found in McDaniel and Hurst (1968, 69–71), from where the main features of this illustration are derived.

The results are as follows: $X_F = \$34M$, $X_T = \$19M$, and $X_E = \$45M$. Thus for each industry the total production required is very much more than the figure for final demand, because of the interindustry flows necessary to achieve the given quantities of output for the final consumer. The *multipliers*, indicating the number of dollars of total production generated by one dollar of final demand in each section, are 6.8 in the food industry, 9.5 in textiles, and 4.5 in engineering.

In addition to those showing dollar flows and input-output coefficients, there is a third kind of input-output table that can be very useful. This is the table of *inverse coefficients,* obtained by the inversion of the matrix of input-output coefficients. While the input-output coefficients measure the direct contribution of inputs of one industry to total output in another, the inverse coefficients express for the industry in whose row the cell appears that portion of the industry's total output required directly and indirectly to meet one unit of final demand for the product of the industry in whose column the cell appears (Leontief, 1965, 34).

Once this inverse matrix has been obtained it can be used to answer questions that otherwise would involve much computation. Solution of the kind of problem considered above, where it was required to find the effect of a certain volume of production for final demand in one industry (i) on the level of output in another (j), simply involves multiplying the final demand figure for i by the inverse coefficient in column i and row j. The impact of a change in the demand for a product can be calculated in a similar way. The inverse coefficients are thus very useful in helping to predict the effect of specific levels of consumption on output in each industrial sector, within the general model of the interconnected industrial system.

There are many practical and conceptual problems involved in input-output analysis. A major one is the need to adopt a sensible industrial classification at an appropriate level of aggregation before input-output tables can be compiled. When this has been done there arises the problem of acquiring the necessary data. The number of pieces of information needed can be enormous; for example, in the 81×81 input-output table prepared for the United States economy in 1958 there are 6561 cells, and a fifty-industry ten-region model would require a 500×500 matrix with 250,000 cells (Garrison, 1960). Compiling any kind of input-output table is thus a difficult and expensive procedure, and for an interregional system the task is generally so great that it is prohibitive.

On the conceptual side, the input-output model can be quite far from the reality it purports to replicate, because of some of the simplifying assumptions that must be used to make the device operational. Particularly important is the need to keep the coefficients constant irrespective of the scale of production, which means that there is no substitution between inputs and that there are constant returns to scale. An interregional framework requires additional assumptions, particularly with regard to the trading relations between different components of the system. The nature of all these assumptions, and their implications, are set down more fully elsewhere, for example in Isard (1960, Chapter 8) and Richardson (1969, 237–246).

21.2 AN ILLUSTRATION FROM THE UNITED STATES INPUT-OUTPUT TABLES

As an illustration of actual input-output tables to supplement the simplified imaginary examples of the previous section, Tables 21.6, 21.7, and 21.8 present extracts from the tables for the United States economy in 1958. They show the nine industries making up the basic metals section. It must be emphasized that these are only very small parts of the whole tables, which comprise 81 × 81 matrices and are far too complex for reproduction here. However, these extracts are representative of the full tables, and should clarify some of the general points made above.

Table 21.6 shows the dollar flows between the nine basic metal industries. The most obvious feature is the importance of intraindustry interconnections; the two largest flows are within primary nonferrous metals and primary iron and steel. As might be expected, there is virtually no direct transfer of the output of the two ore-mining activities to the fabricating industries (groups 31–35). The mineral finds its way into metal stampings, containers, and so on via the two primary metal industries, both of which get the bulk of their inputs from the appropriate mining sector. The fairly general interchange of outputs and inputs between all the industries except 37 and 39 emphasizes the closely interconnected nature of the various branches of metal manufacturing. This is expressed in the tendency of many of these industries to be associated spatially with one another.

The input-output coefficients for the same nine industries are shown in Table 21.7. This is more useful than the previous table in showing up the relative importance of different inputs in a given industry or the same input in different industries. In six of the nine industries, output from the primary iron and steel sector is the largest source of inputs, comprising roughly one-fifth of the total value of output in four cases and as much as 44 percent in the manufacture of metal containers. In industries 36 to 39 a relatively large share of the inputs comes from within the industry itself, but this is very much less the case in the fabricating activities.

These input-output coefficients provide a very effective way of measuring industrial linkages. A recent example is in a paper by Richter (1969), where two sectors are regarded as linked if one sells $1/n$th or more of its output to the other or if one purchases $1/n$th or more of its inputs from the other, n being the number of sectors in the input-output

Table 21.6 Input-Output Table for the Basic Metals Section of the United States Economy 1958: Dollar Flows ($1M)[a]

Industry Producing	Industry Purchasing								
	... 31	32	33	34	35	36	37	38	39 ...
31 Heating, plumbing, and structural	201	4		39	76	4	1	62	2
32 Machine shop products	44	142	13	18	26	45		192	
33 Metal containers	4		4	17	6				
34 Stampings, screw products, etc.	208	11	37	133	171	125	1	167	1
35 Other fabricated metal products	339	44	11	130	330	143	2	447	2
36 Primary nonferrous metals	785	163	27	320	582	3959	9	425	53
37 Nonferrous metal ores mining					2	1059	306	9	
38 Primary iron and steel	2570	168	1219	983	1680	158	68	5395	28
39 Iron etc. ores mining						29	17	1396	84

Source. Leontief (1965).
[a] Flows of less than $0.5M are not included.

Table 21.7 Input-Output Table for the Basic Metals Section of the United States Economy 1958: Input-Output Coefficients (Value of Inputs, Dollars per $1000 of Output)[a]

Industry Producing	Industry Purchasing								
	...31	32	33	34	35	36	37	38	39...
31 Heating, plumbing, and structural	18.7	1.9	4.8	8.0	8.9	0.3	0.5	2.5	1.5
32 Machine shop products	4.1	67.5	4.8	3.8	3.0	3.7	0.1	7.6	0.1
33 Metal containers	0.4		1.6	3.5	0.7				
34 Stampings, screw products, etc.	19.3	5.2	13.3	27.1	20.0	10.2	0.6	6.6	0.4
35 Other fabricated metal products	31.5	21.1	4.0	26.6	38.5	11.7	1.3	17.6	1.1
36 Primary nonferrous metals	73.0	77.6	9.6	65.3	67.9	324.8	6.2	16.7	2.3
37 Nonferrous metal ores mining					0.3	86.9	224.5	0.4	50.3
38 Primary iron and steel	239.0	80.0	439.1	200.6	195.9	13.0	45.6	212.0	26.4
39 Iron etc. ores mining						2.4	12.4	54.9	80.5

Source. Leontief (1965).
[a] Figures of less than 0.05 are not included.

Table 21.8 Input-Output Table for the Basic Metals Section of the United States Economy 1958: Inverse Coefficients (Dollars of Inputs Required Directly or Indirectly per Dollar of Delivery to Final Demand)

Industry Producing	Industry Purchasing								
	...31	32	33	34	35	36	37	38	39...
31 Heating, plumbing, and structural	1.024	0.005	0.009	0.011	0.013	0.003	0.003	0.007	0.004
32 Machine shop products	0.010	1.076	0.012	0.009	0.008	0.007	0.002	0.013	0.001
33 Metal containers	0.002	0.001	1.003	0.005	0.002	0.001	0.001	0.001	0.001
34 Stampings, screw products, etc.	0.030	0.012	0.022	1.037	0.029	0.019	0.004	0.015	0.003
35 Other fabricated metal products	0.048	0.032	0.021	0.042	1.053	0.024	0.008	0.031	0.006
36 Primary nonferrous metals	0.140	0.140	0.044	0.123	0.128	1.500	0.022	0.050	0.011
37 Nonferrous metal ores mining	0.018	0.017	0.008	0.015	0.016	0.169	1.294	0.012	0.072
38 Primary iron and steel	0.365	0.140	0.590	0.301	0.296	0.594	0.103	1.307	0.583
39 Iron etc. ores mining	0.022	0.009	0.036	0.019	0.018	0.010	0.024	0.079	1.092

Source. Leontief (1965).

table. In other words, industries are deemed linked if their interconnections are greater than would be the case if all inputs and outputs were evenly distributed between all sectors of the economy. Leontief (1963, 1965) emphasizes the usefulness of this definition of linked activities, and employs it diagrammatically to indicate something of the input-output structural characteristics of different economic systems.

Finally, Table 21.8 lists the inverse coefficients for the basic metals industries. The diagonal stands out with very high values, indicating the dominant contribution of inputs from within the industry itself in most cases. Among the other features of this table is the importance of inputs from the primary metal industries to the fabricating activities (31 to 35), which is an even more prominent characteristic of this table than it was in Table 21.6.

This brief illustration of actual input-output tables is sufficient for the purpose of this chapter. More detailed and complete empirical applications of this technique can be found elsewhere; for example, in the reports of a major project on the Philadelphia region (Karaska, 1966, 1968; Isard, Langford, and Romanoff, 1967), and in a study of the spatial structure of the Indian economy (Berry et al, 1966, 257–234).

PART SIX

Industrial Location, Economic Development and Public Policy

Thus far this book has been concerned almost entirely with the ways in which economic factors influence industrial location. In both the theoretical and empirical sections the focus of attention has been on the locational choice of the entrepreneur operating within a competitive economic system regulated by market forces. Except for a brief reference to planning in Chapter 6, and the integration of areal subsidies and taxation into the theoretical framework developed in Part Three, the direct effects of public policy have been virtually ignored. The reason for this approach is that an examination of the economic framework within which business decisions are made is a necessary prerequisite to the discussion of government intervention. Now that the groundwork has been laid, the relationship between industrial location and public policy may be considered directly and in some detail, in the general context of the planning of economic development.

The expression *public policy* refers to any program of action set forth by the people, or by their elected or appointed representatives, in pursuit of some economic or social objectives. Such programs can vary considerably in their spatial scale, in the actual measures or strategy adopted, and in the objectives that the policy is designed to achieve. The spatial framework can range from a small community to a group of nations. The measures can be negative in the sense of going no further than restricting freedom of locational choice, or positive in that they attempt to induce development in certain areas. The strategy can be anything from uncoordinated local attempts to stimulate new businesses in a depressed area to complete regional economic and land-use plans based on sophisticated econometric model building. The objectives of public policy may be entirely economic, entirely social, or a combination of the two.

The planning of economic development is a subject that encompasses much more than simply the location of industrial activity. It transgresses interdisciplinary boundaries, to impinge on the fields of government, sociology, operational research, and others, as well as geography, economics, and regional science. This book is not the place for a comprehensive treatment of economic development problems and policies, which is offered in a number of existing texts. The concern here is only with the location of industrial activity in development planning, a subject that itself requires at least book-length treatment if anything beyond a few broad generalities are to be offered.

At the outset it is important to make a distinction between public policy as a cause and as a consequence of industrial development, that is, as an independent or as a dependent variable. As an independent variable, public policy and areal-planning strategy can greatly affect the spatial arrangement of industrial activity, by modifying the economic conditions under which choice of plant location is made. But the locational characteristics of industry in its turn affects public policy as a dependent variable, imposing constraints on what the planners can reasonably propose and hope to achieve. The cause-and-effect relationship is seldom in one direction only, however; most public intervention in economic affairs is a response to the consequences of a particular course of industrial development, and leads to measures designed to influence the future structure and location of industrial activity.

The reciprocal relationship between public planning policy and industrial location, and the inseparability of the two, is the central theme of Part Six. Most of the argument is couched in terms of "regional" problems and "regional" planning, although it is generally also applicable at the national, city, or local level. The discussion begins with a general review of regional problems and types of problem regions (Chapter 22), and this is followed by a chapter on industrial planning strategy (Chapter 23), supported by a number of case studies (Chapter 24). Then there is a brief review of industrial planning as a land-use problem, a subject which is often neglected in the literature on economic development (Chapter 25). Next, a discussion of location theory in relation to the planning of industrial development (Chapter 26) provides a link back to the analysis of Parts Two and Three. Finally, some reflections are offered on the role of industrial development in contemporary society (Chapter 27).

The emphasis is on the strategy of planned industrial development as an instrument of public policy rather than with the effects of this on actual locational behavior. The orientation of Part Six thus departs somewhat from the direction established in the other parts of the book, where attention has been confined almost entirely to the circumstances in which choice of location is made.

22

Regional Problems and Problem Regions

What constitutes a regional problem, and what defines a problem region? A regional problem, like any other economic or social problem, is determined by the nature of the society and its value system. It is society that decides whether a certain condition constitutes a problem, by referring observed facts to whatever goals or conception of social justice the people uphold. It is also society that distinguishes between conditions that are considered to be unsatisfactory but where public concern is not expressed in public policy, and conditions that are recognized as so serious that some kind of remedial program is initiated. As an illustration, there is a general consensus that the level of unemployment among the black population of large American cities has serious social consequences but as yet this has not led to positive public intervention, whereas the economic stagnation of certain regions such as Appalachia has stimulated the formulation of a national regional development policy. These differences, which reflect societal attitudes and degrees of concern, help to determine not only which are the regional problems but also which are the problem regions.

A regional problem may be broadly defined as some unsatisfactory condition which is associated with a subnational area or areas. A problem region is an area in which some specific problem or set of problems is identified. The problems may be recognized simply as existing within the area in question viewed in isolation, or they may arise partly from the relationship between this and other regions; the problems of a single region as a closed system may be quite different from those of the same region considered as an open system within a wider system of regions.

For example, in a metropolitan region considered in isolation large-scale population growth need not be a problem as long as congestion and diseconomies of scale are avoided, whereas if this growth is connected with the decline of other regions this may constitute a problem.

There are many adjectives in common use to describe problem regions. These include depressed, distressed, lagging, backward, unfortunate, declining, deprived, underprivileged, undeveloped, underdeveloped, overdeveloped, overcrowded, congested, and so on. Applied indiscriminately, these terms can be a source of great confusion, but much of this can be avoided by the recognition of three broad categories of problem regions: (1) the underdeveloped region, (2) the depressed region, and (3) the congested region. Each has a distinctive set of problems, which may require different policies and spatial strategies of remedial action.

The term *underdeveloped region* refers to an area that has yet to be fully developed and in which resources are underused. Industrial activity is primitive or nonexistent, the region not having experienced a period of widespread industrialization involving factory production with power-driven machinery. Such regions are characterized by low incomes and standards of living, and may be thought of as playing less than their full part in the economic advancement of the nations to which they belong.

Industrialization is generally regarded as the key to the acceleration of economic growth in underdeveloped regions. But there are a number of serious obstacles. There is generally a shortage of capital for industrial investment and an inadequate infrastructure, while the lack of effective demand on the part of the existing population means that the home market for manufactured goods is severely restricted. Physical resources may be in short supply, and there are also problems of lack of enterprise, education, and technology. In addition, underdeveloped regions may suffer from purely locational disadvantages: most of the underdeveloped parts of Europe are remote from the major transport routes and centers of population, and the same is true of the backward areas in the so-called developing countries of Africa, Asia, and South America.

A recent United Nations publication (Economic Commission for Europe, 1967) summarizes the decision that must be made in the process of industrializing an underdeveloped region under four headings. The first is timing, involving the determination of when and at what stage of economic development a successful policy of promoting rapid growth can be initiated. The second is the role that industry should play in the overall process of economic transformation. The third is the pattern of distribution of industrial investment. The fourth decision is the role of the large plant in an industrialization program. The third is the distinctively spatial decision, in which industrial location analysis has the major part to play, but the fourth decision also has important spatial implications. These matters will be examined in later chapters. Further discussion of the general problems of industrialization in underdeveloped regions can be found in Mountjoy (1963), and in a number of shorter reviews such as that by Rosenstein-Rodan (1961), while a series of case studies in Ward (1967) underline many of the practical difficulties faced by the individual firm.

The *depressed region* is one that has already achieved a high level of industrial development but which now has an unsatisfactory economic performance when compared with other regions or with some national norm. This is typically a problem of the advanced industrial nations, in which highly specialized industrial regions developed during the nineteenth century. Changes in demand, in world trade, and in comparative locational advantage have worked to the detriment of many such regions, slowing or halting their growth and depriving them of major sources of income and employment. This kind of problem is likely to be the unhappy experience of an increasing number of countries, for despite the tendency toward more diversified industrial regions less sensitive to the fortunes of single industries, changing economic circumstances will always work to the advantage of some regions and to the disadvantage of others.

Unemployment was the first condition to draw attention to the problem of depressed regions. The level of unemployment is still an important criterion in the identification of such regions in most countries, although more attention is now being given to such matters as the rate of industrial growth, the structural characteristics of the economy, population migration, and the quality of the environment. The criteria adopted by any particular country will depend on how society perceives the problems, and on the objectives of their regional planning policy (if they have one).

The problems of depressed or backward regions in advanced industrial nations are well known, and only summary observations are required here. There is a characteristic sequence of events, beginning with rapid industrialization and the indiscriminate exploitation of resources, progressing through changes in technology and demand conditions, and ending with the decline of the leading industry bringing unemployment, age-selective outward population migration, and general economic stagnation. The air of economic depression combines with the outworn towns and cities, and with other environmental problems such as the dereliction of land, to create a situation repellent to new industrial development. Market forces certainly could be allowed to take their natural course, but in most countries faced with this kind of problem public policy has been to attempt to revive the depressed region.

Depressed regions and their problems differ from underdeveloped regions in some important respects. In one way the depressed regions are easier for the planner to deal with, since there are already pools of labor, substantial investments in social overhead capital and entrepreneurial experience to be drawn upon, and generally some industries are still reasonably prosperous. The problem is thus one of economic redevelopment and conversion rather than of de novo industrialization. But in another sense these problems are more complicated than those of underdeveloped regions, for industrial reconstruction involves changes in an outdated but well-established economic structure and the replacement of industries that are in decline and reducing their employment.

The *congested region* is one in which economic development has reached a scale at which diseconomies (economic or social) can be detected. This is a problem of the major metropolitan area in advanced industrial nations—for example, in northern France centered on Paris and in southeast England centered on London. The diseconomies arise from continuing increases in the intensity of use of resources, in particular the transportation system, and this eventually leads to reduced industrial efficiency. Pressure for metropolitan development can also lead to the spatial expansion of cities and the creation of sprawling megalopolitan urban-industrial regions with all the economic, social, and environmental problems that this implies. However, the effects of congestion are hard to measure, and a major practical difficulty is deciding at what stage economic or social diseconomies of scale begin to operate.

Few regional problems are self-contained, since most of them have implications for other regions. This is especially true in the case of the congested regions, for their rapid growth is generally at the expense of other less prosperous parts of the country. In addition, planning strategies aimed at the relief of pressure on the metropolis require that some of the growth be diverted to other regions. The relationship between congested regions and depressed regions is a particularly important feature of planning in advanced industrial nations, and will be considered further in some case studies in Chapter 24.

Controlling the process of industrial growth in congested regions is difficult for a number of reasons. Industry expands mainly through the extension of existing plants in these regions, and this is more difficult to control than the erection of new factories. Businessmen tend to overestimate the external economies associated with a metropolitan location, but often have greater bargaining power than the planners who are more aware of the social consequences of cumulative industrial expansion (Economic Commission for Europe, 1967, 62). Since the social costs involved in a congested region are notoriously hard to evaluate, it is difficult to support an argument against metropolitan expansion on social grounds. It is similarly difficult to persuade businessmen that the sum of their individual decisions to locate in the metropolitan region, however sound each decision may seem, could be to their collective disadvantage.

An alternative to the trichotomy of underdeveloped, depressed, and congested regions is the more detailed categorization suggested by Friedmann (for example, 1966, 39–44). He recognizes five types of regions: (1) *core regions*, characterized by their high promise for economic growth, and comprising one or more cities and some of the surrounding territory; (2) *upward-transitional areas*, which include all settled regions whose natural endowment and location relative to core regions suggests the possibility of greatly intensified use of resources; (3) *resource frontier regions*, or zones of new settlement in virgin territory which is being occupied and made productive; (4) *downward-transitional areas*, including established settled regions of an agricultural or industrial character which are in decline; and (5) *special problem regions*, where the peculiarity of resources or location requires some special approach to development. Friedmann's scheme stresses the spatial relationships between different kinds of problem regions, in particular between the core and the peripheral areas, and the fact that the problems of one region cannot be sensibly tackled in isolation.

Whatever classification of problem regions is adopted, the planning process requires that they be identified precisely at some stage. It is then that the problem regions can be thought of as *planning regions*, or what Friedmann (1966) terms *development regions* and Boudeville (1966) and others *programming regions*. The problem regions (no matter how defined) need not automatically become planning regions, but this is very often the case, since much regional planning involves drawing a line around an area in which some unsatisfactory condition has been recognized and initiating remedial action within those spatial limits.

In arriving at an areal definition it is important to appreciate that the problem region is a relative concept. This is because the value systems that recognize problems as such vary between nations, and also because the conditions of economic geography differ from one country to another. In addition, society's conception of a problem region changes through time: the less fortunate regions that cause concern in a modern industrial nation with virtually full employment are very prosperous compared with the depressed regions of the 1930s. There are thus no absolute standards that can be applied to the identification of problem regions, and no specific criteria that hold irrespective of place and time.

The regional development policies of the European nations indicate the wide variety of possible approaches to the definition of problem regions (PEP, 1962; European Free Trade Association, 1965; and Area Redevelopment Administration, 1965). Although the level of unemployment is a universal criterion, the percentage rate that is applied differs from one country to another. Other criteria include low incomes and wage levels, low tax yields, population emigration, daily or weekly commuting under unfavorable circumstances, the stagnation of important sections of the economy, other indications of inadequate industrial performance, and low levels of savings. In the United States and Canada employment criteria predominate.

The application of different criteria can obviously lead to different definitions of the problem regions. For example, an areal classification based on levels of unemployment may show little correspondence with one based on other measures of industrial performance. However, the application of multivariate statistical techniques such as principal components analysis, together with appropriate areal grouping procedures, now makes it possible to define regions objectively by using a large number of variables simultaneously. This approach is exemplified by work on the geography of "economic health" (for example, Thompson et al, 1962; Bell and Stephenson, 1964; and Berry, 1965). It has also been applied to the identification of areal variations in industrial well-being (Smith, 1968, 1969a), in an attempt to suggest a more rational basis for the areal allocation of government financial assistance for industrial development. Further discussion of these techniques is beyond the scope of this volume. But they are important, since any improvement in methods of areal classification and spatial organization will help to produce not only a sharper identification of problem regions but also a more effective framework for planned industrial development.

23

Regional Industrial Development Planning

The successful planning of a regional economic development program is one of the most difficult tasks facing the modern world. It is a problem shared by advanced industrial nations and those in earlier stages of development, and it exists in both capitalist and socialist economic systems. The success of general economic and social policy in many countries is now partially dependent on the ability of the central government to influence the location of economic activity in a fairly predictable manner.

When a regional problem or problem region has been identified, the first decision is, of course, whether to take any action at all. In the depressed-area problem this generally involves a choice between "labor out" and "capital in," that is, between allowing outward population migration or to artificially stimulate the declining economy by the injection of new investment. Migration is essentially the laissez-faire solution, permitting labor to react to the areal expression of the market forces of supply and demand. Encouraging or supporting investment in the problem regions is the usual policy of public intervention. Although there are cases where the regional and national interest (no matter how defined) might be served by migration from the problem regions, most countries today prefer some form of government action to letting market forces take their course. The concern here is with the strategy of public intervention in the field of industrial location.

The starting point for the development of any planning strategy should be the setting up of *goals* or targets. The process of identifying the problem itself implies certain economic or social objectives, such as the reduction of local unemployment or the correction of imbalanced regional growth, and these may automatically become the policy goals. In any event, it is important that goals be clearly defined, for otherwise planning is meaningless. The establishing of goals may require the resolution of the conflicting objectives of local, regional, and national planning; for example, the goal of maximizing national income or production may not be consistent with a policy of equalizing regional growth rates and employment levels. The goals that are finally accepted will also reflect political compromise, as various pressures are brought to bear on the public decision-making process.

Achieving a planning goal requires the use of certain *instruments* or tools. These will relate to some of the exogenous variables that affect the operation of whatever system determines the condition which is the subject of the policy goal. This may be clarified by referring to Figure 23.1. Here the goal, or target variable, is on the left and the instrument variables are on the right, while in the middle is the *explanatory model* that defines the functional relationship between the variables which account for the magnitude of the target variable. Thus if the target was a particular rate of industrial expansion the explanatory model would be some kind of regional or national economic growth model, and the instruments would be chosen so as to influence externally how this system operated. If the goal was a particular spatial arrangement of industrial activity the model would have to be derived from location theory, and the instruments would affect such variables as factor costs in alternative locations.

Figure 23.1 indicates the basic form of an econometric model for regional or national planning. Such devices are used quite frequently at the national level, but their application to problems of regional industrial development is severely restricted by the inadequacy of existing explanatory models of industrial location, by the shortage of suitable data, and by the great complexity involved in designing interregional decision models (Siebert, 1969, 185). There is, in addition, some justified suspicion as to the effectiveness of such models, and the reliability of the conclusions drawn from them (Klaassen, 1965, 35). Thus it is not surprising

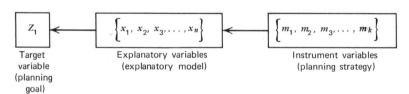

Figure 23.1. The basic model for regional economic development planning. (*Source.* Siebert, 1969, 177, Figure 9.1.)

that public industrial location policy is generally based on less sophisticated approaches, involving concepts that may have more intuitive appeal than theoretical or empirical support. The following review of policy instruments, spatial planning strategy and predictive devices, together with the case studies in Chapter 24, is an implicit recognition of the inadequacy of existing procedures in this field.

23.1 INDUSTRIAL LOCATION POLICY INSTRUMENTS

There are various ways in which a national or local government agency can attempt to influence the location of industry. These range from direct state control of the location decision in the planned economic system of a socialist country to slight alterations of the conditions within which entrepreneurs in a capitalist system make their free choices of location. Which instruments are brought into use in any particular circumstance will depend both on the nature of the problem and society's conception of what constitutes legitimate government intervention. For example, the direction of a major motor-vehicle manufacturer into a depressed area might be a very effective solution to local employment problems, but this would be politically unacceptable in many countries.

The specific instruments that can be used are described fully elsewhere (for example, in Hoover, 148, 251–64; and Orr and Cullingworth, 1969, 20–39), and only a brief review is required here. There are a number of ways in which they can be categorized, but an initial distinction can be made between general areal or regional rehabilitation, on the one hand, and measures designed specifically to attract industrial plants, on the other. The former tends to operate on externalities, while the latter generally takes the form of a direct payment or inducement to the individual firm.

The first of these categories refers broadly to the improvement of the infrastructure. This includes investment in new roads and other means of communication, in technical colleges and other educational institutions, in public utilities, and in various other services. Taken together, these facilities can be an important source of external economies, and their improvement can increase the attraction of a city or region for many kinds of industrial activity. Also under this heading might come regional image-building and other dissemination of information that might induce manufacturers to see a region in a different and more favorable light.

The second category includes the instruments that a government can use to attract private capital to a region, in the form of new industrial plants. These are generally financial subsidies or low-interest loans payable toward the cost of land, buildings, and machinery, but they can also include special tax arrangements, favorable depreciation allowances, help with the retraining of workers, and labor-cost subsidies. In addition, the government may invest directly in fixed capital, by building factories or laying out industrial estates or parks in order to attract industry to specific locations. And in countries where state ownership of industry is possible, the location of a public facility can be used to induce private investment in ancillary activities nearby.

Government industrial-location policy is not always aimed at encouraging development, since there may be a need to discourage further growth in some places. This is the case in some of the congested regions. The most obvious instrument to use in support of such a policy is a legal restriction on development, either by some kind of zoning or by requiring firms to obtain prior approval for building projects in certain areas. Other possibilities include taxing some locations at a higher rate than others, by a payroll tax or what is sometimes referred to as a congestion tax. These restrictions are generally used in conjunction with measures designed to divert industrial growth to other places, such as planned new towns and overspill reception areas in depressed regions in need of additional employment.

Something of the range of instruments available to central governments is indicated in Table 23.1, which refers to six western European countries in the middle of the 1960s. Three categories are recognized—general improvements in the regional infrastructure, measures directed at the individual firm, and those concerned with the retraining and mobility of labor. Further consideration of specific national policy instruments in some of these countries is reserved for the case studies in Chapter 24.

In addition to the measures that the central government may use to influence industrial location, there may be a variety of inducements offered by local communities and development agencies. A recent report (Management and Economic Research Incorporated, 1967) states that there are 14,000 to 15,000 such agencies operating within the United States, and spending hundreds of millions of dollars each year helping to promote the interests of specific areas. The measures used with respect to industrial development tend to be similar to those of the central government: loans from business development corporations, state loans and loan guarantees, municipal bond financing, various kinds of tax exemptions and concessions, and the promotion of industrial parks (Bridges, 1965).

Depending on the planning goals, and on the way the economic system functions, some instruments will be more effective than others. It may seldom be possible to use an econometric model to test the efficiency of

Table 23.1 Central Government Measures for Influencing Industrial Location in Some Western European Countries

Type of Measure	Belgium	Federal Republic Germany	Great Britain	France	Italy	Netherlands
General						
Regional funds, societies for regional developments	X[a]	X	X	X	X	
Improvement of regional infrastructure (roads, etc.)	X	X	X	X	X	X
Accompanying social measures						X
Decentralization of public institutions				X		
Decentralization into new towns			X			
Government orders		X			X	
Establishment license or prohibition			X			
Industry						
Subsidies on land and/or buildings	X		X	X	X	X
Subsidies on industrial equipment	X	X	X	X	X	
Loans, if necessary, at a low rate of interest	X	X	X	X	X	X
State guarantees	X	X		X	X	X
State participation				X	X	
Reduction on transport rates		X			X	
Tax facilities	X	X		X	X	
Exemption from import duty					X	
Labor						
Subsidies on the cost of training or retraining	X	X	X	X	X	X
Subsidies on the cost of moving	X	X	X	X	X	X

Source. Klaassen (1965, 63).
[a] X indicates the use of the measure in question.

specific instruments prior to their application, but there are still rational ways of judging the merits of different measures in relation to a certain goal. For example, if the objective is to reduce unemployment it would seem reasonable to use a labor-cost subsidy to encourage the hiring of more workers or the location of new labor-intensive firms. Grants toward the cost of buildings and equipment could be expected to attract industry which is capital intensive. As Alonso (1968, 38) has noted, there is a certain irony in the use of capital investment inducements by so many governments as an instrument in depressed-region policy. They will tend to favor capital-intensive firms who may have few workers when the stated policy goal is the reduction of unemployment, and such inducements could in fact lead to some substitution of capital for labor. Only recently a few countries, such as Britain and the Federal German Republic, have begun to experiment with labor-cost subsidies.

The use of instruments designed to lower unemployment may not, of course, be the best strategy for the depressed regions in advanced industrial nations. They may help to bring about a short-run improvement in a condition to which both politicians and the general public are especially sensitive, but they may not be able to insure economic revival and self-sustaining growth in the long run. In arguing that relative growth in per capita output is a more rational criterion of the success of planning policy, Richardson (1969, 402) suggests that the relocation of firms should be evaluated in terms of future income growth and the generation of external economies rather than simply in terms of the number of jobs created and what this has cost. For example, a complete transfer of a plant together with its workers may be justified even though it creates few new jobs directly, because it may lead to the inflow of more firms as suppliers to the first one.

This discussion emphasizes again the importance of choosing policy instruments appropriate to the accepted planning goals. It also stresses the significance of the explanatory model in Figure 23.1, between the instruments and the target and relating one to the other. In assessing the likely impact of specific policy measures, this kind of model, no matter how difficult to construct and use, must be regarded as the desired alternative to the intuitive judgment that experience shows is so often at fault.

23.2 THE SPATIAL STRATEGY OF INDUSTRIAL DEVELOPMENT PLANNING

Every development plan involves decisions concerning the spatial allocation of investment. Whatever the problem, the goal, and the instruments selected, some spatial strategies will be more effective than others, and there should be an optimum strategy with respect to any specific objective. It may seldom be possible to identify with confidence anything approaching the optimum pattern of industrial location for a development plan, because of the shortcomings of existing explanatory models and the lack of numerical data on many of the relevant variables. Nevertheless a choice between alternative strategies has to be made, and this involves an initial decision as to whether investment should be evenly distributed or concentrated on certain points or areas, or whether some compromise between these alternatives is desirable.

A policy of even distribution is easy to devise, and relatively simple to apply. The development areas are defined on the basis of some criteria such as percentage unemployment or per capita income, and everywhere within them qualifies for the same level of financial assistance payable to incoming or expanding industrial firms. Faced with a uniform subsidy, the entrepreneur will choose his exact location within the development area just as freely as he would in any other area; public policy influences his general regional selection, but not his final site unless persuasion or local community inducements are brought to bear on his decision. The only selectivity on the part of the central government is with respect to investment in the infrastructure, which may of necessity favor existing urban areas and their interconnections, but again the tendency will be to avoid any differentiation between cities or localities in the amount of assistance given. A policy of even distribution of investment is politically attractive, particularly as applied to the depressed region problem, since it can be claimed by the central government that every community has an equal chance of getting a slice of the cake.

But this kind of policy does have serious drawbacks. In a depressed region it tends to perpetuate the existing form of the space economy, which may be far from optimal with respect to the stated planning goals and may indeed be a serious source of inefficiency. And in an underdeveloped region it ignores such obvious conditions as the uneven distribution of resources and the economic advantages to be gained from initiating industrialization in some places rather than in others.

Areally selective industrial investment policy within problem regions can take a variety of forms, depending as always on the goals. A policy aimed at alleviating some condition such as local unemployment might offer different levels of financial assistance in accordance with need measured by the seriousness of the problem, as is the case in Britain and France (see Chapter 24). A policy directed toward maximizing regional industrial growth might concentrate investment on those places in which industry can operate most efficiently. If some such growth-point strategy is used, as is increasingly the case in regional planning, then there may be any number of different spatial forms which can be adopted.

The concept of *growth points* is so important in the theory and practice of contemporary regional development planning that it requires treatment in some detail here. The concept originated in the work of Francois Perroux (1950), who observed that *pôles de croissance* (growth poles) exist as sectors within an economy. Associated with a growth pole is a *propulsive industry* (or firm), which is characterized by large size, a tendency to dominate others, a high degree of interconnection with other industries or firms, and relatively rapid growth. Initially the concept of the growth pole was nonspatial, the pole simply referring to an industry or interrelated group of industries, and its subsequent extension as something with locational characteristics has led to some confusion. A recent paper by Darwent (1969) helps to clarify the distinction between the economic concept of growth poles and the spatial concept of growth points, and contains a long bibliography. Other useful contributions to the discussion include Parr (1965b), Hansen (1968b), Nichols (1968), and Lasuen (1969). As a matter of definition, the term growth pole may be taken to refer to the original concept of Perroux without any geographical implications, while the terms growth point or growth center refer to a location.

The term growth point can describe both an observed condition and an instrument of planning policy. They are connected, in that a place which is exhibiting vigorous growth may be a good location for further planned growth, and an understanding of how growth points arise naturally in market-regulated economic systems should be of assistance in their artificial creation in planned or partially planned economies. But it is important to bear in mind the distinction in meaning between the two uses of the term. The characteristic of existing growth is neither a necessary nor a sufficient condition for a successful planned growth point, although assumptions to the contrary are often made.

The use of growth points as a sensible instrument of industrial development policy is of course dependent on such a strategy being an effective means of achieving whatever planning goal has been established. If the objective is to maximize regional product or the rate of economic growth, rather than the short-run alleviation of local unemployment, then the concentration of investment at selected points should be more effective than an even distribution, simply because some points will be better locations for industry than others. In addition, pecuniary external economies are more likely to arise from spatially concentrated development than from dispersed plants. Establishing the best location for a single growth point within a region involves the identification of the place where the particular types of industry for which the region has a comparative advantage can operate most profitably, or the place where a planned industrial complex is most likely to be successful. Technically, this may not be too difficult, but determining the optimum spatial arrangement of a system of growth points becomes a highly complicated problem of applied location theory, for which no satisfactory solution has yet been found.

The selection of some places as focal points for investment implies that other areas within the problem regions will get correspondingly less public assistance. This may be perfectly reasonable on economic grounds, as some places well away from the growth points may have so little future industrial potential that their revival is not worth the additional expenditure. However, a growth-point strategy is generally adopted in the hope, and often with the expectation, that the prosperity generated by the growth points will eventually spread outward into the less favored areas. That this will necessarily be true is a common assumption in regional development planning.

This raises the important question of the relationship between the growth center and the surrounding area. Two of the most important and influential statements on this are by Myrdal (1957) and Hirschman (1958), who independently arrived at similar general models of regional economic development. Myrdal argues that once growth has been initiated flows of capital, labor, and commodities develop to support it, and that these operate as a *backwash effect* to the disadvantage of the stagnating areas from which these factors of production are drawn. However, demand for goods from the periphery may lead to a *spread effect*, whereby growth at the core is extended outward. Hirschman's model involves interaction between a growing "North" and a lagging "South," in terms of a *polarization effect* (compare backwash) and a *trickling down effect* (compare spread). The polarization includes the depressing effect of the North's economic strength on industry in the South and the migration to the North of labor and capital, whereas some of the North's growth will trickle down to the South through Northern purchases and investment and the absorbtion of some of the South's unemployed.

The center-periphery model developed by Friedmann (1966) is a partial reformulation and refinement of those of Myrdal and Hirschman. Friedmann proposes that economic growth can be transmitted from the core into the periphery through a hierarchical system of settlements, the creation of which helps to achieve the spatial integration of the economy. There is a certain analogy between the relationship of a growth point to the surrounding area and of the central place to its complimentary region, and it is often argued that growth points are likely to be high-ranking central places (for example, Richardson, 1969, 420). The connection between the urban hierarchy of central place theory and the growth-point strategy in regional economic development is a matter of great current interest, and forms the basis for the spatial planning framework in France (see Chapter 24).

At the level of the individual industry there is also support for the general notion of the spread of activity from a growth center. For example, Hoover (1948, 175) claims that the locational histories of industries have almost typically involved an early stage of concentration followed by a later stage of dispersion. In the early stage technical problems of product development are tackled in some existing industrial center where the necessary business skill and financial backing is available, and it is here that economies of large-scale production are first achieved. But ultimately decentralization will take place, as firms move out in search of cheap labor or some other competitive advantage. Alonso (1968, 27) makes a similar argument in more general terms. He suggests that at an early stage in industrial development a country will tend to have a large proportion of new industry, for which the externalities associated with a city location offer important advantages. However, as economic development proceeds the improvement of the infrastructure in the peripheral areas and the increase in knowledge of their economic possibilities will encourage decentralization.

But despite such support for the idea of the planned growth point as a place from which prosperity will spread outward, there is very little empirical evidence that this does in fact take place. The theoretical basis for this expectation is also rather insecure, dependent as it is on a certain spatial integration between the core and periphery which may have to satisfy rather specific conditions such as the existence of some form of settlement hierarchy. In other words, the functional mechanism required to insure the dispersal of economic development is not fully understood. Looking back to Figure 23.1, if the growth-point concept is a planning instrument there appears to be no general explanatory model to indicate how the spread effect or any other goal can best be achieved, answering the basic questions of the optimum number, size, and spatial arrangements of growth points and their industrial composition. As Darwent (1969, 13) bluntly states, we have "no firm theoretical grounds for planing growth in any particular location."

Even if the existence and operation of centers of relatively rapid growth is imperfectly understood, the growth-point concept is not without value in regional industrial development planning. To quote Darwent (1969, 13) again:

Despite the flimsy theoretical background and the lack of empirical verification, there is nonetheless a great deal of intuitive appeal in the notion of the growth center in which economic and social development is initiated and transmitted to an area around it. Moreover, the most important normative questions of regional economic development, those concerned with the regional allocation of investments in both time and space, can be given some clearer direction if this intuitive notion is adopted. Thus, for example, such a notion would imply that investment is best concentrated in growth centers rather than scattered around in some vague quest for "balance" or "equity." It might also imply that the existing central place structure of a nation could somehow be adapted to serve specific goals of growth initiation and transmission.

In particular, the growth-center idea as generalized by Friedmann into the center/periphery structure may offer a basis for the more formal development of a dynamic spatial theory of economic growth with direct applications in regional planning strategy. At the very least, the recent interest in growth points has widened the perspective of public policy by emphasizing that some places have greater development potential than others. As a result regional planning has been able to move away from the crude prescription of measures for the revival of any isolated pocket of unemployment (Richardson, 1969, 415). Even if there is no clear theoretical guide for the general design of a growth-point strategy, a careful comparison between alternative locations should help in the selection of those with the greatest potential for growth and repercussionary impact on the surrounding areas. Similarly the right industries for a growth point can be selected on the basis of their "propulsive" character, as indicated by such features as size, growth rates and linkages with other sectors.

Returning to the original question of the spatial allocation of investment in industrial development, the concentration at selected points as an alternative to even distribution has gained widespread acceptance in recent years. It is being used as an instrument in the stimulation of depressed regions in advanced industrial nations, such as Britain, France, and the United States. It is being used in the creation of "counter magnets" to relieve congestion in major metropolitan regions, outstanding examples being London and Paris. And it is being used in underdeveloped countries and regions as an essential component of industrial development plans, as for example in southern Italy, Spain, Brazil, and Venezuela. The growth-point concept has become a central and almost essential feature of the spatial strategy of industrial development planning.

However, a growth-point strategy does not necessarily produce the results which are anticipated, particularly with respect to the outward spread of growth. As Lasuen (1969, 137) has pointed out, where the concept is used in planning the failure of policies centered on it are normally attributed to the means of implementation and never to the adequacy of the concept itself. Yet enough has been said in the discussion above to indicate that at the present state of theoretical knowledge the outcome of any particular strategy based on growth points is unpredictable. The fact that so much contemporary industrial development planning rests on such an insecure foundation, although a cause for concern, is an inevitable reflection of lack of understanding of the process of regional economic growth and how industrial development occurs in time and space. The relationship between development planning and industrial location theory will be discussed further in Chapter 26.

23.3 PREDICTING THE IMPACT OF INDUSTRIAL DEVELOPMENT

The degree of predictability of the effects of planned industrial development is clearly very important. If the outcome of a complete regional strategy based on an interrelated system of growth points is still largely a matter for intuitive judgment, the impact of individual development projects can be assessed with much greater accuracy. Some approaches to this problem may be reviewed briefly.

The most common form of impact analysis involves the use of a *regional multiplier*. This is an application of the familiar Keynesian concept, and concerns the way in which an initial rise in income from one industry will multiply by stimulating further income through the expansion of other industries. An increase in industrial production, and hence in regional income, can generally be expected to arise from a change in conditions external to the region, which increases demand for the region's goods and hence its level of exports. In a planning context, such conditions may have been induced by the injection of a new industry into the regional economy, or by investment or subsidies which have the effect of lowering production costs and thus improving the region's capacity to compete in external markets. Alternatively, production can be increased simply by making payments to regional residents to increase their ability to consume the output of local industry.

In general, a change in regional income (dY) can be related to a change in regional exports (dX) by the expression:

$$dY = \frac{1}{1-s} dX,$$

where s is the marginal propensity to consume less the marginal propensity to export, that is, the marginal propensity to consume goods and services produced within the region. The term $1 \div (1 - s)$ is the regional multiplier. The theory behind the multiplier concept is explained fully in texts in general and regional economics (Samuelson, 1964; Nourse, 1969), and a brief history of its application in regional analysis will be found in Keeble (1967).

How such a multiplier is used in practice can best be explained by considering the impact of a single firm. Assume that planning policy is bringing a new enterprise into a depressed region, and it is required to predict the effect of this move on the level of regional income. In the short run there will be three types of impact: the *direct impact* arising from the wages, salaries and profits of the new firm, the *indirect impact* arising from the same kind of payments to regional industries supplying goods and services to the new firm, and the *induced impact* which is the increase in payments to regional consumer-goods industries and their regional suppliers brought about by spending out of the new income.

The way in which these impacts arise can be shown by an illustration, based on an imaginary case described in International Cooperation Administration (1961) and Management and Economics Research Incorporated (1967). The firm in question manufactures lead pencils for a national (external) market. It has 230 workers. Total sales revenue is $3.5M annually, total material costs $1.8M, labor costs $1.1M, other services $0.3M and profits $0.3M. The direct impact of the arrival of this firm will be the sum of wages and salaries, and profits if the entrepreneurs live in the region, which comes to $1.4M. The indirect impact is that part of the $2.1M spent on goods and services which remains in the regional economy. This involves calculating what the new firm itself spends inside the region and subtracting the "leakages" arising from the fact that suppliers may have to purchase some of their inputs from outside. Figure 23.2 illustrates what happens: of the original $2.1M, $1.8M is spent on regional goods and services and $0.3M on imports; in the second round of payments the $1.8M kept in the region generates $0.9M in additional regional income, $0.7M is spent on further regional goods and services, and $0.2M leaks away outside the region; and so on through subsequent rounds. The total indirect impact is the $2.8M which remains in the region less the $1.4M direct impact, that is, $1.4M.

The induced impact of the firm is determined by the regional multiplier. If it is assumed that $0.44 of every dollar of additional regional income is spent on goods and services produced within the region (a representative figure for a large, diversified, metropolitan region), the multiplier is $1 \div (1 - 0.44)$, or 1.8. Arriving at the total income impact is then a simple matter of applying the multiplier to the total additional

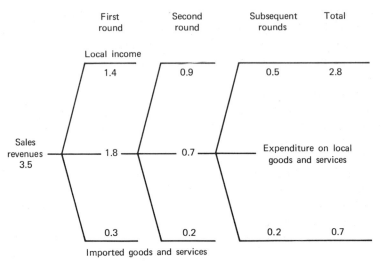

Figure 23.2. The local impact of an industrial development project, indicating the flow of expenditures. (*Source.* Management and Economics Research Inc., 1957, 42, Figure 1.)

income from direct and indirect impacts, that is, $2.8M × 1.8 = $5.04M. The addition to the $2.8M (or $2.24M) is the induced impact.

Unfortunately there are a number of practical problems in this kind of short-run impact analysis, particularly when applied to something more substantial than the arrival of a single firm. One of them is accurately measuring the multiplier. Data on actual income payments are so rarely available that some alternative has to be found, the one most often used being associated with *economic base theory* (see Chapter 7). Employment is generally adopted as a surrogate for production and income, with total regional employment being split up into those producing for the regional or local market (nonbasic employment) and those producing for export (basic employment). The variables in the multiplier equation set down above then become change in total regional employment (dY), change in basic employment (dX), and proportion of nonbasic to total employment (s) as a surrogate for the marginal propensity to consume regional goods and services. If the additional employment arising from planned industrial development is known or can be estimated, and given the basic/nonbasic employment breakdown in the region or city under consideration, then the total impact of the proposed development on the level of employment can be calculated from the multiplier equation. In practice it has been found that the employment multiplier arrived at in this way tends to vary in relation to the size of

Table 23.2 Employment Multipliers for Selected American Communities

Community	Population (1000)	Multiplier
New York	12,500	3.15
Cincinnati	907	2.70
Denver	930	2.54
Wichita	380	2.47
St. Louis Region	2,360	2.43
San Francisco Bay	4,392	2.22
Detroit	2,900	2.17
Albuquerque	116	2.03
Brockton	119	1.82
Madison	110	1.82
Oshkosh	42	1.60

Source. Liu (1969, 56). Most of the figures are from Alexander (1960).

the community in question, as is indicated in Table 23.2. This is because the larger the community the larger the nonbasic (i.e. self-serving) segment of total employment, and the smaller the leakages to other places. More detailed review of this method of impact analysis can be found in Isard (1960, 189–205) and Nourse (1969, 161–3), and in the general literature on economic base theory (Tiebout, 1956, and Pfouts, 1960).

It should be stressed that regional multipliers provide a short-run analysis only. In the long run an industrial development program might be expected to produce more fundamental changes than those reflected in regional income alone, such as changes in economic structure, in the environment, and in comparative economic advantages. These are even more difficult to predict than the short-run impact, because in the long run many of the conditions affecting the outcome of planning policy can change.

Another major difficulty in short-run impact analysis is finding out just where the payments of a new firm or industry go, which requires some form of input-output analysis. In the case of a single plant with a fairly simple input structure this may be reasonably easy, but full interregional models pose much greater problems as was indicated in Chapter 21. If the data were readily available a related set of interarea or intercity input-output tables, with an adequate industrial breakdown, could provide a model within which the impact of alternative spatial and industrial allocations of public investment in a depressed region could be tested out. Payments could be traced from one part of the region to another as well as between industries. However, the cost of assembling the necessary data would probably be prohibitive, and such a model would always be subject to the simplifications involved in compiling input-output coefficients. The intersectoral flow approach, based on much more easily accessible data on industrial sales and employment, may provide an acceptable alternative to full input-output analysis in certain circumstances (Hansen and Tiebout, 1963; Nourse, 1969, 163–176; Yeates and Lloyd, 1970).

Input-output techniques can be used in a variety of ways to assess the impact of change in an industrial system, as was suggested in Chapter 21. Given some target such as the maximization of regional production or income, input-output analysis can be used to help find the sector in which expansion induced by public investment would have the greatest impact, in terms of direct value added and repercussive effects on other sectors. The impact of increased government expenditure in the final demand sector on levels of industrial output can also be examined. Input-output analysis can be used to find which of a range of possible new industries have the capacity to use outputs of existing industries (that is, backward linkages), and which products new industries could provide for those already there (forward linkages). Some simple illustrations will be found in Siebert (1969, 177–182).

As a means of determining the best strategy for public investment, rather than simply the impact of a particular strategy, input-output analysis has one serious conceptual deficiency, however. As Siebert (1969, 182) has emphasized, testing a proposal via input-output analysis is a matter of trial and error, as the planning goal is not built into the model. For this reason a programming approach of the kind outlined in Chapter 20 may be preferred. The linear programming formulation allows a planning goal to be built in as the objective function to be maximized or minimized, and other aspects of public policy can be included in the constraints. To design a spatial industrial development strategy by using a well constructed programming model would no doubt be the best way to ensure that the outcome was both optimal and predictable, but the practical and conceptual problems are formidable. So at present a rather pragmatic attitude tends to prevail: better a clearly suboptimal strategy which is reasonably if not perfectly predictable in its impact than the optimal strategy which cannot be determined.

24

Illustrations of Industrial Development Planning Strategy

A number of case studies have been selected to show how different governments have arrived at a spatial strategy for industrial development planning. These provide specific examples of the kind of approaches referred to in the previous chapter, emphasizing at the same time the uniqueness of the problems of each individual nation. The illustrations are necessarily brief and highly selective. They concentrate on the advanced industrial nations in which a review of recent policy seems most rewarding, but also include an underdeveloped region and a centrally planned economy.

24.1 GREAT BRITAIN

The first western country to recognize regional disparities in prosperity as a major societal problem was Great Britain, and a review of the British experience reveals most of the major difficulties faced in designing a sensible strategy for industrial location and regional planning. Although the emphasis in government policy here has always been on the problems of the depressed peripheral areas, these are closely related to the rapid growth of the metropolitan core of southeast England and hence to the problem of the congested regions. Further details on most of the points discussed below can be found in a recent book by McCrone (1969), and a series of books on contemporary industrial Britain (Smith, 1969a; House, 1969; and Lewis and Jones, 1970) provide more complete surveys of specific regions and industries.

The British government took its first tentative action in the field of industrial location in the 1930s, when unemployment in the older specialized industrial regions of northern England, Wales, and Scotland rose to alarming levels. Two policy objectives were recognized: the alleviation of the short-run employment problem, and the long-run need to strengthen the economic structure of the declining regions. It was assumed that both objectives could be achieved by the same policy—that of taking work to the workers, a proposition which is still largely adhered to despite strong arguments and much evidence to the contrary.

Ever since the designation of the first *Special Areas* in 1934 the problem regions have generally been identified on the basis of unemployment. The rigid application of the figure of $4\frac{1}{2}$ percent unemployed for some years led to a proliferation of small areas qualifying for government assistance, but in 1966 the existing *Development Districts* were replaced by a much smaller number of *Development Areas*. In 1967 *Special Development Areas* were designated covering places with particularly severe problems, and in 1969 certain *Intermediate Areas* were identified, in response to the fact that in some regions economic difficulties are not necessarily reflected in high unemployment. The relationship between the assisted areas and the level of unemployment is shown in Figure 24.1.

The regional development policy instruments adopted in Britain fall into two categories, usually distinguished as "the stick" and "the carrot." The stick comprises the Industrial Development Certificate (introduced under the Town and Country Planning Act of 1947), which requires that any industrial development project over a certain size be officially approved as consistent with the "proper" distribution of industry. Although what is proper has never been defined precisely, the IDC has become a major policy instrument used to restrict development in the prosperous regions and divert it to those with job shortages.

The carrot comprises various financial inducements to locate factories in the problem regions. At the time of writing the main grants in the Development Areas proper are 40 percent of the capital cost of new plant and machinery and up to 25 percent of the cost of new buildings or extensions. In addition the government may itself provide premises for rent or purchase, and there are a variety of special loans and grants for which some firms may qualify. The Development Areas are also entitled to the Regional Employment Premium and an additional benefit under the Selective Employment Premium—flat-rate payments per employee which can reduce labor costs for the average firm by about 8 percent. The Special Development Areas have the extra inducements of a 35 percent building grant, as well as rent concessions in government factories and

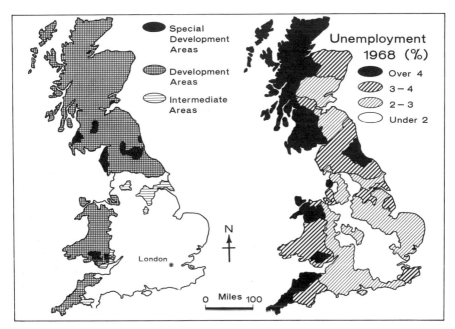

Figure 24.1. Unemployment and the assisted areas in British industrial-location policy. (*Source.* Department of Employment and Productivity, and Board of Trade.)

certain operating grants. The Intermediate Areas qualify for some but not all of the normal Development Area aid, and are treated as Development Areas with respect to the ease with which a firm can obtain an Industrial Development Certificate. There is thus a three-level areal differentiation of industrial incentives, based on need measured largely but not entirely by the unemployment criterion.

In addition to the system just described, the various new towns, expanded towns, and overspill reception centers developed since World War II must be thought of as contributing to government industrial-location policy. As communities planned to relieve population and economic pressures on the major metropolitan areas, these places are de facto growth points, and have been the locations for a large volume of decentralized industrial development in the core regions and to a lesser extent in the periphery.

Much has been achieved by government industrial-location policy in Britain. In most areas unemployment has been kept low, but it must be recognized that national conditions of virtually full employment coupled with labor mobility have been an important contributary factor. Diversification has taken place in all the old depressed areas, and their industrial performance in general has been improved. Nevertheless, the problem regions at present are broadly the same as in the 1930s; the peripheral regions continue to contribute less than their "fair share" to national economic growth, and the tendency toward concentration in southeast England remains a source of concern to regional planners.

A number of important lessons can be learned from four decades of government industrial-location policy in Britain. First, too much attention has been given to unemployment rates in the spatial allocation of public investment. Spending money on any depressed community may be the best short-run solution to unemployment problems, but it is not necessarily the best way to improve regional industrial structure and performance in the long run. Thus policy has not been sufficiently selective from an areal point of view, and the growth-point concept has received little direct application except for the development of the new towns. The fact that centers of relatively rapid industrial growth exist in the peripheral regions is more the result of the collective locational decisions of private entrepreneurs operating within the framework of inducements and constraints laid down by national and local government. This is not an unreasonable basis for the selection of growth points in a mixed (market/planned) economy, but the encouragement of specific growth points may be a more effective means of achieving regional economic revival.

Another lesson is that policy has not been sufficiently selective from an industrial point of view. All industries are treated in much the same way, even though some are more suitable for the problem regions than others. For example, existing policy does not specifically favor the propulsive industry, or the large and dynamic firm with good linkages, which should have the greatest impact on regional economic revival. Very little is known about the effectiveness of different policy instruments as they apply to different types of firms, and about the relative spatial mobility of different industries.

Finally, too much attention has been given to problems of regional industrial structure and not enough to regional locational disadvantages. The emphasis has generally been on structural change induced by industrial movement, rather than on improving regional comparative advantage by investment in environmental renewal, communications, and other aspects of the infrastructure. And the sensible if politically difficult strategy of allowing and planning for the gradual disappearance of places with extreme locational disadvantages for new industrial development has not been considered seriously enough.

At the root of most of these difficulties has been a failure to identify policy goals clearly and pursue them logically and consistently. This, in its turn, is connected with the problem of coordinating industrial-location policy with often opposing policies pursued by government agencies concerned in such matters as local planning, national economic affairs and transportation, and with the problem of reconciling the conflicting aspirations of different regions, cities, and local communities. The ultimate lesson to be learned from the British experience is that it is difficult to pursue a sensible industrial-location policy unless it forms an integral part of a national spatial economic and land-use planning strategy.

24.2 FRANCE

The main interest of industrial development planning in France is the spatial strategy developed around the concept of growth points, and the relationship between regional and national planning. The overriding problems in France are the dominance of Paris over the rest of the nation and the contrast between the prosperous metropolitan region and the poor southern and western peripheral regions. These are commonly referred to as the problem of *Paris et le désert français*. The Paris urban complex contains a quarter of France's industrial jobs and, as in Britain, decentralization and dispersal from the core into the less prosperous periphery are central objectives of public policy. A comparison between the problems of the London and Paris regions will be found in Hall (1966), and useful references on French regional planning include MacLennan (1965), Boudeville (1966), and Hansen (1968c).

Systematic legislation began in 1955, when measures were taken to control industrial development in the Paris region and to encourage decentralizing firms. In 1958 the problem of regional development was formally recognized as an essential part of any program for national economic expansion, and the emphasis of public policy changed from simply the promotion of industrial decentralization to the formulation of regional development plans within the context of a national economic plan.

For the purpose of industrial-location policy, France is divided into five zones, each with a different kind of financial aid (see Figure 24.2). In the first zone, comprising the southern and western periphery, the present (1969) grants are 12 to 15 percent of total investment for a new factory and 6 percent for an extension, with 25 and 15 percent, respectively, in the metropolitan centers. The second zone is largely the old mining and textile districts, and receives an industrial adaptation grant of up to 25 percent of operating costs to encourage industrial conversion. The third and fourth zones are shown as one in Figure 24.2; in the third zone firms qualify for tax exemptions, whereas in the fourth zone—the

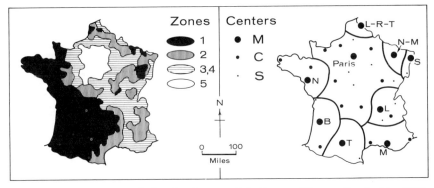

Figure 24.2. The spatial planning framework in France. (*Source.* Boudeville, 1966, 160 and 165.) M, Regional Metropoles; C, Regional Centers; S, Regional Satellite Towns. The metropoles are: L-R-T, Lille-Roubaix-Tourcoing; N-M, Nancy-Metz; S, Strasbourg; L, Lyon-St. Etienne; M, Marseilles; T, Toulon; B, Bordeaux; N, Nantes-St. Nazaire.

relatively rich part of France outside the Paris region—this applies only to decentralizing firms. The fifth zone is the region centered on Paris where industrial development is discouraged.

An essential feature of the French plans for decentralization and regional economic development is its hierarchical system of growth points (Figure 24.2). The country is divided into nine polarized regions, centered on Paris and eight counter magnets termed *metropoles d'équilibrium*. The metropoles were selected largely on the basis of size and central-place status, with the aim of decentralizing some of the functions of Paris. The policy is to concentrate public investment on the eight regional metropoles, and develop an *armature urbaine,* or central-place structure, which will create an interdependence within the peripheral areas of the regions. At the bottom end of the urban hierarchy (not included in Figure 24.2) the smallest villages and hamlets in the most depressed areas will be encouraged to decline through outward population migration. The policy is thus one of increasing the spatial integration of the economy at a regional and national level.

The French approach to regional planning has one major advantage over the British approach described above. This is that the space economy is seen as a system comprising a set of interrelated subsystems, rather than as a number of almost independent problem regions. This has enabled the French to develop a more discriminating strategy for the spatial allocation of investment in the field of industrial location. However, in placing so much reliance on a hierarchical system of growth points as a means of creating spatial integretation and a viable decentralized economy, the French are to some extent experimenting with a spatial structure that is not yet fully understood. As was stressed in the previous chapter, the mechanism by which economic growth is transmitted from core to periphery is uncertain, and the planner can never be sure that encouraging a particular urban hierarchy represents the optimal allocation of resources. Although the growth of the Paris region has certainly been slowed down and some industrial decentralization achieved, it is far too early to evaluate the success of what is essentially a long-term plan for the restructuring of the entire national space economy.

24.3 THE UNITED STATES

The experiences of the United States in the field of regional industrial development planning are of interest from a rather special point of view. As economic leader among the advanced industrial nations, the United States has both the financial resources and the technical skills to develop an effective solution to many social and economic problems which poorer nations would find it difficult or impossible to tackle. Yet despite massive problems of urban and rural poverty, the societal values that support the American "free-enterprise" system impose major constraints on government intervention in economic affairs. How this conflict is eventually resolved is a matter of paramount national concern.

The nature of the major regional problems in the United States is well known, and the background is set down in detail elsewhere (Perloff et al, 1960; Economic Development Administration, 1967; and Cameron, 1968). The structural modifications that have been a feature of all advanced industrial economies have had a particularly severe impact on certain parts of this country. Regions that once supported large agricultural populations have suffered continuing and sizable reductions in the demand for labor. Economic activity in the coal-mining regions (in particular, Appalachia) has been seriously affected by extinction of reserves, falling demand, and indiscriminate exploitation without regard to environmental and social consequences. Certain specialized manufacturing districts have also suffered from industrial decline and outward population migration. Marked regional and subregional variations in prosperity have thus arisen, to which must be added the special poverty problems of the city ghettos and the Indian Reservations.

The setting up of the Tennessee Valley Authority in 1933 represented the first major government intervention in regional economic development. Despite the success of this project in stimulating industrial development, there was very little further organized assistance for the problem regions until 1961 when the Area Redevelopment Administration was established to provide loans and grants for commercial and industrial development in areas with chronic unemployment and low wages. However, the funds made available were meagre, and it was really 1965, with the Appalachian Regional Development Act and the Public Works and Economic Development Act, which marked the beginning of a serious national planning strategy for the depressed regions.

The Appalachian Regional Development Act was a response to the severity of the problems of this particular region, which had become something of a national *cause célèbre* with the "discovery" of large scale poverty and hunger along with thoughtless environmental destruction on the part of the coal-mining corporations. To quote the Act, "the purpose of this Act is to assist the region in meeting its special problems, to promote its economic development, and to establish a framework for joint Federal and State efforts towards providing the basic facilities essential to its growth and attaching its common problems and meeting its common needs on a coordinated and concerted regional basis. The public investments made in the region under this Act shall be concentrated in areas where there is a significant potential for future growth, and where the expected returns on public dollars invested will be greatest." Thus the Appalachia Act explicitly required some form of growth-point strategy.

The Public Works and Economic Development Act (1965), through the Economic Development Administration, set out to cooperate with the states in helping the problem regions by contributing toward the planning and financing of economic development. The Act recognized three major kinds of geographical entities eligible for assistance: redevelopment areas, economic development districts, and multistate economic development regions. *Redevelopment areas* may comprise a county, a labor area, an Indian Reservation, or a municipality of a certain size. The Act prescribes six criteria for qualification: substantial and persistent unemployment with 6 percent as the critical level, population loss, low median family income, sudden rise in unemployment, Indian lands, and finally the requirement that every state must have at least one designated area (an example of the political factor in the design of public policy). *Economic development districts* comprise multicounty areas, designated because single redevelopment areas may not be viable units for economic development. Each district is a group of adjacent counties with three basic characteristics: proper size for effective economic planning and development, at least two redevelopment areas included, and a development center (area or city) of sufficient size and potential to foster the economic growth necessary for the alleviation of distress in the district. *Economic development regions* are the major national problem areas extending across state boundaries and requiring region-wide solutions. The five regions covered are New England, the Coastal Plains of the southeast Atlantic seaboard, the Ozarks, the Upper Great Lakes and the Four Corners comprising most of the states of Utah, Colorado, New Mexico, and Arizona. The extent of the regions, districts and areas as defined in 1969 is indicated in Figure 24.3.

The redevelopment areas and economic development districts are eligible for the full range of benefits under the Economic Development Administration program. These include grants and loans for public works and development facilities, industrial and commercial loans and working capital loan guarantees, and technical assistance. The main provision for aiding industrial development is a loan of up to 65 percent of the total cost of land, buildings, machinery and equipment. The economic development regions have a responsibility to develop a comprehensive long-range economic plan, and are eligible for supplementary grants, administrative expense grants, and technical assistance.

The basic strategy of the United States government is thus to define the problem areas or regions objectively on the basis of need, and then to

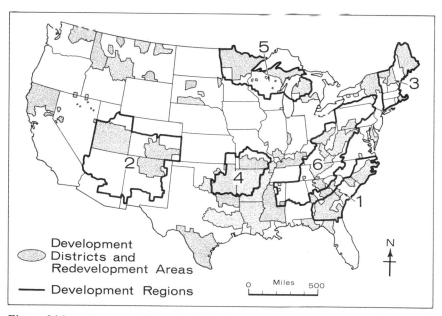

Figure 24.3. Areas qualifying for federal government assistance in the United States in 1969. (*Source.* Area Development Administration, U.S. Department of Commerce.) The regions are: 1. The Coastal Plains, 2. The Four Corners, 3. New England, 4. The Ozarks, 5. The Upper Great Lakes, 6. Appalachia.

concentrate public investment in growth points. Some pertinent questions can be raised concerning both the design of this approach and the way in which it is proposed to implement the two Acts. For example, in Appalachia the states involved have now identified about 125 areas which, it is claimed, have "significant potential for future growth," and growth points have been defined in such a way that each of the region's sixty development districts has at least one. Hansen (1969a) claims that this is not nearly selective enough; it certainly looks very much like an even spread of investment in the guise of a growth-point strategy. A similar criticism has been made of the development-center policy of the EDA: as Duskin and Moomaw (1967) have pointed out, the 1968 allocation of $27M for development-center projects averages only $225,000 to $270,000 per center—"hardly enough for a sewer line."

It is also argued that the chosen development centers are too small to be effective instruments of areal economic regeneration. Their average population is less than 40,000, and by 1968 only two places with over 100,000 had been selected. Berry's analysis of journey to work in the United States (Berry, 1968a; US Bureau of the Census, 1968), which stresses low welfare as a characteristic of intermetropolitan areas on the edge of the commuting fields, suggests that labor markets need a population of more than 250,000 to be viable parts of the national urban system; few cities of under 50,000 appear to influence the welfare of surrounding regions.

Other criticisms are that the policy of helping the worst areas first is in conflict with the selectivity implied in the growth-point concept, and that the emphasis on investment in the infrastructure as against human resources is wrong (Hansen, 1968a). For example, much of the initial expenditure authorized by the Appalachia Act was for highways, yet there is a desperate need for the improvement of education, job training, and health services if life is to be made tolerable and labor more useful. Then there are the problems of the cities and their ghettos—so closely related to migration from depressed regions yet considered largely in isolation from EDA policy.

The major improvements that might be made in United States regional industrial development policy are suggested by European experience as well as on a priori grounds. Greater selectivity in the spatial sense is likely to be more effective than the present policy, with investment in existing growth points and perhaps planned new towns in good locations near the problem areas. This could involve the planned decline of some isolated communities with no industrial potential, or "cutting off the tail" of the urban hierarchy as in France. In addition, more spatial coordination of planning at different levels is required if many of the redevelopment area and development district projects are not to exist in isolation and independent of wider regional and national planning objectives. But such changes would clearly need greater expenditure on induced industrial development, alterations in political attitudes which tend to support an equal-share-for-all policy, and not least a greater national commitment to economic planning than this society is prepared to accept at present.

24.4 SOUTHERN ITALY

The case studies presented thus far have all been concerned with the problems of depressed or lagging regions in advanced industrial nations. Southern Italy provides an illustration of industrial development policy applied to an underdeveloped region characterized by an almost entirely preindustrial economy and society. Southern Italy has a population of 18M and a per capita income somewhat below the average for Latin America. It is largely an agricultural region, hampered by a poor physical environment and lacking mineral resources and other essential bases for industrialization. The low standard of living is reflected in massive outward migration to the north and overseas.

The efforts of the Italian government to stimulate industrial development in the south have attracted a great deal of interest (for example, Lutz, 1962; Chenery, 1962; PEP, 1962; Barbero, 1966, and Rodgers, 1970). A number of different national and international agencies are involved, but by far the most important is the *Cassa per il Mezzogiorno* (Fund for the South). This was set up in 1950 to carry out a major program of infrastructure investment aimed at reducing regional inequalities of economic opportunity, income, and standard of living.

The initial emphasis was on a program of preindustrialization, involving investment in roads, railroads, water supply, and other necessary services as well as in the improvement of agriculture. No provision was made for direct investment in industrial development. The expectation was that the improved infrastructure, increased agricultural production, and the higher purchasing power of the local population would automatically encourage new industry and attract capital and entrepreneurs to the region. The results did not come up to these expectations, however. Private industry was reluctant to move south, and in 1957 a law was enacted providing for direct assistance in the form of subsidies toward the cost of equipment, cheap loans, tax concessions, and various other financial inducements. The total effect of these measures was to reduce the initial capital cost of development by 30 percent and annual depreciation and interest charges by over two-thirds when compared with the north, although a large part of this saving might be offset by higher operating costs in the south (PEP, 1962, 27–28).

This new policy of direct industrial investment raised the question of the best locations for development. An attempt was made to identify those areas most likely to achieve self-sustaining growth, the result being the designation of nine main development areas and a system of growth points (*poli di svillupo*). The growth points were intended to act as focal points for migration from the poorer rural areas as well as centers of concentrated industrial expansion. The combination of this policy with the use of public industry to create a propulsive effect constitutes almost a classic growth-point strategy.

The role of the public sector of industry is of special importance in southern Italy. The legislation of 1957 required state-controlled corporations to make at least 60 percent of their new investments and 40 percent of their total annual investments in the south. The largest state corporation is the Instituto per la Ricostruzione Industriale (IRI), which has important holdings in steel, electricity, shipbuilding, and engineering. Its main project in the south is a large steel complex at Taranto—the first plant of this kind constructed south of Naples, and an essential prerequisite for the growth of an engineering industry in southern Italy. Another national corporation is the Ente Nazionale Idrocarburi (ENI), with diversified interests in petrochemicals, rubber, etc., and responsible for a large plant on the Gela oilfield in Sicily. At the beginning of the 1960s it was estimated that the Taranto and Gela plants alone would represent almost half the investments of the public corporations in southern Italy.

During the 1960s most of the emphasis has been on the development of the capital-intensive basic industry needed to provide a foundation for other activities. Encouragement has also been given to labor-intensive activities using local materials, those with export potential, and anything that might extend the use of the region's mineral and energy resources. However, the industrial investment incentives, as in most other countries, tend to favor capital-intensive projects.

At the end of the 1960s it is clear that the policy of industrialization for southern Italy has had less impact than was anticipated twenty years ago. The difference in living standards between the north and the south still exists, and the industrial take-off hoped for has been confined to a few sharply defined areas. Very simply, the growth-point strategy has failed to produce a spread effect, despite the advantage of propulsive industries subject to state control.

In its search for a more effective approach to industrialization, the government introduced the concept of *contrattazione programmata* in

1969. This involves the coordination of future public and private investment in the south, so as to achieve most efficiently the economic and social objectives of the current national five-year plan. As a result, major expansions have been announced for the early 1970s by a number of firms, but it is too soon to judge the regional impact.

Another approach that has attracted much attention recently has been a proposal to develop a major planned growth point based on a carefully designed industrial complex. The argument behind this is that in a region with very little existing industry it will be impossible to achieve self-sustaining growth without creating the same kind of intricate interindustry linkages that are found in established industrial concentrations. The report of the consultants commissioned to examine this, summarized in Newcombe (1969), proposed an integrated industrial complex based on a combination of heavy and light mechanical engineering and including an appropriate range of ancillary industries providing inputs and others making use of some of the outputs. The site suggested is Bari on the Apulia coast, with a subsidiary location at Taranto about sixty miles away. The initial employment would be 8200 people.

In twenty years the position of the Italian government with respect to industrialization in the south has thus changed considerably. A policy of simply building up the infrastructure and then relying on the private investor has evolved through a growth-point strategy with conventional investment incentives to the prospect of large-scale coordination of public and private development and the creation of a complete planned industrial complex. And still the policy objective is a long way from being achieved. The general lesson is fairly clear: if living standards are to be improved rapidly by economic reconstruction, a large measure of government involvement in the process of industrial development may be the only sensible policy, since anything less is likely to be ineffectual.

24.5 POLAND

The most extensive involvement of the central government in industrial development is in the planned economies of Communist countries. These include the world's second-largest industrial power (the USSR) as well as a number of rapidly emerging industrial nations such as Poland, Czechoslovakia, and Yugoslavia in eastern Europe. Together, these countries account for about one third of the world's population. State control means that industrial location can be much more closely related to the wider requirements of public policy than is possible in a capitalist country. Of particular significance is the fact that the profit of the individual enterprise becomes less important under Communism than the efficiency of the entire economic system or the achievement of social goals. Thus there are major differences between government industrial-location policy in a planned economy and in an essentially capitalist economy like that of the United States. The mixed planned and free-enterprise systems emerging in western Europe and certain other parts of the world occupy the middle ground.

The power of a state planning mechanism to mold the form of the industrial space economy clearly has some advantages in pursuing public policy goals. But it also raises some special problems. Whatever the political system, there are economic constraints on what planners can do with industry, unless it can operate with equal efficiency anywhere. The freedom the state planner may have to follow social rather than economic objectives could lead him to overlook the fact that industry is spatially mobile only within certain limits, and that some patterns of industrial location he may propose are simply not viable economically.

Poland provides a brief illustration of industrial location strategy in a planned economy. There is a large amount of published information on economic structure and planning policy here (for example, Pounds, 1960; Kuklinski, 1964, 1966; and Fisher, 1966), while the work of Hamilton (1967, 381–386; 1970a, 1970b, 1971) provides valuable background on industrial development in Eastern Europe in general. What has happened in Poland in recent years makes an interesting comparison with the previous case studies, for it shows that even with state control of industry, and a national economic plan with fairly well defined objectives, the planning of industrial location is not an easy matter.

The Polish nation that emerged from World War II inherited a high degree of concentration of industrial activity, in Silesia in the southwest and to a lesser extent in the central cities of Warsaw and Lodz. Elsewhere the economy was dominated by agriculture, and living standards were generally very low, indeed. The past quarter of a century has seen a major attempt to restructure the Polish economy, based largely on planned industrialization. Two basic objectives have determined economic development policy and the strategy for plant location—reaching the highest attainable yield from investment and stimulating the growth of the backward areas. The way these have tended to conflict is perhaps the most interesting feature of recent Polish experience in regional development (Economic Commission for Europe, 1967, 44–46).

Postwar planning began in Poland with the Three Year Plan for Economic Reconstruction (1947–1949). During this time capital investment was concentrated on the rebuilding of productive capacity and the adjustment of the economy to new national boundaries. This meant that almost half the national industrial investment went to Upper Silesia, Poland's most industrialized region, despite official recognition even at this early stage that further expansion of industry there should be avoided as far as possible.

Positive changes in the pattern of industrial location were initiated in the Six-Year Plan (1950–1955). A major objective was the economic and cultural improvement of the backward areas, and the main instrument for achieving this was to be the location policy for industrial investment. The plan provided for the building of over 1000 industrial establishments, with those outside the old industrial regions to provide two-thirds of the increase in employment. A planned index of growth of industrial employment was set for each of the country's seventeen voivodships (regions), and the location of new plants was determined in accordance with these targets. As it happened, the general economic situation compelled the government to abandon the building of half the new plants, and most of those whose locations had been determined were in the nonindustrialized areas (Wrobel and Zawadzki, 1966, 436). Since, under the Five-Year Plan (1956–1960) that followed, investment was concentrated on plants existing or started during the Six-Year Plan, choice of location was limited during this period.

The planned dispersal of industrial activity was a response to the need to relieve pressure on the major industrial regions as well as an instrument in the development of the backward regions. Such problems as air and water pollution, water shortage, and the strangulation of the transport system were seen to be raising the cost of industrial production in Upper Silesia. New industrial growth here was restricted to cases where there was a close technological association with the extraction of the local coal, while plants for which proximity to Upper Silesia is an advantage were located around the fringe of the region. The interrelationship between the problems of congested industrial regions and the backward regions in Poland is thus a close parallel of the situation in most advanced western industrial nations.

The achievements of industrial dispersal policies in the 1950s may be summarized briefly. There were high rates of growth of industrial employment in the underdeveloped areas in the north, and to a lesser extent in the east, but in absolute terms most development took place in the existing industrial regions (Figure 24.4). Thus the general results of the location policy aimed at stimulating the economy of the underdeveloped areas, despite some achievements, appear to have been relatively insignificant (Wrobel and Zawadzki, 1966, 437–438). These are high-cost areas compared with the established industrial regions, and in addition plants did not always generate the local multiplier effects which had been

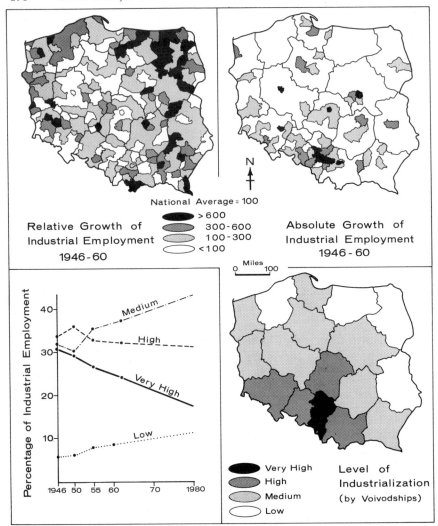

Figure 24.4. Industrial location and regional development policy in postwar Poland. (*Source.* Kuklinski, 1964, 63, and unpublished data.)

expected. As Kuklinski (1964, 67–68) concluded, the assumption of the early 1950s that development of a regional economy could automatically be induced by the location of a few industrial plants in a backward area proved to be incorrect.

The result of all this was a reappraisal of policy at the beginning of the 1960s, in the context of the long-run perspective plan designed to guide the development of the national economy up to 1980. It was recognized that the industrial revolution of the 1950s had achieved only a "take-off" effect in the backward areas, and that the "big push" was yet to come. Much greater emphasis than before was given to investment in infrastructure, to provide the support that many of the plants set up in poor agricultural areas had found lacking in the 1950s.

An important feature of the new location policy was a reduction of the original emphasis on an even distribution of productive activity. The three basic principles outlined in the Five-Year Plan of 1961–1965 were: (1) taking fullest advantage of the natural resources of the different regions; (2) limiting excessive migration of population by locating new plants so as to employ local sources of manpower; and (3) diminishing *within economically reasonable limits* the excessive differences in the economic development of different regions and in the living standards of their inhabitants. Thus the objective of removing interregional variations in the level of development was modified, and relegated to third place in the hierachy of policy goals (Wrobel and Zawadzki, 1966, 439–440). The planned changes in the distribution of industrial employment up to 1980, summarized in the bottom half of Figure 24.4, show that although the proportions in the highly industrialized regions will fall and that elsewhere they will rise the rate of change differs little from that observed during the 1950s.

The Polish experience since 1950 leads to the same general conclusion that is being arrived at independently in Britain and other non-Communist countries: there are limits to the extent to which an industrial space economy can be manipulated in order to achieve the largely social objectives implied in the pursuit of a more even regional distribution of production. Whether the prevailing political framework is socialist, capitist, or a mixture of the two, factories cannot be built in isolated locations with poor infrastructure and still operate with optimum efficiency. The continuing existence of a large enough number of such badly located plants can seriously impair the overall performance of a national economy, which in its turn will affect its capacity to support expenditure on social policy measures. The Polish planners appear to have learned the hard way that their great freedom to determine industrial location on grounds other than the profits of the individual enterprise requires an important ingredient of economic discipline. This lesson should not be lost on other nations where regional planning strategy is based on unrealistic assumptions regarding the spatial mobility of industrial activity.

25

Industrial Location, Land Use, and City Planning

Thus far, Part Six has been concerned with the relationship between industrial location and public policy at a macro-spatial level. The emphasis has been on broad problems of regional development and the national strategies designed to solve them. Now it is necessary to descend to the micro level briefly. At the micro level industrial development planning becomes largely a problem of land use, involving such questions as the projection of industrial land requirements, the siting of industrial plants, zoning, and the relationship between industrial areas, residential areas, and other functional units within the individual city. The discussion of these matters connects industrial location with what is probably the most urgent problem facing contemporary society: city planning.

The mutual interrelationship between industrial location and public policy at the city level is clearly very important. Yet it receives meagre treatment, at best, in most works on location theory, industrial geography, and regional economic development. This is unfortunate because a sound regional plan is dependent on the right kind of land-use planning at the micro level, just as surely as a national plan must incorporate sensibly related regional plans. Furthermore, it is at the community level that industrial development problems express themselves most forcibly with respect to the individual citizen, in terms of shortage of jobs, the desecration of the environment, and other things that stimulate public reaction.

The same kind of issues are likely to arise locally as at the regional and national level. The conflicting aims of social and economic policy have to be reconciled, and within the single city there may be an even greater tendency than on a wider spatial scale for the planner to assume that the location of industry is unimportant and entirely within his control. Some years ago Muncy (1954), in drawing attention to the neglected problem of land for industry, remarked that "little consideration is given to scientifically planning a new industrial area to meet industry's needs," and there is still much truth in this. At the same time it must be recognized that in many communities industry still calls the tune, and in some of the "advanced" industrial nations factories pollute the air, the rivers, the lakes, and the landscape with impunity. Regrettably, this is often the case in the United States.

The discussion that follows is a suggestion of some of the dimensions of industrial location as a city or local planning problem, and the way in which this relates to wider regional and national aspects of public policy. To do full justice to this subject, at least a volume in itself would be required.

25.1 THE LOCAL DEMAND FOR INDUSTRIAL LAND

National public policy objectives have regional implications. Regional plans have an impact on each local community. Thus a national strategy of industrial dispersal may stimulate development in a certain region, which will in turn create a demand for industrial land. National and regional policy can be successful only if some attempt is made to set aside an adequate amount of land for industrial development in places selected for expansion by the planners or likely to be selected by private entrepreneurs.

Some aspects of the relationship between planning policy and the local demand for industrial land are shown in Figure 25.1. The logical starting point is a national plan, or overall strategy for the spatial allocation of population and productive resources. A number of regional plans (1, 2, . . . , n) fit into the national plan, and each of these involves plans for the cities or other areal units within its boundaries (cities 1, 2, . . . , m in region n). A primary task for each city planning authority will be the preparation of a land-use plan, or zoning map, indicating the allocation of land between alternative uses up to some date representing the end of the plan period. The process by which the industrial land allocation may be arrived at is suggested in the figure. First, the city has a target population (that is, the figure expected at the end of the plan period in the light of the regional strategy). This estimate will incorporate the natural increase projection, anticipated migration, and any major development planned in connection with regional population redistribution. The target population and the city's place in the regional pattern of daily labor

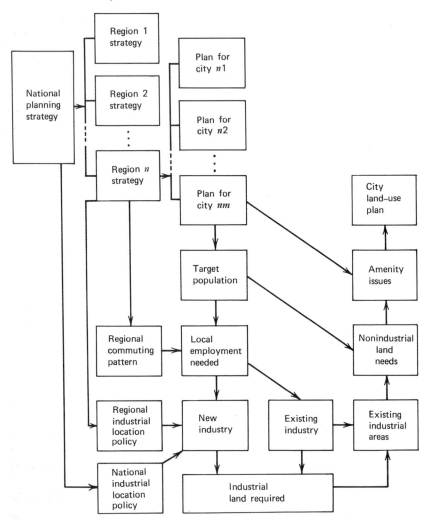

Figure 25.1. Some aspects of the relationship between development planning and the demand for industrial land.

movement leads to an estimate of the local employment required within the city. These jobs can be provided by existing industry and by new industry, the latter depending on the city's position in relation to regional and national industrial-location policy. Then comes the critical question of calculating the amount of industrial land needed, and the implications of making it available.

The calculation of local industrial land requirements can be illustrated by a specific example. The case selected relates to Leek, a small industrial town in the northern part of the English midlands. In 1962 Leek had a population of 19,000, and by 1981, at the end of a twenty-year plan period, it was required to expand the town by 5000 to reach a target population of 24,000. Most of the increase was to be overspill population from the congested city of Birmingham forty miles to the south, as part of a regional strategy of dispersal. This infusion of growth was expected to help revive the stagnating economy of Leek, which had developed during the nineteenth century as a highly specialized silk-manufacturing center. The case under review is thus an example of a planned growth point in the regional periphery, designed to assist in relieving pressure on the metropolitan core as well as achieve a local economic regenerative effect.

One half of the additional 5000 people were expected to want work in the city, which means 2500 new jobs. Since the expansion of the service sector to meet the needs of the new population was expected to generate 500 jobs, this leaves 2000 to be provided by the industrial sector. A survey of existing firms indicated that they could be expected to require 1000 additional workers during the plan period, and at the same time ascertained that the expansion of local industry would create a demand for 25 acres of land to supplement that already held for factory extension within existing curtilages. Thus new industry would be needed to provide the remaining 1000 jobs. An average of 30 employees per acre for new industrial development is a reasonable expectation in this area, which meant an allocation of 34 acres of land for new industry.

The industrial land requirements for Leek are summarized in Table 25.1. The area occupied by existing industry includes the land held for extensions referred to above. The acreage needed in addition to this includes land for the relocation of existing industry as well as for extensions on new sites and for occupation by new industry. Relocation can

Table 25.1 Industrial Land Requirements in Leek, 1962–1981

Class of Land		Area (Acres)
Occupied by existing industry in 1962		107
Net additional land required 1962–1981:		
For extension of existing industry	25	
For relocation of existing industry	5	
For occupation by new industry	34	
Less area to be released by industry	−1	
Total		63
Industrial land in 1981		170

Source. Staffordshire County Planning Department.

arise either because an existing firm is badly located at present and would benefit from a new site, or because it is a "nonconforming use" within an area occupied predominately by residential or commercial property where its continued existence on its present site is undesirable. In the table, the excess of the acreage for relocation over the area released by industry moved from unsatisfactory sites reflects the fact that firms generally need more space after relocation than they originally used.

The allocation of a certain area of land for new industry cannot, of course, ensure that such industry will be forthcoming. The necessary industrial mobility is dependent on regional planning strategy, and on the availability or otherwise of investment incentives built into the national industrial-location policy. However, the allocation of specific sites can help a city to improve its competitive position, particularly if a properly designed industrial estate or park is laid out. In the case of Leek, the town does not qualify for any assistance under national policy, and it has been difficult to attract new industry despite the setting up of an industrial estate because no system of inducements exists at the regional level to support the policy of industrial dispersal. The town's expansion has thus been in jeopardy from the start. This helps to stress again the inseparability of local and regional planning; a town expansion scheme means little outside the context of a regional plan and in the absence of the instruments needed to ensure its implementation.

This brief illustration makes it clear that the requirements of new industry are the critical factor in estimating the demand for land. The needs of existing industry are fairly predictable, and in any event many firms already hold land for expansion. But the area needed for new industry is subject to a number of variables which may be difficult to evaluate, even if regional planning is effective enough to ensure that industry will move to the city.

Although many city planning authorities have different rules for estimating industrial land requirements, the relevant variables are the same and may be summarized in the following expression:

$$A = \frac{(P \times R) - X + Y}{D}$$

where A is the total area of additional land needed for industry
            P is the population increase during the plan period
            R is a projection of the activity rate of the additional population, that is, the proportion likely to be at work
            D is the density of employment which can be expected with new industrial development, in jobs per unit of land area

> X   is the number of jobs that can be expected to arise in services or other nonindustrial sectors of the local economy
> Y   is a figure (positive or negative) for the daily inward or outward migration which can be anticipated.

The derivation of figures for R, D, X, and Y can pose serious difficulty. The activity rate can vary with age structure, type of industry, and local social behavior insofar as it affects wives working and other employment habits. The density of employment can vary considerably with the kind of industry that comes to the city, since some industries will be labor intensive in relation to land while other industries may employ very few workers per acre occupied. Generally, a rule of thumb must be adopted; for example, the Ministry of Housing and Local Government (1955, 22) suggested a likely density of 50 to 60 workers per acre on a large and fully occupied industrial estate in Britain, as a general guide for local planning authorities, although it was subsequently found that a lower figure could be expected in places well away from the major metropolitan areas. The calculation of X requires an estimate of the additional service employment likely to arise from the local multiplier effect. The commuting situation (Y) should be broadly predictable from existing patterns and regional planning strategy, or by some kind of trip distribution model if the planning process is sophisticated enough to use such a device.

The more of these variables that are within the planner's control (or accurately predictable on the basis of known development strategies), the better will a city be able to judge its future industrial land needs. Hence the importance of the relationship between the city plan, on the one hand, and the regional and national plan on the other, as was indicated in Figure 24.1. The planning framework suggested in this diagram is of course idealistic, in that in practice the three spatial levels of planning are seldom if ever as closely integrated as is shown here, but it does help to emphasize that planning at higher levels can reduce uncertainty concerning new industrial development in individual cities. Whatever the planning framework, the demand for industrial land can seldom be predicted with the same accuracy as, for example, land for housing with its more regular densities. Thus the general tendency is for cities to add a safety margin to their estimates to allow for the unexpected.

25.2 THE AREAL ALLOCATION OF INDUSTRIAL LAND

Once the amount of land required for future industrial development has been established, space must be found for it. In certain respects this is a similar problem to that of the spatial allocation of industry regionally or nationally, but taken down to the micro level. However, within the single city the economic and social constraints are generally such as to impose more stringent restrictions on where development can take place, if only because of the nature of existing development and the shortage of remaining space. At the same time, the choice between alternative sites within a city may be less important for most firms than the choice of this city over others in the region or nation. Determining industrial location at the micro level thus involves circumstances different from those at the macro level.

Particularly important within the city is the availability of land at reasonable cost. The cost of land is subject to extreme variation inside a city, and in the free market commercial uses may be able to outbid manufacturers for the best locations. Land already occupied constitutes a major constraint in the search for industrial sites, for although such areas can be aquired and redeveloped by industry this is generally an expensive process. In many cities unoccupied land is in short supply, and the task of the planner is to allocate that which is available between alternative and competing uses in accordance with whatever policy goals constitute the public interest.

Some of the economic considerations in plant site selection are, of course, the same in the city as at other spatial levels. If industrial expansion is planned or anticipated for a given city it should follow that the city itself is a suitable general location for new industry, by virtue of its inherent economic attractions or an adequate level of government subsidy, but the usual considerations of access to factors of production at reasonable cost still apply to choice of the exact site. For example, a location on a railroad, major highway, or waterway may be critical for some industries such as those processing bulky inputs. Other economic considerations include proximity to areas of labor supply, the physical configuration of the land, and the spatial relationship of the site to other existing industrial areas.

The planner deciding on industrial land zoning has an obligation both to the prospective users and the city economy as a whole, quite apart from any amenity issues. Sites must be made available with a view to the particular needs of industry, bearing in mind any special circumstances arising from inter-industry linkages and so on. But the city as a whole must function efficiently, with industrial land located so as to keep intracity labor movement within reasonable bounds and so as not to place under pressure on transport facilities and other services.

Within the city, social considerations are likely to be important in determining which land is used for industry if effective planning is in operation. The objective of the planner should be to balance the purely economic considerations with the need to preserve and improve the quality of the environment and the living conditions of the population. Thus the existence of industrial areas alongside residential areas will be carefully controlled, and the intermixture of industrial and other conflicting uses may be limited as far as possible by the elimination of nonconforming industrial uses and by avoiding spot zoning. Industry of a particularly obnoxious nature is likely to be kept well away from residential districts, and separate areas of land outside the city are sometimes designated for this kind of activity.

It is the conflict between economic and social considerations that makes the planning of industrial location within cities so difficult. In addition to the environmental pollution issue, there are a number of serious problems arising from a growing spatial mismatch between the location of employment and residence. The tendency in recent years for industry to leave the central parts of the city for peripheral locations has not been accompanied by a similar mobility on the part of the inner-city low-income residents who form a major proportion of the industrial labor force. This reaches its extreme in the black ghettos of major American cities, where residential segregation increases the employee's inability to move out with the jobs. The opposite situation has arisen in some European cities (in Britain, for example), where metropolitan industrial dispersal has failed to keep pace with the planned rehousing of slum dwellers in peripheral "overspill" estates. In these conditions, workers are forced to retain their inner-city jobs, thus adding to congestion on the highways or commuter railroads. All this emphasizes the importance of coordinating industrial location with other aspects of city planning.

This discussion of industrial land allocation within a city could be continued almost indefinitely. But, for the present purposes, one illustration is sufficient to round off the argument. Figure 25.2 shows a simplified industrial land-use plan for an imaginary city, distinguishing between existing development and planned expansion. The existing industries around the city center (*CBD*) date from the earliest stages of the city's growth, and allowance is made for a limited amount of expansion in inner-city locations by the redevelopment of an outworn residential area on the south side of the *CBD*. Within the central area itself, existing plants are classed as nonconforming uses, and the plan requires the relocation of those for which the *CBD* is an unsuitable area. Provision is also made for the relocation of nonconforming industry in some of the residential areas, those which remain being of a kind not likely to have a detrimental effect on adjoining property. Most of the new industrial land is toward the edge of the city; in two cases the land allocated is a

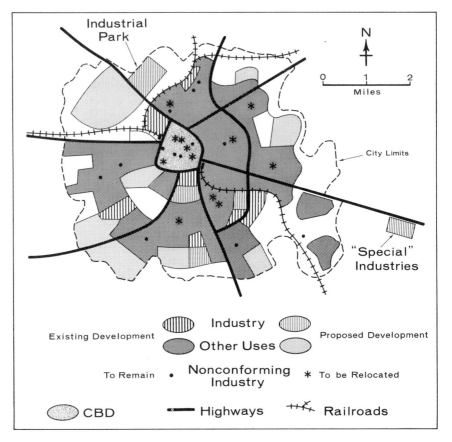

Figure 25.2. A land-use plan for an imaginary city, showing the allocation of sites for industry.

natural extension of existing industrial areas, while in the third it comprises a planned industrial park.

The advantages of a community allocating land for new industrial development in the form of a properly laid out and serviced industrial park have been mentioned already. In the words of Rosenstein-Rodan (1961, 206), an industrial zone or estate "constitutes a strong incentive to invest because it can capture the otherwise volatile external economies of agglomeration. Industrial zones can save a great deal of effort, trouble and expense in erecting a factory; they can realize considerable economies of scales in construction of factory buildings and in the installation of public utility services. They can provide for a better division of labor by securing common technical repair and information services which could not pay for one industrial unit alone but do pay for a series of industrial units." To the city planner, with an eye toward the quality of the environment, they have the additional advantage of helping to confine industrial expansion to particular areas designed for this purpose. Effective development control over such aesthetic matters as factory architecture and forecourt layout is often easier to enforce on a city-owned industrial park where specific standards can be established. The concept of the industrial estate dates from the end of the nineteenth century, with the development of Trafford Park in Manchester, England (1896) and the Clearing Industrial District in Chicago (1899). Their use as industrial planning devices has increased substantially in recent years, and there are now over 1000 operating in the United States and almost half this number in the United Kingdom. There are few countries that do not use industrial estates for planning industrial location at the micro (and macro) level today.

It should be apparent that few if any cities can be viewed in isolation, or as closed systems, with respect to the allocation of industrial land. As Figure 25.1 suggested, each city can be related to every other city by a regional planning strategy, and even if no such plan exists the needs of one place will eventually have repercussions on other places. The areal allocation of industrial land thus ultimately becomes a subregional or regional matter.

As an illustration of this, Table 25.2 shows the additional industrial land allocation in ten places within the West Midlands Conurbation in England. They form part of an old and congested industrial region where there is still considerable pressure for development but an acute shortage of suitable sites. The figures show that when allowance is made for the extension of existing industry and the relocation of badly sited plants, four of the areas have no land remaining for new industry. There are, however, 245 acres available in the other areas, and the use of this land is restricted by the planners to firms already located within the conurbation. As this land is used up, the pressure for further development must be diverted to yet other areas, on the fringe of the conurbation, or beyond in the regional periphery.

Thus industrial growth in one part of a metropolis may eventually absorb all available land, and continuing development will be deflected to other adjoining areas by the planner or by market forces. As pressure on land builds up in the entire metropolitan area the inevitable consequence will be urban coalescence and outward spread, which the planner may wish to control by the imposition of a restrictive instrument like a green belt and a program of industrial and population dispersal. Overspill reception areas or new towns may be designated beyond the green

Table 25.2 Additional Industrial Land (Acres) in Part of the West Midlands Conurbation, for the Plan Period Ending 1971

Local Authority Area	Land for Extensions of Existing Industry (a)	Land for Relocating Badly Sited Industry (b)	Residual Area Available for Redistribution of Industry within Conurbation (c)	Land Released from Industry (d)	Net Additional Land for Industry $(a + b + c - d)$
Bilston	39	28		13	54
Brierley Hill	130	43	127	21	279
Coseley	97	21	17	10	125
Darlaston	42	13		9	46
Rowley Regis	174	36		25	185
Sedgley	11	15	15	10	31
Tipton	68	20	30	23	95
Wednesbury	79	35	25	16	123
Wednesfield	151	14	31	7	189
Willenhall	123	34		16	141
Total	914	259	245	150	1,268

Source. *County Development Plan: Town Maps for South Staffordshire—Summary of Survey Reports and Analysis*, Staffordshire County Council, 1963, 8.

belt and land set aside for new industry there. Some of these growth points may help to revive the economy of depressed or lagging peripheral areas. The discussion thus returns to the regional level, and eventually to national planning strategy.

Local and regional problems of industrial planning are inseparable. Each community or city is but a part of a wider interconnected economic system. To set each local or city plan within a regional and national strategy may be difficult technically and unpalatable politically. But to plan in isolation is to ignore economic and geographical reality.

26

Location Theory and Industrial Development Planning

The relationship between the planning of industrial development and the theory of industrial location thus far has been just beneath the surface in much of Part Six. Any attempt by a central government agency or city planning authority to influence plant location assumes some knowledge of how locations are arrived at in general—knowledge of the nature and operation of the variables that determine locational choice. It follows, then, that industrial location theory and the operational models generated from it should be of considerable assistance to the planner in formulating industrial development strategy in a spatial context.

In practice, however, the connection between location theory and economic development planning is not nearly as strong as might be supposed. Of the major theoretical contributions reviewed in Chapter 8 only Hoover (1948) gives substantial treatment to problems of industrial location and public policy, and the attempt of Isard (1960) to follow up an abstract theoretical treatise (1956) with a set of operational techniques of regional analysis remains unique in the literature in this field. Despite the current interest in regional science and applied geographical analysis, much of the existing literature of a theoretical nature seems to have at best only a tenuous connection with real-world planning problems. The planners, in their turn, are generally guilty of attempting to deal with industry from an inadequate theoretical basis, which means that the outcome of their proposals are often highly unpredictable. Unwarranted assumptions are frequently made concerning the mobility of industry and the extent to which locational choice can be sensibly manipulated in the interests of public policy.

The discussion that follows deals directly with a number of issues that have been raised or implied in previous chapters. It suggests certain ways in which industrial location theory can assist the planner, and points up some of the major inadequacies of existing theory as a guide to public policy decision making.

26.1 THE NEOCLASSICAL THEORETICAL APPROACH

Most of the theoretical sections of this book have been based on what may be termed a neoclassical approach. The framework built up in Part Three was a logical derivation from Weber's original least-cost theory, with a revenue surface and spatial margins to profitability added to the cost surface suggested by Weber. The empirical studies presented in Part Four showed that the identification of single input cost surfaces, and simple representations of demand or revenue surfaces, is by no means as difficult as is sometimes supposed. They also indicated that something approaching a full variable-cost model can be made operational for certain kinds of industry, notably those with a fairly simple input structure, although the inability of such models to incorporate certain at present immeasurable variables has to be recognized.

The comparative-cost approach to industrial location analysis, resting on classical theory, is an appropriate framework within which to examine industrial mobility. And industrial mobility is a critical question in plans for industrial dispersal and the artificial stimulation of economic growth. It is obvious that the success of such plans will be partly determined by the extent to which there is freedom of locational choice, and how far this can be influenced by the type and magnitude of the inducements which the government is prepared to offer.

There appears to be a large measure of agreement on the fact that industry in general is becoming more mobile, or "foot-loose." As a smaller proportion of industrial activity remains concerned with the processing of bulky materials, as improvements in transportation steadily reduce the relative cost of overcoming distance, and as certain external economies of agglomeration become mere geographically mobile, it is argued that very many firms can locate almost anywhere they please within certain fairly broad spatial limits (margins). For example Luttrell (1962) has estimated that something like two-thirds of British manufacturing industry can operate successfully in any of the main regions of the country, and his detailed case studies of firms that have moved show that a branch plant in an unfamiliar area may be able to operate at or below the cost at the parent plant within two or three years providing it is skillfully managed. This helps to explain many of the achievements of British dispersal policy since World War II. In making a comparison between the British experience and the relative failure of the same policy in Italy in the 1950s, Lasuen (1969, 148) points out that "the British firms of the time, already well diversified and managed in a sophisticated fashion, could install their new factories practically anywhere, once the supporting infrastructure was provided. On the other hand, the still primitive Italian firms could not." Industrial mobility may well be a partial function of economic maturity.

Technical changes in the last few decades may have reduced the importance of locational costs in the overall cost structure of the firm. This suggests that in many industries plants of optimum size can operate in a wide range of locations with only minimal differences in production costs, and that profits are largely determined by entrepreneurial skill in making decisions other than on location. But, as Richardson (1969, 398) has stressed, the widespread impression of reduced locational costs has not been sufficiently tested.

If the branch plant of an existing and successful enterprise is the most mobile kind of industry, the advanced industrial nations should be well endowed in this respect. However, by no means all industrial growth takes place in the form of branches even in these countries. A study undertaken for the United Nations (Economic Commission for Europe, 1967) indicates that in industrially developed countries over 60 percent of all industrial development is accounted for by the extension of existing plants, which is not mobile at all. Much development also takes place in the form of new firms, the appearance of which is much more fixed in space (and time) than is the case with branch plants. A small new firm starting up spontaneously in response to some opportunity perceived by the entrepreneur may have very little choice of location; certainly the location and timing of this kind of development is far less susceptible to government control or manipulation than a branch of an existing firm. Another relevant consideration is the growing importance of the very large firm in the modern industrial economy. Such firms often have considerable freedom of locational choice, but as they account for an increasing share of total industrial development it means that industrial investment is allocated to a diminishing number of locations. General claims about the increasing mobility of industry thus involve some oversimplification.

Mobility obviously varies from industry to industry. Some industries are still closely tied to the sources of bulky inputs while others can operate successfully in many different places; for example, in a country the size of Poland there are perhaps fewer than twenty places in which a new cement plant could be built, while there may be over 200 possible locations for a metal-processing factory (Economic Commission for Europe, 1967, 67). The type of industry and its input structure is the main determinant of industrial mobility, but the level of prosperity may also be important. Other things being equal, a growth industry is likely to offer a wider range of locational choice than a declining industry where the spatial margins to profitable operation may be contracting.

As was indicated in previous chapters, national policies of attempting to induce industrial movement are almost invariably supported by uniform financial subsidies irrespective of the type of industry. It requires only an elementary knowledge of location theory to detect the error in this. The need for a more selective approach was stated clearly by Hoover (1948, 246) more than twenty years ago:

Locational policy should be carefully selective in its application to different industries. No locational policy can be intelligently implemented unless its effects on different types of industry are taken into account in advance. Different industries vary widely in their locational responsiveness to possible controls and in the leverage they exert by passing on the effects of locational change to still other industries. If the aim of a policy is to increase or stabilize employment in a specific area, concentration of effort on a carefully chosen group of industries may be essential for success.

He stressed the need to determine the "local profit prospects" of specific industries before implementing a development program for a particular community. The fact that Hoover's comments on this and other matters relating to industrial location and public policy still seem so fresh and pertinent is some indication of the general failure of planners to follow such sound advice.

That comparative-cost analysis provides a sensible basis for the selection of industries for dispersal into depressed or underdeveloped regions is recognized in a number of works on regional development planning. For example, Siebert (1969, 168) suggests that the comparative advantage of the problem region should be determined by comparing the production and transport costs for different industries; the low-cost activities can then be judged with respect to their likely impact in achieving the planning goal. The comparative-cost framework can also be used to examine the production and transport costs of one activity at alternative locations within the region. Other clear calls for a similar approach will be found, for example, in Isard (1960, Chapter 7) and Isard and Reiner (1960).

No matter how obvious a comparative-cost approach may seem on theoretical grounds, it appears to have been almost entirely overlooked in the design of industrial-location policy. During a quarter of a century of subsidized industrial dispersal in Britain no official attempt has been made (as far as is known) to evaluate the cost disadvantage of the peripheral regions compared with the prosperous metropolitan areas, either in general or with respect to particular industries. In Italy there appear to have been no case studies of actual cost differences between the north and the south (PEP, 1962, 28). And in Poland it seems that some of the bad choices of sites for new industry during the 1950s can be attributed to insufficient exploration of all possible locations, and a consequent failure to appreciate how high costs were in some of the underdeveloped areas (Wrobel and Zawadzki, 1966, 437–438). Klaassen (1965, 64), in his survey of the industrial-location policy instruments used in western European countries, came to the following conclusion:

In principle it is possible to calculate the effect of the facilities offered on the cost levels of each branch of industry. Unfortunately, however, it does not seem that such a study has been carried out in any of the countries investigated. The most that can be said is that facilities are offered on the basis of rather vague notions of the effect they may have on an industry. Furthermore, as many different facilities as possible are given; as a result, it is impossible to evaluate the individual effectiveness of the various instruments.

Even when an attempt is made to apply classical location theory to a practical planning problem it may not be appropriate, perhaps because of a too literal interpretation of Weber. An example of this is provided by the development of the iron industry in the USSR. When the choice was being made between expanding the existing capacity in the east (especially the Donbass) and the alternative of building a second base for the industry in the west (the Ural-Kuznetz integrated plant), the theory of Weber was used as an important argument supporting the former and stressing the prohibitive transportation cost of the latter. However, the advocates of the Ural-Kuznetz scheme claimed that the short-run approach of Weber which assumed the existing pattern of population and economic activity was inappropriate where long-run macro-economic decisions designed to change the existing population geography and space economy were involved (Economic Commission for Europe, 1967, 12–13). The Russian planners clearly needed some modified classical framework capable of incorporating the dynamic element of temporal changes in the factors affecting plant location.

The way in which neoclassical location theory can be applied to a problem of planned industrial dispersal may be illustrated briefly by an imaginary case. In Figure 26.1 there is a prosperous metropolitan region

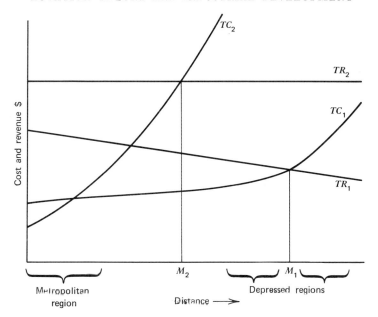

Figure 26.1. Hypothetical space cost and revenue profiles for two industries in an advanced industrial nation with a metropolitan core and depressed peripheral regions.

on the left and two depressed regions on the right. There are two industries, and the government is attempting to decide whether either of these could be induced to move plants from the metropolis to the depressed regions, and if so what kind of subsidies would be needed.

It has already been established that both the industries are the right kind to stimulate economic revival in the depressed regions, provided that they will locate there. Profiles of total cost and total revenue are identified for average or representative firms, these being sections through the appropriate surfaces. Industry 1 has a shallow space cost curve over a broad area, but it eventually rises more steeply with distance from the optimum location in the metropolis. This reflects a bowl-shaped cost surface of the kind which generally arises in a Weber-type analysis and which is also typical of an aggregate travel surface. The slight slope of the space revenue curve suggests that sales are somewhat sensitive to price, which will tend to rise with increasing distance (cost) from the optimum location. Industry 2 has a steeper cost curve, perhaps because it is more dependent on linkages and external economies associated with a metropolitan location. Total revenue for industry 2 is assumed to be a spatial constant.

The first thing that is clear from the diagram is that industry 2 would probably be unsuitable for a program of planned industrial dispersal. The level of subsidy needed to make the depressed regions competitive with the metropolis would be prohibitive. However, industry 1 looks more promising, and only a small subsidy (or perhaps a small investment in the regional infrastructure) would be needed to make the nearer of the two depressed regions a relatively attractive location. Examination of the input structure and service requirements of this industry can help to decide whether the most effective instrument would be a labor-cost subsidy, capital expenditure grants, or some specific local development in the infrastructure such as improving transportation to the metropolis. But the steep rise in costs as the second depressed region is reached indicates that to induce industry 1 to move here would be much more expensive. This is not only a high-cost area but also extramarginal for the industry in question. If economic revival here is to be successful, the subsidy offered to industry 1 must be sufficient to make the region both profitable and competitive with low-cost locations in the metropolitan area. Anything less will be inadequate, and society has to decide whether it is able and willing to bear the necessary expenditures.

This analysis relates to an advanced industrial nation with the characteristic conditions of a prosperous and perhaps congested core and some depressed peripheral regions. Alonso (1968) has recently made some pertinent observations on the differences between cost surfaces in advanced economies and in underdeveloped or developing countries. The advanced nations are likely to have a better integrated transport system, a more dispersed pattern of population and productive capacity, and more complex types of industrial activity with respect to input structure and range of outputs. Thus "the bowl of the transport surface for processes using many materials and yielding several products is likely to be rather flat. By contrast, where the locations of markets and materials are few, the transport surface is likely to have a very distinct low point, and therefore it is likely that there will be a much more definite optimal location in the case of developing countries" (Alonso, 1968, 9). Because value added is generally less than in industries in advanced economies, transport costs are more likely to determine plant location in developing countries.

In Figure 26.2 an attempt has been made to sketch out the kind of conditions existing in a developing country. The core, on the right, is taken to be a coastal city, and constitutes the major port and focal point of national industrial and commercial activity. There are two industries, one serving the personal consumption market concentrated in the major city and the other processing a mineral found in the interior. In industry 1 the optimum location is very obviously in the core, with costs rising fairly steeply towards the interior because of the shortcomings of the

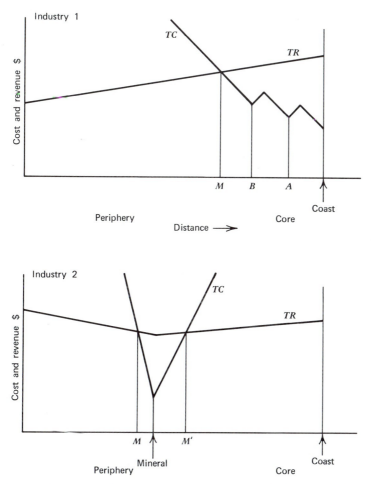

Figure 26.2. Hypothetical space cost and revenue profiles for two industries in an underdeveloped country with a developing coastal city and a backward interior.

transport system. The space cost curve dips at two places A and B outside the city, corresponding with points of good accessibility (one of which also happens to be an input source). The slope of TR reflects the condition that a location in the interior would increase costs to such an extent that sales at the price which would have to be charged would be rather less than from a location in the core. As Alonso (1968, 13) points out, the large coastal cities in underdeveloped countries are the best locations from which to distribute a product to the population at large, and because of limited demand many firms may be serving a nationwide market. In addition, demand for manufactured goods which are typically income-elastic will tend to be concentrated in the core where the more prosperous people live. A port often represents a deep pit in the transport-cost surface, being the best place at which to assemble diverse materials from home and foreign sources especially when it is the focal point of internal communications.

In the circumstances postulated, industry 1 does not have much locational flexibility. However, the planner attempting to induce the spread of development from the core into the periphery might feel that the local low-cost points A and B would be sensible places to start. Comparative cost data would enable him to judge the subsidy needed. In practice these two points might be part of a planned system of growth centers in the periphery, after the style of Friedmann (1966), and would be focal points for infrastructure investment.

The second industry is very closely tied to the source of its major input. Costs rise very steeply away from the mineral deposit, although processing could in fact be done anywhere. Demand for the product is somewhat sensitive to the cost of production, as reflected in the price, although the essential nature of the product to the national economy keeps price-elasticity relatively low. The shallower slope of both TC and TR in the direction of the core reflects the better transport facilities in this part of the region. There is clearly very little scope for the planner to influence the location of this industry. Indeed it would be a mistake to do anything other than ensure its efficient operation at the optimum. Any departure from this point would so increase costs that the performance of the national economy might be adversely affected, and the best course for the planner might be to use this as a propulsive industry in the development of some kind of growth center.

The identification of space cost and revenue curves or surfaces for critical industries thus seems a useful application of location theory to public policy decision making. With a few simplifying assumptions, and given the necessary data, areal variations in comparative locational advantage can be determined with no great difficulty. For many industries in advanced nations there is good reason to expect that over fairly large areas costs will not vary greatly, and within relatively wide spatial limits the planner may be able to influence the entrepreneur's choice of location with quite small subsidies. But eventually costs may rise more steeply; in the terms of the classical Weber model, beyond the locational polygon representing the input sources the cost isolines get closer together as was illustrated in Part Three. It is when these areas of sharply rising costs are reached that industrial planning policies tend to become ineffectual, unless backed by massive subsidies and other local public investment on a scale that may be prohibitive.

Establishing the form of industrial cost and revenue surfaces can thus serve a valuable practical purpose. The position of a problem area with reference to the surfaces for industries which could be expected to help induce economic revival can assist the planner in designing his industrial development strategy. It can also provide society with some indication of the amount of expenditure involved if it decides to meet what it sees as its obligations to the problem areas.

26.2 SCALE, AGGLOMERATION, LINKAGES, AND INDUSTRIAL COMPLEX ANALYSIS

As regional problems become more complex and public involvement in their solution more deeply committed, regional industrial development strategy is tending to become more sophisticated. Although certain areas can be assisted by the subsidized transfer of selected industries, perhaps guided by neoclassical location theory, it is becoming increasingly the case that this kind of approach is too narrow. Greater emphasis is being placed on the search for the optimum spatial allocation of investment in industrial development, generally involving the creation of a system of growth points as a means towards the integration of the space economy. This raises important questions relating to the locational implications of the scale of development, agglomeration economies and industrial linkages, which classical models may be incapable of adequately including without some modification.

The difficulty of arriving at an optimum spatial strategy for industrial development was referred to earlier, in Chapter 24. This is well illustrated in the work of Tinbergen (1961, 1964) and Bos (1965), which was mentioned briefly at the end of Chapter 8. They were concerned with determining how plants in a number of different industries could be combined into industrial centers so structured and located that production and transport costs are minimized, given a closed economic system with an even spread of agricultural population. Tinbergen was able to derive a hierarchy of centers, but he could not find their optimum spatial arrangement. Bos extended this analysis and finally developed a programming model, but it is so complex that it is incapable of mathematical solution (Bos, 1965, 67). Therefore, even given the numerous simplifying assumptions necessary to construct such a model, this line of inquiry is as yet unable to produce results that can be applied directly in the formulation of public policy.

In the absence of an operational general model, the planner faced with pressing problems has no alternative but to adopt a more pragmatic and intuitive approach to the allocation of industrial investment between alternative locations. This partly explains the current popularity of the growth-point concept. In some quarters it is believed that this concept, combined with some notion of hierarchical spatial structure, constitutes an adequate theoretical basis for economic development planning.

The recent evaluation by Darwent (1969, 19–20) of the growth point concept is sufficiently pertinent to be quoted extensively:

A theory of the spatial incidence of development—economic, and perhaps sociocultural, and political—will have to relate a number of previously unrelated theories, hypotheses, and observed empirical regularities. The idea of a process of polarization taking place without reference to geographic space is a suitable starting point, even though it is confined . . . to the economic field. However, in order to account for observed regularities, such as the appearance of a hierarchical structure of central places, we shall expect such a theory to embrace location economics and spatial organization theory, and in particular to account for strong tendencies towards agglomeration, which are apparent in society, possibly via theories of external economies. Moreover, we shall expect such a theory to account for these observed regularities, and hypothetical processes, both through space at one moment in time, and through time in a given space, such as a region or nation. We have seen in the literature various elements or components of such a theory presented in a number of unrelated, simplified, and non-rigorous formulations. We have seen attempts at using the concept of growth pole and growth center in a normative sense, despite the lack of a full explanatory theory on which to base planning actions and policies. (The exigencies of the regional development problem are such that daily decisions must be made despite the lack of an adequate explanatory theory or model.) However, our expectations of a theory of the spatial incidence of growth would include the criterion that any explanations of existing distributions shall by the same formulation be applicable in a normative sense to the solution of planning problems. In other words, the explanatory sense of the theory should be sufficient to identify and quantify the specific areas in which the present structure of economic space falls short of that structure needed to implement the goals of the society under consideration, and to lead to the formulation of policies which will help the society to achieve the optimum distribution of population, industry, investment and urban equipment consistent with the achievement of its goals.

Clearly the notions of growth poles and growth centers reviewed do not constitute a "theory" as defined above, although they do provide some basic elements of such a theory.

This statement, which relates back to some of the observations on theory in the first chapter of this book, stresses again the enormity of the problem posed by the planner seeking theoretical guidance for his decisions on industrial location.

The attention given to the growth-point concept in recent years has had some extremely beneficial results, however. Among these are the growing appreciation of the significance of propulsive industries or firms, and the importance of economies arising from agglomeration and industrial linkages.

The concept of the propulsive firm has helped to direct attention to the type of enterprise that can best initiate economic growth. Branches of existing firms are relatively mobile in some industries, and it may well be that "lagging areas present a low-cost environment for production branches which use simple production techniques, have limited material and human inputs and require relatively limited management control from head office level", as Cameron (1968, 210) suggests. However, the firms most likely to induce self-sustaining regional economic growth are the ones that are at the same time large enough to stimulate ancillary industrial development, through subcontracting and the purchase of materials and components. The major propulsive firm or industry may in fact rely on the existence or creation of a network of small and medium-sized plants to support it and assist its further expansion. As the big enterprise gives rise to other plants by creating or enlarging their markets, so, it is argued, the diffusion effect of induced industrial development takes place; contrary to general historical experience of the process of industrialization, in development planning the large unit can come first and then stimulate the growth of the necessary small units (Rosenstein-Rodan, 1961, 207–208).

External economies of agglomeration and interindustry linkages are becoming increasingly important determinants of plant location in advanced industrial nations. They are tending to strengthen the advantages of a location in an existing industrial or metropolitan area for industries with complex input-output relations with other activities, thus reducing plant mobility to some extent. External economies are also among the most important factors affecting industrial location in developing countries. Their significance in relation to planned industrial development has recently been summarized by Alonso (1968, 20) as follows:

There is considerable evidence that in many cases [external economies] can more than compensate for higher costs of transport, labor, or other factors of production from the point of view of the firm or the project. From the point of view of national regional development policy, an understanding of the elements of external economies probably contains the answer to the crucial questions of whether the principal cities are too big, of how big secondary centers must be to enjoy self-sustaining growth, and of what types of industry are proper subjects for a policy of decentralization and at what stage of their evolution.

In other words, the understanding of external economies is an important ingredient in the solution of most of the major problems of industrial development planning strategy raised earlier in Part Six.

This leads to the critical question of the adequacy of existing location theory to accommodate the economies arising from agglomeration and interindustry linkage. Despite Weber's attempt to build agglomeration into his theoretical framework, and the tendency for industrial activity to concentrate about certain points in Lösch's economic landscapes and Isard's graphic synthesis (see Chapter 8), externalities have certainly not been dealt with as adequately as transportation and other readily identifiable cost items. Wood (1969, 32–33) has stated that "Traditional location theory regards as awkward exceptions the complex agglomerations that are supposed to be based upon the principles of external economies of scale and close functional linkage," and that there is now little to be gained from taking Weber as a theoretical starting point. Such a view expresses vividly the frustration felt by those seeking theoretical guidance for the analysis of important practical problems in which interindustry linkages figure prominently.

However, it can be argued that the difficulties raised by agglomeration and linkage are essentially problems of measurement (Smith, 1970a). If this could be overcome it might be possible to deal with these variables operationally within existing models derived from neoclassical location theory. Agglomeration economies express themselves through reduced operating costs, and conceptually their spatial variations could be treated in the same way as any other cost item, as was suggested in Chapter 12. Industrial linkages are also cost-reducing factors, and could be incorporated into the reformulated Weber model by having each input source (supplying firm) or output destination (purchasing firm) as a corner in the locational polygon. From a practical point of view the solution of a problem in which there were as many input sources as, for example, in a modern motor factory is formidable, even with the use of linear programming and other computer algorithms. But many components contribute so little to total costs that their effect on location is negligible and they can be eliminated, while others may have virtually identical sources and cost/distance functions to further simplify the problem.

This is not to say that no theoretical reformulation may be needed to accommodate agglomeration economies and the effect of linkages more completely. But the most profitable line of inquiry at present appears to be in the empirical investigation and measurement of these conditions, as demonstrated recently by Richter (1969) and Striet (1969), for example. When sufficient information on how these variables actually operate has been accumulated, the directions in which theory might be modified and models redesigned should be a lot clearer.

Meanwhile, problems exist and development has to take place. There seems little doubt now that the most effective strategy for planned industrial development is to create a growth point (or system of such points) based on a carefully selected group of interrelated activities, and large enough to benefit from external economies of agglomeration. What is needed is some conceptual basis for the design of such a strategy, based on a reasonably sound if not perfect theoretical foundation. The best approach at present is industrial complex analysis.

Industrial complex analysis is a compromise between theoretical perfection and practical necessity. Interregional input-output analysis offers the most obvious framework for organizing data on interindustry linkages, but is unable to handle economies of scale, economies of agglomeration and areal variations in production costs arising from different factor prices and combinations. The comparative-cost approach, based on classical location theory, can overcome these difficulties to a large extent, but misses the details of interindustry relations revealed in an input-output table. Industrial complex analysis, as developed by Isard and others (Isard, Schooler, and Vietorisz, 1959; Isard and Schooler, 1959, and Isard, 1960, Chapter 9) is an attempt to provide a hybrid technique which retains the more important interindustry relations while not losing the strength of the comparative-cost approach (Isard, 1960, 376). Its objective is to identify the kind of industrial complex which would be most suitable for a given development program or region.

An industrial complex may be defined as "a set of activities occurring at a given location and belonging to a group (subsystem) of activities which are subject to important production, marketing, or other interrelations" (Isard, 1960, 377). It is unnecessary to describe the detailed procedures involved in an industrial complex analysis here, for they are set down fully in the references in the previous paragraph. Briefly, input-output analysis is used to identify interindustry linkages and the appropriate structure for possible industrial complexes, while comparative-cost analysis evaluates the relative merits of different industries and different locations.

The major application of industrial complex analysis by Isard et al has been in Puerto Rico. The two main resources of cheap labor and access to oil from Venezuela suggested a number of possible programs which could assist the island's economic development, the one with the greatest cost advantage being a refinery-fertilizer-synthetic fiber complex (Table 26.1). The comparative-cost approach used in this case followed closely the traditional Weber framework, modified to include economies of scale,

Table 26.1 Comparative Costs of Selected Industrial Development Programs for Puerto Rico

Production Program	Advantage (Dollars per Year)
1. Refinery alone	−112,000
2. Fertilizer based on fuel oil	−168,000
3. Refinery and fertilizer	−20,000
4. Staple fiber alone	+1,563,000
5. Refinery, fertilizer, and staple fiber	+1,575,000
6. Refinery, fertilizer, chemical, intermediates, and staple fiber	−73,000

Source. Isard, Schooler and Vietorisz (1959), 204, Table 40. The advantages are relative to the best location on the United States mainland.

localization and urbanization as well as labor, power, and other production-cost differentials. The basic structure of the complex with the greatest advantage is illustrated in a simplified form in Figure 26.3, which indicates the major imports and the input-output relations between the various processes. Determining the optimum location for the optimum combination of linked processes in a complex, in terms of maximizing some objective function such as profits, requires linear programming.

This approach to industrial development strategy clearly has very much to offer, despite the relatively high cost and rigorous nature of the analysis required. The proposal for southern Italy by the consulting firm of Italconsult, mentioned in Chapter 24 (Newcombe, 1969), and the industrial complex proposed for a new city in northwest England by Economic Consultants Limited, are major examples of such an approach applied to specific planning problems.

Industrial complex analysis brings together some of the most powerful theoretical concept and operational procedures available in this field of inquiry. As these tools are sharpened, the capacity to design and implement successful industrial development programs should increase. Further work on operational variable-cost models and others derived from neoclassical theory can do much to improve the analysis of comparative locational advantage. Input-output techniques can be extended by attempting to remove some of the simplifying assumptions, and the suggestion by Hoover (1967b, 34) of interindustry tables which show costs per unit of distance of transferring inputs and outputs between different sectors deserves serious consideration, despite the formidable practical and conceptual difficulties. Finally, the development and improvement of computer algorithms can be expected to increase the planner's ability to solve practical problems once they have been stated

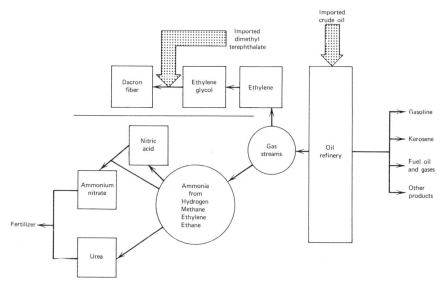

Figure 26.3. A simplified version of the structure of a refinery-fertilizer-synthetic fiber industrial complex. (*Source.* Isard and Reiner, 1961, 30, Figure 1.1.)

in an appropriate form. The closer the theoretician, the empirical investigator and the planner can work together, the sooner these kinds of advances can be expected.

26.3 RISK, UNCERTAINTY, AND THE BEHAVIOR OF THE FIRM

All economic decisions are made in conditions of uncertainty. No firm ever has perfect knowledge, and the consequences of a particular course of action are never completely predictable. And even if risk and uncertainty could be eliminated entirely there is no guarantee that the entrepreneur or decision-making group would always or ever pursue the profit-maximizing location with enough determination to find it.

Considerable emphasis was placed on questions of suboptimal locational behavior in the theoretical sections of this book. In the field of industrial location it is becoming increasingly clear that insufficient attention has been given to the systematic study of exactly how decisions are made under conditions of uncertainty and imperfect knowledge, and how the businessman perceives his environment. This is reflected in the current tendency to depart from normative or deterministic location theory in favor of a probablistic approach. The lengthy treatment of these matters by Pred (1967, 1969), and a spate of recent papers indicates the growing interest in the "behavioral" approach to location analysis.

What are the implications of all this for industrial development planning? One is that an "unsatisfactory" pattern of development may be a result of inadequate or inaccurate knowledge at the disposal of those responsible for location decisions. It is sometimes argued that the general preference for a metropolitan (core) location as against one in a peripheral region can be explained partly by the entrepreneurs' distorted perception of comparative economic advantage. To quote Hirschman (1958, 184–185), "investors spend a long time mopping up all the opportunities around some 'growth pole' and neglect those that may have arisen or could be made to arise elsewhere. What appears to happen is that *the external economies due to the poles, though real, are consistently overestimated by the economic operators*." Alonso takes a somewhat different line, suggesting that there may be great uncertainty as to economic conditions and likely costs in peripheral (underdeveloped) regions, and hence a greater risk to the investor. The neglect of the periphery is thus quite realistic, for entrepreneurs are using "a probabilistic logic which discounts the unproven expectations of the hinterland in proportion to their uncertainty and the delays in their coming to fruition" (Alonso, 1968, 28). "Thus the choice will often be reasonably made in favor of the known opportunities in developed locations now, even where it is recognized that there exists a strong possibility that another location would be better if there were time to look at it" (Alonso, 1968, 19).

If it is true that firms tend to overestimate the cost disadvantages of a peripheral, depressed, or underdeveloped region, this can be counteracted by improving the information at their disposal. Many proponents of planned industrial dispersal argue that interregional cost differences may be both relatively small and decreasing steadily in certain countries, and if this is so the dissemination of knowledge about the less favored areas should induce more firms to consider them as possible plant locations. This is another reason why careful comparative-cost analyses can be so useful to the planner. As well as assisting in the design of an industrial dispersal strategy, they can provide a valuable fund of information which can reduce the entrepreneur's uncertainty as to the outcome of relocation.

Another important implication for development planning is that the failure of industrial-location policy may be partly the result of misunderstandings of how business decisions are actually made. The assumption that all firms will react in a rational, profit-seeking manner is often built into plans for industrial development, whereas it is well known that all kinds of personal and apparently random factors can affect locational choice. In this book great emphasis has been placed on the concept of economically-determined spatial margins within which the entrepreneur is free to substitute psychic satisfaction for pecuniary income and still remain in business. Stafford (1969, 142) has described this as "appealing because it suggests a way out of the maximization box and a path towards bounded rationality. It is a possibilistic answer to the inadequacies of a deterministic model." As such, it might well help the planner to deal with a world of suboptimal decision makers.

One possible approach, arising from this model, is for the planner to try to induce industry to move to certain places within the margin by offering the prospect of psychic satisfaction rather than financial subsidy. Attempts to persuade businessmen that an old and depressed industrial city is not such a bad place to live and that he can play golf and sail his boat nearby are not uncommon, as can be seen in some of the promotional literature of local and regional planning organizations. Such a strategy of city or regional image improvement is another aspect of the dissemination of information, and in some cases it may be more effective and less costly than capital investment. It could be backed up by such schemes as urban renewal, environmental rehabilitation and the development of cultural facilities and other of the intangible personal advantages of life in the prosperous metropolis. However, there is a danger that this kind of approach can become no more than a hollow public relations operation, attempting to persuade the businessman that the region is a better place than it really is. This would be unfortunate; the entrepreneur persuaded to change his location has as much right to the psychic satisfaction offered him as to any financial subsidy to which he is entitled.

Another aspect of this general question is that locational preference may vary with the type of firm, how it is run, and the personal character of the entrepreneur. These matters, discussed at various points in previous chapters, become relevant to public policy when they display some regularity of occurrence. For example, personal factors may play a greater role in the location decisions of firms owned and operated by a single individual than in the modern corporation with more diffuse ownership, and this may distinguish regions or nations in early stages of development from the advanced industrial economies. Even in a completely planned economy with public ownership of industry, the personal factor cannot be disregarded (Hamilton, 1971).

The way firms actually make their location decisions is thus of considerable importance to the planner attempting to influence choice of location. It seems reasonable to expect the behavioral approach to location analysis to become increasingly popular during the next decade, and although it may never be able to yield an adequate alternative to existing theory, based on some satisfying concept, it should at least offer the planner a more sensible view of the businessman than the all-knowing profit-maximizing and entirely rational being of economic fiction. But there are dangers in taking this approach too far, particularly as a basis for public policy. The ultimate task of the planner is to identify the optimum course of action in pursuit of stated objectives, to indicate the consequences of not adopting this strategy, and to offer all this to society for its consideration. In the industrial sphere he is inevitably concerned with economic rationality, for any other kind of plan would be worthless. If society sometimes rejects the plans, or departs from them in a random pursuit of the irrational, then this is part of the price we pay for being creatures of free will.

27

On Industrial Location and Social Well-being

Any discussion of the planning of industrial development inevitably leads to much broader issues of political economy and social well-being. How far the government should intervene in industrial location and other business decisions is one of the critical questions facing contemporary society, involving as it does the relative merits of the market-regulated economic system as against one which is centrally planned. Some reflections on these matters are a necessary conclusion to Part Six.

The case for the free-market economy rests largely on the proposition that in the long run the competitive system will lead to an optimal spatial pattern of economic activity. The optimum is usually thought of in relation to the objective of maximizing national economic efficiency with respect to the production of goods and services, which at the extreme may be equated with the maximization of social welfare. It is argued that the price system is the best available automatic regulatory mechanism for achieving this, by ensuring the optimal spatial allocation of resources. As an industrial economy evolves, industries become localized in the regions with the greatest comparative advantage for the manufacture of the goods in question, which in turn brings economies of agglomeration and scale. In theory, a state of equilibrium is reached when no further increases in the efficiency of the system can be achieved by the shift of factors of production from one industry or region to another.

If demand for the products of a particular region is reduced, then in the free-market model there would be an effective solution without public intervention. In the event of the region possessing comparative advantage for another activity capital would flow in and displaced labor would be reabsorbed. If, however, the region had no advantage with respect to the supply of another good, then capital and labor would move out to areas of greater opportunity to restore spatial equilibrium and maximize the efficiency of the economy. Thus regional economic distress might occur in the short run, but in the long run factor mobility would cure it. The failure of a distressed region to revive its economy would be seen as evidence that it cannot offer a competitive return on new capital invested, and government intervention in support of the region would tend to keep factors in locations with suboptimal returns. Similarly, the existence of an underdeveloped region would be explained by the fact that it is not yet ready for industrialization; when better investment opportunities have been exhausted elsewhere the market mechanism will see to it that capital, labor, and enterprise are drawn in without recourse to regional planning.

The laissez faire argument can be seriously questioned on both economic and social grounds. Its economic validity is dependent on a number of assumptions which do not hold true in the real world. The theoretical basis for the free market in regional economics lies in general equilibrium theory, but this tends to be static rather than dynamic and rests on marginalist assumptions whereas in the space economy locational inertia prevents instantaneous adjustment to marginal changes in costs and revenues (Richardson, 1969, 391). Thus factors of production are not nearly as mobile in space as theory supposes. This means that if a major regional industry declines new capital may be slow to take advantage of other local opportunities, just as labor may be slow in moving out to more prosperous regions.

Another argument against the free-market model is that its efficacy is dependent on the unreal assumption of perfect competition. Tendencies toward monopoly, oligopoly, and a general reduction of free competition are inherent in any economic system governed by the private profit motive. The space economy strengthens this, since distance can be an effective barrier to competition. Thus a process that in the spaceless world of conventional economic theory would ensure the most efficient use of a resource might in practice leave an isolated occurrence underused or underpaid.

Finally, general equilibrium theory is based on the assumption of economic rationality and perfect knowledge. As has been shown already, the fact that this is untrue has important implications for the location of economic activity in the real world. It means that the flow of capital to depressed regions may be impaired by the failure of entrepreneurs to perceive the opportunities which exist there, and by behavioral tendencies such as the choice of security with a satisfactory level of profits instead of the possibility of higher returns under conditions of greater risk. It also means that the unemployed in a depressed region may be unaware of or unimpressed by the opportunities elsewhere. As Cameron (1968, 213) puts it, "for some groups immobility may reflect a crude, though personally satisfying, benefit-cost calculation of the alternatives of migration and of remaining unemployed or underemployed." Like the entrepreneur, they may prefer the known and familiar to the unknown and uncertain. Thus the interregional mobility of labor is much less than is required by the free market to maintain a state of equilibrium.

It can be reasonably concluded, then, that the free play of market forces will not necessarily create an optimal space economy. In the interests of economic efficiency alone some government intervention may therefore be justified. The abolition of the price mechanism altogether and complete spatial economic planning is impracticable, as Lösch (1954, 333) recognized and as some Communist countries have discovered by bitter experience. Yet there are many ways in which the central government can legitimately intervene in the interests of locational efficiency, and indirectly increase social welfare at the same time.

The most obvious way to intervene is to make the free-market mechanism work more effectively. It follows from what was said above that this could be achieved by helping to lubricate interregional factor mobility. Education, job training and financial inducements can assist labor to move from a region where economic revival is out of the question to one with a shortage of workers. The encouragement and subsidy of capital investment in depressed regions with some economic opportunities can raise national output by creating jobs for the unemployed, and induce a fuller use of social overhead capital.

The central government can enhance the efficiency of the space economy in other ways. It can operate some kind of monitoring system, detecting trends making for disequilibrium, such as decreasing returns to scale in congested urban regions, as well as investment opportunities which can be brought to the attention of private business. The government can also reduce the uncertainty in which location decisions are made, by the dissemination of information and by creating conditions of stability in which investments can be made with a minimum of risk. One of the most important functions of a regional plan, particularly in a relatively unknown and underdeveloped area, is to provide some degree of consistency and predictability in economic affairs and thus increase the confidence of the private investor.

The social welfare argument for public intervention is always more difficult to make than the economic argument, because value judgments and personal political philosophy are more obviously involved. However, few informed observers would disagree that the free play of market forces can lead to unfortunate social consequences in the long run as well as the short run. If the individual decisions of profit-seeking businessmen, freely made, do not necessarily add up to the most efficient economic system, it seems even less likely that they will lead to satisfactory conditions of social welfare. The process of rapid industrialization under capitalism in the nineteenth century (and under Communism during the present century) was achieved only by the subjugation of most of the population, and at enormous cost in terms of human misery. The persistence of vast local and regional problems of unemployment, poverty, hunger, environmental pollution, and so on in the most affluent nation in the world is a poor advertisement for the social efficiency of the free-enterprise system. Unless massive government action is directed toward these conditions, the United States may yet confirm the uncomfortable prophesy of Karl Marx (1918) that the capitalist system carries the seeds of its own ultimate destruction.

Thus public action to cure the unfortunate social consequences of industrialization may be necessary if only in the interests of national self-preservation. When considerations of social justice and the Christian ethic of responsibility to society's weaker brethren are added, the case becomes overwhelming. The only question that remains is the form government intervention should take and how far it should lead a nation along the continuum from unencumbered capitalism to complete state planning.

Many nations answer this question by confining public intervention to expenditure on services, infrastructure, and welfare payments to some of the poor. As one writer on regional development puts it, "There is . . . the feeling that social overhead capital is the proper sphere for public investment, while any direct industrial investment would be an improper encroachment on the private sector activities" (Rosenstein-Rodan, 1961, 206). This view is often accompanied by the contention that in any case governments are generally incapable of creating and successfully operating industrial and commercial undertakings, a claim which gets some support from the apparent ineptitude with which certain nationalized industries in Europe have been run. Thus the most profitable activities are kept for private enterprise while society is expected to underwrite the provision of sewerage systems, education, intracity mass transportation and other services which can seldom if ever charge the individual consumer the full economic price.

Some of the problems arising from this position are fairly obvious. Great emphasis has been placed in previous pages on the role of the large plant in regional economic development, and it may be more sensible for the government to create this at the right time and place than to leave it to the uncertainty of private enterprise. There is a good case to be made for public ownership of any industry which in private hands is creating serious economic or social problems, even in an essentially free-enterprise system. As to the quality of public industrial management, a government capable of organizing a visit to the moon should not find it too difficult to manufacture airplanes or mine coal efficiently. If government bureaucracies are indeed incompetent, then it is questionable whether they should even have responsibility for the public sector.

The main lesson to be learned from international experience of public involvement in economic development is that tentative small-scale action is perhaps worse than doing nothing at all. Successful planning in the industrial sphere should be part of some wider grand design for the economy and society. In the words of a United Nations report, "both in the developed and developing countries the problems of industrial location cannot be considered in isolation . . . comprehensive national programming should be recognized as the best framework for the macroeconomic solutions of the problems of industrial location" (Economic Commission for Europe, 1967, 104).

Such statements are, of course, anathema to those who retain their faith in the efficiency of the free market and the sanctity of private enterprise and individual initiative. But it is becoming increasingly apparent that a modern economic system cannot work without a large measure of planning, a function which in advanced nations like the United States is performed mainly by the major private corporations either in their own interests or in the interests of the government as their major market. Many people are reluctant to accept the truth of this; as Galbraith (1967, 396) remarks with his usual perception and wit:

Among the least enchanting words in the business lexicon are planning, government control, state support and socialism. To consider the likelihood of these in the future would be to bring home the appalling extent to which they are already a fact. And it would not be ignored that these grievous things have arrived, at a minimum with the acquiescence and, at a maximum, on the demand, of the system itself.

If the economy has to be planned, it is better that this be done by a government acting for the people at large than by a corporation responsible only to its shareholders and only nominally accountable to most of these.

As has been observed already, there are economic constraints on the extent to which planning can sensibly influence industrial location. There is a limit to the amount of industry any nation can afford to support in suboptimal locations in the interests of social welfare. Too much badly placed productive capacity can seriously reduce the economic efficiency of the nation as a whole, and hence its capacity to finance social measures. Powerful economic forces are encouraging the increasing concentration of economic activity and population in major metropolitan regions, and it would be foolish and impracticable to attempt to reverse this to any great extent. Thus there will always be some places where industry declines and where subsidized economic revival will not be in the national interest on either economic or welfare grounds.

What should be done for such places? Out-migration will not necessarily solve the problem even with monetary inducements; labor is human and does not behave like other factors of production. The firm conclusion of William Beveridge in his *Full Employment in a Free Society* (1945, 169) still bears repetition:

When, through decline of industry in a particular place a third or two-thirds of its working population becomes simultaneously unemployed, to say that they must move in order to find employment is equivalent to destroying the community and wasting the social capital it represents. To say that this must happen because, though demand for new industrial products is arising, businessmen prefer to place their works elsewhere, is to lose sense of proportion.

Industry should be the servant of society, not its master. There are strong arguments on welfare grounds for a negative income tax, simply paying people enough to live on comfortably if they choose to remain in a depressed area with no hope of economic revival. This may also be less expensive than the indefinite support of artificially induced industrial development.

It has been observed that war is too serious a matter to be left to generals. Perhaps the time is approaching when industrial location may be too important to be left to businessmen. If choice of location within fairly broad spatial limits has become largely a matter of economic indifference for many firms, then location might be determined on grounds of public policy without greatly affecting private profits. And if so many location decisions within the margin are made on personal rather than economic grounds it might not be unreasonable to expect the businessman to sacrifice some of his psychic income for the wellbeing of society at large, perhaps by locating in a depressed area or in the ghetto instead of the pleasant town with the country club which is his personal preference. In many advanced industrial nations today, including the United States, planning with respect to industrial location is far too unimaginative and restrictive. There is a failure to fully use industrial development as a positive and creative instrument of public social and economic policy. It is difficult to see how the major problems of regional economic revival, environmental pollution, and minority unemployment in the American city can be solved except by a much greater input of social considerations in the plant location decision. Experience suggests that this input can seldom be left to the businessman.

The discussion of industrial location thus leads directly to some of the major issues facing contemporary society. If this field of inquiry has any meaning outside the pages of academic publications and the abstractions of the classroom, it is in its capacity to help build a new society through the development of new spatial forms of economic activity. As August Lösch, the most perceptive of the great space economists, wrote in his *Economics of Location*, "Not in explaining that which has grown, but where man himself is the creator, lies the real sphere of applicability for the laws of nature and of economics he has discovered". So it is in the study of industrial location.

Bibliography

The following abbreviations are used: AAG, Association of American Geographers; IBG, Institute of British Geographers; RSA, Regional Science Association.

Ackley, G. (1942), "Spatial Competition in a Discontinuous Market." *Quarterly Journal of Economics,* **56**, 212–230.

Airov, J. (1956), "Location Factors in Synthetic Fiber Production." *Papers*, RSA, **2**, 291–303.

Airov, J. (1959), *The Location of the Synthetic-Fiber Industry: A Case Study in Regional Analysis.* MIT Press, Cambridge, Mass.; Wiley, New York.

Alchian, A. A. (1950), "Uncertainty, Evolution, and Economic Theory." *Journal of Political Economy*, **58**, 211–221.

Alexander, J. W. (1944), "Freight Rates as a Geographical Factor in Illinois." *Economic Geography*, **20**, 25–30.

Alexander, J. W. (1954), "The Basic-Nonbasic Concept of Urban Economic Functions." *Economic Geography*, **30**, 246–261.

Alexander, J. W. (1958), "Location of Manufacturing: Methods of Measurement." *Annals*, AAG, **48**, 20–26.

Alexander, J. W. (1963), *Economic Geography*. Prentice-Hall, Englewood Cliffs, New Jersey.

Alexander, J. W., Brown, S. E., and Dahlberg, R. E. (1958), "Freight Rates: Selected Aspects of Uniform and Nodal Regions." *Economic Geography*, **34**, 1–18.

Alexander, J. W., and Lindberg, J. B. (1961), "Measurements of Manufacturing: Coefficients of Correlation." *Journal of Regional Science*, **1**, 71–81.

Alexandersson, G. (1956), *The Industrial Structure of American Cities*. University of Nebraska Press, Lincoln, Nebraska.

Alexandersson, G. (1961), "Changes in the Location Pattern of the Anglo American Steel Industry: 1948–1959." *Economic Geography*, **37**, 95–114.

Alexandersson, G. (1967), *Geography of Manufacturing*. Prentice-Hall, Englewood Cliffs, New Jersey.

Alonso, W. (1964a), *Location and Land Use: Towards a General Theory of Land Rent.* Harvard University Press, Cambridge, Mass.

Alonso, W. (1964b), "Location Theory." Friedmann, J., and Alonso, W., editors, *Regional Development and Planning: A Reader.* MIT Press, Cambridge, Mass.

Alonso, W. (1967), "A Reformulation of Classical Location Theory and Its Relation to Rent Theory." *Papers,* RSA 19, 23–44.

Alonso, W. (1968), *Industrial Location and Regional Policy in Economic Development.* Working Papers, 14, Department of City and Regional Planning and Center for Planning and Development Research, Institute of Urban and Regional Development, University of California, Berkeley.

Andrews, P. W. S., and Brunner, E. (1962–1963), "Business Profit and the Quiet Life." *Journal of Industrial Economics,* 11, 72–78.

Area Redevelopment Administraton (1965), *Area Redevelopment Policies in Britain and the Countries of the Common Market.* U.S. Department of Commerce, Washington, D.C.

Atlas of Illinois Resources (1960), Section 4: *Transportation.* Department of Geography, University of Illinois, for Division of Industrial Planning and Development, State of Illinois.

Ballabon, M. B. (1957), "Putting the 'Economic' into Economic Geography." *Economic Geography,* 33, 217–223.

Barbero, G. (1966), "Development Problems in Southern Italy." Higgs, J., editor, *People in the Countryside: Studies in Rural Social Development.* National Council of Social Service, London, 160–172.

Barloon, M. J. (1954), "The Expansion of Blast Furnace Capacity, 1938–1952: A Study in Geographical Cost Differentials." *Business History Review,* 28, 1–23.

Barlowe, R. (1958), *Land Resource Economics.* Prentice-Hall, Englewood Cliffs, New Jersey.

Baumol, W. J. (1965), *Economic Theory and Operations Analysis.* Prentice-Hall, Englewood Cliffs, New Jersey.

Beach, E. F. (1957), *Economic Models: An Exposition.* Wiley, New York.

Beaver, S. H. (1935), "The Location of Industry." *Geography,* 20, 191–6.

Beckmann, M. (1955), "Some Reflections on Lösch's Theory of Location." *Papers,* RSA, 1, N2–N8.

Beckmann, M. (1968), *Location Theory.* Random House, New York.

Beckmann, M., and Marshak, T. (1955), "An Activity Analysis Approach to Location Theory." *Kyklos,* 8, 125–143.

Bell, W. H., and Stephenson, D. W. (1964), "An Index of Economic Health for Ontario Counties and Districts." *Ontario Economic Review,* 2, 1–7.

Berry, B. J. L. (1965), "Identification of Declining Regions: An Empirical Study of the Dimensions of Rural Poverty." Thoman, R. S., and Wood, W. D., editors, *Areas of Economic Stress in Canada.* Queen's University Press, Kingston, Ontario, 22–66.

BIBLIOGRAPHY 521

Berry, B. J. L. (1967), *Geography of Market Centers and Retail Distribution*. Prentice-Hall, Englewood Cliffs, New Jersey.

Berry, B. J. L. (1968a), "A Summary: Spatial Organization and Levels of Welfare: Degree of Metropolitan Market Participation as a Variable in Economic Development." *Economic Development Administration Review*, June, 1–6.

Berry, B. J. L. (1968b), "A Synthesis of Formal and Functional Regions Using a General Field Theory of Spatial Behavior." Berry and Marble (1968), 419–428.

Berry, B. J. L., et al (1966), *Essays on Commodity Flows and the Spatial Structure of the Indian Economy*. Research Papers, 111, Department of Geography, University of Chicago.

Berry, B. J. L., and Marble, D. F., editors (1968), *Spatial Analysis: A Reader in Statistical Geography*. Prentice-Hall, Englewood Cliffs, New Jersey.

Berry, B. J. L., and Pred, A. (1961), *Central Place Studies*. Bibliography Series, 1, Regional Science Research Institute, Philadelphia; Supplement through 1964 by Barnum, H. G., Kasperson, R., and Kiuchi, S. (1965).

Berry, B. J. L., Tennant, R. J., Garner, B. J., and Simmons, J. W. (1963), *Commercial Structure and Commercial Blight*. Research Papers, 85, Department of Geography, University of Chicago.

Bertalanffy, L. von, (1950), "An Outline of General System Theory." *British Journal for the Philosophy of Science*, 1, 134–165.

Bertalanffy, L. von (1963), "General Systems: A New Approach to the Unity of Sciences." *Human Biology*, 53, 429–440.

Beveridge, W. (1945), *Full Employment in a Free Society*. W. W. Norton, New York.

Bos, H. C. (1965), *Spatial Dispersion of Economic Activity*. University Press, Rotterdam.

Bloom, C. C. (1955), *State and Local Tax Differentials*. Bureau of Business Research, University of Iowa, Iowa City.

Blumenfeld, H. (1955), "The Economic Base of the Metropolis." *Journal of the American Institute of Planners*, 21, 114–232.

Boudeville, J- R. (1966), *Problems of Regional Economic Planning*. Edinburgh University Press, Edinburgh.

Böventer, E. von, (1961), "The Relationship Between Transportation Costs and Location Rent in Transportation Problems." *Journal of Regional Science*, 3, 27–40.

Böventer, E. von, (1962a), *Theorie des räumlichen Gleichgewichts*. Mohr (Siebeck), Tübingen.

Böventer, E. von, (1962b), "Towards a United Theory of Spatial Economic Structure." *Papers*, RSA, 10, 163–187.

Bramhall, D. F. (1961), "Projecting Regional Accounts and Industrial Location: Reflections on Policy Applications." *Papers*, RSA, 7, 89–118.

Bramhall, D. F. (1969), "An Introduction to Spatial Equilibrium." Karaska and and Bramhall (1969), 467–476.

Bridges, B. (1965), "State and Local Inducements for Industry." *National Tax Journal*, 18, 1–14 and 175–92.

Britton, J. N. H. (1969), "A Geographical Approach to the Study of Industrial Linkages." *Canadian Geographer*, 13, 185–198.

Brown, L. (1968), *Diffusion Processes and Location: A Conceptual Framework and Bibliography*. Bibliography Series, 4, Regional Science Research Institute, Philadelphia.

Brown, R. (1963), *Explanations in Social Science*. Aldine Publishing Co., Chicago.

Bunge, W. (1962), *Theoretical Geography*. Lund Studies in Geography, Series C, 1.

Burstall, R. M., Leaver, R. A., and Sussams, J. E. (1962), "Evaluation of Transport Costs for Alternative Factory Sites—A Case Study." *Operational Research Quarterly*, 13, 345–354.

Cameron, G. C. (1968), "The Regional Problem in the United States—Some Reflections on a Viable Federal Strategy." *Regional Studies*, 2, 207–220.

Cao-Pinna, V. (1961), "Problems of Establishing and Using Regional Input-Output Accounting." Isard and Cumberland (1961), 305–338.

Campbell, A. K. (1958), "Taxes and Industrial Location in the New York Metropolitan Region." *National Tax Journal*, 11, 195–218.

Carrothers, G. A. P. (1956), "An Historical Review of the Gravity and Potential Concepts of Human Interaction." *Journal of the American Institute of Planners*, 22, 94–102.

Casetti, E. (1966), "Optimal Location of Steel Mills Serving the Quebec and Southern Ontario Steel Market." *Canadian Geographer*, 10, 27–34.

Chamberlain, E. H. (1936), *The Theory of Monopolistic Competition*. Harvard University Press, Cambridge, Mass.

Chapman, J. E., and Wells, W. H. (1958), *Factors in Industrial Development in Atlanta*. Bureau of Business and Economic Research, College of Business Administration, Georgia State University.

Chenery, H. B. (1962), "Development Policies for Southern Italy." *Quarterly Journal of Economics*, 76, 515–547.

Chenery, H. B., and Clark, P. G. (1959), *Interindustry Economics*. Wiley, New York.

Chicago and Eastern Illinois Railroad (1953), *Industrial Potentialities of Southern Illinois*. Chicago.

Chinitz, B. (1961), "Contrasts in Agglomeration: New York and Pittsburgh." *Papers and Proceedings, American Economic Review*, 51, 279–289.

Chinitz, B., and Vernon, R. (1960), "Changing Forces in Industrial Location." *Harvard Business Review*, 38, 126–136.

Chisholm, M. (1962), *Rural Settlement and Land Use*. Hutchinson, London; Aldine Publishing Co., Chicago.

Chisholm, M. (1966), *Geography and Economics*. G. Bell & Sons, London; Praeger, New York.

Chisholm, M. (1967), "General Systems Theory and Geography." *Transactions and Papers*, IBG, 42, 45–52.

Chorley, R. J., and Haggett, P., editors (1966), *Frontiers in Geographical Teaching*. Methuen, London.

Chorley, R. J., and Haggett, P. (1967), *Models in Geography*. Methuen, London.

Christaller, W. (1933), *Die zentralen Orte in Suddeutschland*. Translated by Baskin, C. W. (1966) as *Central Places in Southern Germany*. Prentice-Hall, Englewood Cliffs, New Jersey.

Clark, C. (1967), *Population Growth and Land Use*. Macmillan, London.

Cleef, E. van (1949), "Maps for Appraisals." *The Appraisal Journal*, 17, 219–231.

Cohn, E. J. (1954), *Industry in the Pacific Northwest and the Location Theory*. Kings Crown Press, Columbia University, New York.

Cole, J. P. and King, C. A. M. (1968), *Quantitative Geography*. Wiley, London.

Committee of New England, National Planning Association (1954), *Freight Rates and New England's Competitive Position*. Report No. 12, Boston.

Common Carrier Conference of Domestic Water Carriers (1964), *Freight Rate Discrimination in the United States: A Catalog of Typical Current Rate Comparisons*. Chicago.

Conkling, E. C. (1962), *A Geographical Analysis of Diversification in South Wales*. Studies in Geography, 7, Northwestern University, Evanston, Illinois.

Conkling, E. C. (1963), "South Wales: A Case Study of Industrial Diversification." *Economic Geography*, 39, 258–272.

Conkling, E. C. (1964), "The Measurement of Diversification." Manners, G., editor, *South Wales in the Sixties*. Pergamon Press, London, 161–183.

Copper, L. (1963), "Location—Allocation Problems." *Operational Research*, 11, 331–343.

Cooper, L. (1964), "Heuristic Methods for Location—Allocation Problems." *Society for Industrial and Applied Mathematics Review*, 6, 37–52.

Cooper, L. (1967), "Solutions of Generalized Locational Equilibrium Models." *Journal of Regional Science*, 7, 1–8.

Cooper, L. (1968), "An Extension of the Generalized Weber Problem." *Journal of Regional Science*, 8, 181–197.

Cotterill, C. H. (1950), *Industrial Plant Location: Its Application to Zinc Smelting*. American Zinc, Lead and Smelting Co., St. Louis.

Cox, K. R. (1965), "The Application of Linear Programming to Geographic Problems." *Tijdschrift voor Economische en Sociale Geografie*, 56, 228–236.

Craig, P. (1957), "Location Factors in the Development of Steel Centers." *Papers, RSA*, 3, 250–265.

Crum, R. J. (1967), *Simulated Interregional Models of the Livestock-Meat Economy*. Agricultural Economic Reports, 117, Economic Research Service, U.S. Department of Agriculture.

Czamanski, S. (1964), "A Model of Urban Growth." *Papers, RSA*, 13, 177–200.

Czamanski, S. (1965), "Industrial Location and Urban Growth." *Town Planning Review*, 36, 165–180.

Daggett, S. (1950), *Principles of Inland Transportation*. Harper, New York.

Daggett, S., and Carter, J. P. (1947), *The Structure of Transcontinental Railroad Rates*. University of California, Berkeley.

Darwent, D. F. (1969), "Growth Poles and Growth Centers in Regional Planning—A Review." *Environment and Planning*, 1, 5–31.

Devletoglou, N. E. (1965), "A Dissenting View of Duoply and Spatial Competition." *Economica*, 32, 146–160.

Dorfman, R., Samuelson, P. A., and Solow, R. M. (1958), *Linear Programming and Economic Analysis*. McGraw-Hill, New York.

Dodge, F. W. Company (1969), *Dow Building Cost Calculator and Valuation Guide*. McGraw-Hill, New York.

Due, J. F. (1961), "Studies of State-Local Tax Influences on Location of Industry." *National Tax Journal*, 14, 163–173.

Duncan, O. D., Cuzzort, R. P., and Duncan, B. (1961), *Statistical Geography: Problems of Analysing Areal Data*. The Free Press of Glencoe, New York.

Dunn, E. S. (1956), "The Market Potential Concept and the Analysis of Location." *Papers, RSA*, 2, 183–194.

Duskin, G. L. and Moomaw, R. L. (1967), *Economic Development Centers: A Review*. Office of Economic Research Staff Paper, Economic Development Administration, U.S. Department of Commerce, Washington, D.C.

Economic Commission for Europe (1967), *Criteria for Location of Industrial Plants*. United Nations, New York.

Economic Development Administration (1967), *Regional Economic Development in the United States*, Parts 1, 2, and 3. U.S. Department of Commerce, Washington, D.C.

Enke, S. (1951), "Equilibrium Among Spatially Separate Markets—Solution by Electric Analogue." *Econometrica*, 19, 40–47.

Estall, R. C., and Buchanan, R. O. (1961), *Industrial Activity and Economic Geography*. Hutchinson, London.

European Free Trade Association (1965), *Regional Development Policies in EFTA*. Geneva.

Eversley, D. E. C. (1965), "Social and Psychological Factors in the Determination of Industrial Location," Wilson, (1965), 102–114.

Ezekiel, M., and Fox, K. A. (1959), *Methods of Correlation and Regression Analysis* (third edition). Wiley, New York.

Fantus Company (1962), *Cost Comparison Study*. Manitoba Department of Industry and Commerce, Winnipeg.

Fair, M. L., and Williams, E. W. (1959), *Economics of Transportation*. Harper, New York.

Fetter, F. (1924), "The Economic Law of Market Areas." *Quarterly Journal of Economics*, 38, 520–529.

Fisher, J. C., editor (1966), *City and Regional Planning in Poland*. Cornell University Press, Ithaca, New York.

Florence, P. S. (1948), *Investment, Location, and Size of Plant*. Cambridge University Press, Cambridge.

Florence, P. S. (1962), *Post War Investment, Location and Size of Plant*. Cambridge University Press, Cambridge.

Florence, P. S., Fritz, W. G., and Gilles, R. C. (1943), "Measures of Industrial Distribution." *Industrial Location and National Resources*, U.S. National Resources Planning Board, Washington, D.C., 105–124.

Floyd, J. S. (1952), *Effects of Taxation on Industrial Location*. University of North Carolina Press, Chapel Hill.

Freeman, J. W., and Rodgers, H. B. (1966), *Lancashire, Cheshire and the Isle of Man*. Nelson, London.

Friedmann, J. R. (1966), *Regional Development Policy—A Case Study of Venezuela*. MIT Press, Cambridge, Mass.

Fulton, M. (1955), "Plant Location—1965." *Harvard Business Review*, 33, 40–50.

Fulton, M. (1960), "Where to Locate Your Plant." *American Machinist / Metalworking Manufacturing*. December 12, 1960, 121–128.

Fulton, M., and Hoch, L. C. (1959), "Transportation Factors Affecting Locational Decisions." *Economic Geography*, 35, 51–59.

Fuchs, V. R. (1962a), "The Determinants of the Redistribution of Manufacturing in the United States Since 1929." *Review of Economics and Statistics*, 44, 167–177.

Fuchs, V. R. (1962b), *Changes in the Location of Manufacturing in the United States Since 1929*. Yale University Press, New Haven, Conn.

Fuchs, V. R. (1962c), "Statistical Explanations of the Relative Shift of Manufacturing Among Regions of the United States." *Papers*, RSA, 8, 105–126.

Fuchs, V. R. (1967), "Hourly Earnings Differentials by Region and Size of City." *Monthly Labor Review*, 90, 22–26.

Galbraith, J. K. (1967), *The New Industrial State*. Houghton Mifflin, Boston.

Gambini, R., Huff, D., and Jenks, G. F. (1968), "Geometric Properties of Market Areas." *Papers*, RSA, 20, 85–92.

Garner, B. J. (1966), *The Internal Structure of Retail Nucleations*. Studies in Geography, 12, Northwestern University, Evanston, Illinois.

Garner, B. J. (1967), "Models of Urban Geography and Settlement Location." Chorley and Haggett (1967), 303–360.

Garrison, W. L. (1959a), "Spatial Structure of the Economy: I." *Annals*, AAG, 49, 232–239.

Garrison, W. L. (1959b), "Spatial Structure of the Economy: II." *Annals*, AAG, 49, 471–482.

Garrison, W. L. (1960), "Spatial Structure of the Economy: III." *Annals*, AAG, 50, 357–373.

Garrison, W. L. and Marble, D. F., editors (1967), *Quantitative Geography, Part I, Economic and Cultural Topics*. Studies in Geography, 13, Northwestern University, Evanston, Illinois.

Ghosh, A. (1965), *Efficiency in Location and Inter-Regional Flows: The Indian*

Cement Industry During the Five Year Plans 1950–1959. North-Holland Publishing Co., Amsterdam.

Goldman, T. A. (1958), "Efficient Transportation and Industrial Location." *Papers*, RSA, 4, 91–106.

Greenhut, M. L. (1951), "Observations of Motives to Industrial Location." *Southern Economic Journal*, 18, 225–228.

Greenhut, M. L. (1952a), "Integrating the Leading Theories of Plant Location." *Southern Economic Journal*, 18, 526–538.

Greenhut, M. L. (1952b), "Size and Shape of the Market Area of a Firm." *Southern Economic Journal*, 19, 37–50.

Greenhut, M. L. (1955), "A General Theory of Plant Location." *Metroeconomia*, 7, 59–72.

Greenhut, M. L. (1956), *Plant Location in Theory and in Practice*. University of North Carolina Press, Chapel Hill.

Greenhut, M. L. (1957), "Games, Capitalism and General Economic Theory." *The Manchester School of Economic and Social Studies*, 25, 61–88.

Greenhut, M. L. (1959), "Space and Economic Theory." *Papers*, RSA, 5, 267–280.

Greenhut, M. L. (1960), "Size of Market vs. Transport Costs in Industrial Location Survey and Theory." *Journal of Industrial Economics*, 8, 172–184.

Greenhut, M. L. (1963), *Microeconomics and the Space Economy*. Scott Foresman, Chicago.

Greenhut, M. L. (1964), "When is the Demand Factor of Location Important?" *Land Economics*, 40, 175–184.

Greenhut, M. L. (1967), "Interregional Programming and the Demand Factor of Location." *Journal of Regional Science*, 7, 151–160.

Gregory, S. (1963), *Statistical Methods and the Geographer*. Longmans, London.

Haber, W., McKean, E., and Taylor, H. (1959), *The Michigan Economy: Its Potentials and Problems*, W. E. Upjohn Institute for Employment Research, Kalamazoo, Michigan.

Hägerstrand, T. (1967), "On the Monte Carlo Simulation of Diffusion." Garrison and Marble (1967), 1–32.

Haggett, P. (1965), *Locational Analysis in Human Geography*. Edward Arnold, London; St. Martin's Press, New York.

Hagood, M. J., and Price, D. (1952), *Statistics for Sociologists*. Holt, New York.

Hague, D. C. and Dunning, J. H. (1954), "Costs in Alternative Locations: The Radio Industry." *Review of Economic Studies*, 22, 203–213.

Hague, D. C., and Newman, P. K. (1952), *Costs in Alternative Locations: The Clothing Industry*. Occasional Papers, 15, National Institute of Economic and Social Research, Cambridge University Press, Cambridge.

Hall, P. (1962), *The Industries of London Since 1861*. Hutchinson, London.

Hall, P. (1966), *The World Cities*. Weidenfeld & Nicolson, London.

Hall, P., editor (1966), *Von Thünen's Isolated State*, translated by Wartenburg, C. M. Pergamon Press, Oxford.

Hamilton, F. E. I. (1967), "Models of Industrial Location." Chorley and Haggett (1967), 361–424.

Hamilton, F. E. I. (1969), *Regional Economic Analysis in Britain and the Commonwealth.* Weidenfeld & Nicolson, London.

Hamilton, F. E. I. (1970a), "Changes in the Industrial Geography of East Europe since 1940." *Tijdschrift voor Economische en Sociale Geographie,* forthcoming.

Hamilton, F. E. I. (1970b), "Planning the Location of Industry in East Europe." *Economics of Planning,* 6, No. 2, 3–7.

Hamilton, F. E. I. (1971), "Locating Industry in East Europe: An Approach to Spatial Decision-Making in Planned Economies." *Transactions and Papers,* IBG, **52,** forthcoming.

Hansen, N. M. (1968a), "Public Policy and Regional Development." *Quarterly Review of Economics and Business,* 8, 51–60.

Hansen, N. M. (1968b), *Growth Centers and Regional Development: Some Preliminary Considerations.* Discussion Papers, 5, Program on the Role of Growth Centers in Regional Economic Development, University of Kentucky, Lexington.

Hansen, N. M. (1968c), *French Regional Planning.* Indiana University Press, Bloomington, Indiana.

Hansen, N. M. (1969a), *Growth Center Policy in the United States.* Discussion Papers, 14, Program on the Role of Growth Centers in Regional Economic Development, University of Kentucky, Lexington.

Hansen, N. M. (1969b), "French Regional Planning Experience." *Journal of the American Institute of Planners,* 35, 362–368.

Hansen, W. L. and Tiebout, C. M. (1963), "An Intersectoral Flows Analysis of the California Economy." *Review of Economics and Statistics,* 45, 409–418.

Harris, B. (1968), "Quantitative Models of Urban Development: Their Role in Metropolitan Policy-Making." Perloff and Wingo (1968), 363–412.

Harris, C. D. (1954), "The Market as a Factor in the Localization of Industry in the United States." *Annals,* AAG, 44, 315–348.

Hartshorne, R. (1926), "The Economic Geography of Plant Location." *Annals of Real Estate Practice,* 7, 40–76.

Hartshorne, R. (1927), "Location as a Factor in Geography," *Annals,* AAG, 17, 92–99.

Hartshorne, R. (1939), *The Nature of Geography.* AAG, Washington, D. C.

Hartshorne, R. (1959), *Perspective on the Nature of Geography.* Rand McNally, Chicago, for AAG.

Harvey, D. (1967a), "Models of the Evolution of Spatial Patterns in Human Geography". Chorley and Haggett (1967), 549–608.

Harvey, D. (1967b), "The Problem of Theory Construction in Geography." *Journal of Regional Science,* 7, 211–216.

Harvey, D. (1969), *Explanation in Geography.* Edward Arnold, London.

Havlicek, J. Rizek, R. L. and Judge, G. C. (1965), *Spatial Structure of the Livestock*

Economy: II. Spatial Analyses of the Flow of Slaughter Livestock in 1955 and 1960. North Central Regional Research Bulletins, 159, Agricultural Experiment station, South Dakota State University, Brookings, South Dakota.

Hawley, A. H. (1955), "Land Value Patterns in Okayama, Japan, 1940 and 1952." *The American Journal of Sociology*, 60, 487–492.

Hecock, R. D., and Rooney, J. F. (1968), "Towards a Geography of Consumption." *Professional Geographer*, 20, 392–395.

Henderson, J. M. (1958), *The Efficiency of The Coal Industry: An Application of Linear Programming*. Harvard University Press, Cambridge, Mass.

Highsmith, R. M., and Northam, R. M. (1968), *World Economic Activity: A Geographic Analysis*. Harcourt, Brace and World, New York.

Hill, L. E. (1964), "Rates of Return on Municipal Subsidies to Industry: Comment." *Southern Economic Journal*, 30, 358–359.

Hirsch, S. (1967), *Industrial Location and International Competitiveness*. Clarendon Press, Oxford.

Hirschman, A. O. (1958), "The Strategy of Economic Development." Yale University Press, New Haven, Conn.

Holt, R. A. (1964), *The Changing Industrial Geography of the Cotton Areas of Lancashire: A Study of Mill Conversion and Employment Structure*. Unpublished MA thesis, University of Manchester.

Hoover, E. M. (1936), "The Measurement of Industrial Localization". *Review of Economics and Statistics*, 18, 162–171.

Hoover, E. M. (1937), *Location Theory and the Shoe and Leather Industries*. Harvard University Press, Cambridge, Mass.

Hoover, E. M. (1948), *The Location of Economic Activity*. McGraw-Hill, New York.

Hoover, E. M. (1964), *Spatial Economics: The Partial Equilibrium Approach*. Occasional Papers, 2, Center for Regional Economic Studies, University of Pittsburg, prepared for publication in the *International Encyclopedia of the Social Sciences*, The Crowell-Collier Co., New York.

Hoover, E. M. (1966), *Computerized Location Models for Assessing of Indirect Impacts of Water Resource Projects*. Institute for Urban and Regional Studies, Washington University, St. Louis.

Hoover, E. M. (1967a), "Some Programmed Models of Industry Location". *Land Economics*, 43, 303–311.

Hoover, E. M. (1967b), "Some Old and New Issues in Regional Development". Economic Development Administration, *Regional Economic Development in the United States*, Part 1, 4, 19–40, U.S. Department of Commerce.

Hoover, E. M., and Vernon, R. (1959), *Anatomy of a Metropolis*. Harvard University Press, Cambridge, Mass.

Hotelling, H. (1929), "Stability in Competition." *Economic Journal*, 39, 41–57.

House, J. W. (1969), *Industrial Britain: The North East*. David & Charles, Newton Abbot, Devon, England.

Huntsberger, D. V. (1961), *Elements of Statistical Inference.* Allyn and Bacon, Boston.

Hyson, C. D. and Hyson, W. P. (1950), "The Economic Law of Market Areas." *Quarterly Journal of Economics,* **64,** 319–327.

International Cooperation Administration (1961), *Plant Requirements for Manufacture of Lead Pencils.* Washington, D.C.

Isard, W. (1948), "Some Locational Factors in the Iron and Steel Industry Since the Early Nineteenth Century." *Journal of Political Economy,* **56,** 203–217.

Isard, W. (1949), "The General Theory of Location and Space Economy." *Quarterly Journal of Economics,* **63,** 476–506.

Isard, W. (1951), "Distance Inputs and the Space-Economy." *Quarterly Journal of Economics,* **65,** 181–198.

Isard, W. (1952), "A General Location Principle of an Optimum Space Economy." *Econometrica,* **20,** 406–430.

Isard, W. (1956), *Location and Space-Economy.* MIT Press, Cambridge, Mass.

Isard, W. (1957), "General Interregional Equilibrium". *Papers,* RSA, **3,** 35–60.

Isard, W. (1958), "Interregional Linear Programming: An Elementary Presentation and a General Model." *Journal of Regional Science,* **1,** 1–59.

Isard, W. (1960), *Methods of Regional Analysis.* MIT Press, Cambridge, Mass.

Isard, W. (1967), "Game Theory, Location Theory and Industrial Agglomeration". *Papers,* RSA, **18,** 1–11.

Isard, W. (1969), *General Theory: Social, Political, Economic, and Regional.* MIT Press, Cambridge, Mass.

Isard, W., and Capron, W. H. (1949), "The Future Locational Pattern of Iron and Steel Production in the United States." *Journal of Political Economy.* **57,** 118–133.

Isard, W., and Cumberland, J. H. (1950), "New England as a Possible Location for an Integrated Iron and Steel Works." *Economic Geography,* **26,** 245–259.

Isard, W., and Cumberland, J. H., editors (1961), *Regional Economic Planning: Techniques of Analysis for Less Developed Areas.* Organization for European Economic Cooperation, Paris.

Isard, W., Langford, T. W., and Romanoff, E. (1967), *Preliminary Input-Output Tables for the Philadephia Region.* Regional Science Research Institute, Philadelphia.

Isard, W., and Kevesh, R. (1954), "Economic Structure Interrelations of Metropolitan Regions". *American Journal of Sociology,* **60,** 152–162.

Isard, W., and Reiner, T. (1961), "Regional and National Economic Planning and Analytical Techniques for Implementation." Isard and Cumberland (1961), 19–38.

Isard, W., and Schooler, E. W. (1955), *Location Factors in the Petrochemical Industry.* Office of Technical Services, Area Development Division, U.S. Department of Commerce, Washington, D. C.

Isard, W., and Schooler, E. W. (1959), "Industrial Complex Analysis, Agglomeration Economies and Regional Development." *Journal of Regional Science*, 1, 19–33.

Isard, W., and Schooler, E. W., and Vietorisz, T. (1959), *Industrial Complex Analysis and Regional Development*. MIT Press, Cambridge, Mass.; John Wiley, New York.

Isard, W., and Smith, T. E. (1967), "Location Games: With Applications to Classic Location Problems." *Papers*, RSA, 19, 45–80.

Isard, W., and Smith, T. E. (1968), "Coalition Locational Games: Paper 3." *Papers*, RSA, 20, 95–107.

Isard, W., and Whitney, V. (1950), "Atomic Power and the Location of Industry." *Harvard Business Review*, 28, 45–54.

Johnson, B. L. C. (1958), "The Distribution of Factory Population in the West Midlands Conurbation". *Transactions and Papers*, IBG, 25, 209–223.

Johnson, R. E. (1958), "Application of Linear Programming to Plant Location Decisions". *Engineering Economist*, 4, 1–16.

Judge, G. C., Havlicek, J., and Rizek, R. L. (1964), *Spatial Structure of the Livestock Economy: I. Spatial Analyses of the Meat Marketing Sector in 1955 and 1960*. North Central Regional Research Bulletins, 157, Agricultural Experiment Station, South Dakota State University, Brookings, South Dakota.

Kaplan, A. (1964), *The Conduct of Inquiry*. Chandler Publishing Co., San Francisco.

Karaska, G. J. (1966), "Interindustry Relations in the Philadelphia Economy." *East Lakes Geographer*, 2, 80–96.

Karaska, G. J. (1968), "Variations of Input-Output Coefficients for Different Levels of Aggregation." *Journal of Regional Science*, 8, 215–227.

Karaska, G. J. (1969), "The Partial Equilibrium Approach to Location Theory: Graphic Solutions." Karaska and Bramhall (1969), 22–41.

Karaska, G. J., and Bramhall, D. F., editors (1969), *Locational Analysis for Manufacturing*. MIT Press, Cambridge, Mass.

Katona, G., and Morgan, J. N. (1950), *Industrial Mobility in Michigan*. University of Michigan Survey Research Center, Institute for Social Research, University of Michigan.

Katona, G. and Morgan, J. N. (1951), "The Quantitative Study of Factors Determining Business Decisions." *The Quarterly Journal of Economics*, 66, 67–90.

Keeble, D. E. (1967), "Models of Economic Development." Chorley and Haggett (1967), 243–302.

Kennelly, R. A. (1954–5), "The Location of the Mexican Steel Industry." *Revista Geografica*, 15, 109–129; 16, 199–213;17, 60–77.

Kerr, D. and Spelt, J. (1960), "Some Aspects of Industrial Location in Southern Ontario." *Canadian Geographer*, 15, 12–25.

King, L. J. (1966), "Approaches to Location Analysis: An Overview". *East Lakes Geographer*, 2, 1–16.

King, L. J. (1969), *Statistical Analysis in Geography*. Prentice-Hall, Englewood Cliffs, New Jersey.

Klaassen, L. H. (1965), *Area Economic and Social Redevelopment: Guidelines for Programmes.* Organization for Economic Cooperation and Development, Paris.

Knos, D. (1962), *Distribution of Land Values in Topeka, Kansas.* Lawrence, Kansas.

Koch, A. R. and Snodgrass, M. M. (1959), "Linear Programming Applied to Location and Product Flow Determination in the Tomato Processing Industry." *Papers, RSA,* **5,** 151-64.

Koopmans, T. C., and Beckmann, M. (1957), "Assignment Problems and the Location of Economic Activity". *Econometrica,* **25,** 53-76.

Krumme, G. (1969), "Towards a Geography of Enterprise." *Economic Geography,* **45,** 30-40.

Krutilla, J. V. (1955), "Locational Factors Influencing Recent Aluminum Expansion." *Southern Economic Journal,* **21,** 273-288.

Kuenne, R. E. (1968), "Approximate Solution to a Dynamic Combinatorial Problem in Space." *Journal of Regional Science,* **8,** 165-180.

Kuhn, H. W., and Kuenne, R. E. (1962), "An Efficient Algorithm for the Numerical Solution of the Generalized Weber Problem in Space Economics." *Journal of Regional Science,* **4,** 21-33.

Kuklinski, A. (1964), "Progress and Change in the Industrialization of Poland." *Geographia Polonica,* **3,** 57-70.

Kuklinski, A. (1967), "Changes in Regional Structure of Industry in People's Poland." *Geographia Polonica,* **11,** 97-109.

Lasuen, J. R. (1969), "On Growth Poles." *Urban Studies,* **6,** 137-161.

Launhardt, W. (1885), *Mathematische Begründung der Volkwirtschaftslehre.* Leipzig.

Launhardt, W. (1882), "Die Bestimmung des Zweckmässigsten Standorts einer Gewerblichen Anlage." *Zeitschrift des Vereins Deutscher Ingenieure,* **26,** 106-115.

Lean, W. (1969), *Economics of Land Use Planning: Urban and Regional.* The Estates Gazette, London.

Lefeber, L. (1958), *Allocation in Space.* North-Holland Publishing Co., Amsterdam.

Lefeber, L. (1966), *Location and Regional Planning.* Training Seminar Series, **7,** Center of Planning and Economic Research, Athens, Greece.

Leontief, W. W. (1951), "Input-Output Economics." *Scientific American,* **185,** 15-21.

Leontief, W. W. (1963), "The Structure of Development." *Scientific American,* **209,** 148-166.

Leontief, W. W. (1965), "The Structure of the U.S. Economy." *Scientific American,* **212,** 25-35.

Leontief, W. W., et al (1953), *Studies in the Structure of the American Economy.* Oxford University Press, Oxford.

Lerner, A. P. and Singer, H. W. (1937), "Some Notes on Duopoly and Spatial Competition." *Journal of Political Economy,* **45,** 145-186.

Lewis, P. W. (1969), *A Numerical Approach to the Location of Industry.* Occasional Papers in Geography, 13, University of Hull.

Lewis, P. W., and Jones, P. N. (1970), *Industrial Britain: Humberside*. David & Charles, Newton Abbot, Devon, England.

Lindberg, O. (1951), *Studier över Pappersindustriens Lokalisering*. Almqvist & Wiksells Boktryckeri, Uppsala.

Lindberg, O. (1953), "An Economic-Geographical Study of the Localization of the Swedish Paper Industry." *Geografiska Annaler*, 35, 28–40.

Lindsay, R. (1956), "Regional Advantage in Oil Refining". *Papers, RSA*, 2, 304–317.

Liu, B. (1969), *Employment Multipliers and Employment Projections: An Economic Base Study for the St. Louis Region*. St. Louis Regional Industrial Development Corporation.

Lloyd, P. E. (1965a), "A Method for Conducting Rapid Reconnaissance Surveys of Manufacturing in Australian Cities." *Australian Geographical Studies*, 3, 31–38.

Lloyd, P. E. (1965b), "Industrial Changes in the Merseyside Development Area 1949–1959." *Town Planning Review*, 35, 285–298.

Lloyd, P. E., and Dicken, P. (1968), "The Data Bank in Regional Studies of Industry." *Town Planning Review*, 38, 304–316.

Logan, M. I. (1966), "Locational Behavior of Manufacturing Firms in Urban Areas." *Annals, AAG*, 56, 451–466.

Lösch, A. (1938), "The Nature of Economic Regions." *Southern Economic Journal*, 5, 71–78.

Lösch, A. (1954), *The Economics of Location*; translated by Woglom, W. H., from *Die räumliche Ordnung der Wirtschaft* (1940). Yale University Press, New Haven, Conn.

Lowry, I. S. (1965), "A Short Course in Model Design." *Journal of the American Institute of Planners*, 31, 158–165.

Luckerman, F., and Porter, P. W. (1960), "Gravity and Potential Models in Economic Geography." *Annals, AAG*, 50, 493–504.

Luttrell, W. F. (1952), *The Cost of Industrial Movement*. Occasional Papers, 14, National Institute of Economic and Social Research. Cambridge University Press, Cambridge.

Luttrell, W. F. (1962), *Factory Location and Industrial Movement: A Study of Recent Experience in Great Britain*. National Institute of Economic and Social Research, London.

Lutz, V. (1962), *Italy: A Study in Economic Development*. Oxford University Press, Oxford.

Machlup, F. (1949), *The Basing-Point System*. The Blakiston Co., Philadelphia.

MacLennan, M. C. (1965), "Regional Planning in France." Wilson (1965), 62–70.

Malinowski, Z. S., and Kinnard, W. N. (1961), *Personal Factors Influencing Small Manufacturing Plant Locations*. University of Connecticut, for the Small Business Administration.

Management and Economic Research Incorporated (1967), *Industrial Location as a Factor in Regional Economic Development*. Economic Development Administration, U. S. Department of Commerce, Washington, D. C.

Manners, G. (1964), *The Geography of Energy*. Hutchinson, London; Aldine Publishing Co., Chicago.

Maranzana, F. E. (1964), "On the Location of Supply Points to Minimize Transport Costs." *Operational Research Quarterly*, 15, 261–270.

Martellaro, J. A. (1965), *Economic Development in Southern Italy*. Catholic University of America Press, Washington, D. C.

Martin, J. E. (1966), *Greater London, An Economic Geography*. G. Bell & Sons, London.

Marx, K. (1918), *Capital: A Critique of Political Economy*. William Gliesher, London.

Massey, D. B. (1968), *Problems of Location: Linear Programming*. Working Papers, 14, Center for Environmental Studies, London.

Maxfield, D. W. (1969), "An Interpretation of the Primal and the Dual Solutions of Linear Programming." *Professional Geographer*, 21, 255–263.

Mayhew, A. (1969), "Regional Planning and the Development Areas in West Germany." *Regional Studies*, 3, 73–79.

McCarty, H. H. (1940), *The Geographical Basis of American Economic Life*. Harper, New York.

McCarty, H. H. (1954), "An Approach to a Theory of Economic Geography." *Economic Geography*, 30, 95–101.

McCarty, H. H. (1959), "Towards a More General Economic Geography." *Economic Geography*, 33, 283–289.

McCarty, H. H., and Hook, J. C., and Knos, D. S. (1956), *The Measurement of Association in Industrial Geography*. Department of Geography, University of Iowa, Iowa City.

McCarty, H. H., and Lindberg, J. B. (1966), *A Preface to Economic Geography*. Prentice-Hall, Englewood Cliffs, New Jersey.

McCrone, G. (1969), *Regional Policy in Britain*. Allen & Unwin, London.

McDaniel, R., and Hurst, M. E. E. (1968), *A Systems Analytic Approach to Economic Geography*. Commission on College Geography Publications, 8, AAG, Washington, D. C.

McNee, R. B. (1959), "The Changing Relationships of Economics and Economic Geography." *Economic Geography*, 25, 189–198.

Meehan, E. J. (1968), *Explanation in Social Science: A System Paradigm*. The Dorsey Press, Homewood, Ill.

Mennes, J. B. M., Tinbergen, J., and Waardenburg, J. G. (1969), *The Element of Space in Development Planning*. North-Holland Publishing Co., Amsterdam.

Miehle, W. (1958), "Link-Length Minimization in Networks." *Operations Research*, 6, 232–243.

Miernyk, W. (1965), *The Elements of Input-Output Analysis*. Random House, New York.

Miles, C. (1968), *Lancashire Textiles: A Case Study of Industrial Change*. Occasional

Papers, 23, National Institute of Economic and Social Research, Cambridge University Press, Cambridge.

Miller, R. E. (1963), *Domestic Airline Efficiency: An Application of Linear Programming.* MIT Press, Cambridge, Mass.

Ministry of Housing and Local Government (1955), *The Use of Land for Industry.* Technical Memorandum No. 2, London.

Morgan, M. A. (1967), "Hardware Models in Geography." Chorley and Haggett (1967), 727–774.

Morrill, R. L. (1970), *The Spatial Organization of Society.* Wadsworth, Belmont, California.

Moses, L. N. (1958), "Location and the Theory of Production." *Quarterly Journal of Economics,* 73, 259–272.

Moses, L. N. (1960), "A General Equilibrium Model of Production, Interregional Trade, and Location of Industry." *Review of Economics and Statistics,* 42, 373–399.

Mountjoy, A. B. (1963), *Industrialization and Under-Developed Countries.* Hutchinson, London.

Muncy, D. A. (1954), "Land for Industry—A Neglected Problem." *Harvard Business Review,* 32, 51–63.

Murata, K. (1959), "A Viewpoint on Economic Geography from Location Theory." *Proceedings of the IGU Regional Conference in Japan 1957,* 434–439.

Murphey, R. E. (1966), *The American City.* McGraw-Hill, New York.

Murphey, R. E. and Spittal, H. (1945), "Movements in the Center of Coal Mining in the Appalachian Plateaus." *Geographical Review,* 35, 624–633.

Myrdal, G. M. (1957), *Economic Theory and Underdeveloped Regions.* Duckworth, London.

National Building Agency (1968), *Land Costs and Housing Development.* London.

National Coal Association (1968), *Bituminous Coal Facts 1968.* Washington, D. C.

Neft, D. S. (1966), *Statistical Analysis for Areal Distributions.* Monograph Series, 2, Regional Science Research Institute, Philadelphia.

Netzer, R. (1968), "Federal, State, and Local Finance in a Metropolitan Context." Perloff and Wingo (1968), 435–476.

Newcombe, V. Z. (1969), "Creating an Industrial Development Pole in Southern Italy." *Journal of the Town Planning Institute,* 55, 157–161.

Nichols, V. (1968), *Growth Poles: An Investigation of their Potential as a Tool for Regional Economic Development.* Discussion Papers, 30, Regional Science Research Institute, Philadelphia.

North, D. C. (1955), "Location Theory and Regional Economic Growth." *Journal of Political Economy,* 63, 243–258.

Nourse, H. O. (1967), *The Electronics Industry and Economic Growth in Illinois.* Department of Business and Economic Development, State of Illinois.

Nourse, H. O. (1968), *Regional Economics.* McGraw-Hill, New York.

Noyes Development Corporation (1965), *Investment and Plant Location in Canada 1965*. Plant Location Study No. 3, New York.

Olsson, G. (1965), *Distance and Human Interaction*. Bibliography Series, 2, Regional Science Research Institute, Philadelphia.

Orr, S. C., and Cullingworth, J. B. (1969), *Urban and Regional Studies*. Allen & Unwin, London.

Palander, T. (1935), *Beitrage zur Standortstheorie*. Almqvist & Wiksells Boktryckeri, Uppsala.

Parr, J. B. (1965a), 'Specialization, Diversification and Regional Development." *Professional Geographer*, 6, 21–25.

Parr, J. B. (1965b), *The Nature and Function of Growth Poles in Economic Development*. University of Washington, Seattle (mimeo).

PEP (1962), *Regional Development in the European Economic Community*. Allen & Unwin, London.

Perloff, H. S. (1963), *How a Region Grows: Area Development in the U.S. Economy*. Supplement Paper No. 17, Committee for Economic Development, New York.

Perloff, H. S., et al (1960), *Regions, Resources and Economic Growth*. The Johns Hopkins Press, Baltimore.

Perloff, H. S. and Wingo, L., editors, (1968), *Issues in Urban Economics*. The Johns Hopkins Press, Baltimore, for Resources for the Future.

Perroux, F. (1950), "Economic Space, Theory and Applications". *Quarterly Journal of Economics*, 64, 89–104.

Pennsylvania Economic League (1960), *Comparative Tax, Water and Sewer Costs for Philadelphia and 81 Other Municipalities in Pennsylvania, New Jersey, Delaware and Maryland*. Philadelphia.

Pfouts, R. W., editor (1960), *The Techniques of Urban Economic Analysis*. Chandler-Davis, New Jersey.

Pincus, J. A. (1961), "Discussion Paper." Isard and Cumberland (1961), 217–220.

Ponsard, C. (1955), *Economie et Espace: Essai d'Integration du Facteurs Spatial dans l'Analyse Economique*. Observation Economique, 8, Ecole Practique des Haute Etudes, Paris.

Ponsard, C. (1958), *Histoire des Theories Economique Spatiales*. Etudes et Memoires, 41, Centre d'Etudes Economique, Paris.

Pounds, N. J. G. (1960), "The Industrial Geography of Modern Poland." *Economic Geography*, 36, 231–253.

Pred, A. (1965), "Industrialization, Initial Advantage, and American Metropolitan Growth." *Geographical Review*, 55, 158–185.

Pred, A. (1966a), "Some Locational Relationships Between Industrial Inventions, Industrial Innovations, and Urban Growth." *East Lakes Geographer*, 2, 45–70.

Pred, A. (1966b), *The Spatial Dynamics of U.S. Urban-Industrial Growth, 1800–1914: Interpretive and Theoretical Essays*. MIT Press, Cambridge, Mass.

Pred, A. (1967), *Behavior and Location: Foundations for a Geographic and Dynamic Location Theory, Part 1*. Lund Studies in Geography, Series B, 27.

Pred, A. (1969), *Behavior and Location; Foundations for a Geographic and Dynamic Location Theory, Part 2.* Lund Studies in Geography, Series B, 28.

Predöhl, A. (1928), "The Theory of Location in its Relation to General Economics." *Journal of Political Economy,* 36, 371–390.

Rawstron, E. M. (1951), "The Distribution of Steam-driven Power Stations in Great Britain." *Geography,* 36, 249–262.

Rawstron, E. M. (1954), "Power Production and the River Trent." *East Midland Geographer,* 2, 23–30.

Rawstron, E. M. (1958a), "Some Aspects of the Location of Hosiery and Lace Manufacture in Great Britain." *East Midland Geographer,* 9, 16–28.

Rawstron, E. M. (1958b), "Three Principles of Industrial Location." *Transactions and Papers,* IBG, 25, 132–142.

Rawstron, E. M. (1966), "Electric Power Generation." Edwards, K. C., editor, *Nottingham and its Region,* prepared for the meeting of the British Association for the Advancement of Science, Nottingham, 310–314.

Rawstron, E. M. (1970), "Where x, then abc: Some Thoughts upon a Comprehensive Theory of the Geography of Production." Osborne, R. H., Barnes, F. A. and Doornkamp, J. C., editors, *Geographical Essays in Honour of K. C. Edwards.* Department of Geography, University of Nottingham, 242–247.

Ray, M. (1965). *Market Potential and Economic Shadow: A Quantitative Analysis of Industrial Location in Southern Ontario.* Research Papers, 101, Department of Geography, University of Chicago.

Reifler, R. M. (1957), "Estimating Wage Rates in Different Areas—A Plant Location Technique." *Industrial Development,* September 1957, 5–9.

Renner, G. T. (1947), "Geography of Industrial Localization." *Economic Geography,* 23, 167–189.

Renner, G. T. (1950), "Some Principles and Laws of Economic Geography." *Journal of Geography,* 49, 14–22.

Richardson, H. (1969), *Regional Economics.* Weidenfeld & Nicolson, London.

Robertson, C. W. (1956), "The Löschian Landscape: A Review." *Scottish Geographical Magazine,* 72, 81–84.

Richter, C. E. (1969), "The Impact of Industrial Linkages on Geographical Association." *Journal of Regional Science,* 9, 19–28.

Rizek, R. L., Judge, G. C. and Havlicek, J. (1965), *Spatial Structure of the Livestock Economy: III, Joint Spatial Analyses of Regional Slaughter and the Flows and Pricing of Livestock and Meat.* North Central Regional Research Bulletins, 163, Agricultural Experiment Station, South Dakota State University, Brookings, South Dakota.

Robinson, A. H. (1956), "The Necessity of Weighting in Correlation of Areal Data." *Annals,* AAG, 46, 233–6.

Robinson, E. A. G. (1967), *Location Theory, Regional Economics and Backward Areas.* Papers presented to the International Economic Association, Conference

on Backward Areas in Developed Countries, Varenna, Italy, 1967, Macmillan, London.
Robinson, J. (1934), *The Economics of Imperfect Competition*. Macmillan, London.
Rodgers, A. (1952), "Industrial Inertia—A Major Factor in the Location of the Steel Industry in the United States." *Geographical Review*, 42, 56–66.
Rodgers, A. (1957), "Some Aspects of Industrial Diversification in the United States." *Economic Geography*, 33, 16–30.
Rodgers, A. (1970), "Migration and Industrial Development: The Southern Italian Experience." *Economic Geography*, 46, 111–135.
Roepke, H. G., editor (1967), *Readings in Economic Geography*. Wiley, New York.
Rosenstein-Rodan, P. N. (1961), "How to Industrialize an Underdeveloped Area." Isard and Cumberland (1961), 205–211.
Russell, J. (1959), "Geography of Industrial Costs." *Industrial Development*, 128, November 1969, 6–10.
Sampson, R. (1961), *Railroad Shipments and Rates from the Pacific North West*. University of Oregon, Bureau of Business Research, Eugene.
Sampson, R. J. and Farris, M. T. (1966), *Domestic Transportation—Practice, Theory and Policy*. Houghton Mifflin, Boston.
Samuelson, P. (1964), *Economics: An Introductory Analysis* (6th edition). McGraw-Hill, New York.
Serck-Hanssen, J. (1963), "A Programming Model for a Fishing Region in Northern Norway." *Papers*, RSA, 12, 107–118.
Shakashita, N. (1968), "Production Function, Demand Function and Location Theory of the Firm." *Papers*, RSA, 20, 109–122.
Siebert, H. (1969), *Regional Economic Growth: Theory and Policy*. International Textbook Co., Scranton, Pennsylvania.
Siegel, S. (1956), *Nonparametric Statistics for the Behavioral Sciences*. McGraw-Hill, New York.
Slater, L. J. (1967), *Fortran Programs for Economists*. Occasional Papers, 13, Department of Applied Economics, University of Cambridge.
Smith, D. M. (1962), "The Cotton Industry in the East Midlands." *Geography*, 37, 256–269.
Smith, D. M. (1963), "The British Hosiery Industry at the Middle of the Nineteenth Century: An Historical Study in Economic Geography." *Transactions and Papers*, IBG, 32, 125–142.
Smith, D. M. (1964), "Birmingham's Gun Quarter and its Workshops." *Journal of Industrial Archaeology*, 1, 106–119.
Smith, D. M. (1965), *The Industrial Archaeology of the East Midlands*. David & Charles, Newton Abbot, Devon, England.
Smith, D. M. (1966), "A Theoretical Framework for Geographical Studies of Industrial Location." *Economic Geography*, 42, 95–113.

Smith, D. M. (1968), "Identifying the 'Grey' Areas—A Multivariate Approach." *Regional Studies,* **2**, 183–193.

Smith, D. M. (1969a), *Industrial Britain: The North West.* David & Charles, Newton Abbot, Devon, England.

Smith, D. M. (1969b), "Industrial Location and Regional Development: Some Recent Trends in North West England." *Environment and Planning,* **1**, 173–191.

Smith, D. M. (1970a), "On Throwing Weber Out with the Bathwater: A Note on Industrial Location and Linkage." *Area,* 1970, No. 1, 15–18.

Smith, D. M. (1970b), "The Location of the British Hosiery Industry since the Middle of the Nineteenth Century." Osborne, R. H., Barnes, F. A. and Doornkamp, J. C., editors, *Geographical Essays in Honour of K. C. Edwards.* Department of Geography, University of Nottingham.

Smith, D. M., and Lee, T-H. (1970), *A Programmed Model for Industrial Location Analysis.* Discussion Papers, 1, Department of Geography, Southern Illinois University, Carbondale, Ill.

Smith, R. H. T., Taaffe, E. J., and King, L. J., editors (1968), *Readings in Economic Geography: The Location of Economic Activity.* Rand McNally, Chicago.

Smith, W. (1952a), *An Economic Geography of Great Britain* (second edition). Methuen, London.

Smith, W. (1952b), *Geography and the Location of Industry.* Inaugural Lecture, University of Liverpool.

Smith, W. (1955), "The Location of Industry." *Transactions and Papers,* IBG, **21**, 1–18.

Smith, W. (1968), *An Historical Introduction to the Economic Geography of Great Britain.* G. Bell & Sons, London.

Smithies, A. F. (1941), "Optimum Location in Spatial Competition." *Journal of Political Economy,* **49**, 423–439.

Spiegelman, R. G. (1964), "A Method for Determining the Location Characteristics of Footloose Industries: A Case Study of the Precision Instrument Industry." *Land Economics,* **40**, 79–86.

Spiegelman, R. G. (1968), *A Study of Industry Location Using Multiple Regression Techniques.* Agricultural Economic Reports, 140, Economic Research Service, U.S. Department of Agriculture.

Spence, N. A. (1968), "A Multifactor Uniform Regionalization of British Counties on the Basis of Employment Data for 1961." *Regional Studies,* **2**, 87–104.

Stafford, H. A. (1960), "Factors in the Location of the Paperboard Container Industry." *Economic Geography,* **36**, 260–266.

Stafford, H. A. (1966), "Population as a Determinant of Industrial Type." *East Lakes Geographer,* **2**, 71–79.

Stafford, H. A. (1969), "An Industrial Location Decision Model." *Proceedings,* AAG, **1**, 141–145.

Steed, G. P. F. (1968), "Commodity Flows and Interindustry Linkages of Northern

Ireland's Manufacturing Industries." *Tijdschrift voor Economische en Sociale Geografie.* September/October 1968, 245–259.

Stefaniak, N. J. (1963), "A Refinement of Haig's Theory." *Land Economics,* 4, 428–433.

Stevens, B. H. (1958), "An Interregional Linear Programming Model." *Journal of Regional Science,* 1, 60–98.

Stevens, B. H. (1961a), "Linear Programming and Location Rent." *Journal of Regional Science,* 3, 15–26.

Stevens, B. H. (1961b), "An Application of Game Theory to a Problem in Location Strategy." *Papers,* RSA, 7, 143–157.

Stevens, B. H. (1968), "Location Theory and Programming Models: The Von Thünen Case." *Papers,* RSA, 21, 19–34.

Stevens, B. H., and Brackett, C. A. (1967), *Industrial Location: A Review and Annotated Bibliography of Theoretical, Empirical and Case Studies.* Bibliography Series, 3, Regional Science Research Institute, Philadelphia.

Stevens, B. H., and Coughlin, R. E. (1959), "A Note on Inter-areal Linear Programming for a Metropolitan Region." *Journal of Regional Science,* 1, 75–83.

Stillwell, F. J. B. (1969), "Regional Growth and Structural Adaptation." *Urban Studies,* 6, 162–178.

Stocking, G. W. (1954), *Basing Point Pricing and Regional Development.* University of North Carolina Press, Chapel Hill.

Stopler, W. F. (1958), "Economic Development, Taxation and Industrial Location in Michigan." *Michigan Tax Study Staff Papers.*

Strasma, J. D. (1959), "Taxation of Industry." *Federal Reserve Bank of Boston, New England Business Review,* February, 1–4; March, 1–4.

Striet, M. E. (1969), "Spatial Associations and Economic Linkages Between Industries." *Journal of Regional Science,* 9, 177–188.

Taaffe, E. J., Morrill, R. L. and Gould, P. R. (1963), "Transport Expansion in Underdeveloped Countries: A Comparative Analysis." *Geographical Review,* 53, 503–529.

Taylor, M. J. (1970), "Location Decisions of Small Firms." *Area,* 1970, No. 2, 51–54.

Thomas, E. N. and Anderson, D. L. (1965), "Additional Comments on Weighting Values in Correlation Analysis of Areal Data." *Annals,* AAG, 55, 492–505.

Thoman, R. S., Conkling, E. C., and Yeates, M. H. (1968), *The Geography of Economic Activity* (second edition). McGraw-Hill, New York.

Thompson, James H. (1961), *Methods of Plant Site Selection Available to Small Manufacturing Firms.* University of West Virginia, for the Small Business Administration.

Thompson, J. H. (1955), "A New Method for Measuring Manufacturing." *Annals,* AAG, 45, 416–436.

Thompson, J. H. (1966), "Some Theoretical Considerations for Manufacturing Geography." *Economic Geography,* 42, 356–365.

Thompson, J. H., Surfrin, S. C., Gould, P. R., and Buck, M. A. (1962), "Towards a Geography of Economic Health: The Case of New York State." *Annals*, AAG, 52, 1–20.

Thompson, W. R. (1957a), "The Coefficient of Localization: An Appraisal." *Southern Economic Journal*, 23, 320–325.

Thompson, W. R. (1957b), "Importance of State and Local Taxes in Industrial Costs." *National Tax Association Proceedings*, 185–190.

Thompson, W. R. (1965), *A Preface to Urban Economics*. The Johns Hopkins Press, Baltimore, for Resources for the Future.

Thompson, W. R. (1968), "Internal and External Factors in the Development of Urban Economies." Perloff and Wingo (1968), 43–62.

Thompson, W. R., and Mattila, J. M. (1959), *An Econometric Model of Postwar State Industrial Development*. Wayne State University, Detroit.

Tiebout, C. M. (1957), "Location Theory, Empirical Evidence and Economic Evolution." *Papers*, RSA, 3, 74–86.

Teitz, M. B. (1968), "Locational Strategies for Competitive Systems." *Journal of Regional Science*, 8, 135–148.

Tinbergen, J. (1961), "The Spatial Dispersion of Production: A Hypothesis." *Schweizerische Zeitschrift für Volkswirtschaft and Statistic*, 97, 1–15.

Tinbergen, J. (1964), "Sur Une Modele de la Dispersion Geographique de l'Activite Economique." *Revue d'Economie Politique*, 74, 30–44.

Törnqvist, G. (1962), *Transport Costs as a Location Factor for Manufacturing Industry*. Lund Studies in Geography, Series B, 23.

Toulmin, S. (1953), *The Philosophy of Science—An Introduction*. Hutchinson, London; Harper & Row, New York.

Townroe, P. M. (1968), *Industrial Location and Regional Economic Policy: A Selected Bibliography*. Occasional Papers, 2, Centre for Urban and Regional Studies, University of Birmingham.

Townroe, P. M. (1969), "Locational Choice and the Individual Firm." *Regional Studies*, 3, 15–24.

Tulpule, A. H. (1969), "Dispersion of Industrial Employment in the Greater London Area." *Regional Studies*, 3, 25–40.

Ullman, E. L. and Dacey, M. F. (1960), "The Minimum Requirement Approach to the Urban Economic Base." *Papers*, RSA, 6, 175–194.

United Nations (1963), *A Study of Industrial Growth*. Department of Economic and Social Affairs, United Nations, New York.

U.S. Bureau of the Census, (1968), *Metropolitan Area Definitions: A Re-Evaluation of Concept and Statistical Practice*. Working Papers, 28, U.S. Department of Commerce, Washington, D.C.

Vajda, S. (1961), *The Theory of Games and Linear Programming*. Methuen, London; Wiley, New York.

Valavanis, S. (1955), "Lösch on Location: A Review Article." *American Economic Review*, 45, 637–644.

Vergin, R. C. and Rogers, J. D. (1967), "An Algorithm and Computational Procedure for Locative Economic Facilities." *Management Science,* 13, 240–254.

Walker, H. M., and Lev, J. (1953), *Statistical Inference.* Holt, Rinehart & Winston, New York.

Ward, R. J., editor (1967), *The Challenge of Development: Theory and Practice.* The Aldine Publishing Co., Chicago.

Warntz, W. (1957), "Contributions Towards a Marco-economic Geography: A Review." *Geographical Review,* 47, 420–442.

Warntz, W. (1959), *Towards a Geography of Price.* University of Pennsylvania Press, Philadelphia; Oxford University Press, London.

Warntz, W. (1965), *Macrogeography and Income Fronts.* Monograph Series, 3, Regional Science Research Institute, Philadelphia.

Weber, A. (1929), *Alfred Weber's Theory of the Location of Industries;* translated by Friedrich, C. J. from *Über den Standort der Industrien* (1909). University of Chicago Press, Chicago.

Williams, W. V. (1967), "A Measure of the Impact of State and Local Taxes on Industrial Location." *Journal of Regional Science,* 7, 49–59.

Wilson, T., editor (1965), *Papers on Regional Development.* Blackwell, Oxford.

Wise, M. J. (1950), "On the Jewellery and Gun Quarters of Birmingham," *Transactions and Papers,* IBG, 15, 59–72.

Wonnacott, R. J. (1963), *Manufacturing Costs and the Comparative Advantage of United States Regions.* Study Papers, 9, Upper Midwest Economic Study, University of Minnesota, Minneapolis.

Wrobel, A. and Zawadzki, S. M. (1966), "Location Policy and the Regional Efficiency of Investments." Fisher (1966), 433–440.

Wood, P. (1969), "Industrial Location and Linkage." *Area,* 1969, No.2, 32-39.

Yaseen, L. C. (1956), *Plant Location.* American Research Council, New York.

Yeates, M. H. (1965), "Some Factors Affecting the Spatial Distribution of Chicago Land Values, 1910–1960." *Economic Geography,* 41, 57–70.

Yeates, M. H. (1968), *An Introduction to Quantitative Analysis in Economic Geography.* McGraw-Hill, New York.

Yeates, M. H. and Lloyd, P. E. (1970), *Impact of Industrial Incentives: South Georgian Bay Region, Ontario.* Geographical Paper No. 44, Policy Planning Branch, Department of Energy, Mines and Resources, Ottawa.

Zelinsky, W. (1958), "A Method for Measuring Changes in the Distribution of Manufacturing Activity in the United States, 1939–47." *Economic Geography,* 34, 95–126.

Index

Advertising, 62, 65
Aesthetic considerations, in industrial development, 489
Agglomeration, 82–88, 136, 151, 154–155, 269, 501–507
 and basing-point pricing, 67
 economies of, 82–88, 94, 319, 354, 360, 385–387, 398, 501–507, 511
 and elasticity of demand, 140, 144–145
 diseconomies of, 87–88
 in the variable-cost model, 211–212
 in Weber's theory, 117–118, 124, 129
Agglomeration theory, the, 110
Aggregate travel model, 297–301, 303–304, 327–329, 378, 497
Agricultural land use, 154
Agricultural location, 206
Airov, J., 317–319
Alexander, J. W., 76–77
Alonso, W., 156, 158, 189, 213, 217, 220, 225, 238, 280, 452, 456, 498, 499, 503, 508
Aluminum industry, 43, 315–317
Amortization, 317, 325
Analogue models, 163; *see also* Varignon's mechanical model
Appalachia, 441, 469–472
Appalachian Regional Development Act, 470, 472
Areal classification, 446
Areal studies, 6–7
Areal units for data collection, 8, 405
 as they affect statistical analysis, 394, 395
Area Redevelopment Administration, 470
Autocorrelation, 395

Backwash effect, in economic development, 455
Barloon, M. J., 354–360
Barlowe, R., 206
Basic cost, as opposed to locational cost, 190–191, 194, 198–202, 286
Basic industries, 100–101

Basic-nonbasic (B/N) ratio, 100–101
Basing-point pricing, 67–68, 349
Beckmann, M., 412
Behavioral approach, 92, 105–109, 158, 209, 507–510, 512–513
Behavioral matrix, 106–108, 209, 234
Berry, B. J. L., 98, 472
Beveridge, W., 516
Birmingham, England, manufacture of jewelry and guns in, 39, 84
Black Americans, problems of, 441, 487
Blanket freight rates, 73–74, 79
Bos, H. C., 157, 501
Boundaries, locational significance of, 129
Böventer, E. von, 157, 413
Branch plants, mobility of, 493–494
Breakeven points, 229–231
Break of bulk points, 80
Building costs, 40, 86, 282–284, 365
Buildings, industrial, 38–40
Bunge, W., 109
Business climate, 54, 55

Calibration, of models, 160, 298, 302, 328, 368–370
Cameron, G. C., 503, 513
Canada, cost of land in, 34–35
 cost of manufacturing electronic goods in, 320–326
 Ontario, comparative locational advantage in, 31
 United States business in Ontario, 328–330
Canals, 70
Capital, 37–40, 329, 330
 cost of, 38
 equipment, 38–40
 financial, 37–38
Capitalist economic systems, 447, 449
Capron, W. H., 349–351
Cassa per il Mezzogiorno, 473–475
Cement industry, 417–420, 495
Center-periphery (or core-periphery) model, 445, 455–457, 497–500, 508

543

544   INDEX

Central business district, 487–488
Central place theory, 98, 107, 132–134, 305, 455–456
Chain of production, 401
Chamberlin, E. H., 140
Changing role theory, the, 110
Cheap-labor locations, 116–117, 129; see also Labor, cost of
Chinitz, B., 38, 56
Chisholm, M. 62, 66
Chi-square test, 396
Christaller, W., 98, 132, 134
Christian ethics, 514
C.i.f. pricing, 66–67, 239
Cities, problems of , 441, 472, 487, 517
City planning, 87, 88–89, 480–491
Classification, 7–9, 430
Classification, the, in transportation, 74–75
Clearing Industrial District, Chicago, 489
Clothing industry, 29–30, 39, 83, 84, 337–341
Coal, cost of, 357–358
Coefficient of geographical association, 394–395
Combination indifference line, 217–219
Combination indifference point, 216
Combination of factors or inputs, 25–29, 156, 212–221; see also Substitution between factors or inputs
Commodity freight rates, 75
Communist countries, industrial planning in, 475–479, 496, 513
Comparative-cost analysis, 328, 368
  applications of, 312–326, 330–345, 349–360, 362–367
  as a basis for industrial development planning, 493–496, 508
  theoretical basis for, 181–235
Competition, 60–61, 114, 273, 512
  spatial, 156, 245–248, 254–258, 354, 367–374
Computer algorithms, 100, 115, 163–164, 168, 506–507
Computer mapping, 280
Concentration theory, the, 110
Congested regions, 444–445, 450, 463, 477, 489–491
Congestion tax, 210, 450
Conindustrialization, 99
Conjunctive simbiosis, 99

Construction costs, see Building costs
Container systems, 70
Contingency coefficient, 396
Control points, for cost surface analysis, 337, 376–377
Cooper, L., 163
Correlation and regression analysis, 160, 162, 269–270, 304, 365–370, 393–405
Cost comparisons in alternative locations, see Comparative-cost analysis
Cost curves, 58–61, 167, 227–230, 260
Cost/distance functions, see Space cost curves
Cost/distance profiles, see Space cost curves
Cost gradients, see Space cost curves
Cost isolines, 193–206, 219–221; see also Cost surfaces; Isodapanes
Cost structure, 26, 29–31, 103–104, 354–355, 378, 399
Cost surfaces, 48–51, 189, 194–206, 248–249, 251, 259–261, 271, 279–295, 328, 330–345, 357–360, 376–383, 386–389, 493, 497–500
  building-cost surfaces, 282–284
  labor-cost surfaces, 48–51, 288–292, 379
  land-cost surfaces, 280–282
  material-cost surfaces, 284–288, 334–337, 357–360
  occupancy-cost surfaces, 381
  taxation surfaces, 292–295, 382
  transport-cost surfaces, 298–301, 309–311, 334–338, 379, 497
Cotterill, C. H., 313–315
Cotton industry, 46; see also Textile industry
Craig, P., 351
Critical isodapane, 116, 117
Crystal manufacturing, 319–320
Cumberland, J. H., 352–354
Cycle theory, the, 110
Czamanski, S., 102

Dacey, M. F., 100–101
Darwent, D. F., 454, 456–457, 502
Darwinism, economic, 273
Data, collection and arrangement of, 7–10
Decentralization, industrial, see City Planning; Regional Planning
Decision makers, availability of, 55
Deductive theory, 19–22, 95, 178
Deglomeration, 87
Demand, 57–66, 388–389

elasticity of, 60, 139–142, 144–145, 238–239, 500
  in location theory, 130, 144–145, 147, 164, 233–231, 236–261, 268, 388–389, 415
  as a variable in empirical research, 296–311, 327–330, 354, 360, 369, 388–389
Demand cones, 240–242, 251
Demand curves, 58–61, 302
Demand functions, 165, 169–170, 173, 239–241, 330
Demand space potential, 304
Depressed regions, 443–444, 463–464, 483, 491, 497–498, 508, 512
Description, 6–10, 16
Descriptive techniques, 10
Deterministic models, 18, 107
Development Areas, in British planning, 464–465
Development Districts, in British planning, 464
Development regions, 445
Devletoglou, N. E., 142
Dichotomous variables, 396–397, 398
Differential growth theory, the, 110
Diffusion of innovation, 89–90
Discrimination, in freight rates, 80–81
  in pricing, 66
Diseconomies of scale, 58, 87–88, 442, 444
Disjunctive simbiosis, 99
Dispersal of industry, *see* City planning; Regional planning
Distance inputs, 149
Diversification, industrial, 465–466
Downward-transitional areas, 445
Dresses, manufacture of, 29–30
Dual, in linear programming, 412–415, 420–422
Dunn, 327–328
Duopoly, 138

Econometric models, 448–449
Economic-base theory, 100–102
  minimum requirement approach, 100–101
  as a predictive device, 102, 460–461
Economic Consultants Limited, 506
Economic Development Administration, 470–472
Economic development districts, in United States, 470–472
Economic development regions, in United States, 471

Economic health, 446
Economic landscapes, 134, 154
Economic restriction, principle of, 102–104
Economics, theory in, 18–19
Economic-shadow effect, 329–330
Economies, of localization, 83–84, 154
  of scale, 58, 82, 85, 319, 354, 360, 501–507, 511
  of urbanization, 83, 84–87, 154
Efficiency frontier, in linear programming, 409
Elasticity of demand, 60, 139–142, 144–145, 238–239, 500
Electrical appliances, manufacture of, 284–286, 361–374
Electric analogue models, 163
Electricity industry, in East Midlands, 104–105
Electric power, 43–45, 333–334, 380
Electronics industry, 320–326, 374–387
Empirical generalizations, 14
England and Wales, cost of land in, 33–34; *see also* Great Britain
Ente Nazionale Idrocarburi, 474
Enterprise, 54–56, 329–330
Entrepreneurial skill, 207–210, 255–256, 260
Entrepreneurs, personal character of, 91–92, 146, 509
Environment, problems of, 88, 443, 469, 470, 480, 487, 489, 507, 514, 517; *see also* Pollution
Equal outlay lines, 27–28, 149–150, 214–215, 217, 223–225
Equal product curves, 27–28, 214–215, 216–217, 223–225
Equal product lines, 408–409
Equal profit lines, 186
Equilibrium, locational, 122, 130, 132–134, 140, 147, 149–152, 156–157, 273, 511–512
Europe, city problems in, 487
  identification of problem regions in, 446, 464–466, 467–468
  planning instruments in, 450–451, 464–466, 467–468
  regional industrial development strategy in, 463–469, 473–479, 496
Eversley, D. E. C., 91
Evolution, of industrial location patterns, 269–273

Expansion path, 28
Explanatory models, in development planning, 448, 453
Explanation, 10–15
External economies, 82–88, 93–94, 211–212, 385–387, 444, 452, 497, 501–507
  of agglomeration, 82–88, 94, 319, 354, 360, 385–387, 398, 501–507, 511
  of localization, 83–84, 154
  or urbanization, 83, 84–87, 154
Extractive industries, 125–127

Factor analysis, *see* Principal components analysis
Factors of production, combination of, 25–29, 156, 212–221
  mobility of, 28, 512–513
Factory construction, cost of, *see* Building costs
Fantus Company, location consultants, 31, 38, 306, 322, 361, 375
Fashion effect, 142
Fetter, F., 138
Florida, market potential and transport costs in, 327
Flour milling, 29–30
F.o.b. pricing, 67, 239
Food, consumption of, 63–65
Food industry, cost of labor in, 289, 291–292
Foot-loose industries, 493
Footwear industry, 83, 129
Ford, Henry, 56, 89
Forklift truck operators, wages of, 289–290
France, industrial development planning strategy in, 467–469
Free-market model, the, 511–514
Free will, 18, 510
Freight costs, *see* Transportation, costs
Freight rates, 71–81, 123, 284–286, 305–311, 322–323, 369–370
  blanket rates, 73–74, 79
  commodity rates, 75
  effect of changes in, 265–266, 268
  mileage rates, 74–76, 79
  postage-stamp rates, 72–73
  service tariffs, 75
Friedmann, J. R., 445, 455, 457, 500
Fringe benefits, in labor costs, 322–323

Galbraith, J. K., 234–235, 515
Game theory, 154–155, 156
Garment industry, *see* Clothing industry
Garner, B. J., 36
Gases, industrial, manufacture of, 29–30
General equilibrium theory, 156–157, 511–513
General systems theory, 109–110
Geograqhical expansion paths, 225
Germany, Federal Republic of, 452
Ghettos, problems of, 469, 472, 487
Ghosh, A., 417–420
Gini coefficients, 394–395
Goals, in planning strategy, 447–448, 452, 453, 466–467, 479, 495
Goldman, T. A., 412
Great Britain, availability of executives in, 55
  cost of land in, 33–34
  costs in alternative locations in, 319
  industrial development planning in, 463–467, 494, 496
  industrial estates (parks) in, 489
  labor costs in, 45–46
  labor-cost subsidies in, 452
Green belts, 32, 489–490
Greenhut, M. L., 142, 143–147, 148, 164, 231–232, 238, 241, 415
Growth points, in regional industrial development, 453–458, 483, 501, 502–503, 508
  in France, 468
  in Great Britain, 466
  in Southern Italy, 474–475
  in the United States, 472
Growth poles, 454, 508
Guns, manufacture of, 39, 84

Haggett, P., 109
Hamilton, F. E. I., 109, 476, 509
Hansen, N. M., 472
Harris, B., 52
Harris, C. D., 297, 299–300
Hartshorne, R., 98
Harvey, D., 20
Hecock, R. D., 64–65
Hexagonal market areas, 132–134, 151
Highways, 70
Hirsch, S., 319–320
Hirschman, A. O., 455, 508
Historical accident, 89–90

Historical studies of industrial location, 330–334, 388
Hoover, E. M., 125–130, 137, 138, 151, 164–167, 205, 272–273, 305, 367, 388, 456, 492, 495, 506
Hotelling, H., 138–140, 142, 145–146, 155, 156, 247
Hunger, 470, 514
Hydroelectricity, 315
Hypothesis, testing of, 16, 393; *see also* Quantitative methods

Ideal weight, in Weber's Theory, 116
Illinois, cost of coal in, 286–288
Impact studies, 458–462
Imperfect competition, 60–61, 138, 187
Index, of labor cost, 116
  of location, 327
India, cement industry in, 417–420
Indian Reservations, 469, 470
Inductive theory, 20–22
Industrial classification, 7–8, 430
Industrial complex analysis, 319, 475, 505–507
Industrial development agencies, 450
Industrial Development Certificates, in Britain, 464–465
Industrial development incentives, *see* Instruments; Subsidy
Industrial development planning, *see* Regional planning
Industrial inertia, 39
Industrialization, of underdeveloped regions, 442–443; *see also* Regional planning
Industrial linkages, *see* Linkages
Industrial nurseries, 40
Industrial parks (or estates), 94, 450, 484, 488–489
Industrial Revolution, the, 33, 38, 46, 70
Industrial simbiosis, 99
Inertia, industrial, 39
Information, as an input, 385–386
Infrastructure, 84
  improvement of, 449, 453, 456, 466, 472, 473, 475
Innovation, diffusion of, 89–90
Input coefficients, 29, 161–162, 198–202, 369, 407
Input costs, effect of changes in, 264–268
Input-output analysis, 412, 423, 435, 461–462, 505, 506

coefficients, 426–430, 431, 433
  inverse coefficients, 430, 434–435
Inputs, combination of, 26–29, 212–221
  mobility of, 28, 512–513
Instituto per la Riconstruzione Industriale, 474
Instruments, in industrial development planning, 448, 449–452, 454–456, 496
  in Europe, 450–452
  in France, 467–468
  in Great Britain, 404–405, 406
  in Poland, 475
  in Southern Italy, 473–475
  in the United States, 471
Interest rates, 38, 86–87
International cost comparison, 319–320
Intermediate Areas, in British planning, 464–465
Interregional input-output analysis, 425, 430, 461–462, 505
Interregional linear programming, 410–411, 417–420
Intersectoral flow analysis, 462
Iron and steel industry, 31, 68, 313, 341–345, 346–390, 496
Iron ore, cost of, 357–358
Isard, W., 20, 85, 119, 148–155, 157, 159, 189, 258, 276, 319, 349–354, 428, 492, 495, 504, 505–507
Isochrones, 122–123
Isodapanes, 116–119, 122, 123, 127, 129, 151, 193, 205, 343–345
Isodistantes, 122
Isoline techniques, *see* Cost surfaces; Isodapanes; Potential surfaces; Profit surfaces; Revenue surfaces
Isotantes, 122, 123
Isotims, 123, 125, 127–128, 129
Isovectors, 123
Isovectures, 331, 334–337
Israel, cost of manufacturing crystals in, 319–320
Italconsult, 506
Italy, industrial development strategy in, 473–475, 494, 496, 506

Japan, machinery manufacturing in, 401, 403–404
Jewelry industry, 39, 84
Johnson, R. E., 416–417
Joint action space, in a locational game, 155

Kaiser Aluminum Company, 317
Kaplan, A., 14–15, 18
Karaska, G. J., 158

548 INDEX

Kenelly, R. A., 341–345
Kerr, D., 328–329
Keynes, J. M., 458
Krutilla, J. V., 315–317
Kuklinski, A., 478

Labor, 44–52, 93
  cost of, 40, 44–52, 86, 288–292, 322–323, 329, 347, 365, 377–379, 384–385
Labor coefficient, 117, 118
Lace industry, 29–30, 39, 84
Lancashire, reoccupation of mills in, 39
Land, 32–37
  areal allocation of industrial, 485–491
  cost of 33–37, 86, 280–282, 325, 365, 486
  estimating needs for, 482–485
Land-use competition, 129
Land-use planning, 467, 480–491
Lasuen, J. R., 458, 494
Launhardt, W., 113, 123, 151, 152, 343
Laws, 11, 13, 14, 17, 18, 21, 99–100
Least-cost (or variable-cost) theory, 113–130, 136, 137, 143, 146, 147, 149–151, 158, 161–162, 165, 182–184, 186–187, 188–235, 238, 248, 259–261, 263–268, 279, 330, 346, 354, 373, 387–390, 493–501, 504–505
  major applications of, 330–345, 362–367, 374–387
Leek, Staffordshire, industrial land-use planning in, 483–484
Lefeber, L., 156–157
Leontief, W. W., 423, 426, 435
Lewis, P., 111, 396
Limestone, cost of, 357, 359
Lindberg, J. B., 206
Lindberg, O., 330–337, 353
Linear programming, 157, 164, 103, 216, 406–422, 464, 504, 506
Line-haul freight charges, 71, 74
Linkages, between industries, 84, 94, 401–402, 426, 431, 435, 457, 462, 466, 497, 501–507
Local industrial development inducements, 450
Locational cost, 103–104, 190–191, 194, 197–198, 285–286, 494
Locational games, 154–155
Locational interdependence, 131, 137–143, 144–147, 154, 156, 165, 187, 238, 245–248, 254–258, 305

Locational lines, 315
Locational polygons, 163, 203, 343–345, 500, 504
Locational triangles, 113, 114–118, 123, 128, 149–151, 163, 190, 194–197
Location factors, changing importance of, 92–94
Location leaders, 209
Location rent, 413–415, 420–422
Localization, economies of, 83–84, 154; see also External economies
Logan, M. I., 281–282
London, cost of land in, 33–34, 35–36
Lösch, A., 130–137, 138, 140, 146, 148, 151, 154, 157, 159, 181, 205–206, 209, 231, 235, 240–242, 251, 258, 262–263, 276, 305, 504, 513, 517
Lowry, I., 160
Lumber industry, 73, 79
Luttrell, W. F., 493–494

Machinery, cost of, 40
Machinery industry, 400–404
Macroeconomic geography, 109
Maintenance costs, for buildings, 325
Margin lines, 126, 151
Margins to profitability, spatial, as an analytical device in industrial development planning, 493–495, 497–501, 506
  as a basic theoretical construct, 184–186, 205–206
  difficulty of empirical identification, 388–389
  in dynamic models, 262–269, 271–273
  in linear programming, 421–422
  as no-rent margins, 206, 415
  in Pred's theory, 107–108
  in Rawstron's theory, 103–105
  in variable-cost theory, 176, 188, 197–206, 208–212, 220, 229–231, 233–235
  in variable-demand theory, 244, 254, 260–261
Market, the, 62–66, 296–311, 354, 398, 400, 404
  increasing importance of, 93, 348–349, 360
Market areas, empirical identification of, 165, 304–311, 367–374
  in location theory, 119–122, 123, 125–128, 132–136, 137–143, 151, 156, 158, 187, 239–258
Market potential, 300–304, 327–330
Markov Chain model, 270–271
Marshak, T., 412
Marx, K., 514
Material handling laborers, wages of, 289–290

Material index, 115, 118
Material orientation, 144, 337
Materials, 25–26, 41–43, 93
  cost of, 284–288, 330–345, 357–360, 365
Mathematical models, *see* Linear programming; Multiple correlation and regression analysis; Operational models
Matrix algebra, 391, 429
Maxfield, D. W., 420–422
McCarty, H. H., 20, 21, 206, 400–404
McNee, R., 19
Measurement, 9
Meehan, E. J., 11, 15
Metal industries, 312–317, 431–435, 495; *see also* Iron and steel industry
Metropoles d'equilibrium, in French planning, 468
Mexico, steel industry in, 341–345
Migration, of population, 443, 447, 469, 474, 479
Mileage freight rates, 74–76, 79
Military research contracts, 386
Minimum aggregate travel, point of, 162–163, 298–299, 328
Minimum requirement approach, to economic-base theory, 100–101
Ministry of Housing and Local Government, in Britain, 485
Mobility, of factors of production or inputs, 28, 512–513
  of industry, 479, 484, 492–496
Models, 13, 16, 18, 20–21, 159–162
  aggregate travel model, 297–301, 303–304, 327–329, 378, 497
  analogue models, 163
  calibration of, 160, 298, 302, 328, 368–370
  deterministic models, 448–449
  in development planning, 449, 453
  input-output analysis, 412, 423–435, 461–462, 505, 506
  linear programming, 157, 164, 193, 216, 406–422, 462, 504, 506
  locational polygons, 163, 203, 343–345, 500, 504
  locational triangles, 113, 114–118, 123, 128, 149–151, 163, 190, 194–197
  market potential model, 300–304, 327–330
  Markov chains, 270–271
  Monte Carlo models, 270–271
  operational models, 20, 159–176, 276, 279, 297–304, 330, 367–374, 388–389, 506

probabilistic models, 18, 270–271
Varignon's mechanical model, 114–115, 151, 163, 197, 343–344
Monclova, Mexico, steel plant at, 341–345
Monopoly, 60–61, 138, 512
Monte Carlo models, 270–271
Monterrey, Mexico, steel plant at, 341–345
Morrill, R. L., 109
Moses, L., 156, 213, 215, 222, 224–225, 412
Multiple correlation and regression analysis, 162, 304, 395, 397–405
Multipliers, 429, 458–461, 477–478, 485
Multivariate statistical techniques, 446; *see also* Multiple correlation and regression analysis; Principal components analysis
Myrdal, G. M., 455

Narrowing down of locational choice, concept of, 104–105
National plans, 467, 473, 477–479, 481–482, 515
Negative income tax, 516
New England, as a location for an iron and steel works, 352–354
  textile industry in, 305–306
Newspaper industry, 29–30
New towns, 465–466
New York, cost of land in, 37
  levels of taxation in, 53
Nonbasic industries, 100–101
Nonconforming industries, 484, 487–488
No-rent margins, 206, 421
Northwest England, cost of land in, 281–282
  new city and industrial complex in, 506
Nottingham, lace industry in, 84
  large firms in, 89
  reoccupation of lace warehouses in, 39
Nourse, H. O., 82, 241, 385, 386

Observation, 6–10, 16
Occupancy costs, 323–325, 380–381
Oil refining, 319
Okayama, Japan, cost of land in, 35–36
Oligopoly, 145, 512
Ontario, comparative locational advantage in, 31, 328–330
Operational models, 20, 159–176, 276, 279, 297–304, 330, 367–374, 388–389, 506
Overspill, 483, 487

Pacific Northwest, cost of aluminum production in, 315–317

550 INDEX

Palander, T., 119–124, 125, 127, 128, 129, 130, 137, 138, 151, 152–153, 154, 205, 305, 330, 343, 345
Paperboard container industry, 404–405
Paper industry, 111, 306–308, 330–337
Parameters, calculation of, 160, 369–370
Payroll tax, 210, 450
Pennsylvania, market areas in, 308–310
Perfect competition, 61
Perroux, F., 454
Personal factors in industrial location, 89–92, 145–146, 147, 231–235, 508–510
Petrochemicals industry, 319
Philadelphia area, input-output study in, 435 taxation in, 292–295
Phosphate industry, freight rates in, 80–81
Physical restriction, principle of, 101–102
Pipelines, 70
Pittsburgh plus system of basing-point pricing, 68, 349
Planning industrial location and development, 157, 210–211; *see also* City planning; Regional planning
Planning regions, 445
Point biserial correlation coefficient, 396–397
Poland, industrial development strategy in, 475–479, 495, 496
Polarization effect, 455
Political factors, 448, 470
Pollution, 88, 477, 481, 487, 514, 517
Ponsard, C., 157–158
Potential surfaces, 300–304
Pottery industry, 56, 83
Postage-stamp freight rates, 72–73
Poverty, 469, 470, 514
Power, 43–46
Pred, A., 98, 106–108, 209, 233, 272
Prediction, 16, 18–19
  of the impact of industrial development, 458–462
Predohl, A., 148
Price, 57–68, 242–244, 372–374
  effect of changes in, 135–136, 142–143, 263–264
Pricing policies, 42, 66–68, 134
Principal components analysis, 446
Principles of industrial location, 102–105, 181–187, 266, 269
Probabilistic models, 18, 270–271
Problem areas (regions), 441–446
  criteria for identification of, 446, 464–466, 467–468, 470–471
Production functions, 220
Production theory, complimentary with location theory, 229–231, 261
Product moment correlation coefficient, 395
Profit surfaces, 254, 259–261, 271
Programming regions, 445
Propulsive industries, 454, 457, 503
Psychic income, 145, 232–234, 366, 509
Public policy, 129, 437–438, 441, 493, 495, 500; *see also* City planning; Regional planning
Public sector, 474, 514–515
Public Works and Economic Development Act, 470–472
Puerto Rico, industrial complex in, 319, 505–507

Quantitative methods, chi-square, 396
  coefficient of geographical association, 394–395
  contingency coefficient, 396
  correlation and regression analysis, 160, 269–270, 304, 365–370, 393–405
  Gini coefficients, 394–395
  point biserial correlation coefficient, 396–397
  principal components analysis, 446
  product moment correlation coefficient, 395–396
  Spearman's rank correlation coefficient, 365–366, 396
Quantitative revolution, the, 110
Quasi laws, 18, 21

Railroads, 70
Random elements in location patterns, 255, 273, 276, 374, 388; *see also* Personal factors in industrial location
Random processes, 270–273
Rawstron, E. M., 102–105, 184
Ray, M., 329–330
Redevelopment areas, in United States, 470–472
Regional Employment Premium, in Britain, 464
Regional industrial development problems, 441–*see also* Regional planning
Regional multipliers, 458–461
Regional planning, 88–89, 443, 445, 447–479, 481–482, 484, 493, 496–507, 508, 512, 513
  instruments, 449–452
  relationship to city and national planning, 481–
  spatial strategy, 452–458, 462, 463–479, 501
Regional science, 148, 423, 492
Regression analysis, 160, 162, 269–270, 304, 369–370, 393–405

Reifler, R., 292
Relative location, the factor of, 98
Relocation, industrial, *see* City planning; Regional planning
Renner, G. T., 98–100
Rent, 206; *see also* Location rent
Rent gradients, 414–415
Rent surfaces, 189, 414–415, 421, 422
Reoccupation of industrial premises, 39
Residuals from regression, 405
Resource frontier regions, 445
Retail trade, in the United States, 63–65
Revenue cones, 241
Revenue curves, 59–61, 227–230
Revenue domes, 251
Revenue surfaces, 237, 238, 242, 248, 251, 252, 259–261, 271, 296, 328, 493, 500, 501
Richardson, H., 158, 241–242, 452, 494, 512
Richter, C. E., 431
Rodgers, A., 348–349
Rooney, J. F., 63–65
Rosenstein-Rodan, P. N., 514

Sakashita, N., 156, 215, 217
Sampson, R. J., 73
Scale, 25–26, 57–61, 125–126, 222–231, 501–507
 diseconomies of, 58, 87–88, 442, 444
 economies of, 58, 82, 85, 319, 354, 360, 501–507, 511
Scale lines, 28
Scrap, cost of, 353
Selective Employment Premium, in Britain, 464
Service freight tariffs, 75
Shoe and leather industries, 83, 129
Siebert, H., 448, 462, 495
Simbiosis, industrial, 99
Simulation models, 270–271
Smith, T. E., 154–155
Smithies, A. F., 142
Social costs, 445
Socialism, 515–516
Socialist economic systems, 447, 478–479
Social justice, 441
Social policy, 476, 479, 480, 486–487, 511–517
South, the textile industry in, 305–306, 319
Southern Italy, industrial development in, 374–375, 494, 496, 506

Space cost curves, 182–185, 195–203, 206, 208–212, 229, 231, 253–254, 263–268, 497–501
Space demand profiles, 244
Space revenue curves, 184–185, 229–231, 244, 251–254, 497–501
Spatial margins to profit ability, *see* Margins to profitability, spatial
Spearman's rank correlation, 365–366, 396
Special Areas, in British planning, 464
Special Development Areas, in British Planning, 464–465
Special problem regions, 445
Spelt, J., 328–329
Spiegelman, R. G., 398–399
Spread effect, in growth-point strategy, 455–457, 474
Stafford, H., 102, 404–405, 509
State control of industry, 88, 449, 450, 474–475, 475–479, 514, 515
Statistical tests, 393; *see also* Quantitative methods
Steel industry, *see* Iron and steel industry
Stepwise regression analysis, 400
Stevens, B. H., 156, 410, 412, 413–415
Stochastic models, 270–271
Stochastic processes, 270
Stopler, W., 130
Sub-optimal decision making, 106–109, 145–146, 185, 188, 206, 208–209, 231–235, 273, 507–510, 516
Subsidy, of locations, 52, 88, 210–212, 233, 449–452, 453, 464–465, 467–468, 471, 484, 493, 495, 500, 509, 513
 of labor costs, 452, 464, 498
Substitution between factors or inputs, 26–27, 156, 212–221, 222–225
Substitution principle, 148–152
Supply and demand, 57–62
Supply space potential, 304
Surrogates, use of, 160, 398, 404, 460
Sweden, clothing industry in, 337–341
 paper industry in, 330–338
Sydney, Australia, cost of land in, 281–282
SYMAP computer mapping system, 280
Synthetic fiber industry, 317–319
Systematic studies, 6
Systems, 109–110, 161

Targets, in planning strategy, *see* Goals
Tariffs, 136

INDEX

Taxes, 52–54, 88, 210–211, 292–295, 317, 325, 365, 380, 383, 450, 516
Taylor, M. J., 389
Technical restriction, principle of, 104
Technology, changes in, 262, 267, 331–333, 347, 494
Technostructure, the, 55
Teitz, M. B., 156
Tennessee Valley, cost of aluminum production in, 315–317
Tennessee Valley Authority, 469
Terminal charges, 71, 74, 196
Texas Gulf Coast, cost of aluminum production on, 315–317
Textile industry, 33, 38, 46, 83, 305–306
Theory, 14–15, 17–22, 95, 178
  central place, 98, 107, 132–134, 305, 455–456
  economic base, 100–102, 460–461
  game, 154–155, 156
  industrial location, *see* names of individual theorists, and contents pages
Thompson, J., 110
Thompson, W., 87–88
Thünen, H. von, 148, 151, 154, 407
Tiebout, C. M., 158, 234, 259–260, 273
Time factor, 124, 262–273
Tinbergen, J., 157, 501
Törnqvist, A., 337–341
Total revenue dome, 250–251
Trade, 135
Trafford Park, Manchester, 489
Transformation lines, 149–150
Transportation, 25, 69–81, 93
  costs, 65, 71–81, 103, 114–118, 122–123, 128–129, 144, 171, 181, 244, 269–280, 284–286, 297–301, 305–311, 313–314, 316–317, 322, 323, 334–345, 348, 378–380
  line haul charges, 71, 74
  methods, 69–71
  systems, 109, 203, 498–499
  terminal charges, 71, 74, 196
Transportation problem, in linear programming, 411–412, 416–417
Transport cost gradients, 74, 75–79, 81, 125, 160, 202, 369–370; *see also* Space cost curves
Transport inputs, 149–151
Transport lines, 123

Transport orientation, 144, 165, 341, 347
Transport points, 123
Transport surfaces, 123; *see also* Cost surfaces; Isodopanes
Transshipment, 70, 128
Travelling salesman problem, 164
Trickling down effect, 455

Ullman, E. L., 100–101
Underdeveloped regions, 442–443, 473–475, 477, 498–500, 508, 512
Unemployment, 441, 443, 446, 452, 457, 464–466, 514
Unionization, 52, 93, 353
Uniqueness, 17
United Kingdom, industrial estates (parks) in, 489
  labor costs in, 45–46
  see also Great Britain
United States, building costs, 40, 282–284
  consumption, 63–65
  contemporary problems, 514, 515
  crystals, manufacture of, 319–320
  electric power, 44
  electronics industry, 361–374, 374–387
  freight rates, 72–81
  industrial cost structures, 29–31
  industrial development agencies, 450
  industrial development planning, 469–473
  industrial parks, 489
  input-output tables, 431–435
  interest rates, 38
  iron and steel industry, 346–360
  labor costs, 47–52, 288–292
  machinery industry, 400–404
  managerial employees, availability of, 55
  markets, 298–301, 302–304
  materials costs, 41–42
  paperboard container industry, 404–405
  pollution, 481
  wheat industry, 420–422
Upward transitional areas, 445
Urban hierarchy, 455–456, 468–469, 472
Urbanization economies, 83, 84–87, 154
USSR, 496
Utilities, cost of, 325, 365

Values, of society, 88, 441, 445, 469
Variable-cost theory, *see* Least-cost theory
Variable-demand theory, 236–261; *see also* Demand; Locational interdependence

Varignon's mechanical model, 114–115, 151, 163, 197, 343–344

Wage rates, 45–52, 288–292, 322–323, 329; *see also* Labor, cost of
Warehouses, location of, 164, 166
Warntz, W., 109, 304
Waste disposal, land for, 104
Water, for industrial use, 93, 104
Water power, 331–333
Waterways, 334
Weber, A., 113–119, 122, 123, 124, 127, 128, 129, 130, 131, 137, 138, 148, 151, 152, 154–155, 156, 163, 188, 190, 196–197, 198, 213, 232–233, 249, 259, 330, 334, 343–345, 348, 354, 387, 407, 493, 496, 497, 500, 504, 505
Weberian Locational Game, 155
Wedgewood, Josiah, 56
Weight triangle, 152; *see also* Locational triangles
West Midlands Conurbation, England, 489–491
Wheat industry, 420–422
Wonnacott, R. J., 48–50, 289
Wood, P., 504

Zinc manufacturing, 29–30, 313–315
Zoning, of land, 32, 88, 450, 480, 481, 486